CONTEMPORARIES
OF
BULSTRODE WHITELOCKE
1605-1675

RECORDS OF SOCIAL AND ECONOMIC HISTORY
NEW SERIES XIV

CONTEMPORARIES
OF
BULSTRODE WHITELOCKE
1605–1675

Biographies, Illustrated by Letters and other Documents

BY

RUTH SPALDING

an Appendix to

The Diary of Bulstrode Whitelocke

Published for THE BRITISH ACADEMY
by THE OXFORD UNIVERSITY PRESS

Oxford University Press, Walton Street, Oxford OX2 6DP
Oxford New York Toronto
Delhi Bombay Calcutta Madras Karachi
Petaling Jaya Singapore Hong Kong Tokyo
Nairobi Dar es Salaam Cape Town
Melbourne Auckland

and associated companies in
Berlin Ibadan

Oxford is a trade mark of Oxford University Press

Published in the United States
by Oxford University Press, New York

British Library Cataloguing in Publication Data
Spalding, Ruth
Contemporaries of Bulstrode Whitelocke 1605–1675:
biographies, illustrated by letters and other
documents. — (Records of social and economic history.
New series; 14)
1. Great Britain, 1603–1714 — Biographies —
Collections
I. Title II. Whitelocke, Bulstrode. Diary of
Bulstrode Whitelocke 1605–1675 III. British Academy
IV. Series
941.06′092′2
ISBN 0–19–726081–0

Typeset by J&L Composition Ltd
Printed in Great Britain by
Billings & Sons Ltd,
Worcester

Introductory Note

The Diary of Bulstrode Whitelocke 1605–1675, edited by Miss Ruth Spalding, constitutes Volume XIII of the New Series of Records of Social and Economic History. To complement that volume and to elucidate the activities and backgrounds of some of the extremely large number of people mentioned in the diary, Miss Spalding has prepared the present Volume XIV in the New Series. It consists of biographical information, supplemented by many previously unpublished letters and other documents, covering approximately one thousand of those referred to in the diary. All sorts of persons – monarchs and family servants, preachers and politicians – figure in this assembly of biographical detail, shedding new light on various social, political and economic topics of the period. It can be used separately or in conjunction with Volume XIII.

D.C. Coleman
*Chairman, Records of Social and
Economic History Committee*

Contents

The Acknowledgements, Family Tree, Sources and other information listed above, repeat those provided in the *Diary*. This is to save the reader having to refer from one volume to the other.

List of Illustrations
with acknowledgements

ix

Acknowledgements

My deep thanks go in the first place to Lord Bute, not only for generously allowing the publication of his manuscript, but also for the consideration he has shown throughout the time I have been working on it. Having allowed me to borrow the two volumes of the 'Diary' for a considerable length of time, he later agreed to my having a photocopy and microfilm made of them. To Miss Catherine Armet, his former Archivist, I am indebted for all her prompt help and encouragement. I am also very grateful indeed to Lord Bath for allowing me both to study and to quote from his great collection of Whitelocke manuscripts at Longleat. I am greatly indebted to Miss Jane Fowles, formerly his Archivist and Librarian, for her unflagging help on my numerous visits to Longleat, not only in fetching and carrying the 30 folio volumes from the muniments room but sometimes, too, in deciphering seemingly illegible passages, particularly in Edward Hyde's letters. Her successor, Miss Kate Harris, has also been most helpful and efficient on my later visits, and I record my gratitude to her.

Next, I wish to thank the British Academy, and in particular members of the Records of Social and Economic History Committee, who undertook this publication. Their patience and support, professional and financial, have been invaluable. In particular I am grateful to Professor Donald Coleman, Chairman of the Committee, and to Dr. Joan Thirsk, my link with the Committee, who has read and commented on the whole script, and who has always found time to discuss my editorial problems and to give me her very wise advice. I am also grateful to the British Academy's former Publications Officer, Mr. Hagan Powell, and subsequently to Mr. James Rivington, for valuable help, and to the printers who had the exacting task of setting up the book.

The people who share in the toil of bringing a book like this into existence are normally mentioned at the end of the acknowledgements, under a 'last but by no means least' heading. Without their massive help there would be no book, so I thank them all at this point: Marjorie Wyatt has pursued Whitelocke with me relentlessly from the time I started writing about him; she has typed the full text of *The Diary* twice and the footnotes once with meticulous care and at considerable sacrifice in terms of

4

domestic and social freedom; she has also given me invaluable help as a research assistant, and in the mammoth task of compiling the index. When Marjorie was going on a visit to Australia, I asked the Institute of Historical Research if they knew of a first-class secretary to type the last draft of the footnotes, also the chapters and the whole of the biographical appendix (the companion volume to this edition). Unaware of any connection, they recommended a Mrs. Jeanie Moyo so, despite an inborn dislike of nepotism, I decided on their recommendation that I had better hire her, although she happens to be my daughter. Her editorial flair for spotting inconsistencies and bad turns of phrase while typing, has been of the greatest possible service. The late Ingrid Fernyhough, in a wheelchair with multiple sclerosis, retained the eye of a hawk and the memory of a computer; with these endowments she checked every stage of *The Diary*, notes and chapters with me; for Whitelocke she has been known to sacrifice both Wimbledon and the Test Match on T.V. Phyllis (Phil) Edwin has sustained Ingrid and me with food and drink, has looked up points in her own books and researched items (chiefly genealogical) in London and at various county record offices; she has helped with the translation of French and Latin letters and in transcribing copies of documents, for all of which I am most grateful. In later stages of the work I had a timely and unexpected offer from a neighbour, Lesley Brenner, to help in any capacity. This led to her scrutinizing over 900 pages of footnotes from which she made lists of abbreviations and books, and tracked down suspected inconsistencies of style, a formidable and boring job which she tackled with high intelligence. In addition, for many months, while she was free, she checked the early part of this volume with me. At the last, vital lap, another neighbour, Jacqueline (Jacky) Johnston, volunteered to continue with this work, with other checking and with proof-reading, and has brought a fine critical faculty and skills which she describes as 'nit-picking' to the final stages of the work. The kind of dedication shown by these colleagues brings disruption to household routines, and I am grateful to all the husbands or households who have put up with the Whitelocke Nuisance in their homes, and have manfully helped with domestic and culinary chores. I also thank P.W.P., Welwyn, for retyping numerous amended pages at short notice; and Vera and John Crossman at Mill Farm, for their great kindness on my many visits to Longleat, not least for allowing me to spread my papers all over their sitting-room floor, and Vera for her help with decoding letters to Thurloe written in number code.

I am grateful for the generous help given to me by many scholars and am only sorry that I cannot acknowledge them all. I am deeply indebted: to Dr. Christopher Hill for suggesting first that I ought to edit the 'Diary' and later that I should offer it to the British Academy; to Mr. Robert Latham for advising me in detail on the general lay-out, before I started work, and to Dr. Ian Roy who read the typescript of *The Diary* and footnotes and made valuable suggestions. I am also immensely grateful to Dr. Gerald Aylmer who generously offered to read *The Contemporaries*, and who has picked up numerous very helpful points. Mr. Peter Hasler, General Editor of the *History of Parliament*, has been painstaking and generous in replying to tiresome questions, and so have Mr. Nicholas Pointer of the Search Department of the Public Record Office, and Mrs Lena Dahlkvist of the Swedish Embassy Information Section. Mrs. Grace Hogarth read my early draft of chapter I (*Diary*), which was bothering me, and gave me the shrewd advice of an experienced editor, even though her field is quite a different one.

I wish to thank the following people for specialist advice: Mr. R.H. Adams on Dr. Baylie and St John's College, Oxford; the late Commander Philip Aubrey on matters concerning John Thurloe's letters; Mr. Stephen Black on certain legal points; Mr John Ferris on the identification of some of Whitelocke's friends; Dr. G.E. Fussell and Dr. Bernard Tinker on agricultural matters; the late Sir Noel Hall on his ancestor, Whitelocke's friend Bartholomew Hall; Dr. George Hammersley on questions of timber; Dr. J.C. Hayward on Thomas Triplet; Mr. Norman Hidden on Jethro Tull, sen., and others living near Hungerford; Mr. C.P. Hill on the Hill family, into which Whitelocke's daughter Anne married; Dr. Eric Sams and through him Mrs. Ann Payne on Whitelocke's shorthand, some of which Ann kindly transcribed; Mr. John Sharp on 'sympathetic ink'; my brother, Dr. John Spalding, on medical and sailing questions; Mr. Robert Temple on the judges at the trial of King Charles I, and in particular the regicides (and Robert's wife Olivia for her patience whenever we talked shop); Dr. Colin Tite on manuscripts borrowed by Whitelocke from the Cotton Library; and Dr. Blair Worden for some useful comments on the text of *The Diary*. I am also indebted to Brigadier Peter Young, Mr. Anthony Kemp of the Study of Forts Group, and to Dr. Alan Borg, Keeper of Blades at the Tower of London, for their attempts to date the curious pieces of metal-work which I excavated near the ramparts of Henley Garrison, but which remain a mystery.

On visits to France and Sweden I received helpful information from Professor Olivier Lutaud and Dr. P. Grillon, both of the Sorbonne, and from M. Charles Rowe, Curator of the J.-J. Rousseau Museum at Montmorency; also from M. Pierre Bazin, Curator at the Castle Museum in Dieppe; from M. François Burckard, Chief Curator of the Upper Normandy Archives and Mme. Dominique Lebeltel of the City of Rouen Archive Services. Members of the History Departments, and others, at the

Universities of Gothenburg, Stockholm and Uppsala, which I visited for research and to speak on Whitelocke, were most helpful and hospitable. In particular I thank Dr. Åke Holmberg and Professor Gunnar Olsson who both introduced me, early one morning, to the University Library in Gothenburg. Gunnar has since answered a number of letters from me asking time-consuming questions. I had the great pleasure of staying with Professor Gunnar and Mrs. Mavis von Proschwitz, who also answered many questions, showed me places in Gothenburg referred to in *The Diary*, and helped with some translating. In Stockholm I spent a delightful evening with Professor Herman Schück, his wife and daughter; I had the pleasure of meeting Professor and Mrs. Linberg with them, and they all helped to shorten my list of questions arising from Whitelocke's Swedish Embassy, and provided me with useful introductions. Of these, Fil. dr. Birgitta Lager-Kromnov in particular gave me valuable biographical details of Swedes whom Whitelocke met; the staff in Riksarkivet were also very helpful. At the University of Uppsala Dr. Stellan Dalgren, at the History Institute, entrusted me with a key to the library, answered numerous questions and he too gave me some useful introductions; I was glad to be able to consult Professor Sven Nilsson and I am grateful for the help given to me by the staff at Carolina Rediviva (the University Library) and at Landsarkivs Bibliotek, in the Castle. I also wish to thank Dr. Spies, City Archivist of Lübeck, who answered my questions about Whitelocke's journey home through North Germany, also Miss Brigit Strand and Mrs. Agneto Kirkby for prompt help with some Swedish translating, and Mrs. Susanne Gregersen for translating material concerning prominent Danes who appear in *The Diary*. For help with translations from the Latin and with Whitelocke's classical allusions, I am much indebted to Beryl Williams, Gwen Walter, Joyce Hayward and finally to Peter Mason.

Incidents in *The Diary* have caused me to visit many houses and churches in this country. Knocking on doors I have been struck by the friendly hospitality shown to a perfect stranger enquiring about seventeenth-century inhabitants. In the Henley-on-Thames, Fawley and Hambleden area I have received great help from old friends and new: from Mr. Gordon Claisse, Bursar of Greenland; from Father Paul Jasinski, Superior at Fawley Court, now a Polish school, and from Mr. Paul Rosewarne, formerly Chairman of Phyllis Court Club. These properties formed Whitelocke's three Thames-side estates. Members of Henley-on-Thames Archaeological and Historical Society have been generous with their help. In particular I am grateful to Mr. John Crocker who has made an extensive study of Henley, and the late Miss Ann Flinders-Petrie who wrote on Yewden Manor (alias Greenland); also Mr. Harold Hussey, Commander A.H. Piggott (Hon. Archivist to the Rector of Hambleden), and Mrs. Elizabeth Young, who have all provided me with useful details.

In other areas I have received help from Mr. Bill Ackworth of the Chilton Estate Office; Mr. Hughes, tenant farmer of North Hidden (a farm on Whitelocke's Chilton Park estate) and the Revd. E.G.F. Swinnerton, Rector of Chilton Foliat; from Mrs. Barton of Knaith Hall, Lincs.; the Revd. Canon Arthur Bennett of Little Munden, Herts.; Mr. Leslie Bailey of Little Rollright, Oxon.; Mrs. Morag E. Barton, Assistant Curator of Weybridge Museum; the Revd. Francis B. Cutler, Rector of Crowland, Lincs.; Mr. Bernard Griffin, Chairman of the Parslowe Charity, Watlington, Oxon; the Revd. David Hemsley, Rector of Quainton; Mr. Ralph Hall who has made a study of Raunds, Northants.; Mrs. Kinloch of Blunts Hall, Essex; Lady Pemberton of Trumpington Hall and Mr. Jeremy Pemberton of Granchester concerning the Hall, where Whitelocke's eldest son, James, lived with his wife; the Sister Archivist at Newhall, Essex; the Revd. William J.T. Smith, Vicar of Boreham; and the Revd. Canon A.J. Watts.

I have had great help, by correspondence and in person, from the staff of numerous county record offices, in particular those of Cambridgeshire, Cardigan, Clwyd, Gloucestershire, Hampshire, Hertfordshire, Lincoln, Northamptonshire, Oxford, Surrey, Wiltshire and N. Yorkshire. Librarians and their staff have been very kind and patient in dealing with my questions, particularly: at the British Library; at the Institute of Historical Research; at the Archives Department of Reading University Library, which houses the interesting Chilton Estate Papers; and at Dr. Williams's Library where I have been allowed some long-term borrowing and the staff have not been too precise as to the number of books borrowed at one time. I am also indebted to the following institutions for the help their staff have given me and for permission to quote from their archives: the Bodleian Department of Western Manuscripts; the British Library Department of Manuscripts; the Public Record Office for permission to quote from papers in which Crown-copyright subsists; the House of Lords Record Office, and the Royal Historical Society. I also wish to thank Lord Mostyn for permission to quote from his manuscripts in the University of Bangor Archives and in the Clwyd Record Office, and Mr. and Mrs. P.J. Radford for allowing me to quote from manuscripts concerning Sheffield Park, Sussex, when it was owned by Whitelocke's son-in-law, George Nevill.

Finally, I must acknowledge that after receiving all this massive help, I alone am responsible for any errors in the book, whether of judgement or of fact.

Ruth Spalding

Abbreviations

A. & O.	*Acts and Ordinances of the Interregnum*
A.B.B.	A.B. Beaven *The Aldermen of the City of London*
A Voyce	*A Voyce from the Watch Tower* by E. Ludlow (ed. A.B. Worden)
Add.Mss	Additional Mss, B.L.
'Annales'	'Annales of his Life and Labours remembered for his Children' by Bulstrode Whitelocke, Add.Mss
bapt.	baptized
B.L.	British Library
Bt.	Baronet
bur.	buried
c.	*circa*
C.	century
Cal.Com.Adv. Money	*Calendar of the Committee for Advancement of Money*
Calamy Revised	*Calamy Revised* by A.G. Matthews
Capt.	Captain
C.J.	*Commons Journal*
C.L.D.	*Concise Law Dictionary*
Col.	Colonel
C.S.P. Dom.	*Calendar of State Papers, Domestic*
C.S.P. Ven.	*Calendar of State Papers, Venetian*
C.U.L.	Cambridge University Library
cwt.	hundredweight
d.	pence; died
D.	Duke
dau.	daughter
D.N.B.	*Dictionary of National Biography*
E.	Earl; East
ed.	editor; edited
edn.	edition
Eg.	Egerton Mss, B.L.
E.H.R.	*English Historical Review*
fl.	*floruit* – flourished – used where date of birth and death is not known

fol.	folio
G.E.C.	G.E.Cokayne *The Complete Peerage*
Gen.	General
Harley Mss	Harleian Mss, B.L.
Hist. of Parl.	*History of Parliament. House of Commons 1660–1690*, 3 vols.
ib.	*ibidem* – in the same place, i.e. source
J.M.H.	*Journal of Modern History*
Journal	*A Journal of the Swedish Embassy* by Bulstrode Whitelocke (2nd edn. 1855)
jun.	junior
K.	King
Kt.	Knight
Lansdowne Mss	Lansdowne Mss, B.L.
Liber	*Liber Famelicus* by James Whitelocke
L.J.	*Lords Journal*
Long. Cal. W.P.	Longleat, Calendar of Whitelocke Papers
Long. W.P.	Longleat, Whitelocke Papers (Mss)
Lt.-Gen.	Lieutenant-General
m.	married; mile
M.	Monsieur
Memorials	*Memorials of the English Affairs* by Bulstrode Whitelocke (1853 edn.)
M.F.K.	M.F. Keeler *The Long Parliament, 1640–1641*
mls.	miles
Ms/Mss	Manuscript/Manuscripts
N.	North
n.d.	no date
n/nn.	note/notes
N.S.	New Style, i.e. using the Gregorian Calendar
O.E.D.	*Oxford English Dictionary*
O.S.	Old Style, i.e. using the Julian Calendar
par.	paragraph
Pepys	*Diary of Samuel Pepys* (ed. Robert Latham & William Matthews)
Pepys X	*Diary of Samuel Pepys*, Vol. X, *Companion*
Q.	Queen
q.v.	*quod vide* – which see: referring to a further entry, in *The Contemporaries*
R. Hist. S.	Royal Historical Society
Rawl. Mss.	Rawlinson Mss, Bodleian Library (Department of Western Manuscripts)

Restoration	*Restoration of Charles II* by G. Davies
R.O.	Record Office
s.	son; shilling
S.	South
s. & h.	son and heir
S.B.L.	*Svenskt Biografiskt Lexikon*
sen.	*senior*
Shaw's Knights	W.A. Shaw *Knights of England*
Sloane Ms	Sloane Mss, B.L.
S.M.K.	*Svenska Män och Kvinnor*
suc.	succeeded
Thurloe S.P.	*John Thurloe, State Papers* (ed. Thomas Birch)
T.L.S.	*Times Literary Supplement*
trans.	translation
v.	verso; verse
V.C.H.	*Victoria County History*
vs.	versus
W.	West

Principal Manuscript Sources
with notes

THE MARQUESS OF BUTE'S COLLECTION

Ms 196 D.13 '1605–1675'. The Diary of Bulstrode Whitelocke. Vol. i 1605–1659, Vol. ii 1659–1675.

THE MARQUESS OF BATH'S COLLECTION

Bulstrode Whitelocke's Collected Papers. 30 folio vols. also Index and Calendar; 9 parcels, Muniments Room, Longleat.

Ms 124 'Book of Expenses attending Sir Bulstrode Whitelocke's Embassy to Sweden'.

Ms 124a 'Journal of the Swedish Embassy'. The original version. Incomplete. Library, Longleat.

BODLEIAN LIBRARY, Department of Western Manuscripts.

Rawlinson Collection: numerous letters written by Whitelocke from Sweden to John Thurloe, Oliver Cromwell etc., most of them printed in *Thurloe State Papers*.

BRITISH LIBRARY MANUSCRIPTS

(1) *Judge Sir James Whitelocke*
Stowe Mss 297 fols. 87–142 and 298 fol.2. 'An Argument upon the Questions of Impositions ... by Sir Davyes Knight ...' These fols. give the Remonstrance from the Commons after the King's instruction to them not to examine his right to make impositions without the assent of Parliament; consideration of the question and the King's answer. James Whitelocke is not named but was a prime mover.

Add. Ms 36082 fols. 101–105, 174v.–176v. Hardwicke Papers. Legal treatises by Sir John Davyes Knight on impositions, etc.

Stowe Ms 569 fols. 35–39. Tract 3 on private and public duels; in Latin.

Harley Ms 4176 fols. 11v.–18. Tract 3 on private and public duels; in Latin.

Add. Ms 25247 fols. 93–95. 'Of the antiquity, use, and ceremony of Lawfull Combates in England written by Mr James Whitelocke of the middle temple'.

Hargrave Ms 237. Turn volume upside-down and read back to front, fols. 1–95. [James] 'Whitelocks Reading on 21 Hen. 8. *de Facultatibus Beneficiorum*'. Bartholomew Hall's copy.

Add. Ms 53725. 'Liber Famelicus'. Autobiography, incompletely published by the Camden Society, 1858.

Add. Ms 24481 fols. 62–75v. Roughly copied extracts from 'Liber Famelicus' with additional family trees based on the text.

(2) *Bulstrode Whitelocke*
Add. Ms 64867. Whitelocke's Letter-book and journal compiled while he was one of Parliament's Commissioners to the King at Oxford, Mar./Apr. 1643. (Acquired in 1987.)

Add. Mss 15622 and 15623. 'Whitelockes History of Parliament'. Vol. i autograph Ms, vol. ii in another hand. A treatise on Parliament's antiquity, constitution and privileges etc. Fols. 102–102v. refer to the Petition and Advice offered by 'the last Parliament', indicating that this Ms was completed in 1657.

Add. Ms 4993. 'Whitelockes Treatise of Government'. Title on spine only. Part-autograph. Some chapters correspond with chapters in Add. Mss 37341 and 37342. Chapter 15 refers to Writs of Summons issued in December 1658 in the name of Richard, Lord Protector of the Commonwealth 'to this present Parliament 1658/59'.

Add. Mss 4749–4754. 'Whitelockes Notes Uppon the Kings writt for Choosing Members of Parlement 13. Car. 2'. Written for Charles II; details in *Diary*. Published 1766.

Add. Ms 21099. 'The Kings Right to graunt Indulgence in matters of Religion'. Small volume on toleration, written in March 1662/63 at the request of Charles II.

Add. Mss 37341 and 37342. 'Whitelockes Annales of his own Life Dedicated to his Children'. Transcribed in retirement from his earlier work. Whitelocke explains in the Preface why he inserts this 2-volume 'History of the Parlement of England' (in effect a treatise on government) at the beginning of his 'Annales'. Numbers 1 and 2 on the fore-edge do not correspond with those on the next volumes of 'Annales'.

Add. Ms 53726. 'The Annales of his own Life Dedicated to his Children'.

Marked 1 on the fore-edge, this volume runs from Whitelocke's birth in Aug. 1605 to Aug. 1634. The Preface in Add. Ms 4992 belongs to this manuscript, as Whitelocke's paging shows. Dr. Charles Morton (the first under-librarian of the British Museum) presented Add. Ms 4992 to the British Museum between 1770 and 1780; he also borrowed (and thought he had been given) the volume now numbered Add. Ms 53726. It seems likely that while it was in his possession the Preface fell out of the borrowed manuscript and was bound into the other.

Add. Ms 37343. 'Annales'. Aug. 1634 to 1645, marked 2 on fore-edge. Add. Ms 37344. 'Annales'. Aug. 1645 to 1649, marked 3 on fore-edge. Add. Ms 37345. 'Annales'. Aug. 1649 to 1653, marked 4 on fore-edge. Add. Ms 4992. 'Annales'. July 1653 to Apr. 1656, marked 6 on fore-edge. Although the years run continuously in the 'Annales' there is no volume marked 5. Whitelocke wrote two volumes, listed below and bound as 'Annales', which cover the period of the Swedish Embassy, 1653–1654. The greater part of the 'Annales' was published as *Memorials of the English Affairs*, from 1625–1660, heavily edited and cut. The Ms 'Annales', 1656–1660 is missing.

Add. Ms 37346 autograph, and 37347 part-autograph. 'The History of Whitelockes Ambassy from England to Sweden'. Bound as 'Annales', numbered 1 and 2 on fore-edge. Vol.i Sept. 1653 to Feb. 1653/54. Vol. ii Mar. to June 1654. Written after Whitelocke's return from Sweden but before the Restoration. Passages favourable to Cromwell or hostile to monarchy heavily deleted by Carleton Whitelocke. Material in some chapters overlaps with that in the works on parliament and government.

Add. Mss 4991A and 4991B. 'The History of Whitelockes Ambassy from England to Sweden with Notes theruppon And touching the Governement Publique Councells and Persons in those and in other Countries'. Transcript from Add. Mss 37346 and 37347. Formerly in 4 vols. Vol. i marked 1 and 2 on fore-edge, vol. ii marked 3 and, upside-down, 4.

Add. Ms 4995. 'Papers relating to Whitelockes Swedish Embassy'. Title on spine only. Mainly transcripts.

Add. Ms 4902. 'A Journall of the Swedish Ambassy in the yeares 1653 & 1654', edited by Dr. Charles Morton, published 1772; 2nd edn. edited by Henry Reeve, published 1855.

Add. Ms 31984. 'Whitelockes History of the fourty eight year of his Age ... Dedicated to his Children, For their instruction in private & publique duetyes, & in the Governement of their Countrey ...' 1 to 31 Aug. 1653.

Eg. 997. 'Whitelockes History Of the fourtey eight year of his Age'. Aug. to Nov. 1653. Notes addressed to his children.

Add. Ms 53727. 'September 1653'. No title page. A diary supplementing the other versions of Whitelocke's preparations for the Embassy.

Add. Ms 4994. 'Passages in November. 1653'. 1 to 12 Nov. 1653.

Eg. 1048 fol. 160. Draft of the 'Commission of Bulstrode Whitelocke as Ambassador Extraordinary to Queen Christina of Sweden, 21 Oct. 1653'; in Latin and English.

Stowe Ms 189 fols. 59–59v. Bulstrode Whitelocke's 'Commission to treat with the Queen of Sweden 1653'; in Latin.

Eg. 2542 fol. 108 endorsed 108v. 'Whitelockes Speech to the Queene of Sweade at taking his leave at Upsal. May 12. 1654'; in Latin.

Add. Ms 59780. 'Lectures Uppon perticular Occasions By a Father to his Family'. 1666.

Add. Ms 53728. 'Lectures Uppon perticular Occasions By a Father to his Family'. 1667.

Stowe Ms 333. 'Whitelockes Historie of the Parlement of England. And of some Resemblances to the Jewish & other Councells'. Incomplete. Several chapters overlap with Add. Mss 4993 and 37341. See Whitelocke's draft letter to Lord Ashley on his intention to write a history of England and seeking the King's command and encouragement, Add. Ms 32094 fol. 265, Feb. 1671/72.

Letters from Whitelocke:
    Add. Ms 32093 fol. 54, to Edward Hyde from Paris, ¹⁶/₂₆ May 1634.
    Sloane Ms 1519 fol. 135, to John Rushworth, 9 June 1646.
    Lansdowne Ms 821 fols. 300–300v., to Henry Cromwell, 2 Mar. 1656/57.
    Add. Ms 32093 fol. 420, to The Speaker, Harbottle Grimston (copy), 22 May 1660, applying for the King's pardon for himself and his son James.
    Add. Ms 32094 fols. 265–265v., to Lord Ashley (copy), Feb. 1671/72, applying for permission from Charles II to write a History of England.
Letters to Whitelocke:
    Add. Ms 32093 fols. 207–208, from John Ridley, Mar. 1644.
    Ib. fol. 276, from Walter Strickland, ¹⁷/₂₇ Jan. 1650/51, from The Hague.
    Ib. fol. 302, from B. Gerber, 1 Mar. 1652/53.
    Ib. fols. 316v.–317v., from Sir Charles Wolseley, 7 Jan. 1653/54.

Ib. fol. 328, from John Selden, 2 Mar. 1653/54, amended draft.

Ib. fols. 329–329v., from Sir John Holland, 28 Mar. 1654.

Ib. fols. 341–341v., from John Dury, 15 Apr. 1656.

Ib. fols. 343–343v., from William Swyfte, ¹⁶/₂₆ July 1656, serving Ambassador William Lockhart (and Col. James Whitelocke) in France.

Ib. fols. 416–417v., from Algernon Sydney, 13 Nov. [1659].

From John Thurloe 1653–1654, see entry in the present volume.

Sundries:

Add. Ms 6194 fol. 64v., warrant to the officers of the ordinance at the Tower of London for the provision of army quarters in Gresham College and elsewhere, including 450 beds etc., 10 Aug. 1659.

Sloane Ms 645 fol. 46, a tantalizing list of about 25 signatures, including those of Whitelocke and of 11 regicides. Probably *c.* 1659/60.

Loans to Whitelocke from Sir Thomas Cotton's Library: Cotton Mss loans lists. Cotton Appendix xlv, art. 13, fol. 13. Ib. fol. 14v.; Nero B iii, iv, v.

Royal Ms ICII fol. 1. Whitelocke's autograph Jan. 1654/55, illuminated Ms of the Bible in Latin.

UNIVERSITY LIBRARY, CAMBRIDGE

Ms Dd 12. 20–22. A Parliamentary Diary for 1626. Whitelocke's signature is on the inside cover and there is a marginal note on fol. 30: '*Me B.W. Absente*'.

Ms Mm 6. 57 fols. 92–94. Copy of a document from Charles II to Sir Bulstrode Whitelocke granting, or confirming, and defining Whitelocke's entitlement to lands in Ireland.

UNIVERSITY LIBRARY, LUND

Whitelocke's pocket Phrase Book for use in Sweden, with sentences in Latin, French and English. Photocopy B.L.: R.P. 209.

UNIVERSITY OF READING, ARCHIVES DEPT.

Papers in connection with Chilton Park estate and family marriage settlements etc., BER. 36/5/18–39, *passim*.

WINDSOR CASTLE

'Windsor Castle Governors' Book 1668–1671', pp. 1–7: 'Certain Particulars Relating to the Office of Constable of Windsor' collected by Sir

Bulstrode Whitlock' (*sic*). Transcript of Whitelocke's report to Prince Rupert, 1671.

MRS. M.A. HAWKSLEY

Sundry letters and papers concerned with Sir William Whitelocke.

MOSTYN PAPERS: UNIVERSITY OF BANGOR ARCHIVES and CLWYD RECORD OFFICE

Manuscripts relating to Whitelocke's sister Elizabeth Mostyn.

MR. & MRS. P.J. RADFORD

Papers drafted, signed or sealed by Whitelocke in connection with Sheffield Park, Sussex.

MRS. MADELEINE WHITELOCKE

'August 1653'. Diary notes and meditations during the month in which Whitelocke heard he had been nominated as Ambassador.

GLOUCESTER RECORD OFFICE

Freeman Family (FF) papers include Whitelocke family estate papers,[1] mortgages on Fawley Court from 1654, FF70. Also a copy of a picture of the north view of Phyllis Court during the time of the Civil War (garrisoned) from the original, which is thought to have been drawn in the early 18th C., and was found behind panelling at Phyllis Court, ref. FF76.

---

[1] Further documents concerning Fawley Court and the Whitelocke family, are in a private collection.

Bulstrode Whitelocke's Published Work, including Speeches

(Listed according to the date of first publication)

The Speech of Bulstrode Whitelocke Esquire to the ... Lords at a Conference of both Houses ... 17 Feb. 1641 ... concerning ... the speedy reducing of the Kingdom of Ireland (London. 1642).

Three Speeches made to ... the Lord Maior, Aldermen, and Common Council of London, by the Lord Whitlock, Lord Fleetwood, Lord Disbrowe, at Guildhall etc. (London. 1659).

Memorials of the English Affairs ... (ed. Arthur, Earl of Anglesea, London. 1682). 2nd edn. (1732) a fuller text; 3rd edn. (O.U.P. 1853); the work covers the reign of Charles I, the Interregnum and the Restoration of Charles II.

Essays Ecclesiastical and Civil ... To which is subjoined a Treatise of the Work of the Sessions of the Peace (ed. Carleton Whitelocke, London. 1706).

Memorials of the English Affairs from the Suppos'd Expedition of Brute to this Island to the End of the Reign of King James I (London. 1709); 2nd edn. (1713) re-named *The History of England; or, Memorials of the English Affairs* ... Both include an account of Whitelocke's life by William Penn.

Quench not the Spirit (London. 1711). 2nd edn. (1715). Introduction by William Penn. Sermons preached by Whitelocke in Conventicles at Chilton Lodge.

Mr. B. Whitlocks Account of his Embassy to Sweden delivered to the Parliament in ... 1654 together with the Defensive Alliance concluded ... in ... 1700 (London. 1714).

Two Tracts on the benefit of Registring Deeds in England I. 'The draught of an Act for a County Register.' By the Lords Commissioners Whitlock and Lisle ... (London. 1756).

Notes uppon the King's writt for choosing members of Parlement ... (ed.

C. Morton. London. 1766) 2 vols. Writen in 1660–1661 for the use of Charles II.

A Journal of the Swedish Ambassy ... (ed. C. Morton. London. 1772). With an appendix of original papers. Transcribed from Add. Ms 4902. 2nd edn. revised (ed. H. Reeve. London. 1855). Both versions in 2 vols. *B. Whitelockes Dag Bok* (Upsala. 1777) is a shortened text in Swedish with notes, 1 vol.

Collectanea Juridica ... (London. 1791–2), ii Tract x, pp. 332–339. 'Of the Places of Meeting of Public Councils of this Kingdom ...'

RELATED WORK

Piscatoris Poemata ... Vel Panegyricum Carmen (London. 1653 onward) Includes panegyrics to Cromwell, Bradshaw, Ireton, and Ambassador Whitelocke; also elegies by Robert Stapylton and others on the death of Whitelocke's daughter Frances from smallpox.

Preface

The biographies which follow provide about one thousand portraits of people named in Bulstrode Whitelocke's *Diary*. They range from thumbnail sketches to full-length portraits. The people include close friends and colleagues (as well as a few enemies), with Kings, Queens and Protectors, leading politicians, military men and scholars, judges and diplomats, also legal clients, bishops, preachers and tenant farmers; there are Royalists and Parliamentarians among them, aristocrats and Levellers, along with members of Whitelocke's large family (he had two surviving sisters, three wives and seventeen children); his secretaries, coachman, a sculleryman and a washerwoman also put in an appearance.

Whitelocke's inability to throw away papers from his files was obsessive. Not only did he keep letters from his many correspondents but he hoarded drafts, bonds and receipts, all kinds of manuscript ephemera, along with documents of historic importance. This magpie's collection covers over forty years, from the 1630s (and even earlier) until 1675, the year in which he died. More surprising than his own hoarding instinct, is the fact that his family did not make a bonfire of these papers after his death. The Whitelocke manuscripts (the greater part of them in the vast collection at Longleat, also in the British Library and in the Bodleian) have supplied most of the original information used in these biographies, but other unpublished material (not from the Whitelocke collections) has also been used. In most cases, reference is made to the person's connection with Whitelocke; where this is not so, the link is probably unimportant, but in any case it can be traced in *The Diary*, through the index. Inevitably, an enormous amount of the material studied has had to be ignored, but sources are often given for papers which, although not transcribed, are relevant and interesting from a historical or from a purely human point of view.

Ruth Spalding

Biographical Entries
With selected letters and other documents

ABERCORNE (ABERCORN), James Hamilton, 2nd E. of (c.1604–c.1670). G.E.C.; *D.N.B.* (in his father's entry). Son, heir and namesake of the 1st Earl, he succeeded to the title in 1618; he inherited large estates in Scotland from his grandfather, Lord Paisley, and succeeded to that title in 1621. He married Catherine, Dowager Duchess of Lennox (some 12 years his senior), in about 1632; she died in 1637. He was by that time deeply in debt. As a Roman Catholic, he was excommunicated by the General Assembly of the Church of Scotland in 1649, and expelled from Scotland. On two occasions he turned to Whitelocke for support in connection with parliamentary and property matters, *Diary* 4 Dec. 1656; 19 Apr. 1657, with notes.

ABERGAVENNY (BERGAVENNY), George Nevill, 12th Lord of (1665–1695). G.E.C. Son of George Nevill, 11th Baron, he succeeded to the title in 1666, being one year old. Nephew of John the 10th Baron (below). A parliamentary Bill for the sale of entailed lands, which had been initiated successfully in the lifetime of his uncle, was further pursued on behalf of the infant, and was opposed, on both occasions, by Whitelocke in the interest of his young son-in-law, another George Nevill (q.v.), and of Nevill's son and heir of the same name, *L.J.* xii, 84, 89, 90; *Diary* 12 Dec. 1666. The 12th Baron was succeeded by his cousin (Whitelocke's grandson), see NEVILL, George, jun., later 13th Baron and the first Protestant to hold the title.

ABERGAVENNY (BERGAVENNY), John Nevill, 10th Lord of (c.1614–1662). G.E.C. Uncle of the above and brother of the 11th Lord, he was related to Whitelocke by marriage (as shown above). Whitelocke, on behalf of his son-in-law, opposed the Baron's attempt to sell entailed lands, by means of a private Bill in Parliament, but after 'some satisfaction' was arranged with Whitelocke's son-in-law George Nevill, the Bill was apparently enacted, *Diary* 27 May 1657.

ADOLF JOHN (JOHAN), Prince, Count Palatine of the Rhine (1629–
1689). *S.B.L.* Brother of Charles X of Sweden (q.v.); Grand Master at the
Court of Queen Christina (q.v.). His very cordial letter in Latin,
welcoming Whitelocke to Sweden, is translated in *Journal* i, 197–198; the
original, dated 28 Nov., received 9 Dec. 1653, is in Long W.P. xiv, 208.
Whitelocke encountered Prince Adolf John several times in Uppsala, and
most of their meetings were very friendly, *Diary* 23, 27 Dec. 1653; 11 Mar.
1653/54, *passim*. The Prince however showed much displeasure when, on
one occasion, Whitelocke failed to welcome him at the door of his
residence, ib. 6 Jan. 1653/54. After returning to England, Whitelocke
received news of the Prince breaking his leg in a fight, ib. 4 Apr. 1656; in
the next decade, when Adolf John was becoming inactive, his eccentricity
increased, along with the quarrelsome and litigious side of his character.

ALBEMARLE, George Monck (Moncke), MP, 1st D. of (1608–1670)
G.E.C.; *Hist. of Parl.*; A. Woolrych *Commonwealth to Protectorate*,
passim; *D.N.B.* Prime mover in bringing about the Restoration. Whitelocke's
earliest references to meeting Monck occur in *Diary* 12, 19 Oct. 1653;
these mention him only by rank as 'Generall' or 'Generall at Sea', with
Blake (q.v.), when the two of them talked to Whitelocke, at a banquet,
about providing ships for the voyage to Sweden; a few days later Monck is
named by Whitelocke for the first time, when the General attended a
dinner in the City, ib. 24 Oct. He next appears some 16 months later
sending a letter to Whitelocke, but this is not mentioned in *The Diary*; the
General was writing about George Bilton (Deputy Treasurer of the forces
in Scotland); at that time Monck considered him highly suitable for the
post, but by 1658 Bilton was found to have misappropriated £46,000; the
letter also refers to military events in Scotland, 6 Feb. 1654/55, Long. W.P.
xvii, 23.

The following year Monck importuned Whitelocke, as a Governor, to
nominate his nephew for a place at Charterhouse, for he had been
informed: 'there is no publique schoole where children are so vertuously
educated as in that', 12 Apr. 1656, ib.144. He also wrote that his brother-
in-law, Thomas Clarges (q.v.), had told him that Whitelocke was willing to
procure him (Clarges) a Commissioner's place in the Navy, for Monck's
sake; the General expressed effusive gratitude for this proposed help and a
desire to reciprocate the kindness, 20 Mar. 1656/57, ib.xviii, 29. An
undated report from a Committee refers to the estates of William, late
Duke of Hamilton, and the implications of his legacy for the Dowager
Duchess; certain lands, settled on the Duchess, had been granted to
Monck, who had sold them to George Bilton (the scoundrel referred to

earlier), who refused to restore them for less than £143,000, although he had paid much less for them, ib.96.

When Thomas Povey (q.v.), of Hounslow, helped to obtain a seat for Whitelocke's son William, as Burgess of West Looe, *Diary* 6 Jan. 1658/59, Whitelocke tried to repay him by finding him a Scottish seat; Monck wrote, however, that he had received Whitelocke's letter of 14 Jan. but he could not have Mr. Povey chosen as a candidate since most of the elections were over, except in remote parts of Scotland where his letters would arrive too late. He promised, however, to do all in his power to get Povey chosen for some future vacancy, ib.1 Feb. 1658/59; Long. W.P. xix, 5, undated.

The tone of the next letter is significant. While it is improbable that Monck was planning the Restoration as early as June 1659, a few months later, when he *was* doing so, he may well have expected Whitelocke to be an ally – and been bitterly disappointed. The second part of the letter suggests that Monck may have received Cromwellian grants of land in Ireland, which were at risk under the restored Rump:

> My Lord
>
> My Brother Clarges often acquaints me w[i]^th y[ou]^r Lor[dshi]^ps great and carefull remembrance of me w[hi]^ch I despair ... to meritt ... but ile assure yo[u]^r Lord[shi]^p you have not a person in the world that loves and hono[u]^rs you moore than I doe and I heartily wish I were as well able to doe yo[u]^r Lord[shi]^p Service as I am sensible that I owe much to you. I hear at this time the Conduct of the Union w[i]^th Scotland is in the managery of yo[u]^r Lord[shi]^p w[hi]^ch is a work worthy of you and I could be gladd I might have the hono[u]^r [to] see yo[u]^r Lord[shi]^p heer (although but for a little time) [to] dispose the nation to that Setlement the Parliament [intends] for it, w[hi]^ch will require some such heads and hearts as y[ou]^r Lord[shi]^ps to doe it well. I find by the ordinary intelligence I meet w[i]^th, that Ireland is in the same posture as we are w[hi]^ch is somewhat (if possible moore) pressing because the whole disposition of the lands in that Country hath bin by power since your interruption. I am myselfe a little concern'd there and I know not whether my absence in this Service may not render me helpless but I hope yo[u]^r Lord^s[hi]^p will give my Brother Clarges asistance when he shall address himselfe unto yo[u]^r Lord^s[hi]^p in my behalfe, I am very much ashamed of this importunity w[hi]^ch threatens you for my Concernments for w[hi]^ch I earnestly beseech yo[u]^r Lord^s[hi]^ps pardon too.
>
> My Lord,
> yo[u]^r Lord^s[hi]^ps most humble and obliged Servant
> George Monck
>
> Dalkeith the
> 24th of June 1659.   Ib. 26.

(Part of the manuscript is stained and some words are lost. An entry in *Diary* 21 June 1659 is clearly a wrongly-dated reference to this letter.)

Soon afterwards Monck thanked Whitelocke for his letters, and for being mindful of his servant in that remote place and offered to serve him to the best of his poor power, Long. Cal. W.P. xix, 57, no date; *Diary* 19 July 1659. The following month he asked Whitelocke (who was by that time Lord President of the Council), to arrange that when Captain Talbot's officers approached Parliament, he would see to it that their petition was read; Whitelocke would receive the text of it from Thomas Clarges. Monck also asked him to stand the friend of the four officers who were honest, faithful and stout men, and there were not better left in the Army. (Parliament had been interfering with the composition of Thomas Talbot's regiment of foot), Long. W.P. xix, 78; *Diary* 29 Aug. 1659.

After the tables were turned, in Jan. 1659/60, Whitelocke wrote saying that someone near to Monck had written to an MP aggravating the crime of the Committee of Safety, and hinting that an example should be made of him (Whitelocke), because he had served on it. He appealed for clemency. In acting after the interruption of Parliament, his intention had been to prevent 'extravagancies' and to oppose the common enemy, but his mistakes had brought him, after long service, to the condition of expecting a sentence for his errors; if Monck judged it fit to write to the Speaker, interceding on his behalf for pardon, Whitelocke would ever be obliged to him, Long. W.P. xix, 114; also 116, 28 Jan. 1659/60 (drafts). In an undated reply Monck wrote that he knew nothing of the letter to an MP, but that he resented the speech Whitelocke had made at Guildhall, where the sincerity of his actions 'were more traduced that I deserv'd from any Man, but especially from yo[u]^r Lo[rdshi]^{ppe} of whose friendshippe I have ever had a great Esteeme.' Nevertheless, he would not increase Whitelocke's troubles on account of any particular unkindness to himself, but would endeavour to lessen them. It would not be proper for him to write to the Speaker, but he understood that the Speaker was well inclined to serve Whitelocke and he would encourage him to persevere in that, ib.118. In a servile draft of 6 Feb. 1659/60, Whitelocke thanked Monck for his great condescension in writing, and assured him that his own remarks at Guildhall had been misreported and misprinted (see *Diary* 8 Nov. 1659; Whitelocke had warned the City of Monck's intentions but had not, in fact, cast a slur on his sincerity); to have traduced Monck in public he wrote: 'had bin barbarous', Long. W.P. xix, 120. Monck's generous attitude soon altered and, according to Colonel William Willoughby (q.v.), his conduct after the Restoration became very overbearing and made many enemies for him in Parliament, *Diary* 6 June 1660.

That ends the Longleat correspondence between Whitelocke and Monck. Whitelocke wrote to Vice-Admiral John Lawson, soliciting support for his letter to Monck of 28 Jan. 1659/60 (above), and asking him to try to procure the letter from Monck to the Speaker, Long. W.P. xix,

126 (rough draft). Several diary entries concerning Monck appear around the time of the Restoration. Three years later, on 7 Nov. 1663, Whitelocke was consulted by the 2nd Duke of Buckingham (q.v.), about conveyancing the great estate of Newhall, Essex, to George Monck, by then 1st Duke of Albemarle. The sales particulars show the total valuation as £108,750.15s.0d. for the house with 2,600 acres, ib.xxv, 133, 133v.

ALLEYNE (ALLEYN, ALLEN, ALLIN), Sir Thomas, Bt. (d. 1690). A.B.B. ii, lv, 81, *passim*. A grocer; he served the Commonwealth and was Lord Mayor of London in 1659, yet was knighted and created Baronet by Charles II in 1660. He is referred to half a dozen times, not by name but as Lord Mayor, around the time of the Restoration, *Diary* 25 Apr. 1660, *passim*.

ALSTON, Sir Edward, MD (1595–1669). W. Munk *Roll of the Royal College of Physicians*; *D.N.B.* President of the College of Physicians. He and his daughter appear briefly in *Diary* 20 Sept., 18, 28 Oct. 1661.

ALURED, Col. Matthew, C. Firth and G. Davies *Regimental History of Cromwell's Army*; T. Carlyle *Letters and Speeches of Oliver Cromwell* (ed. S.C. Lomas. Methuen. 1904); *Restoration* p.19, *passim*. Brother of the regicide, Colonel John Alured. He is only referred to by Whitelocke, in 1659 and 1660.

ANDREWES (ANDREWS), Sir Thomas (d.1659). A.B.B. ii, xxvii, lv, 66, *passim*. G.E. Aylmer 'Check-list of Central Office-holders' (1976). A leatherseller. He served as Treasurer at Wars from 1645–1651/2 and as Treasurer for various land sales from 1649–1654. Lord Mayor of London in 1649 (for part of the year), and in 1650–1651. Knighted by the Protector in 1657; he had been in Court when sentence was passed on Charles I. Earlier, his signature as Lord Mayor and Treasurer, appeared on a certificate in connection with the advance of money (by Thomas Knight and Bulstrode Whitelocke) for lands in Ireland, 9 June 1649, Long. W.P. x, 14. Whitelocke refers to Andrewes in his capacity as Lord Mayor, *Diary* 5 Apr., 7 June 1649.

ANGLESEY (ANGLESEA), Arthur Annesley, 1st E. of (1614–1686). G.E.C.; *D.N.B.; Hist. of Parl.* (under Annesley).

ANNESLEY, George. Add. Ms 4995, appendix 5 fol. 12. Son of Viscount Valentia and brother of the 1st Earl of Anglesey (above). A gentleman of the first rank attending Whitelocke in Sweden.

ANTRIM, Randal MacDonnell, 1st Marquis of (1609–1683). G.E.C.; *D.N.B.* A Roman Catholic; arrested on a charge of high treason, *Diary* 8 July 1660.

APSLEY, James, *D.N.B.* (entry for his brother Sir Allen, 1616–1683). A Royalist; he attempted to murder Ambassador St. John (q.v.) at The Hague, *Diary* 14 Apr. 1650.

ARCHER, Judge John (1598–1682). *D.N.B.* He appears in *The Diary* briefly, on and between 28 Nov. 1658 and 23 June 1660.

ARGILE (ARGYLE), Archibald Campbell, 1st Marquis of (1598–1661). G.E.C.; *D.N.B.* He put the crown on the head of Charles II at Scone in 1651, but was later charged with high treason, *Diary* 8 July 1660, and was executed in Edinburgh.

ARLINGTON, Sir Henry Benet (Bennet), later 1st E. of (1618–1685). G.E.C.; *Hist. of Parl*; *D.N.B.*; *Pepys* x; J. Evelyn *Diary, passim.* Secretary of State. An unpleasant, ambitious man. Related to Whitelocke's first wife, Rebecca Benet. Created Baron in 1665 and 1st Earl in 1672.

ARUNDELL (ARUNDEL) and SURREY, Thomas Howard, 4th E. of (1628–1677). G.E.C. Suffered brain damage from a fever in 1645; he was one among several men, about whom Queen Christina (q.v.) spoke to Whitelocke, *Diary* 31 Dec. 1653. Arundell was pronounced a lunatic, and his estate was committed to the custody of the Earl of Northumberland and others, ib.15 Feb. 1654/55; Order from Chancery, 16 Feb. 1654/55, Long. W.P. xvii, 25. He was restored to the Dukedom of Norfolk in December 1660.

ASHBURNHAM, John, MP (1603–1671). M.F.K.; *Hist. of Parl.*; *D.N.B.*; *Pepys* x. A devoted Royalist. One of the King's Commissioners at Uxbridge, *Diary* 22 Feb. 1644/45.

ASHBURNHAM, William, MP (*c*.1604–1679). M.F.K.; *Hist. of Parl.*; *D.N.B.* Brother of John (above). Cofferer to Charles II. Whitelocke had troublesome encounters with him over the payment of wood bought for the King, *Diary* 30 Aug. 1661, 6, 18 Feb. 1661/62, *passim*.

ASHFIELD, Col. Richard. *Restoration* p. 19, *passim*. A Republican. Politically active as an army officer, *Diary* 6 May, 27 Oct. 1659, *passim*.

ASHLEY, Anthony Ashley Cooper, MP, 1st Baron (1621–1683). *Hist. of Parl.*; G.E.C.; *D.N.B.* Brother of George Cooper (q.v.). Whitelocke wrote to Lord Ashley about his intention to write a History of England, Add. Ms 32094 fols. 265–265v. Ashley was created 1st Earl of Shaftesbury in 1672. He appears in *The Diary* in 1659 and 1660.

ASHMOLE, Elias (1617–1692). *D.N.B.*; *Elias Ashmole ... His Auto-biographical Notes* etc. (ed. C.H. Josten. O.U.P. 1966). As Windsor Herald, he wrote to Whitelocke about the Swedish Order of Amaranth, *Diary* 16 Feb. 1670/71. He recorded Whitelocke's death, *Elias Ashmole ...* (above), iv, 1436.

ASHTON (ASSHETON), Sir Ralphe, Bt., MP (*c*.1605–1680). M.F.K.; D. Underdown *Pride's Purge* pp. 21, 106, *passim*; *Hist. of Parl.* Active in Parliament against Whitelocke; this was in retaliation for an alimony order made against him, earlier, by Whitelocke and others, *Diary* 1 June 1660.

ASTLEY, Sir Jacob, later Baron (1579–1652). *D.N.B.* A Royalist, incorrectly identified by Whitelocke as Governor of Oxford, *Diary* 22 Nov. 1644, with note.

ATKINS (ATKYNS), Sir Edward (1587–1669). *D.N.B.* A Baron of the Exchequer and Judge of Common Pleas. Knighted at the Restoration and reappointed a Judge. When riding the Oxfordshire Circuit, he stayed with the Whitelockes at Phyllis Court, *Diary* 29 July 1647; after Frances Whitelocke's death in 1649, the Judge tried to find a new wife for his friend, and was very kind to him, ib. 13 May 1650.

AUDELEY (AUDLEY), Hugh (d.1662). *D.N.B.* A trained lawyer and a money-lender. Referred to as 'Rich Mr Audeley' by Whitelocke, *Diary* 8 Apr. 1657, *passim*. It was said that he died worth £400,000.

AUGIER, René. G.E. Aylmer *King's Servants* pp. 358, 359 note, and *State's Servants* p. 19. The King's and later Parliament's Agent in Paris from about 1629 to 1649. Referred to in that capacity when Whitelocke visited France, *Diary* 1633. 1634. fols. 22, with note, and 23v. For newsletters addressed to Augier by Monsieur Petit in Paris (mainly on successful Huguenot protests, and on commercial matters), Feb., Mar. 1651/52, see Long. W.P. xii, 46, 50, 55.

AVERY, Richard (*c*.1634–1687). *Calamy Revised* pp. 19–20; *Alumni Oxonienses*. Chaplain to Richard Cromwell's wife, Dorothy. He visited his friend James Pearson (q.v.), tutor to Whitelocke's youngest children, and stayed the night at Chilton Lodge, returning to Newbury the next day, *Diary* 7, 8 Nov. 1671.

AXTELL, Col. Daniel (d.1660). *D.N.B.*; *Pepys* i, 268, with note, and 269. He commanded the soldiers at Westminster Hall during the King's trial. Colonel of a regiment in Ireland, *Diary* 20 Aug. 1659. In 1660 he was sent to the Tower and was executed for high treason.

AYSCUE (ASCUE, ASCUGH), Admiral Sir George (d.1671). *D.N.B.*; article by P. Le Fevre, 'Sir George Ayscue, Commonwealth and Restoration Admiral', *Mariner's Mirror* vol. 68, May 1982, pp. 189–202. Weybridge Museum, Surrey, has files on the Admiral and his moated house, Hamm Court, where he entertained the Swedish Ambassador, Christer Bonde (q.v.), accompanied by Whitelocke, *Diary* 13 Aug. 1656.

BACKWELL (BAKEWELL), Alderman Edward, MP (c.1618–1683). *Hist. of Parl.*; *D.N.B.*; A.B.B. i, 40, *passim*, ii, 187, *passim*; *Pepys* x. Beaven corrects some mistakes in the *D.N.B.* entry. An eminent Goldsmith-Banker, during both the Commonwealth and the reign of Charles II, Backwell was a founder of the English banking system; he lent small sums of money to Whitelocke and vast sums to the King and the Government.

BAGSHAWE (BAGSHAW), Edward, MP (d.1662). *D.N.B.*; M.F.K. A Middle Temple lawyer, he worked with Pym, but later joined the King in Oxford.

BALDWIN, Timothy (1620–1696). *D.N.B.* Civil lawyer, Royalist and Oxford academic. He sent Whitelocke his book, *Diary* 19 Feb. 1655/56, presumably *The Privileges of an Ambassador ...* (1654) concerning the charge of manslaughter brought against the Portuguese Ambassador's brother. He was knighted in 1670.

BALMERINO (BALMERINOCH), John Elphinstone, 2nd Baron (d.1649). G.E.C.; *D.N.B.* A leading Covenanter, active against Charles I. Whitelocke's client, *Diary* 14 Oct. 1645.

BALTIMORE, Cecil Calvert, 2nd E. of (c.1606–1675). G.E.C. Referred to only once by Whitelocke *Diary* 9 Aug. 1656.

BAMFIELD (BAMPFIELD), Col. Joseph (d.1685). *D.N.B.* Royalist officer; later a spy in Cromwell's service. Imprisoned, *Diary* 31 May 1660; released in 1661.

BAMFIELD (BAMPFIELD) Thomas, MP (1623–1693). *Hist. of Parl.*; *D.N.B.* Temporary Speaker of the House of Commons, *Diary* 16 Mar. 1658/59; then chosen as Speaker, ib. 14 Apr. 1659.

BANÉR (BANNIER), Gustav Persson (1618–1689). A Swedish Senator from 1652–1682.

BANÉR (BANNIER), Svante, the younger (1624–1674). Governor of Uppsala from 1652 to 1654.

BANKES, Sir John (1589–1644). *D.N.B.* Attorney-General, later Chief Justice of Common Pleas. A Royalist. He corresponded with Whitelocke over the appointment of Thomas Napper (q.v.); in 1638 he bought Kingston Lacy, in Dorset, from Bartholomew Hall (q.v.).

BAREBONE (BARBON), Praise, or Praise-God (c.1596–1679). *D.N.B.* (as Barbon); A. Woolrych *Commonwealth to Protectorate*; *Pepys x.* An ardent Anabaptist; member of the 'Little' or 'Barebone's' Parliament of 1653. Referred to in *Diary* 9 Feb. 1659/60; 31 Mar. 1660. He was sent to the Tower in 1661.

BARKER, Matthew (1619–1698). *D.N.B.*; *Restoration* p. 175. A Pastor, he was sent to Holyrood, with another Pastor and two former Officers, to try to persuade General Monck to a 'right understanding, of things, & to prevent effusion of blood', but the mission failed, *Diary* 1, 20 Nov. 1659.

BARKER, Nathaniel. *Liber* and 'Book of Bulstrode', for his ancestry. Of Sonning. He was related to Whitelocke by the marriage, in 1541, of Thomas Bulstrode to Anne, daughter of Ambrose Barker of Sonning. Nathaniel wrote in September 1653, of his 'weake estate' and begged his kinsman to take his son to Sweden as a member of the retinue, Long. W.P. xiii, 240. An entry in *Diary* 6 Aug. 1655 is presumed to refer to Nathaniel.

BARKER, 'Nephew'. He married Whitelocke's 'Niece Dixon'; possibly the son of Nathaniel (above). He negotiated to purchase Greenland from Whitelocke, but did not complete the deal; this did not, however, deter him from cutting down trees on the land at a great pace, *Diary* 4 Dec. 1666; 23 Feb. 1666/67; 7, 9, 16, 23, 25, 29 May 1667, *passim.*

BARNARDISTON, Sir Nathaniel, MP (1588–1653). *D.N.B.*; M.F.K. A Parliamentarian; only referred to once, acting with Sir Henry Vane, jun., in connection with the letter from Lord Savile, E. of Sussex (q.v.), *Diary* 8 July 1645.

BARNEWALL (BARNEWELL, BERNEWELL), Nicholas, 1st Viscount (1592–1663). G.E.C.; *D.N.B.* A Roman Catholic with royalist sympathies. He fled to Wales from Ireland. Whitelocke helped him, at the request of his sister, Elizabeth Mostyn, probably over a Sequestration Order by the Protector and a charge that Barnewall had been connected with a plot against Cromwell in 1654, *Diary* 10 Sept. 1656; 30 May 1657.

BARTLETT, Dr. Add. Ms 53726 fol. 97v., *passim*; Long. W.P. vi, 88, 101. A physician, who practised in Bow as a specialist in treating emotional disorders. He demanded £200 in 1634 to cure Rebecca Whitelocke, plus £2. 10s. 0d. a week for her keep. His wife, Mary Bartlett, is referred to by Whitelocke as being his cousin.

BASENET, Nathaniel. A Presentation deed by Whitelocke to the Bishop, to institute Basenet as Rector of Fawley, is in the Lincolnshire Archives Office, Diocesan Records P.D./1668/13. After his induction, Basenet continued to preach in conventicles at Ditton Park, for Anne and Richard Winwood (q.v.).

BASTWICK, Dr John (1593–1654). *D.N.B.*

BATCHELOR (BATCHELER), JOHN (d.1674). *Calamy Revised* p. 34. An ousted minister, he preached at the Winwoods' home and also for Whitelocke's family in 1667 and 1671.

BATEMAN, —. A kinsman of Whitelocke's and curate of Chilton Foliat in 1671.

BATES (BATE), George, MD (1608–1669). *D.N.B.*; W. Munk *Roll of the Royal College of Physicians* pp. 228–229. Physician to Charles I and Charles II, and to Cromwell. One of several doctors consulted when Frances Whitelocke (q.v.) was dying, *Diary* 4, 8, 9 May 1649. He wrote probably the earliest contemporary history of the Civil War, *A Compendious Narrative of the late Troubles in England*, or *Elenchus* (London. 1652). Translated from his original version in Latin. Reprinted in London in 1902.

BAYLIE (BAYLY), Dr Richard (c.1586–1667). W.C. Costin *History of St. John's College Oxford 1598–1860* (O.U.P. 1958). President of St. John's from 1633–1648, and 1660–1667. Dean of Salisbury from 1635 until his death. A revealing conversation, which took place in about November 1634, between Dr. Baylie and a very outspoken Whitelocke, followed Laud's rebuke to Whitelocke for his runaway marriage:

D^r [Baylie]	When were you with our old friend my Lords Grace of Canterbury?
Wh[itelocke]	our old friend hath gott new friends, & is so great & angry a man, that so meane a fellow as I am, cannot take much pleasure in waiting on him.
D^r	... he hath a great kindnes for you, & the oftener you apply yourselfe to him, the better, for no man is more able than he to doe you good ... he loves you, & tooke the care of your education in our Colledge, & he was your fathers old friend.
Wh.	Butt when you great Doctors come to be made Bishops it doth much impayre your memories of old acquaintance & new Sycophants that flatter & humor you most, are by some of you most respected.
D^r	You were alwayes wont to have a puritannicall jerke att the Church.
Wh.	I hope that I am as much one of the Church, as any man that weares a Canonicall coate or a silke girdle.
D^r	This comes uppon the same straine, & you will not leave your puritan perswasions.
Wh.	I shall begin to thinke it better to be a Puritan, then a proud & angry Prelat.
D^r	Methinkes you are very angry, I pray tell me, hath there bin lately any unkindnes between my Lord of Canterbury & you, that hath putt you into this passion?
Wh.	I will tell you all D^r as my old friend ... [he proceeds to do so]
D^r	Shall I tell him your words, that he used you more like a porter then a gentleman?
Wh.	Yes, if you please, ... & that theruppon I resolved to come no more att him, till I were assured of better treatment ...
D^r	You must not be too stout, especially with a person of his condition.
Wh.	... I have no dependance uppon his Grace, nor expect any preferrement by him either in Church or State ... butt Mr President, English gentlemen are distasted att nothing more, then att reproaches from their superiors whom they have knowne not so much above them, till the Kings favour made the distinction ... Mr President I am much obliged to you, for your antient friendship, & favour to a St Johns man.

Add. Ms 37343 fols. 11–12v.

The outcome was an invitation to dine at Lambeth, when Laud went out of his way to put matters right.

BEAKE (BEKE), Capt., later Major Richard, MP. Add. Ms 4995 appendix 5, fol. 12. A gentleman at Whitelocke's table and Captain of his Guard in Sweden; described as '... of the army ... eldest son of an esquire, of a good estate in Buckinghamshire ...', *Journal* (1st edn. 1772) ii, 463. In July 1654 he was supported by Whitelocke as a parliamentary candidate for Buckinghamshire, Long. W.P. xvi, 74; ib. Parcel 4, No. 29; he was knighted by Richard Cromwell, *Diary* 6 Dec. 1658. On the evidence, he appears to have been Captain Richard Beke (1630–1707), of Dinton, Bucks. (eldest son of Henry Beke of Haddenham, Bucks.) who served as an MP before and after the Restoration, see *Hist. of Parl.*

BECHE, de la, family of: Whitelocke's ancestors. See chapter 1 of *The Diary*.

BEDFORD, William Russell, 5th E. of, created 1st D. of in 1694 (1613–1700). G.E.C.; *D.N.B.* He left Parliament's Army for the King's in 1643, but returned in the same year.

BEDINGFIELD, Sir Thomas, MP (*c.*1593–1661). *D.N.B.*; M.F.K. A Justice of Common Pleas.

BELLASIS (BELASYSE) of WORLABY, John, MP, later 1st Baron (1615–1689). G.E.C.; M.F.K. (which refers to errors in the *D.N.B.* entry). A distinguished royalist Commander; G.E.C. shows him as Governor of Hull from 1661 to 1673; *Diary* refers to him in that office in August 1660.

BENET (BENNET), Dorothy (formely MAY), of Cheapside and Mortlake, Long, W.P. v, 244. Sister of Sir Humphrey May (q.v.) and widow (by the time she appears in *The Diary*) of Alderman Thomas Benet, mercer and Sheriff of London; see *Complete Baronetage* iii, 130 (in the entry for her son Sir Thomas Benet, q.v.). Her other children named in *The Diary* and in this volume, were Richard and Sir Humphrey Benet, also Whitelocke's first wife, Rebecca, whose disastrous marriage was celebrated in the private chapel of Dorothy Benet's country house in Mortlake. Rebecca's sister, Mrs. Amcotes, is mentioned once only, at the time of Rebecca's death in 1634, and is described as being 'in the same condition' as Rebecca (i.e. mentally disturbed) and in the care of the same doctor.

BENET (BENNET), Sir Henry, see ARLINGTON, 1st E. of.

BENET (BENNET), Sir Humphrey (Humfry), Kt., MP (c.1605–1667). *Hist. of Parl.*; *Liber* p. 110. Son of Thomas Benet, Sheriff, and of Dorothy Benet (above); brother of Richard Benet (q.v.), Sir Thomas Benet Bt. (q.v.), and of Rebecca Whitelocke (q.v.). Although a Royalist, he rescued Whitelocke, his brother-in-law, from attack by Royalists in the streets of Oxford, *Diary* 1642.1643. fol. 61v. Benet, in turn, was helped by Whitelocke when charged with conspiracy, *Diary* 9 June 1658.

BENET (BENNET), Sir Levinus, 2nd Bt., MP (c.1631–1693). *Hist. of Parl.*; *Complete Baronetage* iii, 130–131. Eldest son of Sir Thomas Benet 1st Bt. (q.v.) and of Lady Mary Benet (below); heir to Babraham, in Cambridgeshire. He was Whitelocke's client in 1669 and 1670.

BENET (BENNET), Lady Mary, daughter of Levinus Munck (Monke), one of the Clerks to the Signet. Wife of Sir Thomas Benet, 1st Bt. (q.v.), who died in 1667; she became Whitelocke's client in 1668.

BENET (BENNET), Richard (c.1595–1658). *V.C.H. Cambs.* vi, 21. Of the Inner Temple, later of Chancery Lane; elder brother of Sir Thomas Benet (below). A monument in St. Peter's Church, Babraham, states that he and his brother Thomas were both Baronets, but this does not seem to be confirmed elsewhere. He was helped by Whitelocke with his sequestration in 1647 and was able, in return, to lend his brother-in-law £500 in 1657, Long. W.P. xviii, 66. He and his brother, Sir Thomas, married the daughters of Levinus Munck (Monke).

BENET (BENNET), Sir Thomas, created 1st Bt., 1660 (c.1597–1667). *Complete Baronetage* iii, 130. Of the Inner Temple; owner of Babraham, Cambridgeshire, which his father, Thomas Benet, Mercer, of London, had bought in 1620. Sir Thomas was Whitelocke's brother-in-law. For further details, see the entries for his mother, Dorothy Benet, for his brothers Sir Humphrey and Richard (above) and for his son, Sir Levinus (q.v.).

BERESFORD, Christopher. Add. Ms 37343 fols. 136v.–137. Agent to the 7th Earl of Rutland, but busy with the King's affairs when Whitelocke and Frances stayed at Belvoir Castle in August 1635, hoping to secure Frances' inheritance from the trustees to her father's Will. For a Bill in the Court of Wards on a similar matter, naming Beresford among others, Oct. 1637, see Long W.P. vii, 131v.

BERKLEY (BERKELEY), George, 8th Baron (1601–1658). G.E.C.; *D.N.B.* Son of Sir Thomas Berkley and Elizabeth, daughter of George Carey, 2nd Baron of Hunsdon. Four months after the death of Whitelocke's wife, Frances, Lord Berkley lent Whitelocke his 'house near Hunstone', *Diary* 21 Sept. 1649.

BERKLEY (BERKELEY), George, 9th Baron and 1st E. of, Viscount Dursley (1628–1698). G.E.C.; *D.N.B.*; *Pepys* x. Sent as a Commissioner to Charles II in May 1660; the following month he was present at the Lord Mayor's Banquet for the King; in July, he was deputed to thank the King for raising Monck to the peerage. He was one of the original Fellows of the Royal Society.

BERKLEY (BERKELEY) of STRATTON, John, 1st Baron (c.1606–1678). G.E.C.; *D.N.B.*; *Pepys* x. Comptroller of the Duke of York's household in exile. He later consulted Whitelocke, *Diary* 21 Apr. 1663.

BERKMAN (BARKMAN), Jean. See Baron Leyonbergh.

BERKSHIRE, Thomas Howard, 1st E. of (c.1590–1669). G.E.C.; Long. W.P. viii, 85, Jan. 1640/41 gives an abstract of his patent for the farm of post fines. He pressed Whitelocke to join him in developing a new type of malt-kiln (for which he had acquired the patent) and wanted him to persuade Henley men to use it; for some reason Whitelocke judged this to be illegal and dishonourable, and so made an enemy of the Earl, *Diary*

1636.1637. fol. 43. Later, receiving instructions from Parliament to prevent the Earl and others from executing the King's Commission of Array in Watlington, Oxfordshire, Whitelocke captured the Earl. Attempting to show his prisoner courtesy on the ride to Henley, Whitelocke found him 'very proud & peevish, sullen & empty in his discourse', so left it to the guards to escort him to London on the following day; the House of Lords committed the Earl and his associates to prison, where he 'lay a long time, not enquired after nor missed or condoled by his Countrey [i.e. County], where he had not much love', ib. 1642.1643. fol.56. In 1649 Whitelocke replaced the Earl as High Steward of Oxford but when, at the Restoration, the tables were turned the Earl had his revenge, *Diary* 30 May, 7 June 1660.

BEUNINGEN, Coenraad (Conrad) van (1622–1693). His diplomatic activities were the subject of a doctoral thesis by M.A.M. Franken, at the University of Utrecht; there are many entries relating to him in *Thurloe S.P.*, and in Long. 124A fols. 125–128v., 134–135v. As Netherlands Ambassador to Sweden, his letters to the States General were frequently intercepted by Thurloe's agents, and translations were sent to Whitelocke in Uppsala. He was Ambassador Extraordinary to England in the 1670s.

BIRKENHEAD (BERKENHEAD), Sir John, MP (1617–1679). *Hist. of Parl.*; *D.N.B.* He devised the royalist news-sheet, *Mercurius Aulicus*, in 1642. More than 20 years later, he was helpful to Whitelocke in Parliament, *Diary* 7, 8 May 1663.

BISHOP, Capt. George. G.E. Aylmer *State's Servants* p. 21, *passim*. Secretary to the Intelligence and Examinations Committees. His letter to Whitelocke in Sweden, 10 Nov. 1653, Long. W.P. xiv, 182, enclosed an alarming paper, ib. 181: this reported a discussion between royalist agents who thought Whitelocke 'must have great fortune if he scaped the fortune of Dorislaus and Ascham'. There were two in Sweden already 'that were used to that sport [assassination] & would attempt him.' Bishop intended to look after Whitelocke's safety, although just 'putting foot in stirrup for Bristol' where he hoped to live retired, serving the public in a private capacity. He confirmed that Whitelocke's wife had been delivered of 'a brave boy'. Some years later, Captain George Bishop was named by an informant as having conspired 'soon after his highness was declared lord protector', at meetings with Colonel Sexby, Major Wildman (q.v.), George Cokayn (q.v., Independent Minister and Whitelocke's close friend) and

Captain (Vice-Admiral) Lawson (q.v.), 27 Feb. 1657, *Thurloe S.P.* vi, 829–830.

BISHOP (BYSHOP), Richard, of the Manor of South Warnborough. *V.C.H. Hants* iii, 378–379; for an Ordinance of Parliament that Bishop should pay Whitelocke £500, plus interest, 18 Sept. 1644, see Long. W.P. ix, 31–32; Bishop owed money to the delinquent William Sandys, who was in debt to Whitelocke, *Diary* Sept. 1644, fol. 66v.

BLAGUE (BLAGGE, BLAKE), Col. Thomas (1613–1660). Musgrave *Obituary* i, 191; Stow *Survey of London* (revised J. Strype. 1720) ii, Book vi, 15. *Memorials* ii,55, records Blague's financial malpractice as royalist Governor of Wallingford Castle. He was a Groom of the Bedchamber to Charles I and Charles II, and was buried in Westminster Abbey. Whitelocke considered him haughty and quarrelsome, *Diary* Nov. 1644 fols. 67v., 68, *passim*.

BLAKE, General Robert (1599–1657). *D.N.B.* Admiral and General-at-Sea. Whitelocke wrote that Blake was 'a man of as much gallantry & sincerity as any in his time' and that he himself lost a great friend by the General's death, *Diary* 10 Aug. 1657. Blake was buried in Westminster Abbey; Whitelocke attended the funeral, ib. 4 Sept. 1657. The body was disinterred after the Restoration.

BLANDY (BLUNDY), John, of Inglewood, Kintbury, Berks. Whitelocke signed a bond to Blandy in 1663, receipts are dated 1666 and 1669, Long. W.P. xx, 104–104v., 119. See also *Diary* 30 Aug., 7 Oct. 1664. (A Mr. Blandy from Wantage was a client of Whitelocke's, ib. 13 May 1672; 5 May 1673.)

BODVILE, Anne. M.F.K. Daughter of Sir William Russell; she deserted her husband John Bodvile, MP for Anglesey. She and Mrs. Winwood (q.v.) visited Whitelocke when his doctors said he was too ill to have visitors, *Diary* 19 Dec. 1649.

BONDE (BOND, BUNDT), Count Christer (Krister) (1621–1659) *Swedish Diplomats at Cromwell's Court . . . The Missions of Peter Julius Coyet and Christer Bonde* (translated and edited by M. Roberts. Camden 4th series. 1988). The work contains interesting references to Whitelocke. Bonde was a Swedish Senator and Ambassador Extraordinary to England. Known to Whitelocke in Uppsala and London. He wrote to Whitelocke about the anxiety of King Charles X of Sweden to be on friendly terms with the Protector, 5 May 1655, Long. W.P. xvii, 45, (Latin); reply, fol. 46.

BONNEL (BONNEALE, BONNELL, BONELE), Benjamin. Commissioner for Trade from Queen Christina of Sweden. He had extensive correspondence with the Council, pressing for the release of captured Swedish ships and their cargoes in 1653 and 1654, ib. xiii, 40–41, *passim*; xiv 5–6, *passim*; xv, 53; xvi, 125; Long. 124A, 157–157v.

BOOTH, Sir George, Bt., MP, later 1st Baron Delamer (1622–1684). *Hist. of Parl.*; *D.N.B.* A disillusioned Cromwellian, he led the Cheshire rising before the Restoration, in 1659. There are numerous diary references in connection with his rising.

BORLACE (BORLASE, BURLASE), Sir John, Bt., MP (1619–1672). M.F.K.; *Hist. of Parl.* Of Marlow, Buckinghamshire. Grandson of Sir Francis Popham, sen.; son-in-law of Sir John Bankes (q.v.). In 1640, Whitelocke stood against him in a bitterly-contested election for the Long Parliament. As neighbours they had many encounters, social and professional, the last one recorded being in *Diary* 26 Apr. 1666.

BOTELER (BUTLER), Hugh. *Calamy Revised* pp. 92–94. Ejected as Rector of Beaconsfield in 1660, he preached in Whitelocke's bedroom (when the latter was ill in London), and later wrote about Whitelocke's mother-in-law, *Diary* 19 Feb. 1664/65; 25 Mar. 1669.

BOTELER (BUTLER), William. C. Firth and G. Davies *Regimental History of Cromwell's Army*; P.H. Hardacre 'William Boteler: A Cromwellian Oligarch' *Huntingdon Library Quarterly* Vol. xi, No. 1, Nov. 1947 pp. 1–11; *Restoration* pp. 48, 72–73, *passim*. A hated Cromwellian Major-General. Under great pressure from Charles Fleetwood (q.v.) Whitelocke,

when reappointed Keeper of the Great Seal, reluctantly appointed Colonel
Boteler as Secretary to the Seal, instead of his own faithful and experienced
Secretary, Daniel Earle (q.v.), *Diary* 2 Nov. 1659. Later references,
however, show that Whitelocke and Boteler were on good terms after the
Restoration, ib. 10 Dec. 1668, *passim*.

BOULTE (BOLTE, BOLT), Michael (Mykell). Paid Whitelocke his first
fee; Mayor of Henley in 1643; he wrote offering the services of his son, a
soldier who had served the Commonwealth faithfully, for Whitelocke's
security in Sweden, 22 Sept. 1653, Long. W.P. xiii, 226.

BOYLE, The Hon. Robert (1627–1691). *D.N.B.* A distinguished scholar
and scientist, he formulated 'Boyle's Law'. Brother of Baron Broghill
(later E. of Orrery, q.v.), and of Lady Ranelagh (q.v.), with whom he
lived in London. Whitelocke met him at Lady Ranelagh's house, *Diary*
20 Jan. 1669/70 with note; 26 Mar. 1670.

BOYS (BOIS), Sir Edward, MP (1579–1646). M.F.K. Royalist Governor
of Greenland Garrison (adjoining the Fawley Court estate) near Henley-
on-Thames.

BRADSHAW (BRADESHAW, BRADSHAWE), John, MP (1602–1659).
D.N.B. A Barrister; President of the High Court of Justice which
condemned Charles I to death. Whitelocke was walking in procession near
to Bradshaw, at the funeral of Col. Rowland Wilson (q.v.), when the
crowd of bystanders yelled: 'heer is the Rogue that judged the King, Kill
him, Kill him, Lett us teare him in pieces'. Much shaken, Bradshaw
appealed to Whitelocke not to leave him, and together they slipped down a
lane, before reaching the Church, and went home, *Diary* 5 Mar. 1649/50.
As a staunch Republican, Bradshaw opposed the Protectorate; Whitelocke
refrained from taking sides but tried to lessen the hostility between
Bradshaw and Cromwell, ib. 3 Dec. 1657.

BRADSHAW, Richard. Nephew of John (above). He was appointed
Agent to the King of Denmark in Nov. 1652, then Resident in Hamburg
and 'Deputy' there in charge of the English Company of Merchant
Adventurers. He corresponded with Whitelocke in Uppsala in Nov. 1653,

Jan. 1653/54 and Apr. 1654, Long. W.P. xiv, 195; xv, 19, 110, 113 (enc.); xvi, 45; moreover, he cordially invited Whitelocke to stay in the Merchant Adventurers' house in Hamburg, on the journey home from Sweden to England, with his retinue. Shortly after Whitelocke's visit, hostility towards Bradshaw erupted, inspired by an ambitious young merchant, Francis Townley. Vitriolic letters were sent by both factions to Samuel Avery (Governor of the Merchant Adventurers in England), also to Cromwell and to Whitelocke. After Bradshaw's allies had left a particular meeting, Townley was swiftly voted into the post of Deputy by his supporters. The Bradshaw faction wrote of the 'destructive combination' of Townley's friends, of 'clandestine and disorderly proceedings' and of the threat to their immunities and privileges in the City, ib. 57–57v., 61, 63, 65, 80 (Avery's reply to Bradshaw), 87–87v., 95, 102. See also *Royal Commission on Historical Manuscripts*, 6th Report, appendix pt. i, 426; this entry refers to a conspiracy to murder Bradshaw, to his being despatched in April 1657 on a mission to Russia, after the troubles in Hamburg, and to his later returning there. Bradshaw continued to ask Whitelocke for help in 1657 and 1659, Long. W.P. xviii, 45; xix, 33. Earlier letters from Bradshaw on trade matters etc. appear in *Thurloe S.P.* ii, 123, 180, 209–210, with complaints against Townley in iv, 103, *passim*; see also *C.S.P. Dom.* 1655–1656 pp. 283–284.

BRAHE, Count Per (1602–1680). Provost-Marshal of Sweden; Governor of Finland; said to have been the richest man in Sweden. His *Tänkebok* (i.e. memoirs) was published in 1806.

BRAMSTON (BRAMPSTON), Francis (d.1683). *D.N.B.* A Bencher and Reader of the Middle Temple in 1668; in that year Whitelocke was deprived of his Temple Chambers, which were given to Bramston.

BRAMSTON, Sir John, sen. (1577–1654). *D.N.B.* A King's Bench Judge and a Keeper of the Great Seal.

BRIDGEMAN, Sir Orlando, Bt. (1609–1674). M.F.K.; *D.N.B.* A Royalist. Lord Chief Baron of the Exchequer; he presided at the trial of the regicides, and served as Lord Keeper after Clarendon's fall. Whitelocke believed that Bridgeman was unfriendly towards him in a Chancery case, *Diary* 10, 22 July 1669.

BRISTOL, George Digby, MP, later 2nd E. of (c.1612–c.1677). G.E.C.; D.N.B.; M.F.K. A Royalist. One of Whitelocke's Committee which handled the evidence against the Earl of Strafford (q.v.). Digby opposed the third reading of the Bill of Attainder against the Earl. He was impeached during his absence, in 1642. Many years later he attempted to impeach the Earl of Clarendon (q.v.), Diary 10 July 1663. As a young lawyer, Whitelocke had taken notes on the impeachment of Digby's father, the 1st E. of Bristol, Long. W.P. iii, 42, 1626.

BROGHILL, Baron, see ORRERY, 1st E. of.

BROMAN, Lars (1615–1669). S.B.L.; H. Almquist Göteborgs Historia i, 369–379, passim. Studied at Uppsala University. He was one of Göteborg's (Gothenburg's) three Presidents who were entertained to dinner by Whitelocke, Diary 25 Nov. 1653; Broman wrote the next day to Erik (Eric) Oxenstierna (q.v.), describing the meal: glasses of apple juice with bread and sugar in them, followed by delicious English food, good beer and 'lovely French wine'. Whitelocke drank to each of his guests but there were no official toasts to the Swedish or the English government. After dinner, as they sat round the fire, Whitelocke offered each of his guests a pipe of tobacco, and members of his household played violin music, H. Almquist (above) p. 544.

BROOKE, Lady Catharine (d. c.1676). G.E.C.; D.N.B. (entry for Robert Greville, 2nd Baron BROOKE). Daughter of Francis Russell, 4th Earl of Bedford.

BROWNE (BROWN), Major-General, later Sir Richard, Bt., MP (d.1669). Hist. of Parl.; D.N.B.; Memorials i, 356, passim; ii, 469; Pepys i, 64, passim. A woodmonger of Whitefriars. He became a parliamentarian officer who turned Royalist; he was subsequently knighted and made Lord Mayor of London in 1660. In the first entry for Browne, Whitelocke refers to him as an honest-dealing woodmonger, Diary 1638. 1639. fol. 47. Later he noted 'the height [i.e. haughtiness] of Brown', by then a Major-General sent by Parliament to effect the surrender of Greenland, a royalist Garrison. This achieved, Browne would do nothing to help Whitelocke recover possessions which Parliament's soldiers had looted (presumably from Fawley Court) and sold in Henley and the neighbourhood, ib. 1643.

1644. fols. 65, 65v. Yet later, Browne frequently turned to Whitelocke for advice and help, ib. fols. 66, 70v.–71, *passim*.

BROWNE (BROWN), Samuel, Kt., MP (*c*.1598–1668). *D.N.B.*; M.F.K.; *Hist. of Parl.* A Commissioner of the Great Seal. As a Judge, he refused to act under the Republic. Earlier, he had been Chairman of the Committee which dealt with Lord Savile's charges, in 1645, against both Denzil Holles (q.v.) and Whitelocke.

BRUNNIUS, Dr. Erik (1597–1664). *S.B.L.* A learned scholar; Super-intendent of the Church in Gothenburg. He sent a letter to Whitelocke congratulating him on his successful journey towards Uppsala and giving an introduction to his brother-in-law, Jacobus Lenæus, son of the Archbishop of Uppsala, 14 Dec. 1653, Long. W.P. xiv, 228, (Latin).

BUCKINGHAM, George Villiers, 1st Marquess then 1st D. of (1592–1628). G.E.C.; *D.N.B.* He was created Marquess in 1617/18, and was appointed Lord High Admiral of England in 1618/19. The instructions he gave for the government of H.M. Navy laid down the duties of those serving at all levels: officers, comptrollers, porters, boatswains etc., Long W.P. Parcel 4, No. 25 (six folios of a manuscript book). An outspoken letter from Thomas Alured (q.v.) to the Marquess, in 1623, deplored the proposed match between Prince Charles and the Spanish Infanta and its likely effects on England and the protestant religion, Long. W.P. ii, 118–120v. An account of the reception accorded to Prince Charles at Madrid (escorted by Buckingham who was sent to negotiate the match) and of the Duke's unpopularity, is given in a letter from Madrid of 20/30 Sept. 1623, ib. 106. (Buckingham was created Duke in May 1623, while he was still in Spain.) A Commission for the Duke to receive Henrietta Maria is dated 6 May 1625, ib. Parcel 3, No. 13 (Latin).

There is also a paper headed 'One man the generall cause of all our ills', with six short headings, 11 Mar. 1625/26, ib. No. 15; the rough draft of a letter from young Whitelocke (mistakenly attributed, in the Calendar, to Judge Sir James Whitelocke, to whom it appears to have been addressed) describes events connected with the Duke's impeachment by the Commons in Charles's second Parliament; it refers to the declaration against Buckingham which the King refused to receive, to Charles dissolving Parliament in June 1626, and to an order that anyone possessing a copy of the declaration or notes on it must burn them, Long. W.P. iii, 46; a draft

PLATE I

George Monck, 1st Duke of Albemarle.

PLATE 2

Ambassador Coenraad van Beuningen, by Caspar Netscher.

PLATE 3

Roger Boyle, Baron Broghill and 1st Earl of Orrery.

PLATE 4

Charles X of Sweden.

letter to someone in Paris covers the same events with additional details, ib. 46v. After Buckingham's assassination, and seven years after his abortive crusade on behalf of the Huguenots, the Duke's adventure still rankled in Frenchmen's memory (see a compressed account of a tense conversation at sea, *Diary*, summer 1634, fols. 26v–27):

Wh[itelocke]:	Gentlemen, I am sorry you have such a leisure time being becalmed, will you give me leave to discourse, and take a pipe of Tobacco with those of you who I see take it?
[French] Marryner:	You may sitt downe among us if you will, but perhaps our discourse will not be very pleasing to you.
Wh.	Why? What unpleasant discourse have you undertaken?
Ma.	We are discoursing of the base action of your Countrymen, when without any cause they invaded our Kings territories, & landed an Army att the Isle of Rea. [i.e. Ré]
Wh.	I confesse I cannot justify that action, nor many actions of our State, butt we poore inferior men, neither understood them, nor had any hand in them.
Ma.	It was a Warre & enterprise of your Nation, & you are all guilty of the french bloud which was shed there & by the Hugenots, whom you assisted, in rebellion against their King, & revenge may be taken uppon any of you English for it.
Wh.	The Hugenots had no great advantage by the English, nor did the English gaine much by that action ... butt prithee take a pipe of my tobaccoe, tell me whither thou likest it or not ...
Ma.	I care not if I tast of your tobaccoe, butt that action of the English will never be forgot by us, & it were just to be revenged uppon any of you, wheresoever we meet you.
Wh.	... If you meet with any that were ingaged in that action ... you might have more to say to them ...
Ma.	You are all concernd in it, for it was the action of your Nation, & every Englishman is lyable to suffer for it ... your action att the Isle of Rea was very bad & bloudy & you are all guilty of it.
Wh.	... Those that did it, lett them suffer, I assure you, most part of the Nation, disliked the designe, & were against it ...

Add. Ms 53726 fols. 106–107v.

The conversation, of which this is only an excerpt, was presumably conducted in French.

BUCKINGHAM, George Villiers, 2nd D. of (1628–1687). G.E.C.; *D.N.B.* He was helped by Whitelocke with his sequestration. After his involvement in the second Civil War, July 1648, he fled to Holland and was declared a traitor by the Commons. Buckingham welcomed it when Whitelocke (his relative by marriage, see below) was given a share of his Chelsea house with John Lisle (q.v.); this was granted to them by Parliament in July 1649. The Duke married Thomas Fairfax's daughter Mary in 1657; he was committed to the Tower in August 1659, but his estate was restored to him in May 1660. He appears to have gone back on his word to reimburse whatever money Whitelocke laid out on the upkeep of his Chelsea house: Whitelocke applied for £2,000 and was advised to accept £1,000, *Diary* 16 July 1661, *passim.*

BUCKINGHAM, Katherine, Duchess of (d.1649). G.E.C. Daughter of Francis Manners, 6th Earl of Rutland, and cousin of Whitelocke's second wife, Frances; she was the wife of the 1st Duke of Buckingham (q.v.). The *D.N.B.* (John Williams's entry) states that in 1620, when Williams (q.v.) was Dean of Salisbury, he persuaded her to renounce the Roman Catholic faith, without which James I would have forbidden the marriage; she later resumed her previous faith. In a letter of 14 May 1636, addressed to 'my loving Cusin Mr Whitelocke', she asked him to lend £20 to her cousin Mrs. Thynne (q.v., who had helped Whitelocke with his runaway marriage), since the Duchess's own rents had not come in and there were many demands on her money, Add. Ms 37343 fol. 147 (transcript). The letter is signed K. Buckingham, despite the fact that in April 1635 she had married Randal MacDonnell, Marquess of Antrim.

BULL, Anthony. *Liber* pp. 21, 45. A gentleman of Judge Sir James Whitelocke's household for 40 years, he knew how to manage his sometimes irascible master, Add. Ms 53726 fol. 68v.

BULL, Mrs. Anthony. As a widow, she appealed to Whitelocke for financial help, *Diary* 15 Sept. 1656.

BULLER, Col. Anthony, MP (1613–1679). *Hist. of Parl.*; C. Dalton *English Army Lists and Commission Registers* (London. 1892) i, 67. The fifth son of Sir Richard Buller, MP, of Shillingham, Cornwall, near Saltash, see M.F.K. A staunch Parliamentarian but not a Republican, the Colonel was Governor of the Scilly Isles from 1647 to 1648, and Deputy Governor from 1666 to 1667. He wrote suggesting a match between Whitelocke's son James and a niece of Colonel Popham (q.v.), *Diary* 25 May 1656. With the help of his eldest brother, Francis Buller, MP (*c*.1603–1677), see M.F.K., and of his nephew Francis (below), he procured a seat for Whitelocke's son William (q.v.) as MP for West Looe, Cornwall, *Diary* 6, 11 Jan. 1658/59. A very cordial note from the Colonel states that he called at Bishopsgate Street on the previous day (10 Jan.) to present his nephew's and his own respects and to tell Whitelocke of the seat procured for William. He gave his assurance that if there were 'any Commands further wherin My Rellations May be . . . servisable . . . you will find them ready . . . ' but that none was more desirous to serve Whitelocke than himself, from Dean's Yard, 11 Jan. 1658/59, Long. W.P. xix, 3.

BULLER, Francis, MP (1630–1682). *Hist. of Parl.* Son of Francis Buller and nephew of Anthony (above). Of Shillingham. He studied at the Middle Temple. Elected MP for Cornwall in 1659; for Saltash in 1660 and 1661. Five days before his uncle Anthony Buller's letter and visit to Bishopsgate Street, Francis wrote that he and his brother (unnamed) had called at Whitelocke's lodgings, but had not had the happiness of finding him at home. They had wished to express their willingness to serve him 'in any thing in o[u]^r power'. Having heard that it would be acceptable to Whitelocke if young William were to become an MP '. . . and being well assured of the qualities and abilities of your sonn for that service; we have used o[u]^r interest [i.e. influence] at West Looe (of which Towne my Brother is Recorder) [his brother John Buller MP is shown in *Hist. of Parl.* as the Town's Recorder 'c.April 1660'] & he [William Whitelocke] was yesterday (nemine contradicente) elected Burgesse . . .' The letter is signed 'Fran: Buller jnr.', 6 Jan. 1658/59, Long. W.P. xix,1, Shillingham. Below his letter, in a different hand, is a note evidently written by his father. This concerns difficulties with Thomas Povey (q.v.) who had made out that William was to be found a seat in Reading; this had delayed the proceedings in Cornwall: 'hee [Povey] will waite on you w[i]th excuses, & it may bee reflexions on mee . . . [but] after hee hath beene angry enough, y[ou]r Lordship may please to lett him see this letter', signed 'F. Buller', ib.

BULSTRODE family (below). Bulstrode Papers, Buckinghamshire R.O.; some details taken from 'The Book of Bulstrode', compiled by H.W. Bulstrode in 1939; Ms Rawl. B.73 fol. 163 provides a 17th century pedigree.

BULSTRODE, Judge Edward (1588–1659). *D.N.B.* Son of Edward Bulstrode of Hedgerly Bulstrode south-east of Beaconsfield, and brother of Henry (below). Whitelocke's maternal uncle. He studied at St. John's College, Oxford. An Inner Temple lawyer, and Reader in 1632. A discharge by the Committee of Sequestration was issued for him on 3 December 1647; later the Committee for Compounding ordered that he be permitted to enjoy his estate if there was no new matter against him, 24 February 1652. He was appointed a Commissioner for the Security of the Protector in 1656, see *A. and O.* He was buried in the Temple Church.

BULSTRODE, Col. Henry (1579–1643). *Liber* pp. 16, 28–29, *passim*; Long. W.P. ii, 200; iii, 1. Born and buried at Upton, near Windsor. Of University College, Oxford, and the Inner Temple. He was Whitelocke's uncle and godfather. High Sheriff of Buckinghamshire. He married Mary, daughter of Thomas Read, and lived at Horton. He served as Governor of Aylesbury during the first years of the Civil War. Some of his receipts and payments survive, in ib. vi, 82, 248; vii, 55, 74.

BULSTRODE, Sir Richard (1610–1711). *D.N.B.*; *Original Letters . . . Memoirs and Reflections . . .* Sir Richard Bulstrode's letters (when he was the Resident in Brussels) to Henry Coventry, Secretary of State, between 1674 and 1686, are in Long. Coventry Papers xxix–xxxii; Henry Coventry's letter-book contains copies of his letters to Sir Richard in Brussels, between 1674 and 1680, ib. lxxxviii (published posthumously). A Royalist, soldier and diplomat; Richard was a son of Judge Edward Bulstrode (q.v.), and Whitelocke's cousin. His *Memoirs . . .* tell nothing of his non-royalist activities during the Interregnum. He begged Whitelocke, in vain, to take him to Sweden, writing: '. . . I shall esteeme it as the greatest happinesse that has ever befallen me that I may have the honour of wayting upon your Lo[rdshi]p though in the meanest employment', 27 Sept. 1653, Long. W.P. xiii,244. On Whitelocke and Fleetwood's recommendation, he was elected Steward of Reading in 1656; Whitelocke saved him from a financial predicament in Reading, *Diary* 22 July 1658 with note. Richard held diplomatic appointments after the Restoration, notably in Brussels. A Roman Catholic, after the Revolution he followed King James II to St. Germain.

BULSTRODE, Col. Thomas (1602–1676). Son and heir of Henry Bulstrode of Horton (q.v.); Whitelocke's cousin. Of St. Alban's Hall, Oxford, and the Inner Temple. A Bencher. Sheriff of Buckinghamshire in 1643. An Officer in the 9th Regiment of Foot of the New Model Army. Briefly Governor of Phyllis Court (i.e. Henley) Garrison in 1644. In 1645, two years after his father's death, he was made Governor of Aylesbury, a post which his father had held. He wrote to Whitelocke in Sweden on 25 April 1654 (four months after Cromwell took power as Protector), describing him as '. . . the Almightyes Chiefe Instrument, in the supporting of us in these late dismall times . . . In the great change which hath bin in England, . . . many that are most cordially affected to the Commonwealth, have bin so amused [i.e. puzzled], that they would have rejoyced to have waited on your honor though in a region so farre remote . . . amongst many others, my condition is changed, & I am reduced to a private life agayne . . .' He asked that if Whitelocke had no other nominee, he would appoint Captain Hall (who had served in Phyllis Court Garrison) as a Clerk of the Peace for Buckinghamshire, Add.Ms 37347 fol.234v. (transcript). In 1656 Colonel Bulstrode was made a Master in Chancery.

BULSTRODE, Whitelocke (1651–1724). *D.N.B.* Son of Sir Richard (q.v.), he was confusingly named after his father's cousin, Bulstrode Whitelocke, with the Christian name and surname in reverse. Of the Inner Temple. Lord of the Manor of Hounslow. Unlike his father, he was opposed to the Pretender and refused to be converted to Roman Catholicism.

BURGES (BURGESS), Daniel (1616–1679). *D.N.B.* (in the entry of his son and namesake); *Calamy Revised.* Son of William Burges of Marlborough. Rector of Collingbourne Ducis, Wiltshire, until he was ejected in 1662. His patron, the Duke of Somerset (q.v.), tried to persuade him to conform. Retiring to Marlborough, he continued to preach. He consulted Whitelocke in 1669 about being bound over in connection with a Conventicle.

BURGES, Capt. Isaac, MP (d.1679). Brother of Daniel (above). Twice High Sheriff of Wiltshire.

BURGES, Samuel. A gentleman of first rank in Whitelocke's retinue for Sweden; son of Dr Burges, who was known to George Cokayn (q.v.), Long. W.P. xv, 107; Add.Ms 4995, appendix 5, fol.12v.

BUSHELL, Thomas (*c*.1594–1674). *D.N.B.*; J.W. Gough *The Superlative Prodigall* (Bristol. 1932). He had served under Francis Bacon; he held the lease of royal mines (notably lead and silver mines) in Wales and elsewhere, under Charles I, the Protectorate, and Charles II. Shortly before the Swedish embassy, he sent Whitelocke a velvet-lined cabinet full of glass bottles with silver tops, containing medical 'cordials' and instructions for their use. In his covering letter he wrote:

> ... When the weight of State affaires had opprest the vitall spirits of yo[u]ʳ Predecessor [Lord Bacon] I observed in my dayly attendance upon his Lo[rdshi]ᵖᵖˢ person that his recourse was to such Cordiall Waters as are here inclosed within this Cabinett, and now[,] knowing that the welfare of this Comonwealth consisteth [i.e. depends] upon your Lo[rdshi]ᵖᵖˢ health and Embasy to that cold and frozen Country of Sweden[,] makes me presume to present your lo[rdshi]ᵖᵖ with a small present theirof as a mite of my gratitude for past favors ... 18°Oct. 1653

Long. W.P. xiv, 108.

Enclosed, was an engraved list of the cordials and their uses, plus an endorsement listing other available cordials. The main list is headed:

> Sir Walter Rawleighes cordialls made by John Phillips att the Well and Bucketts att the Lower end of Milkstreete Butt he is now att the goulden harty-choke over against Middle-Temple-Gate now in Fleete-streete.

Beazor   Is an approved Antedote against all contagious diseases as the Plague, Purples[,] Smale pox and the like[,] for preventing wherof 2 spoonefulls is to be mixt with an indifferent draught of beere to be dranke in the morning fasting[.] But to the infected therewith three good spoonefulls mixt with six of cardus [i.e. carduus, cardoon] or Angelica water that is distild cold onelie of the herbe &[,] for want of those waters[,] in cleare possett drinke which by provokeing a moderate sweate will expell the mallignitie of the malladie[,] the patient being kept temporatelie warme. It is likewise an experienced remedie in a violent surfett and when the stomacke is oppressed with winde[,] cold flegme or anie superfluitie[;] it is effectuallie disgestive and in these cases to be drunke of it selfe without anie other mixture.

Spirit of   Is an excellent restorative in anie kinde of weaknes[.] But chiefelie
clary   for that of the back which it much enableth, it recovereth those that are in (and preserveth such as are incident to) consumptions[,] comforteth the harte[,] healeth the ulcerated longues [i.e. lungs,] increaseth the radicall humour and is a greate strengthner of women after their deliverance[,] to be taken morning and evening[,] 2 good spoonefulls.

The remaining cordials were: Spirit of Mints for 'infirmities of the stomacke', used to stop vomiting and to cure digestive ailments; Treacle

Water for diseases of the spleen and to 'expell the malignitie of anie manner of contagion . . .'; Spirit of Saffron, 'a great comforter of the heart' and a remedy against melancholy; Spirit of Rosemary Flowers for stomach trouble, to suppress 'malignant vapours assending from thence into the head', also to be used against apoplexy and vertigo; Spirit of Roses opened the lungs, healed their ulceration and preserved them from putrefaction; finally, Adrian Gilbert's Cordial Water expelled poison from the heart and all infections, and helped with wind, cholic and vomiting of meats. It was admirable as a treatment for consumption and for delivering women in labour, as well as being:

> exselent in . . . time of the measels and smalle pox and for a surfett . . . for swoundings[,] for Rhumatique persons and cold bodies . . . maie be given in a burning feaver and to a child new borne . . . tis good [for] all diseases and hurtfull to none . . .
>
> ib. 110v.–111v.

See also N. le Febre *A discourse upon Sr Walter Rawleigh's Great Cordial* (London. 1664). For the draft of an Act to establish a College of Philosophers for improvement of mineral works in 1662, see Long. W.P. xiv, 212–211v., endorsed 'Mr Bushell'; his letter of religious expostulation to Lord Downes, who had deprived him of certain land, is in ib. xxiv, 427–430.

BUTLER, Thomas (d. 1690). A wealthy neighbour in Whitelocke's last years, repeatedly named in *The Diary* as his surety. An ironmonger with connections, probably business interests, in Bristol. For Butler's receipt to Whitelocke for £100, see Long. W.P. xx, 163. He was Constable of Hungerford in 1667.

BUTTON, Sir Robert, Bt. (1622–c. 1679). *Complete Baronetage* i, 193. Sheriff of Wiltshire. Whitelocke's client in Jan. 1673/74.

BYRON, Sir Ernestus. Son of Sir Nicholas Byron, Bt. He petitioned the House of Lords, unsuccessfully, to exclude Whitelocke from the Act of Pardon and Oblivion, *Diary* 9 June 1660.

BYRON, Sir John, MP, created 1st Baron Byron of Rochdale in 1643 (c. 1599–1652). G.E.C.; *D.N.B.* A Royalist, he defended Oxford unsuccessfully in 1642, and fought at Edgehill. Shortly afterwards his regiment was quartered at Whitelocke's house, Fawley Court, near Henley-on-Thames. Although instructed not to damage the property, his cavalry plundered the place with enthusiasm.

BYRON, Sir Richard, Kt., succeeded as 2nd Baron Byron of Rochdale in 1652 (*c*.1606–1679). G.E.C.; *D.N.B.* (in the entry for his brother John, the 1st Baron). A Royalist. Whitelocke's client in 1664 and 1665; see also *Diary* 5 May 1665; 23 Apr. 1666.

BYRON, Sir Thomas (d.1644). *D.N.B.* A Royalist. Brother of John and Richard (above). When Sir John's regiment overran Fawley Court, Thomas was quartered with Whitelocke's tenant farmer, William Cooke (q.v.), who attempted (for their safety) to pass off his landlord's five young children as his own grandchildren. Sir Thomas was not deceived but kissed and petted them, saying it would be barbarous to hurt them, *Diary* 1642. 1643. fol. 58v.; Add.Ms 37343 fols.259–260.

CAPEL OF HADHAM, Arthur, 1st Baron (*c*.1610–1649). G.E.C.: *D.N.B.* One of the King's Commissioners at Uxbridge, he was active in the second Civil War and was executed by Parliament in March 1649. An interesting, hearsay account of his death appears in *Memorials* ii, 551, and his earlier plea, ib. 539. For the statement of the case of the trustees and creditors of the late Lord Capel see Long. W.P. x, 94.

CAREY, John, of Poyle Farm. For the long-lasting legal dispute between him and Anne Cromwell (q.v.) see *Diary* 13 Nov. 1651 with note, and 28 Dec. 1666 with note, *passim*.

CARLETON family (below): they may well have been related to Sir Dudley Carleton, diplomat (d.1632), judging by an application to Whitelocke from Thomas Carleton to help him purchase Sir Dudley's birthplace, Baldwin Manor, Brightwell Park, Oxfordshire, 11 Oct. 1651, Long. W.P. xi, 72; related papers ib. 87, 89, 93, 170, 172.

CARLETON, Mrs. (*c*.1598–1672). *Diary, passim*; *D.N.B.* (entry for her son-in-law, Colonel Rowland Wilson, q.v.). Widow of Bigley Carleton, grocer; mother of Whitelocke's third wife Mary, the widow of Colonel Rowland Wilson.

CARLETON, John, of Addington, Surrey, son of Mrs. Carleton (above); Whitelocke's brother-in-law. With Rowland Wilson sen. (q.v.), Samuel Wilson (q.v.) and others, he signed a letter to Whitelocke from the Guinea Company 6 Apr. 1654, Long. 124A, fol. 268v. (transcript).

CARLETON, Rowland. Probably another brother-in-law of Whitelocke's.

CARLETON, Samuel. Whitelocke's brother-in-law.

CARLISLE (CAERLISLE), Col. Charles Howard, MP, 1st E. of (1628–1685). *Hist. of Parl.*; G.E.C.; *D.N.B.*; A. Woolrych *Commonwealth to Protectorate, passim*; G.E. Aylmer and R. Cant (eds.) *History of York Minster* (O.U.P. 1977) p. 448. Four times MP in the 1650s, he also sat in the Convention Parliament of 1660. Of royalist leanings, yet he fought for Parliament at Worcester, was Captain of the Protector's Lifeguard and was created Viscount by Cromwell in 1657. He married Anne, daughter of Edward, 1st Baron Howard of Escrick, in December 1645, when he was 17, so the proposal for their daughter to marry James Whitelocke, *Diary* 9 Apr. 1656, must have been for the betrothal of a child aged about 10. Colonel Howard would have known Whitelocke in Parliament, and as a member of George Cokayn's congregation at Pancras, Soper Lane. In March 1659 Whitelocke referred to him as 'Earl' (Cromwell had called Howard to the Upper House as a Viscount), but the diarist reverted to 'Colonel' when Howard, Ingoldsby and Lee pressed him, as late as 23 December 1659, to go to the King with the Great Seal (a previous attempt by others having failed because of Fleetwood's indecision). Colonel Howard was created 1st Earl of Carlisle in April 1661. In May 1663, before being sent as Ambassador to Russia, Poland, Sweden and Denmark in 1664, the Earl invited Whitelocke to visit him. Whitelocke's son Bigley (q.v.) went to London in 1673, hoping for the Ensign's place in the Earl's regiment.

CARTERET, Sir George, 1st Bt., MP (c.1610–1680). *Hist. of Parl.*; *D.N.B. Pepys, passim.* A wealthy and powerful Royalist. Governor of Jersey; Treasurer of the Navy etc. He and the Earl of Norwich consulted Whitelocke in his Temple Chambers, but neither client gave him a fee, *Diary* 17 Dec. 1662.

CARYL (CARYLL), Joseph (1602–1673). *D.N.B.*; A.G. Matthews *Calamy Revised*. Preached to the Long Parliament; a member of the Assembly of Divines. He was sent with others to Monck, to try to 'prevent effusion of blood'; they could, however, 'perswade nothing with him, nor have any butt generall & uncertaine answers from him', *Diary* 1, 20 Nov. 1659. He was ejected from his living in 1662.

CASTLEMAINE, Roger Palmer, E. of (1634–1705). G.E.C.; *D.N.B.* A diplomat and Roman Catholic. He corresponded briefly with Whitelocke, whose son-in-law George Nevill (q.v.) had died tragically, and whose estate owed the Earl some money, *Diary* 22 June 1665; 18 Feb. 1665/66. Castlemaine's wife, Barbara, was one of Charles II's many mistresses.

CATHERINE OF BRAGANZA (1638–1705). *D.N.B.* Queen Consort of Charles II. Her journey from Salisbury to Oxford caused great trouble to local people. She stayed with the Popham family (q.v.) at Littlecote, where Mary Whitelocke went to see her and kissed her hand, *Diary* 25, 26 Sept. 1665.

CELY, John, lawyer of Clifford's Inn, an Inn of Chancery belonging to the Inner Temple. A friend and colleague of Whitelocke's father and a gentleman of the Judge's household. The 'Liber Famelicus' manuscript (not the printed text) records 'of Cely for endictm[en]ts [£]5.0.0[;] of him for writts [£]2.0.0' April 1623, Add.Ms 53725 p. 145. Whitelocke, in his late twenties, left England while his wife Rebecca (whose mind was violently disturbed) underwent expensive treatment in the house of a doctor in Bow, her family and friends being forbidden to visit her for at least five months, *Diary* 1633. 1634. fol. 21v. He wrote several letters to Cely from Paris. They tell a good deal about Whitelocke and about the trustworthiness of the older man:

> I received your letters att Paris with much gladnes, but cannot write to you being hindered by the unapt[n]es of my right arme where I was lett blood this

morning to prevent a feaver wherinto I was hastning through [a] could [i.e. cold] I caught a shipboard and extreame raging of the toothache ... I am most gladd to heare of the continuance of the hopes of my wifes recovery and of my childes being well, every notice of it will much refresh me.
May 6/16 1634

Long. W.P. vi, 90.

Eight days later, Whitelocke wrote about a report that the King of France was sending the Duc de Rohan as Ambassador to England, to treat about 'a new league intended by divers princes against the Spaniard' into which they wished to draw the King of France. He wrote of the King's Army in Lorraine and of 'Monsieur frere du Roy' in Brussels having a Spanish bodyguard, ostensibly for his safety but said in Paris to be 'to hinder his returne w[i]'hout their licence.' He went on:

> Wee may take example in England by an Edict of the King heere verifyed in the parlement for reformation of habits [i.e. dress,] that no person shall weare any gold or silver lace or imbroidery nor of silke butt two fingers in breadth in each seame. This new plaine fashion makes me desire your trouble to send me a present for a Lady heare to whom I am much ingaged ... [He wanted six dozen yards of ribbon] such as gentlewomen usually weare in knotts, one dozen yards black, one other dozen yards scarlett colour, the other 4 douzen yards of severall light coulours, butt all plaine & w[i]'hout any gold or silver.

Ib. 93.

(*The Diary* refers to the charm, the lady-like qualities and the comfort afforded by the Innkeepers' wives in Dieppe and in Paris).

Whitelocke entrusted his next letter to Monsieur Piccar, a Parisian goldsmith, who considered placing his son in Whitelocke's service. Terms had been agreed. If Piccar decided to leave his son at Salisbury Court, Fleet Street, after making enquiries about Whitelocke, the boy was to 'ly by himselfe and diet and be there as my servant', Long. W.P. vi, 96. In another letter to Cely, of the same date, Whitelocke wrote that the key to his study in the Temple was in his study at home.

> ... I pray do not stick to goe into either of them for any paper or uppon any other occasion ... I would they did conteine such treasure as I should willingly trust with you ...

Whitelocke had been addressing some of his letters, written in Paris, as if from Cilcain, North Wales, in order to mislead his mother-in-law:

> It would much rejoice me if the rumor of my travell might be dashed ... The mischiefe my wife's mother hath done us in speaking to her daughter, doth add extreamly to my griefes ... [see *Diary*] there wants nothing to make up a sea of troubles ...

(Was he quoting from *Hamlet*?) He gave directions for 'a new Mawdlyn cup to be sent to Bow' for his wife's use and for Mrs. Hinkson, a member of his household, to:

> order things discreetly concerning my wifes clothes, and not submitt to the controwle of my wife's mother ... I can never reade enough concerning my domestic affairs ...

Whitelocke reported that after the edict on dress reform 'the officers in the streete mett with some germans in clothes laced with gold and silver laces, and supposing them to be french[,] arrested them ...' This had led to a scuffle in which the chief officer, a commissary and two sergeants were killed and the Germans, both masters and servants, were in prison awaiting trial. He also sent political and military news and added, after his signature:

> I would faine know what perticular scandalls my wifes mother layes uppon me w[hi]^{c}h I weigh not[,] neither I hope will they be beleeved by any that know us.
>
> Long. W.P. vi, 99–99v.

In March 1637 Cely wrote to Whitelocke about records relating to the Wychwood Forest case, Add. Ms 37343 fol. 148 (transcript). Many years later Cely met Whitelocke at Fawley Court, *Diary* 15 May 1665.

CHARLES I, King of England (1600–1649). Whitelocke first met the King in connection with 'The Triumph of Peace', the Royal Masque staged in the Banqueting House in February 1633/34. Papers concerning the Commons' negotiations with Charles, shortly before the outbreak of the Civil War, may be found: (1) in Long W.P. viii, 292–295; partly in Whitelocke's hand, this document is an early (probably the first) draft of the 19 Propositions sent to the King on 1 or 2 June 1642. The numbering is drastically revised on the draft, and there are 23 instead of 19 Propositions, some of which tally with those in the final document as printed in *Constitutional Documents of the Puritan Revolution 1625–1660* (ed. S.R. Gardiner. O.U.P. 1962) pp. 250–254. *The Parliamentary History of England* (London. 1762) x, 400, *passim*, shows that there were, at one stage, 25 Propositions. Several of the 23 draft Propositions, mentioned above, attacked the Queen and her advisers, demanding that she take an oath not to meddle in matters of religion and government nor in placing and displacing the King's Councillors and other great officers. The Queen's name and the attacks on her were omitted from the more tactful version of the 19 Propositions which was sent to the King. These papers are calendared and bound out of order in relation to (2) Long. W.P. viii, 235–239 which should follow, not precede, the draft Propositions. This second document consists of interesting scribbled notes, in Whitelocke's hand, of the Commons' debate on 23, 24 June 1642 (the debate continued for a week); a Committee of the Whole House, with Whitelocke in the chair, considered the challenging 'Preamble of his Majesty's Answer to the Nineteen Propositions' and referred the matter to a sub-committee, from which he reported back to the House. *C.J.* records the decisions but not the speeches. C.C. Weston in her *English Constitutional Theory and the House of Lords 1556–1832* (Routledge and Kegan Paul. 1965) p. 33, regrets the lack of detail from the discussions in the Committee. The Longleat document provides some speeches and enough tantalizing snatches to indicate the stand taken in the House by different MPs.

For impressions of the King and of events surrounding him between the summer of 1646 and the spring of 1647, see the entry for Sir John Holland, who wrote letters to Whitelocke from Newcastle and Holdenby. In the summer of 1647, Whitelocke received the following letter from Sir John Coke jun., MP:

> ... The King removed yesterday from Hatfeild [*en route* from Royston] to Windsore, where Collonel Whitchcott [Christopher Whichcote, q.v.] is governor of the Castle. He hath his commission immediat[e]ly from the Parliament & not from the General & being commander of the present guards within his own garison[,] he hath willingly received our orders to remove all of the Kings party from about his person, w[hi]^{ch} Collonel [Edward] Whaley [q.v.] would not take upon him without the Generals expresse com[m]and. It is said here that the King removes to morrow to Caversham if the resolution hould. I pray you S[i]^r[,] favor your freinds with a right representac[i]on of them in those things ... w[hi]^ch will oblige us all & very much
> your affectionate freind to serve you
> John Coke
> Windesower
> 2 July 1647
> I shall be very gladd to heare where S[i]^r John Holland is ...
> Long. W.P. ix, 144.

The identity of the writer as 'Sir' John Coke is confirmed by Whitelocke's endorsement.

The Diary tells of earlier meetings with the King in Oxford, when Whitelocke was negotiating as one of Parliament's Commissioners; of Whitelocke's understandable evasiveness, *Diary* 13 July 1647, when the King proposed coming to Henley from Caversham, to play bowls and to dine with him at Phyllis Court, and of the diarist's refusal to take any part in the King's trial and execution. A waistcoat, said to have been worn by

Charles on the scaffold, is on view at Longleat and was apparently already there in the reign of Charles II; it seems to have a sound provenance; some of its tiny buttons are missing, having perhaps been distributed as relics.

CHARLES II, King of England (1630–1685). The first reference to Whitelocke meeting Charles II was at an informal, private audience on 8 June 1660, ten days after the Restoration. There are many diary references to him before that date, including a record of: (1) a conversation initiated by Queen Christina about a rumour that she was to marry Charles Stuart, and (2) separate approaches made to Whitelocke on 22 and 23 Dec. 1659, urging him to go to Charles at Breda with an offer to restore him to the throne on reasonable terms, before Monck could make him an unconditional offer. Soon after the Restoration, Whitelocke took it on himself to compile 'Whitelockes Notes Uppon the Kings writt for Choosing Members of Parlement', a collection of information on the constitution, which he gave to the King through Clarendon, *Diary* 12 Nov. 1660 with note. At Charles's request, Whitelocke wrote 'The Kings Right to graunt Indulgence in matters of Religion', in support of toleration, *Diary* 13, 14, 15 Mar. 1662/63, 25 Mar. 1663. A decade later, in 1673, Parliament compelled the King to rescind the Declaration of Indulgence and to pass the Test Act, which resulted in Roman Catholics being expelled from any office under the Crown. This may explain the following scrappy message, but there is no clue as to how it came into Whitelocke's hands:

> I am servant to a papist Lord and one my self[.] I was told last night we must suddenly be in arms and that the King was to be kil[l]ed[,] so was the parliment[.] I abhor their bloody Cosins[;] look about you quickly or els[e] you are all loste[.] I am in haste . . . it is either with powder or masacre[,] god preserve you. [no date.]
>
> Long. W.P. Parcel 4 No. 33.

Possibly this was connected with information (attached) from Thomas Rous of Kingston, Surrey, about his sister-in-law, Mrs. Margaret Kent, 17 Jan. 1673/74.

CHARLES X (KARL X GUSTAV), King of Sweden (1622–1660). Son of John Casimir, Count Palatine of Zweibrücken and of Catherine, sister of Gustav Adolf; a cousin of Queen Christina, whom he succeeded after her abdication in 1654. He married Hedwig Leonora of Holstein-Gottorp. In May 1654 he showed great courtesy to Whitelocke in Uppsala, and gave him a jewel with his portrait set in diamonds; Whitelocke gave the Prince seven bay coach-horses. In 1654 (?) the King enquired, through Benjamin Bonnel (q.v.), about the treatment of his subjects in England (evidently those whose ships and cargoes had been seized). Whitelocke replied to the King in French, Long. W.P. xiv, 73, making excuses for delays in the Admiralty Court, which was not yet re-established, and referring to pressures between the Protector and his Parliament which had now been resolved with good accord. For letters touching on the King and his wars see entries for: FLEETWOOD, Sir George; POTLEY, Andrew, and WRANGELL, Carl Gustav.

CHARLES LOUIS (LEWIS), Prince (1617–1680). Second son of Frederick V, Elector Palatine, and Elizabeth of Bohemia; nephew of Charles I; elder brother of Prince Rupert and Prince Maurice; despite these relationships, the Prince supported Parliament in the 1640s. It was rumoured that he hoped for the English crown, if his uncle were deposed. He became Prince Elector after his elder brother's death in 1629, and heir to the Palatinate; the Lower Palatinate was restored to him after the Peace of Westphalia, in 1648, when an eighth Electorate was created for him. *The Diary* shows that the Prince was Whitelocke's client between 10 Sept. 1645 and 22 Nov. 1648, *passim*.

CHAUNCY (CHANCEY), Ichabod (c.1634–1691). W. Munk *Roll of the Royal College of Physicians*; J. Savage *Genealogical Dictionary of the First Settlers of New England* (Little, Brown & Co., Boston, 1860); *D.N.B.* gives the latter part of his life only, not mentioning that his father was Charles Chauncy, Vicar of Ware, in Hertfordshire, later President of Harvard College, Cambridge, Massachusetts, where Ichabod studied. Arriving in England, he became tutor to Whitelocke's sons in London, *Diary* 8 Oct. 1660, but was dismissed in August 1661 for being too harsh, after striking Carleton on the head with a heavy book. His signature appears on a bond, Long. W.P. xix, 158. He became a dissenting minister and later a physician in Bristol, where Whitelocke wrote to him, *Diary* 1 Aug. 1670 with note.

CHESTERFIELD, Philip Stanhope, 1st E. of (1584–1656). G.E.C.; *D.N.B.* He suffered sequestration as a Royalist. In a Commons debate on a resolution to stop the Earl from using the Prayer Book at home, Whitelocke opposed the motion as being against liberty of conscience, *Diary* 1 Mar. 1646/47; *C.J.* v, 102 (same date) only records information received that the Earl was maintaining malignant Ministers to preach in his house.

CHRISTINA, Queen of Sweden (1626–1689). For a bibliography see *Catalogue, Christina Exhibition* (Council of Europe. 1966) pp. 582–586; S. Stolpe *Christina of Sweden* (Burns and Oates. 1966); G. Masson *Queen Christina* (Secker and Warburg. 1968); *Drottning Kristina Maximer* (ed. S. Stolpe. Bonniers, Stockholm. 1959). Among Whitelocke's papers are: a letter from the young Queen Christina to the English Parliament, sending Israel Lagerfeldt (q.v.) on a well-meaning mission, to mediate in the Anglo-Dutch War, 20 Jan. 1652/53 (this seems to be wrongly calendared), Long. W.P. xv, 23–25 (English translation from Latin), with a belated reply from Barebone's Parliament, of 29 Oct. 1653, ib. xiv, 168v.–169, (copy, in Latin); Whitelocke's Commission, Instructions and Letters of Credence as Ambassador to Sweden, the instructions including proposals for a stricter alliance, the Ambassador to protest against the Queen receiving any Ambassador from Charles Stuart, son of the late King, and to remove misrepresentations respecting Parliament's proceedings etc., 21 Oct. 1653, ib. 115–125; an Order for Whitelocke to appear, to receive his Commission for Sweden, 28 Oct. 1653, ib. 142; Ambassador Whitelocke's speech to the Queen at his first audience, 23 Dec. 1653, ib. 234 (Latin draft). A closely observed description of the Queen at this audience is given in Whitelocke's draft letter, probably to Henry Lawrence, Lord President of the Council of State:

> Her habit was a plaine gray stuffe Coate to the grounde[,] and over that a plaine close horsemans Coate of the same stuffe w[i]^th a black scarfe about her neck tyed w[i]^th a little black ryband, her haire put in a dresse more like a mans then a woman.
> 30 Dec. 1653.
>
> Long. 124A, fol. 52

After a visit from the soldiers of the Queen's guard, the Queen's coachmen came to Whitelocke expecting New Year's gifts:

> ... butt to come in this manner is very unworthy themselves, & dishonourable to their Mistris, butt they all love money with greedines ...
> 1, 2 Jan. 1653/54.
>
> ib. fols.62–63

Christina's reply to Charles Stuart, politely turning down his appeal for help (conveyed by Ballendin as go-between), was shown to Whitelocke by the Spanish Envoy, Don Antonio Pimentel de Prado (q.v.), *Diary* 2 Jan. 1653/54; (Whitelocke believed that the Queen contrived to let him see this secret communication). An edited version of the letter appears in *Journal* i, 280 and an earlier transcript in Long. 124A, fols.62v.–63. A draft letter from Whitelocke to the Queen explains that the change in the English government to a Protectorate would in no way alter the nation's good intentions towards Sweden, 14 Jan. 1653/54, Long. W.P. xv, 16. There is a draft (in English and French) of Whitelocke's covering note to the Queen with the gift of an English grammar, 6 Feb. 1653/54, ib. 43. An undated copy of Whitelocke's letter (in French) to the Queen, thanked her for her favours and especially for investing him with the Order of Knighthood of Amaranta or Amaranth, ib. 69; (this was promised early in 1654, when he was in Uppsala, but was not delivered until the end of the year). For Christina's authority to Chancellor Axel Oxenstierna (q.v.) and his son Eric (Erik) (q.v.) to negotiate with Whitelocke and to conclude a treaty of commerce and navigation, 14 Mar. 1653/54, see ib. 90. A copy of Whitelocke's letter to the Queen (in French), praised her strength of character and accomplishment in the sciences, but stated boldly: '*Rien ne vous manque que l'estude du principal Livre, que je me suis enhardi de presenter en Anglais a vostre majest[i]*'; he suggested that perhaps it was not the custom in Sweden to spend much time on private Bible-reading, and that it might be thought enough to hear the Bible read in Church; he knew that ill-natured people made a mock of him for his views and because, although he was not a priest, yet he preached sermons; their reproaches troubled him no more than a dog barking at his horse as he rode through a village, but he humbly begged the Queen to set a good example to her subjects by not travelling on Sundays, 24 Apr. 1654, ib. xiv, 41–43v.

Whitelocke kept: the Warrant (in Swedish) for the delivery of 200 ship-pounds of copper to Ambassador Whitelocke as a present from Queen Christina, 6 May 1654, ib. xv, 164; a copy (in French) of the Queen's speech to the Four Estates at Uppsala announcing her plan to abdicate, 11 May 1654, ib. 172–173, and of her proposals to the Four Estates at the above assembly, with his corrections, ib. 174–177; his own farewell speech to Christina, 12 May 1654, ib. 145 (in French), 178 (in Latin), and three drafts of his letter of thanks to her, written from Hamburg, with a description of his homeward journey, 14 June 1654, ib. xiv, 52–52v., 54–54v., 55v.

There is a letter from Christina to Whitelocke, written from Antwerp after her abdication:

> Monsieur[,] permetez que je vous face souvenir par la presente, d'une personne a quis vous avez autrefois donné part en vostre amitié. J'espere que vous conservez encores les mesmes sentiments pour moi. Et je vous puis asseurer que je ferai toute ma vie profession de vous estimer. Je vous prie

d'assister Monsieur Sested [Sehested q.v.] auprez de Monsieur le Protecteur et d'asseurer son Altesse de ma part qu'il n'y a personne au Monde qui l'honore et l'estime a l'esgal de moi. Et a vous Monsieur[,] souffrez que je vous proteste que je suis tres affectionnée a vous obliger en toutes occasions
Christine
1 Oct. 1654.

Ib. 59.

An undated draft of Whitelocke's business-like reply, in French, is written on the back of Christina's letter, ib. 59v.

Christina's servant, H. de Wulffen, wrote in French that, on her instructions, he was sending Whitelocke the Order of the Amaranth which she had promised him in Uppsala; de Wulffen reminded Whitelocke '. . . je suis le mesme qu'il [sic] avoit l'honneur de retrouver vos Lunettes perdues à la Chambre de la Reyne à Upsall.' (The only reference to Whitelocke wearing spectacles), 24 Nov./4 Dec. 1654, ib. xvi, 151. The Diary gives a transcript of a letter from Christina dated 26 Feb. 1655 (new style) in which she apologised for the delay in sending the Order of the Amaranth. Whitelocke had written to her saying that, at the turn of the year, he wished to renew his offer to be of service to her. He sent news of Hannibal Sehested (q.v.), 29 Jan. 1654/55, Long, W.P. xiv,64. Christina replied from Brussels, asking for his help in releasing the St. Michael, a ship from Hamburg, which had been captured by an English Admiral off the coast of Barbados, as far back as 1651; she finished the letter 'Votre tres affectionnée amie Christine', 4 Feb. 1655 (new style), ib. xviii,138–138v. An undated draft of Whitelocke's answer was probably written in April, May or June 1655 (he having resigned as Keeper of the Seal in April), before his appointment as a Commissioner to the Treasury. He commented on his low condition; being out of public service, owing to his resignation, he was less able to be of help to her than he had been, but within his poor capacity he was anxious to do whatever he could for her, ib. xiv, 65v. An undated draft letter (in French) written by Whitelocke around 8 July 1655, told the Queen that he had taken the earliest opportunity to accompany Hannibal Sehested to an audience with the Protector and that the warmth with which Cromwell received Sehested was proof of the high regard he felt for her Majesty; Whitelocke had never seen him receive even an Ambassador with more respect, ib. Parcel 3, No. 26 (see Christina's letter of 1 Oct. 1654 above). On 11 Mar. 1657/58, Whitelocke wrote expressing, in warm terms, the honour he felt in knowing Christina, and he made elaborate excuses for the Protector's delay in replying to propositions brought by her Secretary, Passerini (q.v.), ib. xviii, 123–123v. For the ruthless side of Christina's nature see: MONALDESCHI, Giovanni.

In discussion with Whitelocke, Christina had expressed doubts as to the wisdom of showing toleration in matters of religion. It is interesting to see how radically she had moved in his direction, after Whitelocke's death and many years after her conversion to Roman Catholicism; this is reflected in her reply to a letter from the Chevalier de Terlon on the extirpation of heresy in France. She wrote, for example:

> I am not over well persuaded of the success of that great design and ... I cannot rejoice at it as something of great advantage to our holy religion ... In good earnest, are you truly convinced of the sincerity of those new converts? ... Soldiers are strange apostles and I think them more expert at killing, ravishing and robbing than at persuading ... I look upon France as it is now as upon a sick body whose arms and legs are cut off to cure him of a distemper that, with a little patience and gentleness, might have been cured without. But I much fear lest the sore should fester and finally become incurable ... since our Saviour never used this way to convert the world, it certainly cannot be the best ...
> Rome, 2 Feb. 1686
>   B.L. Harleian Ms 6848, fols. 147–148v. (copy) in English

The author is indebted to Father Francis Edwards S.J. for this reference.

CHUTE, Chaloner MP (d. 1659). *D.N.B.* A distinguished barrister, of the Middle Temple. First elected an MP in 1656. He served as Speaker of the House of Commons briefly in 1659, shortly before his death. Edward Hyde wrote to Mordaunt that he did not believe Chute would have accepted the office of Speaker if he had not hoped to be able, thereby, to serve the King. But Whitelocke, after referring to him as an excellent orator, a man of great parts and generosity, whom many people thought would not join the Protector's party, added 'butt he did heartily ...', *Diary* 31 Jan. 1658/59. When Chute was ill, Whitelocke recorded that the Speaker had 'so much gained the affection of the House that he swayed much w[i]'h them ...', ib. 19 Mar. 1658/59. Entries from 1644 onwards describe Whitelocke's friendly encounters with Chute. Several times they met over a meal with other lawyers, including Speaker Lenthall, Solicitor-General St. John, Attorney-General Prideaux and Sir Thomas Widdrington. After Chute's death Whitelocke wrote that he was a kind friend and eminent in his profession, ib. 14 Apr. 1659.

CLANRICARDE (CLENRICARD), Anne, Marchioness of. G.E.C.; *D.N.B.* Daughter of William Compton, 1st Earl of Northampton, she married Ulick de Burgh, 5th Earl, later created Marquess of Clanricarde, a Royalist. There is only one diary reference to her; this concerns money for her, when she was a widow, 20 Dec. 1658. Her jointure and house were restored to her in 1661. Earlier, an application from her husband in Galway, to the Commander-in-Chief of the Parliamentary Forces in Ireland, solicited a safe-conduct for Commissioners negotiating a Treaty, 14 Feb. 1651/52, Long. W.P. xii, 46.

CLARE, John Holles (Hollis), 2nd E. of (1595–c.1665). G.E.C.; *D.N.B.* Brother of Denzil Holles (q.v.). A moderate, he left Parliament for the King in 1643, but returned in 1644. His land had been sequestrated in his absence. An undated paper refers to several reasons why Clare should not pay a 20th part, in view of the losses he had suffered, Long. W.P. xx, 162; he was discharged from his delinquency by an Order of July 1644. Clare consulted Whitelocke, Prideaux (q.v.) and Bartholomew Hall (q.v.) on legal affairs between 1644 and 1659. He wrote from Drury Lane to Whitelocke in Sweden: the letter referred to his difficulty in arranging to see Lambert (q.v.) about Whitelocke's claim for £2,000, since Lambert often refreshed himself at his villa, his 'country palace' in Wimbledon, but things were now 'stirring'; Clare described Christina as 'the matchless Queen, the most exact copy of Queen Elizabeth, whose perfections are not only admirable but impossible for any other to attain to', 1 Mar. 1653/54, ib. xv, 71. *Diary* 26 Aug. 1659 refers to Clare's letters 'in the great buisnesses', presumably the trouble over his new buildings between Lincoln's Inn Fields and Drury Lane, erected by licence under the Great Seal; Clare wrote that he had reserved an open market where the country people could sell their produce, and that he would have built a church there, had he not incurred heavy debts through the loss of his country fortune for four years (in the Civil War), Long. W.P. xxiv, 172v.–173. In a letter, probably written a day or two later, Clare apologized for causing Whitelocke to receive 'a clowdy look' from the Board, and begged him not to press 'their business' further for the time being since the Council was, perhaps, dealing with other matters which might 'sour them', ib., 200.

CLARENDON, Edward Hyde, 1st E. of (1609–1674). G.E.C.; *D.N.B.*; *Pepys* x; *Diary of John Evelyn*; B.H.G. Wormald *Clarendon: Politics, History and Religion 1640–1660* (University of Chicago Press, Midway Reprint. 1976); Hugh Trevor-Roper 'Clarendon' (lecture marking the tercentenary of Clarendon's death), text in *Times Literary Supplement* 10 Jan. 1975. He was appointed Lord Chancellor (in exile) in 1657; three years later, at the Restoration, he became the effective and powerful Chancellor. He was created Earl of Clarendon in 1661; impeached of high treason and banished, in 1667, he proceeded to write his *Life* and to rewrite and finish his *History of the Rebellion*.

Hyde first knew Whitelocke (who was four years his senior) at the Middle Temple; the affection and admiration he displayed for his friend, before their political paths parted in the 1640s, appear in his letters below (see also *Diary* chapter 1). In spite of some lack of cordiality towards his former friend and idol, Clarendon allowed Whitelocke surprisingly free access to him after 1660.

When Whitelocke left England secretly for France in 1634 (forbidden by Dr. Bartlett to see his wife Rebecca during her six months' treatment at the Doctor's house in Bow) Hyde wrote reproachfully:

> If I had not a stronge sense of my owne unworthinesse . . . I should tell you I suffered much when I found your remoove without the bestowinge one lyne upon your servant: Assure your Selfe you have not transported all your troubles with you, parte of your griefes stay with me, and I suffer deeply in your afflictions: I shall pray that the Change of Ayer may recreate your mind too, and that the Language of France may expell your English distractions: though I feare . . . that Paris hath as few Antedotes against a troubled soule as London: Indeed Passions that cannot be forgotten must be mollifyed, and then the conversat[i]on of frends is the only remedy; if your wife were deade I should be of your mind, to absent my selfe from the mourners . . . [Hyde's first wife had died six months after they were married; he was to marry Frances, daughter of Sir Thomas Aylesbury, two months after writing this letter] but your condit[i]on I feare is not comforted in beinge tormented with a thousand feares and doubts and hopes . . . which were removed . . . if your abode were neere . . . I could wish you heare againe, but truly tis with noe other thought but of robbinge you of some [of] your cares . . .
> Middle Temple this
> 7th of May [1634]
>
> Long. W.P. vi, 91

Transcribed by Whitelocke, with minor amendments to spelling and punctuation, Add.Ms 53726, fols. 101v.–102.

An apologetic letter from Whitelocke to Hyde, dated 9 May, ib. fol. 102 (transcript), probably crossed Hyde's letter. Whitelocke wrote again on ¹⁶/₂₆May in reply to Hyde's reproaches, apologizing again and admitting:

> I find not what I hoped for in . . . ease to a sick mind. It is my greatest happines to heare from my friends, and how it fares with my poore wife, w[hi]ᶜh is all the comfort I could receive of her though I continued in the same house where she is, bicause I am barred her sight for 6 moneths, this will plead excuse for my absence and for my neglect of so worthy a friend as your selfe att my going away, lett the many distractions and extreamities wherin I was att that time obteine my pardon. . . . I intreate you to silence the rumour w[hi]ᶜh I beleeve you may heare of my journey . . .
> Add.Ms 32093 fol.54 (transcript).

Hyde wrote a letter of condolence on the death of Rebecca Whitelocke, starting not 'Sir' but 'My deare Friend'; he assured Whitelocke that he should not be troubled by criticism from his mother-in-law and the Benet family, on account of his leaving the country:

> ... the best part of the worlde ... know your reputation is much above the reach of their impotent malice. If you stand fast uppon your own virtue you are fully vindicated from any shadow of blame by that journey, butt if you thinke by any complyance to prevayle with people of such compositions, you butt expose your selfe to the mischiefs of insolency ... [Whitelocke must decide, in his wisdom, whether or not to return at once.] My little friend at Salisbury Court [James, nearly three years old] is lusty, & shall live your Comfort.
>
> If there be any clamours att court (as your Madde mother [-in-law] threatens) I ... shall easily prevent any mischiefs ... Amongst your afflictions, suffer not your selfe ... to forget your fayre proportion of blessings too, among which your fame with all good men will find a chiefe place, & lett the share we beare of your griefes ease your too heavy burden ...
>
> Add.Ms 53726 fols.103v.–104, 21 May (transcript).

Whitelocke's prompt reply seems to indicate that Hyde's letter from London to Paris was delivered in two days, ib. 104, 23 May (transcript).

Among Hyde's next letters is one written in the same decade from Westminster; it refers cryptically to Whitelocke's suit to the Earl of Northampton (probably in connection with the Earl's ownership of the Manor of Henley). Hyde had solicited Lord Grandison's support and he referred to Whitelocke's 'brother Willoughby' (q.v.) and to the Earl of Rutland (q.v.), who might be helpful in the suit; Hyde's wife thanked Whitelocke and his second wife, Frances, for their gift of cider, 7 Dec. (as usual no year is shown), Long. W.P. vi, 166. An undated letter from Hyde apologized abjectly for his failure to send venison as promised; his Keeper had had a fall which had confined him to bed, but Hyde promised an even better doe later, ib. 168.

From Westminster, Hyde wrote to Whitelocke and his wife at Fawley:

> My good Frendes.
> ... I must excuse my selfe not only to you, but to your honest Waterman, whome I promised the last weeke a letter to you: but the truth is, I was in the disorder of my remoove to my new chamber and forgott it, for w[hi]^{ch} I beate my boy, whome I commaunded to remember me: Since Thursday I have obay'd the D^r ... who hath eased me of a full pound of my bloode so that I looke like a pale gyrle newly recover'd of the greene sicknesse. Our best Newes is, that wee have good wyne aboundantly come over, and the worst, that the plague is in Towne, and no Judges dye, the old absurd [transcribed 'observed' in *Memorials*] Baron out of meere frowardnesse resolvinge to live ...

I must give you both many thankes for my very free and herty entertainment ...
12 Apr. [1636].

This letter is transcribed in Add.Ms 37343 fols. 146v.–147, and a few lines
from it appear in *Memorials* i, 73, introduced by Whitelocke as one in
which Hyde 'drolls'.

An undated letter from Hyde starts: 'My deare[,] I am glade you prosper
so happily in issue male, god send the good woman well agayne ...' This
may be dated around January 1636/37, after William's birth. Hyde wrote
that his own wife was encouraged 'for her journey, which shee will shortly
be ready for', but their first son, Henry, was born in June 1638, so it would
appear that Frances Hyde either gave birth to a daughter or lost her first
child. The letter ends: 'I am very prowde that you are a freend to your most
affectionate Serv[an]ᵗ ...' Long. W.P. vii, 196; *Memorials* i, 74 gives the
full transcript and confirms the year as 1637.

A letter from Hyde of 27 February could have been written in 1636/37 or
(more probably) in 1637/38:

> My dear Frende
> I can not infuse courage enough into my wife to think on London ..., but
> she is now preemptorily resolved to disburthen herselfe in the Country, so
> that I am to desyre you as soone as you please to convay your long'd for
> Syder to Wyndsor and cause it to be left at Fryths house the London
> Bargeman ... send me worde what tyme this Lent you are to bestir from your
> owne house, that when my wife will spare me, I may be free to find you at
> home ... you have a fuller power over no man, then over ... your most
> affectionate Serv[an]ᵗ
>   Edw[ard] Hyde
> Cranborne Lodge
> in Wyndsor Forrest

In another undated letter Hyde wrote:

> ... This noble messenger will only allow me tyme, to write me name to you,
> if you find some convayance to the George at Wyndsor, your letter will
> quickly find me; send me worde then the tyme when you would have your
> Doe, for tis not fitt in the Winter you send a man purposely ...

He entreated Whitelocke to send his 'pretious Syder by the next convoy to
Windsor'; he would refund the freight and Whitelocke's ferryman should
leave it with the Mistress of 'The George', ib. 278.

Hyde proposed paying a visit to Whitelocke, when they would 'be soe
merry ... that you shall perceave you have much of my hearte in your
keepinge ... I am in Dʳ Moores disposall for one weekes phisicke ...' but

the treatment was postponed because, as Hyde wrote satirically, '. . . my L[or]^d Treasur[er]s sicknesse confin'd him to an attendance solely there, and he [Dr. Moore] would not undertake two persons of such quality togither. . .' 13 Mar. [1637/38?]. Ib. 191, transcribed in Add.Ms 37343 fol. 153; *Memorials* i, 76 omits an obscure but intriguing passage about Frances Whitelocke's aunt (presumably the Countess of Sunderland q.v.), and a composition to be made on reasonable terms, which Hyde considered should not exceed £1,500.

In another letter Hyde wrote:

> . . . I leave this towne with no other remorse then what concernes the want of your lov'd conversac[i]on . . . I wayted yesterday [on] my L[ord] Chamberlyne, who is still the same brave man [Philip, 4th Earl of Pembroke, q.v., who had helped Whitelocke at the time of the Royal Masque] and in particular [he] enquir'd how Mr Whitlocke did, I told him you were buisy in the Country getting of money; I hope you will not omitt to see him shortly, such a frende is noe burthen . . . Justify your first error by continuinge to love your most affectionate Serv[an]^t . . .
>
> Long. W.P. vi, 276

The letter was written in November 1638, according to the transcript in Add.Ms 37343 fols. 196v.–197. The next letter was probably written in 1639, judging by a reference to troubles in Scotland, and to the likelihood that even victory would prove 'Melancholique enough.' Hyde wrote:

> I wounderd to receave your Cydar without a letter, which made me believe you were fallen to your old trade of rydinge Circuite agayne . . . I am hugely inclyned to doe myselfe a good turne in grantinge your wifes Suite, and I assure you it shall be a quarrell betweene my wife & me if I visitt you not, but I must see my poore gyrle recover'd of her Ague before I stirr . . . If ther be any faulte in your Cydar, you shall heare of it when wee meete . . .
>
> Long. W.P. vii, 351.

Another undated letter of 1639 is endorsed by Whitelocke 'Ned Hyde':

> . . . your letter was so longe in findinge me, that . . . I sent my boy as soone as I was setled at Crannborne, to . . . know when you could commaunde your Bucke[;] the same day he returned . . . he brought me from Windsor your letter so that I was utterly innocent in your missinge your vinison: now I have casually met this gentleman of Henly who assures me you are returned fro[m] your Welsh progresse . . . believe me I infinitely longe to injoy you some howers, this weeke I intend to make a visit to Gwyder [Gwydir Castle, home of the Wynn family, q.v., who were related to the Mostyns] . . . if you finde some way to convey any letter to Windsor, or to the Gray hounde at Maydonheade & derect it to be sent forthwith to me, I shall know how you dispose of your selfe . . . Only let me tell you that ther is no doubt of a Parlyament [the Short Parliament, after Charles's eleven years of personal

rule], and very shortly, therfore if your owne interest [i.e. influence] at Abington will not provyde for you, take some course with the L[ord] Danvers who by his brother (for ther is no hustinge to his owne I know) cannot fayle[;] in good Fayth I would not you should be absent fro[m] that Assembly, for ther will be much to be done for good men ... My best Frend, if to love you very passyonately, can any way meritt me, you ought in justice to continue your favour & good opinion.
This Mundy,
What day of the moneth I know not.

Ib.353.

On 2 October [1640] Hyde wrote about elections to what was to become the Long Parliament:

> ... you must give me leave to be very angry with you or your messenger, you call me to Maydenheade at 4 of the clocke & tis full 3 when your letter comes, if you had vouchsafed me notice of your being at Maydenheade, the last night, or early this morning I know nothinge I desire more then to speake with you an hower ... I have bene alwayes told my L[or]^d Wenman [q.v., of Thame Park] would carry that parte of the County [Oxon.] against all men & I am confident Mr Fynes [James Fiennes, son of Lord Say and Sele q.v.] must carry the other: for amongst the peticioning^e Lords the very procuring^e this Parlyam[en]^t will be imputed to my L[or]^d Say: so if they two stand I would rather you should suffer W. Walter, Mr Doyly & S[i]^r Rob[er]^t Dormer to be canvassed the[re] [than] runn[?] the hazard your selfe: I should chuse[,] if I might advise you[,] to write to my L[or]^d Wenman (with whome I have only acquaintence enough to believe him a civill man and S[i]^r Fr[ancis] Penman's [?] worde that he is a very honest man) to know if he would stande, and to offer him your service, with intimati[o]ns that if he declyned it, you would be glad^e under his favour to offer your service to the County ... if he signify to you that he will not stande, then with his assistance joynd with Mr Fynes for sure he will carry it ... by no meanes accept of Bedwyn [Wilts.], for my L[or]^d of Hartford is now obliged to vindicate that place against S[i]^r L[?] D ... be sure you fayle not to be of the house ...

Ib. viii, 25

An undated note, calendared '1642?', refers to Hyde's reluctant journey into the country and to his leaving all papers that needed Whitelocke's attention with a trustworthy man, Tom Hughes, ib. 209. That appears to be the last letter from Hyde to Whitelocke.

Curiously, a letter dated 1 May 1654, written by Hyde from Paris, to Sir William Curtius in Frankfurt, is endorsed by Whitelocke (who was in Uppsala) 'rec. 11 May 1654.' Letters of interest to Ambassador Whitelocke were often intercepted by Thurloe's agents and copies were sent to him via London. This letter of Hyde's is, however, the original, and the dates make it clear that the letter did not go via Thurloe. The letter starts with comments on postal delays, on the negligence of the Postmaster at Frankfurt, and on packets from Curtius and Lord Rochester:

> For the Queene of Sweden[,] I know not what her designe may be upon travayling, but I cannot imagine she hath any thought of marriage, and if the report be true ... of Cuningmarke's having taken the fort by Bremen, methinkes she does not leave her Successer such a Legacy of Peace, as might be expected from a Queene, who gives over her Government for quyetness sake.
>
> I know not what to say of this people [the French] who pretend to beleive that their Treaty with Cromwell is almost finished, yet my l[ette]rs from London are very confident that Cromwell does not intend to make a Peace w[i]^{t}h them, and methinks their carryage on either side to each other are but untoward preambles to a Peace[;] the French having very lately stopt the delivery of an English ship at Marseille, w[hi]^{ch} upon Cromwell's Interposit[i]on they [the French] had lately given order to discharge ... two other rich Ships of London are taken and brought into Tolloon [Toulon]; ... Newes came yesterday from St Maloe that a squadron of the English Frigates mett with a fleete of Ships belonging to that Towne w[hi]^{ch} are always richly laden, and sunck some and tooke the rest[,] of w[hi]^{ch} the Newes noe soon[er] arrived there, but all the English were turned out of the Towne, and their Goods seized upon [then, satirically]: If these mutual Addresses produce a good Intelligence betweene each other, Cromwell will introduce a new method of Treatyes as well [as] of Governem[en]^t. We are soe farr advanced towards our Journey that the King hath received part of his Money, and is promised the rest very speedily, and then undoubtedly we shall draw towards your partes, and I am soe farr from despayring upon this Peace that I hope this Sum[m]er will improve the Kings condit[i]on, and that the temper of our owne Country [England] will by degrees recompence for the ill spiritt w[hi]^{ch} hath possessed it for these last yeares. Methinkes the Protector does not hasten towards a Parliam[en]^t[,] as if he were not enough confident of the good will of his Subjects ...
>
> Ib. xv, 154–154v.

CLARGES (CLARGE, CLERGES), Dr Thomas, MP (c.1618–1695).

Hist. of Parl.; *D.N.B.* Brother-in-law of George Monck, D. of Albemarle. In 1660 Clarges' name appears in *The Diary* for the first time but it occurs earlier in Whitelocke's correspondence with Monck, when Whitelocke was in a position to help both men (see entry: ALBEMARLE). When the Restoration was imminent, Whitelocke solicited Monck's help in connection with obtaining a pardon, and at the same time drafted a humble letter to Clarges, telling of the action he had taken and saying 'I am glad so good a friend as your selfe is now with him ...' He hoped for an early reply and added: 'I shall never forget the favour of a friend especially in a day of streights ...', c.28 Jan. 1659/60, Long. W.P. xix, 116 (draft).

CLAYPOLE, Elizabeth (1629–1658). *D.N.B.*; T. Carlyle *Letters and Speeches of Oliver Cromwell, passim*. Second daughter of Oliver Cromwell; she married John Claypole (below). Although she was believed be to Cromwell's favourite daughter she affirmed, indiscreetly, that Whitelocke was found 'hon[ora]^{ble} imployement' (as Ambassador Extraordinary to Sweden) so that he 'might be no obstacle or impediment to Crom[wells] ambitious designs . . .' and even 'that he might never returne again . . .' but she herself was always courteous and friendly to Whitelocke '& she was glad when [he] came home safe', *Diary* Nov. 1652 fol. 125; 7, 8 Aug. 1658.

CLAYPOLE (CLEYPOLE), John, MP (d.1688). *D.N.B.* Only referred to twice in *The Diary*, at the second instalment ceremony of his father-in-law as Protector, 26 June 1657.

CLEVELAND, Thomas Wentworth, 1st E. of (1591–1667). G.E.C. (under Wentworth); *D.N.B.*; J. Thirsk 'The Sale of Royalist Lands during the Interregnum', *Economic History Review*, second series v, 2, 1952, pp. 195–199, *passim*; J.H. Blundell *Toddington, Its Annals and People* (Toddington. 1925) pp. 52–54, *passim*. There is only one diary reference to Cleveland, on 17 Oct. 1661; this concerns the Earl's creditors consulting Whitelocke. The Earl had started amassing debts and encumbering his lands in the 1620s–1630s. As a Royalist, he was captured after the battle of Worcester in Sept. 1651, was committed to the Tower and narrowly escaped the death sentence. Starting in Oct. 1651, he and his agents sent Whitelocke massive particulars of the Manors of Toddington and (initially) of Harlington, Bedfordshire, which were part of the Earl's estates north-west of Dunstable, offering him a pre-emption on them and urging him to buy out the State's interest for the sake of the Earl's creditors, for whom he had 'an honest care'. It appears that Whitelocke had made a tentative overture, referred to both by the Earl himself and, more positively, in *Love Letters of Dorothy Osborne to Sir William Temple* (King's Classics. 1903) p. 172, in which she wrote that Whitelocke '. . . was making a purchase of one of the best houses in the county. I know not whether he goes on with it; but 'tis such a one as will not become any thing less than a lord.' No evidence has appeared that he showed more than a passing interest, probably when staying with the Cokayns at Cotton End, Bedfordshire. For papers from the Earl and his agents see Long. W.P. xi, 81; xii, 3, 5, 15, 37, 51, 57 and 59 (the Earl's pressing letter of 16 Mar. 1651/52), 93, 95, 99, and 101 (Mary Whitelocke's letter, with a message that her husband would lose his pre-emption if he took no action, Apr.

1652), 103, 104 and 106v.–113 (a schedule of encumbrances on Toddington Manor and lands, which were appointed, by Act of Parliament, to be sold for payment of the Earl's debts; the schedule lists mortgages, bonds, bills etc. totalling £31,828, including £100 to Sir Anthony Van Dyck, whose full-length portrait of the Earl was exhibited in South Kensington in 1866); 115 (a schedule of debts to the Earl's former servants and dependants, including £38.5s.6d. due to the clerk to the kitchen, £90 to the gardener, £257 to the poor of Toddington parish etc.); fols. 117v.–124 show debts on the estate, from 1619 onward, with a claim on the property as security for £5,000 lent by the Earl's son-in-law, Lord Lovelace (q.v.); 126; 127 gives a short review of the estate, which had come under the control of Parliament, because of the Earl and his son's delinquency; it refers to payment of the Earl's debts, and states that building Toddington House was said, by tradition, to have cost Lord Cheney (husband of the Earl's aunt) £52,000, ib. 132–134, 136, 138–138v.

CLOTWORTHY, Sir John, MP, later 1st Lord Massereene (d.1665). G.E.C.; *D.N.B.*; M.F.K. From Antrim. MP for Maldon, Essex, in the Long Parliament. He befriended Whitelocke in connection with the Savile case, in 1645.

COGHILL family (below): of Bletchington (Bletchingdon), Oxon. J.H. Coghill *Family of Coghill 1377 to 1879* (Cambridge. 1879); *V.C.H. Oxon.* vi, 57, 59, *passim*; Oxfordshire C.R.O. Misc. Bru. 1/1 *passim* and Dash. xi/i/1–4; *Royalist Ordnance Papers* ii, 358, 505; the Coghill family memorial, St. Giles's Church, Bletchington; *Diary* 1640, *passim*. Related to Whitelocke, probably through the Dixons (q.v.).

COGHILL, Elizabeth (d.1675). Née Sutton, of Aldenham, Herts.; heiress to The Sutton, Surrey. Whitelocke's kinswoman, Add.Ms 37345 fol.79. In 1622 she married Thomas (below) who was knighted in 1633. The receipt for a black box containing three leases connected with Lady Coghill, is dated 13 July 1656, Long. W.P. xvii, 176. Other related documents are in the Oxfordshire C.R.O. (above).

COGHILL, Sir Thomas (d.1659). Younger son of a London merchant. Coghill built Bletchington Manor House, Oxfordshire, in about 1630; he quarrelled with the Rector and later with his fellow-Royalist Colonel

Francis Windebank when the latter was Governor of Bletchington House, which was garrisoned during the Civil War. Against Whitelocke's advice, Coghill arranged the conveyance of his estate to his son Thomas, to avoid sequestration, *Diary* 30 June 1647; this resulted in bitter family disputes in the 1650s. Coghill tried to sell Bletchington to Whitelocke, ib. 26 Sept. 1654, but Whitelocke, in a letter thanking Coghill for his hospitality, declined to buy it, 5 Jan. 1654/55, Long. W.P. xvii,1. Sales particulars of the Manor give detailed valuations, totalling £28,193, ib., 3, 5–7v., 9. A note from Coghill's agent, sending further particulars to Whitelocke's representative, expresses the desire both that Sir Thomas should have a full value set on his lands and that Lord Whitelocke should get 'a pennyworth for a penny', ib. 11, 13. After quarrelling with his eldest son and namesake, Sir Thomas left the Manor and lands to his younger sons, John and Sutton; in spite of this, the Manor went to his eldest son in the year after Sir Thomas's death.

Whitelocke may well have met the young Christopher Wren with the Coghills, for Wren's sister married Dr. William Holder, Rector of Bletchington, who had grounded Wren in mathematics; in 1669 Wren married Faith Coghill, who was either Sir Thomas's daughter (*V.C.H. Oxon*, vi, 58; *Family of Coghill* ... p. 42), or the daughter of Sir John Coghill, and grand-daughter of Sir Thomas (*D.N.B.* in Wren's entry).

COKAYN (COKAYNE, COKAIN), George, (1619–1691). *D.N.B.*; *Calamy Revised*; *Bedfordshire Times* 26 Aug. 1932 (article, 'George Cokayn: a forgotten Bedfordshire man', based partly on documents in the Bedfordshire R.O.); references and biographical note in B. Capp *Fifth Monarchy Men*; Add.Ms 37345 fols. 190, 220, 228, Cokayn took his BA at Sidney Sussex College, Cambridge. An Independent Minister, he served as Rector of Pancras (St. Pancras), Soper Lane, until he was ejected at the Restoration; and was also appointed Chaplain to Charles Fleetwood (q.v.) in August 1651; he is said to have conducted John Bunyan's funeral. Sporadically a Fifth Monarchist, he was sometimes in political trouble under the Protectorate, and later under Charles II. Marchmont Nedham (q.v.) reported on a seditious meeting at Blackfriars, 19 Dec. 1653, at which Cokayn preached after the Fifth Monarchists, Christopher Feake and Vavasour Powell. Cokayn's text was Hosea 5 verse 2: 'And the revolters are profound to make slaughter, though I have been a rebuker to them all.' He attacked priests, kings and, by implication, the Protector, who had only assumed power a week earlier, *C.S.P. Dom.* 1653–54 pp. 304–308. See also a report on Cokayn as a conspirator with Captain George Bishop and others, in Bishop's entry. Cokayn's letters to

Whitelocke, however, suggest that he soon became reconciled to the new regime.

He became a life-long friend of Whitelocke's after they met in 1650. Whitelocke stayed with Cokayn's parents, John (q.v.) and Elizabeth, at Cotton End, Bedfordshire, while courting his third wife, Mary; the secret marriage, in Bromham Church, was undertaken from their house and with their knowledge. He also knew George Cokayn's wife Abigail, their daughters Abigail and Elizabeth (?), and their son William.

When Whitelocke went to Sweden, he left George Cokayn and Bartholomew Hall (q.v.) in charge of his affairs, under Mary's overall direction. Cokayn, the famous preacher with a humorous, benign face, knew the ways of the political world and wrote racy letters to Sweden, full of news. In one (an extract from which appears in *Journal* ii, 232–234) he wrote:

> ... I thinke (as I have hinted ... in former letters) it will not be amiss if you draw good store of bills uppon us though but pro forma that wee may gett as much money as wee can for you before y[ou]^r return and that you may have a sufficient overplus to pay off servants wages which I beleeve will amount to a considerable sume. & uppon this peace [with the Dutch] I hope it will be noe hard matter to gett y[ou]^r bills payd[,] especially if your excell[en]^{cy} please ... to write to my Lord prot[ector] & Mr Thurloe [q.v.] & some of the Councell about it. I could wish that you would make what hast[e] you can home for I am informed by a speciall hand that theier is great Labouring to make a Chancellore ... & to take the opportunity to put you by, whome I believe they doubt to be too much a Christian & an Englishman to trust in theier service ... [After signing the letter, dated 2 Apr. 1654, he continued] turn over to the other side of the paper. Since the writing of my Letter[,] extraordinary newes from the other end of the Town came to us viz: the Lord prot[ector] sending for the Lords Commiss[ione]^{rs} of the great seale and taking away the seale ... onely telling them that he had occasion to make use of the seale for signing the articles between us and the Dutch ... But I having had many hints before ... did partly know the meaning ... & my heart akeing for feare of an affront to be putt uppon your Lor[dshi]^p in your absence I went immediately to Whitehall & between nine and ten a clock at night I had the favouer to speake w[it]^h Mr Thurloe[,] whoe was pleased to acquainte mee that it was his Highness & the Councells pleasure to make some alteration in that Court [Chancery] & that it was determined that your Lor[dshi]^p and S[i]^r Tho[mas] Widdrington [q.v.] & my Lord Lisle [q.v.] should have the seale comitted to you ... but I perceive this ... was not done w[it]^{h}out some tugging, but my Lord prot[ector] & John Thurloe were true to you & now I am out of all feares that any affront should be offerd you ... which I confess makes mee sleepe better then I did. Mr Mackworth [q.v.] deserves a Letter from you but not a word in it about this business ... Mr Thurloe hath played his part gallantly, & like a true Frinde for which I shall Love him as Longe as I Live ... in the meane time ... whatsoever falls out

... whatsoever Cottened [Cotton End] will afford is your Lor[dshi]^{ps} for 6 yea almost seaven Lifes ... [,] whether you have the seale or noe for it is not the greatness of your place but the worth of your persone that hath made us your servants ...

Long. W.P. xv, 107–108, endorsed by Whitelocke 'r[ec]d May 11 54', ib. 108v.

Cokayn wrote in his next letter:

... wee question not but by the beginning of June ... wee shall have the happ[i]n[e]s to wayte uppon y[ou]^r excell[en]^{cy} at Graves end whither some of us that love not Gunnes, others that love not water shall be brought in a coach w[i]^{t}h six horses if the new executor [Cromwell?] keep his word ...

A short extract from this letter appears in *Journal* ii, 233–234 and reflects the affection in which Whitelocke was held. His old servant Abel refused to be tempted into the Protector's service, as chief falconer, without his master's explicit permission, for:

... he would not serve the greatest prince in the world except he might wayte uppon you w[i]^{t}h a cast of Hawkes at the beginning of Sept[ember] every yeere into Bedd[ford]sh[ire]. It is pitty that gallantry should hurt any man[,] I shall therfore endeavower w[i]^{t}h Mr Thurloe ... to gett the place referred for him till your returne ... it is a noble profession that inspires ... such a spirite ...

Cokayn had his ear to the ground in matters political and legal; he reported that there were no more changes at Westminster Hall but:

Judg[e] Jermayn [q.v.] since his putting out is deade, and my Lord Keeble [q.v.] is not well[,] he is much troubled at his being layd aside. there is a constant meeting at the M[aste]^r of the Rolles his house by the judges and the greate Lawyers about reforming the Law[,] which must be done before they have another terme. they much complayne of the want of your Lor[dshi]^{ps} assistance in that business. [He went on, sarcastically] The French Ambassadouer is likely to return home againe *re infecta* because all London and Westminster and the Lines of Communication will not [provide] an house good enough to hide his heade in, York house and Lycester house being but ordinary stables in his account, ... Mr Peters [q.v.] adjourned his death till next week and[,] by what I could gather from him this day[,] resolves to doe soe *de die in diem* till the Law be reformed, or y[ou]^r excell[en]^{cy} returne, in the meane time he can neither stand nor goe nor sitt nor ly nor ride nor speake nor heare nor eate nor drinke nor write nor reade nor understand English or Lattin, therefore I judg[e] it not yet convenient to show him the verses or the Queenes Letter ...

Long. W.P. xv, 138–138v., endorsed 14. April 1654 recd. 11 May 1654.

In the next letter, Cokayn wrote regretting the trouble Whitelocke put himself to in writing long letters:

... yet considering the content my Lady [Whitelocke's wife Mary] takes therein and what a diversion it is of sad afflicting thoughts[,] I know not how to entreat y[ou]ʳ Lor[dshi]ᵖ to abate of your trouble ... wee all Longe to see you heere ... On Wednesday last the peace between us and Holland was publiquely proclaymed at Whitehall[,] Temple Barre, and the old Exchange ... It is hoped trading will be much quickened by it. Yesterday his Highness Feasted the Dutch Ambassadours and their Ladyes[,] he gave them an exceeding greate entertaynment, especially w[i]ᵗʰ musick which was the best England afforded. His Highnes hath passed an Act for making England and Scotland one Com[m]onwealth and the Sᵗ Andrewes Cross is now to be added to the Armes of England. an act is alsoe passed for the pardoning of all Delinquents in Scotland excepting some greate ones whose names I have herew[i]ᵗʰ sent ... I have bin this day w[i]ᵗʰ some of the Grandees to prepare them for the newes of some very great bills of exchange ... and I finde that wee shall (though I doubt not w[i]ᵗʰout some difficulty) gett them payd. when the bills come I shall cheerfully ... lay out myself in your ... service ... and shall be glad ... to show ... what a grateful resentment [i.e. appreciation] I have of all y[ou]ʳ favoures and what true affections I beare to the persons of you and yours ... I cannot complement but what I am and have is yours ...

Ib. 141, 28 Apr. 1654, endorsed recd. 25 May.

The next week, active as ever, Cokayn wrote:

... I waited this afternoon upon my Lady to Whitehall about the Ships and I finde the Councell have passed an Ord[e]ʳ to the Com[missione]ʳ of the Admiralty to appoint two good frigats for y[ou]ʳ L[ordshi]ᵖᵖˢ Service, I went to the Admiralty and found Gen[eral] Desborow with the Councells ord[e]ʳ in his hand & he promised to move it instantly, but it being post day, I could not stay[;] the Secretary hath promised this night to send me a Coppy of their Ord[e]ʳ and I hope it will come before our pacquett be made upp ... The Officers in Ireland[,] except some few[,] have signed a pap[e]ʳ in approbation of the present Government ... [After giving other political news he went on, teasingly] I have this day challenged my Lady [Mary Whitelocke] to goe to Hamborough [Hamburg] in those shipps that are appointed for yo[u]ʳ Ex[cellen]ᶜⁱᵉ but I doubt Gravesend will serve our turne & then the grand queston in debate among us is whether it be Lawfull after we heare ... of your ... arrivall ... to stay to take M[ist]ʳⁱˢ Earle [wife of Whitelocke's secretary] a longe with us[;] my Lady holds it absolutely in the negative, and [all] the arguments in the world cannot convince her ... but wee sent very gravely to S[i]ʳ Oli[ver] fleming [q.v., Master of Ceremonies] to know whether [you] ... might ... come home privately or no according to the Law of Nat[i]ons, he answered ... [it] was most proper so to doe, ... w[hi]ᶜʰ spoyles a most Learned disputat[i]on and now lest we should be surprized ... wee are getting all thinges ready at Chelsey a pace ... where we shalbe Longing & praying for yo[u]ʳ safe returne ...

5 May 1654,

Add.Ms 37347 fols. 263v.–264; endorsed recd. [in Stockholm] 25 May (transcript)

PLATE 5

Edward Hyde, 1st Earl of Clarendon.

PLATE 6

George Cokayn, Independent Minister of Pancras Church, Soper Lane, London.

PLATE 7

Queen Christina, by Sébastien Bourdon.

PLATE 8

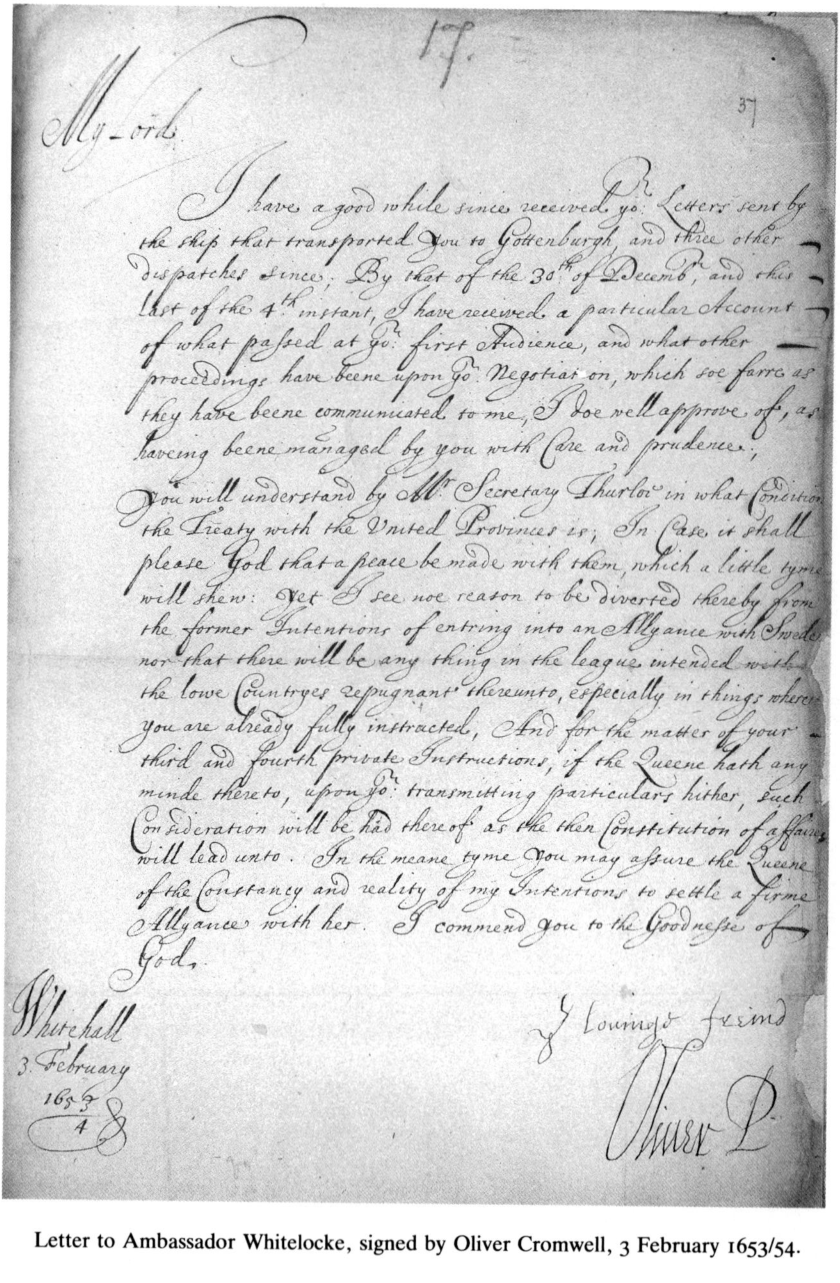

17.

37

My Lord,

I have a good while since received yo:r Letters sent by
the ship that transported you to Gottenburgh, and three other
dispatches since; By that of the 30:th of Decemb:r, and this
last of the 4:th instant, I have received a particular Account
of what passed at yo:r first Audience, and what other
proceedings have beene upon yo:r Negotiation, which soe farre as
they have beene communicated to me, I doe well approve of, as
haveing beene managed by you with Care and prudence;

You will understand by M:r Secretary Thurloe in what Condition
the Treaty with the United Provinces is; In Case it shall
please God that a peace be made with them, which a little tyme
will shew: Yet I see noe reason to be diverted thereby from
the former Intentions of entring into an Allyance with Swede
nor that there will be any thing in the league intended with
the lowe Countryes repugnant thereunto, especially in things wherein
you are already fully instructed, And for the matter of your
third and fourth private Instructions, if the Queene hath any
minde thereto, upon yo:r transmitting particulars hither, such
Consideration will be had thereof as the then Constitution of affaires
will lead unto. In the meane tyme you may assure the Queene
of the Constancy and reality of my Intentions to settle a firme
Allyance with her. I commend you to the Goodnesse of
God,

Y:r Loving freind

Oliver P.

Whitehall
3 February
165 3/4

Letter to Ambassador Whitelocke, signed by Oliver Cromwell, 3 February 1653/54.

Cokayn's last letter was presumably among those Whitelocke received on his way to Hamburg:

... I received your Excell[en]^{cyes} of the 28th of Aprill this morning and immediately repayred to Whitehall and had the opportunity to dine privately w[i]th Mr Thurloe and soe to speake fully w[i]th him ... concerning the Queene of Swedens goods which are detayned here, he did assure me they should be instantly discharged, and delivered to Mr Boneale [Bonnel, q.v.] ... This morning ... the councell have passed an order for mee to receive 1200^l for y[ou]^r Excell[en]^{cyes} use of the Com[missione]^{rs} of the Custome house ... soe that I hope w[i]thin a few dayes to deliver y[ou]^r money to my Lady the faythfull Casheere [Mary Whitelocke]. Wee might as well have had as much more money if your bills had not bin soe moderate ... butt wee submitt to y[ou]^r ... greater wisdome, though wee would have bin glad to have presented you w[i]th something at home that might have made upp the loss y[ou]^r Excell[en]^{cy} will have by your good nature in that cold country, It is well we have so greate an affection to your person for wee now playnly perceive wee shall never receive you with your feathers but it will be a sufficiently joyfull day wherein wee see y[ou]^r Excell[en]^{cy} though on Foot, having newly bought a payer of black coach horses[,] speciall good ones[,] to present to your Excell[en]^{cye} uppon your returne ... I judg[e] that this letter will not come to y[ou]^r ... hands therfore I forbeare to write any thinge of secresy though at this time somethinge of that nature offers itself but our water [i.e. secret ink] being bad I dare not use it, therfore I shall onely trouble y[ou]^r Lor[dshi]^{pp} w[i]th the ordinary newes. This week a desperate persone should have assassinated his Highness and his Councell, seised Whitehall and proclaymed Cha[rles] Stuart there and all England over[,] and in all parts to have risen to a bloody Masacer of all the honnest people in the nation. [Vowel and Gerard's Plot, of May 1654, see D.E. Underdown *Royalist Conspiracy in England 1649–1660*, Yale U.P. 1960, pp. 101–102; T. Carlyle *Letters and Speeches of Oliver Cromwell*, ed. S.C. Lomas, ii, 333, 335] this might easily have bin effected, ... because soe many men have bin sent into Scotland and on shipboard, insomuch that the drumes beate upp this day for Volunteeres to be listed under Col[one]l Ingolsby[,] that is a thing not known for some yeares ... past. It is beleeved by some of the Councell ... that Cha[rles] Stuart is now in London which occasioned the enclosed proclamation, the partyes already Com[m]itted for this conspiracy are in a list enclosed but others are brought in dayly and severall partyes are gone out to apprehend more of them in divers places in England and Mr Thurloe tells mee many considerable men are engaged in this develish designe. And certaynly there is something more then ordinary in this plot for it makes them look sadly at Court and some stout men look as if they were extreamly affrighted[.] I see not indeed the old parliamentary mettle ... Yesterday the old man [Judge Jermyn] was buryed[.] Mr Sedgwick preached but spake not a word in his com[m]endations[;] the reason was because he could say nothing but that he dyed a rich man[,] which the younge la[w]yers knew better then himself, next Monday wee [with Mary Whitelocke and the children] remove

to Chelsy ... I am halfe undon[e] if you arrive not in England before May be ended ...
26 May 1654

Long. W.P. xv,195–195v.

COKAYN (COKAIN), John. Father of George (above). Whitelocke described admiringly

> ... the mediocrity ['the mean' in Aristotle's sense] & middle estate & condition, of that private family of M[r] Cokain where I was now intertained. They were people not given to vanity, or lyes, ... of a smalle Estate, yett having sufficient to live comfortably & conveniently, not riotously, yett plentifully ... The Master & Mistris of the family ordering ... affayres of the household, more by themselves, then by serv[an][ts] who were few butt carefull, their provisions were in season sweet & good, yett not delicate nor superfluous ... cleanly, well drest and after the English fashion. the meat & drinke, the company & conversation was not exceeded by the stately neighbouring pallaces ...

See CLEVELAND, 1st E. of, for Dorothy Osborne's description of the Earl's house at nearby Toddington, as fit only for a Prince; Whitelocke's vignette of the Cokayn household, in Add.Ms 37345 fol.224, is followed by a meditation on Proverbs 30 verse 8: 'Remove farre from me vanity & lyes, give me neither poverty nor riches ...' John Cokayn sent his son George, at Lord Whitelocke's lodging in Whitehall, particulars of a property named Rowney which he could have for £12,000 (evidently meaning Whitelocke rather than George) and the old man wrote that it was a very good bargain, 24 Nov. 1651, Long. W.P. xi,130.

COKE, Clement, MP. S.R. Gardiner *History of England 1603–1642* vi, 76; Cambridge University Library, Ms Dd 12.20–22 fol.43, *passim* (Whitelocke's Parliamentary Diary, 1626). 'Fighting Clem', youngest son of Sir Edward Coke (below) was, like Whitelocke, a member of Charles I's second Parliament.

COKE, Sir Edward, MP (1552–1634). C.D. Bowen *The Lion and the Throne* (Hamish Hamilton. 1957); *D.N.B.*; *Liber, passim.* Of Clifford's Inn (an Inn of Chancery dependent on the Inner Temple). The brutal prosecutor at the trials of Essex, Walter Raleigh and the gunpowder plotters; an eminent and contentious Lord Chief Justice, he courageously opposed James I's inflated claims for the royal prerogative. Hated and condemned by some contemporaries, he was admired by his young friend, Whitelocke's father, for his outstanding integrity, ib. p. 50. Whitelocke claims that, as a young man, he himself was 'admitted into perticular acquaintance' with Coke and other eminent lawyers and politicians, *Diary* 1625. 1626. fol.7.

COLE, Robert. *Middle Temple Admission Register*. Third son of George Cole of Petersham. A contemporary of Whitelocke's at the Middle Temple, he was called to the Bar in February 1630/31, and went as Whitelocke's travelling companion to France, in 1634.

COLLADON, Sir John, MD. W. Munk *Roll of the Royal College of Physicians* i, 321. Nephew of the distinguished physician Sir Theodore de Mayerne (q.v.), Add.Ms 37345, fols.33v.–34. As Deputy from Geneva (with which City he retained connections), he brought congratulations to Charles II, *Diary* 2 July 1660. Naturalized by the King, he became one of the Queen's physicians. He attended Whitelocke from time to time, both as a doctor and as a client; a troublesome prospective purchaser of Greenland, he paid a deposit and sealed an agreement, but never completed the deal, ib. 25 Apr. 1668 with note, *passim*.

COLLINS, John (1632–1687). *D.N.B.*; *Calamy Revised*. A Congregational Minister, educated in America where he was made a Fellow of Harvard; Chaplain to George Monck in 1659, whom he is said to have accompanied from Edinburgh to London; after that however, in March 1660, it was reported that Monck dismissed his Independent Ministers in favour of Presbyterians. On the other hand *Diary*, 21 Nov. 1659, records that Whitelocke was informed by letter at that date that many of Monck's men were dissatisfied, and that Mr. Collins had left him. Collins was later referred to as 'one of the best preachers in or about London ... some say the best.' A large congregation came to hear his sermon at the house of Nathaniel Ponder (q.v., John Bunyan and Whitelocke's publisher, and Whitelocke's landlord at the time), ib. 13 Dec. 1668.

COMBE, Thomas. Whitelocke termed him an ungrateful and dishonest man, formerly of Henley. According to *The Diary*, a petition from Combe against Whitelocke was postponed from 31 January and dismissed by the Lords on 7 February 1661/62. No reference to this has been found in *L.J.*, the Lords being concerned nearly all day on 7 Feb. with regicides being brought to the Bar, attainted of high treason.

CONSTANTINE, Sir William, MP (1612–1670). M.F.K.; *Master Worsley's Book on ... the Middle Temple* (ed. A.R. Ingpen. 1910). A Middle Temple lawyer; brother-in-law of Whitelocke's friend Bartholomew Hall (q.v.); disabled by Parliament and deprived of the recordership of Poole, Dorset. He was reinstated and knighted after the Restoration, and became Middle Temple Treasurer in 1688. He supported Sir John Colladon (q.v.) in Sir John's proposal to purchase Greenland from Whitelocke.

COOKE, William (d.1653). Copyholder at Fawley Hill (probably Fawley Court Farm), Add.Ms 37343, fol.259v., where he was a tenant farmer and was also employed on the Fawley estate by Whitelocke, as by Judge Sir James Whitelocke before him; Cooke was 'trusted in his Countrey affayres ... & held the ablest man for such buisnes in those parts', *Diary* 1632. 1633. fol.18. Whitelocke not only heeded his tenant's forthright advice on estate management, but also on personal and professional matters such as marriage, and acceptance of appointment as a Keeper of the Great Seal, and as Ambassador Extraordinary to Queen Christina of Sweden. Cooke died in his cart, returning home from London (where he refused to stay overnight) after delivering a load of wheat, apples, butter and other provisions for Whitelocke's journey across Sweden. Whitelocke wrote: 'I have a great losse of him espetially att this time & I know no man alive whom I cann trust more or speake [to] so freely as I could to him', Long. 124A fol.20.

A précis of the old countryman's advice to his master to remarry after Rebecca's death, even to his naming a suitable young lady, is given in *The Diary*, early in 1634. 1635. fol.29v., and a note refers to the vivid, dialogue version in the 'Annales'; this led to Whitelocke meeting and falling in love with Frances Willoughby, and to their runaway marriage. A shortened transcript is given in R. Spalding *Improbable Puritan* pp. 58–60.

Among a number of memoranda between Cooke and Whitelocke are: Whitelocke's note about sheep and the profit from their wool, Long. W.P. v, 200v.; a receipt for £30 from Cooke for the cows ('kine') 'about the house' (i.e. around Fawley Court or the Farm?); Whitelocke was to supply hay for them until May Day; Cooke was also to rent Horseleas Close at £15 p.a., but he was to sell back the cows and give up the Close, if required to do so within a year; below this is a note about Cooke sowing Rogers field, Rogers Hill and Foxholes Close in 't[w]o halfes', Whitelocke finding half

the seed and lending Cooke £100 for one year, 4 Apr. 1634, ib. vi, 80.
Cooke was a witness to a bond for £20, signed by William Lewys of Henley
to Whitelocke, 4 Jan. 1635/36, ib., vii, 1. Whitelocke and Cooke signed a
bill to John Clarke in £300, 1 May 1639, ib. 326. A receipt concerning 300
loads of billets, and 200 of stackwood, at £27.10s.0d. and £30 a hundred,
respectively, 2 Aug. 1639, is in ib. 338. There is a further reference to
Cooke as tenant of Fawley Court, 17 July [1650], ib. x, 157.

Three letters from Cooke have been traced. They reflect both his
affection for the Whitelocke family and his freedom in speaking his mind.
His spelling is bizarre, even in 17th century terms. The first letter, written
in about March 1644, tells of damage done by Parliament's soldiers to
Whitelocke's property, the Bell in Henley, Add.Ms 37343 fols. 290–290v.,
transcribed in R. Spalding *Improbable Puritan* p. 99. The next concerns
Whitelocke's loss of his wife Frances, nearly nine months earlier. Cooke
thought his master seemed even more distressed the last time they met,
than before. He recalled his own grief at

> the losse of my three Dames [Whitelocke's mother, wife Rebecca, and then
> Frances, all three] sorllye mist & specially my last Dame ... M[aste]^r I doe
> find that some that be neer you, hath no desier that you should marie with no
> woman nether good nor bad, butt ... M[aste]^r I desier you ... if you can,
> meet with a good onest woman doe not be daunted with no man nor woman

1 Feb. 1649[50].

Add.Ms 37345 fol.45 (transcript).

See *Diary*, same date. The last note can be dated around 14 February
1649/50, since it concerns Robert D'Oiley's letter of that date offering to
sell Whitelocke a property for £1,300, Long. W.P. x, 121. *The Diary*
ignores these particular negotiations, which refer to 344 acres of farmland
and woodland with four farms, belonging to Greenland Manor, at
Woodend, north-east of Hambleden, Bucks.; the tenants' rents totalled
£311.16s.6d. p.a. These details are given at the top of a paper on which
Cooke wrote:

> M[aste]^r I have a great desier that you should deall with Mr Doylie for this
> bargin & give it to your litell prattilling boy at my house[;] let that be his
> porcion ... I do thinke that it is a very good bargin at xii hundred poundes[;]
> these livinges maie stik by him when you & I have did [i.e. died] & gone & If
> thear should be a diferrance betw[i]xt Mr Doylie & you for a hundred
> poundes I would make som shifte orother to agre w[it]h you that you should
> not parte I rest your sarvant to command to you or yourne ...

Long. W.P. x, 120.

The 'litell prattilling boy' was presumably Whitelocke's third son, Bulstrode
jun., then aged two; the elder brothers, James and William, were to inherit

Fawley Court and Phyllis Court but no provision had been made for the (at that date) youngest son. Two months after Whitelocke's second wife's death he had left five of his younger children in the care of William and 'Good wife' Cooke, *Diary* 30 July 1649, and it may appear from Cooke's letter that little Bulstrode was still with them.

COOPER, Anthony Ashley, see ASHLEY, 1st Baron.

COOPER, George. G.E. Aylmer *State's Servants* pp. 131–132. Brother of Anthony Ashley Cooper, 1st Baron (q.v.). He had married the widow of Alderman John James. Cooper pursued Whitelocke in 1671 and 1672 for £40, which had been lent to Whitelocke's improvident son James by the late Alderman, on Whitelocke's promise to repay it.

COOTE, Sir Charles, MP (d.1661). G.E.C.; *D.N.B.* Initially, a Parliamentarian; Commander in Ireland and President of Connaught. He turned Royalist after Richard Cromwell's fall, was appointed President of Connaught, and created Earl of Mountrath in 1660.

CORBET, Miles (1595–1662). *D.N.B.*; M.F.K. His execution is not mentioned in *The Diary*, so he does not appear in a footnote with other regicides. After Whitelocke's refusal to serve on Corbet's committee to draw up charges against Archbishop Laud (q.v.), in 1643, diary entries only concern news of Corbet in England, Ireland and Wales; they do not suggest any further personal contact.

CORRALL (CORALL), Sebastian. Described by Whitelocke as one of his servants for the Swedish embassy: 'an honest old fellow, the sculleryman', Add.Ms 4902 fol.20. In 1655 Corrall petitioned:

> L[or]^d Whitelocke one of the Governors of Westminster Colledge ... your Pet[itione]^r having bin a soldier for the present Governement both by sea and land. And ... was your Honors humble servant in the time of your Ambassage in Swedland [in the previous year]. And being stricken in age ... humbly flyeth unto your Honor ...

He appealed for a letter of recommendation to the Governors for an almsman's place in the College. This, Whitelocke procured for him,

Add.Ms 4992 fol.128; *Diary* 4 Aug. 1655. Eighteen months later, Corrall petitioned Whitelocke for a place for his son in Sutton's Hospital, ib. 2 Feb. 1656/57.

COTTON, Sir Thomas, Bt. (1594–1662). *D.N.B.* (in his father Sir Robert's entry). He inherited the great Cotton Library. A note of Whitelocke's borrowings from it appears in this volume under 'Manuscript Sources, B.L. . . . Cotton Library'. Whitelocke refers to having Sir Thomas Cotton exempted from being Sheriff of Bedfordshire, which he did readily in gratitude for 'the freedom of his excellent Library'. A year later he performed the same service, at Sir Thomas's request, 'for his own [Cotton's] sake & for Mr Selden their friends sake', *Diary* 25 Oct. 1656; 2 Nov. 1657.

COYET (COYETT, KOYET), Sir Peter Julius (1618–1687). *Swedish Diplomats at Cromwell's Court* . . . (translated and edited by M. Roberts. Camden 4th series. 1988). Swedish Resident or Envoy from Charles X, concerned with trade negotiations; (described in *Shaw's Knights* as Ambassador). He was knighted by Cromwell, before his departure, and given the Protector's portrait, with a chain or jewel worth £400 or £500, *Diary* 1 Apr., 3 May, 5 Aug. 1656. Later, Coyet wrote long letters to Whitelocke, explaining the grounds of Sweden's dispute with Denmark and giving reasons why the King could not agree to the terms which the Commissioners, negotiating peace talks, were trying to impose, ^{16}/$_{26}$ Dec. 1659, Long. W.P. xix, 98 (Latin); 30Dec.1659/9Jan.1660, ib. 108 (French); both letters sent from The Hague. Whitelocke, out of office and on the run, did not reply until 25 Feb. 1659/60. His letter, also in French, explained that the reason for his silence was that he had been indisposed. He had tried to promote the Swedish King's interests, but the troubles and displeasure falling on him after the recent changes in England (his collaboration with the Committee of Safety, followed by the restoration of Parliament) had made it impossible, ib. 125.

CRAVEN, William, 1st E. of (*c.*1608–1697). G.E.C.; *D.N.B.* Created Baron Craven of Hampsted Marshall in March 1626/27 then Viscount and Earl in March 1664/65. His properties included Combe Abbey near Coventry, Hampsted Marshall in Berkshire (where Whitelocke saw the Earl's new house in 1665), and Caversham Park. Craven, known as 'the little Earl', was immensely rich. He was known for his generosity towards

Elizabeth of Bohemia and her family. A sequestration order on his property had excluded Combe Abbey. Whitelocke claims to have done him service, *Diary* 9 Nov. 1654 (when Craven was attempting to have a judgement against himself reversed). Later, the Baron (as he then was) made a direct appeal to Whitelocke, ib. 28 July 1659, with note.

CREW, John, MP (1598–1679). G.E.C.; *D.N.B.*; M.F.K.; *Hist. of Parl.*; *Pepys* x. He served with Whitelocke in the Long Parliament and as a parliamentary Commissioner to negotiate with the King at Uxbridge; Crew was also a Commissioner in Newcastle, at Holdenby, and on the Isle of Wight. Like Whitelocke, he was opposed to the King's trial and execution. There is no diary reference to Crew after he sent Whitelocke a present of venison and showed him great respect, *Diary* 11 Jan. 1647/48. He was created Baron Crew of Stene in 1661.

CRIPS (CRISP), Capt. John. Appointed to Whitelocke's household for the Swedish Embassy and described by him as '... a discreet grave fashionable Man, Clerke of the Stable, and one of the Gentlemen Servers ...', Add.Ms 4995 appendix 5, fol.11v. One of 13 members of the Ambassador's household who received a gold chain with Christina's portrait on a medal. Referred to as 'Crisp' by Whitelocke, but he signed his name 'Crips' on a long letter sent from Uppsala to Robert Blackburne, Secretary to the Admiralty Commissioners. This letter complements the diary account of the journey across Sweden:

> His [the Ambassador's] Jorney was tedious[,] full of hardships & very Chargable: from Gotten Burgh was sent a man of breeding ... the shendick [i.e. Syndic] w[hi]^ch is one that keeps the Records of the Cittye [i.e. Recorder] togeather w[i]^th the Secretary of Lord lagerfelt [Jean Berkman] sent immediately from the Queene Impowered to press Carrages & Horses from stage to stage, ... our Baggage was soe great that my lord was at the Charge of paying neare 200 horses every day, not w[i]^thstanding he left behind all his Beare & Wine & gross & ponderous stoufes ... his large traine of Baggage ... Togeather w[i]^th his retinue seemed in their March like to a petty Army[;] the first day we pasd ... a Dirty & a myrie way[;] at night ... a homely dyett & worse lodging but our straw was cleane, three days we marched in a Rockey, barren Contry but furnished w[i]^th ... gallant springs desending from the Rockes, then for Fower days we traveled through the most pleasant woods that ever I beheald ... the trees are all greene now as in the midst of summer. It pleased god to give us such brave weather that we thought we had left the winter & were traveling in the greene woods as in the spring[;] for the Townes I can speake little ... in praise of the Accommodations

... made for travelers on the road ... my lord was forced to repose him selfe in [a room] the Swine uses to sport them selves, in the best of the Booer houses the kittchins generally on the Road were Hoggs styes, against his Ex[cellen]^{cie} Coming they killed a Leane scragged Beife & put it in a readyness in the kittchin wher it had p^r[e]ferment next the Hogship ...' [Crips went on to describe the school house at Scarow i.e. Skara] ... w[hi]ch is both scoole & Collidge. In he[e]r wer[e] some 3 hundered scollers some 20 some 30 years of age[,] all subject to the rod[;] the Higher read Phylosophy lodgicke & soe down [to] greeke[,] lattin &c ... & soe downeward to the beginning of lerning ... The next Citty was Osbro [Örebro] ... ther my lord had hansom Accommodation & his retinue very good quarters[,] I meane good beds w[hi]ch is a rare thing & much prised in our travells; the next Cittye was Westrass [i.e. Västeras; but according to *The Diary*, Köping was the scene of the Mayor's insulting behaviour, an account of which follows] where the Praeter of the Citty was very negligent in Assisting ou[r]^e quarterm[aste]^r & was over heard by a boy that was the quarterm[aste]^r[s] guide to say that since the King was kild ther was none in Authority in England but Coblers & Tinkers w[hi]ch was told my Lord[,] who Civelly yett Austeerly declared his dyslike of that uncivell depp[o]rtment of the Praetor or Maior, the Gentlemen promised strickt inqui[r]ey should be made of the truth[;] the Maio[r]^e was sent for [and] Came that night to my Lord[.] Excused the words by another Gent[le]man[,] his frend[,] for he could not speake him selfe he did soe tremble & weepe for feare some Exemplary Justice shou[l]d have fallen uppon him, pleading he tould One that stood by him that he read such a thing in a Holland news booke & said that he said the Hollander[s] were lyers & that he saw my Lord was a Noble person & came Attended w[i]th an honorable retenue[,] he heartyly begged his p[ar]don, w[hi]ch was granted & the poore Pretor very Joyfull ... [Crips finished with an account of the Ambassador's reception outside Uppsala and preparations for the first audience]
22 Dec. 1653.

P.R.O. S.P. 95 5A 9919.

CROKE family (below). Related to the Whitelockes through Bulstrode's mother's mother. A distinguished name in 17th century legal circles. Some details are taken from A. Croke *Genealogical History of the Croke Family originally named Le Blount*, 2 vols. (John Murray & Joseph Parker. 1823).

CROKE, Charles. A younger son of Unton Croke, Serjeant-at-Law; brother of Sir Richard and of Colonel Unton Croke. He served as a page in Whitelocke's retinue, on the Swedish Embassy.

CROKE (CROOK, CROOKE), Judge Sir George (1560–1642). *D.N.B.*; *V.C.H. Oxon.* vii, 221, 223, *passim*; family monument in the Church of St. Mary the Virgin, Chilton, Bucks., near Thame. Third son of Sir John Croke and Elizabeth née Unton; he was the brother of Sir John Croke, jun., (who was Speaker of the House of Commons and a King's Bench Judge), and of Whitelocke's maternal grandmother, Cicely Bulstrode. He owned Waterstock Manor, west of Thame, in Oxfordshire. Whitelocke was born in Sir George Croke's house in Fleet Street, London. They referred to each other as 'uncle' and 'nephew' but Sir George was in fact Whitelocke's great-uncle. A further, more distant, family connection came through Whitelocke's first marriage: in middle age, Croke had married Mary Benet, second daughter of Sir Thomas Benet (Bennet) Kt., Lord Mayor of London; Mary Croke's cousin (and the Lord Mayor's nephew) Alderman Thomas Benet, Sheriff of London, was the father of Whitelocke's first wife, Rebecca (q.v.), and of Richard and Sir Thomas Benet Bt. (q.v.). For Lord Mayor Sir Thomas Benet Kt. and Alderman Thomas Benet (Bennet) see A.B.B. ii, 175, 177, *passim*. George and Mary Croke's eldest daughter, also Mary, married Harbottle Grimston jun. (q.v.); *Diary* 1627. 1628. fol.8 records how Whitelocke 'in a youthfull frollicke' played coachman to the young couple after their wedding. The Crokes' second daughter, Elizabeth, married (1) Thomas Lee (q.v.), of Hartwell near Aylesbury, and (2) Sir Richard Ingoldsby (q.v.), a regicide who was pardoned after the Restoration.

In 1638 Croke, a King's Bench Judge, challenged the legality of Ship Money levied by the Crown on John Hampden, without Parliament's consent. Earlier he had resisted royal interference with the judiciary.

Whitelocke, with Bartholomew Hall (q.v.) and Ralph Freke (q.v.), signed a bond in £1,600 to Sir George and Alexander Croke, for payment of £800 on 13 May 1639, Long. W.P. vii, 291.

Croke's famous reports on law cases were first published in 1641, shortly before his death, and were later translated from Norman-French into English by his son-in-law, Sir Harbottle Grimston jun. (q.v.). A letter from Croke (by then retired), concerned Whitelocke's regular communications reporting on parliamentary business, and particularly on the Commons' proceedings against Judges and Bishops; Croke appealed for support for the Judges, 1 Nov. 1641, Add.Ms 37343 fol.232v. (transcript); an inexact synopsis is given in *Memorials* i, 143–144.

CROKE, Sir Richard, MP (1625–1683). *Hist. of Parl.* Grandson of Judge Sir John Croke; son of Serjeant-at-Law Unton Croke, and brother of Colonel Unton Croke below. Recorder of Oxford.

CROKE, Unton, jun. (*fl*.1650s and 1660s). *D.N.B*. (in his grandfather Sir John Croke's entry, below that of his father Unton Croke, Inner Temple barrister and Serjeant-at-Law); there, his *father* seems to be mistakenly identified as the Unton Croke who accompanied Whitelocke to Sweden, but the retinue list names Whitelocke's kinsman as 'Capt. Unton Croke of the Army ... Son of Serg[e]ant Croke ... ', Add.Ms 4995 appendix 5 fol.11; subsequent diary entries confirm the identity. Unton Croke jun. was a Captain, later Colonel, in Parliament's Army, but shortly before the Restoration he and his regiment declared their obedience to Monck, *Diary* 29 Feb. 1659/60. Brother of Sir Richard and of Charles Croke (q.v.).

CROMWELL, Anne. Daughter of Sir Philip; a cousin of Oliver Cromwell, who harassed Whitelocke to find in her favour in protracted litigation against John Carey (q.v.) over Poyle Farm, Middlesex. Whitelocke intimated that, being under oath as a Judge, he could not oblige Cromwell; he noted that his colleagues were more compliant, *Diary* 21 Feb. 1648/49; 13, 20 Nov. 1651; 20 Feb. 1651/52.

CROMWELL, Henry (1628–1674). *D.N.B*. Fourth son of Oliver Cromwell. From 1650 onwards, he made his military career in Ireland, where he was appointed Commander-in-Chief in 1654; and Lord Deputy in 1657. He was handsomely entertained at Mostyn, in North Wales, by Whitelocke's royalist nephew Roger Mostyn, *Diary* 11 July 1655.

CROMWELL, Lord Protector Oliver (1599–1658). T. Carlyle *Letters and Speeches of Oliver Cromwell* (ed. in 3 vols. by S.C. Lomas. Methuen. 1904); *D.N.B*.; W.C. Abbott *Bibliography of Oliver Cromwell* (Harvard U.P. 1929); *Writings on Oliver Cromwell since 1929* (Chicago. 1961), a reprint from *J.M.H*. 33 No. 1. *The Diary* contains innumerable references to him, the first occurring in 1642. Later, Whitelocke noted that 'Cromwell & his party courted ... & shewed great respect to him', *Diary* 25 May (near the end) 1647. Entries in the 1650s indicate that Cromwell often consulted Whitelocke, particularly on foreign affairs; that he was some-times put out by Whitelocke's blunt advice, but that at other times he seemed to welcome a respite from flattery, ib. 11 July 1649; 7, 22 Jan. 1651/52; 16 June 1652; Mar. 1652/53; 30 Oct. 1655; 2–3 Apr. 1656, *passim*. In November 1653, a year after advising Cromwell not to take the title of King, Whitelocke found himself despatched to Sweden as Ambassador Extraordinary, to be out of the way (as he later believed) when Barebone's

Parliament resigned their powers to Lord General Cromwell on 12 December. Four days later, in Westminster Hall, Cromwell assumed the title of Lord Protector. Whitelocke's opposition to Cromwell becoming King of England is referred to in Chapter 1 of *The Diary*, yet he was among those who, in 1654, prepared the Lord Protector's oath, with its pledge to preserve the peace, safety and just rights of the people, according to law, Eg. 1048 fol.115.

The Diary describes how Cromwell liked to relax after hours spent in consultation: 'laying aside his greatnes', often in the company of Whitelocke, Lord Broghill (later E. of Orrery q.v.), young Sir Charles Wolseley (q.v.) and John Thurloe (q.v.); he would play bowls, write verses with them, sometimes smoke a pipe with Whitelocke, and enjoy 'some frollickes of diversion', *Diary* 12 Sept. 1655; 2 May, 18 Oct. 1657.

Most of Whitelocke's letters to Cromwell and Thurloe from Sweden are in Mss Rawl. and appear in *Thurloe S.P.* A notable exception is the inside page of a letter written in secret or 'sympathetic' ink, which Birch failed to transcribe since it had already faded by the 18th century. Largely illegible until photographed with an ultra-violet process, it is now transcribed for the first time. The covering page of the letter, which is printed in *Thurloe S.P.* ii, 133–134, ends: 'I beseech your Highnesse to make use of the water on the other leafe of this letter.' In an earlier letter he wrote that if Cromwell had lost the bottle of water for washing over the invisible ink, Mary would let him have another one. Queries occur in the transcript where dried splashes show that Cromwell or his Secretary put on too much of the liquid, washing out some of the writing:

> I find the Queene [Christina] much sett uppon it to have Spayne ... in the Treaty with England & Sweden wh[ich] I presume commetn from Don Piementel the Spanish Resident heere who is in greatest favour with her, & hath lodgings in her house & dayly waites uppon her; I have given an account of this in my letters to Mr Secretary Thurloe. As to the buisnes of the Sound I perceive that her M[ajes]^{ty} hath a fancy if the Isle of Zeland cann be gayned from the Dane that she would make that her retreit for a private life & have the[?] Island to herselfe, which will bringe no great advantage[?] to England. I asked her if she w[ould] not be contented to have some honest English Gent[le]men to commaund the Castles [Elsinore etc.], & some forces there such as your Highnesse should appoint, she say[d] Y[es] & if I were appointed by your Highnesse that she would be gladde of my Company; I told her that I had another [emplo]yment[?] in England w[hi]^{c}h would not permitt me. She desired me to write word to your Highnes that the Kinge of Denmarke was preparing some shippes to send to Guinne, & that it would be a great prejudice to the En[glish] [marc]h[ants][?] & she hoped that you would not permitt [it]. As soone as I may receive the happines of your Highnes p[ermission] to leave it to me to returne! I shall not stay longer then

my buisnes require, nor shall I prejudice that by making too much hast
from hence.
3 Mar. 1653/54

Ms Rawl. A.12, 143.

Christina's fantasy of eliciting Cromwell's help to capture the island of
Zealand, on which Copenhagen stands, was first mentioned by Whitelocke
six weeks earlier, *Diary* 21 Jan. 1653/54; a fuller account appears in *Journal*
i, 355–356. It was either not recorded in the original 'Journal', Long. 124A,
or it has disappeared from the manuscript. The project was evidently
encouraged (if not inspired) by the dissident Dane, Count Corfitz Ulfeldt
(q.v.), spelt 'Woolfeldt' by Whitelocke, *Diary* 12 Apr. 1654; *Journal* ii,
124–125. Christina's dream anticipated the empire-building adventures of
her successor, Charles X (q.v.).

The Long. W.P. Index lists numerous entries under Cromwell, many of
them being reports on his actions or references to him in letters. The
papers include: a copy of Cromwell's renewal and confirmation of
Whitelocke's instructions as Ambassador after the Protectorate was set up,
23 Dec. 1653, Long. W.P. xiv, 232; a signed letter in which Cromwell
acknowledged a letter from Whitelocke and stated that he had also '...
received a particular Account of what passed at y[ou]^r first Audience' – an
indication that members of the Ambassador's retinue sent their own
reports to the Protector '... and what other proceedings have beene
communicated to me, I doe well approve of, as haveing beene managed by
you with care and prudence ...' After referring to negotiations for a peace
treaty with the Netherlands, Cromwell continued reassuringly: 'I see noe
reason to be diverted thereby from the former intentions of entring into an
Allyance with Sweden ...' Nothing in the new treaty would be repugnant
to that. 'In the meane tyme you may assure the Queene of the Constancy
and reality of my Intentions to settle a firme Allyance with her ...' He
ended the letter 'Y[ou]^r lovinge freind Oliver P.' 3 Feb. 1653/54, Long.
W.P. xv, 37. See Plate 8, facing p. 55.

Additional Instructions, headed 'Oliver P.', ib. 114–114v., are published
in *Thurloe S.P.* ii, 218; Birch seems to have transcribed them from
Thurloe's copy. A copy of Cromwell's belated acknowledgment of
Christina's letter, delivered by Signor Passerini (q.v.), is dated 18 Feb.
1657/58; this prompted Whitelocke to write making excuses for the
Protector on 11 Mar., Long. W.P. xviii, 118, 123.

Whitelocke wrote bitterly about Cromwell casting people like himself
aside when they had served their turn, and criticized him for unwarrantably
dissolving Parliament, but he commended the Protector (even writing after
the Restoration) for not having acted from personal ambition.

CROMWELL, Richard (1626–1712). *D.N.B.* Third son of Oliver. He is first mentioned in *The Diary* at his father's 2nd inauguration as Protector, in June 1657. Whitelocke normally referred to him as 'Richard' but seldom referred to the older Cromwell as 'Oliver', and then usually in moments of annoyance. Whitelocke took a fatherly interest in the young Protector, was pleasantly surprised when he conducted himself with more poise than was generally expected, and was frequently consulted by him, *Diary* 18 Oct., 5 Nov. 1658, *passim*. Richard only survived as Protector for eight months; the beginning of his fall was seen by Whitelocke as dating from 14 April 1659, when the Army became restless over their pay etc.

Richard's regal-sounding letters patent appointed, as Lord Commissioners of the Treasury: Whitelocke 'Constable of our Castle of Windsor', Edward, Lord Mountagu (Montagu) 'one of our generalls at Sea', William, Lord Sydenham 'Captaine Governor of our Isle of Wight' and Sir Thomas Widdrington Kt. 'Chiefe Baron of our Excheq[ue]r', 18 Sept. 1658, Long. W.P. xviii, 151v.–152, (copy). 'Tumbledown Dick' was the nickname given to Richard by his enemies. By nature he was a country gentleman, with a liking for field sports, who did his best to give a sound performance in the part for which he was cast, and who had the character to say, at the time of his fall: 'I will not have one drop of blood spilt for the preservation of my greatness.'

CULLEN, Charles Cokayne, created Baron and Viscount (1602–1661). G.E.C. Of Tipperary. Said to have lost over £50,000 in the royalist cause; he compounded for £7,515. There is only one reference to Cullen, when Lady Cullen (Mary, daughter of Henry O'Brien, 4th E. of Thomond, q.v.) an old acquaintance of Whitelocke's, earnestly solicited his help for her husband. Whitelocke responded, 'butt they were little gratefull for it', *Diary* 1643.1644. fol.65v.

CULPEPER (CULPEPPER), Sir Cheney (Cheny), KB (d. *c.*1663). *D.N.B.* (in his father's entry). Eldest son of Sir Thomas Culpeper and Elizabeth née Cheney. Of Hollingbourne, Kent, he inherited Leeds Castle, Kent. One entry only, *Diary* 28 June 1656.

DALBIER, Col. John (d.1648). *D.N.B.* (Supplement); J. Rushworth *Historical Collections, passim*; T. Carlyle *Letters and Speeches of Oliver Cromwell* i, 223, 231 with note, 322. Of Dutch birth; he was said to have instructed Cromwell in the mechanical techniques of war and to have helped to train the Ironsides but see note above. He was with Cromwell at the storming of Basing House in October 1645, but joined the Royalists for the abortive Second Civil War, and was hacked to pieces by Parliament's soldiers. Only his death is noted by Whitelocke, *Diary* 5 July 1648.

DANBY, Henry Danvers, 1st E. of (1573–1644). G.E.C.; *D.N.B.* Of Dauntsey, Wilts., SE. of Malmesbury. A Royalist; brother of Charles with whom, as a young man, he murdered Henry Long of nearby Corsham, in a feud; for this the brothers were banished to France, but were later pardoned. Charles was beheaded as an accomplice in Essex's plot against Queen Elizabeth. Henry's younger brother, Sir John Danvers (below), was a regicide. Henry himself fought in the Netherlands and in France. He became Lieutenant of Wychwood Forest; Whitelocke, in his early 30s, was retained as Counsel against the Earl by several Oxfordshire landowners. Danby '. . . sought to promote his perticular interest as Lieutenant of that forest, though to the prejudice of gentlemen & freeholders there in the liberties & priviledges claymed by them'. Whitelocke studied the ancient forest laws, aided by Bartholomew Hall (q.v.) and others; he fought the case effectively and made an enemy of the Earl, *Diary* 1635.1636. fols. 41v., 42v., 43v.; 1637.1638. fol.44. See J.C. Cox *Royal Forests of England* (Methuen. 1905). Whitelocke outlined the case, writing of Danby's 'pretensions of power & privilege as Lieutenant of that forest', Add.Ms 37343 fols.148–149. Commenting to his children on the disadvantages of having to oppose a powerful man, he wrote of the need to be sure of your ground, to be just and honest and then to 'doe your worke roundly yett civilly', ib. 140v.–141. The fame that this case brought to Whitelocke no doubt contributed to his being appointed, soon after his election to the Long Parliament, as chairman of the distinguished committee which was to handle evidence for the impeachment of the Earl of Strafford (q.v.).

DANVERS, Sir John, MP (*c.*1588–1655). *D.N.B.*; J. Aubrey *Brief Lives.* A regicide, who did not live to be tried. Brother of the 1st Earl of Danby (above). He retained Whitelocke as his lawyer in 1645, in connection with a protracted legal case against his sister Catharine, Lady Gargrave; she had been the beneficiary under their brother the Earl of Danby's Will, because she was a Royalist, whereas Danvers had adhered to Parliament. Danvers brought the case to the Commons, who referred it to the Committee of Lords and Commons for Sequestration, *C.J.* iv, 403, 520; vi, 211, *passim*; P.R.O. S.P. 20/2 (vol. 2) 243, 20 Mar. 1645–46. Later, in another connection, Danvers wrote an unsigned paper to Whitelocke nominating men, in particular John Sadler (q.v.), for the work of 'supervising or contracting of the Laws' (through the Hale Commission on Law Reform), 26 Dec. 1651, Long. W.P. xi, 159–159v.; the manuscript was endorsed by Whitelocke 'Sir Jo Danvers Law'. See also B. Worden *Rump Parliament* pp. 272–273.

DAVENANT (D'AVENANT), Sir William (1606–1668). M. Edmond *Rare Sir William Davenant ...* (Manchester University Press. 1987); K. Sharpe *Criticism and Compliment ...* (C.U.P. 1987); *D.N.B.* His mother was the wife of a vintner, who was the proprietor of an Oxford tavern. A poet and a Royalist, Davenant consulted Whitelocke both about his poetry and about an opera, and later about arranging his release from the Tower, *Diary* 4 Sept. 1656; 16 Aug. 1659 with notes, including one on the rumour that he was William Shakespeare's son.

DAVIES, John (c.1625–1693). *Dictionary of Welsh Biography*; *D.N.B.*; D. Hook 'John Davies of Kidwelly: a neglected literary figure of the seventeenth century', *Carmarthenshire Antiquary* xi, 104–124 (1975). This article corrects some points in the *D.N.B.* A translator and writer, Davies studied at Jesus College, Oxford (until Oxford became a royalist garrison), and at St. John's College, Cambridge. He dedicated his *Treatise against the Principles of Descartes* (1654) to Whitelocke. He was probably the 'Mr Davys' who wrote to Whitelocke, *Diary* 27 Aug. 1658.

DEANE, Christopher. Boatswain of the *Elizabeth*, a frigate in Whitelocke's convoy for Sweden, in 1653. Later, he asked Whitelocke to recommend him for a gunner's place, ib. 17 Apr. 1657.

DEANE, Col. Richard (1610–1653). *D.N.B.*; G.E. Aylmer *State's Servants* p. 262, *passim*. Comptroller of the Train of Artillery in Fairfax's Army; Lieutenant of Artillery in Ireland, *C.J.* v, 176, 18 May 1647. Shortly after Pride's Purge, Whitelocke met, by appointment: Speaker Lenthall (q.v.), with Cromwell (q.v.), Cromwell's relative Colonel Deane, and Sir Thomas Widdrington (q.v.), when they discussed 'the present affayres, wherin Cromwell desired their advice ...', *Diary* 18 Dec. 1648. Deane was a regicide but did not live to be tried. In February 1649, he was one of three Commissioners (later styled Generals-at-Sea) appointed to command the fleet, jointly with Edward Popham and Robert Blake (q.v.). He was killed in action in the first Anglo/Dutch war.

DEANE, Mr ——. An acquaintance of Whitelocke's son James who, like James, borrowed money from Whitelocke.

DELL, William (1). H.R. Trevor-Roper 'William Dell', *English Historical Review* lxii (1947). The devoted secretary of Archbishop William Laud (q.v.); he is distinguished, in the above article, from the academic puritan (below). Although Whitelocke only refers to him once, he describes Laud's secretary as his 'old friend Mr Dell', *Diary* 1635. 1636. fol. 41v.

DELL, William (2), (d.1664). *E.H.R.* article (above); E.C. Walker *William Dell: Master Puritan* (Heffer. 1970); *D.N.B.*; *Calamy Revised*; C. Hill *Change and Continuity in 17th Century England* pp. 136–143, *passim*; B.S. Capp *Fifth Monarchy Men, passim*. A dissenter with a radical, religous fervour for equality. Chaplain in the New Model Army. As the 'intruded' Master of Gonville and Caius College, Cambridge, he envisaged a widespread extension of university education; he held the post of Master alongside that of Rector of Yelden, Bedfordshire, but lost these appointments in 1660 and 1662 respectively. Dell is not named when Whitelocke approached the Protector for a favour to Gonville and Caius, *Diary* 6 Feb. 1657/58. Eighteen months later he appealed to Whitelocke on behalf of some Bedfordshire men held prisoner, ib. 11 Aug. 1659, and four months after that he wrote, in characteristic terms, deploring Whitelocke's service on the Committee of Safety:

My Lord
   out of the intire respects I beare to yo[u]^r Hon[ou]^r, I could not choose but signify to you the great hazard you certainly runn, by joyning in with the Nine officers & their Adherents, for as their treacherous & rebellious Act is highly displeasing & di[s]honourable to o[u]^r righteous Lord God, so hee will in due tyme certainly judge them for so doing; yea & pursues them at the very heels, whilst they like drunken men are pursuing & prosecuting their friends[.]
   The infatuation of these officers is so great, that all men stand wondering at them, to see their ridiculous[,] incongruous, brainelesse actings, whilst they set at liberty S[i]^r George Booth, the Earle of Northamp[ton][,] Lord Bellasis, & other rebells, but newly ingaged in the highest Treason against Gods Cause & People, & imprisson Okey, Wagstaffe & other faithfull Officers, because they oppose them, in their horrid Treason & Rebellion

against the Parliament. And by this & the like Actions, the welaffected see, what they must by degrees expect from these officers ...

My Lord let no man deceave you, by telling you the godly people are satisfyed with this Act of the Armyes for I assure you, that all godly & sober people in all places where I come (& I learne from others, that it is so generally in all places) do abhor & detest this Act & look uppon these officers as the betrayers of Gods cause & people, for their owne unworthy ends sake ...

Wherefore my Lord as you tender the glory of God[,] the preservation of the cause & people, & therein y[ou]^r owne, use y[ou]^r ... utmost indeavo[u]^r for the setting downe of the longe Parliam[en]^t againe: for these officers must either be subject to their [i.e. Parliament's] just Authority, or abide the Tyranny of Charles Stuart. And all the blood & ruin of the honest party, will be uppon your heads ... Therefore my Lord come out from amonge them in due tyme ... I hope yo[u]^r Lordship will pardon my great boldnesse & plainesse with you[,] seeing what I have written [is] in uprightnesse of heart ... being grieved to see ... so wise & understanding & usefull a person, intangled in the snares of ruin, with giddy & unstable men ...

I remaine

Yo[u]^r faithfull servant in the Cause of Christ & the Com[m]onwealth
Ye[l]den December 19th [1659].   Will. Dell

                                              Long. W.P. xix, 105–104v.

DENBIGH (DENBY), Basil Feilding, 2nd E. of (c.1608–1675). G.E.C.; D.N.B. Nephew of the 1st Duke of Buckingham (q.v.). He served the Crown in the 1620s and 1630s, but fought for Parliament at Edgehill in October 1642, and was appointed Commander-in-Chief of Parliament's forces in Warwickshire, Worcestershire, Staffordshire, Shropshire, Coventry and Lichfield in June 1643. In the following year he headed Parliament's Commissioners (including Whitelocke) at the peace negotiations with the King in Oxford, and served again as a parliamentary Commissioner (once more with Whitelocke) at Uxbridge in Jan.1644/45. He supported Hollis and Whitelocke with evidence, in the Savile affair, *Diary* 12 July 1645 (having earlier cleared his own name, under suspicion of being disaffected, *L.J.* vii,51, 8 Nov. 1644). Although Denbigh's loyalty was questioned again in Dec. 1649, *C.S.P. Dom. 1649–1650*, pp. 444–447, he continued as a member of the Council of State from 1649 to 1651. Years later he came to Whitelocke as a client, *Diary* 17 Apr. 1662. In February 1664/65 he was created Baron St. Liz.

DENTON, Dr. William MD (1605–1691). W. Munk *Roll of the Royal College of Physicians*; *D.N.B.* Physician to Charles I and Charles II. A

Royalist, he wrote on political matters. Whitelocke was his patient in 1649, 1650 and 1665.

DERBY, Charles Stanley, 8th E. of, and Lord Strange (1628–1672). G.E.C. Mentioned by Whitelocke for his support of Sir George Booth's rising, his disguise as a serving man and his capture, *Diary* 5, 24 Aug. 1659.

DESBOROUGH (DISBROWE, DISBOROW), Major-General John (1608–1680). *D.N.B.* Brother-in-law of Oliver Cromwell but active, as Whitelocke was aware, in bringing about the fall of his nephew, Protector Richard Cromwell, *Diary* 14, 21 Apr. 1659. Whitelocke made numerous diary entries concerning the Major-General, including some on his activities with other officers in 1659. At the end of that year it was Desborough, with Vane and Berry, who prevented Whitelocke from being sent to Breda to negotiate terms for the Restoration, ib. 22 Dec. 1659. In June 1660, Desborough's name was among those listed in the Second Exception to the General Pardon.

D'ESPAGNE (D'ESPAIGNE), Jean (1591–1659). *D.N.B.* The French Pastor of a Huguenot congregation in London. He wrote in French from 'St Giles-fields', recommending, as physician for the Swedish Embassy, a friend who not only spoke French and Latin 'perfectly' but who also spoke good English and Italian; he stated that the doctor had spent three years in Sweden, Norway and Denmark, was a sincere and judicious man, and had formerly been Secretary for foreign affairs to the Chancellor of Denmark, 21 Sept. 1653, Long. W.P. xiii,215–216. In the event, Whitelocke took Daniel Whistler (q.v.) as his physician. A letter in French, offering medical advice in Latin under the heading *Cautiones Medicae vel Antidotus*, came to Whitelocke from the unsuccessful candidate, ib. xiv, 16–22.

DEVONSHIRE, Countess of. G.E.C.; *D.N.B.* Née Lady Elizabeth Cecil, second daughter of William Cecil, 2nd Earl of Salisbury; she married William Cavendish, 3rd Earl of Devonshire.

DEWY (DEWEY, DEWYES), James. G.E. Aylmer 'Check-list of Central Office-holders' (1976). Dewy appears on two lists of Whitelocke's retinue for Sweden, although not on the list in *The Diary*. Described as 'M^r

James Dewy, menial Servant to Wh[itelocke]. Gent[leman] Ussher, a sober proper young Man, industrious to Study Law, and a good Scholar; he had the Latin Tongue readily', Add.Ms 4995 appendix 5, fol.11v.; Long. 124A, 361v. In 1652, he was Clerk of Warrants in Chancery, where Whitelocke no doubt knew him; later he was Clerk to the Commissioners of Oyer and Terminer at Exeter, *Diary* 16 Mar. 1654/55, then Solicitor to the Treasury Commissioners (of whom Whitelocke was one), in 1657. References to him occur up to ib. 7 May 1663.

A copy letter to Whitelocke indicates Dewy's affection and gratitude:

> I can scarce passe through any place, butt where I am putt in minde of your L[ordshi]ᵖˢ great & many favours to me, your L[ordshi]ᵖ hath bin pleased in so honourable a way to interest your selfe in my behalfe, I could in no wise stay till my returne, nor any longer protract the humble acknowledgement of a deeply sencible heart . . . who as Æschines did to Socrates (having nothing else) freely & wholly give myselfe without any mentall reservation or power of revocation.
>
> Blandford [Dorset]   Your L[ordshi]ᵖˢ for ever
> Mar. 12 1655[56]   devoted servant
>   Ja[mes] Dewy.
>   Add.Ms 4992 fol.146; also *Diary*, same date.

DIGGES, Sir Dudley, Kt., MP (1583–1639). *D.N.B.* A diplomat and a Judge, he supported the Commons in claiming their rights. Whitelocke met him in Charles I's second Parliament, when Digges angered the King by his speech against Buckingham, *Diary* 1625.1626.fol.7v. A fuller account is given in Add.Ms 53726 fols. 20v.–21v.

DIXON, Anne (d.1660). The wife of Henry Dixon (q.v.), she resented her husband's generosity towards the Whitelocke family, *Diary* 13 Aug. 1655; 12 Jan. 1655/56. She and Whitelocke were joint executors to her husband's estate; a small account for disbursements names them both in that capacity, Long. W.P. xix, 135.

DIXON, Cecilia (Cislye), (1608–1647). *Liber* p. 17. Whitelocke's younger surviving sister, she married Edward Dixon (below). Her 'milliner's' bill before the wedding amounted to £46. 18s. 3d. which included: rolls of taffeta to line, £1. 1s. od.; 'Left unpaid of the last workinge £7. 3s. 3d.'; binding for petticoats 2s.; making petticoats and waistcoats 3s. 6d.; 20½ yards of straw-yellow satins £15. 7s. 6d.; three rolls of taffeta to line, 'at

14d the elle', £1. 4s. 6d.; 16 yards of material for Lady Muston (i.e. Mostyn, Cecilia's elder sister), 3 Feb. 1631/32, Long. W.P. v, 201.

Whitelocke recalled the delicate problem of Cecilia's £2,500 portion, of which her father had paid £1,200 in advance, without deleting it from his Will, *Diary* 1631.1632. fols. 16–16v. Cecilia and Edward Dixon's final receipt for £2,500 from Whitelocke, as executor, dated 2 July 1632, Long. W.P. v, 240, is the release he insisted they should sign when he paid the balance, *Diary* 1632.1633. Cecilia died in sad circumstances, ib. 24 July 1647. A monument in Little Rollright Church, Oxfordshire, commemorates Cecilia in flowery terms, but depicts Edward's second wife (making her look like Cecilia's twin) without a word about her character, nor does it even give her first name.

DIXON, Edward. 'Brother Dixon', son of Henry (below) and brother-in-law of Whitelocke. Of Hildenborough, near Tonbridge, Kent, and Little Rollright, Oxfordshire. He recommended Captain Beston to Whitelocke as a member of the retinue for Sweden, describing him as an honest, valiant man and a true servant to Parliament (the Rump), Long. W.P. xiii, 246.

DIXON, Henry (*c*.1581–1656). 'Old Mr Dixon' or 'Cousin Dixon' of Hilden (Hildenborough), Kent, of Wandsworth, and of Braughing, Herts. He is also shown in the church at Little Rollright, Oxfordshire, as Patron of the living in 1622, 1630, and 1640. Husband of Anne (q.v.) and father of Edward (above); he was an old friend of Judge Sir James Whitelocke (q.v.). Whitelocke signed a bond to him for £2,000, conditioned for payment of £1,400, June 1632, Long. W.P. v, 238. Dixon, in due course, borrowed from Whitelocke and, in return, settled land in Wandsworth and Braughing on Whitelocke's son Willoughby, *Diary* 1641.1642. fol.55v.

DIXON – 'Nephew' and 'Niece'. No first names are given, but Whitelocke's 'Nephew Dixon' may have been Thomas, whose name appears on the Earl of Portland's Act of 1663. 'Niece Dixon' became Mrs. Barker.

DIXWELL, Col. John, MP (d.1689). *D.N.B.* A regicide, he escaped to the Continent after the Restoration and later to America, under the name of James Davids. Whitelocke only makes two short references to him, *Diary* 31 Dec. 1659; 20 June 1660.

D'OILEY (DOILEY, D'OYLY, D'OYLEY) family (below). Burke *Extinct & Dormant Baronetcies* (for lineage only); W.D. D'Oyly *Account of the House of D'Oyly* (1848); *V.C.H. Bucks.* iii, 49, *passim*; iv, *passim*. Of Chislehampton, Oxon., Greenland House near Hambleden, and Turville, Bucks. (Some printed information on Greenland House conflicts with Whitelocke's record of his selling it and with evidence in Long. W.P., shown in *Diary* notes.) For interesting reports on Greenland, garrisoned for the King in the Civil War, and owned at that time by John D'Oiley, see *Journal of Sir Samuel Luke* (ed. I.G. Philips, Oxfordshire Record Society. 1950–1953), *passim*.

D'OILEY (D'OILIE), Col. Charles. Son of Sir Cope D'Oiley (below). He served briefly as parliament's Governor of Phyllis Court (alias Henley) Garrison, until his soldiers mutinied and nearly killed him, *Diary* 13 Aug. 1645.

D'OILEY, Sir Cope, Kt. (d.1633). A Commissioner of Oyer and Terminer, and a Deputy Lieutenant for Oxfordshire. Of Greenland, next property to Whitelocke's home, Fawley Court. When Whitelocke was 18, Sir Cope gave him 'a good Nagge, the first wherof he was master . . .', ib. 1623.1624. fol.5v.

D'OILEY, Henry. Of Turville, Bucks. Son of Robert D'Oiley (q.v.). Whitelocke does not refer to Henry until after the Restoration. Nearly all the entries concerning him include the term 'difference' (i.e. dispute) or 'ill-dealing'. Whitelocke composed some of the differences with tenants, but he himself also suffered from Henry D'Oiley's 'ill dealing', ib. 1 Apr., 12 Aug. 1661; 18 Feb. 1661/62; 24 June 1662. An uncontentious letter from a Mr. D'Oiley, about the purchase of property in Northamptonshire, is probably from Henry, ib. 21 Apr. 1663.

D'OILEY, John. Eldest son of Sir Cope (q.v.). He offered to sell the Greenland estate to Whitelocke for £14,000, ib. 1637.1638. fol.44; later, he and his brother Robert (below) successfully negotiated the sale to him at the much lower price of £6,500, after the house had been battered in the Civil War, ib. 27, 29 Oct. 1651.

D'OILEY, Robert, of Turville Court, Bucks. (which he built in 1635). Brother of John (above), and father of Henry (q.v.) who caused friction over tenancies after the Restoration. For bonds, payments and receipts between Robert D'Oiley and Whitelocke, dated: Dec. 1636, see Long. W.P. vii, 84; 18 Feb. 1651/52, see ib. xii, 48; 29 Nov. 1652, see ib. 181v.–182. Earlier, D'Oiley wrote to Whitelocke, urgently:

> I being to pay two thousand pounds unto my kinsman Doiley by the first of February next, causeth me to put to sale fowre farmes or tenements ... I have profered them unto the Tennants but they[,] not being able to buy them, desire me to proferr them unto your honor, w[hi]^ch imboldeneth me to write unto you, being willing to let you have the forsaling of them, (and cheaper) than any other, I having occasions for ready monyes my price shall be but thirtene hundred pounds for them ... (desiring an awnswer ... by this bearer if it may stand w[i]^th your conveniency) ...
> 14 Feb. 1649/50
>
>   Ib. x, 121.

For further details see COOKE, William.

DORMER, Sir Robert (d. 1649). *V.C.H. Oxon.* viii,59, *passim*; ib. *Bucks.*, iv, *passim*. (Not to be confused with Robert Dormer, Earl of Caernarvon). Dorton, in Buckinghamshire, was settled on him at his marriage, by his father Sir John Dormer, MP for Aylesbury. Later, Robert inherited Chinnor (or the 'Manor of Overcourt'), near Watlington. Whitelocke, with Hampden and Goodwyn, pursued the Earl of Berkshire (q.v.) from near Watlington to Sir Robert's house at Chinnor, in August 1642, *Diary* 1642.1643. fol.56. Five years later, Sir Robert sent Whitelocke a present of a fat doe, and consulted him on legal business, *Diary* 18, 21 Sept. 1647.

DOUGLAS, Gen. Robert (1611–1662). *S.M.K.* A Scottish soldier of fortune, he served the Swedish Crown in and after the Thirty Years War, and was made a Baron and Master of Horse in Sweden. He was well-disposed towards Whitelocke in Uppsala and towards Christopher Potley (q.v.), whom he had known in the Swedish Army. He subsequently wrote congratulating Whitelocke on his safe return to England, Long. W.P. xvi, 106, and asking help for his kinsmen, Lord Lauderdale (q.v.) and Lauderdale's son, *Diary* 4 Apr. 1655.

DOWNING, Sir George, Bt., MP (1623–1684). *Hist. of Parl.*; *D.N.B.*; *Pepys* x; E. Ludlow *Voyce from the Watchtower* pp. 297–298. He went to

New England with his parents, and studied for the ministry at Harvard College. Returning to England, he became an army chaplain, then a politician and diplomat during the Interregnum and after the Restoration. He earned himself a reputation as an able, mean, avaricious and treacherous man but as a legislator he argued on behalf of the poor. Disliking the Dutch, he was for many years Resident (later Commissioner or Agent) at The Hague, where the antipathy became mutual. Among other duties, he was charged with that of encouraging the formation of a Protestant Union in Europe. After the Restoration, he was active in promoting the capture of three regicides in Delft: Barkstead, Corbet (q.v.) and Downing's former Colonel, Okey, whom he tricked. (A 'Judas' came to be known as an 'arrant George Downing'.) A grant of land to him by Charles II, in the Whitehall area, resulted in his name being given to one of the most famous streets in London.

Whitelocke must have known Downing in Parliament and crossed swords with him when Downing was zealous to punish James Naylor (q.v.), yet there are only two colourless entries, *Diary* 30 Nov. 1659, and 18 Jan. 1659/60. Some of Downing's despatches from Holland appear in *Thurloe S.P.* vi, 759, 790–791, 818–819, *passim*; and in *C.S.P. Dom.* 21 June 1659, *passim*. His untidily-written, obsequious letters to Whitelocke, from The Hague, focus mainly on his financial straits. In contrast to a letter from George Cokayn (q.v.), of 26 May 1654, complaining that Ambassador Whitelocke's 'bills had . . . bin soe moderate . . . ' Downing wrote:

I had ere this written to y[ou]^r Lordship, but th[a]^t I am very fearfull of being troublesome[,] yet understanding from my wife [Frances, sister of Charles Howard whom Charles II later created E. of Carlisle, q.v.] th[a]^t undeserved goodwill by you expressed for me, I have . . . presumed, & truly they whose hap it is to be long absent will . . . find need of friends, for out of sight is out of mind, thow it be in publique service, & . . . that I have been in hath been dangerous & troublesom enough. once some came from Bruxells on purpose to murder me, but . . . I knew not of it till afterwards. & truly it hath been . . . a chargable employment for I have spent of my owne 1000^l p. annum [the amount of his salary] more th[a]^n was allowed me. This is I think the dearest place in Europe & I have endeavoured to live in such a manner as may uphold the credite and inte[r]est of my Countrey, & . . . I have not gone about any thing for the Com[m]onwealth the w[hi]^{ch} I have not carryed throw, w[hi]^{ch} is a mercy . . . espetially considering the Constitution of the Government of this Countrey [Holland] & how much against the grayne hath been w[ha]^t I have . . . been . . . employed about . . . I am now about 500^l in arreare of my sallery, & also I was . . . commanded . . . to mayntayn an intelligence in flanders both in Ch[arles] Stuart[s] & the Spaniards court[,] for the w[hi]^{ch} & sundry expenses I am out[,] out of my owne purse[,] 700^l w[hi]^{ch} is . . . disbursed by me & of w[hi]^{ch} a great dale hath been layd out since the sitting of this Parl[ia]m[en]^t[,] as Mr Thurlow well knowes, & will avowe, for I did not at such a Crisis w[i]^th draw, & not getting any monyes of a long time from England & the noyse coming hither of my being to returne for England, every one to w[ho]^m I owed a penny came presently for payment, & there is no making any ... disputes heer upon such accounts, so one may have his house pulled downe about him as the Polish Envoye was lately in danger of ... so th[a]^t having no other way in the world I was forced for present exigency to take up 600^l upon a certayne parcell of plate w[hi]^ch I had in my hands, of w[hi]^ch I doubt not th[a]^t you have heerd, & now I find the Councell hath ordred this plate to be delivered to the Assigne of Mr Backwell the goldsmith [q.v.], the w[hi]^ch I am willing to do, ... but as to the mony allready borrowed on it[,] I had no other shrift & being abroad ... in the Commonwealths Service I could not longer be w[i]^th out mony, I must have brought a dishonorable cry upon the Commonwealth w[hi]^ch it needs not here, if men had the least occasions against me heer are thousands in this towne will be ready to embrace it to make a stirre, may be pull down my house or deface it, may be serve me as Dorislause. [Assassinated at The Hague by Royalists in 1649]. This is the naked truth ... so truly w[i]^th out first th[a]^t mony be payd its impossible for me to give it aw[a]y [i.e. part with the plate] & interest is also by me payd for th[a]^t mony, but I hope ... th[a]^t ... the Councell will not order any of the plate from me till I am fully payd the whole th[a]^t is due unto me.

He congratulated himself on his success in averting a naval incident by having the Hague Treaty signed on 21 May; he was unable to believe that the Council would fail to pay him or that they would demand the return of the plate before satisfaction was given for his debts, and he appealed to Whitelocke for his assistance, Long. W.P. xix, 59–60, 1 Aug. (n.s.) 1659.

A week later, Downing wrote with further excuses for his financial predicament and complained of the fact that he was at The Hague in the capacity of a mere Commissioner, 29 July/8 Aug. 1659, ib. 68.

Nearly three weeks later he wrote again:

My Lord,
It was too much for me to have a line from y[ou]^r Lordship while in the chayre [as Lord President of the Council] & so much busines upon you. I humbly thank you for y[ou]^r thoughts of my poor wife, which truly had so ill a labour of her last child w[he]^n absent from me ... & truly apprehension itselfe ... is very much[,] espetially at such times. Tis a high mercy th[a]^t the enemy gott not to a head in any other place[;] I hope the next [letter] will give me a good account of th[at]^t of Cheshire & Lancashire [Sir George Booth's rising; yet within eight months Downing sent humble messages to Charles II, blaming his disloyalty to the Crown on his early years in New England]. I am sensible of the states necessitys as to mony^es yet such as are abroad ... cannot live upon tickett ... I cannot dowpt but th[a]^t the Councell will take care of me ... but truly my Lord P[resident,] thow at first I was not willing in the least to demurr upon the title ... of bare Commissioner yet truly I hope the Councell & Parl[ia]m[en]t will now in th[a]^t think upon me, tis very very low,

& the esteem a State hath to such as they employ is judged by the world by these things, besides th[a]ᵗ it bereaves me of those ceremonyes of respect w[hi]ᶜʰ are necessary for their Service, & ... I cannot at present come in company w[i]ᵗʰ other publique Ministers for I cant stoop so low as that character would putt me, & its taken notice of th[a]ᵗ Monsieur Lockert [William Lockhart, q.v.] from Amb[assador] is made Amb[assador] Ext[raordinary] & I from Res[i]d[en]ᵗ made simple Commissioner[,] w[hi]ᶜʰ is the le[a]st th[a]ᵗ can be, & w[he]ʳas I was this time 4 years Com[missione]ʳ Ext[raordinary] to the King of fraunce I cannot but a little touch upon this ... even for the Parliament their service sake ... I doupt not to bring things to a happy settlement between England & this State ... I forbeare particulars because my letters to S[i]ʳ Henry Vane [q.v.] I know came to y[ou]ʳ knowledge ... Hague, Aug. 28.[n.s.]59

ib. 72–72v.

DRAKE, Frauncis (Francis), MP (b.c.1610). M.F.K. Of Walton-on-Thames. Younger brother of Sir William Drake (below); both were Middle Temple lawyers and both were MPs for Amersham in the Long Parliament, where no doubt both brothers were acquainted with Whitelocke, but the only four references to Frauncis in *The Diary* occur between Dec. 1657 and Jan. 1658/59.

DRAKE, Sir William, Bt., MP (1606–1669). *Hist. of Parl.*; *Complete Baronetage* ii, 107–108; M.F.K. Of Shardeloes, west of Amersham. Brother of Frauncis (above). He supported Parliament initially, spending two spells abroad 'for his health'; he was secluded at Pride's Purge. Chirographer of the Court of Common Pleas from 1652–1659. He sat again for Amersham, from 1661 until his death. A scholarly, wealthy friend of Whitelocke's, mentioned twice: (1) when he gave Whitelocke a coach and pair by way of a fee in 1643 (Whitelocke being at Highgate without his own transport, his coach and horses having been plundered at Fawley Court, by the King's soldiers); (2) when he left Whitelocke £20 in his Will, enabling his old friend to settle pressing domestic bills, *Diary* 1643.1644. fol.63; 25 Jan. 1669/70.

DUNCH (DUNCHE), Edmund, MP (1603–1678). M.F.K. Of Little Wittenham, north-west of Wallingford. A cousin, through his mother, of Oliver Cromwell and John Hampden; he married Bridget Hungerford of Down Ampney, a wealthy woman whom Whitelocke found insufferably proud and foolish, *Diary* 17 Dec. 1647. He was related to John Lisle (q.v.), ib. 24 Mar. 1650/51.

DUNGARVAN (DUNGARVEN, DUNGARVON), Richard Boyle, Viscount, MP; later 2nd E. of Cork; created E. of Burlington (Bridlington) in 1664 (1612–1698). G.E.C. (as Cork); *D.N.B.* and M.F.K. (as Boyle). Son of the 1st Earl of Cork; brother of Roger Boyle, Lord Broghill 1st Earl of Orrery (q.v.). MP for Appleby in the Long Parliament, until he was disabled in 1643. Named on the King's safe-conduct for Parliament's Commissioners to Oxford in Jan. 1642/43, *Memorials* i, 195, but this appointment does not appear in the reference books above. At his father's death, he joined the King at Oxford, in September 1643.

DURY (DURIE), Alexander Gibson, Lord (d.1656). *D.N.B.* A Scottish Judge.

DURY (DURIE, DUERY), John (1596–1680). *D.N.B.* An ecumenist and librarian. Born in Edinburgh, he worked abroad for some years; returning to England he was ordained in 1634 and became a Chaplain to Charles I; he preached before Parliament in 1645. Between appointments he devoted his life to protestant unity, but his extensive journeys in Europe (including Sweden, from which he was ejected), his talks and correspondence, achieved no positive results. His large output of writing is listed in the *D.N.B.* He married the aunt of Whitelocke's friend, Lady Ranelagh (q.v.). After the King's execution Dury, a lukewarm supporter of the Rump Parliament, was appointed Library Keeper, under Whitelocke, of the Royal Library at St. James's Palace, where he was given lodgings. He declined an invitation to accompany Whitelocke to Sweden, on grounds of his wife's and his own ill-health, 26 Sept. 1653, Long. W.P. xiii, 236; writing from 'Bishops Gate Street at Mr Wilsons' (i.e. Samuel Wilson's) he sent Whitelocke manuscripts on the Swedish constitution and on the Peace Treaty between Poland and Sweden, the latter borrowed from Sir George Douglas's secretary, 11 Oct. 1653, ib. xiv, 96.

Within a month of the Protectorate being set up, he wrote about it non-committally to Whitelocke in Sweden, but gave other information likely to be of use to the Ambassador:

> I know th[a]^t I can adde nothing to y[ou]^r information in matters of public concernment, because you will have things fro[m] the fountaine: yet I am willing to shew my dutifull respect, & acquaint y[ou]^r Excell[en]^{cie} with some matter of circumstance w[hi]^{ch} perhaps elsewhere you will not meet with all, in reference to this breaking off of the Treatie w[i]th the Low Country Deputies, w[hi]^{ch} is thought to have a speciall Mysterie in it; for although it seems th[a]^t all is broken off ... yet I know where the Deputies ... [were]

before they went away; all three being together, to take their leave of one who is a public Minister from a forrein state; did in plaine terms declare unto him (sub sigillo silentii) [under the seal of silence, i.e. in strict confidence] th[a]^t wee & they were come to an agreement in all things; & that the only remaining difference was concerning Denmark; whether he should bee taken into the Defensive League, which is agreed upon between the two Commonwealths; w[hi]^ch they did desire & wee would not yeald unto ... I was told th[a]^t Mons[ieu]^r Bevering did tell Mons[ieu]^r Bordeaux [French Ambassador] th[a]^t the Treatie was wholly Broken & without effect, when hee tooke his leave of him ...

[St.] James house this 6 January 1653/4   John Dury

ib. xv, 3.

Two years later he wrote about the subject on which he was an expert: a proposed embassy to the German Protestants, for which Samuel Hartlib told him the State intended to employ Whitelocke. (Besides his works on reformed husbandry, Hartlib had written earlier on ecclesiastical peace among Protestants.) Dury wrote tactfully that it was certainly a most worthy design for England and that Whitelocke had the ability for it, but such a mission would be in vain and would do more harm than good:

... because the mindes of the Lutheran Princes are not yet prepared to entertaine any motion of th[a]^t kinde ... & lesse from England, then from any other, except a due preparation & ... gradual proceeding bee used ...

As matters stood, the approach would be unseasonable; if the purpose were to remove the causes of religious differences, beginning with the King of Sweden and moving on, with his concurrence, to the Elector of Saxony and other Lutheran Princes and Divines, that would be worth attempting; but if there were no such foundation of confidence it was senseless to alarm enemies

... who are in a fitter disposition to bee united ... against us then wee are against them ... It is not to bee believed, how much this negotiation of mine, (w[hi]^ch is ... meerly theologicall, & only with our owne Reformed partie hitherto) doth startle them, & w[ha]^t ... industrie they use to obstruct them ... [As to trying to reconcile Lutherans and Calvinists, or foreign Protestants and those in England] they are so alarmed, th[a]^t they will bee on horseback before wee can know where to find our horses ... nor will Protestants ever mind the Civil part of their Common interest, till a good intelligence in reference to the profession of Religion bee wrought ...

15 Apr. 1656.

Add.Ms 32093 fols. 341–341v.

The letter came from Cassell, in Hesse, which Dury was to make his home after the Restoration.

DUWALL (du VALE, du VAL), Marshall Sir Gustaf (Gustav), Kt. (1630–1692). *Svenska Män och Kwinner*. Steward and, as such, one of the chief gentlemen attending the Swedish Ambassador Extraordinary, Count Christer Bonde (q.v.), on his mission to England. Whitelocke entertained him, with the Ambassador, *Diary* 20 Sept. 1655; 13 Mar. 1655/56. When Cromwell knighted Duwall (July 1656), Whitelocke was taken aback, reflecting, rather sourly, that Queen Christina had knighted him, England's Ambassador Extraordinary, while the Protector bestowed the same honour on the Swedish Ambassador's servant, ib. 5 Aug. 1656. Sir Gustaf returned to England as Swedish Envoy, to congratulate Richard Cromwell on his succession, ib. 19 Oct. 1658, *passim*. He took his leave of the new Protector, ib. 13 Nov. 1658, but apparently stayed in England, with his retinue, until 28 Dec. 1658, *C.S.P. Dom. 1658–1659* p. 497.

EARLE, Daniel. For many years Whitelocke's chief secretary; shown in *The Diary* as entering that service on 16 Sept. 1645, but he was first described (no doubt with hindsight) at negotiations between Parliament's and the King's Commissioners in Oxford, and again at Uxbridge where: 'Mr Thurlo, & Mr Earle Wh[itelockes] servant, were servants for the Parlem[en]^{ts} Com[missione]^{rs}, *Diary* 1642.1643. fol. 60v. (Mar. 1642/43); ib. 30 Jan. 1644/45, fol. 71v.; *Thurloe S.P.* i, 59. Sir John Holland (q.v.) obtained Earle's services temporarily, during negotiations with the King at Newcastle and Holdenby; Earle was still employed in that business when the King moved from Holdenby via Royston, Hatfield House, and Windsor to Caversham, *Diary* 16 Jan. 1646/47; 19 July 1647. Signing a bond with Whitelocke, he appears as 'Daniel Earle of the Middle Temple, London. gent.', 8 Feb. 1651/52, Long. W.P. xii, 48. Descriptions of him, given on lists of Whitelocke's retinue for Sweden, indicate his standing: 'Receiver and Chiefe Secretary Daniel Earle, Esq; his [Whitelocke's] menial [i.e. of the household] servant', *Journal* i, 77;

> ... an antient faithfull and affectionate servant, who left his wife and children and a good fortune, to follow his Master, resolved to run the same hazards, and was att great Charge in fitting himselfe for this journey, which he did not sparingly, butt to his Masters honour and his own Credit. He had the French tongue and understood Latine, and had gained much Experience as Secretary to the Commissioners of the Seale.
>
> Add.Ms 37346 fol. 30v. and ib. 4995 fol. 11v.

Eventually, when Whitelocke reluctantly appointed Fleetwood's nominee, instead of Earle, as Secretary to the Keepers of the Seal, his old servant showed great bitterness, in spite of Whitelocke explaining his predicament, and offering the choice of any other post connected with the Seal, *Diary*

2 Nov. 1659. The last entry for Earle shows Whitelocke visiting his old secretary, who was ill, ib. 30 Apr. 1662.

EARLE, Erasmus, MP (1590–1667). *D.N.B.* Bencher and Reader of Lincoln's Inn. Serjeant-at-Law in 1648, and again in 1660. He served under Oliver and Richard Cromwell and under Charles II. *D.N.B.* states that he was Secretary, with Thurloe, to the English Commissioners at the Uxbridge negotiations (apparently confusing him with Daniel Earle, above).

EARLE, Thomas. A Bristol merchant, he took Whitelocke's son Bigley as an apprentice and sent him to Spain as his factor (i.e. agent), but later sent him home for bad behaviour, *Diary* 30 Sept. 1670; 4 July 1671; 23 Oct. 1672.

EARLE, Sir Walter, MP (1586–1665). M.F.K.; C.V. Wedgwood *Thomas Wentworth, First Earl of Strafford, passim*; *Hist. of Parl.* A member of the Select Committee, chaired by Whitelocke, which prepared evidence against the Earl of Strafford; he said derisively that Whitelocke, as a gownsman not a swordsman, was unfit to deal with military matters in the impeachment. His own inadequacy played into Strafford's hands, for example when Sir Walter implied that soldiers could be marched into England from Ireland – which he clearly thought was joined to the mainland.

ELIOT, (ELLIOT) Sir John, MP (1592–1632). *D.N.B.* Sat in two Parliaments of James I; he turned against his patron, the 1st Duke of Buckingham (q.v.), after the Cadiz expedition. A leading opponent of court policies in the first three Parliaments of Charles I, he was imprisoned several times and died in the Tower. Whitelocke, as a young member of Charles I's second Parliament, refers to being 'admitted into perticular acquaintance' with Eliot, among others, *Diary* 1625.1626. fol. 7. Two papers containing legal arguments about Eliot's committal, for words spoken in Parliament, appear in Long. W.P. xxiv (not foliated), pp. 575–578 and 579–586; also part of a speech made in the King's Bench, challenging the power of the Courts to question MPs for words spoken in the House, ib. 465–468, *passim*. See also ib. xxi, 5v.–7v.

ELIZABETH, Queen of Bohemia (1596–1662). *D.N.B.* Known as 'the Winter Queen'; sister of Charles I (q.v.); she married Frederick, Elector Palatine of the Rhine, in 1613. Following his loss of Bohemia and the Palatine, and his death in 1632, she continued to live overseas until after the Restoration. She was sometimes short of funds but was usually subsidized by the States General or by the Earl of Craven (q.v.). Whitelocke records that he helped to obtain an annual allowance of £10,000 for her, *Diary* 20 Apr. 1646; *C.J.* iv, 515 records the Resolution. Her sons Charles Louis (or Lewis) Elector Palatine, Prince Rupert, and Prince Maurice all feature in *The Diary*.

ELLIS, Edward. Coachman. He was an old 'menial' servant (i.e. of the household), and was with Whitelocke at the Uxbridge negotiations in January 1644/45 and with him in Sweden in 1653 to 1654. Years later he wrote for arrears of his £10 p.a. annuity, *Diary* 20 May 1669.

ELLIS, William. Organist, and a Gentleman of the Household to Judge Sir James Whitelocke, he was retained by Whitelocke for a short time, after the Judge's death. Later, Ellis sent Whitelocke information from Saint-Omer, south-east of Calais, *Diary* 1632.1633. fol. 18 with note (only described there as 'Organist'); 1634.1635. fol. 30v.

ELSYNGE (ELSING), Henry, sen. (1598–1654). *D.N.B.* G.E. Aylmer 'Check-list of Central Office-holders'. Clerk to the House of Commons. He pleaded ill-health as an excuse to resign his place before the trial of Charles I, confiding to Whitelocke that he would have no hand in it, *Diary* 26 Dec. 1648. He did, however, hold other offices, serving as Registrar and Keeper of Records for the sale of Bishops' lands, from 1646 to 1654, and as an Appeals Commissioner, from 1653 to 1654. Described as a friend, a man of extraordinary abilities and learning, and of great integrity, ib. 17 July 1654.

ELSYNGE (ELSING), Henry, jun. Page to Whitelocke in Sweden.

ELTONHEAD (ELTENHEAD), Edward (d.1660). G.E. Aylmer *State's Servants* p. 93. A Master in Chancery. Appointed Middle Temple Treasurer in 1652, after Bartholomew Hall (q.v.), *Master Worsley's Book on the ... Society of the Middle Temple* (ed. A.R. Ingpen) p. 172. He frequently wrote to Whitelocke about hawks. Some months after Frances Whitelocke's death in 1649, he wrote on behalf of the Earl of Suffolk, inviting Whitelocke to stay at Audley End. Eltonhead was described by Whitelocke as 'good Company' and as a 'kind & cheerfull friend', *Diary* 6 Jan. 1649/50; 16 Dec. 1660. He also wrote from Audley End on behalf of the Countess of Suffolk, recommending a Gentleman Usher for the Swedish Embassy, 3 Oct. 1653, Long. W.P. xiv, 3. Whitelocke's transcript of another letter from Eltonhead is introduced as coming 'from his hearty & cheerfull friend ... who [during Whitelocke's absence in Sweden] expressed much kindnes & affection to his wife & children, whome he often visited ... ' The letter runs:

> ... First ... give me your pardon for using my servants hand to you, my eyes having bin lately troubled with rhume I cannot hold downe my head to write. Butt my eares are open to heare the many loud prayers ... for your ... returne, & ... an obser[va]tion of one of your servants that it had pleased God to withdrawe both the Sun, & your selfe from us a long winter, that we might the better value both your ... returne, your opinion [i.e. the good opinion of Whitelocke] is not greater in the happy wishes of the people, then in his Highnes the Lord Protectors bosome, for ... when he delivered the great Seale, it was to your L[ordshi]P in the first place [,then] my Lord Widdrington & my Lord L'Isle, Another observation of his Highnes favour is, that ... [when] your Clerke of the Peace dyed about a Moneth since, and the countey came up, & petitioned his Highnes to putt in a Clerke of the Peace, he asked who was their Custos Rotulorum, they answeared my Lord Whitelocke, he told them he would not meddle therwith, butt leave it to your L[ordshi]ps disposall, which answear satisfyed them not, butt replyed that they could not hold the sessions, without a Clerke of the Peace, & your absence might obstruct justice, My Lord Protector wished them to satisfy themselves ... that he would not meddle therwith, & that you would be heere sooner then they were aware of; the most coolest of your friends can admitt no longer your absence ... the ... Dutch Pease ... was most sumpteously proclaimed att London, & in all the Porte Townes uppon Wednesday last, with great acclamations of joy of both English & Dutch, the Ambassadors caused great bonfires to be made ... [Eltonhead added, after his signature] My M[aste]rs of the bench of the Middle Temple doe unanimously present their dutyes and services unto you.
>
> My Lord Rich[ard] Cromwell whom I waited upon yesterday commanded me to present his humble service to your Lords[hi]P and did it with much expressions of joy [and] affect[i]on
> rec. Stockholm 25, transcribed under 26 May, 1654.

Add.Ms 37347 fols. 236–237.

ELWAY, Sir John. Of Weston, Berkshire, north-east of Hungerford. A trustee of the Hussey estate, Chilton Park, which Whitelocke bought in 1663.

EMOT (EMOTT), [Richard?]. Musician and old retainer of Judge Sir James Whitelocke's, 'a cheerfull man ...' He accompanied Whitelocke and Frances on a visit to Lincoln and to Belvoir Castle and later to 'Sister Mostyn' in Wales, *Diary* 1634.1635. fol. 36v.; 1637.1638. fol. 45v. The name Richard Emott (*sic*) of 'Cheping Wicombe' (High Wycombe) appears on a bond for £200, signed by Whitelocke, and on a receipt, Oct. 1637; Apr. 1648, Long. W.P. vii, 129–129v.

ESSEX, Robert Devereux, 3rd E. of (1591–1646). G.E.C.; *D.N.B.* Son of the 2nd Earl of Essex, Queen Elizabeth's favourite, who was executed for his plot against her. As General of Parliament's Army, the 3rd Earl invited Whitelocke 'often to his Table, & to much intimacy' but Whitelocke was not uncritical of him in the field, for example at Turnham Green. The General jokingly called Whitelocke 'Mr Dean' in the Commons, because he wore a long robe like a cassock, *Diary* 1641.1642. fol. 54; 1642.1643. fols. 59–60; 1643.1644. fol. 64; 23 Nov. 1645, *passim*.

EVELYN, Col. [Arthur]. C. Firth and G. Davies *Regimental History of Cromwell's Army*; D. Underdown *Pride's Purge* p. 95; G. Davies *Restoration* p. 151. He served as a Parliamentary General, and was appointed Governor of Wallingford Castle, after the fall of Oxford, succeeding the Royalist, Col. Thomas Blague (q.v.). Brother of Sir John Evelyn (below); the assumption that the Colonel's brother was Sir John Evelyn of Wiltshire, not Sir John of Surrey, is based on their ages. Later, as a Major, Arthur Evelyn commanded the Life Guards, *Diary* 31 Mar., 20 July 1648; 13 Oct. 1659, with note.

EVELYN, Sir John (of Wilts.), Kt., MP, JP (1601–1685). M.F.K.; P. Crawford *Denzil, First Lord Holles, passim*; *Hist. of Parl.* He supported Holles in seeking peace with the King. Brother of Arthur (above) and cousin of Evelyn the diarist. He was secluded at Pride's Purge, in 1648, but sat again in the Convention Parliament of 1660.

EXETER (EXCESTER), Frances, Countess of (c.1580–1663). G.E.C.;
D.N.B. (under CECIL, Thomas, 1st Earl of Exeter, d. 1623). Daughter of
William Brydges, 4th Baron Chandos of Sudeley and widow of Sir Thomas
Smith, she became the Earl's second wife in 1610, being 38 years his junior.
Whitelocke described her as 'froward' about money she owed him, *Diary*
8 Dec. 1645, but she gave handsome entertainment to him and John Lisle
(q.v.), when accompanied by her 'grandchild' (her husband's great
grandson) the regicide, Thomas 3rd Baron Grey of Groby (q.v.), 2nd Earl
of Stamford, ib. 21 Apr. 1649.

EYRES (EYR), Lady Dorothy. *Liber* pp. 25–26. Whitelocke's aunt;
without parental consent she married Sir John Eyre who was, according to
Judge Sir James Whitelocke, '... on [i.e. one] of the most dissolute,
unjust, and vitious reprobates that livethe upon the face of the earthe.'
There are only two entries for Lady Eyres in *The Diary*, and a comment
from Whitelocke to his children: '... I received letters from the Lady Eyres
my Aunt, your Grandmothers Sister, full of kindnes, she was one of the
best accomplisht women in her time for witt and behaviour, & a fine
schollar for a woman', Add.Ms 37343 fol. 150.

FAIRFAX, Sir Thomas, later 3rd Baron, MP (1612–1671). *Hist. of Parl.*;
G.E.C.; *D.N.B.* Eldest son of Ferdinando, 2nd Baron Fairfax (d.1648).
From Jan. 21 1644/45 he was Commander-in-Chief of the New Model, *C.J.*
iv, 26. He refused to take part in the King's trial. Whitelocke describes the
events leading to Fairfax's resignation, in *Diary* 24 June 1650. The
numerous diary entries include (1) Fairfax's request to the Speaker to
allow Whitelocke to join him for the siege of Oxford, ib. 12 May 1646 and
(2) a description of Fairfax taking Whitelocke in his coach to the Earl of
Essex's funeral and, characteristically, retaining his composure when the
coach nearly crashed into a ditch, ib. 22 Oct. 1646. He was justly described
by Whitelocke as '... of a generous & Coragious spirit, yett meek & civil &
not given to insulting ...', Add.Ms 37343 fol. 262v. An Order from Fairfax
of 31 Mar. 1645 is in Long. W.P. Parcel 2 No. 8; a letter he wrote on 17
June 1646 from Water Eaton, south of Bletchley, Buckinghamshire, begs
Whitelocke to present another letter to the Speaker, petitioning the House
of Commons to be lenient with Mrs. Chamberleyne, following the surrender
of Sherborne House (Dorset); he remarked that he had received no reply to
his former letter, Long. W.P. ix, 82; *C.J.* iv, 568 refers to the earlier letter,
dated 18 May, being read to the House on 6 June; see also *C.S.P. Dom.*, 10
Jan. 1645/46 for the plan to capture the House, which was a royalist garrison.

FALKLAND (FAWKLAND), Henry Cary (Carey), MP, 4th Viscount (1634–1663). *Hist. of Parl.*; G.E.C. Son of Lucius, 2nd Viscount (below). He succeeded his elder brother in 1649 and, as a Scottish Peer, was elected MP for Oxfordshire in 1659, for Oxford City in 1660, and again for the County from 1661 to 1663 (see G.E.C. v, 239, note d). Cromwell had once rejected an appeal from Whitelocke on Falkland's behalf, considering the young Viscount untrustworthy; at the Restoration, Falkland (apparently blaming Whitelocke for the incident) attempted to have Whitelocke's name included in the Second Exception to the Act of Pardon and Oblivion, preventing him from ever holding office again, but was foiled in this attempt by William Willoughy (q.v.), *Diary* 7 June 1660.

FALKLAND (FAULKLAND, FAWKLAND), Lucius Cary (Carey), 2nd Viscount (*c.*1610–1643). G.E.C.; *D.N.B.* In the 1630s his home, near Chipping Norton, was the meeting place of the Great Tew circle, which discussed academic, political and religious issues rationally and with toleration. The tone of his letter (below) suggests that Whitelocke may sometimes have joined the circle, perhaps when staying with his sister at Little Rollright. Long after Falkland's death, aged 33, Whitelocke remembered him as his 'great friend ...', *Diary* 7 June 1660. A man of peace, Falkland initially supported the Long Parliament against the Court but soon joined the King. Hating the choices imposed by revolution and civil war, he threw his life away at the first Battle of Newbury. Later, Dr. Thomas Triplet (q.v.) wrote to Whitelocke about him.

The undated letter below clearly concerns the litigation over Wychwood Forest, and the Earl of Danby's pretensions, *Diary* 1635.1636., *passim*. The Forest is about 10 miles south-west of Great Tew:

> To my very worthy and much respected friend Mr Whitlocke ... These.
> S[i]^r
> The businesse of this is to put you in mind of the Justice seate which is to be held on Thursday in Easter weeke, against which it is requisite that the Country [i.e. County] bee not found unprovided ... If therefore you will be pleased to lett mee know what way[?] will be requisite for searching either more Records (if more neede) or other requir'd Charges, I will take care that it bee suddenly provided, and desire you that (in continuance of that care for which wee are all allready bound to you) you will please to retaine for us both what Councell and what Sollicitour you shall in your discretion thinke fitt, upon w[hi]^ch wee are willing to Rely: so with my Thankes to you for y[ou]^r past Industry, and my request that you will (which I doubt not) goe on in it for the Common good, I remaine
> S[i]^r   your Servant
> Falkland
> Long. W.P. vi, 178, undated.

Whitelocke records receiving a courteous letter of thanks from Lord Falkland (untraced) for these services, *Diary* 1638.1639. fol. 47.

FANSHAWE, Sir Thomas, KB, MP, later created Viscount Fanshawe of Dromore (1596–1665). *D.N.B.*; M.F.K.; *Hist. of Parl.* A Royalist, from Ware, in Hertfordshire. The King's Remembrancer in the Exchequer from 1619 to 1641 and again from August 1660 until his death. Whitelocke, Palmer (q.v.) and Hale (q.v.), with their wives, rented Sir Thomas's house in Ivy Lane, London, in 1642, until political pressures made the joint tenancy impossible. Whitelocke refers to 'Lord' Fanshawe being released from prison on 1 December 1659 but, in fact, Sir Thomas was not created Viscount until September 1661.

FAUCONBERG (FALCONBERG; FALCONBRIDGE – Whitelocke's error), Thomas Belasyse, 2nd Viscount (*c*.1627–1700). G.E.C.; *D.N.B.* From a royalist, Yorkshire family. He accepted the Interregnum, and married Cromwell's third daughter, Mary, in 1657. A staunch Royalist at the Restoration, he was created an Earl in 1689.

FELL, Thomas, MP (1598–1658). *D.N.B.* A student and later a Bencher of Gray's Inn; he was elected MP for Lancaster in 1645 and was nominated Vice-Chancellor of the Duchy of Lancaster and Attorney for the County Palatine, in 1649. He was also appointed an Assize Judge. There is only one diary entry for him; this records his death. Whitelocke refers to Fell as his 'kind friend . . . a good lawyer & a good man . . .', *Diary* 13. Oct. 1658. Although not a Quaker himself, Fell protected them, and his widow Margaret, a convert, married George Fox.

FETTIPLACE (FETTEPLACE, FETYPLACE), family of. They do not appear in *The Diary* until the Whitelockes moved to Chilton Lodge, west Berkshire, in the 1660s. Staunch Royalists. They were distantly related to the Whitelocke family, see references to 'Cousen Fettiplace', *Diary* 9 Aug. 1672, *passim*. John Fettiplace of Childrey, Berkshire, and Swinbrook, Oxfordshire (nephew and heir of John Fettiplace, MP, whose details appear in M.F.K.) was created Baronet in March 1661 for 'services and sufferings for Charles I' and Sheriff of Berkshire from 1667–1668; he died in September 1672, leaving 10 children, all of them minors, see *Complete Baronetage* iii, 182; *V.C.H. Berks.* iv, 275–276; *Extinct & Dormant*

Baronetcies 195–196. Other Fettiplaces mentioned in *The Diary* are difficult to identify since few forenames are given; they include 'Old Mʳ Fettiplace' (Whitelocke's client), who died in 1674; his widow; 'Mʳ Fetteplace of Letcomb' (Regis or Bassett?), and Charles Fettiplace, Sir John's second son, who succeeded to the title on his brother Edmund's death in 1707; Charles stayed with Whitelocke's young family, to play cards.

FIENNES, James, MP, later 2nd Viscount Say and Sele (*c.*1602–1674). M.F.K.; *Hist. of Parl.*; G.E.C. Eldest son of William, 1st Viscount Say and Sele (q.v.). He was elected to the Long Parliament; Whitelocke withdrew, rather than stand against Fiennes (who had been an MP since 1625) and Thomas, Viscount Wenman (q.v.). Fiennes succeeded to the Viscountcy in 1662 but never sat in the Lords.

FIENNES, John, elected MP in 1645 (*fl.* 1657) *D.N.B.* Third son of the 1st Viscount Say and Sele and brother of James (above). A Parliamentarian; he was active in the Army during the Civil War.

FIENNES, Nathaniel, MP (*c.*1608–1669). G.E.C. (entry for his son William, 3rd Viscount Say and Sele); *D.N.B.*; M.F.K. Second son of the 1st Viscount Say and Sele. He was secluded at Pride's Purge but was appointed a Keeper of the Great Seal from 1655 to 1659. He and Whitelocke both negotiated with the Swedish Ambassador in 1656. He was a member of the Council throughout the Protectorate, until the fall of Richard Cromwell.

FINCH (FYNCH), Sir Heneage, Bt., MP, later 1st E. of Nottingham (1621–1682). *Hist. of Parl.*; G.E.C.; *D.N.B.* Of the Inner Temple. A Royalist, who took no part in the Civil War; he practised as a lawyer during the Interregnum, and was subsequently appointed: Solicitor-General on 6 June 1660 (wrongly shown in *Diary* under 1 June); Attorney-General in 1670; Lord Keeper in November 1673; Lord Chancellor in 1674. He was created Earl of Nottingham in 1681. He attempted, unsuccessfully, to have Whitelocke excepted from the Pardon, *Diary* 1 June 1660. Serving as one of the prosecuting Counsel against the regicides, he showed no sympathy for dissent nor for freedom of conscience.

FINCH (FYNCH), Sir John, MP, later created Baron Finch of Fordwich (1584–1660). Uncle of Sir Heneage Finch (above). Of Gray's Inn. He served as MP for Canterbury in 1620, for Winchelsea (briefly) in 1623/24, for Canterbury in 1625, and was elected Speaker of the House of Commons in 1627/28. In 1626 he had been appointed King's Counsel and Attorney-General to the Queen, and in 1634 was appointed Lord Chief Justice. He was conspicuous for his support of the King, and for his brutal sentencing. Whitelocke encountered him in connection with the Royal Masque, *Diary* 1633.1634. fols. 20, 21; a few years later he recorded that Finch procured the private opinions of the Judges on the Ship Money issue, ib. 1636.1637. fol. 42v.

FITCH, Col. Thomas. C. Firth & G. Davies *Regimental History of Cromwell's Army*; G. Davies *Restoration*. A leading Commonwealth man, described by Whitelocke (when Fitch's name was put forward for appointment as Lieutenant of the Tower) as 'Hese[l]riggs Creature', *Diary* 10 June 1659.

FITZWILLIAM of MERRION, Oliver, 2nd Viscount; created, in 1661, Earl of Tyrconnel (d.1667). G.E.C. (main entry under Fitzwilliam of Merrion). A Royalist, he fought at Naseby. Brother-in-law of Denzil Holles (q.v.). He applied to Whitelocke for help over a case in Parliament, *Diary* 2 Apr. 1657. His undated Declaration (not mentioned in G.E.C.) sought to justify his conduct during the Civil War; he had been accused of putting Protestants to death, during his short tenure of a command in Ireland; he claimed that Queen Henrietta Maria (q.v.) had wished him to command 10,000 men, to be sent from Ireland to England for the service of Charles I, Long. W.P. xviii, 100.

FLEETWOOD (FLETEWOOD) family (below). Genealogy in Ms Rawl. B.263 fols. 241–242. Sir William, Sir George (later Baron), and Charles Fleetwood were the first, second and third sons of Sir Miles Fleetwood. Miles Fleetwood, jun., was Sir William's son; Colonel George Fleetwood, the regicide, was a second cousin of the three brothers.

FLEETWOOD, Charles, MP (1618–1692). *D.N.B.* Of Gray's Inn. A Colonel in the New Model; later Commander-in-Chief in Ireland, then Lord Deputy in 1654; Major-General for the Home Counties and East

Anglia, in 1655; Commander-in-Chief in England, 1659. His second marriage, in 1652, was to Cromwell's eldest daughter, Bridget, widow of Henry Ireton (q.v.), the regicide. There are numerous entries for Fleetwood in *The Diary*. George Cokayn (q.v.) had served as Chaplain to his Regiment, *Diary*, 3 Apr. 1650, and was appointed his personal Chaplain, 19 Aug. 1651 (*C.S.P. Dom.*).

FLEETWOOD, Sir George (Georg), later Baron (1605–1687). *S.M.K.*; *D.N.B.* Like General Robert Douglas (q.v.), he had been a soldier of fortune with the Swedish Army, also a diplomat. He was made a Swedish Knight in 1632, and a Swedish Baron in 1654. Sir George's brother William (q.v.) wrote to him when Whitelocke was going to Sweden as Ambassador Extraordinary. Sir George was friendly towards the Ambassador and kept in touch with him after the Embassy, writing from Sweden:

> Ower King [Charles X] hath bin very inquisitive after your excellencie, and seemed to be very well contented that your Honor was safely come on in Englande which I informed him yesterday. Concerning our late resignation [Christina's abdication] and coronation I dare not particularise ... it is in print in all languages. Ower noble Kinge (who gaineth the affection daily of all men by his affable carriage) is involved in new troubles before he is once settled. A war fomented by the Bremers ... [Bremen, south-west of Hamburg, was a Swedish Duchy]

He went on to say that Chancellor Oxenstierna (q.v.) had been very ill but was 'reasonable well recovered'; Count Gabriel Oxenstierna (q.v.) was planning, with the hot weather past, to send the six or seven reindeer to the Protector (the gift had been discussed with Whitelocke in Uppsala); those reindeer from Lapland that had survived the heat were 'very svelt and lustie' and Whitelocke could have as many of them as he pleased, for himself. Fleetwood added that Count Gabriel Oxenstierna had implored him to remind Whitelocke 'of the English horses and doges hee pretended [were] promised ...' 22 July 1654, Ms Rawl. A.27. fol. 533. A few months later, Sir George wrote to Sir William Fleetwood (q.v.) at Woodstock Park, starting: 'Dearest Brother'. He told of how homesick he felt since his wife's death; he had a gracious King in Charles X but was away from his native soil, absent from his kinsfolk and among strangers. While his Swedish wife Brita was alive, he had felt at home. He believed

> ... it could bee, by my Lord Whitelockes meanes[,] I mought finde some intisements to come over, which I must confes would be very welcome[;] he was pleased to make many large promises at his being heare; I pray pardon my plainenes, I haveing noe friend in this world to open my harte to above you and expect ... your advise in this buisnes.

He added in a postscript that Count Erik (Oxenstierna, q.v.), the new Chancellor, sent apologies for not writing by that post but would not fail by the next, and wished to report: '... how highly his Majestie hath accepted your intimation of doing all good offices betwixt his Majestie and my Lord Protector ...', 7 Oct. 1654, Long. W.P. xvi, 127–127v. The King's message about Cromwell is surprising, in view of the fact that Sir William Fleetwood was a Royalist.

A week after writing to his brother, Fleetwood wrote at some length to Whitelocke, acknowledging a letter of 3 August, and referring to other letters (apparently unanswered) and to correspondence with Richard Bradeshaw (q.v.) of Hamburg. He gave an account of the King of Sweden's movements, of

> ... the Muscoviters greatt army with which hee is saled into Poland, and of his greate progresse[,] ower last newes report his retirement towards Smolenske (which some write is taken, others not) ... The russe [i.e. Russian] taketh greate titles uppon him, which causeth everyone to looke about ... [A cryptic passage follows, perhaps containing a diplomatic message: it was reported that the Polish King had refused to give the Swedish King his bible] wondering [that] the King of Sweden should write to an other, but now the report goeth hee hath done it, onely will write a French bible backe againe, which how accepted I know not: but beleive this next spring will produce a new warre ... [He sent news of an ambassador coming with the wrong credentials, made out to Queen Christina, and of events at Court.] His majestie hath often asked after youer Excellencie and is often inquisitive after the affaires in England. Hee is a noble Prince, and giveth mee (I must confes) greate[r] respect then I can deserve ...
> 14 Oct. 1654.
>
> Ib. 129–129v.

In the same month he acknowledged Whitelocke's letter of 28 September, received on 19 October, with enclosures for Erik Oxenstierna, the new Chancellor, and for Count Douglas (q.v.), Grand Master of the Horse:

> ... wee have boath acquainted his Majestie of youer Excellencies resolutions of doeing all good offices betwixt this Court and his Highnes the Lord Protector, which his Majestie taketh for a high engagement, asuring the recompence with all Kingly favor, which I am commaunded to write to youer Excellencie ...

Referring to 'the buisnes of Breme' the 'last eruption' was caused by their obstinacy, 'and not ... religion as they now pretende ...' Among other matters he referred to the arrival of Sweden's new Queen (Hedwig of Holstein-Gottorp) at Stockholm Castle, to the wedding on 24 October and to her coronation two days later, in Stockholm.

... this next weake will bee most spent in shewes[,] running at the ringe and dancing. The Queene is of little stature but verie handesome, and they say of as good conditions ... his majestie seemeth extra pleased in his lot ...

I am glad to heare my brother hath waited uppon youer Excellencie, and humbly thanke you for puting [i.e. having] mee in minde of retiring to my native soile ... and I shall let slipe noe occation ... where in ... I can demonstrate ... how much I am youer creature ...
Stockholm 28 Oct. 1654.

Ib. 138–138v.

In a letter dated 13 January 1655 (presumably New Style, since by the next January, 1655/56 he was in England), Fleetwood wrote of Charles X receiving a letter from Whitelocke and of the King's respect for him. Fleetwood sent condolences to Whitelocke (whose beloved daughter, Frances, had died in December 1654) and went on to give news of events in the Swedish war, ib. xvii, 134–135. Three months later he wrote:

... ower whole time [is] taken up with preparations for a new warre, and it seemeth ower doeings have bin much misconsieved [i.e. misunderstood] ... His Majestie being informed of some misreportes of his intentions was much moved at it, and openly, in discourse with mee[,] utterly disclaimed ever haveing such thoughts ... [Fleetwood was confident that a communication from General Douglas would give Whitelocke] a sufficient satisfaction of our Kings intentions and thereby you will easily judge which way ower storme bendeth. I dare not particularise any newes, not questioning Count Douglas will give you a farre better account then I can ... god willing I hope in a shorte time to kisse your handes, my dispatch being all ready, onely the allmoast unpassable ill wayes and some private affaires uppon the lande may a little detaine mee ... I travell as a private person to see my friendes, but I beleive there by shall have a commission to his Highnes ... [He added] Privy Counselour Christerne Bonde (q.v.) shall folow mee ... as Extraordinarie Ambassadour ...
14 Apr. 1655.

Ib. 37–37v.

Fleetwood came to England in 1655, principally to justify Sweden's military activities. His stay in England is touched on by Whitelocke, *Diary* 18 Jan., 20 Feb. 1655/56, *passim*. He was knighted by Cromwell in September 1656.

FLEETWOOD, Col. George, MP (*c*.1622–*c*.1672) *D.N.B.* (Second cousin to the three brothers.) Of the Vache, near Chalfont St. Giles, Buckinghamshire. A Militia Colonel in that County. He was a regicide while still in his 20s. As a suitor for the hand of Mary Wilson (who later became Whitelocke's third wife) he requested the lady's permission to fight his older rival; but years later, when he was in prison, he became Whitelocke's client, *Diary* 11 Nov. 1663. He was discharged from the Tower on 31 Mar. 1664, and was pardoned for his part in the King's death, *C.S.P. Dom.*, 1664, p. 536.

FLEETWOOD, Sir William, MP, JP (1603–1674). *Hist. of Parl.*; Burke *Extinct & Dormant Baronetcies*; *D.N.B.* (briefly, in Charles Fleetwood's entry). In 1641 he succeeded his father, Sir Miles Fleetwood of Aldwinkle, Northamptonshire, as Receiver-General of the Court of Wards. A Royalist. Of High Lodge, Woodstock Park, Oxfordshire. Whitelocke helped him over his composition, *Diary* 18 June 1649, and he is referred to in Whitelocke's 'defence', ib. 6 June 1660. Earlier, when Whitelocke was appointed Ambassador Extraordinary, Sir William wrote:

> I am extreeme sorry to receive it from your one [i.e. own] penne, that you are to goe into Swedland but since it must be, there shall be noe person more dilligent w[i]th his prayers & good wishes for your safe jurney & returne then my selfe ... I have written this inclosed to my brother [Sir George, q.v.] nowe at Stockholme whoe I am sure will be reddy to serve you there ... I feare you will finde a colde jurney, you had need be well provided w[it]^h Furs & hottwaters, & warme clothes & a stronger body then I feare your Lord[shi]^p haithe at present, but I feare necessety haithe no remedy ... Northampton this 26th [September 1653].
>
> Long. W.P. xiii, 242–243.

FLEMING (FLEMMING), Sir Oliver. Master of Ceremonies for Parliament from 1643 to the end of the Protectorate, T. Carlyle *Letters and Speeches of Oliver Cromwell* (ed. S.C. Lomas), *passim*; G.E. Aylmer *State's Servants* p. 19; p. 351 note 11, in that work, gives, among other references: *The Humble Narrative of Oliver Fleming Knight*, reprinted in *Somers Tracts*, 3rd collection, II (1751), 232–240. For a letter to Fleming from Amerigo Salvetti, Florentine Agent, 21 Aug. 1651, see Long. W.P. xi, 47.

FORSTER (FOSTER), families. *The Diary* has a number of entries for Sir Humphrey Forster (below) and his family, mainly between 1645 and 1657; also several for a Mr. Forster, son-in-law of Robert Gough (q.v.) and for that young man's father, in the 1670s. No connection between the families has been traced. Judge Forster and Alderman Forster have one brief entry each, *Diary* 2 June 1660; 29 Apr. 1662. Captain Nicholas Foster (q.v.) was always mis-spelt 'Forster', by Whitelocke.

FORSTER, Sir Humphrey, Bt. (c.1595–1663). Burke *Extinct & Dormant Baronetcies*. An inscription to his mother, on the south wall of the Chancel in the Church of St. Mary the Virgin, Aldermaston, Berkshire, gives his details; see other family memorials and an armorial window showing alliances of the Forster family. Sir Humphrey was the son and heir of Sir William Forster and of Mary, daughter of Sir Mark Stewart. Forsters were Lords of the Manor of Aldermaston from 1490–1711. Sir Humphrey inherited the Manor in 1618; he sold Harding (alias Harpsden) Court near Henley-on-Thames to Whitelocke, who bought it for Bartholomew Hall (q.v.), *Diary* 25 Dec. 1645. Harpsden had come into the Forster family, through marriage, some time before 1500. Sir Humphrey was Sheriff of Berkshire in 1619; he was created Baronet in 1620. After offering to sell Watchfield Manor (north-east of Swindon) to Whitelocke, he changed his mind, ib. 13 Sept. 1648. Whitelocke wrote of being 'highly feasted' on visits to Aldermaston, and although Sir Humphrey 'constantly was silent att Meales' the splendid hospitality 'spake his bountey ...', ib. 11 Aug. 1648. When Whitelocke took the Swedish Ambassador to Aldermaston, they were nobly entertained with hawking, hunting, fishing and card games, ib. 22 Sept. 1655. In the year of Sir Humphrey's death his widow, Lady Anne Forster (d.1673), daughter of Sir William Kingsmill, came to Whitelocke as a client, ib. 1 June 1663; Mrs. Forster 'the widdow' (who also consulted Whitelocke and invited him to Aldermaston) was presumably Elizabeth, daughter of Sir John Tyrrell and widow of Sir Humphrey's son and heir, William (d.1660, aged 36), ib. 11 Oct. 1666. Sir Humphrey and his wife Anne had 16 children. Burke states that Sir Humphrey Forster's sister married Elias Ashmole (q.v.); he was her third husband.

FORTH, Alderman John. A.B.B. ii, 102, 190, *passim*. A Brewer. Alderman in 1668; Sheriff from 1670 to 1671. Brother of Alderman Dannet Forth. He married Albinia, daughter of Sir Henry Vane, and Lady Vane consulted Whitelocke about the marriage, *Diary* 26 Mar. 1668. Forth's niece married Oliver St. John's son. Known for his hot temper. It was noted that, being 'noe lover of the Church of England ... he hath a consecrated chapell in his owne house ... a nonconformist and a brewer officiating ...', A.B.B. (above).

FORTH and BRENTFORD, Patrick Ruthen (Ruthven), E. of (c.1573–1651). G.E.C.; *D.N.B.* He served in the Swedish Army; was appointed General-in-Chief by Charles I after Edgehill, and was with the King at Oxford. Whitelocke records that Forth made overtures for peace to Essex, in the summer of 1644; Forth was wounded at the second Battle of Newbury on 22 Oct. that year, and in the following month he was superseded by Prince Rupert, who was appointed Commander-in-Chief.

FOSTER (FORSTER), Nicholas. Captain of the frigate *Phoenix*, in which Whitelocke sailed to Sweden. He was instructed to convey any orders given by Whitelocke, to Capt. Myngs (q.v.) and to other officers in the convoy. Instructions to Foster for the transport of Lord Ambassador Whitelocke and his retinue are signed by Robert Blake (q.v.) and George Monck (later Duke of Albemarle, q.v.), 24 Oct. 1653, Long. W.P. xiv, 128 (copy); a letter from Foster to Whitelocke, after the Captain had left the Ambassador at Gothenburg, is at once chatty and overflowing with piety and admiration, written aboard the *Phoenix*, 24 Nov. 1653, ib. 204.

FOUNTAIN (FOUNTAINE), Judge John (1600–1671). *D.N.B.*; G.E. Aylmer *State's Servants*. Of Lincoln's Inn. Initially a Royalist, he was viewed with some suspicion by the Rump, yet he served as a Law Reform Commissioner from 1652–1653, and was appointed a Commissioner of the Great Seal (although his appointment was contested) for five months, and the appointment was later renewed, by the restored Rump, *Diary* 3, 4 June 1659; 18, 19 Jan. 1659/60. He was made a Serjeant-at-Law before and after the Restoration, ib. 16 June 1659; 23 June 1660. Whitelocke visited the Serjeant some years later, ib. 9 Nov. 1669.

FREAKE (FREKE) family (below). 'History of Parliament 1604–1629' (draft typescript biography at the time of writing. Permission to quote from this unpublished source, here and elsewhere, is gratefully acknowledged); *The Ancestor* (quarterly Review) x, 179, *passim*, July 1904; *V.C.H. Dorset* ii, *passim*; J. Hutchins *History and Antiquities of the County of Dorset* 3rd edn. (1861–1870) iv, 86–87 pedigree (this shows relationships of this well-known Dorset and Wiltshire family, but a printing error makes Sir Thomas and his eldest son John die in the same year, the one aged 69 and the other 70). Related to Sir John Meller (q.v.) of Phyllis Court, Henley, and of Little Bredy, Dorset, through Meller's stepmother Margaret, sister of Sir Thomas Freake.

FREAKE (FREKE), John, MP (1589–1641). Eldest son of Sir Thomas Freake (q.v.) and brother of Ralph (below). He owned: Westbrooke

House, Upwey, north-west of Weymouth, Dorset; Peper Harow, south-east of Farnham, Surrey, and Cerne Abbas, Dorset, north of Dorchester. He entered the Middle Temple in 1600, Hart Hall, Oxford, in 1605, and became Sheriff of Dorset in 1636. His wealthy second wife, Jane née Shirley, of Ifield, married Denzil Holles (q.v.), the year after Freake's death, P. Crawford *Denzil Holles* (Royal Historical Society. 1979) pp. 71, 72 note 1. An undated account of 'The Deamens of Cerne Abbas' (which Freake bought from the Crown in 1625) has Whitelocke's seal on it and is addressed, though not in Whitelocke's hand, to his worthy friend John Freake 'att his house att Cerne . . .', Long. W.P. v, 285.

When buying out Sir John Meller's interest in the Phyllis Court estate, Whitelocke wrote in the 'Annales' more fully than in *Diary* 1635.1636. fol. 41:

> I made use of my Noble friend Mr John Freake to treate with S[i]^r John Miller [i.e. Meller], about the purchase of Phillis Court, which S[i]^r John had now offered to sell, & no man had more interest with him then this great friend & kinsman of his . . . who was a very faithfull friend to me like wise.
>
> Add.Ms 37343 fol. 139v.

In a brief abstract of title to 'Fillets' (i.e. Phyllis Court), John Freake is mentioned as son and executor of Sir Thomas, and as being 'possessed of the premises in trust' (it had previously been assigned to the trusteeship of his father and Henry Swynerton); in the Trinity Term, 11 Car. (i.e. 1636), Sir John Meller, his wife and children exhibited a bill in Chancery against John Freake, to assign the residue of the term of his interest, 1636 (?), Long. W.P. vii, 249–250.

FREAKE (FREKE), Ralph (1596–1684). *Register of Admission to the Middle Temple*. Third son of Sir Thomas Freake (below). Of Hannington, Wilts. A contemporary of Whitelocke's at the Middle Temple, he was called to the Bar in 1628. Bartholomew Hall (q.v.) and Benjamin Tichborne (q.v.) witnessed a bill of Whitelocke's for payment of £100 owed to Ralph Freake, 9 Feb. 1634/35, Long. W.P. vi, 189. Whitelocke and Henry Bulstrode signed a bond to him in £400 for payment of £208, 26 May 1636, Long. W.P. vii, 45; when Whitelocke was borrowing money to buy Phyllis Court, Ralph Freake was bound with him and Bartholomew Hall to Sir George Croke (q.v.) and Alexander Croke, in £1,600 for payment of £800, 12 Nov. 1638, ib. 291.

FREAKE (FREKE), Sir Thomas, Kt., MP (1563–1633). Burke *Extinct &
Dormant Baronetcies* (for lineage). Of Iwerne (Ewern) Courtney, alias
Shroton (Sherevton), Dorset, south of Shaftesbury. There is a large
monument to him in the Church. His sister was the second wife of Sir
Robert Meller (of Dorset and of Phyllis Court, Henley), and stepmother of
Sir John Meller (q.v.). Whitelocke recorded that the first fees he earned as
a lawyer were paid by Michael Bolt or Boulte (q.v.) and the next by Sir
Thomas Freake, *Diary* 1628.1629. fols. 10v.–11.

FREAKE (FREKE), Thomas, jun. (1599–1643). Fifth son of Sir Thomas
(above); he does not appear in *The Diary*, but Whitelocke was bound with
Henry Bulstrode in £400 for payment of £208 to him, 23 Apr. 1635, Long.
W.P. vi, 202.

GARDIE, Ebba Sparre, Countess de la (1626–1662). *S.M.K.*; B.
Whitelocke's *Dag-Bok* p. 377, note. Wife of Count Jacob Kasimir de la
Gardie, known as '*la belle comtesse*'. Lady-in-waiting to Queen Christina.
Reputedly the most beautiful woman in Sweden, she was introduced to
Whitelocke by the Queen as: 'this lady my bed-fellow', *Journal*, i, 405,
8 Feb. 1653/54, *passim*; this passage was omitted from *The Diary*.

GARDIE, Count Magnus Gabriel de la (1622–1686). *S.M.K.*; *Sweden's
Age of Greatness 1632–1718* (ed. M. Roberts. Macmillan. 1973). A
cultured man and an able negotiator. While he remained a favourite,
Queen Christina showered him with gifts. He was appointed: Ambassador
to France in 1646; Councillor of the Realm, and a member of the War
Council in 1647. He married the sister of the future Charles X of Sweden,
and was made High Treasurer in 1652, but was expelled from Court in
1653; Whitelocke was given a detailed description of the Count's fall from
favour, *Journal* i, 340–347 (referred to briefly in *Diary* 20 Jan. 1653/54).
The Count remained under a cloud until after the Queen's abdication. He
served his brother-in-law, Charles X, in the Baltic, ib. 16 July 1657, and
became leader of the Regency during the minority of Charles XI,
1660–1672.

GARRARD (GARRET), Sir John, Bt. Burke *Extinct & Dormant
Baronetcies*. Of Lamer House, north of Wheathampstead, Herts.
Advanced from Knight to Baronet in 1622. He was connected with

Aldermen and Lord Mayors of London, both through his own family and through that of his first wife, Elizabeth Barkham, A.B.B., *passim*. In 1629, Judge Sir James Whitelocke tried to negotiate a match for Bulstrode with Garrard's daughter Jane, but the treaty broke down. The draft agreement shows a marriage portion of £2,700, to be paid by instalments; Jane was to be provided with jewels, apparel and £200 in lieu of two years' board; the Judge was to provide, as jointure for the couple: lands and tenements to the value of £300 p.a. etc., Long. W.P. iv, 45. Six months after these negotiations had failed, Bulstrode married Rebecca Benet. No doubt Garrard thought he could do better for his daughter: in 1634 she married Sir Justinian Isham, 2nd Bt. (*D.N.B.*), but she died in childbirth in 1638.

GATES, Judge [Thomas] (*c.*1587–1650). E. Foss *Judges of England*. Misnamed 'Yate' by Whitelocke, who refers to his being sworn a Baron of the Exchequer, *Diary* 22 Nov. 1648. Gates's term as a Judge was short, and apparently undistinguished.

GAYTON, Edmund (1608–1666). *D.N.B.* Author and playwright. Three years Whitelocke's junior; educated, like him, at Merchant Taylors' School and at St. John's College, Oxford, of which he was elected a Fellow. He lived in poverty for much of his life and was in a debtor's prison in 1655; Whitelocke was asked to do a favour to his old acquaintance, *Diary* 10 Apr. 1657.

GERHARD, Lord, probably Charles Gerard, 1st Baron of Brandon and E. of Macclesfield (d.1694). G.E.C.; *D.N.B.* An active Royalist, he was involved in a chancery dispute in 1661. The next year he obtained a pension and, later in the year, was sent as Envoy Extraordinary to France. That year 'Lord Gerhard' consulted Whitelocke twice, as a client, the first time about conveyancing; the second time may have been about his embassy to France, *Diary* 19 Feb. 1661/62; 18 June 1662.

GERRARD (GERARD), Sir Gilbert Bt., MP (1587–1670). M.F.K.; R. Somerville *Office Holders of the Duchy ... of Lancaster* (1972), *passim*; Burke *Extinct & Dormant Baronetcies*; G.E. Aylmer *King's Servants*. Of Gray's Inn. Created a Baronet in 1620. He owned Flambards (Flamberds), Harrow-on-the-Hill, and later Aston Clinton, Bucks., and is mentioned when he came with others 'to conclude Christmas' with the Whitelockes, i.e. to celebrate Twelfth Night, *Diary* 6 Jan. 1647/48. He was appointed Chancellor of the Duchy of Lancaster, of which Whitelocke was Attorney '& glad of so good a friend to be Chancellor there', ib. 7 Mar. 1647/48. (Actual date of appointment: 4 Apr. 1648.) He was secluded at Pride's Purge and imprisoned for a short time, but was later reappointed Chancellor of the Duchy, ib. 14 Mar. 1659/60.

GIBBONS, John (d.1651). P. Crawford *Denzil Holles* pp. 181–182 with notes. Holles's servant, perhaps his secretary. Gibbons was executed with the Presbyterian Minister Christopher Love (q.v.), in connection with a royalist uprising. Whitelocke's friends. feared that he too might be implicated, because of his friendship with Holles, but he saw no cause for alarm, *Diary* 19 July 1651.

GIBBONS, Robert. T. Carlyle *Letters and Speeches of Oliver Cromwell* i, 322, 323 with note. A Major, later Colonel. In the Second Civil War he led a party which defeated a band of Royalists from Kingston, Surrey, as they rode towards Reigate.

GLANVILLE (GLANVILE), Sir John, the younger, MP (1586–1661). *D.N.B.*; M.F.K. (in the entry for his son William). Speaker of the House of Commons in the Short Parliament. King's Serjeant. As a Royalist he made his composition and, after a spell of imprisonment, was released from the Tower. Whitelocke gave him some unspecified help, *Diary* 27 July 1648. Many years later Glanville's widow Winifred, née Bourchier, came to Whitelocke as a client, ib. 18 June 1672.

GLEMHAM, Sir Thomas, Kt. (d.c.1649). *D.N.B.* A Royalist Colonel-General; Governor of York, and later of Oxford until its surrender. He showed his humanity when, after the capitulation of Winchester, six of Cromwell's troopers violated the terms of surrender, by plundering their enemy; at their trial by a Council of War, all were condemned to death, apparently by Cromwell, but afterwards were allowed to draw lots for one to die; the other five were delivered as prisoners to Glemham, then Governor of Oxford, who was free to execute or to punish them as he thought fit: '. . . which was so well received by the enemy . . . that sir Thomas Glemham returned the prisoners . . . with an acknowledgment of the lieutenant-general's nobleness', quoted in C.H. Firth *Cromwell's Army* p. 293.

GLOUCESTER, Henry, D. of (1639–1660). G.E.C.; *D.N.B.* The youngest son of Charles I (q.v.). He was cruelly treated by his mother, Queen Henrietta Maria (q.v.), in 1654, when he resisted attempts to convert him to her faith. Most of the diary references to the Duke occur between his brother's Restoration on 25 May 1660, and his own death from smallpox a few months later, when Whitelocke wrote: 'There was much sorrow for his death, being a Courteous & good natured P[rince]', *Diary* 14 Sept. 1660.

GLYN (GLYNNE), Sir John, MP (1603–1666). *Hist. of Parl.*; *D.N.B.* (both under Glynne); M.F.K. Of Lincoln's Inn. Politically he was a moderate; Recorder of the City of London from 1643 to 1649. As one of the 11 members who attempted to disband the Army in 1647, Glyn was expelled from Parliament and imprisoned in the Tower, but was later appointed Chief Justice of the Upper Bench, under Cromwell; in spite of this, he was knighted by Charles II, soon after the Restoration. He played an active part as MP for Caernarvonshire in the Convention Parliament of Apr. 1660, and subsequently in the Courts as King's Serjeant, *Diary*, *passim*.

GODDARD family. Of the Manor of South Standen or Standen Hussey, W. Berks., *V.C.H. Berks.* iv, 196. Mrs. Sarah Goddard was a widow by the time the Whitelockes moved to Chilton Lodge (her husband, Francis, having died in 1652). Their son, Edward Goddard (buried in Hungerford, 1684), inherited the Manor from his father. Sarah Goddard's brother, Henry Hungerford (q.v.), lived with Sarah and his nephew Francis, see his entry in *Hist. of Parl.* Mrs. Goddard appears frequently in *The Diary*, from 29 July 1663 onward. No indication has been found that other Goddards known to Whitelocke, in the same area, were related: Mr. Goddard of Woodhay, Berkshire; Mrs. Goddard of Clopcot; young Elizabeth Goddard, daughter of Vincent Goddard, and described as Mrs. Tull's daughter (see Jethro Tull); or Mr. Thomas Goddard, who regularly repeated sermons but 'prayed wonderfully well.'

GODDARD, Jonathan, MD (*c.*1617–1675). *D.N.B.* Whitelocke consulted him in London, and the Doctor prescribed drops for Mary Whitelocke. He does not appear to have been connected with the Goddard family above.

GOFFE, see also GOUGH.

GOFFE (GOUGH), Col., later Major-General, William (d.*c.*1679). *D.N.B.* A regicide and a religious fanatic. He and three others were sent to Monck to try to prevent bloodshed, *Diary* 1 Nov. 1659. He escaped overseas at the Restoration.

GOFFE (GOUGH), William (b.*c.*1626). A.G. Matthews *Calamy Revised.* Rector of Inkpen, Berks., until he was ejected in 1662. He preached twice to the Whitelocke family, in conventicles at Chilton Lodge, *Diary* 12 July 1674.

GOODGROOM (GOODGROOME), [? Capt. Richard.] B.S. Capp *Fifth Monarchy Men* p. 250, *passim.* A yeoman and preacher. He was sent to the Tower, *Diary* 29 Sept. 1660 (this date does not quite tally with that given by B.S. Capp). Possibly he was the Digger whose name appeared with 14 others (his own directly under that of Gerrard Winstanley), on *The True Levellers' Standard Advanced,* 26 Apr. 1649, see *Winstanley: the Law of Freedom* ... (ed. C. Hill. Penguin Books. 1973), p. 75. A man named Goodgroom had opposed the Protectorate but served in Robert Overton's regiment; later, a Cornet Goodgroom was moved to a Chaplaincy, *C.S.P. Dom.* 27 July; 4 Oct. 1659. The possibility that there was more than one Richard Goodgroom is explored by J.G.A. Pocock *Political Works of James Harrington* (C.U.P. 1977), pp. 11–12, 58, 125 note 4.

GOODWYN (GOODWIN), Col. Arthur, MP (*c.*1593–1643). *D.N.B.*; M.F.K. One of the Knights for Buckinghamshire, in the Long Parliament. A Deputy-Lieutenant for the County, and close friend of John Hampden, with whom he had been a student at Magdalen College, Oxford. The House of Commons appointed a party of Goodwyn's regiment of horse and of Hampden's foot, to support Whitelocke in preventing the execution of the King's Commission of Array in Watlington, Oxfordshire, *Diary* Aug. 1642.

GOODWYN, Ellis, of Moulsford near Wallingford.

GOODWYN (GOODWIN), John (*c*.1594–1665). *D.N.B.* A controversial republican divine. Vicar of St. Stephen's, Coleman St.; later, he set up an Independent Church there. His book, *The Obstructours of Justice*, was burned with two of John Milton's, on 27 Aug. 1660; the proclamation and the event are referred to in *Diary* 16 June, 13 Aug., 5 Sept. 1660.

GOODWYN (GOODWIN), Thomas, DD (1600–1680). *D.N.B.*; B.S. Capp *Fifth Monarchy Men*, *passim*. President of Magdalen College, Oxford; he was deprived of the post in May 1660. A prominent Independent Minister, he discussed liberty of conscience with Whitelocke and at a meeting arranged by Whitelocke with Chancellor Clarendon, *Diary* 14 May 1661; 24 Mar. 1661/62; 1 Apr. 1662. In the following year, Whitelocke signed a bond to Thomas Goodwyn DD for £200, conditioned on payment of £103, and another, nine months later, for £400, 8 July 1663, Long. W.P. xx, 82; 5 Apr. 1664, ib. 100.

GOODWYN (GOODWIN), Capt. –. Knew Whitelocke, Bartholomew Hall (q.v.) and Sir Humphrey Forster (q.v.) of Aldermaston; he is referred to in *The Diary* between 1 Oct. 1645 and 11 Sept. 1648.

GOUGH (GOFFE) family. Samuel, Whitelocke's eldest son by his third marriage, married Elizabeth Gough, daughter of Robert Gough. The family lived in Vernham, Hants, within riding distance of Chilton Lodge. Having three daughters but no son, Robert Gough offered a marriage portion of £3,000 plus a share of his estate when he died, *Diary* 8, 9 Nov., 12, 20 Dec. (with note), 1671, *passim*. Gough's other daughters married a Mr. Foster and a Mr. Godfrey. Mr. Godfrey sent a salmon to his 'Sister Whitelocke', b. 1 Apr. 1672. Robert Gough's wife and his brother Francis appear in *The Diary*, also an unidentified Mr. or Major Gough, of Marlborough.

GRANDISON, William Villiers, 2nd Viscount (d.1643). G.E.C. Great-nephew and heir of Oliver St. John, the 1st Viscount. He is described in *The Diary* as a special friend of Lord Willoughby (q.v.); Edward Hyde (later Earl of Clarendon, q.v.), approached Lord Grandison after Whitelocke's runaway marriage to Frances Willoughby in Nov. 1635, asking him to put matters right with her family.

    Grandison's daughter was Barbara Villiers, later Lady Castlemaine, mistress of Charles II.

GREEN (GREENE), John, JP (d.1687). There is a monument to Green in Hambleden Church. He was a substantial 'woodmonger' or timber-merchant, who owned Mill End Wharf, Hambleden, in Buckinghamshire, near Fawley Court, and died as Lord of Yewden Manor, alias Greenland, *V.C.H. Bucks.* iii, 49. He supported Whitelocke in parliamentary elections, 24 June 1654, Long. W.P. xvi, 55; *Diary* 5, 7 Aug. 1656, *passim.* Whitelocke had him appointed a JP, ib. 7 Oct. 1658.

After the Restoration, Green contracted to buy standing timber from Whitelocke's estate; this led to a prolonged dispute. Green was related to George Monck, Duke of Albemarle's wife Nan, the daughter of a blacksmith, who was Monck's laundress when he was imprisoned in the Tower, in 1643. According to Whitelocke, Green had given her some money, had then been made an officer in the King's stables, and was supplying wood for the King's use, ib. 24 May 1661. Details of transactions between Green and Whitelocke include: a receipt for £357.12s. od. paid by John Green and his brother George, as early as 16 July 1649, for 1,192 loads of billets and stackwood, Long. W.P. x, 21; an unsigned draft bond from the Green brothers to Whitelocke for £3,000, conditioned for payment of £1,500, 17 Aug. 1661, ib. xix, 156; a bond of Green's to Whitelocke for £500, conditioned for payment of £280 on 29 Sept. [1661?] at Whitelocke's house in Coleman St., London, ib. 160; these last two items relate to articles of agreement specifying Whitelocke's woods

> which lye most convenient for carryage to the wharfe of the sayd John Green called Mill end wharfe in Hambleden ... & ... woods ... which lye most convenient for carryage unto the wharfe in Henley called Fortunes wharfe

Green was to pay £2,000, by instalments, for 6,000 loads of billets and 1,000 stacks of wood, ib. 153 (draft, with date left blank, about 18 June 1661). Whitelocke's attempts to find a legal loophole in the agreement are described in *Diary* 13 Nov. 1662 with note.

GRENVILLE (GRANVILLE, GREENVILLE), Sir John, Kt., later 1st E. of Bath (1628–1701). G.E.C. *D.N.B.*; *Restoration, passim.* Third son of Sir Bevil Grenville of Cornwall, who was an MP in the Long Parliament. Sir John, like his father, was a Royalist; he was a kinsman of George Monck (later Duke of Albemarle, q.v.). Sir John was arrested in July 1659, in connection with a royalist rising in the West Country, planned for 1 August, but he was released on parole, *Restoration* pp. 133–134. Described, by Whitelocke, as a Gentleman of the Bedchamber to Charles II at Breda; he also carried letters and messages between the King and

General Monck, and brought the King's letter and the Declaration of Breda itself to both Houses, with copies to Monck (who was to inform the officers of it), and to the Lord Mayor and Aldermen of London; for these services he was suitably rewarded, *Diary* 1, 2, 3 May 1660; he was created 1st Earl of Bath in April 1661.

GRENVILLE (GRENVILE, GREENVILL), Richard, MP (not to be confused with Sir Richard, a Cornish Royalist). A Deputy-Lieutenant of Buckinghamshire, *Diary*, 1641.1642. fol. 54v. He was appointed to represent that County on the Committee of the Three Counties, *C.J.* iv, 294, 30 Sept. 1645, and later was elected one of the Knights for Buckinghamshire, in Cromwell's second Parliament, *Diary* 21 Aug. 1656; (*Return of Members of Parliament* i, 499 shows that no return was found for Buckinghamshire in that Parliament).

GREY of GROBY, Thomas, styled Lord, MP (*c*.1623–1657). G.E.C.; *D.N.B.*; M.F.K. A regicide. Whitelocke visited Groby's grandmother (the Dowager Countess of Exeter) with him, *Diary* 21 Apr. 1649. For the Commons' decision after the Restoration, concerning the regicide's estate, see *Diary* 9 June 1660 with note.

GREY of WARKE (WERKE), William, Bt., MP, later 1st Baron (*c*.1593–1674). G.E.C.; *D.N.B.* Of Chillingham, and of Wark, in Northumberland; he was created Baron in 1624 and bought the Manor of Epping in 1636, *V.C.H. Essex* v, 119. He supported Parliament, serving as Speaker of the House of Lords in 1643 and as a Commissioner of the Great Seal with the Earl of Kent (q.v.), Thomas Widdrington (q.v.), and Whitelocke, in 1648. Whitelocke stayed with him at Epping, *Diary* 11 Aug. 1649. There are numerous other diary entries for him. Lord Grey withdrew from public life in 1649; although elected a member of the Council of State after the King's execution, he did not serve on it, as he refused to qualify by subscribing to the engagement of loyalty.

GRIMSTON, Sir Harbottle, 2nd Bt., MP (1603–1685). *Hist. of Parl.*; Burke *Extinct & Dormant Baronetcies*; *D.N.B.*; M.F.K. He succeeded to the Baronetcy, on the death of his father of the same name, in 1648. Of Lincoln's Inn. Grimston was related to Whitelocke by his first marriage, to Mary, daughter of Whitelocke's great-uncle, Sir George Croke (q.v.).

Whitelocke gives a lively account of the journey, after this wedding, when he acted as the young couple's coachman, *Diary* 1627.1628. fol. 8v. Grimston, a Presbyterian, served as Speaker of the House of Commons, in the Convention Parliament of 1660; he assisted at the trial of the regicides, and was rewarded with a life-patent as Master of the Rolls. When Grimston was Speaker, Whitelocke wrote to him on behalf of himself and his son James, applying for the King's pardon within the prescribed 40 days, Add.Ms 32093 fol. 420 (copy), 22 May 1660. When Grimston was Master of the Rolls, Whitelocke dined with him on a number of occasions, *Diary* 4 Feb. 1661/62; 2 Jan. 1662/63, *passim*.

GURDON (GOURDEN), John, MP (1595–1679). M.F.K.; *Hist. of Parl.*; *D.N.B.* P.Crawford *Denzil Holles*. Of Gray's Inn. He served on numerous parliamentary committees. Active against Whitelocke and Holles (q.v.) in the Savile case, *Diary* 2, 5, 7, 8 July 1645. He opposed the plans to disband the New Model, but refused to take part in the trial of Charles I. A Councillor of State from 1650 to 1652.

HALE, Sir Matthew, MP (1609–1676). *Hist. of Parl.*; *D.N.B.* Of Lincoln's Inn. As a young man he was influenced, as Whitelocke was, by John Selden (q.v.). A Judge under the Protectorate and after the Restoration, he ultimately became Chief Justice of the King's Bench. By inclination a Royalist, he was active in promoting the Restoration but argued for a treaty to be negotiated with Charles II. He shared a house in Ivy Lane, London, with Whitelocke, Palmer (q.v.) and their three wives, in the Autumn of 1642. Palmer and Hale's wives were Margaret and Anne Moore (an aunt and niece), see: MOORE. For an Order of some significance, signed by Hale on 13 Feb. 1651/52, see *Diary* 31 Jan. 1651/52, with note. Whitelocke's last meeting with Hale recorded in *The Diary*, was on 18 Feb. 1665/66.

HALL, Bartholomew (c.1592–1677). *Middle Temple Admission Register*, i; *Master Worsley's Book on the History and Constitution of . . . the Middle Temple* (ed. A.R. Ingben); *Dorset Standing Committee 1646–1650* (Exeter. 1902), *passim*; R. Somerville *Office Holders of the Duchy . . . of Lancaster* (1972); *V.C.H. Oxfordshire*, iv.; a memorial slab, on the floor of Harpsden Church, north-west of the altar. Second son of Thomas Hall of Kingston Lacy, Dorset. Of the Middle Temple. He married Frances (c.1613–1663), sister of Sir William Constantine (q.v.). Hall was about 13 years Whitelocke's senior. Although not related, Whitelocke normally referred to 'Father and Mother Hall'. Bartholomew and his brother, Thomas Hall, sold Kingston Lacy to Sir John Bankes (q.v.), Wessex Regional Office, Bankes Mss 48/3. Bartholomew Hall succeeded Whitelocke as Attorney of the Duchy of Lancaster from 1649 to 1653. He was made Treasurer of the Middle Temple in 1650; Recorder of Abingdon from 1649 to 1656 (again succeeding Whitelocke), but was replaced in that post on the pretence that 'he liveth far remote [some 20 miles away, at Harpsden Court near Henley-on-Thames] and by reason of his [other] great ymployment, the Mayor and Principal Burgesses . . . are destitute of his assistance and counsell', A.C. Baker *Historic Abingdon* (Abbey Press, Abingdon.1963) pp. 12, 74. As Recorder of Oxford, Hall was invited to resign in 1660, unless he would move nearer to the City, *V.C.H. Oxford* iv, p. 149. Years earlier, Whitelocke bought Harding alias Harpsden Court on behalf of Hall, who wished to live near to him at Fawley Court, *Diary* 25 Dec. 1645.

Although there are many diary entries (some of the later ones unflattering to Hall), surprisingly little correspondence between the two has been traced, and that mainly in transcript. Whitelocke wrote to Hall from Paris: 'I received a great deale of joy in the lines of so true a friend . . . as your selfe, which I know is . . . from so good a hearte . . .' He wanted his whereabouts to be kept a secret, and explained in a postscript why he had left England so abruptly, on Rebecca's account: '. . . my wifes doctor persuaded me to this journey, that I might not desire to see her [all family visits were forbidden by Dr. Bartlett, q.v.]. She is fallen much worse as I heare uppon sight of her mother lately . . .', May $^{16}/_{26}$ 1634, Long. W.P. vi. 95.

Some nine months after Whitelocke's runaway marriage to his second wife, Frances Willoughby, Hall accompanied the couple to Belvoir Castle as their legal adviser. They stayed with the 7th Earl of Rutland (q.v.) and attempted to secure from him, as one of the Trustees, Frances Whitelocke's legacy from her father, William, 3rd Baron Willoughby of Parham; Hall drew up a lengthy report, 10 Aug. 1635, Long. W.P. vi, 251v.–256.

More than a decade later, Whitelocke was nominated as one of Parliament's four Keepers of the Great Seal, newly struck as a defiant substitute for the King's Great Seal. The appointment was potentially dangerous, but it took Whitelocke to the top of his profession. Whitelocke suspected that Hall was thinking of his own career in wishing him to accept the post, *Diary* 6 Mar. 1647/48. He recorded:

> Father Hall wrote a few lines in my wife's letter in characters [i.e. shorthand] to My dear Son,
> You are like now to be a father of the lawe, we can not advise you whither best to returne or proceed in your journey, [riding the Circuit] butt thought

best to acquaint you with it, that you may consider of it your selfe, the question is whether it be necessary to be in London, in case the Ordinance be past the Lords house, wherof we heare nothing yett ... Your grave father [three words transcribed in shorthand] BH.

[Whitelocke went on] Mother Hall wrote also in my wife's letter, thus.

Although these learned Scribes, have writ, as they thinke, much to the purpose, yet my advice is not the worst, which is to come home as soon as you can, for we want you very much, & be carefull of your selfe, these daungerous times for robberies. F.H. Rec. 6 Mar. 1647/48.

Add.Ms 37344 fols. 136–136v. (transcripts).

Frances Hall's positive advice won the day.
Later, Hall wrote to Whitelocke in Sweden:

Deare Sonne
I cannot forbeare writing though I have no more newes to send you then what I writ the last weeke, only my Lord Protector is now removed to Whitehall, most of the Gownemen [i.e. lawyers] are gone home a gaine, & those that remai[ne] here are at ease by reason of the adjour[n]ment, and we all hope of your safe returne before the Terme ... My Lord of Clare [q.v.] & S[i]ʳ Humphrey Foster [q.v.] are both out of Towne ...

It is wondred heere of the Queens [Christina's] resolution to Part of that which is so ambitiously desired of many, but *ar cana Imperii* [i.e. state secrets], are not to be searched into ... she has shewed herselfe to be a Lady of much wisdome and Civility in her carriage towards you. Judge Jermine is dead & Baron Nicholas is very sicke ... & not like to recover, there is hopes of my L[or]ᵈ Sᵗ Johns recovery, my Lady [Mary Whitelocke] was with us yesterday whoe is very well and she and we hope to see you here shortly ... Tom [Hall's eldest son, d.1656] wishes himselfe often with Mʳ Whitelocke now his mother is reasonable well, he hath bene a great comfort to her in hir affliction.

Your faithfull
friend & Gravefather
B. Hall

14 Apr.
1654
... I must needs trouble you with my scrible to present my service & continuall wishes to see you heere. Received in Stockholm 26 May 1654.

Add.Ms 37347 fols. 237–237v. (transcript).

By September 1654, Whitelocke had again taken up his appointment as a Lord Commissioner of the Great Seal, but this time under the Protector; Hall addressed him under that title, writing from Houghton, in Nottinghamshire, where he was the guest of the royalist Earl of Clare (q.v.) to whom, from time to time, Whitelocke and Hall gave legal advice. Hall wrote:

... I must needs say I have heer as kind wellcome from the highest to the lowest, as can be wished, yett I must needs crave leave of my Lord of Clare, to come for London, the next Monday ... I understand that your L[ordshi]ᴾ was pleased to see my wife the day after you came to Towne, which was a great comfort to her, in the time of her solitarynes; Mʳ William Pierrepont [q.v.] inquired of your L[ordshi]ᴾ very affectionately ... [Whitelocke noted that the Earl of Clare added, in his own hand] My Lord I must loose no opportunity to present you with the Service of

Your humble un-
profitable servant
Clare

[date smudged, Aug.] 1654

Add.Ms 4992 fols. 98v.–99 (transcript).

Whitelocke's bonds to Hall, others in which Hall was bound with him, and details of 'adventuring' money together in the 1630s, occur between 1630 and 1652, Long. W.P. iv, 128, 161, 189; vi, 18; vii, 259, 261, 264, 274, 291, 293; ix, 95, 97, 99, 153; xii, 186.

Whitelocke records the death of Frances Hall in *Diary* 10 April 1663. Of the Halls' seven children three died in infancy or childhood. Thomas (1632–1656), was only referred to at his death, *Diary* 6 Dec. 1656; William died unmarried; Henry (1637–1700), who was admitted to the Middle Temple on 1 Nov. 1658, became Commissioner of the Peace and High Sheriff of Oxfordshire; Bartholomew jun., usually referred to as 'Bat' (*c*.1639–1717), was admitted to the Middle Temple on 30 March 1660; he became the owner of Barkham Hall, Berkshire, and married Mary Owen, niece of Dr. John Owen (q.v.), Vice-Chancellor of Oxford University.

HAMEY, Baldwin, jun., MD (1600–1676). W. Munk *Roll of the Royal College of Physicians*; J.J. Keevil *The Stranger's Son* (London.1953). A distinguished physician; he was active as a doctor during the Interregnum, although a convinced Royalist. He is referred to twice by Whitelocke: when Dr. Hamey 'advised' with him and, in the same month, when Whitelocke consulted the doctor about his daughter Cecilia Harvey's health, *Diary* 10, 23 May 1662.

HAMILTON, James, 3rd Marquess, 1st D. of (1606–1649). G.E.C.; *D.N.B.* Inept both as a soldier and as a negotiator. He supported King Gustav Adolf of Sweden in Germany, but most of the 6,000 or more men he had brought with him died of famine or plague. Gustav Adolf's letters of credence, presumably carried by Hamilton when he returned to England, were addressed to Charles I, Long. W.P. v, 247. In 1638

Hamilton was sent to Scotland, in a vain attempt to quell or pacify the Covenanters. On 8 July 1648 he led a force of some 20,000 men in a march on England. In spite of his superior numbers he was defeated at the battle of Preston and was executed on 9 March 1648/49, with others responsible for the Second Civil War. He is referred to posthumously in *Diary* 24 June 1650.

HAMPDEN, John, MP (1594–1643). *D.N.B.* MP for Wendover in Charles I's first three Parliaments; he supported Sir John Eliot (q.v.). Whitelocke mentions getting to know him in 1626, in the second Parliament of the reign. Famous for his opposition to the second Ship Money Writ, of 1635, Hampden consulted Whitelocke, among other lawyers, *Diary* 1636.1637. fol. 42v. He was MP for Buckinghamshire, in the Short and Long Parliaments; in the latter, in 1641, he spoke up in memory of Whitelocke's father, ranking him with Judge Croke as a Judge who had opposed the forced loan and irregularities in court procedure, ib. 1640.1641. fol. 50v. Hampden served on the Select Committee to manage articles against the Earl of Strafford (q.v.), under Whitelocke's chairmanship; they served together as Deputy-Lieutenants of Buckinghamshire in 1642, and Whitelocke served under Hampden at Turnham Green. Whitelocke wrote that he lost a kind friend and kinsman when Hampden died the week after being shot in battle at Chalgrove Field, near Watlington, ib. 1642.1643. fol. 63.

HARRINGTON (HARINGTON), Sir James, Bt., MP (c.1607–1680). *Complete Baronetage* i, 53; D. Underdown *Pride's Purge*; B. Worden *Rump Parliament*; G. Davies *Restoration*. (Not to be confused with James Harrington, author of *Oceana*). Of Lincoln's Inn; MP for Rutland from 1646 to 1653; he replaced one of Parliament's Commissioners to the King at Newcastle, *C.J.* v, 45; MP for Middlesex from 1654 to 1655. A radical himself, he worked for reconciliation between moderates and radicals. He served on the Council of State from 1649 to 1652, and again from May to October 1659; also on the Committee of Safety, but he is only mentioned in *Diary* 17, 26 Oct. and 16 Nov. 1659. After the Restoration he was stripped of the titles of Baronet, Knight, Esquire and Gentleman, and was imprisoned in the Tower.

HARRISON, Col., later Major-General Thomas, MP (1606–1660). *D.N.B.*; C. Firth and G. Davies *Regimental History of Cromwell's Army*; A. Woolrych *Commonwealth to Protectorate*; B.S. Capp *Fifth Monarchy Men*

p. 251, *passim*. Of Clifford's Inn. A regicide; a recruiter MP for Wendover in 1646, he served in the Rump and in Barebone's Parliament. He was one of the most prominent of the Fifth Monarchy men, for which he was cashiered and imprisoned under the Protectorate. After the Restoration he was executed as a regicide. The numerous entries in *The Diary* include references to two untraced letters to Whitelocke, 5 July 1656 and 1 April 1657, the latter soliciting help for Lady 'Shandos', presumably the wife of William, 7th Baron Chandos, whose daughter Rebecca married the regicide Colonel Thomas Pride (q.v.).

HARTCLIFFE, John (d. *c*.1676). *Calamy Revised*. Rector of Harpsden, near Henley-on-Thames, Oxon., in 1654. (Bartholomew Hall, q.v., lived at Harpsden Court.) Later, he was curate of Stadhampton with Chislehampton, also in Oxfordshire. He was suspended in 1662. Brother-in-law of Dr. John Owen (q.v.). He first appears as a correspondent, *Diary* 21 Aug. 1656, *passim*; then as a preacher at conventicles in the parlour at Fawley Court, ib. 6 Jan. 1660/61; four days later he set off on horseback for London, with Mary Whitelocke riding behind him, to see if the Whitelocke children were safe after the Coleman Street riots (these had arisen from the fanatical fervour of Thomas Venner, q.v., who, supported by a band of Fifth Monarchy men, made a violent attempt to establish the Kingdom of God on earth). Hartcliffe's 'heart fayled him, by the way', however, and Mary finished the journey in a stagecoach with her manservant. Hartcliffe is described as Mary's Chaplain, ib. 10 Jan. 1660/61. There are only two more references to him: when he preached at Whitelocke's house in Coleman Street, and at Samuel Wilson's house in Greenwich, ib. 21 Apr. 1661; 13 May 1666.

HARVEY, Cecilia (Cecill) née Whitelocke (1641–1662). Fifth daughter of Whitelocke and his second wife, Frances. At 17 Cecilia married Samuel Harvey, son of the notorious Edmund Harvey (below), *Diary* 26 Sept. 1658. Whitelocke stated that her father-in-law settled the Manor of Fulham (Fulham Palace, residence of Bishops of London until 1972) on any children of the marriage, ib. 1 Nov. 1660, but two days later he recorded that it was settled on Samuel. Gilbert Sheldon (q.v.), Bishop of London, amiably negotiated with Whitelocke for the return of Fulham Palace, assuring him that he would not send in soldiers to take possession, Cecilia being some four months pregnant and 'a tender & fearfull young woman', ib. 3 Nov. 1660. Two days before Christmas, however, soldiers appeared, sent on the Bishop's instructions; they forced their way in, plundered the house and terrorized Whitelocke's daughter; the incident is recorded, ib. 24 Dec. 1660. When her baby (born 2 June 1661), her husband and Cecilia herself all died, within 18 months of this event, Whitelocke recorded with unwonted bitterness: '. . . all their blood lyes att the doore of this B[isho]P', ib. 27 May 1662.

HARVEY, Col. Edmund, MP (d.1673). *D.N.B.*; A.B.B.; G.E. Aylmer *State's Servants* pp. 161–162 (background), 388 note 83 (bibliography); *C.S.P. Dom.* 1655.1656., *passim*. A draper, with an unsavoury reputation. After serving as Colonel of Horse under Essex, he was charged with plunder and extortion. A recruiter MP for Great Bedwin, Wiltshire, in 1646, he sat in the Rump. Around 1648 he invested extensively in property, including Fulham Palace (Manor of Fulham), which had come on the market as a former episcopal estate, for which he paid £7,617. 2s. 10d., *Collectanea Topographica et Genealogica* (London. 1834) i, 3. As one of the King's judges, he was enraged that the King was not allowed to defend himself. He was appointed First Commissioner of Customs, and also a Naval Commissioner, but a few days after entertaining Cromwell royally at Fulham, in November 1655, Harvey's accounts were investigated and he was sent to the Tower for defrauding the Commonwealth of at least £30,000; he was later dismissed from his post. Figures mentioned in this major fraud, involving up to £57,722, are considered by Dr. Aylmer (above); finally, a mere £326. 6s. 8d. was levied on Harvey's goods and chattels.

In September 1650, years before the scandal and before Harvey's first appearance in *The Diary*, he wrote from Fulham Palace, acting as a friendly agent between Cornelius Burgess, DD (see *D.N.B.*) and Whitelocke; the puritan minister had been appointed that year as preacher in Wells Cathedral and was anxious to sell his house in the City; Harvey wrote sending Whitelocke Burgess's note on the subject; it was written with the urgency common to house-vendors:

> . . . another person of quality now enforced to live in the Citty sent by a special friend his desires to see my house, & to bee a Chapman.
> I prayed the party to tell him that I am at present ingaged to my best friend [Harvey] to let another [Whitelocke] have the first view & refusall . . .

He hoped that Whitelocke's 'great affairs' would permit him to see the house on the following day or on Saturday, 19 Sept. 1650, (St.) Paul's, Long. W.P. x, 168.

The first diary entry for Colonel Harvey occurs when he wrote a 'very civill & kind letter' about £1,500 due to Whitelocke from the

Commissioners of the Customs; curiously, this is dated 16 months after the Customs scandal broke, *Diary* 6 Mar. 1656/57. About 18 months later, Whitelocke's daughter Cecilia (above) and Colonel Harvey's son Samuel (below) were married, ib. 26 Sept. 1658. Whitelocke later recorded that it was Dr. Thomas Hodges (q.v.), Minister of Kensington, who had proposed the match, ib. 29 Nov. 1658. There are two more entries concerning money for Whitelocke and money to be borrowed, ib. 19 July; 1 Oct. 1659. Subsequent entries concern Harvey's surrender and imprisonment as one of the King's judges, and Whitelocke's negotiations to restore Fulham Palace to Bishop Sheldon (q.v.). Whitelocke is silent as to the Colonel's character. Nothing positive has been traced to suggest a connection between Harvey's lucky escape from his financial scandal and Whitelocke's position as a Commissioner at the Treasury, and later as Lord President of the Council, but Harvey's reminder of the £1,500 payable to Whitelocke from Customs, plus the marriage of his son to Cecilia Whitelocke, certainly raise a question as to Harvey's strategy. Whitelocke, for his part, tried to procure Harvey's pardon, ib. 9 Nov. 1660.

HARVEY, Samuel (d.1662). Son of Edmund Harvey (above); Whitelocke's son-in-law, described by him as '. . . a sober[,] discreet young man, & a kind husband . . .' and later as '. . . a very honest gent[leman]' – no doubt in contrast to his father, ib. 10 Nov. 1658; 1 Nov. 1660. After the soldiers ransacked the house at Fulham, ib. 24 Dec. 1660, Samuel Harvey (or more probably Whitelocke) prepared a report of the incident, stating that, under pretence of searching the house for arms, Captain Raymond, with other soldiers from the Life Guards, had entered his house and gone off with his money and other effects, no date, Long. W.P. xx, 117, endorsed by Whitelocke 'Son Harveys narrative'. Samuel died on 8 Jan. 1661/62. After Cecilia's death on 27 May 1662, Charles Harvey opposed the administration of his brother Samuel's estate, *Diary* 5, 20 June 1662.

HAVERGILL, Thomas. Of Fawley, Bucks. Son of Anne Havergill (d.1658), and grandson of William Cooke (q.v.). Havergill, like his grandfather, was a servant and tenant farmer on the Fawley Court estate. He was a young man of uncertain temper. Francis Sharpe, a rival tenant, wrote of Havergill's debauchery, threats to kill the servants at Fawley Court and of his beating his grandmother (Cooke's widow?), ib. 27 Oct. 1656. In spite (or because) of his intimidation, Mrs. Cooke wrote to Whitelocke on Havergill's behalf, ib. 13 Feb. 1656/57; later, although Whitelocke tried to dissuade her, widow Cooke gave her grandson all her stock and moved out of Fawley Court Farm, leaving him as the new tenant, ib. 22 Oct. 1661. Whitelocke, with his young sons and their tutor, James Pearson (q.v.), went hunting with him and 'had very good sport when Tho[mas] Havergill was in a good humor ...' ib. 3, 6 Sept. 1662, but on 9 Sept. Havergill and his wife 'carryed themselves very doggedly to Wh[itelocke] & his wife & the children' and on the next day it was recorded that he was often 'in disorder & full of debauchery.' When Havergill 'In a sullen humor' said he was tired of the farm and wished to leave, Whitelocke 'tooke him att his word' and would not relent when Havergill changed his mind, ib. 15, 17 Sept. 1662.

HAYES, Sir James, Kt. Bachelor, MP. *Shaw's Knights*; *Alumni Oxonienses*; *Lincoln's Inn Admission Register*. Of Beckington, Somerset. Possibly 'James Hayes, gent.' who matriculated in Feb. 1648/49; of Corpus Christi College, Oxford. In the same year, James Hayes of Beckington was admitted to Lincoln's Inn, Oct. 1649; he was probably a friend at that time of Whitelocke's son William, who had then been at the Middle Temple for two years (see below). Recorder and MP for Marlborough in 1659, he was knighted in 1670. Secretary to Prince Rupert (q.v.). Two letters from Hayes (one supported by Lord Willoughby, the other sent via William Whitelocke) ask for Whitelocke's advice on behalf of the Prince, *Diary* 28 Feb. 1668/69; 14 June 1671. A letter not mentioned in *The Diary*, also addressed to William Whitelocke at his chambers in the Middle Temple, was written between the other two letters, on 13 Jan. 1670/71. These approaches indicate that even as an old man, out of office for a decade, Whitelocke was still regarded as a powerful authority on legal matters. In the January letter Hayes wrote:

> ... The Prince my Master hath commanded me to send to y[ou]ʳ Father S[i]ʳ Bulstrode Whitlock to desire his opinion under his hand in a Case that his Highnesse thinks doth nearly concern him as Constable of Windsor Castle, or rather as Keeper of the Forest. The Great Parke of Windsor[,] lately disparked [railings removed during the Interregnum] is now reassumed by the King and reparked, and there is a Walke therein called the Paddock Walke which his H[ighne]ˢˢ hath a mind to dispose of [to] a Servant of his[,] one Dowcett, whose Father had a Grant of it from the late King [Charles I] as far as he was able in the Isle of Wight under his Ma[jes]ᵗⁱᵉˢ hand[,] which is still to be produced for the terme of 3 Lives; And the Earle of Holland before[,] when he was Constable[,] had given the same Walke to the same Person. Now ... there is a Person hath preferr[e]d a Petic[i]on to the King [Charles II] for the Custody of the said Walke, and his desires are so powerfully seconded that the King may be induced to comply with it. Yet if it be a reall breach upon his Highnesses [Rupert's] Interest there, and that

attested by so learned and honourable a Person as S[i]^r Bulstrode, there will probably be no further endeavours used, wherefore I must desire you in his H[ighne]^{ss} name, to obtaine yo[u]^r Fathers opinion in this matter, as soon as may be[.]

My Lord Mordaunt at his leaving that Government [of Windsor Castle] presented the Prince [with] some Papers which y[ou]^r Father wrote, at the instance of my Lord Willoughby y[ou]^r Unkle, concerning the Powers of the Constable and amongst other things therein, he doth say that he hath power to dispose of the Walks of the Forest ...

13 Jan. 1670[71]

Long. W.P. xx, 159-159v.

HEATH, Lord Chief Justice, Sir Robert, MP (1575-1649). *D.N.B.*; G.E. Aylmer *King's Servants.* Of Clifford's Inn and the Middle Temple. A Royalist, Judge, MP for East Grinstead, Sussex, from 1623 to 1624 and in 1625; he supported the King's claims of royal prerogative, and was later impeached by the House of Commons, *C.J.* iii, 567, July 1644. Heath was distantly related to Whitelocke through the marriage of his eldest son, Edward, to a niece of Sir George Croke (q.v.); Whitelocke gives her father's name as Paul Croke, *Diary* 1636.1637. fol. 43v., but *D.N.B.* gives it as Ambrose Croke.

HENRIETTA MARIA, Q. (1609-1669). *D.N.B.*; C. Oman *Henrietta Maria* (Hodder & Stoughton. 1936). Queen Consort of Charles I (q.v.). Whitelocke's contacts with her were (1) in connection with the Royal Masque of February 1633/34 (for which he borrowed four musicians of the Queen's Chapel), and (2) many years later when, as Queen Mother, Henrietta Maria sent her physician and surgeon to tend Whitelocke's young son-in-law, George Nevill, who was dying of stab wounds, *Diary* 18 Apr. 1665. She was noted, during her husband's life-time, for interfering in state affairs, yet she appears in a different light as quoted in a letter to Whitelocke from Sir John Holland (q.v.) at Holdenby Manor, written in March 1647. By that time the Queen was tactfully trying to soften the King's self-righteous obstinacy and notion of honour, which impaired negotiations. The letter appears in Sir John's entry.

HERBERT of CHIRBURY, Edward, 3rd Baron (*c.*1633-1678). G.E.C.; *D.N.B.* (in the entry for Edward Herbert, 1st Lord). Succeeding to the title in 1655, he joined forces with the Royalists under Sir George Booth in 1659, and was imprisoned; shortly afterwards, however, Lord Herbert was one of the Lords released 'to ingratiate w[i]'h the Cavaliers', *Diary* 2 Nov. 1659. Although that is the first diary reference to Herbert, Whitelocke evidently knew him earlier, as a comment in Whitelocke's 'Case or Vindication' of himself shows, ib. 2 June 1660. Lord Herbert's second wife tried to retain Whitelocke as his Counsel against William Herbert, 6th Earl of Pembroke (q.v.), ib. 10 Aug. 1674. This second wife (married in 1673), was Elizabeth, daughter of George Brydges, 6th Baron Chandos of Sudeley; her maternal grandfather was Henry Mountagu, Earl of Manchester.

HERTFORD, William Seymour, 1st Marquess of, restored in 1660 as 2nd D. of Somerset (1588–1660). G.E.C.; *D.N.B.* A Royalist, scholar and soldier. He was appointed governor of the Prince of Wales in 1641 and Lieutenant-General for the Western Counties in 1642. He married (1) Arabella Stuart (2) Frances, daughter of Robert Devereux, 2nd Earl of Essex. He served as Chancellor of Oxford University from 1643 to 1647 and again in 1660. Whitelocke encountered him at the Uxbridge negotiations, *Diary* 31 Jan. 1644/45. Mistakenly shown in *The Diary* as receiving the Garter from Charles II on 13 June 1660, he actually received it in Canterbury on 26 May, the day after Charles landed at Dover.

HESILRIGE (HESELRIGGE, HASELRIG), Sir Arthur, Bt., MP (d.1661). *Pepys* x; *D.N.B.*; *Complete Baronetage* i, 202; M.F.K. A prominent Republican and upholder of Parliament's rights. He enriched himself by purchasing episcopal lands in the See of Durham, but refused to take part in the trial of Charles I. He opposed the Protectorates of both the Cromwells, as usurpation, was excluded from Oliver Cromwell's Parliaments and, in 1657, refused the place offered to him by Cromwell in the reconstituted House of Lords. His influence in the restored Rump of 1659 was considerable, and he continued to exert power up to the first months of 1659/60. Ludlow, in *Voyce from the Watchtower*, gives an account of Hesilrige's fall, and of his misjudgement and loss of nerve at the approach of the Restoration. Whitelocke warned Charles Fleetwood (q.v.) that Hesilrige would easily be deluded by Monck, *Diary* 22 Dec. 1659, and his prediction was soon proved to be correct. Sir Arthur died in the Tower in 1661. In the same year Whitelocke (who had not been on good terms with Hesilrige, since the time of Savile's accusation against himself and Holles) gave legal advice to Hesilrige's son, ib. 25 June 1661 and again on 27 May 1664.

HEVENINGHAM (HEVININGHAM), William, MP (1604–1678). *D.N.B.*; M.F.K.; Ludlow *Voyce from the Watchtower* (ed. A.B. Worden). One of the King's judges, he was sentenced to death but was spared by the King. He owned extensive property in Norfolk and Suffolk, see M.F.K. 214, n.308; Whitelocke refers to the sale of some of Heveningham's land, *Diary* 5 Feb. 1662/63.

HEWET (HEWITT), John, DD (1614–1658). *D.N.B.* A powerful preacher. One of Charles I's Chaplains at Oxford, where Whitelocke probably knew him, although he only refers to Dr. Hewet's trial and death, *Diary* 25 May; 8 June 1658. Although openly royalist in sympathy, Hewet conducted the private wedding of Mary Cromwell to Lord Falconbridge in 1657; in 1658 another of Cromwell's daughters, Elizabeth Claypole (q.v.), pleaded for Hewet's life after his arrest and trial for his part in a royalist plot; in spite of this, he and Sir Henry Slingsby (q.v.) were beheaded. Whitelocke was told that Hewet's conduct at his trial was imprudent – a reference, no doubt, to the Doctor's refusal to plead before Cromwell's High Court of Justice (on which Whitelocke refused to serve), to his demand for trial by jury and perhaps to his plea, which was drafted by William Prynne (q.v.).

HEWSON, Col. John, MP (d. 1662). *D.N.B.*; A Woolrych *Commonwealth to Protectorate*, 182–183, *passim*. A regicide, who had been a substantial shoemaker, supplying the army; he became a Colonel by merit, and an MP in Barebone's Parliament of 1653, and in the Protectorate Parliaments of 1654 and 1656. He was knighted by Cromwell in 1657 and appointed to the Committee of Safety in 1659. Later, he was referred to contemptuously by the Earl of Berkshire, in conversation with Whitelocke, as one of the 'base mechanicke fellowes' who had served in Cromwell's House of Lords, *Diary* 7 June 1660. He died in exile.

HILL, Abraham (1635–1721). *D.N.B.*; *The Royal Society; its Origin and Founders* (Royal Society. 1960); papers in the possession of Mr. C.P. Hill (a descendant of Alderman Richard Hill's brother William). The family came from Shilstone, Devon; Abraham, son of Alderman Richard Hill (below), was a scientist of some distinction. He entered his father's business and, by the age of 24, was managing director and foreign correspondent of the family firm. He was on the Council of the newly-formed Royal Society, being named in the King's Charter of 1663, and he became its first Treasurer. His portrait is on permanent loan to the Royal

Society. In 1665 Hill bought St. John's Jerusalem, Sutton-at-Hone, Kent. There is a family monument in the local church. His first wife, née Anne Whitelocke (1640–1661), was 17 when they married, *Diary* 12 Nov. 1657, with note. They had two children, Frances and Richard. Anne's burial is recorded in the parish register of St. Dionis Backchurch, but the Church was destroyed in the Fire of London. After her early death, there is no further mention of Hill until the last weeks of Whitelocke's life, *Diary* 16, 20 July 1675. The only correspondence traced between Hill and his father-in-law is an affectionate letter from Whitelocke, warmly approving the purchase of some unspecified property, and advising Hill to get in touch with George Nevill (q.v.) 28 Jan. 1659/60, Long. W.P. xix, 117.

HILL, Alderman Richard (d.1660). A.B.B. (ii). Father of Abraham (above). A cordwainer (i.e. shoemaker). One of the Treasurers of Sequestrations at Guildhall in 1643. A Parliamentarian and friend of Cromwell's. Whitelocke wrote, with hindsight, that Hill 'was esteemed a more wealthy man then he appeared to be att his death . . .', *Diary* 12 Nov. 1657 (around the time of Anne Whitelocke's wedding in Chelsea Old Church to Abraham Hill, above); yet the *D.N.B.* records that the Alderman left an 'ample fortune' to his son, and Abraham's purchase of the estate in Kent seems to confirm the fact.

HILL, Roger, MP (1605–1667). *D.N.B.*; M.F.K. Of the Inner Temple. He served in the Long Parliament, and continued to sit in the Rump; Baron of the Exchequer in 1657, he was transferred to the Upper Bench in Jan. 1659/60.

HOBY, Peregrine, MP (1602–1679). M.F.K.; *Hist. of Parl.*; *D.N.B.* (entry for Sir Edward Hoby). Natural son of Sir Edward Hoby but, being accepted as his heir, Peregrine inherited Bisham Abbey near Marlow, Buckinghamshire. He was a candidate for Great Marlow, in 1640 (as Whitelocke was, without knowing it), at the elections for the Long Parliament. Although their two names were shouted the loudest, they were not shown on the returns as having been elected; this was reported to the Committee of Privileges who ordered a new election, at which both men were successful. Hoby sat until Pride's Purge; he regained his seat in 1659 and sat again in 1660 and 1661. A couple of neighbourly letters have survived: Hoby wrote praying that Ralfe Newbery, his former servant, be given a warrant as gamekeeper at New Lodge (presumably in Windsor

Park), succeeding Sir Charles Haward, with 'power to take Guns and Netts from destroyers and Dogs and that he may have the allowa[nce]s of wood that formerly was to the Lodge[;] he is now living in it[;] he can informe you of the destruction th[a]^t hath binn this year ...', 12 Feb. (1650/51?), Long. W.P. xi, 26. Shortly before Whitelocke left for Sweden, Hoby's wife, an eccentric speller, wrote:

> My Lord
>
> I canot but blush th[a]^t I should againe trouble you^r Honore, Espesualy in this so busey a time w[i]th you, but the ernest desire of this berer (who hath ben Mr Hobys servant this two year) prevaild with me too trouble you with thes lines ... he writes a good hand, and kepes a counts well ... and is an honest ye[o]mans Sonn in Buckingame Sheer, and if you have any occasion for such a one I should take itt as a favour if your Lordship will Imploye him ...
>
> Kat[harine] Hoby
>
> Mr Hoby desier you to pardon his not waiting on you when you were att henelly, [i.e. Henley;] hee did not thinke your Staye had ben so short and intended to have see you had your stay ben but the day you went.
> Bisham. 23 Oct. 1653.
>
> Ib. xiv, 126.

HODGES, John. P. Crawford *Denzil Holles* p. 209, n. 6. Ejected as a minister. Hodges was described by Richard Baxter as 'a grave, ancient, godly moderate divine', and was recorded by him in 1679 as having lately lived with Holles, see D.R. Lacey *Dissent and Parliamentary Politics* (Rutgers University Press. New Jersey. 1969) p. 467. Hodges is referred to in *The Diary* as preaching, in conventicles, to members of the Wynwood family.

HODGES, Thomas, DD (d.1672). L. Sanders *Old Kew, Chiswick and Kensington* (Methuen. 1910) p. 200; *History of Hereford* (London. 1717). Rector of Kensington; he preached before Parliament, was a member of the Assembly of Divines, and a Covenanter. He was a distant relative of his patron, the Earl of Holland (q.v.), whom he attended day and night after sentence of death was pronounced on the Earl, and also ministered to him on the scaffold. After the Restoration, Hodges became Rector of St. Peter's, Cornhill; he was preferred to the Deanery of Hereford in 1661. Earlier, he recommended a servant to Whitelocke and proposed the match between Whitelocke's daughter Cecilia and Samuel Harvey (q.v.), *Diary* 9 June 1657; 29 Nov. 1658.

HOLAC (HOLACK otherwise HOHENLOHE, HOHENLOE), Louis, or Ludovic Gustav, Count of. He and Whitelocke met as guests of the Swedish Ambassador, 20 Feb. 1655/56. He subsequently sent newsletters from The Hague and Amsterdam, in French or Latin. Thanking Whitelocke for favours received when he was in London, Holac reported on the strength of feeling in Holland against the Protector and the English, especially on account of the damage to Dutch trade, arising from England's recent treaty with Sweden. He also recorded that the Prince of Orange's party was very moderate, and that state affairs in Poland were very bad, $^{14}/_{24}$ Nov. 1656, Cal. Long. W.P. xvii, 213. Two weeks later he wrote of the Dutch fleet sailing to the Mediterranean under De Ruyter, in a pretence of sailing against Turkish pirates, and he gave an exposition of Dutch policy, and news from Poland and Sweden, $^{28\ Nov.}/_8$ Dec. 1656, ib. 215; the Count complained that, in spite of his promises, the Protector had given someone else a company of cavalry which should have come to him. He appealed to Whitelocke to procure enough money to enable him to return to Germany, ib. xviii, 108; next he wrote of conditions in Germany and of the misery resulting from Spanish tyranny and persecution, ib. 109. The Council having considered a paper from Holac, voted him £200 for his journey, C.S.P. Dom. 1655.1656. pp. 283, 588, 17 Apr., 12 June 1656 (the grant is shown in Cal. Long. W.P. as £100). Holac then asked Whitelocke to procure immediate payment of his money (no date), Cal. Long. W.P. xviii, 111. He proposed sailing on the following Saturday, if he could obtain a despatch from Secretary Thurloe (q.v.) and prayed Whitelocke to put Thurloe in mind of his promises, 1656, ib. 112. No trace of Thurloe's support has been found, but the following year Holac (named in the letter 'Earl of Hohenloe', and by that time at the Court in Heidelberg) was highly recommended to Thurloe 'for his great understanding, activity, and zeal for the protestant interest . . .', Thurloe S.P. v, 789, 2 Feb. 1657 (new style).

HOLLAND, Henry Rich, MP, later 1st Earl of (1590–1649). G.E.C.; D.N.B.; P. Crawford Denzil Holles, passim. Second son of Robert, 1st Earl of Warwick, and his wife Penelope, daughter of the 1st Earl of Essex. MP for Leicester in 1610 and 1614; created Baron of Kensington in 1623, and Earl of Holland in 1624. A devastatingly handsome courtier, but a second-rate negotiator and soldier. In spite of these drawbacks Whitelocke, as will be shown, found reasons for admiring him. Among numerous other offices, Holland was appointed Constable of Windsor in 1629, the first Governor of the Providence Company the next year, and Chancellor of the University of Cambridge from 1628 to 1649. As High Steward of Abingdon he showed himself 'a favourer of the Puritans': when Whitelocke (at that time Recorder of Abingdon) was summoned to attend the Council in London, to answer complaints that he refused to punish dissenters for not conforming, Holland supported him, *Diary* 1634.1635. fol. 32. As Chief Justice in Eyre, South of the Trent, from 1631, Holland 'shewed much respect & favour' to Whitelocke in litigation over Wychwood Forest and the claims of the Earl of Danby (q.v.), ib. 1637.1638. fol. 44.

In the 1640s Holland wavered between giving his allegiance to Parliament or to the King, crossing the boundary more than once and apparently leaving the Court for reasons of pique rather than principle. After sitting in the Lords at the start of the Long Parliament, he joined the King as Captain-General North of Trent; then he fell out with Charles, who had denied him the nomination of a new Baron. On his return to London he often invited Whitelocke to his house in Whitehall (i.e. at Charing Cross) to consult about public affairs, ib. 1641.1642. fol. 53v. He served with his kinsman the Earl of Essex at Turnham Green, in November 1642, and was appointed one of Parliament's Commissioners from the Lords (as Whitelocke was from the Commons) to treat with the King at Oxford early in 1643. A leader of the peace party, he turned Royalist again, and fought in the King's Regiment at the First Battle of Newbury; but when a post that he wanted was given to the Marquess of Hertford (q.v.), Holland returned to London at Essex's suggestion; he was arrested but, at the request of Essex and of Holland's brother the 2nd Earl of Warwick, Whitelocke worked with Holland's friends to have him restored to his place in the Lords, and succeeded in this 'though with much difficulty . . .'; that was after they had had the sequestration order on Holland's estate reversed, ib. 1643.1644. fol. 64; Add.Ms 37343 fols. 285–285v. Between Oct. 1645 and June 1648, Holland and Whitelocke paid each other several social visits, heard sermons together at Kensington (no doubt preached by Thomas Hodges, q.v.), and dined together. The Countess of Holland (Isabel, daughter and heiress of Sir William Cope of Kensington) visited Whitelocke when he was ill and offered him, for his convalescence, 'her little house att Kensington', *Diary* 25 Sept.; 19 Oct. 1645; the stately mansion built for her father in 1607, was originally called 'Cope Castle', later 'Kensington House' and finally 'Holland House', after the Countess and her husband's title, see G.E.C., Holland's entry, pp. 538 note c. and 540 note a.

The Earl of Holland paid Whitelocke the compliment of sending him a buck, *Diary* 23 July 1647. Then, on 5 July 1648 (only two weeks after a long discussion with Whitelocke, ib. 22 June), Holland, with others involved in the Second Civil War, declared for the King, 'expecting great numbers to joyne with them, butt very few came.' Instead, the Earl was captured with many others. Whitelocke recalled Holland's recent visit to his house when the Earl had hinted at what he had in mind and Whitelocke had dismissed it, saying 'it would be a desperate & rash attempt ...' ib. 5 July 1648. Holland was beheaded on 9 Mar. 1649, with James, 1st Duke of Hamilton (q.v.) and Arthur, 1st Baron Capel of Hadham (q.v.). Thomas Hodges (q.v.), Rector of Kensington, though a preacher before Parliament, slept in his patron's room after sentence was passed, and later described the agony of mind the Earl had suffered while preparing for death: how he could not even bear to see his wife or children; how he could neither eat nor sleep until, on the day before the execution, he told Hodges that his prayers had been answered. He then supped and went to bed, and slept so soundly that they had trouble in waking him for his execution; on the scaffold, he forgave the executioner and made him a generous gift of £10 in gold, *Memorials* ii, 549–551.

The serious side of Holland's nature appealed to Whitelocke but this has usually been ignored; most descriptions of him dwell on his good looks, lack of judgement and love of money, the latter neatly noted by Clarendon; they ignore the dilemma of a man with little grasp of politics, fumbling in his search for peace in a revolution. Whitelocke's brief recollections of him, recorded in 'Annales', around Dec. 1643 and Jan. 1643/44, are almost entirely omitted from *Memorials* i, 243:

> The Earle of Holland being my very noble friend ... they [Holland's relatives and friends] ingaged my furtherance of his restitution to be a member of the Lords House ... Holland demeaned himselfe with great prudence & submission. He was a person of much honor & ingenuity, & constant in his way of devotion ... I have seen in his study a great volume in folio of Sermon notes, all written with his own hand [,] which he told me he did after he had heard a good sermon, & was retired in his closet, he used to write down what he remembred of it, & I believe many of his notes were better then the Sermons themselves.
>
> Add. Ms 37343 fols. 285–285v.

HOLLAND, Sir John, Bt., MP (1603–1701). M.F.K.; *Hist. of Parl.;* *Complete Baronetage* ii, 74; D. Underdown *Pride's Purge, passim.* Of the Middle Temple. Holland has been described as 'a tolerant Presbyterian' and as an 'Erastian conformist'. He married a Roman Catholic, who withdrew to Bergen op Zoom in the Netherlands. Holland sat in the Short Parliament of April 1640; in the Long Parliament, from November 1640 until shortly before Pride's Purge of 1648; in the Convention Parliament of 1660, and in the Cavalier Parliament of 1661.

A notebook of Holland's, which starts during the Short Parliament, but contains records mainly connected with the Long Parliament, is in the Bodleian Library, Ms Tanner 321; so is his parliamentary diary running from 22 May to 8 Aug.1641, with other material, Ms Rawl. D. 1099. These volumes contain: letters, speeches by Holland, a few pleasant drawings, and some verses, including lines which he evidently copied following the execution of the Earl of Strafford (q.v.). The verse is bold and deliberately ambiguous:

> Here lyes wise, & valyant Dust,
> Hudled up, twixt fitt & Just,
> Strafford, who was hurryed hence,
> Twixt Treason, & convenyence ...
> His Princes nearest Joy & Greif
> Hee had, yett wanted [i.e. lacked] all releif
> The Prop, & rayne [i.e. ruin] off the State;
> The Peoples' vyolent love, and hate,
> One in Extreames loved & abhord ...

> ib. fol. 190.

The full text of this epitaph on Strafford, attributed to John Cleveland (1613–1658), appears in *The Oxford Book of Seventeenth Century Verse*. (This Rawlinson volume is awkward to study and to quote from: to keep the sequence, it has to be read straight through from the recto folios, then the volume must be turned upside down, before reading the un-numbered verso folios.)

In 1643, Sir John Holland and Whitelocke were among those appointed as Parliament's Commissioners to negotiate with the King at Oxford; there they shared a room in Merton College, and Whitelocke described Holland at that time as his 'Noble friend and Bedfellow ...'(see letters below). When Whitelocke fell ill, during the negotiations, his companion 'tooke great care of him ...', *Diary* 1642.1643. fol. 61. Sir John and the Whitelocke family continued the friendship, ib. 13 Dec. 1645.

Holland was again appointed one of Parliament's Commissioners to the King when Charles was in Newcastle, and later accompanied him to Holdenby (Holmby Manor) and to Caversham. (For the text of Parliament's version of the Propositions, sent to Newcastle on 13 July 1646, with the King's first and second answers, see S.R. Gardiner *Constitutional Documents of the Puritan Revolution* pp. 290–309.) Holland was accompanied to Holdenby by Whitelocke's experienced secretary, Daniel Earle (q.v.); *The Diary* gives 16 Jan. 1646/47 as the date for Whitelocke lending Earle's services to the Commissioners, but the opening passage of the letter below (written in London) indicates that Earle had joined Holland and the others some months earlier. (Initially, the Earl of Pembroke wrote asking Whitelocke if he would allow Daniel Earle to accompany him to Newcastle, see PEMBROKE, Philip, 4th E. of.) The letter from Sir John in London (with its characteristically bizarre punctuation) is included here, although it is rather incoherent, for the light it sheds on the Commissioners' reports to Parliament in the summer of 1646, and for the sake of continuity with his later and more interesting letters:

Deare Bedfellow.
M[r] Secretary y[ou][r] Servant [Daniel Earle] importunes [,] by your directions, an Account of what have passed with us since y[ou][r] departure, I inclyne off my selfe, to give you satisfaction in all things; my affection leads mee to it. & shortly I shall tell you that much time have binn spent to littel purpose; Upon Thursday [12 Aug. 1646], after we had made some entrance upon the Scotch paper; as to the order off our proceedings; before we came to any resolution; The Lords desired a Conference, att w[hic][h] they communicated; the Kings answer [,] The Scotch paper, the Commission[er][s] report. & the resolutions upon the paper; w[hi][ch] were in Generall wordes; only to the first off the propositions[,] touching the vindication off the nation from those Aspersions that was cast upon them by Scandalous papers & Pamphletts[,] the Lords deliverd to us an Ordinance; that only lookt forward to prevent the like for the time to come. & left the punishment to the parliam[en][t] against the offend[e][rs]. This Ordinance tooke up much time . . . & by [a] division was Comitted [i.e. referred to a Committee] & some general directions were given, that provision might be made as well with respect to us [the Commons] as them [the Lords] that the press might not be shutt only off one syde; we have enterd likewyse upon the 2[n]d proposition touching the rendring off our townes &c; & after a longe debate whether . . . a Comittee should have a generall power so great . . . or that the House should first vote to propose to them 100,000[l] . . .

(This sum was eventually paid to the Scots on 30 Jan. 1646/47, as a first instalment of the money owed to them, and on that day they left Newcastle for Scotland, abandoning Charles to the parliamentary Commissioners; for the earlier vote, see *C.J.* iv, 642, 644; Thurs., Frid., 13, 14 Aug. 1646, *passim*; *L.J.* viii, 699, *passim*.)

. . . wee adjourned until Tuesday morn. w[hi][ch] hath given mee this liberty to express my . . . service to y[ou][r] Lady. If you had binn with in 20[ty] myles [the letter was addressed to Whitelocke 'att his house neere Henley'] I had seene you both hir in this Vacation. I believe I shall leave towne before you returne. I am now going to Kensington to dinner wher I shall wish you [probably with the Earl of Holland, q.v.]; At the Conference [of the two Houses] the Lo[rd] off Pembroke [q.v.] by direction from the Lords, did Harangue it most earnestly for our Bretheren [the Scottish Commissioners]. And cryed up the faythfulnes & galantry off ther carriage in the busines off the propositions. W[hi][ch] have done them more good then himselfe; with some men[.] It is here reported th[a][t] Pendennis, & Ragland are both in but I doe not tell it w[i]^th confidence. [Pendennis surrendered on 17 and Raglan Castle on 19 Aug. 1646].

Y[ou]^rs most affectionately
J. Holland.

(No date)

Long. W.P. ix, 100.

The background to negotiations with the King at Newcastle (and after) is given in S.R. Gardiner *History of the Great Civil War*, iii 1645–1647.

A tantalizing letter to Whitelocke, from Newcastle, refers to the likelihood of the King going to Holdenby with the Parliamentary Commissioners, and to the King's wry comment that 'it was, as good for him to goe w[i]^th those that bought him, as w[i]^th those that sould him ...',25 Jan. 1646/47, Long W.P. ix, 118, sealed with a stag's head; the signature has been heavily deleted; the letter was endorsed by Whitelocke 'E. Newcastle'; it was almost certainly written by the above-mentioned Daniel Earle (q.v.).

This was followed by a letter from Sir John Holland, also from Newcastle:

S[i]^r

Since my last[,] Lanerick [William, E. of Lanark, later 2nd Duke of Hamilton] is come Post hether out of Scotland. what busines have brought him in such hast in this point off time few know, nor can wee learn, whether he have brought new Arguments to perswade the King to give that Kingdome satisfaction by taking the Covenant & [to] grant the Propositions touching Religion & Ireland; wee cannot tell; but if hee yet can bee soe farre prevayld with I perswade my selfe that 70 [evidently number code for the King] shall not march 14.15.53.12.11.13.8.25.5 [Northward?] but most men are confident that he is hardened against it. the Scotch Preachers have given him great offence by the liberty they have taken in personating [i.e. mimicking] him in ther Pulpitts; even to his face rayling ther against him, hee is very desirous to have a Chapleyn off his owne to attend him in his Journy & at Homby [i.e. Holdenby]. & have underhand intimated as much to us; but it is but wisdome not to take notice off what wee cannot grant, nor answer. Many yett dispute whether he shall, or will, goe alonge with us or noe; but it is generally beleeved hee shall & will. He hath binn cajolling the Scotch Co[mm]iss[ione]^rs the last night late & early this morning, & would as I heare have them frame his answer for him; w[hi]^ch they refuse. Hee sayd likewyse[,] as I heare[,] that ther was one worde in the Message that stook with him; viz to receive his person[;] & sayth hee[,] if I must be received I must be delivered! I pray who shall deliver me[?] To all such Questions I like wyse heare that the Scotts lye att ther Gaurd [i.e. are on their guard]. & tells him th[a]^t att parting ... they will give him a full answer to all demands whatsoever. but desires to bee excused for the present. this latter part I pray communicate to that Noble frend, with whom wee suppt att parting. for I have not tutched [on] it[,] as I remember[,] in my lett[e]^r to him nor have I leysure to com[m]unicate to you somthinges I have [written] to him; wee are now sent for to attend the King at fower this Evening … My service to all, great and small in the Middel & Inner Temple. Yonge & old; Hott & Cold, the wyse & eke the Simple; If ther bee any; In the next verse.

I pray strok my Bitch for mee. Shee is much more beautyfull then those off Scotland. I longe for the opertunity to bring us towards the Sunn againe. yet wee have not wanted [i.e. lacked] good weather; I shall leave open my lett[e]^r, untill my return from the King; purposely to give you an Account off our enterteynm[en]^t; & I ame now returned, & hee still continues his civility towards us & growes more familiar with us. & is resolved to goe alonge with us to Holmby & proposed some Questions to us; w[hi]^{ch} we have perticularized in our lett[e]^{rs} to the speaker & I will not trouble you heere with the repetition. Wednesday next is designed to begin our Journey. of w[hi]^{ch} I now hope wee shall give a good Account. upon Saturday next I thinke he will fall into our Hands; for the Scotch I perceive will avoyde the delivery off him … w[hi]^{ch} he himselfe well understands. I pray attend the Howse when our lett[e]^r is redd, for I doubt not how cautious soever wee have binn in our answers with respect to our Instructions yett possibly all men may not be of that opinion. nor will bee pleased with whatsoever is done … by us, how faythfully soever wee performe our trust; once more I pen in much greater hast then by my length I appear to bee   I rest

> Y[ou]^r most faythfull frend
> & Servant
> JH.

28 Jan; 1646[/47]

ib. 119–120.

Two days later he wrote, with undisguised relief, about the agreed handover by the Scots:

Sir.

The good newes of our happy progress in our troublesome imployment I know will be welcome to you. & therfor how short soever the time is you must not want it; the Towne of NewCastle was this day about 4^r in the afternoone delivered to Major Generall Skippon [q.v.] & the King left with us. without noyse or distraction; or trouble more then by releiving off Guardes; Noe ill accident have as yet faln out in the conduct off this affayer; w[hi]^{ch} wee have good cause to esteeme a very great blessing; & must … attribute very much to the candide carriage off our Bretheren [the Scots] towards us; The Scotch Horse marched through this Towne [in the] morning & the Lieutenant Generall in the Head off them. They wer about 4000, proper Men[,] Good Horse & every way well Appointed; The Scotch Commission[e]^{rs} att ther departure kist the Kings Hand & delivered him a Declaration in the Name of the Parliam[en]^t of Scotland, the Coppy wherof they delivered to us & wee send to the Howses [see L.J. viii, 699–700]. Att our Comming to the King, hee acquainted us with this declaration. & was somwhat distempered with it, Hee told us that it conteyned that w[hi]^{ch} was false & that although hee was unfortunate yet hee would ever be honest; Hee knew well upon what tearmes hee came to the Army & how since his

Comming hee had binn used by them; He hered the world did not beleeve that he came to them as a foole or Jugler; It was true hee had promysed to give both his parliam[en]^{ts} all just satisfaction. If hee differed from them in what was just; & mistooke[,] that was but the fault of his understanding not of his Will, and notwithstanding any thinge expressed in that Declaration [he] doubted not but to vindicate him selfe by legall proofes.

Most off those assigned for his Attendants have kist his Hands, but he declared to us that notwithstanding hee had noe exception against the person off such as might bee putt upon him; yet they could not bee acceptable to him; Hee have exprest his good opinion off our Chaplynes. but is very unwilling to have them officiate the Directory [compiled in 1644 by the Westminster Assembly] not being setled in England by his Authority; but is content they should Saye grace & willing to heare them argue for his satisfaction & have even now sent for them for that purpose. Upon Wedsenday [*sic*] wee intend to remove from this place towards Homsby where within 10 or 12 dayes wee Hope the King shall arrive in Safty & wee [be] speedely discharged off this troublesome imployment; for it is much more delightfull to mee to bee in the Temple then at Court; & I pray bee you ready to contribute towards o[u]^r deliverance & communicate this Good Newes to my Worthy frends at the Inner Temple to whom I know it will be welcome. I hope yet to see Mr Kytely & my Mother before they see Hertingfordbury Parke [near Hertford; bought by Thomas Keightley sen., d. 1663, see *D.N.B.*, entry for Thomas Keightley jun.; *V.C.H. Hertford* iii, 465]. My Service to ... Father Hall [i.e. Bartholomew Hall, q.v.] & his good wife, that is older then my Mother [this cannot be true; Frances Hall was born in 1613] & Colder then the Winter. My Service even to all ... in more hast then you can thinke[,] bei[n]g called to attendance ...

NewCastel 30 Jan: 1646[/47]

Ib. 121–121v.

Some two weeks later, Sir John wrote a flamboyant but insecure letter from Holdenby, addressed to his noble friend Bulstrode Whitelocke, a Member of the House of Commons, London:

Why how now Bedfellow. What? but one lett[e]^r in five weekes absence, & that in the States Service too. Have Mr Lylly [astrologer William Lilly, q.v.] given us for lost[?] & soe you looke upon all you shall doe this way as fruitless to you; or have wee carryed our busines soe, as that you are not willing to hold correspondence with us[?] Say. What is the matter ... but more earnestly (I earnestly desire you) that wee may now be recalled. wee have born the burthen off this service longe enough; & I ame confident that every day will bring new difficultyes upon us ... reserve all y[ou]^r excuses untill wee meete; to tell you the King is come safe to Homsby, is noe newes; nor that at Nottingham the Generall [Fairfax] mett him upon the way with about 200 Officers; that the King was very civill to him; but yet not many wordes passed betweene them; that Multitudes of people thronged him in many places in his passage hether; but whether out off curiosity or affection I know

not; that hee refuseth still to heare our Chaplynes; & desireth some of his owne w[hi]^ch it is possible that lett[e]^r he have now sent to the Howses expresseth; wherof hee offered us to take a view before hee sent it; but that wee thought fitt to excuse; soe as wee are noe wayes privy to the contents off it; but yett could not refuse to send it; It being noe part off [our] duty to hinder any Intercourse betwine the King & Parliam[en]^t; yet wee conceived our selves in some kind off difficulty heerin but hope a candide construction will be made off all our actions; amongst you; to whom wee have binn very faithfull in this service; & I pray take care off us ... My Service to y[ou]^r lady, & good father Hall & his ...
Homsby
17 Feb: 1646[/47]

Ib. 125.

Eight days later, he wrote:

My Deare Bedfellow
   Wee have once more upon the return off S[i]^r Walter Earle [q.v.] ... addressed ourselves to the Howse for our speedy recall from this Service; & I cannot doubt y[ou]^r assistance therin; I cannot bee fond off my continuation heere; how sweet soever the place is. How powerfull soever wee are in the command off it. or How civill soever the King is in his carriage towards us all; I know the severall hazards wee must & doe dayly runn; & how new difficultyes will be multiplyed upon us dayly; & what unavoydable jealousyes will bee contracted by the resedency off any whatsoever longe heere; how faythfull & innocent soever they are; & therfore I doe earnestly intreat that you will bee solicitous for our return.
   From hence you cannot now expect much; I can only tell you that the King walks, Eates & talks as hee was wont to doe; only upon this day wee prevayl[e]d with him to observe the Fast; (It being ordeyned by his consent & published by his proclamation); which I believe hee hath not done off many Months before; but hee will not yett come to our Chaplynes Sermons; He came not out into the Presence [i.e. company] untill the Evening; nor did hee Eate untill supper; Hee expects now to heare from you [i.e. Parliament] dayly; but I cannot yett discover any inclinations in him to give you satisfaction upon the propositions; He have binn heard to say; that hee had now only his Honour & honesty left w[hi]^ch hee would not depart from; That hee was rationall; & must be convinced by reason; otherwyse hee would not part with any considerable part off his Crowne whatsoever hee suffered; but would submitt to Gods pleasure ... with patience; which resolution some will call magnanimity in him; whylst others call it obstinacy; My Lord off Pembrok is somwhat amended since the departure off his servant; My Service to y[ou]^r lady; to Father Hall & I heartily wish his good wives recovery; if I have any time that I can call mine owne heere I intend to see y[ou]^r children [James and William, q.v.] at Scoole & to take our Secretary [Daniel Earle] with mee; My Service amongst them att the Inner Temple ...
25 Feb. 1646[/47]

Ib. 126.

The next day he wrote again with a new worry, laying on his appeal with 'thee' and 'thy':

> Deare Bedfellow.
> I writt to thee last night by S[i]ʳ Walter Earle & I importuned thy assistance amongst other frends for our recall; & my thoughts are not att all changed. I thinke it would bee of very great advantage to us now to come off; for I ame confident the worst part off the Service is ... behind; for I see littel hopes off the speedy sending off the Propositions; nor off ther good speed heere when they come; soe ... the imployment will not only bee very hazardous but uncomfortable att best; but I heare off some intention ther hath binn to recall only three of us[;] who they are I know not; nor whether it [be] intended in favour or otherwyse; but I beleeve the world would make the worst construction of it; If three only should be recall'd ? & the other continued ... how earnest soever I ame of my return & you know it much concerns mee in mine owne private affayres; yet I would not willingly come upon such tearmes, that the imploym[en]ᵗ now should become my disadvantage; & I thinke wee are all of this opinion heere ...
> 26 Feb: 1646[/47].
>
> Ib. 127.

The next letter traced was probably written at the end of March 1647. In it, Holland recalled that in his previous letter he had asked for help in arranging his release from the appointment, so that he could come to London and proceed to Hampshire to despatch his affairs:

> ... some may suspect (in this Jealous world how innocent soever I ame) that I desire to come thither ... in design upon the lett[e]ʳ brought by this messenger from the King, w[hi]ᶜʰ (I protest upon the word of an Honest man & gental man ...) I never heard ... mention of untill wedsenday noone last[,] when the King appointed us all to attend him & then asked us, how it came abut, the Scotch Commiss[ione]ʳˢ being come to London, that the [new] propositions came not to him[;] wee answered that wee expected them dayly! Hee told us, wee had done soe Longe, & soe had hee[,] with much patience, but that hee could not doe soe longer, least the world should thinke him insensible off his owne and the Kingdomes condition & therfore for the Setlem[en]ᵗ of the Kingdomes peace hee was resolved to give an Answer to the Propositions that remeyned w[i]ᵗʰ him; It was true (hee sayd) that hee had publish[e]ᵈ his intentions to most of us, that hee would give noe answer in the condition he was; & this hee had formerly done likewyse by Lett[e]ʳˢ to the Queene from NewCastele[,] foreseeing his condition; but by those lett[e]ʳˢ th[a]ᵗ he had received from hir [from France] by Boswell, shee had intreated him againe to weigh that resolution, not that shee would undertake to advyse him what answer to give, but submitted it, to his owne Judgment & Conscience [&] ... offered it to his consideration that if in a Puntilio of Hon[ou]ʳ, with relation to his condition, hee should absolutely refuse to give any answer to the Propositions; it might be thought hee had more tender regard to himselfe in a point of hon[ou]ʳ then to the distracted & bleeding

condition off his Kingdomes; wherupon hee confessed that hee tooke a review of his owne intentions heerin; & finding many other more prevalent reasons, then what the Queene had shortly represented to him, hee came to a resolution in himselfe to give an Answer, and would doe it speedely, that ther might bee noe defect in anythinge in him that might contribute to the peace off the Kingdome, although it were littel hee could doe in the condition hee was & therfore [hee] desired that wee would assigne him some body to transcribe what he had prepared; as well for his ease as th[a]^t it might goe in the third person; otherwyse hee would bee his owne Secretary, & doe it this after noone; upon w[hi]^{ch} wee withdrew & tooke into consideration whether ... wee should send a message of this nature, when the propositions were expected with some alterations[,] & not being able to come suddaynly to a rsolution ... wee desired time to consider of what his Ma[jes]^{ty} had proposed. Hee told us what hee desired was easly answered; whether ... wee would alow him any[one] to ease him & write for him. for the sending of his lett[e]^r, hee knew wee could not; wee durst not deny it him. wee had sent lett[e]^{rs} of his formerly; & if wee should refuse this; what strictures soever ther was or might bee put upon him; hee would find meanes to divulge it to all the world; After much consideration among our selves wee came to a resolution to send this lett[e]^r; without any differing in opinion; but with all wee told the King freely that wee would write up to them that entrusted us, to lett them know what wee conceived the Contents off the lett[e]^r was; & M^r [Thomas] Herbert[,] one sent downe by you[,] was assigned to write for him. The lett[e]^r wee received sealed [,] without ... knowing any thinge off the Contents; & ... is soe ordered that it is to arrive ther [at Westminster] upon Fryday night. Soe as you [are] not sitting upon Saturdayes; you may have three dayes to consider what is best to bee done w[i]th the best advantage to y[ou]^r affayers. And all hope noe exceptions can bee taken to what wee have done heerin; wee having formerly sent two lett[e]^{rs} from the King to both Howses, enclosed in others from our selves wherin wee earnestly desired ther directions for the future ... & not having received any directions, wee still conceive it our duty ... not to interrupt any intercourse betweene the King & the Parliam[en]^t. & if it bee objected that the Contents of this lett[e]^r differs much from that off the former[,] wee desire it may bee considered that wee dare not in the Capacity wee are heere, take upon us to Judge what is fitt or unfitt to be Sent to the Parliam[en]^t; wee are only Ministeriall; & I ame confident all those that have any sence of us, will easely exonerate us in a time, when ther is such diversity off opinion both within & without the Howse; and especially ... when the publication therof by any other meanes might ... make impressions of greater disadvantage amongst the people ... Our difficultyes encreaseth dayly ...

I have referred our Noble frend Mr Perrepont to the perusale of this[,] wherin I have binn as particular as I could in soe short time alowed ... I pray communicate it to him ...

Undated; '47' [added by Whitelocke].

Ib. 130–131v.

Sir John Holland's speeches, after he left Holdenby, are in the Bodleian, Tanner Ms 321, fols. 24–25. They express confidence in the possibility of negotiating with the King.

Some years later, he wrote to Whitelocke in Uppsala:

> My Lord
> I endeavoured to have kissed y[ou]ʳ lo[ordshi]pps hands before y[ou]ʳ journy[,] but without success. Since such time I have heard Nothing of y[ou]ʳ lo[rdshi]pp, but by the Printed Bookes ... I had some hopes now at my return out of Flanders (wher I have binn to visite my wife by my Lord Protect[o]ʳˢ leave), to have heard of y[ou]ʳ lo[rdshi]pps dispatch & preparation for England ... Since my returne I have attended his Highnes [Cromwell], who obliges all I thinke that comes neere him ... Hee was pleased to give mee very ready admittance, even the first, though many attended that morning to make address to him. His Highnes was pleased to alow mee above half an Howers discourse ... & to command mee at parting, to be noe stranger ther.
> I believe his Hignes have very good thoughts of y[ou]ʳ lo[rdshi]pp, He was pleased to say somwhat of y[ou]ʳ lo[rdshi]pp to mee ... I doe not doubt, but y[ou]ʳ lo[rdshi]pp will by y[ou]ʳ prudence in the manage[ment] of the treaty with that fam[e]d Queene lay a firme Foundation of Interest in the favour of his Highnes, & Gover[n]ment heere ... I ame now going to attend y[ou]ʳ Lady in London, & to desire the favour of these in hir Packett for the safer conveyance ...
> London 28 Mar 1654.
>
> Add. Ms 32093 fols. 329–329v.

After the Restoration, Holland spoke in support of Whitelocke in the indemnity debates, *Hist. of Parl. 1660–1690*, ii, 557.

HOLLES (HOLLIS) of IFIELD, Hon. Denzil, MP, later 1st Baron (1599–1680). *Hist. of Parl.*; P. Crawford *Denzil Holles* (R. Hist. S. 1979); *D.N.B.* Second son of the 1st Earl of Clare and brother of the 2nd Earl; he sat in Parliament in March 1624. In the Long Parliament, he was initially a supporter of John Pym (q.v.) in opposing Court policies, and in 1642 he was one of the five MPs whom Charles I attempted to arrest in the House of Commons; concerned with preparations for the Civil War, he commanded a parliamentary regiment. In April 1642 he married Jane, the wealthy widow of John Freke (q.v.). By the end of November that year he was active in the peace party, seeking reconciliation with the King, and by mid-December was among the foremost Parliamentarians favouring peace negotiations. Like Whitelocke, he was one of Parliament's Commissioners to the King in Oxford, March 1642/43 and again in November 1644. A private conversation between the King, Holles and Whitelocke, at the second Oxford negotiations, led to the accusations made against both MPs by Thomas, 1st Viscount Savile, Earl of Sussex (q.v.), *Diary* 2 July, 1645, *passim*. After their names had been cleared in the Commons, Whitelocke distanced himself from Holles and the moderates. Holles did not sit in Parliament after Pride's Purge, until 1660. Later, when Whitelocke visited his former colleague (by that time Lord Holles) he was very courteously received, ib. 9 Nov. 1669.

HONYWOOD (HONEYWOOD), Col. Sir Robert, Kt. (1601–1686). *D.N.B.* Of Charing, Kent. Steward to Elizabeth of Bohemia (q.v.); he married Frances, daughter of Sir Henry Vane, the elder. Later, he was sent by the Council of State, with Col. Sydney (q.v.), to negotiate a peace treaty between Denmark and Sweden, *Diary* 5 June 1659; 15 Mar. 1659/60.

HOWARD, Col. Charles, see CARLISLE, 1st E. of.

HOWARD, Lady Mary. In 1639 she was examined by Whitelocke for her part in the rising led by Sir George Booth (q.v.); Whitelocke signed the warrant for her committal, but later helped her, ib. 30 July; 14 Sept. 1659. After the Restoration her father, Thomas Howard, 1st Earl of Berkshire (q.v.), and her brother, Sir Robert Howard (q.v.) demanded £500 and £1,000 respectively from Whitelocke, on her behalf, by way of reparation, ib. 7 June 1660.

HOWARD, Hon. Philip, MP (1629–1717). *Hist. of Parl.* Seventh son of the 1st Earl of Berkshire and brother of Lady Mary Howard (above). He brought a letter from The Hague to the House of Lords, *Diary* 23 May 1660; or a letter to the House of Commons, according to *Hist. of Parl.* At the Restoration, he joined the household of the Duke of York (q.v.).

HOWARD, Sir Robert, MP (1626–1698). *Hist. of Parl.*; *D.N.B.* Sixth son of the 1st Earl of Berkshire; brother of Mary (q.v.) and of Philip Howard (above). He served the King in the Civil War and was helped by Whitelocke during the Interregnum, *Diary* 11 Feb. 1656/57; 9 Aug. 1659. He was active as an MP in seven Parliaments, starting in 1661. Knighted in the Civil War, he was made a Knight of the Bath after the Restoration. Forgetting his promises of hearty friendship and good offices, made when he was weak, Sir Robert, when he was strong, pressed Whitelocke to pay £1000 to his sister, Lady Mary Howard, and £250 to their friend the Chancellor, ib. 7, 21 June 1660. Sir Robert acted as go-between when Charles II wanted Whitelocke's free advice on the King's right to grant indulgence (i.e. toleration) in matters of religion, ib. 13 Mar. 1662/63, with note.

HOWARD, Hon. Thomas, MP (1621–c.1681). *Hist. of Parl.* Second son of Theophilus Howard, 2nd Earl of Suffolk. A Royalist, he was helped by Whitelocke, *Diary* 3 Sept. 1654, perhaps because he was a brother-in-law of Roger Boyle, Baron Broghill, 1st Earl of Orrery (q.v.).

HOWELL, [Francis] (c. 1625–1680). *Calamy Revised*; *D.N.B.* A puritan divine. Principle of Jesus College, Oxford. After being ejected, he became co-pastor of a congregation in Lime St., London. Assumed to be the 'Mr Howell' who paid Whitelocke a fee of 20s. in London, *Diary* 22 Nov. 1669.

HOWELL, James (c. 1594–1666). *D.N.B.* Fellow of Jesus College, Oxford. A versatile author, a somewhat inaccurate historian and a good linguist. He was sent on various foreign missions, commercial and political, and served both the King and Parliament. He may have become acquainted with Whitelocke through the Dowager Countess of Sunderland (q.v.), since he had been secretary to Emanuel Scrope, Earl of Sunderland, in 1626. The diary references to Howell occur during the Interregnum, and concern his writing; he consulted Whitelocke about some of his work before publication and sent copies of his books, *Diary* 8 Aug. 1654, 12 June 1658, *passim*.

HUNGERFORD family (below) of Wiltshire, Berkshire, Somerset, and Oxfordshire. R.C. Hoare *Hungerfordiana*; Add.Ms 33412 fols. 77–79. (The servants Betty, q.v., and John, q.v., are presumed not to be members of this family.)

HUNGERFORD, Anthony, MP (c. 1608–1657). M.F.K.; *D.N.B.* Of Black Bourton, Oxfordshire; he entered the Middle Temple in 1625. Half-brother of Sir Edward Hungerford, MP. He was disabled, as a Royalist, and imprisoned in 1644. Presumably this was the Mr. Hungerford whom

Whitelocke helped, *Diary* 30 Sept. 1645. He compounded for his delinquency in 1646.

HUNGERFORD, Betty. Assumed to be Mary Whitelocke's maid, Betty Heyward, who married John Hungerford (q.v.), a servant in Whitelocke's household at Chilton Lodge, *Diary* 3 Apr. 1673 with note, *passim*.

HUNGERFORD, Sir George Kt., MP (*c.* 1637–1712). *Hist. of Parl.* Of Cadenham, Bremhill, Wiltshire; son of Edward Hungerford. He studied at Christ Church, Oxford, and in 1656 entered Lincoln's Inn. He is only mentioned twice, briefly, *Diary* 1 Apr. 1671; 5 Jan. 1671/72.

HUNGERFORD, Giles (Gyles), MP, JP (1614–1685). *Hist of Parl.* Fifth son of Sir Anthony Hungerford, and younger brother of Henry Hungerford (below); half-brother of Sir Edward Hungerford KB, MP, owner of Corsham, Wiltshire, and of Farleigh Hungerford Castle, Somerset (now a spectacular ruin). Giles Hungerford was a Middle Temple barrister. Of Freefolk, Hampshire, and East Coulston, Wiltshire. In 1654 he married Frances, daughter of Whitelocke's great-uncle Sir George Croke (q.v.), and widow of Richard Jervoise MP, of Freefolk. Giles was one of the trustees of Thomas Hussey's estate, from whom Whitelocke bought Chilton Park, near Hungerford, see University of Reading Archives BER.36/5/18,19,20,21,23.

HUNGERFORD, Henry, MP (1611–1673). *Hist. of Parl.* Fourth son (the third by the second wife) of Sir Anthony Hungerford of Stokke House, Great Bedwyn, Wiltshire; a brother of Giles Hungerford (above), and of Mrs. Sarah Goddard (q.v.). A Lincoln's Inn barrister. He was elected a recruiter MP for Great Bedwyn in July 1646. Although re-elected in 1656 and 1659, it appears that he did not sit after Pride's Purge in December 1648, until he was readmitted on 21 February 1659/60. He was subsequently elected to the Convention Parliament of 1660, in which he seems to have been fairly active. He lived, after 1652, at Standen, Berkshire, in the house of his nephew, Edward Goddard (q.v.). A neighbour of Whitelocke's at Chilton Lodge, they hunted and dined together, *Diary* 7 Sept. 1644; 8 Nov. 1671, *passim*. Whitelocke recorded Hungerford's death, ib. 22 May 1673. There is a memorial to him in the Church of St. Lawrence, Hungerford.

HUNGERFORD, John. A servant in the Whitelocke household, trusted with responsible duties; he married Mary Whitelocke's maid Betty (q.v.). Whitelocke sealed a bond to him, ib. 29 Oct. 1673; Hungerford, with the tutor James Pearson (q.v.), witnessed a promissory note of Whitelocke's to Thomas Withers for £6, in connection with 'two beasts commons' (i.e. quarters and food) in Chilton Marsh, 20 Oct. 1667, Long. W.P. xx, 134.

HUNGERFORD, [Letitia]. Gentlewoman to Whitelocke's second wife, Frances; her first name is given on a receipt for £10.7s.6d. from Peter Huggeford (sic), by appointment of his cousin Mrs. Letitia Hungerford (sic) from John Joy, 25 Nov. 1639, ib. vii, 349, endorsed on 349v., by Whitelocke's wife Frances: 'Grocer for sugar'. Mrs. Hungerford has only one entry, Diary 29 Sept. 1648; this refers to her ill-usage of Whitelocke's daughter Frances. In spite of this lapse she was still in the family's service the next year; this is shown on a receipt for 14s., paid by Mrs. Hungerford for two rubies and for 'trimming up' a jewel with diamonds, dated six days after Whitelocke's wife died, 22 May 1649, Long. W.P. x, 12. A few days later, Edmund Clarke and Walter Bigg signed a receipt to Mrs. Hungerford, amounting to £4.11s.6d. '... for all beer and ale to this day', endorsed by Whitelocke: 'Hungerfords bill', 2 June 1649, ib. 13. She was presumably paying household accounts, after her mistress's death. Without mentioning any names Whitelocke recorded later, when he remarried, that he had been '... miserably plundred ... by his former wife's waiting woman after her [Frances's] death, in his Temple Lodgings', Diary 17 Sept. 1650.

HUNGERFORD, Margaret, Lady (d.c. 1673). M.F.K. & D.N.B. (in the entries for her husband, Sir Edward Hungerford, KB, MP, 1596–1648, a parliamentary commander); V.C.H. Wilts., xi, xii. A daughter of Alderman William Hollidaie (Halliday), see A.B.B.; her sister married Sir Henry Mildmay (q.v.). Widowed the year before Whitelocke lost his second wife, Frances, Lady Hungerford inherited, among other estates, Westwood Manor, south-west of Bradford-on-Avon, also Upavon Manor, south-west of Pewsey, and Corsham, north-east of Bath. She was stated, in a Chancery suit of 20 November 1649, to have inherited from her husband a personal estate of at least £20,000, and to have had £2,000 a year settled on her. These sums and her legacies are listed in Add. Ms 33412 fols. 78v., 79v., 79 (sic), 7 May 1673. Within a year of Whitelocke's bereavement, match-making friends described Lady Hungerford to him as: '... a widdow of excellent parts & vast fortune', Diary 2 Jan. 1640/50. At first, he wrote: '... my thoughts were againe strangely disturbed, & my griefe renewed for

... my deceased Companion', Add.Ms. 37345 fol.38. He visited the widow several times, however, and began to find her attractive, but at that point the regicide, John Lisle (q.v.), claiming to be a relative of Sir Edward's, indicated that he should have been called upon as an intermediary. He then proceeded to hinder the courtship, at which point Lady Hungerford, turning to the Scriptures, quoted I. Timothy 5 verse 11 as an argument against a young widow remarrying. Sir Henry Mildmay (q.v.) and his wife, Lady Hungerford's sister, were approached and promised their support, but '... they[,] gaping for her Estate ...' stood in the way of Whitelocke or of anyone else marrying the widow, *Diary* 11, 14, 16 Jan. 1649/50. Many years later, Whitelocke's wife Mary stayed with Lady Hungerford at Corsham, ib. 3 Sept. 1669.

HUSSEY (HUSEY), William. His name appears on an indenture of 12 June 1663, as '... of Anvilles in the parish of Hungerford ... son and heire of Thomas Husey the elder late of Hungerford parke in the same County Esquire deceased and brother and heire of Thomas Husey the younger Esquire deceased who was son and heire of the said Thomas Husey th[e] elder ...', University of Reading Archives BER.36/5/18; his name or signature appears on several other documents in the same collection, relating to Whitelocke's purchase of Chilton Park, Berkshire, and adjoining properties. His wife Ann is named with him, ib. 36/5/22. The Whitelockes dined with Hussey at Anvilles, *Diary* 3 Aug. 1663; when that property was offered for sale, Bartholomew Hall (q.v.) and later John Thurloe (q.v.) considered buying it, ib. 16 Feb. 1665/66; 14 Dec. 1667.

HUTTON, Judge Sir Richard (c.1561–1639). *D.N.B.* Of Gray's Inn. Whitelocke recorded that Hutton and Croke were the only Judges who failed to support the King over Ship Money in the Court of Exchequer, *Diary* 1636.1637. fol. 42v. The *D.N.B.* gives a rather different account of Hutton's position, showing a change of attitude although he gave judgement in Hampden's favour in April 1638.

HYDE, Anne, see entry for YORK, James D. of.

HYDE, Edward, see CLARENDON, 1st E. of.

HYDE, Henry. Of Dinton, Wiltshire. Father of the 1st E. of Clarendon (q.v.).

HYDE, Laurence, MP, later E. of Rochester (1642–1711). *Hist. of Parl.*; *D.N.B.* Second son of the 1st Earl of Clarendon (q.v.). Of the Middle Temple. He consulted Whitelocke on a legal matter, *Diary*, 4 Nov. 1663. Created Earl of Rochester in 1682.

HYDE, Judge Sir Robert, MP (1595–1665). *D.N.B.*; M.F.K. Whitelocke, although 10 years his junior, knew him at the Middle Temple, *Diary* 1622.1623. fol. 5. A cousin of the 1st Earl of Clarendon (q.v.); Hyde sat briefly in the Long Parliament until he was disabled as a Royalist. He was knighted and made a Judge in May 1660. With Clarendon's help, he became Chief Justice of the King's Bench in 1663.

INGELO, Nathaniel, DD (*c.*1621–1683). *D.N.B.* Of Bristol. A Fellow of Eton. He accompanied Whitelocke on the Swedish Embassy as one of his Chaplains and as *rector chori*. They are said, in *D.N.B.*, to have become acquainted when Whitelocke was Recorder of Bristol; Ingelo's name does not appear in *The Diary* before the Embassy, but Whitelocke wrote to him urgently:

> ... I do make it my earnest suit to you, that you would be pleased to accompany me in that journey [to Sweden], according to your former resolutions to go with my Lord Viscount Lisle in the same service ... no person in my company is more desired ... than yourself, by your affectionate friend ... B. Whitelocke.
> Chelsea, September 21, 1653.
>
> *Journal* i, 44.

See also draft letters addressed to him in the same month, Long. W.P. xiii, 206, 208. Whitelocke described Ingelo as

> ... a Person of admirable Abilities in the Work of the Ministery and ... a well Studied Scholar, perfect in the Latin Tongue, Conversant in the Greek and Hebrew and could speak good Italian, he was much delighted in Musick . . . and carried persons and Instruments with him for that Recreation . . .',
>
> Add. Ms 4995, appendix v, 11.

Ingelo is quoted in the *D.N.B.* as saying 'Take away Music, take away my life.' There are numerous diary entried for him in connection with the Swedish Embassy, and finally a reference to a letter, *Diary* 8 Sept. 1658.

INGOLDSBY (INGOLESBY), Col. Sir Henry, Bt., MP (1622–1701). *D.N.B.* (in the entry for his elder brother, Sir Richard, below); *Restoration, passim.* He served with Henry Cromwell (q.v.) in Ireland, and was returned as MP for Kerry, Limerick and Clare, in 1654, 1656, 1659, but was dismissed from the Army for his attitude to Parliament, which he said he would withstand 'to the wearing out of his old shoes'; eventually he withdrew to Ireland via Dieppe, *C.S.P. Dom.* 10 July 1659. Parliament thanked him when, with Major Wildman (q.v.) and 300 volunteer horsemen, he caused Colonel Whichcote (q.v.), Governor of Windsor, to surrender the Castle to Parliament, *C.J.* vii, 798; 28 Dec. 1659. He was created a baronet both by Cromwell and by Charles II.

INGOLDSBY (INGOLESBY), Col. Sir Richard, KB, MP (1617–1685). *Hist. of Parl.*; *D.N.B.* A regicide. Related through his mother to Cromwell, and distantly to Whitelocke: Ingoldsby's wife Elizabeth (widow of Thomas Lee) was the second daughter of Whitelocke's great-uncle, Judge Sir George Croke (q.v.). Ingoldsby studied at Gray's Inn; later, he served as a Captain under John Hampden (q.v.) and as a Colonel in the New Model. After the fall of his kinsman, Richard Cromwell, he turned Royalist, and was one of those who urged Whitelocke to take the Great Seal to Charles II, *Diary* 23 Dec. 1659. Following the Restoration, he not only earned his pardon as a regicide but was made a Knight of the Bath in April 1661. Later in Whitelocke's life, proposals for a match between the Ingoldsbys' daughter and the Whitelocke's son Samuel came to nothing, because the Whitelockes could not meet the required terms, *Diary* 3 May 1671, *passim.*

INGRAM, Sir Arthur, Kt., MP (c.1570–1642). *D.N.B.*; *M.F.K.*; A.F. Upton *Sir Arthur Ingram* (O.U.P. 1961); G.E. Aylmer *King's Servants, passim.* A Yorkshireman and wealthy London merchant (a linen draper). He had held office in the Customs and as Secretary to the Council in the North etc. Aspiring to a profitable place as Cofferer at the Court of James I, he received something of a royal snub (see G.E. Aylmer, above, pp. 86–87). He showed kindness to Whitelocke, *Diary c.* Jan. 1641/42, fol. 54, and '. . . old S[i]ʳ Arthur Ingram the great feaster had me often with him', Add. Ms 37343 fol. 239v. Earlier, no doubt with the snub from the former monarch in mind:

> . . . S[i]ʳ Arthur Ingram, resolving to intertaine the K[ing] [Charles I] att Yorke [in his costly home, on the King's return from Scotland] & to make such musicke as should be worthy of the Kings ease, [as] part of his

intertainement, he wrote to me to borrow one of my servants Mr Wensley, who was a very excellent Musitian, & had a very rare voice, to come downe to him, no lesse journey then from Fawley Court to Yorke.

                                                    Add. Ms 53726 fol. 85v.

INGRAM, Sir Thomas, Kt., MP (1614–1672). M.F.K.; *Hist. of Parl.* Younger son of Sir Arthur (above). A Royalist, disabled in September 1642. Whitelocke only has one entry for him, concerning a letter on Treasury business, in which Sir Thomas acknowledged Whitelocke's favours to him, *Diary* 12 Oct. 1657.

IRETON, Lt.-Gen. Henry, MP (1611–1651). Of the Middle Temple. A regicide. He was married to Cromwell's daughter Bridget, by William Dell, 2 (q.v.), in June 1646. He was made Lord Deputy of Ireland in 1650. Ireton and Cromwell supped with Whitelocke soon after the King's execution, *Diary* 24 Feb. 1648/49, and Whitelocke wrote of Ireton's kindness to him, ib. 17 Mar. 1648/49; he remembered it again when Ireton died, ib. 8 Dec. 1651.

IRETON, Alderman Sir John, Kt. (1615–1689). *D.N.B.* (in his brother Henry Ireton's entry); A.B.B. Knighted by Cromwell, he served as Lord Mayor of London from 1658 to 1659; he also served on the Committee of Safety and, with Whitelocke and others, on a committee to receive accounts from George Downing (q.v.), who was at that time in the United Provinces, *Diary* 26 Oct., 30 Nov. 1659. Ireton was voted in the Second Exception to the Act of Pardon and Oblivion, ib. 13 June 1660, and was imprisoned for a time in the Tower. Later, he visited Whitelocke in connection with a Chancery case and paid him a fee of £1, ib. 9 Sept. 1668; 26 Dec. 1669.

IVE (IVES), Symon (Simon), (1600–1662). *D.N.B.* Composer. Lay vicar of St. Paul's Cathedral until about 1653, after which he gave singing lessons; he was installed as eighth Minor Prebendary at St. Paul's in 1661. Many years earlier, he had helped Whitelocke with music for the Royal Masque, 'The Triumph of Peace', in the Banqueting House, Whitehall, 1633/34, for which he was paid a fee of £100. When Whitelocke's first wife, Rebecca, died a few months later, Ive set as an elegy, for lute and voices, a verse dialogue between two shepherds; the words but not the music, are in

Add. Ms 53726 fols. 108–108v. Apparently around that date, with Rebecca's death in mind, another musician wrote a long and convoluted poem, typical of the period, which included Ive's name. Part of it ran:

> ... Henceforth Let Wheeler, Ive & Quarles bee
> But one continued name, noe longer three,
> Let them bee all united like our harts
> Nay, let us bee one person in three parts
> For Noble Whitlock's hearing; Let us prove
> An heaven composed Trialogue of love;
> Let us subsist one substance, draw one breath
> and let us live one life and dye one death ...

Signed '... your third part Francis Quarles', Long, W.P. Parcel 4, No. 30, undated. For Quarles, see K.J. Höltgen *Francis Quarles, 1592–1644* (Tübingen. 1978). That Whitelocke's friendship with Ive continued for some years, is shown in bonds and receipts between them, 17 May 1637, Long. W.P. vii, 114; 25 Jan. 1639/40 viii, 3, *passim*; the last one is dated 8 May 1645.

JAMES VI, King of Scotland and I, King of England (1566–1625). There are only three references to him in *The Diary*, all of them retrospective.

JAMES II, King of England, see YORK, James D. of.

JAMES, Alderman Thomas (d. *c.*1670). A.B.B. A shipwright. Elected Alderman in June and discharged in July 1669; he was fined £300 and 20 marks. It appears that his widow married Ashley Cooper's brother, George Cooper (q.v.). When short of ready money, Whitelocke was embarrassed by Cooper pressing him to repay £40, which had been sent by Alderman James to Whitelocke's son James, in Paris, *Diary* 21 June, with note, 26 July 1670; 13 July with note, 1 Oct. 1671. Initially, Whitelocke had written to the Alderman, who was evidently well known to him:

> ... you shew a great deale of kindness in being willing to return the money to him [James Whitelocke] that he stands in need off, which is forty pownds, & ... I doe truely promise that I will repay it to you ... within three of fower Moneths att most. I cannot tell you att whose house he lyes in Paris. If you please to send to S[i]ᵣ Theodore De Vaux in Maiden Lane in Covent garden, he can tell how to send to him ... also whither one Mᵣ Boteler who lyes att the Turkes head in Fleetstreet over against Fetter Lane, hath bin with him about the returne of 40ˡ to my son ... butt I doubt that Mᵣ Boteler hath not

done it, & ... unlesse you doe it uppon this promise of mine, I know not what way else he can be supplyed ... I being so farre from London ... with my kind love & service & thankes to you & your good wife, & my blessing to the boyes with you ...
Chilton neer
Hungerford
June. 25. 1670
[Endorsed] for Thomas James Esq[uir]ᵉ att his house att Buntingford in Hertfordshire ...

Long. W.P. xx, 155.

JAMES, William, JP (d. 1669). *V.C.H. Berks.* iv, 213. Of Denford Manor, east of Hungerford, Berks. A neighbour and friend of Whitelocke's between 1664 and 1669. The Bishop's Transcript of the Kintbury parish register shows his burial as 26 June 1669, not 24 June 1666 as in *V.C.H.* above.

JERMYN, Lady Catherine, M.F.K. (in her husband's entry, JERMYN, Sir Thomas, 1573–1645); G.E. Aylmer *State's Servants* pp. 88, 90; *Diary* 15 Mar. 1659/60.

JERMYN (JERMAYN, JERMIN), Judge Philip (d. 1654). E. Foss *Judges of England* vi; G.E. Aylmer *State's Servants* p. 355. Of the Middle Temple. Appointed a King's Bench Judge in 1648. The day after sentence was passed on the King, and two days before the execution, Judge Jermyn and Sir Thomas Widdrington (q.v.), the latter a Commissioner of the Great Seal, consulted Whitelocke; they were evidently concerned as to their legal position if, having sworn the oath of allegiance to the King, they continued in office under the Republic, but '... Judge Jermyn seemed satisfyed to act under the power of the House of Commons only', *Diary* [Sunday] 28 Jan. 1648/49. Accordingly, Jermyn became one of the six Judges who retained their posts; the King's Bench, on which he served, was swiftly renamed the Upper Bench. For legislation enabling the Judges to act, see ib. 9 Feb. 1648/49. In spite of his compliance, Jermyn appears to have been dismissed shortly after Cromwell took power as Protector, and died soon afterwards, see the entry for COKAYN, George, letter of 14 Apr. 1654. E. Foss, in *Judges of England*, recorded cautiously that: 'Peck dates ... [Jermyn's] death on March 18, 1655' but Bartholomew Hall's letter, dated like George Cokayn's 14 April 1654, confirms that Jermyn died in 1654. Cokayn's later comment: 'Yesterday the old man was buryed' is taken, in view of the earlier letter, to refer to Jermyn; never one to mince words, he added that [Obadiah] Sedgwicke, in the funeral oration, '... spake not a word in com[m]endation . . . the reason was because he could say nothing but that . . . [Jermyn] dyed a rich man[,] which the younge la[w]yers knew better then himself . . .' see COKAYN (above) 26 May 1654.

JERNINGHAM (JERNEGAN), Sir Henry, 2nd Bt. (*c.* 1620–1680). *Extinct & Dormant Baronetcies*; *Complete Baronetage*. He inherited the title from his grandfather, Sir Henry, sen., in 1646. Son of John Jerningham (d. 1636) and of Anne, daughter of Sir Francis Moore Kt. (q.v.) see MOORE family, of Fawley, Bucks., where Whitelocke met Sir Henry jun., with his son, probably Francis Jerningham (*c.* 1650–1730), the first surviving son, who later inherited the title, *Diary* 18 Oct., 7 Nov. 1665; see also 14, 31 Aug. 1672.

JERVOICE (JERVOISE), Thomas, MP (1616–1693). *Hist. of Parl.* Of Herriard, Hants, near Basingstoke, at no great distance from Chilton Park. Whitelocke would have known his father, Sir Thomas Jervoice, in the Long Parliament. The circumstantial evidence suggests that Whitelocke's client, identified only as 'Mr Jervoise', who paid the gentlemanly fee of 20s., *Diary* 30 Aug. 1670, was probably Thomas Jervoice jun. He was elected MP in 1680, five years after Whitelocke's death.

JOHNSTON, Sir Archibald, see Wariston.

JONES. Among the characters of this name who appear in *The Diary*, often without a first name, the following have been identified:

JONES, Arthur, see RANELAGH, Lady Katherine.

JONES, Charles (d. 1640). *Lincoln's Inn Admissions*. Son of Judge Sir William Jones (q.v.) of Beaumaris, and himself 'a great practiser' in law. Both of them were kind to the young Whitelocke, *Diary* 1632. 1633. fol. 18v. Charles died in the same year as his father, Judge Jones.

JONES, Elizabeth, née Willoughby, see RANELAGH, 1st Countess of.

JONES, Col. John, MP (*c.* 1597–1660). *Dictionary of Welsh Biography*; *D.N.B.* Of Merioneth. Recruiter MP for that county, in about 1647. A regicide. In July 1650, he was chosen as one of the Commissioners who were to help the Lord Deputy in the government of Ireland, and in 1659 was appointed, by Act of Parliament, as one of the Commissioners who were briefly to govern that country themselves. As a republican he was hostile to the Protectorate, yet he served in Cromwell's Parliament of 1656 as MP for Merionethshire and Denbighshire. In the same year he married, as his second wife, a widow Katherine (or Catherine) Whetstone, sister of Oliver Cromwell, and was in due course summoned to Cromwell's House of Lords, in December 1657. He was executed in 1660.

He wrote a long and respectful reply to a letter from Whitelocke, concerning the Manor of Gogarth in Wales. Whitelocke had evidently suggested that if Jones were selling the property, he should give the first refusal to Colonel (John) Mostyn, at the market rate, Mostyn having, as Colonel Jones wrote, 'the present possession, & Interest in the same . . .', Dublin, 18 Feb. 1651, National Library of Wales, Ms N.L.W. MSC.11, 440D, fol. 39. (The editor is indebted to Robert Temple for this reference.)

JONES, Col. John. Of Nanteos in Cardiganshire, now Dyfed. Jones assisted in the capture of Aberystwyth Castle from the Royalists in 1646, *Aberystwyth 1277–1977* (ed. I.G. Jones. 1977) p.43. Colonel Jones's daughter and coheiress, Ann, married a German Hugenot, Cornelius le Brun; their daughter, Avarina, married a Powell. By then, the Powell family were Lords of Nanteos, see *Dictionary of Welsh Biography* (Powell family, of Nanteos) and information in the Dyfed County Council, Cardigan Record Office. Colonel Jones appears to have been a litigious neighbour of Whitelocke's son-in-law, Sir Richard Pryce (q.v.), described as '. . . a cunning & envious adversary', *Diary* 20 July 1654. The dispute over land, which Whitelocke attempted to resolve, continued for at least three years, with letters of complaint from both parties, ib. 2, 7 Apr. 1657. For papers concerning the dispute see PRYCE, Sir Richard, Bt.

JONES, Lt.-Gen. Michael (d. 1649). *D.N.B.*; T. Carlyle *Letters and Speeches of Oliver Cromwell* (ed. S.C. Lomas), *passim.* Of Lincoln's Inn. Elder brother of Sir Theophilus Jones (q.v.). He fought for Parliament in Cheshire, Wales, and in Ireland where his family had lands; was made Governor of Dublin in 1647, and Cromwell's Lieutenant-General in Ireland. Cromwell wrote to the Speaker saying that Jones, who had never been known even to have an aching finger, had been taken ill '. . . we doubt upon a cold taken upon our late wet march, and ill accommodation . . .' It had turned to a fever from which he died. 'What England lost . . . is above me to speak . . . I lost a noble friend and companion', T. Carlyle *Letters and Speeches of Oliver Cromwell* i, 515. Jones died in Dec. 1649 at Dungarvan, on the south coast of Ireland, and was buried at nearby Youghal in the Earl of Cork's chapel. James Whitelocke, as a young volunteer in Ireland, wrote to his father: '. . . it hath pleased God to call two of my best friends, L^t G[enerall] Jones, & Cap. Lewis Owen, unto him . . .' Whitelocke transcribed his son's letter (which was omitted by the editor of *Memorials* iii, 135) and commented: 'L^t G[enerall] Jones being of my profession, & good acquaintance, expressed great favour & respect to my son, for my sake . . . with a much higher esteeme then I deserved, & by his death both my son & I lost a very affectionate & faithfull friend', Add. Ms 37345 fols. 36v.–37. His character was described in a letter from an unnamed correspondent in Cork: 'His straits, hazards, difficulties, and necessities were very many, and I might add temptations too. Yet he brake through all with unmoved gallantry . . . His temper and disposition were very sweet and amiable', *Memorials* iii, 136, based on a fuller text in Add. Ms 37345 fols. 38v.–39.

JONES, Capt. Richard, see RANELAGH, 3rd Viscount, 1st E. of.

JONES, [Richard]. Of Welford, Berks. Mentioned in connection with Whitelocke's purchase of Chilton Lodge, *Diary* 3 Aug. 1663; identified in a draft conveyance, 20 June 1663, Long. W.P. xx, 20v.–81.

JONES, Col. Sir Samuel, Kt. (*c.*1610–1673). *Hist. of Parl.*; *Shaw's Knights*. Of Courteenhall, south of Northampton, and of Petersham, Surrey. A parliamentary Colonel in the Civil War, yet after the Restoration he was harsh in debate against the regicides, and against Whitelocke and some other former officials. He was knighted in September 1660. For some reason he visited the Winwood family when Whitelocke was staying with them at Fewcot, Oxfordshire, not far from Courteenhall, *Diary* 17 Mar. 1665/66.

JONES, Sir Theophilus, MP (d. 1685). *D.N.B.* Younger brother of Michael Jones (q.v.). Scoutmaster-General of the forces in Ireland. He was appointed Governor of Dublin in 1649 (as his brother had been before him); he collaborated with Lord Broghill, later Earl of Orrery (q.v.), and supported the Earl of Ormond (q.v.). Dismissed as Governor of Dublin in 1659, he declared for a free Parliament. On 13 Dec. that year he helped to capture Dublin Castle from the three Commissioners for the Government of Ireland; this is recorded in *Diary* 19 Jan. 1659/60, when the news reached Whitelocke.

JONES, Judge Sir Thomas, Kt., MP (1614–1692). *Hist. of Parl.*; E. Foss *Judges of England*. Of Shrewsbury. Among his appointments he was made second Justice, North Wales Circuit, from 1662, for eight years. He may have been the Mr. Jones made a Judge in North Wales, according to *Diary* 14 Mar. 1659/60 (his only entry); perhaps this was wrongly dated by Whitelocke. Jones was knighted in 1671.

JONES, Judge Sir William, Kt. (*c.* 1567–1640). *Dictionary of Welsh Biography*; *D.N.B.*; E. Foss *Judges of England*. Son of William Jones of Castellmarch, North Wales. Father of Charles (q.v.). Studied at Beaumaris Free School, Anglesey (now Gwynedd) and at St. Edmund Hall, Oxford; admitted to Lincoln's Inn, 1587; knighted in 1617. After holding high office in Ireland he resigned in 1620, wishing to be recalled. He was appointed a Judge of Common Pleas in 1621 and was transferred to the King's Bench in about 1625. Like Judge Sir James Whitelocke (q.v.) he rode the Oxford Circuit. He showed kindness to Whitelocke, a young lawyer at the time, *Diary* 1632.1633. fol. 18v.; Whitelocke noticed that professional friends were less helpful after Judge Sir James Whitelocke died, ib. 1633.1634. fol. 19, but he received further help, ib. 1634.1635. fol 29v., *passim*. In the House of Lords debate of 1628, over the writ of Habeas Corpus for the five MPs imprisoned in the previous year, for refusing to contribute to the forced loan, Jones said: 'I will neither advance the King's prerogative nor lessen the liberty of the subject'; but about a decade later, he supported the King in the Ship Money dispute.

JONES, Sir William, KC, MP (1630–1682). *Hist. of Parl.*; *D.N.B.* Second Son of Richard Jones, MP, of Stowey Court, Chew Magna, Somerset, whom Whitelocke would have known in the first Protectorate Parliament. Admitted to Gray's Inn, 1647. Of Ramsbury, Wiltshire, near Whitelocke's last home, Chilton Park. A successful lawyer, and protégé of the 2nd Duke of Buckingham (q.v.), he built up an estate on the Wiltshire/Berkshire borders, from his earnings. Knighted in July 1671, he was appointed Solicitor-General in November 1673 and Attorney-General in 1675. Around these dates he negotiated for the purchase of part of Whitelocke's estate (Hidden, near Hungerford), but 'dealt wickedly' and eventually the sale fell through, *Diary* 4 Sept. 1673; 21 May 1674, *passim*; 26 May 1675. (See TULL, Jethro, a landowner whose financial difficulties in 1674 enabled Sir William to buy his land near Hungerford, instead of Whitelocke's.) Sir William is described in *Hist. of Parl.* as being of a 'manic depressive temperament'.

JONES ——. Chaplain and organist to Judge Sir James Whitelocke (q.v.). After the Judge's death, Jones served as Chaplain to the English Agent in Spain, 1637, Add.Ms 37343 fol. 146v.

JUXON, Dr., later Bishop and Archbishop, William (1582–1663). *D.N.B.* Of Merchant Taylors' School, St. John's College, Oxford, and Gray's Inn. Vicar of St. Giles's Church, Oxford; then of Somerton, Oxfordshire, north-west of Bicester. From Somerton he hunted with Whitelocke (at that time a student at St. John's College), *Diary* 1620.1621. fols. 3v.–4; he succeeded William Laud (q.v.) as President of St. John's in 1622, was appointed Bishop of London in 1633 and Lord High Treasurer in 1636; he attended Charles I during the King's last days, and on the scaffold. Deprived of his See in 1649, Juxon retired to Gloucestershire and to his pursuit of hunting. Whitelocke observed of him earlier that '. . . after he had bin a hunting, he would study more in one day then others did in two, he was learned & of a meek disposition . . .', ib. 1635.1636. fol. 41. Charles I called him 'That good man'. After the Restoration, he was appointed Archbishop of Canterbury. Whitelocke's last reference to him concerns questions from a client about a title against the Archbishop, ib. 5 Nov. 1661.

KEBLE, Judge Richard (*fl.* 1640s and 1650s). *D.N.B.*; G.E. Aylmer *State's Servants* pp. 277, 419. Admitted to Gray's Inn, 1609, which indicates that he was some years older than Whitelocke, who described Keble and John Lisle (q.v.), when they were all three Commissioners of the Great Seal, as 'being of small experience', *Diary* 13 Feb. 1648/49. Later, Whitelocke noted his fellow Commissioners' envy of him and attempts to cross him, ib. 29 Jan. 1650/51; 23 Oct., 27 Nov. 1651. Keble's inadequacy is also referred to in the *D.N.B.*; after the trials of Christopher

Lane and John Gibbons, at which he presided in 1651; an opponent is quoted as calling him 'an insolent, mercenary pettifogger', while Echard later described him as a man of 'little practical experience'. Keble was among those who, after the Restoration, were banned for life from holding office, having served on the High Court of Justice which tried the Royalists after the Second Civil War, *Diary* 12 July 1660. He is described by G.E. Aylmer as 'one of the most politically committed of the Judges'.

KELSEY, Lt.-Col. Thomas, MP (d. *c*.1680). *D.N.B.*; T. Carlyle *Letters and Speeches of Oliver Cromwell*. According to Anthony Wood, he started his career as 'a godly button-maker' of Birchin Lane, London. He became a Major in the New Model, later Lieutenant-Colonel and Cromwell's Major-General for Kent and Surrey in 1655. Whitelocke only refers to him in 1659 and 1660.

KENT, Anthony Grey, 11th E. of (1645–1702). G.E.C. Studied at Trinity College, Cambridge; styled Lord Grey until he succeeded to the Earldom in 1651. He consulted Whitelocke about the title of the Barony of Ruthen (Ruthyn), *Diary* 15 Mar. 1663/64; in this connection, the G.E.C. entry for his father, Henry Grey, 10th Earl of Kent (q.v.), states that before the 10th Earl had succeeded to the title, in 1643, he was 'styled (improperly) Lord Ruthyn', from 1639; this is expanded in a footnote: '. . . The Earls of Kent clung tenaciously to the Barony of Grey of Ruthyn, though from 1639 they were no longer heirs thereto . . .'

KENT, Elizabeth Grey, Countess of (1581–1651). G.E.C. (in the 8th Earl's entry); *D.N.B.*; *Aubrey's Brief Lives* (ed. O. Lawson Dick. Peregrine Books. 1962) p. 331. She only appears in *The Diary* as dowager, her husband, Henry Grey, 8th Earl of Kent, having died in 1639. (According to the *D.N.B.*, her husband was 7th Earl; this discrepancy recurs with his successors.) John Aubrey asserts that she let John Selden (q.v.), Solicitor and Steward to the Earl, 'lye with her, and her husband knew it. After the Earle's death he maried her . . . He never owned the mariage . . . till after her death'. Aubrey's statement has been disputed, but whatever the facts were, seven out of Whitelocke's ten references to the Countess link her name with that of John Selden, *Diary* 1642.1643. fol. 61, 28 Sept. 1645; 23 July 1647; 17 May, 4 July, 21 Oct. 1648; 14 Sept. 1649.

KENT, Henry Grey, 10th E. of (1594–1651). G.E.C.; *D.N.B.* MP for Leicestershire, 1640–1643. He succeeded to the Earldom in 1643. That year, Parliament appointed him as First Commissioner of the Great Seal; the diary references to him occur after Whitelocke and Widdrington were also made Commissioners of the Great Seal, working with him and Lord Grey of Warke (q.v.). The Earl served as Speaker of the House of Lords, in February 1645 and from September 1647 to February 1649. Clarendon wrote scathingly of Kent, but he is described by Whitelocke as 'a very honest[,] just, plaine man of good rationall parts & abilities . . .', *Diary* 2 Mar. 1647/48. Whitelocke often dined with his fellow Commissioner, who paid him the compliment of sending him a buck, ib. 10 May, 22 June 1648. A petition addressed to Whitelocke as a Commissioner of the Seal, by the Commissioners of the Peace and for the Militia etc. in Bedfordshire, requested that Henry, Earl of Kent, be removed from office as *Custos Rotulorum* for their county and replaced by Whitelocke, 2 Nov. 1650, Cal. Long. W.P. x, 189. Perhaps the Earl was ill, for he died six months later.

KIFFIN (KYFFIN, KIFFYN), Alderman, Col. William, MP (1616–1701). *D.N.B.*; A.B.B.; *Remarkable Passages in the Life of William Kiffin . . . by himself* (ed. W. Orme. London. 1823); G. Davies *Restoration* pp. 257, 298; A. Woolrych *Commonwealth to Protectorate*. A prominent and controversial Baptist, described as a 'minister' in *D.N.B.*, as a 'lay-preacher' by A. Woolrych (above) p. 350, and as a 'preacher' by A.B.B. He served as MP for Middlesex from 1656 to 1658; a wealthy leatherseller. The *D.N.B.* records Kiffin's arrest and the seizure of arms at his house in Little Moorfields, before the Restoration, and suggests that this may have arisen from his being a Lieutenant-Colonel in the London militia; Whitelocke records: 'A few armes seised in the houses of Lt Col. Kiffin & others', *Diary* 29 Feb. 1659/60. In one entry Whitelocke refers to Kiffin as Leiutenant-Colonel; elsewhere as Colonel. He is shown to have been an acquaintance of Lady Ranelagh (q.v.) who, like himself, was concerned for liberty of conscience, ib. 2 Dec. ; 20 Jan. 1669/70. Colonel Kiffin insisted on paying Whitelocke a fee of £2 for legal advice to the 'Phanatickes', i.e. dissenters, ib. 25 Apr. 1670.

KILLIGREW, Sir Peter, Kt., later Bt., MP (*c.*1593–1668). *Hist. of Parl.*; *Shaw's Knights*; Burke *Extinct & Dormant Baronetcies*. Of St. Budock, Cornwall. Knighted in 1625, he succeeded to the Baronetcy in 1665. Burke (above) notes that he was 'commonly known as Sir Peter the Post for his diligence in conveying messages to Charles I, during the Civil War'. He held office under the Protectorate and sat as MP in 1659 and from 1661 to 1668. A cousin of George Monck (later Duke of Albemarle q.v.), who appointed him Governor of Pendennis Castle, near Falmouth, Cornwall, *Diary* 10 Mar. 1659/60.

KING. Entries under this name offer even fewer clues than those under Jones. An unidentified Mr. King was rich enough to consider buying Yewden Manor alias Greenland; perhaps the same Mr. King paid a fee of £1 as a client, *Diary* 8 Mar. 1668/69; 25 July 1670. Mrs. King, a wealthy widow with a large estate left to her by her husband, was young enough to be considered as a match for Samuel Whitelocke, aged 20; earlier, although it was not recorded at the time, the Whitelockes had encouraged her, in the face of opposition, to marry an untraced Mr. King, ib. 1 Sept. 1671. She could have been the widow of Mr. King above, but another guess, backed by circumstantial evidence, is hazarded at the end of this section. Mrs. King knew Mr. and Mrs. Wynwood (q.v.) of Ditton Park, Buckinghamshire; for some reason, James Pearson (q.v.), tutor to the Whitelocke children, refused to preach in front of her when she visited Chilton Lodge, in the month of Whitelocke's death, ib. 8, 11 July 1675 with note; at that date she was engaged in building almshouses in Buckinghamshire, ib. 12 July 1675. This suggests that she was probably Anne Hannah, widow of John King (d. Mar. 1671), son of Henry King, Bishop of Chichester; under his Will, proved in April 1671, John King left money to found almshouses near the Kings' family home in Worminghall, Buckinghamshire, north-west of Thame, in Oxfordshire, *V.C.H. Bucks.* iv, 125, 130. The widow, Anne Hannah King, later married Thomas Millington (physician to William and Mary, knighted 1680, d. 1704), who helped her found the almshouses, 'Minute Book of the Worminghall Almshouses Trustees' (transcript). She also erected a monument to her first husband and to her father-in-law in Chichester Cathedral.

KING, Col. Edward MP (*c.*1606–1681). *Hist. of Parl.* A parliamentary Colonel; Governor of Boston, Lincolnshire, 1643–1645. MP for Grimsby in 1660. A rigid Presbyterian. He quarrelled with Whitelocke's brother-in-law, Francis, 5th Baron Willoughby of Parham (q.v.). Whitelocke was warned that Colonel King, '... of the Kings party ...' was prejudiced against him, but that his informant, Samuel Wilson, 'tooke him off ...', *Diary* 6 June 1660.

KING, Col. Sir John, later 1st Baron Kingston (d. 1676). G.E.C.; *D.N.B.* Of Boyle Abbey, County Roscommon. Served in the King's Army in 1641; later he served Parliament in Ireland and was knighted by Henry Cromwell, but subsequently worked for the Restoration; he was knighted by Charles II in June 1660, and was created an Irish Peer on 4 Sept., *Diary* 25 Sept. 1660. As Lord Kingston he was a client of Whitelocke's, ib. 18 Jan. 1664/65.

KING, Alderman Richard (d. 23 May 1668). A.B.B. A mercer; Alderman from 1658 to 1661. Just before his death he paid Whitelocke a fee of £2, *Diary* 12 May 1668.

KINGE (KING), Col. (?) Rob[ert]. One of the signatories to the letter from Whitehall summoning Whitelocke to serve on the Committee of Safety, set up by the General Council of Army Officers. Whitelocke's transcript makes Kinge's the next-to-last signature, *Diary* 27 Oct. 1659; on the original, however, his name comes last of all, Long. W.P. xix, 90.

KITSON family (below) *Alumni Oxonienses*. From three generations of Kitsons, Robert and William Kitson (q.v.) became Rectors of Fawley, near Henley-on-Thames, while young Knollys Kitson (below) aspired to the appointment but was rejected as unsuitable. Bonds, receipts, acknowledgements of tithes, etc. from the 1630s indicate transactions between: Sir James Whitelocke and both Robert Kitson, 'Clerk', and William Kitson; also between Whitelocke and Edward Kitson, 'yeoman of Fawley' (related to Robert), one Francis Kitson, and William Kitson (q.v.), Long. W.P. v, 1, 3, 139, 140; vi, 259; vii, 47, 81. Neither Edward nor Francis Kitson appears in *The Diary*.

KITSON, Knollys. Son of William Kitson (below). Young Kitson is referred to confusingly both as 'Mr Knollys Kitson[,] old Mr Kitsons son' and, in the same entry, as 'Mr Knollys', while (even more confusingly) a Mr. Knollys, probably the son of William Knollys (q.v.), a man of some local standing, joined with others in pressing Whitelocke to give young Knollys Kitson the living of Fawley, after the death of William Kitson, his father. Whitelocke, however, who was Lord of the Manor and Patron of the Living, refused on the grounds that Knollys Kitson was very young, was not a good scholar and was reported to be both idle and disorderly, *Diary* 24 Mar. 1667/68.

KITSON, William (c.1609–1667). Studied at Wadham College, Oxford. He succeeded his father Robert Kitson (a Yorkshireman who had studied at Brasenose College, Oxford), as Rector of Fawley, Jan. 1630/31; the presentation deed, signed by Judge Sir James Whitelocke's servant John Oakeley, is in Lincoln Archives Office, PD/1631/92; the living was in the gift of Judge Whitelocke, as Lord of Fawley Manor. On 9 Nov. 1634, when Frances Willoughby eloped with Kitson's new patron Bulstrode Whitelocke, Kitson (aged about 25) conducted the secret marriage ceremony, in Fawley Court Chapel. Later, Kitson looked after some of Whitelocke's books when Prince Rupert's troops occupied Fawley Court, restoring them in October 1644. When Whitelocke was away from home, Kitson kept him informed about events at Fawley. In some of Whitelocke's later entries, 'Mr Kitson' could mean either the Rector or his son, Knollys Kitson (above), but it was presumably William (rather than his very young son) on whose behalf William Knollys (q.v.) wrote asking that Kitson might have the post of schoolmaster at Ewelme, *Diary* 26 Mar. 1659. After William Kitson's death, *The Diary* records: 'He was a learned man, & a good preacher, he was bred up [i.e. educated] by Wh[itelockes] father & was a loving friend to Wh[itelocke] who kept him in his living in the troubles', *Diary* 24 Dec. 1667.

KNIGHT, Isaac. A.G. Matthews *Calamy Revised*. Imprisoned by Archbishop Laud (q.v.) in 1637. Chaplain to Lord General Fairfax (q.v.). He was ejected as Rector of Fulham, in 1660; this was presumably the 'Mr Knight' who preached at the house of Samuel Wilson (q.v.), *Diary* 13 Oct. 1661.

KNOLLYS (KNOWLES), Sir Robert, Kt., JP. *D.N.B.* (in the entry for his uncle, William Knollys, Earl of Banbury); *Hist. of Parl.* (a few details in the entry for his son William Knollys, below). Son of Richard Knollys of Stanford-in-the-Vale, Oxfordshire (formerly Berkshire), near Faringdon; grandson of the famous Elizabethan statesman, Sir Francis Knollys. Admitted to the Middle Temple in January 1610/11. He married Joanna, daughter of Sir John Wolstenholme (q.v.); bought Rotherfield Greys from his uncle, the Earl of Banbury, in March 1630/31; took up the palings at Greys and converted the parkland to tillage. Whitelocke, living nearby, wrote: '... I bought a parcell of those old pales, & caused them to be pieced & sett up about twenty acres of my ground adjoining to Fawley Court', Add. Ms 37343 fol. 142v.; *Diary* 1636.1637. A warrant signed by Sir Robert, as a JP for Oxfordshire, appears in Sept. 1634, Long. W.P. vi,

126; these papers also contain a certificate from Sir Robert to Whitelocke on a paternity case in the village of Harding alias Harpsden, which had been referred to them both by the County Sessions: the mother, Mary Mayne, had changed her evidence and was naming Dr. Webbe as the father as well as his man, Robert Barksten (Dr. Webb was Rector of Harpsden from 1614 to 1639). Sir Robert Knollys, baffled and shocked, entreated Whitelocke to consider the case in which '... a Queane [i.e. harlot] will charge two men to be the father of her childe ...', ib. 195v.–196, 4 Apr. 1635.

KNOLLYS, William, MP, JP (c.1620–1664). *Hist of Parl.* Eldest son of Sir Robert Knollys (above). Admitted to the Middle Temple in 1639. He compounded for £1,100 in 1648. MP for Oxfordshire, April/May 1663 to September 1664. 'Mr Knollys' in *The Diary* is never identified as William Knollys of Greys, but certain clues indicate that he was: William Knollys had studied at St. Edmund Hall, Oxford, which suggests a nonconformist leaning and George Cokayn (q.v.), Independent Minister, appealed to Whitelocke on behalf of 'Mr Knollys' who was in prison, *Diary* 23 July 1658; after the Coleman Street riots, led by Thomas Venner (q.v.), Whitelocke offered to help Mr. Knollys put down any tumults in the county, which points to this being William Knollys, JP, ib. 12 Jan. 1660/61; moreover, the extraordinary contretemps in Henley Church, on the following day, confirms Knollys's standing, when an offending parson 'hardly escaped being sent to prison by Mr Knollys', ib. 13 Jan. 1660/61. Will[iam] Knolles (*sic*) appears in 1660 and 1661 as paying quit rent of 8s. 9d; later, the Lady of 'the Manor of Greys' paid quit rent of 17s. 6d., 1712–1714, as shown in the town of Henley's account book, known as the 'Bridgeman's Bridge book'. No other Knollys or Knolles has been traced who would match Whitelocke's description. If the above assumptions are correct, the Mr. Knollys who pressed Whitelocke to appoint young Knollys Kitson (q.v.) to the Fawley parsonage, ib. 24 Mar. 1667/68, must have been William Knollys's son, since the MP himself had died in 1664.

KNOWLES (KNOLLYS), Hanserd (1599–1691). *D.N.B.*; B.R. White *Hanserd Knollys and Radical Dissent* (Dr. Williams's Trust. 1977). Probably the 'Mr Knowles' who prayed with Frances Whitelocke when she was dying in London, and preached the sermon at her funeral in Fawley, *Diary* 15, 17 May 1649. Although the Baptist preacher was, at that time, based on Suffolk, he had a strong link with Frances' family; he was, or soon would be, a tutor to one of her nephews, preparing him for the university, and in 1656 he dedicated *An exposition of the first chapter of the Song of Solomon* to her brother Francis, 5th Lord Willoughby of Parham (q.v.), explaining that parts of the book had been used in his daily ministry to the Willoughby household, B.R. White (above) pp. 17, 18.

LAGERFELDT, Israël, Israëlsson (1610–1684). *S.B.L.*; *S.M.K.*; *Guide to the materials for Swedish Historical Research in Great Britain* (Stockholm. 1958). The *Guide* ... (above) shows the main collections of Lagerfeldt's papers as being: in the State Papers Office (now in the P.R.O., S.P.); the Bodleian, both in Mss Rawlinson (many but not all of these are published in *Thurloe S.P.*) and Mss Tanner; also in Long. W.P. Lagerfeldt studied at the University of Uppsala; he was appointed tutor to Gabriel, son of Gabriel Gustafsson Oxenstierna, with whom he travelled to Holland, England, France and Italy; he spoke Latin, German and French, and understood Dutch and English. Returning to Sweden in 1640, he was appointed Secretary to Chancellor Axel Oxenstierna (q.v.) in 1641; he was later described by Whitelocke as '... the great creature of the Chancellor', *Journal* i, 338. He sat in the Swedish Parliament, speaking frequently in debates on commercial and financial matters, and was ennobled in 1646, after serving as Secretary at peace negotiations with Denmark, in Brömsebro, from 1644 to 1645.

As a widely travelled man and a commercial expert, Lagerfeldt was appointed Envoy Extraordinary to England, being described by Queen Christina (q.v.), in a letter of credence, as '... Vice-President of the Supream Councell of our Judicature throughout Finland ... Israel Lagerfeldt & Lord of Wigbyholm ...', Christina requested an answer to Lagerfeldt's message 'as soone as possible ... either by Letter or by Expresses, as occasion shall serve ...'. Long. W.P. xv, 25 (translation); a Latin transcript in *Thurloe S.P.* i, is paged 216 but is bound between pp. 223 and 225, dated 20 January 1652/53. Characteristically, the Rump Parliament did not receive Lagerfeldt or his message until 7 April, shortly before the Rump was dismissed by Cromwell on 20 April 1653; a translation of the Swedish Envoy's first speech to Parliament, over the name of Henry Scobell, Clerk to the Parliaments, Long. W.P. xiii, 62, 62v., states that it was read on 8 April. This, the first serious attempt to renew friendship between Sweden and England, after the execution of Charles I in 1649, is considered in chapter 1 of *The Diary*.

Ostensibly, Lagerfeldt brought an offer from Queen Christina to mediate, in the Anglo-Dutch war, between the Commonwealth of England and the United Provinces, to 'testify her Friendly Care & ... Affection ... for the Wellfare & Preservation of the Christian World, but chiefly of the

Evangelicall Dominions . . .' The Queen recalled that her ancestors and indeed her father, Gustav Adolf, '. . . had ever a sincere & faithfull tye of Amity . . .' with England. The lengthy correspondence between Lagerfeldt and the Council of State reflects Sweden's understandable eagerness: to safeguard her ships (some of them carrying rich cargoes) against seizure by the English; to obtain the release of ships already captured, and to negotiate their safe navigation, both in English waters and when sailing to rich lands overseas. The English Council of State had no intention of offending their own wealthy merchants and sea-captains by stopping this piracy; offenders included such a distinguished officer as Vice-Admiral Lawson (q.v.), 6 Oct. 1653, Long. W.P. xiv, 8. Lagerfeldt only made a breakthrough when he offered a pre-emption on vital naval materials, to be brought through the Baltic in Swedish vessels, to a staple at Göteborg (Gothenburg).

When Whitelocke went to Uppsala as Ambassador Extraordinary, Lagerfeldt was recalled and arrived in Sweden before him, to act as intermediary between the Ambassador from England, and the Queen and her Chancellor. Whitelocke suspected that Lagerfeldt tried to 'sift' him, to find out what he was thinking and planning, Diary 19 Jan.; 23 Mar. 1653/54. The Queen appointed Lagerfeldt Vice-President of the College (or Board) of Trade, 18 Feb. 1653/54, a responsible post which he held until 1681. A few letters from Lagerfeldt to Whitelocke, after the Anglo-Swedish Treaty was signed, are listed in the Guide (above) and in the Long. W.P. Index. They concern such matters as the death of Chancellor Axel Oxenstierna (q.v.) and the continued detention of captured Swedish goods.

LAKE, Sir Lancelot, Kt., MP (1609–1680). Hist. of Parl. Son of Sir Thomas and Mary Lake, of the Manor of Canons, Edgware (then in the parish of Stanmore), Middlesex. He was knighted and first elected an MP in 1660. His dates and parentage are taken from Hist. of Parl., in preference to those in D.N.B. (in the entry for Sir Thomas Lake, d. 1630, which shows Sir Lancelot Lake MP as the son of another Lancelot, d. 1646, and as the grandson of Sir Thomas). Lancelot Lake's name appears only once, Diary 1 Jan. 1656/57. The entry concerns a protracted and bitter dispute with de Sabran, who had married Lancelot's niece, Mary Lake. She had died before 1657 and the Frenchman was acting on behalf of their small son Renée (sic). For further information on Lake, see SABRAN, Melchior de.

LAMBERT, Col., later Major-General John, MP (1619–1683). C. Firth & G. Davies *Regimental History of Cromwell's Army*; *D.N.B.*; A. Woolrych *Commonwealth to Protectorate*; *Restoration*; *Pepys* x. He distinguished himself in a courageous but turbulent army career: aggressively ambitious, he suffered from delusions of grandeur; a very able strategist and popular with his men, he was also a military meddler in politics. While still in his 20s he commanded a regiment in the New Model and was appointed a Major-General before he was 30. With Henry Ireton (q.v.) he drafted the well-considered 'Heads of the Proposals', which aimed at a settlement with the King, in July 1647; he later prepared the Instrument of Government for the Protectorate, in 1653, *Interregnum* (ed. G.E. Aylmer) pp. 6–7, 143. He was co-opted to Barebone's Parliament in 1653 but never sat, and was elected MP in 1654, 1656 and 1659, see Woolrych (above) p. 432. After pressing for reform of the Rump he helped to bring about its dissolution, also that of Barebone's Parliament. He was active in helping to set up the Protectorate and he served on the Council. Vehemently opposing the plan to make Cromwell King, and to put the Protectorate on a hereditary basis, he refused to take the oath of allegiance to the Protector and was dismissed, but he was handsomely pensioned off by Cromwell in 1657, at £2,000 p.a., being still in his late 30s. He retired to Wimbledon House as Lord of the Manor, his 'country palace', see the entry for CLARE, John Holles, 2nd E. of. Lambert and his wife were styled 'Lord' and 'Lady', titles used no doubt satirically by Whitelocke, *Diary* 10 July 1654; 4 June 1657.

Lambert had fought at Preston in 1648, Dunbar in 1650 and at Worcester in 1651, serving as Major-General for the five Northern Counties, from 1655–1657.

Lambert was reinstated as an officer by the Rump, when it was restored in 1659 after Richard Cromwell's fall, and he was sent to crush Sir George Booth's rising in Cheshire. At that time Whitelocke, as Lord President of the Council, received two or three daily dispatches from Lambert; later, letters came from the forces to the Council at intervals of two or three hours, ib. 6, 12 Aug. 1659. After Booth's defeat, Lambert was rewarded by a grateful Parliament with a jewel worth £1,000, ib. 23 Aug. 1659. On 12 October, however, he was cashiered by the same Parliament, on account of the Army's Derby Petition to the House. The next day Lambert defiantly drew up his forces outside Parliament, stopped Speaker Lenthall's coach and sent him home, preventing Parliament from sitting. By that means he effectively expelled the Rump which he had helped to restore, and the masters from whom he had received his commission, ib. 12, 13 Oct. 1659.

He then served on the Committee of Safety, set up by the General Council of Officers to govern the country, ib. 26 Oct. 1659. His forcible 'interruption' of Parliament lost him the support he formerly enjoyed from the Army and Navy, and from many civilians; he was already in a weak position when he was sent north, by the Committee of Safety, to check General George Monck on his march south. The General had criticized the disruption of Parliament and the military take-over, ib. 22 Dec. 1659, *passim*. Whitelocke (who was in danger himself, having served on the Committee of Safety) records in some detail events leading to Lambert's arrest, 2,4,6,26 Jan., 13 Feb., 6 Mar. 1659/60. Lambert's escape from the Tower, and his recapture, are also mentioned, ib. 9, 18, 21, 23, 25 Apr. 1660.

After the Restoration, Lambert (although not a regicide) was condemned to death but was reprieved; he was included in the Second Exception to the Act of Indemnity and was imprisoned for life. There are numerous entries for him in *The Diary*, most of them impersonal in character.

He had profited by the revolution: buying the royal palace of Wimbledon for £7,000, and speculating in confiscated estates in Yorkshire, and in soldiers' debentures.

LANE, Sir Richard (1584–1650). *D.N.B.*, *Middle Temple Bench Book* (ed. J. Bruce. London. 1837). Attorney-General to the Prince of Wales in 1634. He ably conducted the defence of the Earl of Strafford (q.v.) when the Earl was impeached in 1641; he was knighted in 1644, and was one of the King's Commissioners at the Uxbridge negotiations; Whitelocke, as one of Parliament's Commissioners, visited him there in January 1644/45. Lane was appointed Lord Keeper of the Great Seal for the King in August 1645; he drafted articles on the King's behalf for the surrender of Oxford to General Fairfax (q.v.), in June 1646, and died in exile four years later. Anthony Wood (quoted in the *D.N.B.*) alleged that when Lane joined the King in Oxford, he entrusted his Middle Temple Chambers, his library and goods to his close friend Bulstrode Whitelocke but that when, after Sir Richard's death, his son Richard asked for their return, Whitelocke denied all knowledge of his former friend. This is a fabrication: an Order of the House of Commons bestowed on Whitelocke the Chambers formerly belonging to the Prince's Attorney, Mr. Lane, with 'all the bookes & the goodes' they contained; goods and books were to be inventoried, 13 Feb. 1643/44, Long. W.P. ix, 18; this is the original Order, signed 'H. Elsyng' (q.v.). When the Order was presented to the Benchers, on 21 May 1644, it was resolved that: 'Mr Whitelocke is admitted for life without fine' (i.e. fee), C.H. Hopwood *Middle Temple Records* (Butterworth. 1904) ii, 930. This last agreement was dishonoured when, as an old man, Whitelocke was deprived of his Chambers. As to the return of the books etc., Whitelocke recorded that when Sir Richard's widow, Margaret, wrote asking for some recompense for her husband's books etc., which the House of Commons had given to Whitelocke, he 'durst not' return them at that time, but that he did so later to her son, *Diary* 1 June 1657; the return of 'a studdy of bookes', manuscripts on the law, and furniture, to Richard Lane, jun., is recorded, ib. 8 June 1660.

LANE, Thomas, MP, JP (d. 1652). M.F.K. Bencher of the Inner Temple. Recorder of Wycombe (High Wycombe), Bucks; he served as MP for that borough in the Parliaments of 1625, 1628 and in the Short and Long Parliaments of 1640, until secluded at Pride's Purge, in December 1648. He 'feasted' Richard Winwood (q.v.) and others, *Diary* 22 Aug. 1648.

LANGHAM, Alderman Col. John, MP, later Kt. and Bt. (1584–1671). *Hist. of Parl.*; A.B.B. An immensely wealthy London merchant (a grocer) of Crosby Place, Bishopsgate, and of Northhamptonshire; a Captain of foot in Parliament's Army from 1642 to 1643, and a Colonel from 1643 to 1645. Whitelocke was retained as Counsel by Captain Limrey (q.v.) in a case against Langham, *Diary* 14 Oct. 1645, and was rewarded with a pearl necklace worth £30, ib. 22 Jan. 1647/48. Langham was imprisoned in 1647 for his opposition to the New Model, yet he served as MP under the Protectorate, after which he helped to promote the Restoration, for which he was knighted in May and created a Baronet in June 1660.

LAUD, Archbishop William (1573–1645). H.R. Trevor-Roper *Archbishop Laud* (Macmillan. 1962); *D.N.B.*; Anthony Wood *Athenae Oxonienses* (ed. P. Bliss. London. 1817) iii, 117–144. Son of a clothier. A contemporary and friend of Whitelocke's father, James Whitelocke, sen. (q.v.), at St. John's College, Oxford; although their opinions diverged, they remained lifelong friends. Laud was appointed: President of St. John's College, in 1611, and Bishop of St. David's, 1621 (which diocese he only visited twice); he was translated to Bath and Wells in 1626 but never visited the diocese (see *Archbishop Laud*, above, p. 92), and was made Chancellor of Oxford University in April 1629. His rigorous Arminian, anti-Puritan convictions won the approval of Charles I (q.v.) and of the 1st Duke of Buckingham (q.v.). He was appointed Archbishop of Canterbury in 1633. In that office he pursued highly authoritarian and oppressive policies, being an honest man of stiff-necked principle who suffered, like

Charles I, from being sure that he was right. A few weeks after the Long Parliament assembled he was impeached by the Commons, on 18 December 1640, imprisoned in the Tower, on 1 March 1640/41, brought to trial in 1644, and sent to the block in 1645, at the age of 71. Whitelocke, at some risk to himself, refused to take part in the trial of the man who had been President of his College and responsible for part of his education, *Diary* 1643.1644. fol. 63v.

Years earlier, when he was Chancellor of Oxford, Laud showed the warmer side of his nature when, soon after Judge Sir James Whitelocke's death in 1632, he stopped at the Bell, in Henley. He sent for the young heir to Fawley Court, his old friend's son and his own former student, and had a long talk with him. Whitelocke wrote in his 'Annales': 'I have thought fitt to sett it downe, dialogue wise ... as neer as I can remember ...' He forgot, when writing it up later (probably from notes), that Laud was Chancellor of Oxford at that time, but was not yet Archbishop:

ArchB^p.   Mr Whitelocke, I am very glad to see you well ... it was my desire, comming into these parts, to see you & speake with you, indeed I purposed to have layen att your house, to have graced you in your own Countrey [i.e. County], butt I was told that you were gone from home, & theruppon, I tooke up my lodging heer, butt when I heard that you were att your house, I sent for you, & I am very gladde to see you.

Wh.   My Lord [a slip, since he was not yet Archbishop; see also 'Your Grace', below] I was very unhappy in that mistake, & misinformation, which was given to your Grace, of my being from home att this time, & I returne my humble thankes for the honour your Grace intended me ... I hope it is not too late for your Grace yet to remove butt a little distance to my house, where you shall have a most hearty wellcome & I hope somwhat more convenient accom[m]odation for your selfe & your retinue, then this place will afforde.

A.   I thanke you very kindly for your invitation, butt now that I am setled, & my people in our Inne, it would be troublesome to remove, & we must take it as we find it.

Wh.   Will your Grace then be pleased, in your returne from Oxford, to honor me with your presence att my house?

A.   I cannot promise that, bicause ... I am partly ingaged if I doe not attend his M[ajes]^{ty}, to lye att a kinsmans house ... att Turville ... I may find some other opportunity, & I assure you ... that I shall be ready uppon all occasions, to doe you any good, for his sake who is gone to God, my old friend your father, & for your owne sake too ... Lett me aske you to what course of life, doe you intend to betake your selfe now, uppon the death of your father ... I shall be willing to give you counsell for ... direction in your way.

Wh.	I shall very readily pursue your Graces directions ... and ... acquaint you with my owne thoughts & inclinations ...
A.	Lett me freely know what they are, & you shall as freely have my opinion therin.
Wh.	Since ... I was brought up in the study of the lawe, & initiated in the practise of that profession, I have thoughts, of continuing in that way ...
A.	I am clearly of that judgement, that it will be best for you, to keep on, in that Course, & still to continue the practise of the Lawe, it will be an advantage to you in all your affayres, & a shield to you in your Countrey against injuries ... butt be not discouraged[,] be diligent in your calling ...
Wh.	It pleased God to blesse my father very much in ... his profession.
A.	your father was a most industrious man, from the first beginning of his studyes, when I came acquainted with him, att St Johns Colledge in Oxford, & so he continued all his time, & I observed when you came a young man to the same Colledge & your father committed you to my care, who was then President ... I had a perticular eye over you, & found that you were not negligent in your studyes nor debauched or idle in your Conversation.
Wh.	I most thankfully acknowledge the great favour & care which your Grace was pleased to take of me, & of my education ... in Oxford ...
A.	I promised your father to take care of you there, & so I did, & will take care of you now that you have lost a good father, & I shall be ready to ... further you in your profession, what may lye in my way ... I know, your father left you a Competent Estate, & sufficient to maintaine you like a gentleman, butt if your Estate were much greater, yett to be in a profession, will be no disparagement, nor diminution to you, butt every way an advantage.
Wh.	I shall be faithfull to my clients, & willing to take pains in my profession.
A.	For matter of labour & pains I shall counsell you to be industrious, yet you need not to sweat so much as others att it[;] make such progresse in your studyes & practise, as may become you, & inable you to serve the King, & your Countrey ... It is an unhappy, & an ungodly life that too many gentlemen doe leade, to spend all their time in hunting, or hawking or in worse things, & often their greatest care is, how to spend their time[;] you will know how to spend your time in your study & profession, and it will keepe you from many inconveniences.

We had much more discourse of this & other matters, till company comming in did interrupt us, & supper being ready, the ArchB[isho]P commaunded me to stay & sup with him ... He was pleasant att supper as he used to be att meales, & after supper, I tooke my leave of him ...

Add. Ms 53726 fols. 73v.–75.

After Whitelocke ran away with Frances Willoughby, Archbishop Laud sent for him and, as Whitelocke observed snobbishly, spoke to him more like a porter than a gentleman, because he had married a nobleman's daughter without permission from the King or the Archbishop. Whitelocke was disdainful, and only the tact and diplomacy of Dr. Richard Baylie (q.v.) brought the warring parties together again, at which point Laud once more exerted his charm at the dinner table, *Diary* 1634.1635. fols.34v.–35.

LAUDERDALE, John Maitland, 2nd E. of (1616–1682). G.E.C.; *D.N.B.* Coarse and capable, he was a Commissioner for the Solemn League and Covenant, and attended the Assembly of Divines at Westminster. As one of the Scottish Commissioners, he attended the peace negotiations in Oxford, 1644, and at Uxbridge in 1645, when Whitelocke, too, was a Commissioner from Parliament. He was styled Lord Maitland by White-locke before the year 1645, when he succeeded to the title. When the attempt to impose Presbyterianism on England failed Lauderdale, like many of his fellow Scots, transferred his allegiance to Charles I; he supported the Engagement in 1647 (the treaty between the King and the Scots, which led to the Second Civil War) and, after the King's execution, he joined Charles II. Like the Earl of Leven (q.v.), he was captured at the battle of Worcester in 1651, was imprisoned in the Tower and later, on Portland and at Windsor. After Lauderdale was excluded from Cromwell's Act of Grace in 1654, Charles X of Sweden (q.v.) appealed on his behalf to Cromwell, while General Douglas (q.v.), a kinsman of Lauderdale's, appealed for him to Whitelocke, who claims to have prevailed with the Protector, *Diary* 4, 7 Apr. 1655. This can only have amounted to improving the Earl's conditions in prison, for Lauderdale was not released until shortly before the Restoration, ib. 3 Mar. 1659/60. The Earl was appointed Secretary of State for Scotland in 1661. He was created Duke of Lauderdale in 1672.

LAUNE (LAWNE), Abraham de. *D.N.B.* (entry for his father). Son of Dr. Gideon de Laune (*c.*1565–1659), the famous and wealthy apothecary to King James I and Anne of Denmark, who devoted himself to practising as an apothecary rather than as a doctor, see W.S.C. Copeman *Worshipful Society of Apothecaries of London* (Pergamon Press. 1967), *passim*; *A.B.B.*; W. Munk *Roll of the Royal College of Physicians.* The doctor, son of a French refugee, acquired property in Roxton, north-east of Bedford, the Manor of Sharsted, in Kent, a mansion in Blackfriars, London, and large estates in Virginia and Bermuda. Colonel William Willoughby (q.v.)

proposed a match between Mr. de Laune (who was to be the heir to a great estate from his father, the rich apothecary) and Whitelocke's daughter Frances (q.v.). She, however, did not like the young man so the treaty was broken off, causing offence to her uncle, Colonel Willoughby, *Diary* 27 Oct. 1651. Instead, Abraham de Laune married Anne, daughter of Sir Richard Sandys of Kent. Years later he consulted Whitelocke about house insurance, some time after the Fire of London, and on other matters, paying fees of £1 or £2 each time, ib. 30 Nov.; 4, 17, 28 Dec. 1669; 18 Jan., 24 Feb. 1669/70; 10 May 1670.

LAWES, Henry (1596–1662). *D.N.B.* A musician. Brother of William Lawes (d. 1645), with whom Whitelocke collaborated over music for the Royal Masque, 'The Triumph of Peace', in February 1633/34. Henry invited Whitelocke to a music meeting, *Diary* 16 Nov. 1655.

LAWRENCE, Col. Henry, MP (1600–1664). *D.N.B.* Elected MP for Westmorland in January 1645/46, he sat for Hertfordshire in 1653, served on the Council of State and became its Chairman. In January 1653/54 he was given the title of Lord President of the Council, under the Protectorate. Whitelocke's references to him occur mainly in 1653 and 1654, in connection with the Swedish Embassy.

LAWSON, Vice-Admiral Sir John (d. 1665). *D.N.B.*; B.S. Capp *Fifth Monarchy Men*; G. Davies *Restoration*. An Anabaptist and a commonwealthman. His declaration, supported by a number of Officers of the Fleet, helped to bring about the restoration (on 26 December 1659) of the Parliament which had been interrupted, by the Army, on 13 October. Lawson was thanked by Parliament for this service. The first entry for the Vice-Admiral concerns this declaration, *Diary* 17 Dec. 1659; Lawson and his Officers made overtures to Monck, ib. 28 Jan. 1659/60. Whitelocke subsequently drafted a letter begging Lawson to speak on his behalf to George Monck (later Duke of Albemarle, q.v.), and to Speaker Lenthall (q.v.), Feb. 1659/60, Long. W.P. xix, 126: this letter is not mentioned in *The Diary* and a fair copy may or may not have been sent.

LECHMORE (LECHMERE), Nicholas, MP (1613–c.1701). *D.N.B.*; E. Foss *Judges of England*; R. Somerville *Duchy of Lancaster Office Holders* p. 22. Of the Middle Temple. Appointed Attorney-General of the Duchy of Lancaster, in succession to Bartholomew Hall (q.v.), perhaps in 1654 (the date shown in the *D.N.B.*, but queried by Sir Robert Somerville, above). He was reappointed in December 1658 and again in March 1660. Lechmore only appears in *Diary* 10 Jan., 14 Mar. 1659/60. After Whitelocke's lifetime, Lechmore was both knighted and appointed a Baron of the Exchequer, in 1689.

LEE, Thomas, MP (1635–1691). *Hist. of Parl.* Of Hartwell Manor, Bucks. His father was Thomas Lee (d. 1643); his mother, Elizabeth (the second wife of Thomas Lee sen.), was a daughter of Whitelocke's great-uncle, Sir George Croke (q.v.), and on this account Lee is referred to as Whitelocke's kinsman. After she was widowed, Elizabeth Lee married the regicide, Richard Ingoldsby (q.v.). Lee was involved in the Aylesbury parliamentary election, *Diary* 21, 24 Dec. 1658, and was himself an active MP, sitting for Aylesbury or for Buckinghamshire, in seven Parliaments after the Restoration. He and Ingoldsby, his stepfather, were among those who tried to persuade Whitelocke to go to the King with the Great Seal, ib. 23 Dec. 1659. His busy parliamentary career began in 1660, after which he never appears in *The Diary*.

LEICESTER (LEYCESTER), Robert Sydney, 2nd E. of (1595–1677). G.E.C. An MP in 1614 and in the 1620s; he succeeded to the title in 1626. After serving as Ambassador to Denmark, Holstein and Paris, between 1632 and 1641, he transferred his allegiance from the King to Parliament, *Diary* 17 Apr. 1645. For his son see LISLE, Philip Sydney, styled Viscount.

LENNOX (LENOX), Mary, Duchess of, see RICHMOND, James Stuart, 4th D. of. Whitelocke referred to Mary, daughter of the 1st Duke of Buckingham, as 'Duchess of Lenox', both in *Diary* 19 Aug. 1656, when she was heavily in debt and wished to sell her estate, and on 25 Nov. 1663 when, as Dowager Duchess, she sought his advice. Esmé, the 5th Duke of Lennox died, aged ten, and Charles, the 6th Duke, was not married in 1663, so it appears that the Duchess of Lennox referred to that year in *The Diary* must have been Mary, the Dowager.

LENNOX (LENOX), James Stuart, 4th D. of, see 1st D. of Richmond.

LENTHALL, William MP (1591–1662). *D.N.B.*; M.F.K. Of Lincoln's Inn. A wealthy lawyer, earning some £2,500 a year, before his election to the Long Parliament, as MP for Woodstock. When Parliament assembled on 13 November 1640, he was elected Speaker of the House of Commons, and was re-elected in most subsequent Parliaments, up to and including that of 26 December 1659. His name was included, at the Restoration, among those in the Second Exception to the Act of Indemnity; he was saved from imprisonment by George Monck, godfather of his son, *Diary* 14 Mar. 1659/60; his son, John Lenthall, was knighted both by Cromwell and by Charles II, *D.N.B.* (in William Lenthall's entry). Lenthall's brother, Colonel Sir John Lenthall, was Keeper of the King's Bench prison, at Royston, and had a reputation for corruption, ib. (same entry); he is referred to by Whitelocke, *Diary* 4 Feb. 1659/60. A letter from John Lenthall, probably the Speaker's brother, not his son, warmly recommends Lord Bridgewater's former coachman, ' . . . I have known him longe . . . ' to accompany Whitelocke to Sweden, 22 Sept. 1653, Long. W.P. xiii, 221; Whitelocke, however, took his own coachman, Edward Ellis (q.v.). Earlier, a warrant signed by the Speaker, William Lenthall, permitted Whitelocke to pass from London to Uxbridge and back to London, with two servants and three horses, 16 May 1643, Long. W.P. ix, 4. A curious letter from John Cole (or Cote?) is addressed to Whitelocke's secretary, Daniel Earle (q.v.):

> at Mr Whitlocks Chamber in the Middle Temple. I was commanded by the Speaker [Lenthall] to returne his fee w[hi]^{ch} y[ou] sent for Mr Whitlocks Ordnance, being 5^l, and my fee (being 10^s) cannot be received fro[m] him to whome I owe farr more then I can ever requite; I have herew[i]th returned 5^l 10^s by this bearer, w[hi]^{ch} I pray you pas one [i.e. pass on] to Mr Whitlock . . . 14 Jan. 1646/47.
>
> Ib. ix, 116.

Five letters from Lenthall to Whitelocke have been traced. They are scrawled and poorly constructed. The first was addressed to Whitelocke in Sweden, shortly after Cromwell took power as Protector:

> My Lord
> I have not left any meanes attempted to finde an opportunity to kisse your handes [before Whitelocke sailed for Sweden], & to give you a very stronge assurance that you have not left any one heere that honors you more or wishes from his hart more happinesse & safety to you: But the journey beinge soe Longe & the time of the yeare soe unseasonable for thes parte . . . I was inforced to stay for a publicke, when I was prevented any privat way of Conveiance.
>   I had alsoe . . . a very great desyer to be the first messenger of our chainge heere, w[hi]^{ch} has binne as great as it was expected & hoped for by every one.

My Lord Generall beinge sworne & p[ro]claimed in a very Solempne Manner our Lord protector of the three nations, w[i]th as much aplause of the people as I thincke hath binne knowne, I was (I confesse) doughtfull of all other Govermente but heerin I cannot but beleeve as I desyer, that it wilbe the occasio[n] of much happinesse & safety to all, (beinge uppo[n] the brincke in my Judgm[en]^t of Confusuo[n] & desolatio[n]) And that it will bringe as much settlem[en]^t to our Lawes & Libertyes & to every p[ar]ticular person, as I am Certaine the publicke wilbe advantaged by it. Tis time to intreat your Lordsh[ips] pardo[n] for this trouble I have given you but I hope you will Looke on it as a testymony that expresseth me p[er]fectly.

My Lord   Your Lordsh[ips] most humble &
faithfull Servant
W[illia]^m Lenthall

23 Dec. 1653.

Ib. xiv, 236.

Endorsed by Whitelocke 'M^r of the Rolles'. rec. 13 Jan. 1653/54.

Ten weeks later Lenthall wrote, again to Sweden, acknowledging a welcome letter from Whitelocke of 3 Feb.:

... It were to[o] great a trouble to presse you w[i]th our affaires heere, when I am aseured, you will reseeave them, by a better hand ... in respect that good newes never wante feathers. I will be bould to pull a quill from that winge & p[r]^esent unto you our generall passages heere.

Our Late Gover[n]m[en]^t heere [the Protectorate] is (as far as I am able to judge) very acceptable & the Spirittes of men much revived in the expectation of a greater ease, then could be imagined when you departed from hence. Our Laws have ther freedome & countenance & property challenges her owne w[i]thout interrupt[i]o[n]. I know new changes affecte the vulgar, but I am Confident the best of Judgmente cannot censure this by any other measure. There is a strange alteration at the black fryers [a centre for dissident groups]. None appeeringe ther & in other partes. Wee can w[i]th boldnesse professe our ancient & true ways of gods worshipp. I (that when you weare heere) was perplexed & troubled w[i]th a p[ar]ty then p[r]^evalent [Barebone's Parliament] can the better judge of ther Conditio[n], that now perchance would be glad of my freendsh[ip] ...

It becomes not me, to enquier the agent for your affaires left behind you [George Cokayn, q.v.]. You may gesse by my former relatio[n] [in an untraced letter], that it will not be unseasonable to fall under your owne Consideratio[n]. [To send in his expenses?]

As [to] what concernes my selfe, I am in the statio[n] you left me [i.e. Master of the Rolls] & have the happinesse to kisse his highnesse [Oliver Cromwell's] hand & w[i]th good incorag[e]m[en]^t & receptio[n]. Pardo[n] ... this Long addresse w[hi]^{ch} tenders more affectio[n] then matter & wisdom ... The excuse must be that it comes from a true hart ...

4 Mar. 1653/54.

Ib. xv, 76, rec. 30 Mar.

A deferential autograph letter, cancelling a meeting, is in ib. xvii, 116; it is undated, but calendared as 1655. A muddled and undated letter, addressed to Whitelocke at Henley, concerns elections for Oxford City and County; Lenthall wrote that he had heard from his 'Cosen Warcopp' that Whitelocke was in 'Hendley', ib. xix, 92. A final letter, ib. 106, desired Whitelocke to attend the restored Parliament (the letter is transcribed, with Whitelocke's minor amendments which clarify the text and improve the spelling, *Diary* 27 Dec. 1659).

Three draft or copy letters from Whitelocke (when he was in hiding) to Lenthall, ask the Speaker to present an enclosed petition to Parliament and to apologize to Members for his absence, owing to illness; one draft refers to a sharp attack of stone, to fits of apoplexy and to other maladies, Long. W.P. xix, 120, 121, both of 6 Feb.; the third, ib. 120v., is dated 19 Feb. 1659/60. (After serving with the Officers on the Committee of Safety, Whitelocke was understandably afraid to show his face in the House.) There is no confirmation in *The Diary* that the letter was sent, but Whitelocke's draft or copy letters to George Monck (later Duke of Albemarle, q.v.), to Dr. Clarges (q.v.) and to Vice-Admiral Lawson (q.v.), all appealing for help with the Speaker, suggest that his letter to Lenthall and his petition were probably despatched.

LEVEN, General Alexander Leslie, 1st E. of (c.1580–1661). G.E.C.; *D.N.B.* He distinguished himself in the Swedish Army, was knighted and made Field Marshal by King Gustav Adolf in the Thirty Years War. Released from service in Sweden in 1638 (at his own request), he returned to Scotland, and, in 1639 led the Covenanters against Charles I; the King put a price on his head of £500. Leslie captured Newcastle with the Scots in 1640 yet, after the negotiations at Ripon, at the request of the Scottish Parliament, the King created him Earl of Leven as well as Lord Balgonie in 1641; Balgonie was part of the General's estate. After Parliament's appeal to the Scots for support in the Civil War, and the signing of the Solemn League and Covenant in 1643, Leven accepted appointment as Lord General of the Scottish forces, his ability in the field and experience in the Thirty Years War making him a valuable ally to Parliament. He was in command of the Scottish Army in Newcastle when Charles fled there, from Oxford, in 1646. Later, with the Scots, he changed his allegiance and supported Charles II. When he was in his seventies he was captured in Dundee in August 1651, and brought to London to be imprisoned in the Tower. His estates were sequestrated by Parliament, but by 1 October his son-in-law, Ralph de Lavall (Delavall), was permitted to take him some necessities and two days later Cromwell, recalling the veteran's earlier record, persuaded the Council to grant him freedom within the Tower, and to allow him his own servant. Shortly afterwards, de Lavall raised £20,000 as security, and Leven was allowed out on parole, to reside at his son-in-law's house at Seaton Delavale, Northumberland, north-east of Newcastle, Nov. 1651, *C.J.* vii, 36.

There are only two entries for Leven, *Diary* 28 July 1656 and 18 June 1659, but he wrote several times to Whitelocke during the same decade: in the first letter, Leven referred to the 'civill respects' shown to him by Whitelocke who, with John Lisle, received his parole. He appealed for 'Furloffe' (i.e. furlough or leave) for eight or ten weeks, to travel from Northumberland to Scotland, in order to settle his affairs in connection with a sequestration order. He apologized for troubling Whitelocke, being 'in a non-capacity to retaliate [*sic*] . . . by any reciprocal returne' apart from gratitude, 17 Mar. 1651/52, Long. W.P. xii, 61. His style of writing and his childish signature (spelt Leuen or Lewen) on letters written in another hand, confirm the suggestion quoted in the *D.N.B.* that he was hardly literate, although a likeable, humble and gifted commander.

In the next communication, Leven referred back to the above letter:

> In my first addresse I made bold to acquaint your Lo[rdshi]^{PP} with what was only intended against me in Scotland, but by this second I must relate . . . how rigorously those in power now, have acted against me, having totally sequestred my Estate both reall and personall, seizing and carrying away all my moveables and furniture out of my houses and yett threatening to forfeitt and make sale of my estate, which the good Providence of god was pleased to bestow upon me as the price of my blood. I shall once more humbly request . . . your Lo[rdshi]^{PP}, knowing your Lo[rdshi]^{PP} has beene a souldier, and is a man of Honour, to consider my condition, and to interpose your best interest [i.e. influence] in seconding my Lord Generall [Cromwell] for procuring me an order for taking of[f] my sequestration from the Parliament.
> Seaton de Lavall.
> 10 May 1652.
>
> Long. W.P. xii, 142.

The next letter, confused in construction, refers to Leven's decision to ask for a pass to travel to London: 'But upon tryall, I found a farre shorter Journey, and in a mour temperate Season, very unequall for that little strength, which my lamenesse, age & frequent infirmityes, have left me.' Instead of attempting to come and see Whitelocke himself, he was sending his 'son' (i.e. son-in-law) Mr. de Lavall, who would tell him of the Earl's sad condition, and of his petition to Parliament, 29 June 1652, ib. xii, 152, endorsed by Whitelocke 'Gen Leven Scot'. An undated note from Balgonie asked Whitelocke to help the bearer, Leven's kinsman (no doubt de Lavall) with his best advice, ib. xxii, 220. Shortly afterwards, Leven's petition was considered by the Commons, 29 Oct. 1652, *C.J.* vii, 204. In the meantime, the Swedes urged the English Parliament to help the veteran General, and after the Swedish embassy Whitelocke wrote to Erik Oxenstierna, promising to do all that a grateful mind could prompt him to do to help the Earl of Leven, 1654(?), Long. W.P. xvi, 113 (Latin).

The last communication, a petition or memorandum from the Earl, is referred to in *Diary* 18 June 1659:

> ... the late deceased Protector[,] well knowing that the s[ai]d Earle did not invade this Nation, either in the yeare 1648 or 1651, & that his estate was never adjudged confiscate; And the King of Sweden [Charles X] in considerac[i]on of the s[ai]d Earles faithfull service done by him in the warres ag[ains]ᵗ the House of Austria [the Thirty Years War], interceding w[i]ᵗʰ the late deceased Protector; he [Cromwell] was pleased to restore the s[ai]ᵈ Earle freely to his Estate againe ... Col Overton having lately presented this Parliam[en]ᵗ w[i]ᵗʰ a Petic[io]n, to be restored to his donative [£500 p.a. voted to the Colonel out of the Earl's estate by Parliament in 1652]; it is humbly prayed, that the p[ar]ticulers before menc[i]oned may be taken in to considerac[i]on, as also the s[ai]d Earles faithfull Services to this Nation in time of their greatest streights ...
>
> [The Earl asked that time might be granted for him to be heard, before Parliament determined his business.]
>
> Long. W.P. xix, 17.

Major-General Robert Overton's petition, referring back to 14 May 1652, was read on 18 June 1659, *C.J.* vii, 688; Leven's petition was read on 29 July 1659, ib. 738, after which the embarrassing case was repeatedly postponed from week to week, ib. 738, 765, 768, 771, *passim.*

LEWYS (LEWIS), [Richard], MP, JP (*c.*1627–1706). *Hist. of Parl.* MP for Westbury, Wilts. His identification is uncertain, since Whitelocke provided no first name. 'Mʳ Lewys' was a regular client between 12 November 1667 and 16 September 1674. His usual fee of £1 to £2 suggests a man of substance, compared with numerous clients who only paid 10s. Lewys sometimes consulted Whitelocke in London but more often at Chilton Lodge, on the border of Berkshire and Wiltshire. This suggests that Lewys was the MP who lived at Edington Priory, north-east of Westbury, some 35 miles from Whitelocke's house, which was almost on his route, when travelling to or from London. In January 1635/36 a Mr. William Lewys of Henley (not the Baronet, q.v.) signed a bond to Whitelocke for £20, Long. W.P. vii, 1, but there is nothing beyond the second name to connect him with Whitelocke's client 30 years later.

LEWYS (LEWIS), Robert. Lackey (or footman) in Whitelocke's retinue for Sweden, 1653–1654. He was chosen, with seven other lackeys, from the Gentlemen's Regiment of Foot, 'Journal', Long. 124A, 361v.

LEWYS (LEWIS), Sir William, Bt., MP (1598–1677). M.F.K.; *Hist. of Parl.*; P. Crawford *Denzil Holles, passim.* Of Lincoln's Inn, created Baronet in 1628; an MP before and after the Restoration. With other Presbyterians, he was friendly towards Whitelocke, and consulted him on policy decisions in the early years of the Long Parliament. He showed himself a staunch supporter of Holles and Whitelocke in the Savile affair, *Diary* 5, 7 July 1645, *passim.* He was one of the 11 MPs impeached by the Army in 1647, and was secluded at Pride's Purge, in December 1648.

LEYONBERGH (LEIJONBERGH), Jean (John) Berkman (Barkman), later Baron. *Guide to the material for Swedish Historical Research in Great Britain* (Stockholm. 1958). Swedish Agent in London in the 1650s, and secretary to Israel Lagerfeldt (q.v.). He unexpectedly joined Whitelocke and his retinue at Gravesend, when they were leaving for Sweden, '... & desired to goe w[i]th him, perhaps as a Spye ...', *Diary* 3 Nov. 1653. In spite of Whitelocke's initial suspicion, Berkman proved himself a helpful escort on the outward and return journeys, and also during the months in Uppsala. His fruitless correspondence with Parliament and the Council of State, appealing for the release of captured Swedish ships before the embassy, and his letters to Whitelocke after it, are listed in the *Guide ...* (above); many of them are to be found in the Long. W.P., Index. In one of his letters to Whitelocke he recorded, boldly, that the warlike nature of Charles X of Sweden was being encouraged by the multitude of military men surrounding him, who flattered him with the prospect of victory, even against the most powerful enemies in the world, 26 Dec. 1654, Long. W.P. xvi, 170 (French).

LIBBE (LYBBE), Richard, son of Richard Libbe. Of Hardwicke House, Oxfordshire, between Pangbourne, in Berkshire, and Henley-on-Thames. Moulsford Manor, nearby, was sold to his son Anthony Libbe in 1668, *V.C.H. Oxon*, iii, 506.

LIDENIUS, Haquinus (Håkan Bengtsson). When Whitelocke visited Göteborg (Gothenburg) in 1653, Lidenius was its Syndic, H. Almquist

Göteborgs Historia i, 390; in a later reference, Lars Broman (q.v.) is named as Syndic at that time, ib. 544, but in fact Broman had held the office from 1645 to 1650. Lidenius, as Syndic (i.e. Recorder), with the three Presidents, Lars Broman, Gerhard von Lengerk and Israel Noræus (Norfelt), called on Whitelocke who was lodging at an inn. Lidenius spoke Latin and French fluently, *Diary* 16, 17 Nov. 1653; *Journal* i, 142–143. He had visited England in 1651 and was appointed to accompany Whitelocke from Göteborg to Uppsala, where he seems to have stayed until the end of the mission, *Diary* 18 Nov. 1653; 1 May 1654. A letter from Lidenius to Prince Adolf John (q.v.) dispatched from Uppsala on 5 Jan. 1654 (new style), provides evidence that it was indeed he who accompanied Whitelocke. The letter complained of indisciplined conduct by Göteborg's garrison soldiers, under the command of one Captain Jacques, at the ceremonial departure of the Ambassador and his retinue; the soldiers had affronted the burghers by attempting to take precedence and marching over muskets which the burghers had laid on the ground, and this could have caused a serious accident. Lidenius appealed to the Prince, and to Queen Christina, to ensure that in future the burghers should enjoy precedence over the soldiers, a right granted to them from the time of the City's foundation. The letter goes on to deal with mundane civic matters concerning flour mills and salmon fisheries, Riksarkivet, Stockholm, Generalguvernörens i Västergötland arkiv, E 379. For another account of this incident see *Diary* 30 Nov. 1653, para. 3.

LIGNE, Claude Lamoral, Prince of. *Pepys* i, 237 with note; 247 with note, *passim*. The Prince was welcomed on his arrival in London, with great pomp and ceremony, when he came as Ambassador Extraordinary, bringing congratulations to Charles II from the King of Spain. A 'suspension of armes' was declared, *Diary* 17 Sept. 1660; *C.S.P. Dom.* 2 Aug.; 28 Sept. 1660.

LILBURNE, Col. Robert, MP (1613–1665). *D.N.B.* A soldier and a regicide; MP for the East Riding of Yorkshire in 1656. He was the elder brother of John Lilburne, the defiant champion of civil liberties. Colonel Lilburne served with Whitelocke on the Committee of Safety from October to December 1659, *Diary* 26 Oct. 1659. At the Restoration, he gave himself up and was tried as a regicide; the death sentence passed on him, by the High Court of Justice, was commuted to life imprisonment. Both before and after his trial he appealed to the King for clemency, retaining Whitelocke as his Counsel over the petition, ib, 13 Oct. 1660 with note. Whitelocke showed considerable courage in advising a regicide who was under threat of execution.

LILLY, William (1602–1681). *D.N.B.*; William Lilly *History of his Life and Times ... 1608 to 1681* (autobiography, ed. K.M. Briggs. Folklore Society. 1974); D. Parker *Familiar to All* (Cape. 1975); *Pepys, passim.* An astrologer and a largely self-taught physician. He prescribed physic for Whitelocke, *Diary* (Autumn) 1641 fol. 53v.; 23 Sept. 1645. Lilly's *Christian Astrology modestly treated in three Books* (1647) is dedicated to White-locke, who helped him when his predictions got him into trouble with Parliament, *Diary* 26 Oct. 1652. Lilly made a generous legacy to Whitelocke's son Carleton, ib. 27 Feb. 1662/63. After the Restoration, Carleton often accompanied his mother and father on visits to Mr. and Mrs. Lilly at Hersham. Lilly's third wife, Ruth, was a Quaker but, to Whitelocke's evident surprise, she entertained them very well, ib. 31 May 1664. If the diary entry for 12 Oct. 1658 is correct, the legacy had already been promised before Whitelocke, anticipating the Restoration, wrote to Lilly:

> My Noble Friend. The great kindnes which you have bin pleased to expresse to me & my family will be remembred by us with all thankfullnes as long as we live, you have bin pleased lately to acquaint me with your further intention of kindnes to me & mine, & it is the more att this time, when your friend is under a clowde, butt I have found your love to be to my person, & that imboldens me to make this request ... that if you shall thinke fitt to settle your land lately purchased ... uppon any of my children, in such a manner as you shall direct, that you would doe it uppon my son Carleton, an ing[e]nious boy, a younger brother [as] yett unprovided for (& as my condition is) uncertain when or how I may be able to doe for him. I only lay it before you to doe as you yourselfe shall thinke good ...
> 8 Feb. 1659/60.
>
> Long. W.P. xix, 122.

Whitelocke was evidently trying to avoid a repetition of the trouble caused when Dr. Winston (q.v.) made a legacy to one of Whitelocke's sons, for whom provision had already been made.

After about 1666 Lilly applied himself to the study of medicine, and Elias Ashmole (q.v.) persuaded Archbishop Gilbert Sheldon (q.v.) to grant Lilly a licence to practise, in October 1670. For a volume inscribed on the title page: 'This is supposed to have been Will[ia]ᵐ Lillys Own Book', see Ms Rawl. D. 145 fol. 20.

LIMREY (LIMBERY, LIMBREY), Capt. John. A Kentish sea-captain and trader, he retained Whitelocke in a case against Alderman Langham (q.v.), *Diary* 14 Oct. 1645, rewarding him with a pearl necklace worth £30, ib. 22 June 1647/48. Whitelocke looked on him as a trustworthy friend as well as '... a man of much honesty and experience in sea matters'; the Captain found a pilot for the ship in which Whitelocke sailed to Sweden, *Journal* i, 60; *Diary* 6 Oct. 1653. He was a victualling officer to the Council of State for supplying provisions to the fleet between London and Hull, *C.S.P. Dom.* 6 Aug. 1652, *passim*.

LINCOLN, Theophilus Clinton, otherwise Fiennes, 4th E. of (*c.*1600–1667). G.E.C. Of Queen's College, Cambridge, and Gray's Inn. A Parliamentarian in the Civil War. He appointed Whitelocke as his Counsel and entertained him, *Diary* 13, 17 Nov. 1645. Speaker of the House of Lords, 1 August 1647.

LINDE ('Vanderlin' in *Diary*), Erik von der (1611–1666). Grandson of a Dutch merchant named van de Linden, he studied at the University of Uppsala. He was Master of Ceremonies or *Introductor* for foreign ministers, when Whitelocke was Ambassador to Sweden, and was eager to put the Englishman in his place, as the representative of a regicidal parliament. His brother, Senator Lawrentz von der Linde (1610–1671), a member of the War Council and later a Field Marshall, also appears in *The Diary*.

LINDSEY (LYNDSEY), Robert Bertie, 1st E. of (*c.*1582–1642). G.E.C.; *D.N.B.* Son and heir of Peregrine Bertie, Lord Willoughby of Eresby, Lindsey succeeded to the Barony in 1601. He was one of three trustees to the Will of William, 4th Lord Willoughby of Parham, which was witnessed on 28 August 1622, Lincs. Archives Office 1617/ii/261. Whitelocke's second wife, a daughter of Lord Willoughby of Parham, was named as a beneficiary but, in spite of Whitelocke's protracted efforts with the trustees, Eresby (created Earl of Lindsey in 1626) appears not to have carried out his trust or his promises, 12 May 1635, Long. W.P. vi, 212v.–213; ib. vii, 306–306v.; ib. ix, 152.

As Vice-Admiral of the Fleet he was sent to the Isle of Ré and, after the murder of the 1st Duke of Buckingham (q.v.), was sent to try to relieve La Rochelle in 1628. The Commission appointing him Admiral of the Fleet to guard the narrow seas (and, annexed to it, lists of the ships under his command with their tonnage, ordnance, commanders and the number of men in each one) are in ib. vi, 215v.–225v. For the hurtful insolence shown by Prince Rupert (q.v.) towards Lindsey, the Commander-in-Chief of the King's Army, before Lindsey died from wounds received at Edgehill, see Clarendon *Great Rebellion* 365, with note, and 366.

LINDSEY (LYNDSEY), Montagu Bertie, 2nd E. of (*c.*1607–1666). G.E.C.; *D.N.B.* Son and heir of the 1st Earl (above). A Royalist, he gave himself up after Edgehill to be with his dying father. Later, he was visited in his lodgings by Whitelocke and Hollis, in November 1644, when they were parliamentary Commissioners to the King in Oxford.

LISLE (L'ISLE), John, MP (*c.*1610–1664). *D.N.B.*: M.F.K.; D. Underdown *Pride's Purge* p. 220, *passim*. Son of Sir William Lisle and Bridget, daughter of Sir John Hungerford of Down Ampney, Gloucestershire (see HUNGERFORD, Margaret, Lady, and the Lisles' interference with Whitelocke's courtship). He was admitted to the Middle Temple in 1626. Whitelocke viewed Lisle as his opponent in the Savile Affair, *Diary* 2, 5 July 1645. At the King's trial, Lisle and William Say (q.v.) sat on either side of John Bradshaw (q.v.), advising him on legal points, C.V. Wedgwood *Trial of Charles I* (Collins. 1964) p. 127. Although not technically a regicide, Lisle was very active in his opposition to the King and drew up the form of the death sentence. After the King's execution, Lisle was appointed a Commissioner of the Great Seal with Whitelocke and Richard Keble (q.v.), *Diary* 8 Feb. 1648/49.

Whitelocke and Lisle were colleagues for years, they shared a house for some time, and occasionally dined or hunted together, yet the two people for whom Whitelocke showed a positive dislike in his record are the royalist, Archbishop Gilbert Sheldon (q.v.), and the revolutionary, John Lisle. Whitelocke described his fellow-Commissioner as '... of smalle experience, butt ... very opinionative', ib. 13 Feb. 1648/49; as taking the best rooms at Syon House for himself and his wife, and also for friends whom he brought in after Whitelocke, as a favour, had agreed to his sharing the place, ib. 7 Aug. 1649. Soon afterwards Lisle's second wife, Alice (a domineering woman who may have inspired the earlier allocation of rooms) did the same, when the two families moved into the 2nd Duke of Buckingham's mansion in Chelsea. Whitelocke had lost his wife Frances in May 1649, and reluctantly agreed to share the house, ib. 20 July 1649; 1 Feb. 1649/50; when the dilapidated building had to be repaired, it fell to Whitelocke to pay the bills, ib. 24 Mar. 1650/51.

Seen through Whitelocke's eyes, Lisle appears thoughtless, pompous and insensitive. Whitelocke was increasingly troubled by his fellow-Commissioner's jealousy; this was shown when suits in Chancery were postponed by lawyers and their clients, if Whitelocke was not in Court; Lisle was apt to show 'Envy & height, and crossnes . . .' ib. 1 Dec. 1650; 5 June, 23 Oct. 1651, *passim*. Like Whitelocke, Lisle was appointed a Treasury Commissioner from 1654 to 1659. He was servile in his attitude towards Cromwell and was rewarded by being summoned (as Whitelocke was) to the Protector's House of Lords. When the Restoration was imminent he escaped to Switzerland, but was later assassinated by a Royalist in Lausanne. His widow Alice (*c.*1614–1685), see *D.N.B.*, survived him. When she was over 70, she was condemned by Judge Jeffreys to be burned alive for harbouring two men after Monmouth's insurrection, although she claimed she had not known of their involvement. On appeal to James II she was beheaded instead of being burned.

LISLE, Philip Sydney (Sidney), styled Viscount, MP, later 3rd E. of Leicester (1619–1698). G.E.C.; *D.N.B.* and M.F.K. (as Sidney). As a boy, in 1632 and again in 1636, he accompanied his father Robert Sydney, 2nd Earl of Leicester, on embassies to Denmark and France. In 1633 he was admitted to Gray's Inn. He served in the Short Parliament of April 1640, and in the Long Parliament, from 1640 to 1653, and was also appointed as Parliament's Lord-Lieutenant of Ireland and as Commander-in-Chief of the forces there, from 1646 to 1647. A Republican. After the King's execution he served on the Council of State for a year, from February 1648/49, and as Lord President of the Council from 1651/52, continuing as a member of the Council until 1659.

He had been appointed Ambassador Extraordinary to Sweden on 31 December 1652, but his instructions were not prepared until March 1653 (shortly before Cromwell dismissed the Long Parliament); at that point he declined to serve, on grounds of ill health, and later that year Whitelocke was appointed in his place. For the Council of State's Order that Henry Lawrence (q.v.) should acquaint Parliament with these facts, 12 Sept. 1653, see Long, W.P. xiii, 194. In spite of his 'ill health', Viscount Lisle was chosen to sit in Barebone's Parliament of 1653 and, despite his republican-ism, and unlike his brother, Algernon Sydney (q.v.), Viscount Lisle was prepared to collaborate with Cromwell; indeed he stood, with drawn sword, near to the chair of state at the Protector's second inauguration, *Diary* 26 June 1657; he was subsequently summoned to the Protector's House of Lords. Just before the Restoration the Lords were informed, presumably by his father, 'That the Lord Viscount Lisle conceiving that some Pictures and Statues are in his Custody which might be the late King's Majesty's, that he would keep them in Safety and be ready at his Majesty's Command, or at the Command of this House, to deliver them as he shall be directed', *L.J.* xi, 34, 19 May 1660. He was granted a pardon in October 1660, and later came to Whitelocke as a client, *Diary* 22 December 1661; 10 February 1662/63; 10 Nov. 1663; 23 Jan. 1664/65; he succeeded to the peerage, as Earl of Leicester, in 1677.

LITTLETON (LYTTLETON) of MOUNSLOW, Sir Edward, MP, later Baron (1589–1645). G.E.C.; E. Foss *Judges of England* vi; *D.N.B.* Of the Inner Temple. When his father, Sir Edward, died in 1621, Littleton succeeded him as Chief Justice of North Wales. He was active in Parliament against the 1st Duke of Buckingham (q.v.); became Recorder of London from 1631 to 1634; Solicitor-General, 1634 to 1640, and was knighted in 1635. Perhaps through John Selden, whose name follows Littleton's in the entry, Whitelocke came to know him in Parliament, *Diary* 1625.1626. fol. 7, and in Whitelocke's early years Littleton, more than anyone, encouraged and instructed him in his profession, ib. 1632.1633. fol. 18v. Littleton argued against John Hampden in the Ship Money case; he was appointed Chief Justice of Common Pleas in January 1640 and Keeper of the Great Seal, January 1641, being created Baron in the following month. He refused, however, to seal the Proclamation for the arrest of the five MPs in January 1642, and further angered the King by upholding the legality of Parliament's Militia Ordinance, *Memorials* i, 171; yet after this, he sent the Great Seal to the King, whom he then joined in York. Littleton's books and manuscripts were seized by the Commons after his death in August 1645 and were bestowed on Whitelocke, *C.J.* iv, 274, 16 Sept. 1645. Whitelocke states that he saved them from being sold, *Diary* 15, 16 Sept. 1645; the incident is more fully recorded in *Memorials* i, 513. In the previous year, the books and goods of Sir Richard Lane (q.v.) had also been given to Whitelocke by the Commons.

LITTLETON (alias Poyntz), Sir Thomas, 2nd Bt. (*c.*1621–1681). M.F.K.; *Hist. of Parl.* Of the Inner Temple. Eldest son of Sir Adam Littleton, Bt. and of Etheldreda, daughter of Thomas Poyntz, and nephew of Lord Keeper Edward Littleton (above), whose daughter Anne he married in 1637, when he was 17 and his cousin 12. An MP in 1640, he was disabled as a Royalist in 1644. He inherited the Baronetcy and his father's estate of Stoke St. Milborough, north-east of Ludlow, in 1647; there he entertained Whitelocke, six months later, *Diary* 14 Mar. 1647/48. Littleton sat as MP for several constituencies after the Restoration.

LITTON (LYTTON), Sir William, MP (1586–1660). M.F.K. Of Knebworth House, Herts. With Whitelocke and others, he was sent as one of Parliament's Commissioners to the King at Oxford, early in 1643.

LOCKHART (LOCKART), Sir William, MP (c.1620–1676). *D.N.B.*; *Thurloe S.P.*, *passim*; S.M. Lockhart *A History of the Lockharts of Lee and Carnwath* (privately published. 1976). He ran away from school at 13 or 14 and escaped to Holland. Later he entered the French Army. Returning to Scotland during the Civil War, he was knighted by Charles I after the King had surrendered to the Scottish Army, in May 1646. Lockhart left the Royalists for Parliament in 1652. His second wife, Robina (whom he married in 1654), was a niece of Oliver Cromwell's. Lockhart was appointed Ambassador to Paris in December 1655, his instructions being to maintain the uneasy alliance between France and England against Spain and, as far as possible, to prevent aid being given to the Stuarts. He took up the appointment in April 1656. Whitelocke's son James (q.v.) and servant William Swyft (q.v.), both of whom had been with him on the Swedish embassy, accompanied Lockhart on his mission. A new Treaty, offensive and defensive, was signed in March 1656/57, leading to a joint attack, in the Netherlands, on Spanish forces in the coastal towns of Gravelines, Mardyke and Dunkirk. Lockhart, in the capacity of General, beseiged Dunkirk in 1658. After its fall on 15 June, Cromwell appointed him Governor of the town. Lockhart continued serving as Ambassador to France under Richard Cromwell, rejecting approaches made to him on behalf of Charles Stuart, and attractive inducements offered by Cardinal Mazarin, in return for the surrender to France of Mardyke and Dunkirk. His governorship ended at the Restoration when he retired to Scotland, but later he was again sent on an embassy to France.

Whitelocke was kept informed of Lockhart's achievements in France in 1656 and 1657, both by the Ambassador himself and, more vividly, in letters from James and Swyft. He received a copy of Lockhart's first speech to France's 'Christian Majesty', Louis XIV, with its references (flowery even by Ambassadorial standards) to that King's '. . . illustrious perfections and most Heroick virtues', Long. W.P. xvii, 151. In a flattering and banal letter (undated), Lockhart apologized to Whitelocke for not having said goodbye, but promised to keep him posted with news from France, ib. 148. Lockhart's letter to Whitelocke of $\frac{4}{14}$ July is referred to in a note, *Diary* 26 July 1656; it mentioned two letters sent by Whitelocke which the Ambassador had not received, and reported that James Whitelocke, serving with the Army in France, had witnessed the action at the siege of Valenciennes, Long. W.P. xvii, 168. Whitelocke's cryptic endorsement in rhyme runs:

achete paix et maison faite
et tu garde de vielle dette

which seems to say:

If you buy peace or a house all set,
You'll burden yourself with a long-term debt.

James Whitelocke showed to best advantage in the Army, whether in Ireland or France. Lockhart wrote:

... as to what may concern your Lo[rdshi]ᵖᵖˢ sone[,] I may assure you his deportment hath been so oblydging and his Converse so advantage[o]us to me, that owing the satisfaction I have received in both to your goodnesse in allowing me the happinesse of his Company[,] I have just reason to esteam myself ... exceedinglie engaged ...
5 Aug. (n.s.) 1656.

Ib., 181.

In a letter of the same date, Lockhart wrote of William Swyft's disappointment at having served the State on several missions without receiving satisfaction (probably in the form of some better appointment). His faithful and diligent service prompted the Ambassador to mediate on his behalf, ib., 185. An empty letter from Lockhart, in reply to one from Whitelocke, begged him to believe that he had not 'a servant living who hath a higher value for the meanest marks of your Lo[rdshi]ᵖᵖˢ favor' than himself, 21 (o.s.), 31 (n.s.) Mar. 1656/57, ib. xviii, 31, from Paris. He sent another letter, full of profound respect but void of news, ib. 49, 18 (o.s.), 28 (n.s.) May 1657, from Boulogne.

A curious, undated memorandum among Whitelocke's papers concerns money borrowed from some English merchants by Monsieur de Cery, French Ambassador in Constantinople, between 1620 and 1624. It was still unpaid in about 1658. Part of the repayment was handed to Ambassador Lockhart, who promptly used it to pay his garrison at Dunkirk, while General Stoakes, under authority from the late Protector, seized certain ships from Marseilles in satisfaction of the balance, ib. 165–165v. For Lockhart's letter reporting the death of William Swyft (q.v.) to John Thurloe (q.v.) see Ms Rawl. A.59, fol. 250. The last letter traced, from Lockhart to Whitelocke, relates to entries in *Diary* 7 June 1658 and 2 May 1659; these concern William Swyft's widow and her pension, more than half of which was being diverted to Swyft's mother and sister. Lockhart showed great zeal in pressing Whitelocke to do the right thing by Swyft's widow, but no sign of adding anything to her pension himself, 2 (o.s.), 12 (n.s.) May 1659. Long. W.P. xix 9–9v.

For further letters about Lockhart's mission to France, see SWYFT, William, and WHITELOCKE, James.

LODER, John (d. 1701). *Hist. of Parl.* (entry for his son Thomas). Whitelocke only names 'Mr Loder' and 'Young Mr Loder', but they can be identified with confidence as John and Thomas, since John owned Welford, in Berkshire, a few miles north-east of Hungerford, and Thomas (1652–1713) was to inherit, from his mother, Balsdon Park, near Kintbury, Berkshire, a few miles south-east of Hungerford, and was elected MP for Great Bedwyn, Wiltshire, in 1685. John Loder attempted to frustrate Whitelocke's sale of Hidden, on the Chilton Park estate near Hungerford, while Samuel Whitelocke, according to his father, drank too much in the company of young Mr. Loder, *Diary* 22 Aug.; 19 Dec. 1674. After the Restoration, John Loder purchased the great house of Hinton Waldrist, in Oxfordshire.

LOE, Lawrence. Referred to as the 'chirurgeon' [i.e. surgeon], who acquired from the New Model, '... one fleabitten nag ... and one bay gelding with a bald face ...', C.H. Firth *Cromwell's Army* (Methuen, University Paperbacks. 1967), p. 243. He attended with Dr. Whistler (q.v.), when Whitelocke's daughter Frances jun. (1) was dying of smallpox, and he was sent for, years later, when Whitelocke's wife Mary was ill; he attended again, with two physicians, when Whitelocke was suffering from piles, *Diary* 9 Dec. 1654; 19 Aug. 1663; 13 Mar. 1664/65. He was also one of the three surgeons who, in 1656/57, carried out part of the autopsy on Miles Sindercombe (q.v.). More surprisingly, it was Mr. Loe who, with others, urged Whitelocke to persuade Charles Fleetwood (q.v.) that he should send someone to negotiate with the King at Breda. A month later, Mr. Loe gave Whitelocke shelter, and later still tried to find employment for Whitelocke's son Willoughby (q.v.), and subsequently for Bigley (q.v.), ib. 22 Dec. 1659; 30 Jan. 1659/60; 1 Dec. 1669; 25 May 1670.

LONG, Sir Lillibone (Lillisbone, Loveban), Kt., MP (1613–1659). *D.N.B.*; G.E. Aylmer *State's Servants* pp. 88–89. A prominent lawyer. Knighted by Cromwell in 1655. Recorder of London, a Master of Requests, and Treasurer of Lincoln's Inn. He is only referred to in *The Diary* when he was appointed Acting Speaker of the House of Commons and after his death, a few days later, *Diary* 9, 16 Mar. 1658/59, but he and Whitelocke had no doubt known each other professionally for many years, and Whitelocke describes Long as his 'kind friend'.

LONG, Sir Walter, MP (d. 1672). M.F.K. Of Whaddon, south-east of Salisbury, Wilts. A presbyterian leader of the House of Commons; with others of his group he urged Whitelocke to persuade Lord Francis Willoughby of Parham not to go as a Commissioner to the Scots Army, *Diary* 21 Dec. 1645; see also 15 Mar. 1659/60.

LOUDOUN, John Campbell, 1st E. of (1598–1663). G.E.C.; *D.N.B.* Appointed Lord Chancellor of Scotland in September 1641. Like Whitelocke, he served as a Commissioner for peace talks at Oxford and Uxbridge.

LOUIS XIII, King of France (reigned 1610–1643).

LOUIS XIV, King of France (reigned 1643–1715).

LOVE, Christopher (1618–1651). *D.N.B.* A Minister of Religion. Executed in August 1651, in connection with the plot which took his name; this involved correspondence with Charles Stuart and the Queen Mother, Henrietta Maria (q.v.).

LOVE, Nicholas, MP (1608–1682). *D.N.B.*; G.E. Aylmer 'Check-list of Central Office-holders'; B. Worden *Rump Parliament, passim.* Of Wadham College, Oxford, and Lincoln's Inn. A wealthy lawyer, he was elected MP for Winchester in November 1645. As one of the King's judges, he helped to draft the death sentence but did not sign the death warrant. From 1644 to 1660, he held the very lucrative office of a Six Clerk in Chancery.

LOVELACE of HURLEY, John, 2nd Baron (1616–1670). G.E.C.; *D.N.B.* (entry for his son, the 3rd Baron, below). Of Hurley, some five miles east of Henley-on-Thames and of Whitelocke's property, Fawley Court. A staunch Royalist. In 1638 he married Anne, third daughter of Thomas Wentworth, Earl of Cleveland (q.v.), of Toddington, Bedfordshire. Supported by Whitelocke's brother-in-law, Francis 5th Baron Willoughby of Parham (q.v.), Lovelace persuaded Whitelocke (against his better judgement) to buy Blunsdon (Blundesdon, Bloundeson, Blountesdon), in

Wiltshire; the object was to save Lovelace from his creditors, including the State, *Diary* 11 July 1652. Whitelocke's misgivings about the entail on the land were fully justified after the Restoration, ib. 15, 17, 25 Jan. 1660/61, *passim*. An attested copy of Lord Lovelace's papers relating to composition for his estate, 24 Sept. 1649, is in Long. W.P. x, 32, 34; particulars of his lands in Aldworth, Berkshire, are in ib. xi, 232, 234, 236. A schedule of deeds concerning Blunsdon shows that Lord Chandos had owned the estate in the reign of Queen Elizabeth; later it came to John, Lord Lovelace, who had use of the entailed property for life; the schedule includes an attested copy of the Act of Parliament, 20 Aug. 1651, which enabled Lovelace to sell the Manor of Blunsdon and raise money to pay the fine for his delinquency; this is followed by deeds showing the transactions between Lovelace on the one part, and Whitelocke with 'brother Willson' (Samuel Wilson, q.v.) on the other, recorded in *The Diary*; the near-compulsory purchase of the property from Whitelocke, after the Restoration, by Edward Hyde, 1st Earl of Clarendon (q.v.) also features in the deeds, one of which includes the name of Laurence (Lawrence) Hyde (q.v.), Wiltshire R.O. 47/3 fols. 1–3; *C.J.* vi, 612, 29 July 1651 and vii, 4, 20 Aug. 1651 relate to the Act enabling Lovelace to sell Blunsdon.

Surprisingly, in a royalist household, the Independent Minister, John Owen, is shown in *D.N.B.* as Chaplain at Hurley between 1640 and 1650. After the Restoration, Lovelace was appointed Lord Lieutenant of Berkshire and a Privy Councillor.

LOVELACE of HURLEY, John MP, 3rd Baron (1642–1693). G.E.C.; *Hist. of Parl.*; *D.N.B.* Son of the 2nd Baron (above). When the 2nd Baron sold the entailed Manor of Blunsdon to Whitelocke, during the Interregnum, he promised to get his son (about 10 years old at the time) to confirm the sale when he came of age, *Diary* 11 July 1652. The promise was unenforceable after the Restoration, ib. 15, 17 Jan. 1660/61; 17 Jan. 1661/62, *passim*. John Lovelace jun. was elected MP for Berkshire in 1661, retaining his seat until 25 September 1670, when he inherited the title. In the Lords, he showed sympathy towards nonconformists and became a Whig supporter. He was on friendly enough terms with Whitelocke to send him a buck from Savernake Forest, ib. 26 Aug. 1673.

LUCAS of SHENFIELD, John, 1st Baron (1606–1671). G.E.C. Of Colchester. A Royalist. Married Anne, daughter of Sir Christopher Nevill KB and granddaughter of Edward, Lord Abergavenny. He was appointed, with Whitelocke and Whitelocke's son William (q.v.), a trustee for the estate of Whitelocke's young son-in-law, George Nevill (q.v.), who was murdered at a tavern in Croydon in 1665.

LUCY, William (1594–1677). *D.N.B.* Of Trinity College, Oxford, and Lincoln's Inn, which he left on 'second thoughts' for Caius College, Cambridge. Rector of Burghclere, Hampshire, in 1619, and Chaplain to the 1st Duke of Buckingham (q.v.). He was consecrated Bishop of St. Davids on 2 December 1660, *Handbook of British Chronology* (ed. F.M. Powicke. R. Hist. S. 1961), p. 280, or on 18 November, according to the *D.N.B.*; he appears to have been a negligent and quarrelsome Bishop. He came to Whitelocke as a client, *Diary* 31 Jan. 1661/62.

LUDLOW, Col. Edmund, MP (1617–1692). *D.N.B.*; *Memoirs of Edmund Ludlow* (ed. C.H. Firth. 1894); E. Ludlow *Voyce from the Watch Tower* (ed. A.B. Worden. R. Hist. S. 1978). Of the Middle Temple. As a regicide and republican, he opposed the Protectorate. He escaped to Switzerland after the Restoration. Among his numerous entries in Whitelocke's record, Ludlow is shown: stag-hunting, *Diary* 21, 23 Aug. 1649 (a letter from Ludlow to Whitelocke about sending him a very good, dead stag, 11 Sept., probably 1649, is in Long. W.P. x, 28); he appears in his military capacity, *Diary* 12, 18 Oct. 1659, *passim*; Articles of Treason against him, seizure of his Irish Estates etc. are noted, ib. 19 Jan. 1659/60; 30 May 1660, and so is the £300 reward offered for his capture, ib. 9 Sept. 1660. Although Whitelocke does not seem to have known Ludlow well, his son James visited the regicide, who was taking refuge at Vevey in Switzerland, *Voyce from the Watchtower* (above), p. 67.

LUMLEY, Prudence. Burke *Extinct & Dormant Baronetcies* and M.F.K. (in her father's entries); A.B.B. ii, 177, *passim* (in her grandfather's entry). Her father, Sir Martin (Martyn) Lumley Bt., MP (*c.*1596–1651), of Great Bardfield (or Bardfield Magna), Essex, sat in the Long Parliament until the purge of 1648. Prudence's mother (Sir Martin's first wife), née Jane Meredith, owned property in Denbighshire; her grandfather, Sir Martin (Martyn) Lumley Kt. (d. 1634), a wealthy draper, was Lord Mayor of London from 1623 to 1624; her great grandfather, a Genoese, had settled in England during the reign of Henry VIII. In 1642, Prudence Lumley married Whitelocke's nephew, Roger Mostyn (q.v.), of Cilcain (Kilken) Hall, south-west of Flint, when Roger was 18 and (in

Whitelocke's opinion) too young to marry; her dowry of £300 was from land in Denbighshire inherited from her mother, *Diary* 15 Feb. 1641/42; this entry anticipates the marriage which was apparently celebrated in about July 1642, see Lord Mostyn & T.A. Glenn, *Mostyn of Mostyn* (1925) p. 151.

LYTTLETON. See LITTLETON, Sir Edward and Sir Thomas.

LYTTON, See LITTON, Sir William.

MACKWORTH, Col. Humphry (Humphrey) sen., MP. *Gray's Inn Admissions Register* 1521–1887, i, 164; J.E. Auden, article in *Transactions of the Shropshire Archaelogical Society*, 1910; H.T. Weyman *Members of Parliament from Shropshire Boroughs* pp. 27–28 (under Thomas Mackworth, MP for Ludlow), also Weyman *Shropshire Members of Parliament* (Memoir No. 158), both being offprints from *Transactions of the Shropshire Archaeological Society*; *D.N.B.* (in the entry for Mackworth's grandson and namesake). A lawyer and soldier; son and heir of Richard Mackworth of Betton, Shropshire. He was admitted to Gray's Inn, October 1621; became a Colonel in Parliament's Army and was appointed Governor of Shrewsbury Garrison; Weyman gives the date of appointment as 1645, but *C.J.* iv, 561 shows he was nominated on 2 June 1646; he held the office until his death. In 1645, he had been appointed both Recorder and Mayor of Shrewsbury and was also Recorder of Wenlock and Bridgnorth. He was described, understandably, as '... a lawyer in greatest practise heer ...' when he accompanied Whitelocke to Shrewsbury Castle '& there in the posture of a soldier shewed Wh[itelocke] the fortifications & stores', *Diary* 21 Aug. 1647. Confusion by several historians between Colonel Humphry Mackworth and his son Thomas, the MP, no doubt stems from errors in the index of *C.S.P. Dom.* (see A. Woolrych *Commonwealth to Protectorate* p. 380 note 72). Thomas was 19 years old at the time of the Governor's appointment – old enough to be elected MP through his father's influence, but too young to be chosen governor of a garrison. Colonel Mackworth was added to Cromwell's Council early in 1654, and was elected an MP for Shropshire in July that year. He is shown in *D.N.B.*, and elsewhere, as dying in December 1654 and his son, according to Weyman, succeeded to the Betton estate in that year; yet Colonel H. Mackworth, Governor of Shrewsbury, appears in the text (as distinct from the index) of *C.S.P. Dom.*, up to 29 April 1656, *C.S.P. Dom.* 1655–1656 p. 300.

MACKWORTH, Thomas MP (1627–1696). The same sources as for his father (above), apart from the first two. His Memoir (biographical note) is No. 162. Eldest son of Colonel Humphry Mackworth (above). MP for Ludlow from 1646, in the Long Parliament and in the Rump. MP for Shropshire in 1656 and 1659. Sheriff of the County in 1669. He was probably the Mr. Mackworth who came to Whitelocke as a client, *Diary* 12 Apr. 1662. Easily confused with Sir Thomas Mackworth, Bt., a post-Restoration MP.

MAITLAND, Lord John, see LAUDERDALE.

MALBONE, Peter (d. 1652). The Seal-bearer when Whitelocke was appointed a Commissioner of the Great Seal. He briefed Whitelocke on appointments to be made or confirmed by the Commissioners, ranging from that of Secretary, worth £500 p.a., to that of messengers attending the Commissioners, worth £53 p.a., *Memorials* ii, 285; the printed text gives the date as 17 Mar. 1647/48, but the manuscript from which it was transcribed enters it under 23 Mar., Add. Ms 37344 fol. 140.v.

MALLERY (MALORY, MALLORY), Thomas. *D.N.B.*; A.G. Matthews *Calamy Revised.* An Independent Minister, appointed Vicar of St. Nicholas, Deptford, in 1644. Later, he moved to St. Michael's, Crooked Lane, from which he was ejected in 1662, under the Act of Uniformity. Whitelocke took down a sermon of Mallery's in shorthand, when staying at the Navy House in Deptford, *Diary* 3 Aug. 1645. After the Restoration, at Chancellor Clarendon's invitation, Whitelocke took Dr. Thomas Goodwyn (q.v.) and Thomas Mallery to the Chancellor's house to discuss liberty of conscience, ib. 24 Mar. 1661/62. See also 1 Apr. 1662.

MALLET, Judge Sir Thomas, Bt. (*c.*1582–1665). E. Foss *Judges of England* vii, 143–146. Of the Middle Temple. Royalist. A King's Bench Judge in 1641. He opposed Parliament's Militia Ordinance, was seized from the Bench by a troop of Parliament's horse in 1642, and was committed to the Tower. At the Restoration, having suffered many losses for the King and although nearly 80 years old, he was reappointed a King's Bench Judge and, after sitting for three years, was awarded a baronetcy and a pension of £1,000 a year.

MANASSEH, see MENASSEH ben Israel.

MANCHESTER, Edward Mountagu (Montague), MP, 2nd E. of (1602–1671). G.E.C.; *D.N.B.*; *Pepys* x; *The Quarrel between the Earl of Manchester and Oliver Cromwell* (ed. J. Bruce and D. Masson. Camden Society. 1875). First cousin of his namesake Edward Mountagu, 1st Earl of Sandwich (q.v.). He sat as MP for Huntingdon in the 1620s; served as a parliamentary Colonel in the Civil War, and was appointed Major-General of the Associated Eastern Counties in August 1643. After the second battle of Newbury, in October 1644, he was charged in the Commons by Lieutenant-General Cromwell, his second-in-command, with military incompetence and reluctance to defeat the King. The Earl's resignation from his command was accepted, in April 1645, but his prestige remained high; he served as Speaker of the House of Lords and was appointed Joint Commissioner of the Great Seal with William Lenthall (q.v.) from 22 January 1646/47 to 17 March 1647/48; these two Commissioners handed over the Seal at the swearing-in of Whitelocke and Sir Thomas Widdrington (q.v.) to that office, *Diary* 12 Apr., 1648; *L.J.* x, 186.

Manchester worked to restore the King and, as Speaker of the House of Lords, welcomed Charles II on his return, 29 May 1660. He held the office of Lord Chamberlain from 1660 to 1671. Before a Governor's Meeting at Sutton's Hospital (i.e. Charterhouse), Manchester and the Earl of Northumberland (q.v.) took their fellow-Governors, Whitelocke and John Thurloe (q.v.), aside and warned them, privately, that Charles II had said they were not fit men to serve, *Diary* 22 Jan. 1660/61.

MANCINI (MANZINI), Lord, *C.S.P. Dom. 1658–1659*. French Agent or Ambassador. A nephew of Cardinal Mazarin. He was rewarded with a jewel after he came to England with the Duke of Créqui, in 1658, to congratulate Cromwell as '... the most invincible of Sovereigns', T. Carlyle *Letters and Speeches of Oliver Cromwell* iii, 198.

MANTON, Thomas, DD (1620–1677). *D.N.B.* A Presbyterian. Rector of St. Paul's Church, Covent Garden, 1656; he led prayers at the investiture of Cromwell as Protector, *Diary* 26 June 1657, yet he was one of the deputation to Charles II at Breda. After the Restoration he was appointed one of 12 Chaplains to the King, and was made a Doctor of Divinity at Oxford in November 1660.

MAPLET, [John], MD (c.1612–1670). *D.N.B.* Studied at Christ Church, Oxford; later, he travelled in France as tutor to the young Lucius Cary, 3rd Viscount Falkland (*D.N.B.* states that this was from about 1648 for two years, but the Viscount died in France, aged about 15, in 1649). During the Interregnum, Maplet practised as a physician in Bath and Bristol. After the Restoration he was appointed Principal of Gloucester Hall (later Worcester College), Oxford, until his retirement in 1662. Initially, he gave discouraging advice to Whitelocke's wife, Mary, when she took the waters at Bath, *Diary* 3 Sept. 1669.

MARCHE (MARSH), Charles de la. *Alumni Cantabrigienses.* Admitted to Emmanuel College, Cambridge, in 1635. Appointed as one of White-locke's two Chaplains in Sweden, with Nathaniel Ingelo (q.v.) as senior Chaplain, *Diary* 7 Oct. 1653. Whitelocke described him as '. . . a native of Guernsey, who had travayled in most parts of Christendome, he had the French naturally, the Latine most readily, he was of an extraordinary hardy Constitution, & good disposition', Add. Ms 4991A fol. 30v.; ib. 4995 appendix 5 fol. 11.

MARCHE (MARCH, MARSH), [John], (1640–1692). *D.N.B.*; *Alumni Oxonienses.* Of Newcastle-on-Tyne. He took his BA at St. Edmund Hall, Oxford, in 1661, and his MA in 1664; Vice-Principal of the Hall and a tutor there to Whitelocke's sons, Samuel (q.v.) and Carleton (q.v.), *Diary* 30 June 1668. Marche became Vicar of Embleton, Northumberland, in 1672.

MARTEN (MARTYN), Henry, MP (1602–1680). *D.N.B.*; M.F.K. A regicide. Son of Sir Henry Marten, MP (1562–c.1641). Of the Manor of Beckett, near Shrivenham, later the home of John Wildman (q.v.), whom Whitelocke visited there. Marten is only referred to briefly, in *Diary* 20 Apr. 1653 and 20 June 1660. 'Mrs Martyn', probably his wife Margaret (widow of William Staunton, a wealthy grocer), paid Whitelocke a fee of 10s., *Diary* 31 May 1670. At that date, Marten was a prisoner in Chepstow Castle.

MARY, Princess Royal of England and (Dowager) Princess of Orange (1631–1660). *D.N.B.* Eldest daughter of Charles I and Henrietta Maria; sister of Charles II (q.v.) and of James II (q.v. as York, James Duke of), whom she helped when they were in exile. For her return to England, see

Diary 23 Sept. 1660 with note; *D.N.B.* gives the date of her return as 30 September, but *Pepys* i, 234, note 4, shows that the Earl of Sandwich sailed from the Downs to fetch her on 7 September.

MASHAM [William], jun., MP (d.1655). G.E. Aylmer *State's Servants* pp. 98, 369–370. Son of Sir William Masham, Bt., MP. Father and son were both members of the Rump Parliament. Masham jun. married Elizabeth, daughter of Sir John Trevor, Kt.; their son, another William, succeeded to his grandfather's baronetcy in about 1656, *Extinct & Dormant Baronetcies*. William Masham jun. was appointed a Treasury Commissioner at the same time as Whitelocke, Widdrington, Lisle and two others, *Diary* 4 Aug. 1654; he died in the following year.

MASON, Sir Robert, MP (1626–1669). *Hist. of Parl.* Of Cannon Court, Kingsclere, Hampshire, north-west of Basingstoke. He married Katherine (Catherine or Carina), widow of Dr. John Vaux and of Thomas Hussey sen. Hussey had owned Chilton Park and Hungerford Park, near the borders of Berkshire and Wiltshire. When Whitelocke bought the Chilton Park estate he negotiated with Sir Robert for Hidden, as part of the purchase, *Diary* 29 June; 14 July 1663; Sir Robert and Lady Mason's names appear with those of other trustees on the conveyance documents for the estate, University of Reading Archives, BER. 36/5/ Nos. 19 & 20. A servant of Whitelocke's had earlier been of service to Sir Robert, *Diary* 16 Mar. 1654/55. Mason was related to Whitelocke's kinsman (by marriage) Sir Humphrey Benet (q.v.).

MASSEY, Sir Edward, MP (c.1619–c.1674). *D.N.B.*; *Hist. of Parl.* A distinguished soldier. He came to Parliament's Army from the King's and defended Gloucester against Prince Rupert (q.v.) in Jan. 1642/43; he was, however, one of the 11 MPs impeached by the Army in 1647, and was imprisoned after Pride's Purge in 1648. An adept at escaping from prison, he rejoined the Royalists, fought with them at the battle of Worcester and took an active part in conspiracies against the Government. He was elected MP in June 1646, in 1660, 1661 and in 1674.

MAURICE, Prince (1620–1652). *D.N.B.* Son of Elizabeth of Bohemia (q.v.) and of Frederick V, Elector Palatine of the Rhine. In England from 1642 to 1646. He and his elder brother, Prince Rupert (q.v.), were in

Oxford with their Uncle, Charles I (q.v.), when Parliament's Commissioners (including Whitelocke) came to negotiate propositions for peace. The 14th proposition listed more than 50 persons who were to be excepted from Parliament's pardon, starting with '*Rupert* and *Maurice* Count Palatines of *The Rhyne*', *L.J.* vii, 55, 8 Nov. 1644. The brothers were present when the 2nd Earl of Denbigh (q.v.), leader of Parliament's Commissioners, read out the list of exceptions, at which the Princes, with other Royalists, 'fell into a rude laughter', *Diary* Nov. 1644 fol. 69v. In 1652, Prince Maurice was lost at sea in the Caribbean.

MAY family (below): *Alumni Oxonienses*; *V.C.H. Sussex* iv, 104; items in the Church of St Nicholas, Lavant, north of Chichester, west Sussex (where material recovered in 1981 from the closed family vault under the Chancel, is now displayed). Richard May, a merchant taylor (d. 1582), had built the mansion of Rawmere (or Raughmere), Mid Lavant, see M.F.K. (entry for Richard May's grandson, Thomas May, MP) and *Hist. of Parl.* (entry for another grandson, Sir Algernon May, MP). The Whitelocke and May families were first brought together through the friendship of James Whitelocke sen. (q.v.) and Humphrey May (q.v.), begun when they were fellow-students at St. John's College, Oxford. This led to Whitelocke's first, unfortunate marriage: the bride chosen for him was Rebecca Benet, a niece of Sir Humphrey May (as he was by then); see also the entry for Rebecca's mother (Sir Humphrey's sister), Dorothy Benet. John May of Rawmere (*c.* 1607–1677), a younger brother of Thomas May, MP, and of Adrian (below), does not appear in *The Diary*, but he consulted Whitelocke from Hampstead, Middlesex, about the distraint of a cow he owned, for payment of a Ship Money levy of 14s.; the cow was sold for £2.10s. 0d., expenses 7s. 6d., balance (after payment of the levy), £1.8s. 6d.; May's letter, Long. W.P. vi, 280 is addressed 'To his very lovinge kinsman and much honored friende Bulstrode Whitelocke Esq'. Whitelocke endorsed it 'Cousen May'; for financial details of the distraint, 23 Aug. 1637, see ib. vii, 127.

MAY, Adrian (b. *c.* 1605). *Alumni Oxonienses*. A Royalist; grandson of Richard May and second son of John May of Rawmere, Sussex; nephew of Sir Humphrey May (q.v.). He served as Groom of the Privy Chamber to Charles I, in 1633, and later to Charles II. Whitelocke helped him over his composition for delinquency, *Diary* 18 June 1649. After the Restoration, Adrian May agreed to serve as Whitelocke's arbitrator in the dispute with Lord Lovelace (q.v.) over Blunsdon, and was accepted (although he was

Whitelocke's kinsman) because he was in the King's service, ib. 17 Jan. 1661/62; 21 June 1662.

MAY, Hugh (c.1622–1684). Information on his coffin plate, St. Nicholas Church, Lavant; *V.C.H. Berks.* iii, 33; *Hist. of Parl.* (entry for his son Richard May, MP, c.1638–1713). He took no part in the Civil War. After the Restoration he was appointed Controller of Windsor Castle and chosen, by Charles II, as 'Sole Architect' in charge of the great alterations to the Castle, a post which he held from 1673 until his death, when he was succeeded by Sir Christopher Wren. Whitelocke consulted him on architectural questions, *Diary* 10 June 1662; 19 Jan. 1666/67; Hugh May came to his kinsman as a client, ib. 6 Nov. 1663. He was buried in the family vault.

MAY, Sir Humphrey (Humfrey), Kt., MP (1573–1630). *D.N.B.*; *Alumni Oxonienses*; G.E. Aylmer *King's Servants*; R. Somerville *History of the Duchy of Lancaster*; J. Hutchinson *Notable Middle Templars* (Middle Temple. 1902); *Hist. of Parl.* (entry for his son, Sir Algernon May MP). Of Carrow Priory, Norfolk, fourth son of Richard May of Rawmere, Sussex. Judge Sir James Whitelocke records that he and Humphrey May, having been fellow-students at St. John's College, moved together from Oxford to the Middle Temple in 1592; there they shared Chambers until May went to Ireland with Lord Mountjoy, around the end of Queen Elizabeth's reign. May bought out a Scotsman to obtain a post as Groom of the Privy Chamber, an office which he later passed to a brother Hugh, see *Liber* pp. 21, 61. Knighted in 1613, he served as Chancellor of the Duchy of Lancaster, from 1618 to 1629, and as Vice-Chamberlain of the Household from 1629 until his death in the following year. He was buried in Westminster Abbey.

MAYERNE, Sir Theodor (Theodore) Turquet de. Kt., MD (1573–1655). *D.N.B.*; *Alumni Oxonienses*; W. Munk *Roll of the Royal College of Physicians*; G.E. Aylmer *King's Servants* p. 360. Son of a French protestant writer. He graduated MD at Montpellier in 1597; although abused by other French doctors for his use of chemical remedies, he became a member of the Council to the King of France for medical matters. He was brought to England in 1606, by an English peer whom he had cured in Paris, and was incorporated MD at Oxford. James I appointed him physician to his Queen, Anne of Denmark. Mayerne returned to Paris and became physician extraordinary to Louis XIII;

recalled to England, he was appointed chief physician to James I, who knighted him in 1624. He continued as royal physician on the accession of Charles I, in 1625.

When Whitelocke's wife Frances was dying, her doctors wrote consulting Sir Theodor; theirs is a very early example of a letter from GPs to a specialist, Add.Ms 37344, 293v. Whitelocke went with Dr. George Bates (q.v.) to ask Sir Theodor's advice, and the famous doctor came to see Frances 'butt it was too late', Diary 8, 15 May 1649. Mayerne lived in St. Martin's Lane before retiring to Chelsea, and was buried in the chancel of the Church of St. Martin-in-the-Fields. For his daughters Elizabeth and Adrienne, see MONTPOUILLAN.

Although the D.N.B. states that Mayerne's descendants became extinct in 1653, it seems that Adrienne survived him, marrying the Marquis of Montpouillan in 1656, and Whitelocke refers to her later, Diary 5, 7 Nov. 1657; 15 Mar. 1660/61.

MAYNARD, Sir John, MP (1604–1690). D.N.B.; M.F.K.; Hist. of Parl.; Pepys x. The date of birth in Hist. of Parl., as given above (two years later than in other sources), is taken from an entry made by Maynard's father, shown in R. Morrice 'Entering Book'. A distinguished and wealthy Middle Temple lawyer, and a staunch Presbyterian, Maynard was elected MP for 12 Parliaments between 1640 and 1689 (although after his exclusion at Pride's Purge in December 1648, he did not sit again until February 1659–60). He was appointed Protector's Serjeant, 1658–1659, and King's Serjeant after the Restoration, was knighted in November 1660, and appointed Commissioner of the Great Seal from 1689 to June 1690. Living into his 87th year, he remained active in Parliament and in his profession almost until the time of his death. A very learned lawyer, he was endowed with a dry humour. Among numerous entries he is described as one of Whitelocke's 'very hearty friends' at the time of the Savile Affair and, more generally, as his 'good friend', Diary 5 July 1645; 1 May 1658.

MAYNARD of WICKLOW, William, 2nd Baron (1623–1699). G.E.C.; Hist. of Parl. (entry for his son the Hon. Banastre Maynard, later 3rd Baron). He succeeded as 2nd Baron in 1640 and sat in the House of Lords during the Civil War, subscribing to the Covenant on 30 Sept. 1644, L.J. vii, 3. He was appointed one of Parliament's Commissioners to take peace proposals to the King at Oxford, ib, 63, 13 Nov.; Diary 20 Nov. 1644. The following year, Whitelocke was his Counsel, ib. 7 Oct., and received a gift of venison from him, ib. 30 Dec. 1645. Maynard was one of seven Lords impeached by the Commons in September 1647, but the prosecution was dropped in June 1648. He attended Charles II on the King's return to London, 29 May 1660, and was Comptroller of the Household from 1672 to 1687.

MAYNE, [Simon], MP (1612–1661). *D.N.B.* A regicide. Of Dinton Hall, Bucks. Studied at the Inner Temple. He is only referred to once, *Diary* 13 June 1660, and his name is clearly spelt 'Meyre', but in the context it is evident that the entry refers to Mayne; moreover, his wife (correctly spelt) and Colonel Robert Lilburne (q.v.) retained Whitelocke as Counsel when preparing petitions to the King, on the day of Simon Mayne's trial at the Old Bailey, ib. 13 Oct. 1660. Mayne died in the Tower the following April.

MAZARIN, Jules (MAZARINI, Giulio) (1602–1661). Italian by birth, he was naturalized a Frenchman in 1642. A Cardinal and a powerful French Minister, he succeeded Cardinal Richelieu. In 1648 he helped to negotiate the Peace of Westphalia, to end the Thirty Years War. He is referred to in connection with the capture of Dunkirk from the Spaniards, *Diary* 15, 21 June, 1658.

MEADOWE (MEADOWES), Sir Philip (1626–1718). *D.N.B.*; G.E. Aylmer *State's Servants* pp. 165, 276, 390 with notes; M. Roberts 'Cromwell and the Baltic', in *Essays in Swedish History* (ed. M. Roberts). A diplomat and protégé of John Thurloe (q.v.); he was appointed Latin Secretary in October 1653, to relieve John Milton (q.v.) of much of that work. *Diary* 30 Dec. 1655, note, refers to Meadowe's humble letter of 10 December which is in Long. W.P. xvii, 110; an entry in *Diary* 7 Feb. 1655/ 56, gives the text of a respectful, routine letter about a meeting. The next reference, ib. 4 Mar. 1655/56, contains a slip: that month Meadowe was appointed to represent the Protector at the ratification of the Anglo/ Portuguese Treaty, and he set sail on 11 March, but the entry states that he wrote to take leave of Whitelocke, being sent as Agent to the King of Denmark; in fact, he was not appointed Envoy to Frederick III of Denmark (at a salary of £1,000 a year) until February 1656/57. He wrote to Whitelocke, a Commissioner for the Treasury, for payment of that sum, ib. 3 May 1657; this entry wrongly shows him as *Sir* Philip, but not long afterwards he was awarded the Danish knighthood of the Order of the Elephant. He was also knighted by Cromwell, in the Spring of 1658. He sailed for Elsinore in August 1657 and was received in Copenhagen, with

considerable ceremony, on about 20 September 1657. The following
March he gave Thurloe an account of the Treaty of Roskilde between
Frederick III of Denmark and Charles X of Sweden (q.v.). Not long
afterwards, however, he was present when the Swedish King attacked
Copenhagen. On 28 August 1659, deeply embarrassed by developments,
Meadowe wrote to Whitelocke from Elsinore:

> My Lord
> I have wrot several Letters to the Council of State humbly supplicating their
> leave to return for England, which I have done upon considerations
> importing me as much as anything that is desirable in this world. To make a
> deduction of al particular reasons would be too great an impertinency to
> trouble your L[o]r^d[shi]^P with[,] amid the multiplicity of so many weighty
> affaires. [Whitelocke, as Lord President of the Council, had been dealing
> with Sir George Booth's rising.] I therfore only crave leave to make this
> humble address ..., emboldned by your former goodness & my present
> extremities, beseeching you either to move the Council or the parlement as
> you shal judg most expeditious & effectual to send me forthwith their
> positive order or permission to return for England. When if it please God I
> arrive I shal alwaies be ready to testify my most thankful resentment [i.e.
> appreciation] of so seasonable a favour ...
>   Ph[ilip] Meadowe.
>   Long. W.P. xix, 76.

MEARE (MEARES), Lewes (Lewis). A tenant on Whitelocke's land in
Ireland. He wrote a letter two months before Whitelocke's death, *Diary*
21 May 1675. (The entry spells the name 'Meares' but the signature is
'Meare'). Another letter from Meare about his rent, and apparently
offering to buy land from Whitelocke with a sitting tenant, in the Barony of
Rathconrath, County Westmeath, is in Long. W.P. Parcel 1, No.7, 1 Jan.
1671/72. For further papers concerning this land and Whitelocke's land in
Kildare, see: ib. No.40, 28 Apr. 1965; No. 6, 8 Feb. 1656/57; No.18, 21
Sept. 1672; Parcel 4, No.27, 15 Mar. 1670 and Parcel 5 (papers unnumbered),
6 Oct. 1672. Whitelocke's title to the lands was confirmed in 1669 by
Charles II, copy in Cambridge University Library, Mm. 6.57 fols. 92–94.
His speech, years earlier, on Adventurers in Ireland, 17 Feb. 1641/42, is
printed in Thomason Tracts E.200 (30).

MELLER (MILLER), Sir John, Kt. (1588–1650). J. Hutchins *History of
Dorset* (Westminster. 1863) ii, 186 *passim*. Son of Sir Robert Meller, Kt.
(1564–1624). Of Little Bredy (Little-Bridy) south-west of Dorchester. In
1611, he married Mary, daughter of Sir John Swynerton (Swynnerton or

Swinnerton), Kt., MP (*c.* 1566–1616), a wealthy Alderman and Lord
Mayor of London from 1612 to 1616, see G.E. Cokayne *Lord Mayors and
Sheriffs of the City of London* (London. 1897). Meller was knighted in
1625, and became Sheriff of Dorset in 1630. His stepmother, Margaret,
was a sister of Sir Thomas Freake MP (q.v.), whose eldest son, John
Freake MP (q.v.), was well disposed both towards Meller, his kinsman,
and towards Whitelocke; he helped the latter to negotiate the purchase of
the moiety of the Manor of Phyllis Court, Henley-on-Thames, from
Meller, Add.Ms 37343 fol. 139v.; *Diary* 1635.1636. fol. 41. Papers
concerning these negotiations include: proposals to be made to Sir John
Meller with details of yearly values, two drafts, May 1637, Long. W.P. vii,
120, 121; an estimated annual value, listing rents and showing the moiety
of the rents at 12 years' purchase, also referring to Henley Park's lawns and
400 acres of woodland, at 18 years' purchase, plus a leased cottage, shown
together as totalling £7,168.16s. od. (although Whitelocke's figures do not
appear to add up to this sum); an undated note at the foot of the page, in
Whitelocke's hand, adds: 'Henley parke as it is now [after damage in the
Civil War?] is worth butt 16 years purchase the leas[e] is worth butt 5 years
purchase the conversion is worth 13 years purchase', ib. 251. Whitelocke's
initial offer to Meller, and related papers are in ib. 252, 253, 255, 257
passim. There are notes on deeds relating to the property when it was in
the hands of Sir William Alford, ib. 310 (Whitelocke's father bought a
moiety of the Phyllis Court lands from Alford for £1,200 in 1622, six years
after buying the adjoining property of Fawley Court from him, *Liber* p.94,
passim).

An abstract of title shows how Phyllis Court came into the hands of the
Meller family of Dorset: early in the 17th century, Alderman William
Masham of London and his son William, had an interest in the property,
which the son assigned to Sir John Meller's father-in-law, Sir John
Swynerton, in consideration of £2,100; Swynerton in turn assigned his
interest to Sir Robert Meller, in consideration of £3,200. Later, the
property (which was presumably part of a marriage settlement) was held in
trust by Sir Thomas Freake and Henry Swynerton, Long. W.P. vii, 249–
250. After Meller's sale to Whitelocke had been agreed, for the sum of
£8,050, several instalments are listed in the 'Annales', and among them is a
curious note on the method of storing a large sum of cash: a receipt from
Thomas Bower, servant to Meller, states that '... threethosand and
threehundred pounds, was all rec by me, & sealed up in several bagges, &
putt into a cheste in the chamber of Bulstrode Whitelocke in the middle
Temple, & the said cheste or tronke was locked up by me, & the key therof
kept by me ...' Below this, a receipt signed by Sir John Meller refers to
part-payment of £8,050 'agreed for Phillis C[ou]rt & Henley Park' with

Bartholomew Hall, Richard Solme and Ralphe Freake, 12 Nov. 1638, Add. Ms 37343 fol. 163; *Diary* 1638.1639. fol.46v.

MENASSEH (MANASSEH) ben Israel. *C.S.P. Dom.* 1655–1656, indexed under Jews, *passim*; T. Carlyle *Letters and Speeches of Oliver Cromwell* ii, 481, 482 n.1. Menasseh is variously described as a physician and as a scholarly Portuguese Jew from Amsterdam. From there he wrote, in Latin, to congratulate Parliament and the Council of State of the Republic of England on their victory (at Worcester), Long. W.P. xi, 59. 29 Sept. 1651. A few years later, he put the case to the Protector and his Council for legalizing the return of the Jews, who had been expelled from England in 1290 during the reign of Edward I. He made 7 requests, namely that: (1) Jews be accepted as citizens and, as such, should receive protection; (2) they be allowed to exercise their religion and attend public synagogues; (3) they be given their own cemetery, out of town; (4) they be allowed to trade freely in all kinds of merchandize; (5) a person of quality be elected to receive their passports, before whom they would swear an oath of fidelity; (6) the chief of the synagogue, with two almoners, be licensed to settle disputes under Mosaic law, with a right of appeal to the civil law; and (7) all laws against the Jewish nation be repealed, *C.S.P. Dom.* 1655.1656, p.15, 13 Nov. 1655 (original in French, with a translation). Cromwell, who presided at the meetings, favoured Menasseh's proposals. The Council, however, nourished a devout antipathy towards any concession towards the Jews, arguing that: (1) Menasseh's recent book on the subject was sinful in a Christian nation; (2) there was a great danger that people of this nation might be seduced in matters of religion; (3) Jewish practices in marriage and divorce would set a bad example; (4) oaths made or injuries done to Christians did not trouble the Jewish conscience; and (5) (predictably) the inhabitants of London suggested that the return of the Jews would be very injurious to trade. Their proposal was, therefore, that: Jews should continue to be treated as strangers; should not be permitted to hold public office; should not be allowed to dishonour the Christian faith nor to employ Christian servants; they must not discourage attempts to convert them; there would, on the other hand, be severe penalties for any apostatizing to the Jewish faith, ib. pp.15–16. Despite Cromwell's failure to win over the anti-Semites, he granted Menasseh a pension of £100 a year, to be paid quarterly, starting on 20 Feb. 1656/57. In the following year, application was made to Whitelocke, as a Commissioner of the Treasury, to pay the £100 to Menasseh, 'the Jewish Rabbi', *Diary* 24 Mar. 1657/58. Further information on this very learned man is given in D.S. Katz *Philo-Semitism and the readmission of the Jews to England 1603–1655*

(O.U.P. 1982), also by D.S. Katz, in an article 'Menassah ben Israel's Mission to Queen Christina of Sweden, 1651–1655', *Jewish Social Studies* (Winter 1983), pp. 57–72.

MESSENGER, [Ralph] (d.1668). Mayor of Henley-on-Thames in 1652 and 1663. Named by Whitelocke, in his written defence of himself after the Restoration, as a witness to the great damage done to his [Whitelocke's] property at Fawley during the Civil War, *Diary* 2 June 1660; there are several other entries concerning Messenger, after that date.

MEYRICKE (MEYRICK), Sir John (d.1659). *D.N.B.* A Presbyterian. He served as a General under Essex. Whitelocke referred to Meyricke as his 'familiar friend', *Diary* 1642, but declined to be influenced in Meyricke's favour and that of his wife Jane, in a Chancery case, saying he would 'doe them right impartially', ib. 18 Feb. 1648/49. They do not appear in *The Diary* after that date. Whitelocke gave a similar rebuff to Cromwell, see entry for CROMWELL, Anne.

MIDDLESEX, Hon. James Cranfield, MP, later 2nd E. of (1621–1651). G.E.C. Of Copt Hall (or Copped Hall), south-west of Epping, *V.C.H. Essex* v, 121–122, *passim*. Immediately after Cranfield succeeded to the Earldom (indeed, on the day of his father's funeral) Whitelocke became his legal adviser, *Diary* 14 Aug. 1645. The Earl supported Parliament but opposed the Army and was imprisoned in 1647. In the following year, however, he was appointed as one of the Commissioners to negotiate with Charles I at Newport, Isle of Wight.

MIDDLESEX, Lionel Cranfield, 3rd E. of (c.1625–1674). G.E.C. Brother of the 2nd Earl (above). Imprisoned in 1659. He was one of the six Peers sent to Charles II in 1660, inviting him to return to England. After the Restoration he entertained the King at Copt Hall, *Diary* 29 June 1660. He was appointed a Gentleman of the Bedchamber in 1673.

MILDMAY, Sir Henry Kt., MP (d.c.1664). *D.N.B.*; M.F.K. He was already in the service of James I when he was knighted in 1617. Master of the King's jewel house in 1620. He was no doubt known to Whitelocke in the Long Parliament, in which Mildmay voted against the Bill of Attainder of the Earl of Strafford. Later, he left Charles I for Parliament and was one of the King's judges; after the King's execution, he was granted £2,000 by Parliament, in July 1649, in repayment (with interest) of a sum he had lent to the King. Six months after that he appears for the first time in *The Diary* when Whitelocke, who was courting Lady Hungerford (q.v.) appealed to Sir Henry and his wife Anne (Lady Hungerford's sister), to help him in his suit. They promised to do so but, 'gaping for her Estate', did the opposite, *Diary* 16 Jan. 1649/50. Sir Henry served as Master of Ceremonies to foreign Ambassadors and Whitelocke refers to this, ib. 24 June 1659. When required, after the Restoration, to say what had become of the King's crowns, jewels etc. which had been in his care, he tried to leave the country but was captured. He was sentenced by the House of Commons to life imprisonment, *C.J.* viii, 26, 37–38, 60, 66, 285–286. In March 1664 it was ordered that he be transported to Tangier but he died in Antwerp, on the first lap of the journey.

MILTON, John (1608–1674). C. Hill *Milton and the English Revolution* (Faber and Faber. 1977); *Life Records of John Milton* (ed. J. Milton French. Rutgens University, New Brunswick, New Jersey. 1954); *D.N.B.* The great republican poet appears in *The Diary* in connection with his work in the Civil Service as Latin Secretary, to which he was appointed in 1649, serving under the Commonwealth and Protectorate: the Swedish Ambassador complained to Whitelocke of the delay caused when articles were sent 'to one Mr Milton a blind man' to be translated; Whitelocke explained that the other Secretaries were out of town, *Diary* 6 May 1656. Later entries concern the burning of three books by the common hangman, at the Old Bailey, after the Restoration: Milton's *Defence of the People of England* and *Eikonoklastes*, with John Goodwin's *Obstructours of Justice;* see *Diary* 16 June 1660, *passim*; the Order to destroy the books may be found in *C.J.* viii, 66, same date. An official letter from Milton to Whitelocke, concerning the Count of Oldenburgh, 12 Feb. 1651/52, Long. W.P. xii, 41, has been reproduced in *Publications of the Modern Language Association of America* XLIX, No. 4, in an article by J. Milton French.

MINNES (MENNES, MYNNES), Sir Matthew (d. 1648). Of Bedfordshire. His brother, Admiral Sir John Mennes (*D.N.B.*), inherited his lands, but they were forfeited the same year because Sir John was in arms against Parliament. When Sir Matthew was dying, it was suggested that his daughter should marry Whitelocke's son James, *Diary* 10 May, 1648, but nothing came of this.

MINNES, Capt. Christopher, see MYNGS.

MISSELDEN (MISEELDEN, MISSENDEN), Samuel. Son of Edward Misselden. Edward, though he does not appear in *The Diary*, wrote a long letter to Whitelocke about Parliament's activities as they affected the Merchant Adventurers:

> ... the strength, Riches, & plenty of the Kingdome, depend on Trade: but more specially on the Cloth-trade: w[hi]^{ch}[,] as the life-bloud, beats strong thro' all the veines of the Body of this Kingdome ... The good effects whereof, sore [i.e. soar] up to the King, & dilate themselves to all degrees of men ...

Trade, he wrote, affected amity with foreign Princes and the nation's standing abroad; it increased customs and advanced navigation, led to improvement of land and the employment of millions of poor people. A list of grievances followed, largely focussed on financial hardships suffered by English traders in comparison with their overseas competitors, also on problems with the Netherlands and Colonies and loss of privileges overseas. The letter ended 'yo[u]^r true friend & Servant Edw[ard] Misselden', 22 June 1642. Long. W.P. viii, 233–233v.

His son Samuel became Secretary to the Merchant Adventurers in Hamburg; when Whitelocke was in Lübeck, on the journey home from Sweden, Misselden jun. brought him a packet of three weeks' letters from England, *Diary* 7 June 1654; with it was a letter of introduction from his father in Bruges, in which Misselden sen. wrote:

> ... because none of the Company there [in Hamburg], I think, knowes yo[u]^r Hono[u]^r better then I, I have writ to the Resident there [Richard Bradshaw q.v.] my ... advice in order to y[ou]^r reception: And [of] the hono[u]^r you did the Company [ie. the Merchant Adventurers], when you were in the Chair of that Com[m]ittee, of Parl[iamen]^t for Trade.

He added that he would leave discussion of other matters, domestic and foreign, to his son, including the question of factions within the Company at Hamburg. He hoped that Whitelocke, in his 'wise & winning way', would bring peace to the Company and give encouragement to the Resident, 2 June 1654, Long W.P. xv, 188. The internal feud is described in the entry for Richard Bradshaw.

MONALDESCHI (MONALDESCO), Giovanni (Gian) Rinaldo, Marchese di (d.1657). Father Le Bel's detailed account of Monaldeschi's death, Sloane Ms 3813 fols. 7–18v., (French); related papers: Add.Ms 16483 fol. 214, Nov. 1658 (Italian) and Harley Ms 3493 fols. 8–15; C. Weibull *Monaldescos död* (Göteborg. 1937); *Catalogue, Christina Exhibition* (1968), Nos. 671–673, *passim*; see also the entry for PASSERINI. Monaldeschi, an Italian courtier, supported French attempts to liberate the kingdom of Naples from Spain, in 1648 and 1654. After her abdication, Queen Christina of Sweden (q.v.) conceived an ambition to conquer Naples herself, with French support, and to assume that crown for life, after which the kingdom would come under French suzerainty. Her agreement on this with Cardinal Mazarin (q.v.), was signed at Compiègne on 22 September 1656, *Catalogue, Christina Exhibition*, No. 666. After her conversion, and when she was first in Rome, Christina appointed Monaldeschi as her Equerry, and as a member of her household, he accompanied her to France, where she was loaned the magnificent Château of Fontainebleau, by the young King Louis XIV. The report of Monaldeschi's execution – or assassination – in the Château scandalized Europe. It is summarized below in some detail because: (1) the events have too often been reworked from secondary sources; (2) many accounts are elaborated or compressed to a degree which distorts the facts; (3) the Priest's eye-witness account illustrates an aspect of Christina's character – the savagery of an otherwise civilized woman, resulting from her invincible conviction of being right.

At 9.15 a.m., on Tuesday 6 November 1657, Christina sent a footman to summon Father Le Bel (Lebel), Superior of the Religious Community of the Château. After describing the Queen's preliminary remarks to him, Le Bel wrote: 'She made me promise, under the seal of the confessional, to keep and hold secret what she was going to entrust to me.' He replied that he was deaf, dumb and blind in small matters, and even more so in regard to a Sovereign's confidences. Christina then handed him a small packet of papers, sealed in three places, with nothing written on the outside. She made him promise to return it to her in the presence of such witnesses as she might decide. She further required him to take careful note of the hour, the date and the place in which she had given him the packet. Le Bel repeated his promise, bowed to Christina and was back in the Community by 10 a.m.

Four days later, on Saturday 10 November, he was again summoned, this time at 1 p.m., and was escorted to the *galerie des cerfs*, where Christina was talking to a man – the Marquis of Monaldeschi. Three other men were present. They were: Francesco Santinelli (not named by the Priest), who was Marshall of Christina's Court and reputed to be Monaldeschi's enemy, and two men-at-arms. The Queen asked Le Bel for the package, which she then handed to Monaldeschi. It contained copies, made by the Queen, of letters written by the Marquis, which had been intercepted. She asked whether he recognized them. Trembling, he said he did not. Christina then produced the originals, bearing his signature and seal, which he could not disown. After trying to blame other people, he threw himself at Christina's feet, asking for pardon. Santinelli and the two soldiers drew their swords. Getting up, Monaldeschi drew Christina first into one corner of the very long, narrow gallery then into another, begging her to listen to him. This she did, showing great patience and no sign of anger. The Priest noted tiny, irrelevant details as, for example, that the young Queen was leaning on a little ebony stick with a round handle, when she told him to witness that she did nothing to hurry the man in his attempt to make a defence; or again that when (at the Queen's insistence) the Marquis handed her some papers with two or three little keys tied together, pulling them out of his pocket he dropped two or three small coins on the floor.

After conferring for two full hours, Christina approached Le Bel, saying 'Father, I am going to withdraw and leave this man with you. Prepare him for death and attend to his soul.' The Marquis flung himself at her feet, as did Father Le Bel, who begged forgiveness for the poor man. Christina, however, replied that this traitor was the more guilty in that she had trusted him as her faithful subject, and had confided many of her private affairs, her thoughts and secrets to him; that she did not reproach him with the favours she had conferred on him, which exceeded those she might have bestowed on a beloved brother, which was indeed how she had always thought of him. With that, she left the gallery. The three men, their drawn swords pointing towards the Marquis, urged him to make his confession, as did Father Le Bel, who was by this time in tears. Santinelli was moved to pity and went after the Queen, but returned sadly. He had been ordered to despatch Monaldeschi. He too was in tears as he said: 'Marquis, think of God and of your soul. You must die.' On his knees, the distraught victim urged the Priest to go to the Queen, which he did. He found Christina alone in her room, her face as serene as if there were nothing wrong. Sobbing, he begged her, by the agony and wounds of Christ, to have pity on the Marquis. She told him she was sorry that she could not grant his request. She had sent many people to be broken on the wheel for lesser treachery. Le Bel tried again, pointing out that she was the King's guest and should consider carefully what she was planning to do and whether the King would approve. Christina replied that the King was not housing her as a prisoner or a refugee; that she was free to exercise justice over her own subjects at all times and in all places (this had been agreed in the terms of her abdication); that she was only answerable for her actions to God, and that what she was doing was not without precedent. The Priest pointed out that if some Kings had indeed taken similar action, it had been in their own domains. Fearing, suddenly, that he had gone too far, he spoke of the respect in which Christina was held in France and of the good that her negotiations could bring to the whole of Europe; he appealed to her to avoid a deed which was, from her point of view, a judicial punishment, but which might seem to others a hasty and violent action. The Queen rejected his suggestions. She would explain her actions to the King and to Cardinal Mazarin, but she could not grant the Priest's request. He noted a weaker tone in her voice, and knew that if she could have done so, she would have changed the course of events.

Returning to the gallery, Le Bel told the Marquis that there was no hope for him in this world; he sat on one of the seats and heard Monaldeschi's confession, which the Marquis made partly in Latin, partly in French and the rest in Italian; but before Monaldeschi received absolution, the Queen's Chaplain came in and the condemned man went over to him, expecting a pardon. They spoke together for quite a long time, in low tones, clasping each other's hands. Eventually, Santinelli and the Chaplain withdrew. When Santinelli returned he told the Marquis he must die; he then struck at the right of the victim's stomach, with his sword. Monaldeschi grabbed the sword in his right hand and three of his fingers were cut off, but the sword did not penetrate his body, for he was wearing a coat of mail-armour (under his tunic) weighing at least nine pounds. His assailant aimed a blow at his face, whereupon the Marquis cried out 'Father, Father!'. The others drew back and, going down on one knee, Monaldeschi confessed something else to the Priest and received absolution. As he threw himself down on the tiled floor, he was given a blow to the top of his head, which cut off some bone. As he lay on his stomach he made a sign to the swordsman to cut his neck, but the coat of mail under his collar checked the executioner's blows. Finally, after another visit from the Queen's Chaplain, Monaldeschi's throat was cut and he spoke no more. He died a quarter of an hour later, at 3.45 p.m. The Queen was at pains to give orders for his burial, she asked that several Masses should be said for his soul, and sent £100 to have prayers said for him. He was buried in the nearby Church at Avon.

Cardinal Mazarin tried to cover up the scandal with a story of a feud between servants, but Christina replied, characteristically: 'We Northerners are rather hard ... I will gladly do ... [anything] to satisfy you ... except for one thing: I will not be afraid', *Catalogue* (above), No. 665 (different translation). Manuscript copies of Father Le Bel's account were widely circulated, and it was published in 1660. Christina also had an Italian version circulated, corresponding closely to Le Bel's. Her secret letter to Cromwell on the subject, brought by Philippi Passerini (q.v.), was in French and it may well have enclosed a copy of Le Bel's report. Her messenger's visit is wrongly entered in *Diary* 3 May 1657, six months before Monaldeschi's execution; for the likely date of this visit see

Passerini's entry. A letter referring to the Pope's displeasure and to that of the Court at Rome is in *Thurloe S.P.* vi, 706, 5 Jan. 1657/58. An unfavourable Italian version of the death refers to Monaldeschi as *'già suo favorito'* – 'formerly her favourite', 16 Nov. 1658, Add.Ms 16483 fol. 214. C. Weibull's theory that Monaldeschi's betrayal concerned the Queen's plans for Naples has much to commend it, yet in human terms there are at least pointers, in the eye-witness account, to suggest that this could have been an ice-cold crime of passion.

MONCK, George, see ALBEMARLE, 1st D. of.

MONDAY, see MUNDY, Dr. Francis.

MONSON (MOUNSON, MUNSON) of CASTLEMAINE (Co. Kerry), Sir William, MP, later Viscount (*c*.1600–*c*.1673). G.E.C.; *D.N.B.*; M.F.K.; *Biographical Dictionary of British Radicals in the Seventeenth Century* (Harvester Press). Wealthy and extravagant as a young man he acquired, through his first marriage (in 1625), the town and castle of Reigate, Surrey. He was MP for Reigate from 1640 to 1653; a protégé of the 1st Duke of Buckingham (q.v.); created Viscount in 1628. He supported the King at Oxford as late as 1646, then joined Parliament; showing a radical outlook, he was appointed one of the King's judges. After the Restoration, although not a regicide, he was brought to the Bar of the House of Commons, was imprisoned in the Fleet, deprived of his honours (the title became extinct) and was sentenced to be dragged on a hurdle, each year, from the Tower of London to Tyburn. He died in prison. He is only referred to by Whitelocke when he gave himself up, *Diary* 21 June 1660.

MONTAGUE, see MOUNTAGU.

MONTECUCCOLI (MONTECUCULY), Count Raymondo (1609–1680). *Catalogue, Christina Exhibition*, Nos. 397, 398, 583. A soldier and diplomat. As a young man, Montecuccoli had fought for Austria against Sweden but he admired Gustav Adolf, King of Sweden. He was held as prisoner-of-war by the Swedes, from 1639 to 1642, yet the Emperor Ferdinand III later sent him on a diplomatic mission to Sweden, which coincided with Whitelocke's embassy. Like the English Ambassador, Montecuccoli kept a diary at the Swedish Court, *Viaggio in Svezia nel mese di Dicembre 1653*. Whitelocke made several entries concerning him, *Diary* 8, 13, 14, 16 Feb., 1, 12 Mar. 1653/54.

MONTPOUILLAN (MONTPELLION, MOUNTPELLION in *Diary*), Armand de Caumont, Marquis of (1626–1701). *Dictionnaire de Biographie Française*. His elder brother, Pierre de Caumont, Marquis of Cugnac, was active in the *Fronde* against Mazarin, 1649–1650, then, escaping to England as a refugee, he married Elizabeth, daughter of the famous physician Sir Theodor Turquet de Mayerne, MD (q.v.). In 1650, Montpouillan himself supported the 2nd *Fronde*, the *Fronde des Princes*; five years later he served in the French Army under Marshal Turenne. In 1656 he married Adrienne, another daughter of Dr. Mayerne. In 1685 he became a Gentleman of the Bedchamber to the Prince of Orange in Holland, and was naturalized an Englishman in 1692. Whitelocke's encounters with him occurred in the year after the Marquis's marriage (although, according to Whitelocke, the marriage followed later). Backed by letters from Louis XIV and Marshall Turenne, the Marquis tried to get his hands on Adrienne's substantial inheritance, hoping thereby 'to make up his smalle fortune'; he appealed to the Protector, but his claims were strongly opposed by Sir John Colladon (q.v.), who made a claim of his own. Whitelocke was obliged to undertake 'many late & troublesom journeys betwixt Chelsey & Whitehall', both to act as interpreter and to advise Cromwell on the case. The outcome was evidently displeasing to the Marquis, for he 'tooke a peek' against Whitelocke, and later tried to do him a great (but unspecified) mischief, *Diary* 7 Nov. 1657.

MOORE family (below). *Extinct & Dormant Baronetcies*; *Complete Baronetage*; *V.C.H. Berks.* iv, 176, *passim*. In 1611 Sir Francis Moore Kt., MP (d.1621) bought Maidencourt, Fawley, in west Berkshire (not Whitelocke's Fawley, in Buckinghamshire). His son Henry (c.1596–c.1635), was created a Baronet in 1627. One of Sir Henry's sisters, Margaret, married Whitelocke's friend Sir Geffrey (Geoffrey) Palmer (q.v.); another sister, Anne, married John Jerningham, and their son Henry (q.v.) inherited the Jerningham Baronetcy in 1646. Sir Henry Moore's daughters, Anne, Elizabeth and Frances, married respectively: Sir Matthew Hale (q.v.), Sir Seymour Pile (q.v.), and Gabriel Pile (q.v.), so Whitelocke was distantly related to the Moore family through the marriage of his daughter Frances to Sir Seymour Pile's son.

The Moores do not appear in *The Diary* until two years after Whitelocke and his third wife, Mary, bought Chilton Park (some five miles from Maidencourt), in 1663; but in 1642 Whitelocke and his second wife, Frances, had shared a home in Ivy Lane, London, with Palmer and Hale (above) and their wives, so Whitelocke evidently knew some members of the Moore family from that date. Moreover, he had among his papers a document concerning Lady Moore (below) and the rating of North Fawley, 12 Jan. 1635/36, Long. W.P. vii, 7; there are also bonds, in the same year, between Whitelocke and both William Moore (q.v.) and Henry Moore (q.v.), ib. 17 and 51.

MOORE, Elizabeth, Lady. Daughter of William Beverley of Bedfordshire; widow of Henry Moore, 1st Baronet, and mother of Henry, 2nd Baronet (q.v.). Lady Moore was referred to by Whitelocke as 'the Lady Moore, the widdow' on his first visit to Maidencourt (Maidencote), *Diary* 6 Nov. 1665.

MOORE, Francis. Son of William (q.v.); cousin of Sir Henry (below).

MOORE, Sir Henry, 2nd Bt. (d. *c.*1699). Son of Henry, 1st Bt., and Elizabeth (q.v.); he succeeded to the title in about 1635. A Commissioner of Oyer and Terminer in the West of England, *Diary* 16 Mar. 1654/55. Whitelocke met him on several occasions between 7 Nov. 1665 and 17 July 1673.

MOORE, Sir St. John, Kt. Brother of Henry, 2nd Bt. (above). Married a Miss Pooley. Whitelocke met him at Maidencourt, and they met again at the wedding between Francis Pile and Frances Whitelocke.

MOORE, William (d.1672). Uncle of Henry, 2nd Bt. (q.v.). Married a Mrs. Blount; they had a son, Francis (q.v.). Moore died in London and his body was brought to Fawley, Berkshire, for burial, ib. 26 Mar. 1672.

MORDAUNT (MORDANT), John, 1st Lord (1626–1675). G.E.C.; *D.N.B.* Second son of John, 1st Earl of Peterborough. As a commoner, he plotted on behalf of Charles I and Charles II. He was tried for treason 1 to 3 June, 1658, but was acquitted on the casting vote of John Lisle (q.v.), President of the High Court of Justice; he was, however, not released immediately, G.E.C. MORDAUNT, p.200, including note d. Francis, 5th Lord Willoughby of Parham (q.v.) successfully appealed to Whitelocke, his brother-in-law, to help Mordaunt, *Diary* 5 June 1658. The next year Mordaunt joined Charles II in Brussels, and was created Baron Mordaunt of Ryegate and Viscount Mordaunt of Avalon in July 1659. Among other rewards for his services to the Restoration, Mordaunt was appointed High Steward of Windsor and Governor of the Castle. After he was impeached by the Commons in January 1666/67 (on the grounds of arbitrary acts he was alleged to have done at Windsor), he appealed to Whitelocke to attend the trial. He received a royal pardon but resigned, see *Diary* 22 Oct. 1667, with note; *Pepys* vii, 386 with note 2. Prince Rupert (q.v.) succeeded Mordaunt as Governor of Windsor Castle, a post formerly held by Whitelocke.

MORGAN, Sir Anthony, Kt., MP (1621–1668). *D.N.B.* Early in the Civil War he served as a Captain in the King's Army but he went over to Parliament's side, apparently in order to save his estate from sequestration. Although he had been on good terms with Henry Cromwell in Ireland, after the Restoration he was knighted by Charles II. He was one of the original Fellows of the Royal Society in 1663, *Pepys* ix, 104 with note 2. Lord Wenman (q.v.), of Thame Park, Oxfordshire, asked Whitelocke to help Sir Anthony in some way unspecified, *Diary* 17 July 1659; Viscount Wenman's letter of that date states that their old friendship emboldened him to write (they had served together, both in the Long Parliament and as Commissioners to the King, and often visited each other, *Diary* 16 Jan. 1648/49, *passim*). He entreated Whitelocke to help Sir Anthony, and to show what 'Lawfull favor' he might, but the nature of that favour was again unnamed, Long. W.P. xix, 53.

MORGAN, General, later Sir Thomas, Bt. (1607–1679). *D.N.B.*; *Complete Baronetage*; *Extinct & Dormant Baronetcies*; C.H. Firth and G. Davies *Regimental History of Cromwell's Army*. He distinguished himself in Parliament's Army in the 1640s and 1650s. After serving in Flanders, in 1657 and 1658, he was knighted by Richard Cromwell, then served in Scotland under General George Monck (later Duke of Albemarle, q.v.), accepting, in due course, Monck's plans to restore Charles II. Morgan served as Commander-in-Chief in Scotland from 1660 until 1662. He was created a Baronet, early in 1661, and appointed Governor of Jersey in 1665. Earlier, he was described as '. . . Wh[itelockes] friend, a very gallant person', *Diary* 26 Nov. 1658.

MORGAN, William, MP, JP (d.1649). M.F.K. Owned the Manor of Brecon. A Middle Temple lawyer, he sat in several Parliaments, including the Long Parliament. Although suspected of royalist sympathies, he was not disabled. Whitelocke refers to Morgan, Sheriff of Monmouth, as his friend and as a friend of his sister Elizabeth Mostyn (q.v.) and her family, *Diary* 9 Mar. 1647/48.

MORICE (MORRICE) [Sir William], Kt., MP (1602–1676). *Hist. of Parl.*; *D.N.B.*; *Pepys* x. A zealous Presbyterian. Of Werrington, Cornwall, which he bought from Sir Francis Drake, 2nd Baronet, in 1651. An MP both before and after the Restoration. Related, through his wife, to George Monck, Duke of Albemarle (q.v.), Morice managed Monck's property in Devon and supported him in the months before the Restoration; living in Monck's house for a time, he was described as the General's 'elbow-counsellor'. Whitelocke noted that Morice was made Governor of Plymouth by Monck, *Diary* 10 Mar. 1659/60. Morice was knighted when Charles II landed in England, in May 1660. Appointments followed, including that of Secretary of State (North). Of the two entries concerning 'Mʳ Morrice' (*sic*), the first refers to letters about the Jews destroying English trade, *Diary* 20 May 1659. Nothing has been found to link this complaint with William Morice, and the letters may have come from Thomas Morrice (*sic*), MP, described after the Restoration as 'formerly a stocking-seller', *Hist. of Parl.* On the other hand, as the entries are quite close together, Whitelocke might have been expected to distinguish between them, for example by referring to William Morice 'of Cornwall'.

MORLAND, Samuel, later Bt. (1625–1695). *Pepys* x; *D.N.B.* Mathematician and inventor. He was Samuel Pepys's tutor at Magdalene College, Cambridge, where Morland was a fellow from 1649 to 1654. His numerous ingenious inventions included a calculator, various water pumps and naval gun-carriages. After the Restoration he was knighted, created a Baronet and granted a pension. A highly gifted man (except in matters of business) he suffered, in the latter part of his life, from chronic insolvency.

Morland had left Magdalene College to join Whitelocke's retinue for Sweden, being recommended for the post by Walter Strickland (q.v.), 21 Sept. 1653, Long. W.P. xiii, 217. The appointment was as a gentleman of first degree and, as such, a gentleman at the Ambassador's table, *Diary* 26 Oct. 1653. Whitelocke described Morland as '... a very Civil Man, an excellent Scholar; modest and respectful, perfect in the Latin Tongue: whom Wh[itelocke] recommended especially to the Society of his Son

William ...', Add.Ms 4995, appendix 5, fol. 12v. Later Morland was appointed as one of John Thurloe's secretaries, *Diary* 3 Feb. 1657/58. He is said to have become a crypto-Royalist in 1659 (while still working for Thurloe), and to have sent information to the King.

MORLEY, Bishop George, DD (1597–1684). *D.N.B.*; *Pepys, passim.* Cultured, witty and a man of principle, Morley was a frequent guest of Lucius Cary, 2nd Viscount Falkland (q.v.), at Great Tew, in Oxfordshire. He became a friend of John Hampden (q.v.) and of Arthur Goodwyn (q.v.). Although Morley's Calvinistic leanings met with Archbishop Laud's disapproval, he was appointed a King's Chaplain and, in 1641, a Canon of Christ Church, Oxford. Made a DD in 1642, he preached before the House of Commons. In 1647 he supported the University in opposing the Parliamentary Visitation; for this he was deprived of his Canonry and of the Rectory of Hartfield, Sussex, and was not restored to the Canonry until after the Restoration. In a letter from Dr. G. Morley to his honoured friend Mr. Whitelocke, he wrote that he knew from Geffrey Palmer (q.v.) and others, how much the whole University of Oxford and he himself were indebted to Whitelocke; he would have sent his thanks sooner, but that any address from those whom Whitelocke had saved would carry '... something of scandal if not of danger to him to whom it is made ...' but Morley added that there was nothing he would not do or suffer to let Whitelocke know of his gratitude. As to the loss of his place, although it was all he had to live on, that did not trouble him since he could not have kept it with a good conscience. It was glory enough for him that Mr. Selden (q.v.) and Mr. Whitelocke were of a different opinion from that of his judges, *Memorials* ii, 149–150, 31 May 1647. (The letter has not been traced in the 'Annales' from which the *Memorials* were transcribed.) Morley subsequently accompanied the Royalist, Lord Capel (q.v.), to the foot of the scaffold. After the Restoration, he was appointed Bishop of Worcester, 1660–1662, and Bishop of Winchester (Winton), 1662–1684. Although Whitelocke had evidently known Morley many years earlier, the only reference to him in the present work is *Diary* 24 May 1673.

MORLEY, Col. Herbert, MP (1616–1667). M.F.K.; *Hist. of Parl.*; *D.N.B.*; *Biographical Dictionary of British Radicals in the Seventeenth Century.* Of Glynde Place, Sussex. An MP before and after the Restoration, he served with Whitelocke in the Long Parliament and was fairly active in the Rump. He opposed the Protectorate. After the Commons revoked the commissions of nine leading officers, including that of Lambert (q.v.), on 12 October 1659, Morley was one of the seven Commissioners appointed to govern the Army. This occurred on the eve of Lambert's military coup which expelled the restored Rump, *Restoration* p.151, *passim*. Whitelocke makes a number of references to Morley between *Diary* 12 Oct. 1659 and 25 Feb. 1659/60. During those months Morley was working with Sir Arthur Hesilrige (q.v.) and Colonel Valentine Walton (q.v.), to restore Parliament. He collaborated with Monck and was appointed Lieutenant of the Tower, in January 1659/60. Obtaining his pardon at the Restoration, he served as MP from 1661 to September 1667.

MORRICE, see MORICE, Sir William.

MOSELEY, Sir Edward, MP (d.1638). R. Somerville *Office-Holders of the Duchy and County Palatine of Lancaster*. Of Gray's Inn. Son of Nicholas Moseley, Lord Mayor of London. Knighted in 1614. Attorney of the Duchy in 1613 and again from 1625; Whitelocke, as a young lawyer, applied for the post when Sir Edward died but was not (at that time) appointed, *Diary* 1637.1638. fol.45v., 46.

MOSTYN family (below). *Dictionary of Welsh Biography*; *Extinct & Dormant Baronetcies*; L.N.V.L. Mostyn & T.A. Glenn *History of the Family of Mostyn of Mostyn* (Harrison, London. 1925); Clwyd R.O., Mostyn Mss; University College of North Wales, Bangor, Dept. of Mss, Mostyn Mss; *Calendar of Wynn Papers, passim*. Of Mostyn Hall and Cilcain, Flintshire (now Clwyd). A wealthy Royalist family, owning coal, silver and lead mines. Whitelocke was related to them through the marriage of his sister, Elizabeth (below).

MOSTYN (MOSTIN), Elizabeth (1603–1669). *Liber, passim*. Whitelocke's elder sister, she married Thomas (later Sir Thomas) Mostyn (q.v.), at Staunton Lacy, near Ludlow, Shropshire, in May 1623. Thomas's father, Sir Roger Mostyn, sen., Kt. (q.v.) sent proposals for the match three years before the marriage, starting aggressively: 'The portion I demand is 3000ᵁ', 17 Jan. 1619/20, Bangor (above) Mostyn Ms 7294. James Whitelocke, who was appointed Justice of Chester in June 1620 (no long ride from Mostyn), summarized the final settlement in *Liber* p.94. He was to provide a marriage portion of £2,500 (£200 of this was remitted, on condition £100 was spent on 'utensils of house' for the young couple); he was also to provide his daughter's apparel and '. . . to give them and theares a yeares enterteynment'; Sir Roger, for his part, undertook to assure to the couple's male issue all his lands in the Counties of Caernarvon, Flint, Denbigh and in the County and City of Chester, worth £3,000 p.a., with his coal mines. The indenture itself is dated 31 Aug. 1623, some three months after the marriage, Clwyd R.O., Mostyn Ms D/M/3608. It differs in some respects from the summary, giving Sir Roger a life interest in the estate. Sir Humphrey May (q.v.), Chancellor of the Duchy of Lancaster, Sir John Wynn of Gwydir and Henry Bulstrode (q.v.), were among the parties to the agreement. In November 1641 Elizabeth, in her late 30s, was left a widow, 'encombred with debts & griefe, & two sons to breed up', *Diary* 1641.1642. fol.53v. During her husband's lifetime Whitelocke, as a young man, made payments to or on behalf of his sister of: £280, on 1 Oct. 1625, Long W.P. ii, 192, receipted by Timothy Tourneur; £30.15.0, on 4 July 1626, ib. iii, 49, receipted by Roger Ellis; £7, in full settlement of her milliner William Bingfield's bill, 21 Oct. 1626, ib. 69, and £10, on 29 Nov. 1637, ib. vii, 195. After Elizabeth was widowed, *The Diary* records numerous letters from 'Sister Mostyn' in Wales, begging for help and favours. Whitelocke received a report that she had married Mr. Owen Wyn[n], '. . . a man of no fortune', *Diary* 7 Nov. 1648; yet he made no further mention of this, and continued to refer to 'Sister Mostyn'; an unsubstantiated statement that Sir Thomas's widow 'married Owen Wynn, son of Sir John Wynn, of Gwydir' appears in *History of the Family of Mostyn of Mostyn* p. 134. Six months after Whitelocke's second wife died, he sent his 10-year-old daughter Elizabeth to Wales, to be brought up by her 'Aunt Mostyn', *Diary* 6 Oct. 1649; later, Elizabeth Mostyn arranged for her niece, then aged 14, to marry Sir Richard Pryce Bt. (q.v.), ib. 5 Aug. 1653.

MOSTYN, John, MP (*c.* 1603–1675). M.F.K.; *D.N.B.* Second son of Sir Roger Mostyn, sen. (q.v.); brother of Sir Thomas Mostyn Kt. (q.v.). Of the Inner Temple. In 1621 he entered the service of John Williams (q.v.), later Bishop of Lincoln, who was a relative of the Wynn family and well disposed towards Whitelocke.

MOSTYN, Mary (d.1662). Daughter of Thomas, Viscount Bulkeley, of Baron Hill, Anglesey. Second wife of Sir Roger Mostyn, jun. (q.v.). After her death Sir Roger, by then a Baronet, married Lumley Coetmor (1642–1684), but she does not appear in *The Diary*.

MOSTYN, Prudence (d.1647). Daughter of Martin Lumley of Great Bradfield, Essex. She married Roger Mostyn, jun. (q.v.), in about July 1642; Whitelocke considered his nephew too young to marry at 18, *Diary* 1641.1642. fol.54. For Prudence's death, see ib. 19 Dec. 1647.

MOSTYN, Sir Roger, sen., Kt., MP (1567–1642). *D.N.B.* (in his grandson and namesake's entry, shown as his son). Of Brasenose College, Oxford, and Lincoln's Inn. He married Mary, eldest daughter of Sir John Wynn, Bt., of Gwydir, was the father of Sir Thomas (q.v.), John, MP (q.v.) and William (q.v.), and father-in-law of Whitelocke's sister Elizabeth (q.v.). Whitelocke visited him at Mostyn, after staying with Elizabeth and Thomas, *Diary* 1627.1628. fol.8v. Earlier in that decade, Judge James Whitelocke (q.v.) signed bonds to Sir Roger (as security for the marriage settlement) for £2,000 and £1,300, Long. W.P. ii, 88 and 126; both were dated 15 May 1623, nine days before their children's wedding. Receipts for various payments made to Sir Roger in 1624 and 1625, by or on behalf of Judge Whitelocke, range from £100 to £300, ib. 174, 185, 191, 192.

MOSTYN, Col. Sir Roger, jun., 1st Bt. (*c*.1624–1690). L.N.V.L. Mostyn & T.A. Glenn *History of the Family of Mostyn of Mostyn* pp.135–155; *D.N.B.* (which makes a slip concerning Roger's parentage, and states in error that Whitelocke married a Mostyn). Of Mostyn. Eldest son of Sir Thomas (below) and Elizabeth (q.v.) née Whitelocke; elder brother of Thomas, jun. (q.v.). Admitted to the Inner Temple in 1637. He married first at the age of 18, some eight months after his father's death in November 1641. The innumerable diary entries for Whitelocke's nephew ignore young Colonel Mostyn's service for the King with some unruly troops in Chester, and afterwards as Governor of Flint Castle. Whitelocke's entries dwell more on family matters. He helped his nephew over his sequestration, *Diary* 4 Jan. 1647/48 and 11 June 1649, and commented, with hindsight, that he received many kind letters from Roger 'who forgott to write to his Uncle when he was out of office', ib. 28 Mar. 1650; many accusations of Roger's subsequent ingratitude occur between ib. 22 Aug. and 2 Feb. 1668/69, when Roger Mostyn refused to help Whitelocke's daughter Hester. After Roger was taken prisoner at Conway, on account of his royalist activities, Whitelocke arranged for his release on parole, ib. 13, 15 May 1658. Earlier, a curious entry refers to Roger nobly entertaining Lord Henry Cromwell (q.v.) at Mostyn, ib. 11 July 1655. His mother (Whitelocke's sister) denied that her son was involved in Sir George Booth's royalist uprising, ib. 29 Aug. 1659, but at the Restoration his services to the royalist cause were recognized by his appointment as a Gentleman of the Privy Chamber, ib. 25 June 1660, and his creation as 1st Baronet on 3 Aug. 1660. An interesting account of the fine entertainment offered at Mostyn, of Sir Roger's silver mines, of his highly profitable lead mines, and of the equipment in the 'Melting [i.e. smelting] houses' with much else is given in *An Account of the Progress of His Grace the First Duke of Beaufort through Wales, 1684* (T. Dineley's account, ed. C. Baker. 1864).

MOSTYN, Sir Thomas, Kt. (*c.* 1598–1641). The eldest son of Sir Roger Mostyn, sen. (q.v.); he died before his father. A brother of John Mostyn MP (q.v.), he married Whitelocke's sister, Elizabeth (q.v.) in 1623, and was knighted at Theobalds in the same year, on the recommendation of the Duke of Buckingham (q.v.). After their marriage, he and his wife lived at Cilcain (Kilken) Hall, some eight miles south of Mostyn. For details of their marriage settlement, see the entry for Elizabeth Mostyn.

MOSTYN, Thomas (d.1665). Second son of Sir Thomas (above) and brother of Sir Roger Mostyn Bt. (q.v.).

MOSTYN, Thomas, 2nd Bt., MP (1651–1692). *Hist. of Parl.* Son of Sir Roger Mostyn, jun., 1st Bt., (q.v.), by his 2nd wife, Mary (q.v.). He studied at Christ Church, Oxford, and lived at Gloddaeth, Caernarvonshire (now Gwynedd) until his father's death. Elected MP for Caernarvon in March and October 1679, and in 1681. A patron of the arts and collector of books, he appears only once in *The Diary*, writing courteously to his great-uncle from Paris, 29 Jan. 1670/71.

MOSTYN, William. A Preacher, at Christleton near Chester. Brother of Sir Thomas Mostyn Kt. (q.v.) and of John Mostyn MP (q.v.). Archbishop John Williams (q.v.) and Elizabeth ('Sister Mostyn') both approached Whitelocke, soliciting his help for William Mostyn, ib. 15 Sept. 1649, with note, and 22 May 1656.

MOUNTAGU (MONTAGUE) family (below). For a 3-branched family tree of male members, see *Hist. of Parl.* iii, 81.

MOUNTAGU of BOUGHTON, Anne, Lady (d. 1684). G.E.C.; M.F.K. (information in the entries for her husband Edward, 2nd Baron Montagu, *sic*, of Boughton). Daughter of Sir Ralph Winwood, former Secretary of State, and sister of Whitelocke's friend Richard Winwood (q.v.). Mother of two post- Restoration MPs, Edward (q.v.) and Ralph Mountagu (q.v.).

MOUNTAGU, Edward, see SANDWICH, 1st E. of.

MOUNTAGU, Hon. Edward, MP (*c.* 1636–1665). *Hist. of Parl.* (4th entry of this name); *Pepys* x. Eldest son of Edward Mountagu, 2nd Baron Mountagu of Boughton (spelt 'Bolton' in *The Diary*) and Anne (q.v.). Aged about 24 in the summer of 1659, the young Edward Mountagu, acting as an intermediary, persuaded his distant cousin, the future Earl of Sandwich (at that time General-at-Sea), to transfer his allegiance from Parliament to the King; moreover, he negotiated favourable terms for his relative and others, with Charles II. Whitelocke had evidently only heard one side of what followed when, with hindsight, he wrote that young Mountagu was not so well requited as those whom he had helped, *Diary* 24 Apr. 1660. In fact, after being elected MP for Sandwich in 1661, Mountagu was sent to Lisbon in January 1662, to escort the new Queen, Catherine of Braganza, back to England, and was then appointed her Master of Horse. He was notoriously extravagant, quarrelsome and ambitious and was dismissed from Court in 1664. The reason for this was covered up, being his attempt to make sexual advances to the Queen. At her request he was replaced in her service by his younger brother Ralph (below) who also earned himself an unpleasant reputation. Neither of the brothers seems to have been known personally to Whitelocke.

MOUNTAGU of BOUGHTON, Ralph, MP, later 3rd Baron, and finally 1st D. of Mountagu (1638–1709). G.E.C.; *Hist. of Parl.*; *Pepys* x. Younger brother of Edward Mountagu MP (above). He succeeded to his father's title in 1684; was created 1st Duke of Mountagu in 1705 and served in the Queen's household from 1665 to 1678. He was reputed to be an unscrupulous politician surrounded, in Pepys's words, by 'scurvey stories'. He only appears in *The Diary* at a date when he was planning to go (or had already gone) as Ambassador to France, where he served from 1669 to 1672. Nathaniel Basenet (q.v.), wrote that Richard Winwood's 'Nephew Mountagu' (i.e. Ralph) would do great things for Whitelocke's advancement, but nothing came of this, *Diary* 29 Jan. 1668/69.

MOUNTAGU, Sir Sydney (Sidney), MP (c. 1571–1644). M.F.K. Sixth surviving son of Sir Edward Mountagu of Boughton. A Middle Temple lawyer; knighted in 1616. Father of Edward Mountagu, 1st Earl of Sandwich (q.v.). As Master of Requests he refused to sell this office when Whitelocke, as a young lawyer, was encouraged to offer to buy it, *Diary* 1632. 1633. fol.19.

MULGRAVE, Edmund Sheffield, 2nd E. of (c.1611–1658). G.E.C.; *D.N.B.* Grandson of the 1st Earl of Mulgrave, from whom he inherited the title in 1646. A moderate in politics, he supported Parliament and later the Protectorate, but had been opposed to the execution of Charles I. He had been appointed a Commissioner of the Navy in 1647. As owner of alum works in Yorkshire, he obtained a ruling from Parliament that the monopoly for the mining and sale of alum, granted by Charles I to Sir John Gibson, was illegal and void, and the Lords ordered that the Earl be entitled to operate the alum mines and works in the Manor of Mulgrave, Yorkshire, *L.J.* X, 243, 4 May 1648, *passim*. Shortly afterwards the Earl approached Whitelocke, and through him John Selden (q.v.), for advice on these works, *Diary* 17 May 1648. He subsequently entertained Whitelocke and John Lisle (q.v.), ib. 13 Mar. 1648/49. When Lisle insinuated himself and his wife into Syon House (lent to the recently widowed Whitelocke by the Earl of Northumberland, q.v.), he brought with him the Earl of Mulgrave and his Countess (Elizabeth, daughter of Lionel Cranfield, 1st Earl of Middlesex) and, according to Whitelocke, they took over the best rooms, ib. 7 Aug. 1649.

MUNDY (MONDAY), Dr. Francis (c.1613–1678). *V.C.H. Berks.* iv, 123, 216; *Terrier and inventory of Church possessions in the Parish of Welford, Berks.* (compiled by Mrs. S. Batson. Newbury. 1892). Rector of St. Gregory's Church, Welford, Berkshire, where there is a marble wall-monument in his memory. A monument to Dr. Mundy's wife Elizabeth (c.1613–1689), next to his own, includes a pleasing effigy of her bonneted head; a further monument lists their children. Mundy appears in documents dated 1663 as 'of Wickham', the parish being Welford with Wickham. The Rector and his wife also had connections with Denton in Berkshire. Welford, Wickham and Denton are north-east and east of Hungerford, and near to the Chilton Park estate. As one of the executors to the Will of Thomas Hussey, sen., Mundy and his fellow-executors sold Chilton Park to Whitelocke, 12 June 1663, University of Reading Archives, BER. 36/5/19 and 20. His daughter was married to Dr. Sheafe (q.v.), Rector of Chilton Foliat, *Diary* 17 Apr. 1671. He was probably the Dr. Monday (*sic*) who, some years before Whitelocke bought Chilton Park, applied for a schoolmaster's position in Henley-on-Thames, and solicited Whitelocke's support, ib. 10, 12 May 1656.

MYNGS (MINNES, MYNNES). Capt., later Sir Christopher, Kt. (1625–1666). *D.N.B.*; C.H. Firth 'Sailors of the Civil War, the Commonwealth and the Protectorate' in *Mariner's Mirror* xii (1926); *Journal, passim*; *Pepys, passim*. A naval Captain under the Protectorate; promoted to the rank of Vice-Admiral after the Restoration. (His name is spelt Minnes in *The Diary*). A skilful and headstrong sailor, aboard the frigate *Elizabeth*, he fought the Dutch at sea in July 1653. Early in October, returning from a mission to Dieppe, he encountered and captured some 20 Dutch ships but two of the *Elizabeth's* masts were damaged and the ship's master was killed in the action; Myngs wrote an account of this to the Admiralty Committee, *C.S.P. Dom. 1653–1654* p.186. Admiral Blake (q.v.) rebuked him: 'I do not love a foolhardy captain . . . temper your courage with discretion . . . undertake nothing hazardous if you can avoid it. So you can come to preferment . . .'; the passage is quoted in Firth's article, above. The admonition was ignored, yet preferment followed: a few weeks later the *Elizabeth*, still under Myngs, was part of the small fleet provided by Blake and Monck, which took Ambassador Whitelocke, his company and horses, to Sweden. Again, Myngs could not resist the urge to chase and capture a Dutch ship, although it caused him to lose touch with the convoy, *Journal* i, 134, 14 Nov. 1653. Next day, he tactlessly arrived with his prize in Göteborg – a bad start to a goodwill mission, and one which led to vehement protests from the Dutch, ib. 136, 152–153, 155–156.

Myngs was one of the Captains sent to meet Whitelocke in Germany, after the embassy, but he took offence because the Ambassador was to sail in the *President* not the *Elizabeth* and, defying orders, Myngs kept his frigate aloof from the other ships. After a near-disaster at sea Whitelocke had him aboard and reprimanded him, but the young Captain held his own and convinced Whitelocke that he was a better seaman than Captain Parkes (q.v.); the dialogue is recorded, ib. ii, 425–427. The incident ended happily, when Myngs entertained the company as the ships lay at anchor that night, with a display of squibs and fireworks.

The following year, when he was recommended for preferment, Myngs was glowingly described as having 'brains on both sides of his head', *C.S.P. Dom. 1655* p. 422. His successful career continued with voyages to the West Indies during the Protectorate, and later in the service of Charles II. His piratical instincts also continued unabated, ib.*1658–1659* pp.57, 123.

The King knighted him in 1665. He was mortally wounded in the Four Days Fight with the Dutch, and Pepys describes the affection and grief shown by Myngs' sailors, at his ill-attended funeral on 10 June, *Pepys* vii, 165–166, 13 June 1666.

NANSON, Joseph. A clerk who had been employed by Sir Arthur Hesilrige (q.v.). On the recommendation of George Cokayn (q.v.), Nanson came into Whitelocke's service, in Coleman Street, *Diary* 6 Oct. 1660. He is described by Whitelocke as having a good handwriting, but not much experience in drafting deeds or bills. There is only this one reference to him in *The Diary*, but his name appears on a bond witnessing Whitelocke's signature, 31 Oct. 1662, Long. W.P. xix, 167, and on a 99-year lease of certain lands on the Chilton Park estate, when Whitelocke bought it, 12 June 1663, University of Reading Archives, BER 36/5/18.

NAPPER (NAPPIER), Col. Thomas. Apprenticed as Whitelocke's clerk in 1633. A trustworthy young servant, to whom Whitelocke wrote the following year from France, when sending two coats for his little son James. No-one (and this meant Whitelocke's mother-in-law) was to know that Whitelocke was in France. He wrote that if anyone suggested the small coats looked like French ones, Napper was to say they were made by the French woman in London. If they were too long, they could be shortened. One coat was for everyday use and the other for holidays. The letter finished engagingly: 'I hope ere long to see my boy playing in one of his new coates, lett nobody know from any of you where you guess I am', 20 May 1634, Long. W.P. vi, 97. When Napper decided to better himself Whitelocke wrote him a testimonial, in a letter to Attorney-General Bankes (q.v.), recommending Napper as 'an honest and civill young man' who had served him as clerk both for his work as a lawyer and as Justice of the Peace, but Whitelocke added that there had been 'the lesse imployment in either bicause my indeavours are more to end buisnes then to make it.' Something had gone wrong with Napper's transfer, and Whitelocke added that he had looked out for a new clerk and did not want Napper back since 'his minde being uppon other hopes his servise to me would be butt unwilling, which seldome proves continuing, therefore I ... shall be very glad for his preferment if you will be pleased to receive him ...' 6 Nov. 1636, ib. vii, 79. Napper's signature appears, witnessing that of his master on bonds, 4 and 9 June 1636, ib. 53, 51, and, as late as 17 May 1637, ib. 114. Napper subsequently became a Colonel in the King's Army during the Civil War, and later commanded a regiment in the French Army.

Some 24 years later, just before the Restoration, a gentleman with a large feather in his hat and a sword by his side accosted Whitelocke on a road in Greenwich. Whitelocke did not immediately recognize his former clerk, *Diary* 11 May 1660. Napper expressed gratitude for the kindness and training he had received and offered to help his former master, with an introduction to the King. He was as good as his word and helped in other ways, but before returning to France, he came for his 'gratuity'. Whitelocke thought £100 a good reward but Napper expected £500, and disdainfully accepted £250, ib. 8 June 1660; 26 Apr. 1661.

NAYLER (NAYLOR), James (*c.* 1617–1660). *D.N.B.*; G.F. Nuttall 'James Nayler, a Fresh Approach', *Friends' Historical Society Journal* (1954). A Yorkshireman. While serving in Parliament's Army he developed his powers as an Independent preacher. When George Fox visited Wakefield in 1651, Naylor was converted and became a fanatical Quaker. In October 1656, in Glastonbury and Wells, doting women strewed garments on the road before Nayler and, when he travelled towards Bristol, cried 'Hosannah' and 'Holy, Holy, Holy, Lord God of Israel', reflecting Christ's entry into Jerusalem, celebrated on Palm Sunday. This led to Nayler's arrest, his trial for blasphemy by a parliamentary committee, and to a brutal and sadistic sentence. Whitelocke, with a few others, considered the proceedings excessive, *Diary* 6, 13 Dec. 1656. Details of the trial are given in Thomas Burton's *Diary*. Three years later Nayler was released, *Diary* 8 Sept. 1659.

NEALE, Sir William, Kt. (1609–1691). *D.N.B.*; *Shaw's Knights*. He was Scoutmaster-General in Prince Rupert's Army and fought at his side in 1644. When he was captured, presumably in connection with the royalist rising inspired by Sir George Booth (q.v.), 'Sister Mostyn' wrote to Whitelocke on his behalf, enclosing 'a very sad letter . . . from his Lady', *Diary* 7 Sept. 1659.

NEDHAM (NEEDHAM), Marchmont (1620–1678). J. Frank *Cromwell's Press Agent: A Critical Biography of Marchmont Nedham, 1620–1678* (University Press of America. 1980). *D.N.B.* Of Burford, Oxfordshire. After studying both the law and medicine, he became a satirical journalist, writing for Parliament's anti-Royalist newspaper, *Mercurius Britannicus*, first issued in August 1643. He was imprisoned in the Fleet on 23 May 1646, for articles obnoxious not to the King, as might be expected, but to

Parliament. Released on bail, on 4 June 1646, he was forbidden to continue with his journalistic career. The next year he begged for and received pardon from Charles I for his earlier, insulting articles and started publishing *Mercurius Pragmaticus* in September 1647, in which he made scurrilous attacks on Parliament. He adopted the technique of abuse which has survived to this day, writing about 'Coppernose', 'Nose Almighty' etc., which his readers knew meant Cromwell. After the King's execution he was again imprisoned by Parliament, in June 1649, but was released three months later and used his skills to defend the Commonwealth from May 1650. He became editor of a new weekly, *Mercurius Politicus* (first published in June 1650) and of the *Public Intelligencer*. Whitelocke only refers twice to Nedham, the first time being when the Council dismissed him from writing the 'weekly intelligence', *Diary* 9 Apr. 1660, but they evidently knew each other in the previous decade.

A newsletter from Nedham addressed 'My Lords' (after the House of Lords had been abolished) was presumably written to Whitelocke and his colleagues, the Lords Commissioners of the Great Seal. It gives information about the Dutch Navy and reports that Prince Rupert was suffering from dysentery at Nantes, 'and hath not as yet obtained leave of the Court to sell any of his stol'n Indie [i.e. Indian] Commodities in France' etc. 22 Mar. 1652/53, Whitehall, Long W.P. xiii, 49–50v. The Commissioners were evidently out of London, for Nedham referred to 'The late French Newes I suppose your Lo[rdshi]^{ps} were made acquainted with before your departure.' Whitelocke's absence from London is not, however, confirmed by the undated, single entry for that month in *The Diary*.

An interesting newsletter in Nedham's hand (neither addressed nor signed) reports letters from The Hague and Amsterdam, again concerned with the Anglo-Dutch war: these recorded a rumour which was rife that the English intended

> to send over an Ambassage, and had . . . Resolutions for Peace; whereof they [the Dutch] have no reall thoughts; notwithstanding their late letter to the Parl[ia]m[en]t. That the designe of that letter is only to feele our pulses . . . That the Dutch seem very little in clined yet to peace. that the States [i.e. the Netherlands] have received a letter from Ch[arles] Stuart [i.e. Charles II] . . . written with his own hands . . . That in his letter he desires to have a squadron of good ships to bear his Flagg, wherewith he would himselfe . . . go to sea against the English. That hitherto holland hath not fully consented to it, though the other Provinces doe not reject it as unfit. That in the mean time, their Ministry and People waile extremely against the present Government in England, saying, they ought wholly to joyn with the King against his Rebels (as they are pleased to stile us;) . . . That . . . they doe more and more incline to the Interest of the Stuarts and that of the Scotch Highlanders . . . and that they [the Scots] want nothing but Arms & Ammunition, wherewith they [the

Dutch] have taken a Resolution to furnish them ... [One hundred Dutch ships were] to block up the Thames [and a standing fleet] to ply continually upon our coasts ... That we had need ... be nimble, in regard the Dutch will be quick ... [That the Dutch were recruiting mariners from Norway, but Queen Christina of Sweden] intends to keep fair with all Part[ie]s, and give assistance to none ... [special Intelligencers had just arrived from Amsterdam with reports] that the drums beat all day [recruiting sailors], ... but few men appear ... [That there was] great joy ... for Rupert's arrival at Nantes: that ... its presumed he will shortly be sent for Ireland, about the Insurrection ... That ... the People are very discontented in holland, missing some thousands of their Friends since the last Engagement, but the Lords stop their mouths, telling them that they are safe in the French Ports ... That their East-Indy Fleet, with a Convoy of 12 men of warr goes off within 10 daies round about Scotland & Ireland ... That Ch[arles] Stuart hath by letter humbly supplicated the Emperor to ... supply him with 200000 Crowns. The Emperor's answer was that his own wants of money were great, and his Affairs at present in a very uncertain posture ...

25 Mar. 1653.

                                                         Long W.P. xiii, 52–53v.

A characteristic letter from Nedham to Whitelocke in Sweden, written soon after the Protectorate was set up, makes it clear that the two men knew each other and that Nedham felt himself in Whitelocke's debt. He apologized profusely for not having kissed the Ambassador's hand before he left; but he dismissed:

verball Professions, which are but empty Returns for your many high Favours; only I humbly beg ... that you would beleve they have not [been] sowne on the sands; nor can the memory of them be lost, unlesse I would lose myself ... The best News wee have here ... at Whitehall is; that your Lo[rdshi]p is safe landed with your whole Retinue; that wee are now under a new Protection in England ... we have a new world formed (like the old) out of Chaos, by the prudence and industry of that excellent person, who may most meritoriously chalenge the stile and Title of Lord Protector ... a Governer, whose high Atchievements have given him a Right beyond all the Tituladoes of hereditary Princes, and made him ... indeed, what most of them are but in name: ... for my owne part ... I would chuse much rather to serve him upon any Terms, than be a Favourite to any of those golden Things that are drop't at adventure into the world, with Crowns upon their heads.

He hoped that the nation was made happy by this change, and thought the Protector most fortunate to have 'so admirable a Tongue' as Whitelocke's to report these developments 'and conquer the affections of that Royall virgin [Queen Christina] ... to the interest of England.'

I would to this ... add somwhat of Intelligence; but being my selfe a person out of dores (though not out of hope) and your Ex[cellen]cy being supplied from such as are within, I shall not pretend to be wiser than becomes me ...

But if your Ex[cellen]^{cy} will vouchsafe an eie upon any of my slender avisoes, I have told my Tale to my dear Friend Mr Stapylton [q.v.] . . . [After a further complimentary paragraph and signing himself 'Mar. Nedham' he added] Just as I was putting pen to paper, Mr Thurloe [q.v.] calls upon me for mine to inclose; so that . . . I cannot salute Mr Stapylton, as I intended. I will next weeke.
6 Jan. 1653[54], Whitehall.

Long. W.P. xv, I–IV.

Nedham survived the Restoration and received a pardon under the Great Seal. After that he earned his living by practising physic; when Whitelocke was very ill, Nedham was one of five medical advisers whom he consulted, and who charged him no fee, *Diary* 29 Mar. 1665.

NEVILL, George (d.1665). Papers in the collection of Mr. P.J. Radford of Sheffield Park, Sussex. George was the son of Richard Nevill (a Groom of the Bedchamber to Charles I), and his wife Sophia, Harl. Ms 3882 fol. 37v. After Richard's death, Sophia married Walter Stuart and by 1657 had been widowed a second time. In that year George, still a minor, married Whitelocke's 18-year-old daughter Mary (q.v.). The bridegroom's mother did not attend the wedding; Whitelocke learned later than she was a recusant, although George was a staunch Protestant, *Diary* 9 May 1657. Whitelocke wrote that the young couple married at Chelsea around that date; in fact, the marriage settlement of 11 June 1657 refers to the wedding as 'intended to be shortly . . . solemnized.' In this settlement Whitelocke paid £3,000 to purchase Sophia Stuart's life interest in Sheffield Park, near Uckfield, Sussex, on behalf of the young Nevills; she agreed to release 'every blade of grass' and the estates, hereditaments, appurtenances etc. in Fletching, Horsted Keynes, East Grinstead, West Hoathly, Lingfield, Uckfield etc.; a tripartite indenture, of 11 June, and Sophia's surrender of her rights, 1 July 1657, are in Mr. Radford's collection (above). Documents show that the settlement on Sophia for life, after her first husband's death, had been made by her father-in-law, Sir Christopher Nevill, KB, who had bought the property in 1623. It was agreed that Whitelocke, with Bartholomew Hall (q.v.) and Daniel Earle (q.v.), should control the estate and that, within six months of George Nevill's coming of age, he should settle the property on his wife Mary, for life, as her jointure in case he died before her. Within eight years the settlement came into operation: Nevill, in his 20s, was stabbed by drunken men in a Croydon tavern and died soon afterwards, *Diary* 17–19 Apr. 166ᴦ Nevill's Will, written after the stabbing, starts: 'being weake in Body t of good and perfect memory . . .' In it, he appointed Whitelocke, Whit's son William (q.v.), and John,

1st Baron Lucas of Shenfield (q.v.) as 'overseers' or trustees to sell Newton
St. Loe, his estate near Bath, to pay his creditors and to see to the bequests
to his children – George (below), Sophia and Mary – as well as to his
servants etc.; his young wife was to be sole executrix. A copy of the Will is
in Mr. Radford's collection, dated 28 Mar. 1665; Whitelocke's dates
(above) do not quite tally with the date on George's deathbed Will.

NEVILL, George, later 13th Lord BERGAVENNY or ABERGAVENNY
(1659–1721). G.E.C.; documents in Mr. Radford's collection (see above,
and entry: ABERGAVENNY). Son and heir of George Nevill (above)
who was killed when the boy was five or six years old. George jun.
inherited the title from his cousin, of the same name, in 1695; a footnote in
G.E.C. states that he was the first Protestant to bear the title. He died at
Sheffield Park. Whitelocke only refers to this grandson in connection with:
(1) a parliamentary bill affecting the Abergavenny inheritance, which he
(Whitelocke) asked friends in the House of Lords to oppose, *Diary* 12 Dec.
1666; (2) sending a servant to collect George from Eton, and (3) George
visiting Chilton Lodge with his mother, Mary (q.v.), and sisters Sophia and
Mary, ib. 26 May 1669; 5 July 1673. The numerous relevant deeds in Mr.
Radford's collection include the 13th Baron's Will of 1708 and his last Will,
dated 16 Dec. 1720.

NEVILL, Henry, MP (1620–1694). *D.N.B.* Not, it seems, related to the
Nevill family (above). A Member of the Long Parliament, for Abingdon,
elected in 1645; MP for Reading in Richard Cromwell's Parliament of
1659. William Whitelocke (q.v.) intended to contest the seat and this,
according to *The Diary*, caused Nevill to become Whitelocke's enemy,
Diary 17 Dec. 1658; 14 May 1659, *passim*. Nevill was further outraged that
Whitelocke had served on the Committee of Safety, ib. 27 Dec. 1659. A
republican and a friend of Sir Arthur Hesilrige (q.v.), he had strongly
opposed the Protectorate.

NEVILL, Mary, sen. (b.1639). Whitelocke's fourth child by Frances, his
second wife. Mary married George Nevill (q.v.), of Sheffield Park, Sussex,
in 1657; his entry gives details of Mary's life-interest in Sheffield Park. She
was 26 when her young husband was murdered in 1665, leaving her with
four (possibly five) children, of whom the eldest, also named George Nevill
(q.v.), the future 13th Lord Bergavenny, was five or six years old; his
sisters, Sophia and Mary jun., appear in *The Diary* while a second son,

Edward, is named in his mother's Will (extracts from which are quoted below). It seems that Mary was only accompanied by George jun. and his two sisters, when she visited her father at Chilton Lodge, *Diary* 5 July 1673, but Whitelocke stated earlier that her husband had left five children, ib. 19 Apr. 1665. Whitelocke, as one of three trustees, went to considerable trouble in connection with the sale of Newton St. Loe, on his daughter's behalf.

In an indenture dated 23 Oct. 1684, between Mary Nevill and Edward Dore the younger, she sold him Little Hidden, near Hungerford in Berkshire, with 104 acres, University of Reading Archives, BER. 36/5/43. There is no reference to her being given this property (part of her father's estate), but perhaps it was conveyed to her in settlement of £1,000 which her father borrowed from her, *Diary* 15 Dec. 1672. Her Will, dated 20 Sept. 1700, refers coolly to her eldest son, Lord Bergavenny, who 'during his life [is] to have only the use of my . . . furniture and household goods in my said house [Sheffield Park] . . .' In warmer terms she bequeaths: '. . . to my loving son Edward Nevill the sum of £2,200 over and besides the portion of £800 . . . left him by his father George Nevill's will.' In a codicil (her son Edward having died in the meantime, leaving his children William and Mary unprovided for) she leaves £2,200 in trust for these grandchildren, see manuscript in Mr. Radford's collection.

NEWDIGATE, Judge Sir Richard, Bt., MP (1602–1678). *D.N.B.*; E. Foss *Judges of England*; *Hist. of Parl.* Of Gray's Inn. Although he fought for Parliament in the Civil War, he was 'no enemy to monarchy.' As a Justice of the Upper Bench (appointed in 1654), he displeased Cromwell by insisting courageously, in a court case, that there was no statute stating it was high treason to levy war against the Protector. He was made Lord Chief Justice in January 1659/60, and MP for Tamworth in the Convention Parliament of April that year. Charles II made him a Baronet in July 1677.

NEWTON of CHARLTON, Sir Henry, Bt., MP (1618–1701). *Hist. of Parl.* (entered as PUCKERING formerly NEWTON, Sir Henry); *Extinct & Dormant Baronetcies* (the information given in these two sources differs substantially). A Royalist. Whitelocke made an offer of £8,000 for Charlton, Sir Henry's fine house near Greenwich, with its contents, but this was refused, *Diary* 1 July 1658. The property was subsequently sold for £8,500.

NICHOLAS, Sir Edward, Bt., MP (1593–1669). *D.N.B.* Of the Middle Temple. Secretary of State to Charles I and Charles II.

NICHOLAS, Judge Robert, MP (1595–1667). M.F.K.; E. Foss *Judges of England*. Of the Middle Temple. MP for Devizes, Wiltshire, in the Long Parliament, from 1640 to 1653. He was made a Serjeant-at-Law in 1648 and a Justice of the Upper Bench from June 1649; he was then moved to the Exchequer, from 1654 to 1658, and returned to the Upper Bench in January 1659/60.

NIXON, John, MP. *V.C.H. City of Oxford.* An Oxfordshire landowner. He wrote, as Mayor of Oxford, stating that Whitelocke had been 'chosen with one voice' as Recorder of Oxford, and begging him to accept the office, 17 Feb. 1646/47, Long. W.P. ix, 123. In the next decade, he corresponded with Whitelocke about the opposition that James Whitelocke would have to face if he stood for election as MP for Oxford, *Diary* 15, 22 Dec. 1658.

NORTH, Sir Dudley, KB, MP, JP (1602–1677). *M.F.K..*; *Hist. of Parl.* Eldest son of Dudley, 3rd Baron North (for whom see G.E.C. and *D.N.B.*). He sat in the 1628 Parliament, then in the Short and in the Long Parliament (until secluded in 1648) and again in 1660. He succeeded to the title in 1666.

NORTHAMPTON, Hon. James Compton, MP, later 3rd E. of (1622–1681). G.E.C.; M.F.K. Of Compton Wyniates, Warwickshire. He was elected to the Long Parliament in 1640 but disabled in 1643, being in arms against Parliament. He succeeded to his wealthy father's title in the same year; his fine for delinquency was reduced from £21,455 to £14,153. He was arrested in 1653 and 1655 and again in September and October 1659, at the time of Sir George Booth's royalist rising; Whitelocke refers to the Earl being released with five other Lords, on security to live peaceably, 'this was to ingratiate w[i]'h the Cavaliers', *Diary* 2 Nov. 1659. A year later, Whitelocke refers to his own earlier purchase of the royalty of the Manor of Henley from the Earl, 'after much labour & trouble', ib. 13 Nov. 1660. This labour and trouble is not recorded in *The Diary* at the time of the negotiations, but a tripartite indenture endorsed 'Bargain & Sale from the Earl of Northampton . . . to Sir Bulstrode Whitelocke' is dated 8 July 1659,

Oxford R.O., D.D. Henley B.11 15 (copy), from Henley-on-Thames Borough Record; this refers back to an indenture of 20 Sept. 1643, which appears to have been executed by the Earl and his widowed mother, to raise money on the Manor of Henley-on-Thames and other properties. Later, a certificate from the County of Oxford, signed by William Lenthall (q.v.) with others, appointed Whitelocke Steward of the Manor, which was described as belonging to the Earl of Northampton, who was in arms against Parliament, 17 Jan. 1645/46, Long. W.P. ix, 77.

NORTHUMBERLAND, Algernon Percy, MP, later 4th (in G.E.C.), but usually named 10th E. of (1602–1668). G.E.C.; *D.N.B.* He inherited the title in 1632, and was appointed Lord High Admiral of England 'during pleasure', serving from 1638 to 1642; the appointment was intended (had the Civil War not intervened) to run until 1655, when James Duke of York (q.v.) would be 22 years old and could take over the office. Northumberland was appointed General of the Forces South of Trent in March 1639 and General of the Army against the Scots in February 1639/40. In spite of these and other high appointments, the Earl left Charles I for Parliament, but worked for reconciliation between the two sides, and was sometimes suspected of being a crypto-Royalist. He was chosen to lead the Commissioners from Parliament to treat with the King at Oxford, in 1642/43, and was a Commissioner again at Uxbridge, in 1644/45. Whitelocke, also a Commissioner on both occasions from the Commons, admired the Earl's 'sober & stout Carryage', recording that on one occasion, when the King interrupted him, Northumberland 'said smartly, your M[ajes]^{ty} will give me leave to proceed', at which the King gave way. While in Oxford, Northumberland lived in his usual style, which was 'hardly . . . exceeded by any subject', bringing with him his own silver, linen and provisions, which included wine, some of which he gave to the King. In the months following the Oxford negotiations, the Earl often invited Whitelocke to dine with him, *Diary* 1642. 1643. fols.60, 60v., 62v.

After Whitelocke had successfully defended himself against Lord Savile's allegations that he and Denzil Holles (q.v.), had conferred privately with the King in Oxford, Northumberland paid Whitelocke the compliment of sending him a fat buck, and two months later a fat doe, ib. 7 Aug., 15 Nov. 1645; there are also references to Whitelocke being 'kindly treated' and being shown 'much kindnes' by Northumberland, ib. 21 Nov. 1645; 10 Jan. 1647/48. A few months after the death of Whitelocke's second wife, Frances, Northumberland (who was living at Petworth, Sussex) lent him Syon House, Isleworth, to prevent it being requisitioned by the Army. The tone of the Earl's autograph letters (on this and other matters) confirms Whitelocke's comments on his friendliness; the letters are neatly penned, and almost Victorian in appearance:

S[i]ʳ

It did very much trouble me that my house att Sion was not sooner free for you, and if I were assured that your being there was a convenience to you as well as . . . an advantage to me, I should receave much satisfaction by haveing it so filled; the consideration you are pleased to have of me and of that house of myne is a very greate favor, w[hi]ᶜʰ shall thankfully be acknowledged and returned unto you if ever it be in the power of

> Your very affectionate
> friend and servant

Pettworth Aug:3
   1649
> Northumberland

Long. W.P. x, 24.

This letter is transcribed, with Whitelocke's appreciative comments, in Add.Ms 37345 fol.2.

Some months later, the Earl wrote very humbly about a matter to be brought to Parliament; this concerned a debt owed by Henry Jermyn, Earl of St. Albans (an unscrupulous Royalist), to Northumberland's sister Dorothy (wife of Robert Sidney, 2nd Earl of Leicester). Northumberland ended his letter with the appeal:

if . . . you finde my sisters desires reasonable, and will please to afford her your assistance in the passing of her acte, you will increase the obligations of

Nov: 29
1649
> Your Lo[rdshi]ᵖˢ very affectionate
> and humble Servant
> Northumberland

ib.x, 69.

(Whitelocke was by then a Lord Commissioner of the Great Seal).

Northumberland also wrote on behalf of a Mr. Goodwin, who had held an appointment in Windsor Forest and who hoped his employment might be continued under Whitelocke (who had been appointed Constable of Windsor Castle and Keeper of the Forest and Great Park in 1649). The letter stated that Goodwin had spent some years in the Earl's family – he did not say in his service. The Earl added, unassumingly:

. . . I am altogether unacquainted how things of this nature are likely to be disposed of, therefore if what I move in the behalfe of this gentleman be either impropper or inconvenient[,] I doubt not but your Lo[rdshi]ᵖˢ favor to me will make you passe by greater faileings in

Feb: 18 1649[/50]
> Your lo[rdshi]ᵖˢ most affectionate
> and faithfull servant
> Northumberland

ib., 122.

Northumberland supported the Restoration, and was Lord High Constable at the Coronation of Charles II in April 1661. His last appearance in Whitelocke's record was when he undertook the embarrassing task, with the Earl of Manchester, of warning Whitelocke and John Thurloe (q.v.), privately, that the King wished to have them dropped from the Governing Body of Sutton's Hospital, *Diary* 22 Jan. 1660/61.

There had been a connection between the Percy and Whitelocke families in the previous generation: Whitelocke's uncle Edmund (q.v.) became an innocent suspect in the Gunpowder Plot, having dined with his friend, the ill-fated Henry Percy, 9th (or 3rd) Earl of Northumberland (Algernon's father) on 4 Nov. 1605, the very eve of the planned explosion, *Liber* p. 9; a footnote states that the elder Northumberland seems to have given Edmund a pension of £40, which was later raised to £60.

NORTON, Col. Richard, MP (1615–1691). *Hist. of Parl.*; C.H. Firth and G. Davies *Regimental History of Cromwell's Army*; *Pepys, passim*. He fought for Parliament; served as an MP for Hampshire, from 1645 until Pride's Purge in 1648; was readmitted in November 1651; sat in 1653, 1654, 1656 and 1660 and, again for Portsmouth or Hampshire, in six Parliaments after the Restoration. Whitelocke, who would have known him in Parliament, exchanged two of his coach horses plus a payment of £40, for four of the Colonel's coach geldings, *Diary* 22 May 1648. Norton was one of the trustees for the insane Earl of Arundell's estate, ib. 15 Feb. 1654/55. Two other entries concern the Colonel's activities in connection with Portsmouth, of which he was Governor from 1645 to 1648, 1655 to 1659 and from April 1660 to 1661, ib. 10 Dec. 1659; 11 May 1660.

NORWICH, George Goring, 1st E. of (1585–1663). G.E.C.; *D.N.B*; *Pepys, passim* (the two last sources under Goring). After service at Court he fought for the King in the Civil War, becoming General of the royalist forces in Kent and Essex. A Privy Counsellor in 1639, he was resworn in 1660. He was distantly connected with Whitelocke by his marriage to Mary (c.1648), second daughter of Edward Nevill, Lord Abergavenny, see: NEVILL, George. Goring was created Earl of Norwich in 1644. The Earl is only referred to in *The Diary* when he and Sir George Carteret (q.v.) consulted Whitelocke at his Middle Temple Chambers, without either of them paying a fee, *Diary* 17 Dec. 1662. He may well have been arranging to have his Will prepared, for it is dated 2 Jan. 1662/63. Norwich died a few days later, on a journey from Hampton Court to London; he was buried in Westminster Abbey, 14 Jan. 1662/63.

NOTTINGHAM, Arabella, Countess of (d.1682). G.E.C. The beautiful daughter of Edward Smith of Abingdon and of the Middle Temple; sister of Sir Edward Smith, MP (see *Hist. of Parl.* as Smythe) and of Dr. Smith (q.v.). She married in 1627 (without their parents' consent) 'a wild young scholar at Oxford', Sir Charles Howard, son of the 1st Earl of Nottingham. (Charles later inherited the title of 3rd Earl, in 1642, on the death of his half-brother.) The wedding ceremony was performed by a clergyman who had been Charles Howard's tutor, without having the banns called or obtaining a licence. When the 17-year-old husband, was threatened with rejection by his mother, he abandoned his wife. Arabella was befriended by Sir Arthur Hesilrige (q.v.) and Lambert Osbaldston (q.v.), who appealed to Whitelocke to have a settlement made on her out of the pension paid to the Earl by Parliament, *Diary* 1643.1644. fol.65. One of the Countess's brothers, Dr. Smith, later sent a well-bound Bible to Whitelocke, in gratitude for his help, ib. 6 Oct. 1649.

NOY (NOYE), William, MP (1577–1634). *D.N.B.* Of Lincoln's Inn. A learned and able lawyer. Elected MP for various Cornish constituencies in 1604, 1623, 1625/26 (Whitelocke's first Parliament), and in 1628. As an MP, he was active against monopolies and other forms of oppression, but after his appointment as Attorney-General to Charles I, in 1631, his name was associated with illiberal measures, including the reintroduction of forest laws, the Ship Money Writ, and brutal Star-Chamber decisions, notably against William Prynne (q.v.). Whitelocke describes an entertaining encounter with him early in 1629, which allows us to hear something of Noy's good-natured, teasing style of speech. The meeting arose from a case described in *The Diary*, and more fully in the 'Annales', in which a young Middle Temple lawyer named Basing died. As he had been a heavy drinker and had lost all his money gambling, the Middle Temple Parliament buried him at their own expense, in the style they considered 'answearable to his quality, & the dignity of his office.' Whitelocke, as their Treasurer, was required to recoup the money; he wrote a civil letter to Basing's father in Dorset, asking him to reimburse the £50 spent on the funeral. Receiving no reply, he wrote more sharply, which prompted 'a froward answear, & churlish, That those who had ordered his sons buryall att that charge, might see it paid, butt he would not.' The Middle Temple Parliament agreed that a bill should be preferred against Basing in the Court of Requests, but before putting in the bill, Whitelocke was instructed to show it to the Lord Privy Seal, who approved it, and then to Noy, '... who left his multitude of company ... & came into his bedchamber, where the discourse ... may be best expressed, & ... understood Dialogue wise.'

Noy thought well of the draft bill and suggested certain amendments. Then:

Noy. As I have given you my advice in your buisnes, so I desire to have your advice in my buisnes, or rather the K[ings] buisnes ... It is a Patent the K[ing] commaunded me to drawe of Association between England & Scotland, concerning the buisnes of fishing.

Wh[itelocke]. I have never had such honor, as to have my advice asked by such a one as your selfe ...

Noy. ... I have forgot my Latin, & I know you write Latin well ...

They went through the Patent, clause by clause, and young Whitelocke suggested some amendments:

Noy. ... to lett you see, that I am pleased with your advice, I will give you a fee for it, out of my little purse, heer[,] take these single pence.

Wh. truely S[i]ʳ, I did not expect a fee from you, nor did I offer you any,

Noy. No, if you had, I should have taken it ill from you, butt you must learne, never to refuse any thing from your friends.

Wh. I thanke you for that profitable rule, & for this extraordinary fee, butt I pray S[i]ʳ why have you given me 11 groats, more then an Atturnyes fee ...

Noy. I give you more then an Atturneyes fee, bicause you will be a better man, then an Atturney – yea then an Atturney Generall.

Wh. I never doubted your opinion in anything so much as this.

Noy. You will find this to be true.

Wh. I doubt you find me troublesome ... I shall humbly take my leave of you.

Noy. You are not troublesome. I pray come to me whensoever there is occasion.

Wh. S[i]ʳ you make me ashamed by ... this complement of bringing me to your doore, which much greater men then I doe not expect from you.

Noy. You are L[ord] Treasurer of the Temple, therfore I will bring you to the Stayres foot ...

They parted, 'After much other drolling, wherin he delighted, & was very good att it ...' and Mr. Basing paid up, with apologies, Add.Ms 53726 fols. 47v.–49.

NYE, Philip (c.1596–1672). D.N.B.; Calamy Revised; G. Nuttall Visible Saints. An Independent Minister; active as a pastor and in public affairs, during the 1640s and 1650s. After the Restoration he signed the declaration against the fanatic, Thomas Venner (q.v.), in 1661. He collaborated with Whitelocke and Dr. Thomas Goodwyn (q.v.) in efforts to obtain liberty of conscience, Diary 14 May 1661; 10 Mar. 1661/62.

OAKELEY (OAKLEY, OAKLY), Richard, MP (d.1653?). *Liber* p.90, *passim*; H.T. Weyman *Members of Parliament for Shropshire Boroughs*, offprint from *Transactions of the Shropshire Archaeological Society*, 'Members of Parliament for Bishop's Castle' (Memoir No. 21). Son of Rowland Oakeley. Of Oakley near Bishop's Castle, Shropshire. He had been a Postmaster (i.e. scholar) at Merton College, Oxford, before entering the service of Whitelocke's father, James Whitelocke (q.v.), as his clerk, in 1609; described by his master as 'a good scholler.' After 10 years Oakeley left to enter the Middle Temple, and was called to the Bar in 1621. In July that year John Williams (q.v.), at that time Lord Keeper of the Great Seal and Bishop-elect of Lincoln, appointed Oakeley as his secretary. Oakeley served as an MP in 1624 and 1626; in 1628 his name was erased from the Return for Boston, in Lincolnshire, and that of Sir Anthony Irbye was substituted.

In view of his position, the 'Mr Oakeley' who lent Whitelocke his house in Dean's Yard, Westminster, was probably Richard, rather than his brother John, *Diary* 1640.1641. fol.51. Described as Whitelocke's 'kinde friend', he supported the King in the Civil War and compounded for his delinquency with a payment of £460. He left £1,200 p.a. from his land to his son, presumably William (below), ib. 7 June 1660. Richard's younger brother, John Oakeley, is not named in *The Diary*, but he had been steward to Judge James Whitelocke's household, and witnessed his master's signature, both on the Judge's Deed of Gift to Whitelocke of all his personal estate, and on his Will, written on a half sheet of paper, Add. Ms 53726 fols.69v. and 70 (transcripts). Richard's or John's signatures appear on a number of other documents between 1622 and 1635, Long. W.P. ii, 76, *passim*. John may well have continued in Whitelocke's service after Judge James Whitelocke's death in June 1632; the last of the Long. W.P. documents mentioned above, contains a message from John Oakeley on domestic matters, including payment of £6, apparently to a French sculptor, William Larson, 'for 8 pictures of stone', 30 June 1635, ib. vi, 247.

OAKELEY (OAKLEY, OAKLY), [William], MP (1635–1695). *Hist. of Parl.* Son of Richard Oakeley (above). Studied at Balliol College, Oxford, and at the Middle Temple. In 1659, aged about 24, he was elected MP for Bishop's Castle, which his father had represented 35 years earlier; William represented it again several times after the Restoration. When Whitelocke was in jeopardy, his brother-in-law, Colonel William Willoughby (q.v.), asked him what he knew of a certain young gentleman, a Knight (i.e. 'Knight of the Shire', or MP) in Shropshire. It appeared that when Whitelocke's name was in question, in connection with the Bill of

Indemnity, this MP had mustered support from all his friends in the Commons, including 20 Welsh and Shropshire MPs, and had persuaded them to vote for the inclusion of Whitelocke's name. The young gentleman turned out to be William Oakeley, who had acted without any appeal from Whitelocke, *Diary* 7 June 1660.

ONSLOWE (ONSLOW), Col. Sir Richard, MP (1601–1664). *Hist. of Parl.*; *D.N.B.* A Parliamentary Colonel. He sat in the Short and Long Parliaments but was secluded at Pride's Purge in December 1648. He sat in the Protectorate Parliaments, and was called to Oliver Cromwell's 'Other House'. His parliamentary career continued in 1660 and after the Restoration. Earlier, he was named as one of the trustees of the Earl of Arundell and Surrey (q.v.), who had suffered brain damage, *Diary* 15 Feb. 1654/55. He wrote to Whitelocke asking a favour for a friend, ib. 20 July 1659.

ORMOND (ORMONDE), James, 12th E. and 1st D. of (1610–1668). *G.E.C.*; *D.N.B.*; *Royal Commission on Historical Manuscripts, Ormond.* A royalist soldier and politician, he was a likeable man with high principles. He served Charles I and Charles II, initially in Ireland, where he was Lord-Lieutenant from 1643 to 1647 and 1649 to 1650. He then joined Charles II in exile from 1651 to 1660. At the Restoration, he took his place in the House of Lords as Marquis of Ormond (a title given to him by Charles I in 1642) and Earl of Brecknock (a title in the English peerage, given to him by Charles II in 1660), *Diary* 28 July 1660. In March 1661 he was created Duke of Ormond in the Irish peerage. Among his numerous offices, he was appointed Lord High Steward of the Household in 1660. Whitelocke was encouraged to petition the Duke, in that capacity, for leave to sue John Green (q.v.) for £2,000, owed for timber that Green contracted to buy from Whitelocke's estate; he had sold the timber for the King's use without paying for it, ib. 1 July 1661.

Ormond's friends took grave exception to a passage in Whitelocke's *Memorials*, when it appeared, posthumously. They wrote indignantly to the old Duke of Ireland, suggesting (quite wrongly) that a slur on his name had been inserted in the printed text by his enemy, the Earl of Anglesey. The offending material indicated that Ormond might, on certain conditions, have gone over to Parliament. (Details are given near the end of chapter 2, introducing Whitelocke's *Diary*.)

ORRERY (ORRORY), Roger Boyle, MP, 1st Baron Broghill, later 1st E. of (1621–1679). G.E.C.; *D.N.B.*; *Hist. of Parl.* (as Roger Boyle); *Pepys* x (Boyle). Third son of the 1st Earl of Cork; brother of Robert Boyle (q.v.) and of Lady Ranelagh (q.v.). A soldier, politician and writer, he was created Baron Broghill in 1627. He served first in the King's Army, then under Parliament's Commissioners in Ireland, but after the King's execution in 1649 he came to London, plotting to cross the channel and see Prince Charles about Restoration plans. When this was discovered by the Council, Cromwell called at his lodgings, saved him from imprisonment and sent him to fight again in Ireland. Broghill, as he then was, went on to become a trusted adviser and friend of Cromwell, *Diary* 2 May 1657. The first diary reference to Broghill concerns his conspicuous kindness to young James Whitelocke, serving in Ireland as a volunteer in Parliament's Army. This kindness was said to be shown for Whitelocke's sake, although Whitelocke commented that he did not know Broghill well at that time, but that later they became friends, *Diary* 1 Jan. 1649/50. Yet it is clear from Broghill's first letter below, of Dec. 1651, that he considered he had already received considerable help from Whitelocke. He was active in the attempt to make Cromwell King, and supported Richard Cromwell as Protector but, after Richard's fall, he worked in Ireland for the Restoration, inviting Charles to land, initially, in Cork. He was President of Munster from March 1660 to 1672, and was created Earl of Orrery in September 1660. Whitelocke, although out of office and out of favour, helped Orrery at the time of his impeachment and in his dispute with the Duke of Ormond (above), ib. 2, 7 Dec. 1669; details of the impeachment may be found in *C.J.* 25 Nov. 1669 and *C.S.P. (Ireland)*, 1669–1670, pp.30–49 (Orrery's defence).

Lord Broghill's letters are written in a large, straggling handwriting:

My Lord
    Having bin informed by my Sister Ranalegh that y[ou]^r Lo[rdshi]^p is pleased to confound me by apprehending th[a]^t I have served y[o]^u in th^e person of y[ou]^r sonn. Give me leave to tell y[ou]^r Lo[rdshi]^p th[a]^t w[ha]^{t}ever service I can performe to him is a short gratetude in Comparison of w[ha]^t I owe y[ou]^r Lo[rdshi]^p for many Noble Favours … [;] if y[ou]^r Lo[rdshi]^p can give me any Comm[an]^d th[a]^t may set me a worke in y[ou]^r service y[o]^u will therby satisfye an earneste desire of myne …

    The very great loss this poore Country [Ireland] in Generall & my selfe in perticular have sustained by the death of our much … lamented De^p[u]^{ty} [Henry Ireton, q.v., d. 26 Nov.] & the Change its like to produce in our affayres here, has made me thinke it fitt to send over a servant of my owne by whome … I have acquainted my Sister Ranalegh w[i]th w[ha]^t I have by divers binn pressed to move for … wherin they think I might both serve the

Publicke & advantage my selfe. I shal bespeeck y[ou]ʳ Lo[rdshi]ᵖ to give her leave to tell you w[ha]ᵗ it is . . .
1 Dec. 1651.

Long. W.P. xi, 148.

In the context, it seems likely that Broghill was aspiring to the vacant office of Lord Deputy of Ireland but the post went, after an interval, to Charles Fleetwood (q.v.) and after him to Henry Cromwell (q.v.). A year later Broghill wrote again, asking Whitelocke to help in preparing a bill, already agreed to, for settling £1,000 a year on him out of Irish estates; he commented that the delay was causing inconvenience, both to him and to those from whom he had borrowed money, 20 Dec. 1652, ib. xii, 188. The bill was not enacted until nearly five years later, *C.J.* vii, 573, 24 June 1657. In the summer of that year, Broghill wrote begging Whitelocke to press for the settlement of arrears of pay, due to soldiers who had served in Ireland before June 1649; the delay was causing great hardship and if Whitelocke would help by persuading the Speaker to read the letter and bill which were enclosed, 'The Poor Army' would be eternally obliged to him, 7 June 1657, Long. W.P. xviii, 64–64v.

Another note introduced its bearer as his niece, 'my owne Sisters Daughter . . . a Person I have a reall Concernement for . . .' 3 Aug. 1657, ib., 75. A further appeal for help concerned 'a reference from his Hig[hnes]ˢ' (Oliver Cromwell), to the Commissioners of the Treasury (of which Whitelocke was one) relating to the Clothworkers, '. . . in wh[ich] a brother of my Wifes is Concerned . . .', 14 Apr. 1658, ib., 125; in 1641, Broghill had married Lady Margaret Howard, daughter of the 2nd Earl of Suffolk.

Apologizing for not taking leave of Whitelocke, Broghill wrote: 'My wife beinge landed [presumably from Ireland] I am goinge to showe I am as kinde a husband as she is a Wife, crossinge to meete her, as much land as she did sea . . .', 29 Apr. [1658?], ib., 129.

After the events surrounding the fall of Richard Cromwell, the 'late Revolutions in England', Broghill, still in sympathy with the Republican Parliament, wrote to his 'Dearest Sister', Lady Ranelagh, describing the merciful calm with which the news had been received in Ireland, where 'probably any divisions amo[n]gˢᵗ ourselves might open too large a doore for our old Com[mo]ⁿ enemye to enter in at . . . I think the Par[liamen]ᵗ may expect al due obedience from hence, wherein my Endeavours shall not be wanting . . . direct y[ou]ʳ letters for me to the Postmaster at Dublin . . .', 25 May [1659], ib. xix, 129; *Diary* 29 May 1659. Lady Ranelagh presumably sent the letter to Whitelocke, who evidently kept it. The following month, Broghill wrote a clearer and more detailed account to Whitelocke, on the same theme:

My Deare Lord

Both as you are a Publike Person, & as you have honored, me with yo[u]ʳ Particular Favor, I owe you an accounte of things heere ... The late Change of the Goᵛ[ernmen]ᵗ did indeed startle many heer, upon severall accounts, but the more Considerable Persons had their Scruples on the score, of their o[a]thes to his late Hig[hne]s warranted by Parl[iamen]ᵗ. But his late Hig[hne]s haveinge, Publikely manefested his acquiessence in the Authority of the Parl[iamen]ᵗ[,] all Scruples in that Action, are wiped away; & all the Army have made now an Adress to the Parl[iamen]ᵗ to evidence their Duty & affection to them. The others in thes Parts are now doinge the like & the Address, when fully subscribed, willbe hastened over to the Parl[iamen]ᵗ to whos Authority all heer, doe willingly submitt.

I know not, whither you may have soe much spare time, as now & then to cast away a letter to yo[u]ʳ Servant; who instead of Conversinge with the most accomplished of men, as my L[or]d Whitlock &c. now talkes with noething but his thoughts, his small Library, his Wife & children; his Plowmen, & Shepherds. & yet ... would not change th[a]ᵗ life, for a Kings, or[,] wh[ich] is more[,] a Genᵗˡ[eman]ˢ. My L[or]d Harry [Henry Cromwell, q.v.] is hasteninge into England & we [?] Preparinge heer to receive our new Go[verno]ʳ. Indeed my L[or]d this nation, thorough mercy[,] is quiet as ever ...

23 June 1659.

Long. W.P. xix, 31.

OSBALDSTON (OSBOLSTON, OSBALDESTON), Lambert (1594–1659). D.N.B.; Alumni Westmonasterienses (London. 1852); Gray's Inn Register.

Appointed joint headmaster of Westminster School in 1621, and sole head in January 1625/26. Reputed to be a good scholar and a good headmaster. Among a number of appointments, he was made a Prebendary of Westminster in 1629, and Rector of Wheathampstead, Herts., with the Chapel of Harpenden. (The Manor of Wheathampstead had been granted by Edward the Confessor, in 1065, not to St. Albans but to the Abbot and Convent, i.e. Monastery, of Westminster. After the dissolution of the monasteries, Henry VIII had granted these estates to the Dean and Chapter of Westminster, V.C.H. Herts. ii, 296–297.)

Osbaldston was ejected from his appointments by the Star Chamber, for criticizing an unnamed person in a letter to Bishop John Williams (q.v.). In the context, epithets such as 'the little urchin' and 'the little meddling hocus pocus' were enough to identify his target as Archbishop William Laud (q.v.). The certificate of Lord Chief Justices Bramston (King's Bench), Finch (Common Pleas), and Judges Jones and Berkley, for the case of the Attorney-General vs. Osbolston (sic), 19 Jan. 1638/39, is in Long. W.P. vii, 313. The trial took place in the following month when Osbaldston was sentenced, among other penalties, to pay £5,000 each to the King and to the Archbishop; to have his ears nailed to the pillory, in the presence of his scholars, and to be imprisoned during the King's pleasure. While the Lord-Keeper (Thomas, 1st Lord Coventry) was giving judgment, Osbaldston managed to slip out of the Court, no doubt with somebody's connivance. He destroyed certain documents at the school and left a note, which successfully put his enemies off the scent: 'If the archbishop inquire after me, tell him I am gone beyond Canterbury.' While officials looked for him in the seaports, he lay low at a house in Drury Lane. He remained in hiding until the Long Parliament reviewed his case; the House of Lords then made an Order, ruling: that neither the Court of High Commission nor any other ecclesiastical court had power to execute a sentence passed by the Star Chamber; that Mr. Osbolston (*sic*) was to be freed from all fines etc. and from corporal punishment; that his prebend and parsonage were to be restored to him and that the sentence of the Star Chamber was to be made void. The earlier damages and costs awarded against Bishop John Williams of Lincoln were also cancelled, 2 Apr. 1641, ib. viii, 115, Order signed by John Browne, Clerk to the Parliaments; *L.J.* iv, 205.

Whitelocke's first diary reference to Osbaldston couples his name with that of Sir Arthur Hesilrige (q.v.), both being friends of the Countess of Nottingham (q.v.), *Diary* 1643. 1644. fol. 65. He is also referred to as actively supporting Whitelocke and Denzil Holles (q.v.) and trying to modify the attacks made on them by Hesilrige, Vane (q.v.) and others, when Lord Savile's accusations against them were considered by a Committee of the House of Commons, ib. 11 July 1645. Later, Sir Arthur Hesilrige joined with Whitelocke in helping Osbaldston at Westminster College (of which the School was and is a part), probably in connection with his prebend, ib. 18 Sept. 1649.

OULSEY, Sir Charles, see WOLSELEY.

OVERBURY family. Of Bourton-on-the-Hill, Gloucestershire, west of Moreton-in-Marsh. Sir Giles Overbury (Will proved 1653), was the brother of Sir Thomas Overbury sen., who had been murdered in the Tower, in 1613. Sir Giles and his wife, Anne, had two children who appear in *The Diary*: (1) Thomas Overbury, jun., knighted 1660 (d.1684), see *D.N.B.* (in the entry for his famous uncle of the same name, referred to above) and (2) Mary. Although a Royalist, Sir Thomas Overbury, jun., was in Anthony à Wood's words: 'a favourer of protestant dissenters.' This was borne out by his twice going to hear nonconformist preachers in

Whitelocke's lodgings, one of them being Dr. John Owen (q.v.), *Diary* 13, 20 Dec. 1668. Sir Thomas was later received into membership of Owen's Congregational Church in Leadenhall Street, P. Toon *God's Statesman* (Paternoster Press. 1971) pp. 154, 155. His wife Hester, née Leach, often visited Whitelocke's wife Mary, *Diary* 26 Nov. 1668. Overbury's sister Mary (q.v.), married Whitelocke's son William (q.v.) at Bourton in May 1659; for details see William's entry. Thomas (not knighted by that date) negotiated the marriage settlement with Whitelocke. His widowed mother (Lady Anne Overbury), is referred to before the wedding, *Diary* 4 Jan. 1658/59; 26 Mar. 1659; she died the next year.

OVERTON, Col. Robert (*c*. 1609–1668). C.H. Firth and G. Davies *Regimental History of Cromwell's Army*; *D.N.B.* A Yorkshireman, Republican, and Fifth Monarchy man; a soldier, scholar, and friend of John Milton. Only referred to in *The Diary* between 18 June 1659 and 12 Mar. 1659/60. He sent Monck a declaration in favour of a free Parliament (unaware, it seems, that the influx of Royalists in a free election must lead to the Restoration of Charles II), yet his stated object was to oppose government by a single person and to defend the nation against arbitrary, kingly rule. He wrote to Monck, who was planning the Restoration, boldly expressing his fear of the country returning to the bondage of kingship, and he persuaded various officers to sign a declaration to that effect. Inevitably, he was dismissed as Governor of Hull, and lost his commission, ib. 15 Feb.; 6, 7, 10 Mar. 1659/60. None of the diary entries indicates that Whitelocke knew the Colonel personally. After the Restoration, although he was not a regicide, Overton spent most of his remaining years in prison.

OWEN, John, DD (1616–1683). *D.N.B.*; *Correspondence of John Owen* (ed. P. Toon. J. Clarke, Cambridge & London. 1970); *The Oxford Orations of Dr. John Owen* (ed. P. Toon. Translated from the Latin. Privately printed. 1971); P. Toon *God's Statesman: the Life and Work of John Owen* (Paternoster Press. 1971); *Calamy Revised*. A distinguished and very influential Independent, well known to Whitelocke. One-time Chaplain to John, Lord Lovelace, sen. (q.v.); later, Chaplain to Oliver Cromwell (q.v.) whom he supported staunchly, although opposing the plan to make him King. Said by Chancellor Clarendon (q.v.) to be Whitelocke's Chaplain, *Diary* 4 Apr. 1664; this was not denied but there is no confirmation of it in other entries, apart from the fact that Owen frequently preached to Whitelocke and his family in the 1660s.

Owen had preached to Parliament on a number of occasions in the

1640s, served as Dean of Christ Church, Oxford, 1651–1660 and as Vice-Chancellor of the University, 1652–1658. His *Oxford Orations* (above) show a good-humoured, devout and humane man, who helped the University to recover from the damage done to scholarship by the Civil War, and supported it against continuing attack by the more extreme radical dissenters.

Owen's niece, Mary, married Bartholomew ('Bat'), son of Whitelocke's friend Bartholomew Hall (q.v.), at whose house, Harding (or Harpsden) Court near Henley-on-Thames, Whitelocke heard Owen preach a month before the King's execution, *Diary* 31 Dec. 1648. After the Restoration Clarendon tried, with offers of preferment, to persuade Owen to conform, but the Doctor courteously declined on grounds of conscience, ib. 4 Apr. 1664; a longer account of the interview with Clarendon (probably based on Owen's report of it) is given in the memoir introducing *A Complete Collection of the Sermons of . . . John Owen D.D.* (ed. J. Asty. London. 1721), pp.xxv, xxvi. Sir Charles Wolseley (q.v.), John Thurloe (q.v.) and Sir Thomas Overbury (q.v.), were among Whitelocke's friends who went to hear Owen preach, *Diary* 22 May 1667, 20 Dec. 1668.

One of Owen's brothers, Philemon, had served as a Captain with Parliament's Army in Ireland, where he was killed, P. Toon *God's Statesman* (above), p. 2 note 2. According to Whitelocke, 'the preacher's son', Captain Lewys Owen (elsewhere referred to as 'son of Mr Owen, the Minister of Harding'), died at that time; he had been a friend of young James Whitelocke's, *Diary* 1 Jan. 1649/50; Add. Ms 37345, fol. 37. 'M^r' Owen (not at that date a DD), was in Ireland as Cromwell's Chaplain.

OWEN, Thankful (1620–1681). *D.N.B.* A learned, Independent preacher. Appointed Senior Proctor of Oxford University in March 1649. A university preacher. Appointed President of St. John's College in 1650. After the Restoration, he became Pastor of an Independent congregation in Fetter Lane. He is only referred to once, when he consulted Whitelocke on a legal matter, around the time of his ejection, *Diary* 2 Nov. 1660.

OXENSTIERNA, Count Axel (1583–1654). *S.M.K.*; M. Roberts *Sweden as a Great Power 1611–1697* (London. 1968), *passim*; D.H. Pennington *Seventeenth Century Europe* (Longman. 1970), *passim*. Swedish Chancellor of the Realm under King Gustav Adolf, he continued in that office throughout the reign of Queen Christina (q.v.). One of Europe's most distinguished statesmen. As a member of the Regency Council, during Christina's minority, he had wielded almost sovereign power; three and later four other members of the Oxenstierna family served under him on the Council, see M. Roberts *Essays in Swedish History* (Weidenfeld & Nicholson. 1967) pp.26–27 and Pennington (above) pp.203–204. Years later, when the Swedish Court received news of Cromwell taking power as Protector, the Queen told Whitelocke that Oxenstierna would like to have done this when she was a young child, and a Dane at the Swedish Court commented that the old Chancellor envied Cromwell for achieving what he himself had failed to do when Christina was young, *Diary* 13, 24 Jan. 1653/54.

Whitelocke's long (and sometimes hard-hitting) discussions with the great Chancellor, are recorded as dialogue in his *Journal*. Oxenstierna asked searching questions about the new regime, the political stability of the English Commonwealth and, in effect, its fitness to sign a treaty with Sweden. Whitelocke held his own with dignity, sometimes defending his position by attacking. At quite an early stage in the negotiations the Chancellor agreed to pay Whitelocke a curious compliment, which he had paid to other prominent men, by calling him his adopted son, *Diary* 12 Jan. 1653/54; *Journal* i, 312. The Chancellor's great wealth (some of it, as Whitelocke suspected, derived from rich cargoes brought home in Swedish ships), was highlighted in a report that John Oxenstierna (q.v.) had £20,000 p.a. settled on him during his father's lifetime, while his brother Erik (below) received £10,000 p.a., apart from what they were to inherit at their father's death, *Diary* 16 Apr. 1654.

OXENSTIERNA, Count Erik (d.1656). Second son of Axel Oxenstierna (above) whom he succeeded as Chancellor in 1654. He served ably under Charles X of Sweden (q.v.) for two years until his own death. Wrongly referred to by Whitelocke as the eldest son, *Diary* 12 Jan. 1653/54, but shown as the second son on the same date in *Journal* i, 308. President of the General College of Trade when Whitelocke was in Sweden, ib. ii, 241 with note. Whitelocke thought him a somewhat aggressive negotiator, on the occasions when Count Erik stood in for his father; but the Count's letters, written in most curious Latin, after Whitelocke left Sweden, were very cordial. Whitelocke wrote a letter of sympathy on hearing of Axel Oxenstierna's death, Riksarkivet E. 1058 fols.57–57v., 29 Oct. 1654. In a letter, here translated, Count Erik wrote:

> ... I snatch at this opportunity of renewing our friendship which ... has been such a pleasure to me ... He [the bearer of the letter] will ... be able to confirm emphatically how great is the respect for your qualities which your Excellency has left behind in this kingdom, particularly in our home ... such an old and close friend of our family ...
> 5th Aug. 1654
> > Long W.P. xvi, 108.

Another letter from the Count, of 13 June 1655, is in ib. xiv, 20v.–21. Later, he reverted to the delicate subject of the English Admiralty Court examining the case of yet another Swedish vessel, alleged to have been engaged in herring fishing, 20 Jan. 1655/56, ib. xvii, 136–137. His last letter in this collection is dated 4/14 Mar. 1656/57. An undated draft from Whitelocke to Count Erik, ib. xvi, 192, is endorsed 'not sent'.

OXENSTIERNA, Count Gabriel (1) (1586–1656). *S.M.K.* Son of Bengt and cousin of Axel Oxenstierana (q.v.). A member of the Regency Government during Christina's minority. Dismissed as Lord High Treasurer in 1645, by the Queen, but appointed Admiral of the Realm in 1652. He knew nothing of naval matters but his deputy, General Wrangell (q.v.), carried the responsibility and later succeeded him. Whitelocke, vigilant for his rights, pushed the Admiral aside in order to stand next to the Queen, at an audience for the Envoy from Moscow, *Diary* 9 Feb. 1653/54. In their later encounters, however, they were courteous to one another. Count Gabriel's nephew, Baron Bengt Horne, was the bridegroom at the long-drawn-out court wedding, in Uppsala Castle, on the very eve of Christina's announcement, to the Four Estates, that she intended to abdicate, *Diary* 10 May 1654; *Journal* ii, 212.

OXENSTIERNA, Count Gabriel (2). Steward of Queen Christina's household. Bearing a silver staff, he received Whitelocke at the foot of the stairs in Uppsala Castle, for the Ambassador's public audience with Christina, *Diary* 23 Dec. 1653. When Whitelocke visited him, he noted that Count Gabriel, with his father and his uncle Chancellor Axel Oxenstierna, and the Chancellor's sons, John and Erik, were all Senators, ib. 7 Jan. 1653/54.

OXENSTIERNA, Count John (1611–1657). *S.M.K.* Eldest son of Chancellor Axel Oxenstierna (q.v.). As a young man he had been sent on several diplomatic missions, including one to England from the Regency Government in Sweden, when he felt he was received with less than the respect due to him from Charles I and the English government. This was still remembered against the Stuarts some 20 years later, and may have been to Whitelocke's advantage as Ambassador from the Commonwealth (later Protectorate), in his dealings with the Swedish Chancellor, *Diary* 9 Jan. 1653/54. Count John, however, resented the English in general rather than the Stuarts, ib. 3, 9 Mar. 1653/54. He had led the Swedish delegation, with John Alder-Salvius, on the mission which culminated in the Peace of Westphalia, 1648; he was created Marshall of the Realm in 1654.

OXFORD, Aubrey de Vere, 20th E. of (1627–1703). G.E.C. Served as a Sergeant-Major in the Netherlands in 1644. He was imprisoned in the Tower for plotting against Cromwell in June 1654. With other royalist Lords, he was later arrested in connection with Sir George Booth's rising, *Diary* 13 Aug. 1659. He was one of the six Peers who formally invited Charles II to return to England, in May 1660, and he took part in the Coronation ceremony of 1661.

PACKE (PACK), Sir Christopher, MP (*c.* 1593–1682). *D.N.B.*; A.B.B. A wealthy wool-merchant, member of the Drapers' Company and a Governor of the Company of Merchant Adventurers before the Restoration. He supported the Protector; was chosen Lord Mayor of London in October 1654 and was knighted by Cromwell in 1655. Serving in the second Protectorate Parliament it was he who, in February 1657, introduced the Remonstrance – the constitutional bill which would have enabled Cromwell to assume the 'name, style, title and dignity of King.' He was called to serve in Cromwell's new House of Lords, in the second session of the second Protectorate Parliament, which assembled on 20 January 1657/58.

Earlier, Whitelocke had been understandably annoyed when Cromwell spoke of sending both him and Sir Christopher as Ambassadors Extraordinary to Charles X of Sweden (q.v.). Colonel William Sydenham (q.v.) and Baron George Fleetwood (q.v.) tried to convince him that Sir Christopher would speak for the City and would be useful in matters of trade, but Whitelocke (having formerly acted on his own, as Ambassador Extraordinary to Sweden) was not to be persuaded; he confided to John Thurloe (q.v.) that he regarded the proposal as disparaging, *Diary* 17, 21, 25, 30 Jan. 1655/56. In spite of this Whitelocke, with other lawyers, supported Sir Christopher's move to make Cromwell King.

PACKER, John, MD. W. Munk *Roll of the Royal College of Physicians.* He qualified in Padua in 1655, and his degree was incorporated at Oxford in the following year. A Fellow of the College of Physicians in 1670. Whitelocke records that the Doctor paid him a visit at Chilton Lodge, to discuss the purchase of land near Hidden. Seven years later Whitelocke's guests, the Winwoods, were invited to dine with the Doctor, who evidently lived within coach-driving distance of Chilton Foliat, *Diary* 27 Sept. 1666; 26 Sept. 1673.

PACKER, Robert, MP (1614–1682). *Hist. of Parl.*; *V.C.H. Berks.* iv, 92. A Presbyterian, of Shellingford Castle, between Faringdon and Wantage, Oxfordshire (both formerly in Berkshire). A member of the Long Parliament from about Sept. 1646, representing Wallingford, Oxfordshire (formerly Berkshire); he was returned for the same seat in 1660 and 1661. Whitelocke and the Winwoods stayed with Packer, *Diary* 5, 7, Mar. 1665/66; later Packer visited Whitelocke as a client, paying fees of £1. and 10s., ib. 10 June 1669; 13 Aug. 1670, *passim.*

PACKER, Major, later Col. William, MP (*fl.* 1644–1662). *D.N.B.*; B.S. Capp *Fifth Monarchy Men,* biographical notes pp. 256–257, *passim.* A Fifth Monarchist in 1652. Noted for his godliness, he was granted a licence by the Council of State, in July 1653, to preach in any pulpit in England. As an active supporter of Cromwell he was made a deputy Major-General for Buckinghamshire, Oxfordshire and Hertfordshire in 1656, but sitting in the second Protectorate Parliament he opposed both the attempt to make Cromwell King, and the Protector's plans to set up a new House of Lords. He lost his commission, was elected to Richard Cromwell's Parliament but was unseated. The restored Long Parliament gave him back his regiment, but he was cashiered by them, with Lambert and other officers, on 12 October 1659, and subsequently became a member of the Committee of Safety. A letter bearing Packer's signature, with those of 11 other officers, informed Whitelocke that the General Council of Officers had appointed him to the Committee of Safety and that he was to report next morning to the Horse Chamber in Whitehall, 27 Oct. 1659, Long W.P. xix, 90. Packer was imprisoned in 1660 and transported in 1662.

PAGET, William, 6th Lord (1609–1678). G.E.C. Of Beaudesert, Staffs. and West Drayton, Middlesex; he inherited the title of 6th Baron in 1628. In 1640, he supported Whitelocke's opponents at the bitterly contested elections for the Long Parliament in Great Marlow (of which Paget had the Lordship); two years later, as Lord-Lieutenant of Buckinghamshire, he appointed Whitelocke, with John Hampden (q.v.) and four others, as his Deputies. In the same year, he left Parliament to join Charles I in York. He fought for the King at Edgehill and was with him in Oxford from 1643 to 1644, but returned to Parliament in September 1644 and took the Covenant in April 1645. In spite of his fluctuating loyalties, he played an active part at the Coronation Banquet for Charles II, in 1661.

PALMER, Sir Geffrey (Geoffrey), Kt., later Bt., MP (1598–1670). *D.N.B.*; *V.C.H. Northamptonshire Families* (ed. O. Barron. 1906); M.F.K.; G.E.C. *Complete Baronetage* iii; J. Hutchinson *Notable Middle Templars* (London. 1902); *Pepys, passim*. Admitted to the Middle Temple in June 1616, where he came to know Whitelocke (some seven years his junior), who was admitted in August 1619. Whitelocke visited Palmer at Carlton (Carleton), Northamptonshire, now known as East Carlton (between Corby and Market Harborough), and was received with 'great intimacy of friendship & Kindness', *Diary* 1637.1638. fol. 45v. A letter from Palmer to Whitelocke (extracts below) reflects an easy-going, close friendship; this was only halted when their loyalties separated them at the Civil War. Before that Palmer, Whitelocke, Matthew Hale (q.v.) and their wives, shared a home on what Whitelocke called a 'joint-stock' basis, renting the house of Sir Thomas Fanshawe (q.v.), in Ivy Lane, London, [Oct.] 1642. ib. fol. 58.

The previous year, in the early hours of 23 November 1641, the vote on the Grand Remonstrance (with its grievances against the King) had been carried by 159 votes to 148, J.R. Tanner *English Constitutional Conflicts of the Seventeenth Century* (C.U.P. paperback. 1961) pp.110, 111. Palmer had stood up and tried to have the royalist protest put on record. This was out of order, since it would have highlighted faction in the Commons. Whitelocke, sitting next to Palmer, vainly attempted to stop his friend speaking and to make him sit down. Palmer was sent to the Tower for his offence, *C.J.* ii, 324, 25 Nov. 1641. When Whitelocke visited him there, they 'drolled about his imprisonment' and Palmer admitted that had he listened to Whitelocke, he would not have found himself in gaol. After a few days, however, and at some expense to himself, Palmer was released and resumed his seat in the Commons, Add.Ms 37343 fols. 234v.–235. When Palmer left Parliament, after the vote on 30 April 1642, to execute the Militia Ordinance, Whitelocke covered up for his absence but added, with hindsight, that this was not remembered later, *Diary* 1641. 1642. fol. 55.

After their ways parted, Whitelocke called on Hyde and Palmer, during the Uxbridge negotiations, when these friends were Commissioners for the King as he was for Parliament, ib. Jan./Feb. 1644/45. Palmer remained in Oxford with King Charles during the siege, and until the City surrendered in June 1646. Suspected of plotting against the Protector, he was imprisoned in 1655. At the Restoration he was knighted, appointed Attorney-General and was created a Baronet on 7 June 1660. At about that time he purchased Carlton Curlieu, in Leicestershire, some 10 miles north-west of his Carlton estate in Northamptonshire. Whitelocke felt that Palmer could have helped him more than he did, when the latter was in a position of power as Attorney-General, but although Palmer never found an appointment for his old friend, from 1660 onwards he allowed Whitelocke easy access to him. Whitelocke thought it politic to offer his Middle Temple Chambers to the Attorney-General, ib. 4 Mar. 1660/61 and noted, only five days later, that it was 'now much adorned & repayred.' In their last years the two men occasionally dined with each other in London, or met at the home of the Moore family (q.v.), in West Berkshire, (Palmer's wife, Margaret, being a sister of Sir Henry Moore, 1st Baronet).

A letter from Palmer to Whitelocke, in the early days of their friendship, is addressed to his 'worthy & much esteemed Cosen Bulstrode Whitelocke Esqu[ir]e att his house att Fawley Court . . .' but this kinship has not been traced. The letter runs:

> S[i]ʳ The elegance for which you make Apologie: growing in elme Court onelie [presumably Fawley Court, with its elm walk], cannot be expected elsewhere; therfor give mee leave to return your heartie thankes For this Continuance of yo[u]ʳ Invitation; my wife hath kept her chamber for the most p[ar]te synce you went but is now I hope recov[e]ʳing; Iff shee be so well that I may leave her; then I shall bee for Northamtonshire; Iff not thither[,] I will make A Sallie to Henley for 3 or 4 daies; And so soone as I can speake with Ned Hide who is yett A stranger att the Temple [,] but about the tyme of choosing officers I looke for him; then will send to you; when & how wee shall come to trouble you. The Newes of the P[ar]liament I knowe is no newes to you; But this may bee[,] that Notwithstanding[,] the shippmonies goes on; my wife and I pʳ[e]sent our Service to yo[u]ʳ Ladie; and y[ou]ʳself; And Bettie hath spoken hers in French but I cannot wright itt.

> To you and yours all hapines so wisheth
>   Y[ou]ʳ most unfeined Frende
>   & Servant
>   Geffrey Palmer
>   Long W.P. vii, 298, addressed on 299v.

Transcribed by Whitelocke, with some variations of spelling and capitalization, and improvements to Palmer's eccentric punctuation, Add. Ms 37343 fol. 162v. Strangely, both the original and the copy are dated 1638 (perhaps this should be shown as 1638/39), but it seems to indicate that rumours were already rife that the new (Short) Parliament was to be called. A bond from Whitelocke to Palmer in £200, for payment of £100, was signed on 5 July 1639, Long. W.P. vii, 337.

There are two legal documents which refer to Palmer when he was Attorney-General: (1) a draft of Whitelocke's undated answers, as one of the defendants, to information offered by the King's Attorney-General (probably the so-called 'English Information', a procedure by which the Crown could recover a debt through the Court of Exchequer). It

presumably relates to a process (i.e. a summons) from the Court of
Exchequer which was left at Whitelocke's house in Coleman Street during
his absence, requiring him to answer a suit of the Attorney-General's
about possession of some of the King's goods, 'whereof he had none att
all', *Diary* 8 Oct. 1662. (2) An order of the Court of Exchequer in a cause
(perhaps the same one, although two years later) between the Attorney-
General and Whitelocke, that no prosecutor appearing against the
defendant as to the royal bill, the cause be dismissed under the Act of
Oblivion, 2 Dec. 1664, Long. W.P. xx, 108.

PALMER [Lewis?], MP (1630–1713). *Middle Temple Admission Register*;
Hist. of Parl. Second son of Sir Geffrey Palmer (above). Admitted to the
Middle Temple on the same day as James and William Whitelocke, 30
October 1647. On this slender evidence it may be supposed that, from
among several possible lawyers named Palmer, it was he whom James
Whitelocke chose to prepare the documents for his marriage settlement,
Diary 10 June 1657. Lewis and his younger brothers, Geffrey and Edward,
served as MPs after the Restoration.

PARGITER, [John?]. A.B.B.; *Pepys* x. A wealthy goldsmith. Pepys
refers to taking his morning cake and ale with Pargiter, whose company he
seems to have enjoyed, although believing him to be a 'cheating rogue';
they joked together about the goldsmith's heavy losses at the King's
Restoration, resulting from his earlier purchase of crown lands, 'of which',
Pepys wrote, '(God forgive me) I am very glad', *Pepys* ii, 199 with note 3,
21 Oct. 1661. A Mr. Pargiter was Whitelocke's client and later wrote about
the rights of Whitelocke's son-in-law, George Nevill (q.v.), in Needwood
Forest, *Diary* 23 Mar. 1662/63; 8 June 1665. This could, however, have
been Francis Pargiter, a merchant connected with the Muscovy Company,
who was also known to Pepys.

PARKE (PARKER), Capt. [Fras. i.e. Francis?]. Captain of the frigate
Great President, referred to by Whitelocke as the *President*. Parke wrote of
receiving an order from General Blake (q.v.) to sail for Hamburg, with
(i.e. along with) the *Elizabeth*, to transport Ambassador Whitelocke back
to England, *C.S.P. Dom.* 18 May 1654, p. 491, see also pp. 579, 583.
Christopher Myngs (q.v.), Captain of the frigate *Elizabeth*, resented
Whitelocke's sailing in the *President* instead of in his ship, and the near
shipwreck that followed satisfied Whitelocke that Myngs was indeed the
better Captain, *Diary* 29 June 1654, *passim*.

PARKER, Judge [John], MP (*c.* 1590–1668). E. Foss *Judges of England*; G.E. Aylmer 'Check-list of Central Office-holders.' Of Gray's Inn. According to Foss, Parker's appointment as a Welsh circuit Judge, in 1647, was confirmed after the King's execution in 1649. Whitelocke does not refer to the original appointment, but writes that he himself procured Serjeants Parker and Elton to be Judges in Wales, *Diary* 5 Mar. 1648/49. Parker was made a Commissioner and Trustee for land sales under the Commonwealth. He was appointed a Baron of the Court of Exchequer in about May 1655; again Whitelocke gives a later reference, naming him as a Baron of Exchequer, ib. 18 Jan. 1659/60.

PARKER, Dr [William] (b. *c.* 1630). W. Munk *Roll of the Royal College of Physicians.* Of Suffolk. He studied at Leyden in 1655, aged 25; a D Med of Padua in 1658, the degree being incorporated at Oxford in 1659. He attended Whitelocke's family at Chilton Lodge, *Diary* 17, 18 Mar. 1673/74; 23 July 1674; and attended Sir Francis Popham (q.v.) on his deathbed, ib. 13 Aug. 1674. The identification is however uncertain, for another doctor of the same name became an Oxford MA (incorporated at Cambridge in 1620) and went on to take a D Med degree at Bourges in 1634; this second William Parker, however, was less likely (being in his late 60s) to have been active as a doctor in the 1670s.

PARSONS, Dr [Philip] (1594–1653). *Merchant Taylors' School Register; Alumni Oxonienses.* A Londoner, educated at Merchant Taylors' School, at St. John's College, Oxford, from 1610, and at Padua from 1624; he took his D Med at Padua, and this was incorporated at Oxford in 1628. Ten years earlier, while still in his 20s, he was appointed a Fellow of St. John's College, and shortly afterwards became Whitelocke's tutor there, *Diary* 1619.1620. and 1620.1621. fol. 3v. Whitelocke, it seems wrongly, referred to him at that time as Doctor, yet when Whitelocke injured his leg, while out beagling, Parsons, in consultation with members of the medical faculty, tried various forms of treatment; when these failed, he sent word to his pupil's parents, who sent the coach, with bedding and pillows, to bring their son home to Fawley, ib.1621. 1622. fols. 4–4v. Dr. Parsons was appointed Principal of Hart Hall, Oxford, from 1633 until his death. When Whitelocke was taken ill during peace negotiations with the King in Oxford, Parsons and another physician attended him regularly, ib. 1642. 1643. fol. 61.

PARTRIDGE, Sir Edward, Kt., MP (b. 1602). M.F.K. Of Greenaway Court and of Bridge, Kent. MP for Sandwich in the Long Parliament, until Pride's Purge in 1648. He and his second wife, Catherine, daughter of Sir Arthur Throgmorton, are mentioned once only, when they visited White-locke at Phyllis Court, *Diary* 30 July 1648.

PASSERINI (PASSARELLI), Filippo. Arriving in London with secret messages from Queen Christina of Sweden (q.v.), a few years after her abdication, Passerini asked Whitelocke to take him to Cromwell. The Council, however, advised Cromwell not to receive him, arguing that Italians were skilful poisoners, willing to be hired for that purpose, and that Passerini might bring poison with the letters. The Protector, with a smile, reported their discussion to Whitelocke, who protested that to refuse an audience to Christina's messenger would cause her great offence, but that he himself was prepared to handle the letters and risk being poisoned. This made Cromwell laugh, but he accepted the offer and arranged an audience at which, according to *The Diary*, only the three of them were present, Whitelocke both receiving the letters and acting as interpreter. The letters included a detailed account of why Christina had caused her Equerry, the Italian Marquis (Giovanni Rinaldo, Marquis of Monaldeschi, q.v.), to be put to death at Fontainebleau in France. This was probably Per le Bel's widely-circulated, eye-witness account (see under Monaldeschi). The date of Whitelocke's entry for Passerini's visit, *Diary* 3 May 1657, is wrong, since Monaldeschi was not put to death until November 1657. Passerini's arrival can be dated, from the following sources, as occurring in January 1657/58: William Lockhart (q.v.), England's Ambassador in Paris, sent a lurid warning against Passerini to Secretary of State John Thurloe (q.v.):

> I have learned from one of the queen of Sweden's servants heare, who is a Protestant, that Philippo Passerini (whom she sends to waite on his highness) is a priest, who ordinarily sayeth masse to her. [Perhaps the Chaplain who figures in Per le Bel's account?] He is her present confident, tho' he hath the esteem of a lewd man, and is said to have been the cheife occasione of that barbarous and unhappy action at Fountainbleaw. I know your lordship will think it fitt, that he met with a civill reception; but whatever his message be, the stay of such a messenger is not [to] be encouraged. Paris 9 Jan. [N.S.] 1657/58.
>
> *Thurloe S.P.* vi, 713.

Towards the end of that month, Francesco Giavarina, the Venetian Resident in England, wrote (in Italian) to the Doge and Senate that because of the secrecy surrounding the visit, he could only send crumbs of unverified information and speculations about Passerini's mission. He informed his masters that an Italian gentleman had recently arrived in the name of Queen Christina, bringing letters for the Protector, for 'Vittlock' (Whitelocke), formerly Ambassador to Her Majesty, and for the Swedish Ministers in London; the gentleman had not, however, received a very favourable response from Cromwell. The letter continued:

> One cannot discover what business he brings and as he bears no title he will not be introduced to audience by the master of the ceremonies in the usual way, but by someone else at Court . . .
> 25 Jan. [1657/]1658.
>
> C.S.P. Venetian, 1657–1659 p. 156.

A week later, Giavarina wrote (basing his information on hearsay) that the gentleman from the Queen of Sweden had recently seen the Protector, but without the formalities customary for an accredited minister; that the letters he brought were in French, but that Passerini had spoken in Italian, and that the only people attending Cromwell were:

> . . . the treasurer, Vitlock and the master of the ceremonies, who was summoned to act as interpreter, the Protector having ordered all the others, usually present, to leave the room, in response to the gentleman's wish . . . [Giavarina wrote that he could not discover the reason for Passerini's visit.] From intimations which reach me from a reliable source I imagine that he has come to suggest some attack to be made jointly by the French and English in the coming campaign, against the kingdom of Naples, which is represented as being easy to conquer . . .

The two powers, he continued, aspired to conquests in Italy; moreover, Christina had in her service numerous Neapolitan refugees, who had escaped to Paris from Spanish rule in Naples; another factor was:

> the presence with her Majesty of the duke of Guise, who on a previous occasion went to Italy to conquer Naples . . . [The Queen's head was full of schemes] which they certainly cherish against our province, unless God, who disposes while men propose, is pleased to deliver it from the threatened scourge . . .
> 1 Feb. [1657/]1658
>
> ib. pp. 158–159.

PAULET (POULETT) of HINTON ST. GEORGE, John, 1st Lord (c. 1585–1649). G.E.C.; D.N.B.; D. Underdown Somerset in the Civil War and Interregnum (Newton Abbot. 1973), passim. A Middle Temple student in 1610; MP for Somerset, 1610–1611 and in 1614; for Lyme Regis, Dorset, 1621–1622; created Baron in 1627. An active Royalist in Dorset and Somerset, during the Civil War, he unsuccessfully besieged his former constituency of Lyme Regis in 1644. In September 1644, the House of Commons made an Order that the Committee for Sequestration grant a lease of Lord Paulet's house and gardens at Chiswick to Whitelocke, 13 Sept. 1644, Long. W.P. ix, 29; *Diary* Sept. 1644. fol. 66. Lord Paulet was taken prisoner in 1646, but being in very poor health and on an appeal from Sir Thomas Fairfax (q.v.), was allowed to return to his house in Chiswick, see *D.N.B.* His delinquency payments are shown in a footnote to his G.E.C. entry.

PEARSON, Dr [?] James. *Alumni Oxonienses*. Studied at Magdalen College, Oxford; BA in February 1658/59; Clerk, 1659/1660. He was appointed, in the following year, as tutor to Whitelocke's youngest sons, *Diary* 14 Sept. 1661 with note. Besides teaching the boys, Pearson frequently preached to the family in conventicles. Described as a congregational teacher, he was eventually granted a licence to preach at Whitelocke's house, Chilton Lodge. This was applied for through Nathaniel Ponder (q.v.), see G.L. Turner *Original Records of Early Nonconformity under Persecution and Indulgence* (T. Fisher Unwin. 1911) ii, 1068 iii, 790–791; *Diary* 26 May 1672. Although no medical qualification has been traced, Pearson began to practise physic, as a sideline, within 10 years of joining Whitelocke's household, ib. 27 Sept. 1671; he attended members of the family and was summoned to visit patients in the neighbourhood, which sometimes prevented him from preaching on Sundays, ib. 31 Dec. 1671; 9, 11 Feb., 16 Mar. 1673/74; 31 May, 16 Aug. 1674; 4 Apr. 1675, *passim*. The title of 'Mr' gives way to 'Dr' Pearson in *The Diary* (with few exceptions), from 10 July 1673 onward. Among his numerous activities, Pearson supervised an experiment in treating wheat before it was sown and also helped to deal with an awkward timber-merchant, John Green (q.v.), ib. 14 Oct., 1 Nov. 1662. He sealed bonds with his master, ib. 18 May 1666; 28 Mar. 1672; 16 Nov. 1674. He wrote a respectful but firm letter to Lord Byron (Richard, 2nd Baron Byron of Rochdale, q.v.), after failing to find him at home; the letter concerns money which Lord Byron owed to Sir John Colladon (q.v.), who in turn had promised money to Whitelocke for the purchase of the Greenland estate. Pearson wrote boldly to Lord Byron '. . . I have the more hopes that you may order some money heer, bicause I understand some considerable some [i.e. sum] to be lately raysed, by the sale of timber in Newstead [north of Nottingham] . . . Fleetstreet May 22. 1666' Long. W.P. xx, 120; also *Diary* 3, 5 May 1665.

Pearson negotiated marriage settlements for two of Whitelocke's children, he bought clothes for the bridegroom (his former pupil, Sam), and a jewel for the bride, ib. 13 Aug., 10, 23 Oct., 16, 18, 23, 26 Dec. 1671, *passim*. He was considered by Whitelocke and his wife an acceptable suitor for their 16-year-old daughter Rebecca (q.v.), but one of the girl's sisters and a sister-in-law persuaded her that he was much too old to be her husband, ib. 8 June 1674.

Pearson was, in short, an uncommonly versatile tutor, and so useful that his ageing master wrote, with unconscious selfishness, 'Dr Pearson went for London about a rich wife & so to leave us who had so much need of him', ib. 3 Dec. 1674. This trip, however, came to nothing and Pearson was still a member of the household at the time of Whitelocke's death in July 1675.

PEARSON (PIERSON), Col. John. C.H. Firth and G. Davies *Regimental History of Cromwell's Army*. An Anabaptist, active in purging the Dunkirk garrison of ungodly officers. He was among those who signed Fleetwood's declaration inviting the Rump Parliament to return, *Diary* 6 May 1659, but was dismissed, without a charge being brought against him, during that summer; he sent letters dissenting from General Monck's policy, when the latter declared for Parliament and against the Army in England, ib. 2 Nov. 1659.

PELL, Alderman Walter (d. 1672). A.B.B. A Master Merchant Taylor. Whitelocke acted as legal adviser to Bartholomew Hall (q.v.), when the latter was negotiating a marriage between his son Henry and Pell's cousin. Whitelocke also attended when the agreements were signed. Soon afterwards, he and his wife Mary were 'invited to the wedding butt afterwards uninvited again', because it was to be a private ceremony, to Whitelocke's slight annoyance. A few days later, however, he and his wife attended a great wedding feast at Alderman Pell's and the next month they dined with him again. After that the Whitelockes returned the invitation, and the Alderman and his company dined with them in London. Two years later, Pell, Hall and other friends dined with Whitelocke and his wife at Fawley Court, ib. 12 Jan., 8, 11, 16 Feb., 8 Mar. 1663/64; 25 Mar. 1664; 8 Jan. 1666/67.

PEMBROKE, Philip Herbert, KB, MP, later 4th E. of (1584–1650). G.E.C.; *D.N.B.* Created Earl of Montgomery in 1605; he succeeded as Earl of Pembroke in 1630. Many years earlier he had matriculated at New College, Oxford, at the age of nine. He received numerous honours and offices from James I and from Charles I until the Civil War, in which he supported Parliament and became, automatically, the butt of royalist abuse. He had the reputation among his political enemies of being brainless and hot-tempered. Clarendon (q.v.) wrote that the Earl pretended to 'no other qualification than to understand dogs and horses', G.E.C., Pembroke p. 415, note e; he was described as 'intolerable, cholerick, and offensive, and did not refraine whilest he was Chamberlaine to break many wiser heads than his owne', ib. p. 416 note f; his second wife, Anne, widow of Richard Sackville, Earl of Dorset, confirmed that he was extremely choleric by nature, but assessed him candidly as being '... of a quick apprehension, a sharp understanding, very crafty ... and of a discerning spirit ...' ib. p. 418 note f. His offices included that of Lord Chamberlain of the Household from 1626 until 1641, when he was dismissed after causing a scene in the House of Lords. Whitelocke's first encounter with the Earl was when he (Whitelocke) and Edward Hyde, later 1st Earl of Clarendon (q.v.), were deputed by the Inns of Court to discuss arrangements for the Royal Masque, *The Triumph of Peace*, to be presented in the Banqueting House, Whitehall. The young lawyers were interviewed by Pembroke, in his capacity as Lord Chamberlain, and by Sir Henry Vane the elder (q.v.), as Comptroller of the Household. It was Vane, not Pembroke, who was quarrelsome, showing 'a scornfull, slighting way of expressing himselfe' and expecting, in accordance with the title of his office, to be 'Comptroller of all other mens judgments ...'; Pembroke acted as peace-maker, and granted the young men their requests, Add.Ms 53726 fol. 90v.; *Diary* 1633.1634. fol.20.

Whitelocke had many more encounters with Pembroke, both officially and socially, and quite an affectionate friendship developed between them. There is no hint in *The Diary* of the Earl's rudeness or of any stupidity on his part, and Parliament frequently employed him in its service, as the two Kings had done earlier. Some months after the performance of the Royal Masque, Pembroke publicly expressed his approval of Whitelocke's runaway marriage, in November 1634, to Frances, daughter of Lord Willoughby of Parham. This was frowned on in some quarters, but the Lord Chamberlain stated publicly 'that he was gladde of it, & he thought his Cousen had done better for her selfe then any of her friends would have done for her ...', *Diary* 1634.1635. fol.33v.–34. The Earl often invited Whitelocke to his house in Whitehall (at the Cockpit), ib. 1641.1642. fol. 53v. Both men served, with others, as Commissioners from Parliament at the Oxford and Uxbridge negotiations. When Pembroke was being sent as a Commissioner to the King at Newcastle, he wrote to Whitelocke, in a clumsily constructed letter:

S[i]^r

Intendinge to sett forward on my Journey to Newcastle ... upon Munday next, I shall be gladd to have such an one with mee (to imploy in such Affayres, as the Com[missione]^{rs} shall have occasion to entrust him with) of whose Experience & Abillityes I have had some knowledge. To this purpose, I now purposely write to you, to desyre you, that you will spare me your Servant, to goe alonge with us, that was formerly with us att Uxbridge [Daniel Earle q.v.], beinge at that Place, sufficiently assur'd of his Fittnes, for such an Imployment. If therefore you will soe farre dispense with his Absence, as to send him to mee ag[ain]st that tyme, you will much oblige

Yo[u]^r very affecc[tio]nate friend
to serve you
Pembroke&Montg[omery]

Whitehall the 9th
of July 1646

Long. W.P. ix, 87.

Daniel Earle appears to have moved from the Earl's service to that of Sir John Holland (q.v.); this is referred to in the first of Holland's letters in his entry. Near the end of that letter Sir John made an interesting reference to a speech of Pembroke's.

The Earl of Pembroke served as Chancellor of the University of Oxford, from 1641 to 1643, and after the City of Oxford capitulated to Parliament, on 24 June 1646, he served in that office from 1647 to 1650. In 1647 Visitors were appointed, by both Houses of Parliament, to regulate and reform the University and to eject Royalists. This led both to fierce attacks on Pembroke, as Chancellor, and to cringing petitions from scholars anxious to save their jobs, as:

The Petition of the friends and ser[van]^{ts} of the sayd univ[e]^r[sity.] ... we will not conspire together to describe [?] the errors and outrages of other men who are as yet (to the greate dishonor and prejudice of our Com[m]on mother the university) of the same body with us. We consider to oppose you[,] our much honord Visitor[,] is to Rebell ag[ains]^t the Houses; to maintaine Prelacy is to uphold Tyran[n]y; and to contend for the Com[m]on Prayer Booke is to contend for a false translation of the Canon[ica]^{ll} Scriptures.

Be pleased to com[m]and every man to pleade his owne Cause and speake for himself, only punish the Heads and Ringleaders of this Rebellious conspiracy and pardon all seduced scollars, who upo[n] better informa[ti]on and more mature dekleration[?] shew that they have erred out of mere simplicity, and doe not have to be reformed ...
June 2. [16]47

Long. W.P. Parcel 2, No. 8 (a small folder of papers), copy.

It seems, however, that not all Oxford scholars were so amenable; some ten months later Thomas Fairfax (q.v.) wrote to Lieutenant-Colonel Kelsey (q.v.):

Whereas the Parl[ia]m[en]t have sent downe Com[m]issioners for the Regulating of the university of Oxford; and whereas divers ill-affected Persons doe fro[m] time to time oppose the putting in execution of the Ord[er] of Parl[ia]m[en]t there; you are on sight hereof ... to send such parties or Companies of your Regiment to Oxford as you shall finde necessarie upon the desire of the Com[m]issioners for the assisting of them ... 30 Mar. 1648

ib.

This show of force was the last straw to Oxford Royalists. Someone, presumably an outraged scholar, wrote a long abusive rhyme (one among many lampoons against Pembroke):

... A hundred Horse his lordship had to boote,
He knew his own wit never else could do't:
Armes are a powerful Ergo, and make schisme
And folly good, maugre [i.e. despite] a syllogisme[.]
Had thou but sense or witt, thou wouldst be slaine
With the inst. [i.e. present] Rymes composed in thy disdaine.

Earlier, the doggerel referred contemptuously to 'good Pembroke', whose 'sacriligious Tutor' was either 'Say [and Seale q.v.] or Cromwell' (q.v.). Pembroke himself was:

... One who we know had neere [i.e. ne'er] bin dipt in treason
Had he been left unto his proper reason,
A mere concurringe Rebell that doth Crie
Like a halfe enterd whelp for Company;
For the greate Doctors of so greate a Schoole,
To be confuted by soe great a foole ... [The couplets ended threateningly]
But we will bridle fancy[,] nor let loose
Too much brave fury on so tame a Goose.
Noe, thou shalt feele the chastening Rod
First of the abused Kinge, next of thie God.
And when inst heaven shall due vengeance take,
And to ingrate thee, an example make,
Apollos Sons shall in a chorus laugh,
And fix upon thie Tombe this Epitaph
          The Epitaph
Pembroke here lies under layd
Whoe his God and Kinge betrayd;
To which sins he joyn'd this other
To Com[m]itt Rape upon his mother [i.e. Oxford, his *alma mater*]
Who soe unto this Gravestone goes
And reads, is pray'd to stop his nose:
His very name, thus blasted must
Be more nautious then his dust. [This was followed by]

Pembrokes Passe
from
Oxford to his Grave [which contains the lines]
Thou Puppit who canst nether speake nor move
If Say or Oldisworth [Michael Oldisworth jun., the Earl's Secretary, see
    D.N.B.] teach[?] not, or approve . . .
O! how would *Pembroke* thy brave brother grieve
To see his Heire to play the under-shreeve [under-sheriff] . . .
And with a borrowed dress of power sit
To crie up ignorance and banish wit . . .

ib.

When Pembroke was appointed Constable of Windsor Castle and Keeper of the Forest, he made Whitelocke his lieutenant or deputy, *Diary* 27 July 1648 (a reference to this in Oct. 1644 appears to be a mistake). In the year 1648, the Earl was made High Steward and Keeper of Greenwich Park. An entry states that Pembroke granted Whitelocke Manor Lodge and Walk, in Windsor Forest, apparently in exchange for the Stewardship of Greenwich, ib. 27 Feb. 1648/49.

After the abolition of the House of Lords, Pembroke was elected MP for Berkshire, and on 16 April 1649, he made a triumphal entry into the House, B. Worden *Rump Parliament* pp.192–193. When the Earl died, in the following year, Whitelocke wrote that he had 'lost a very good & kind friend', *Diary* 23 Jan. 1649/50. Without any other reference to the move, Whitelocke states that his son Carleton was born at the family's lodgings in Whitehall 'w[hi]ᶜh were formerly the E[arle] of Pembrokes', ib. 13 July 1652; the Earl had died at his house in the Cockpit, Westminster.

PEMBROKE, William Herbert, MP, later 6th E. of (1640 or 1642 – 1674) G.E.C.; *Hist. of Parl.* Grandson of the 4th Earl of Pembroke (above). MP for Glamorgan, 1661 – Dec. 1669, when he succeeded to his father's title. *The Diary* shows that Whitelocke was Pembroke's legal adviser from early in 1670 until the young Earl's death, four years later, and received from him a present of a buck from Gravely Chase, and fees ranging from £1 to £4. These were usually paid by Dr. Caldecot, who was evidently in the Earl's service. The incoherence of the following autograph letter suggests that the young nobleman was barely literate, or else was drunk when he wrote it:

S[i]ʳ
    I received your letter & accepted[?] & directed to Docter Coldecott at present is absent. I expect him owerly I am not fullier resolved by your kind proseedings to me which I tacke in great respect to me. I will undertake to

tacke in my punishment the justice of peace knowes not his acctions what it is to question a Peers, they are apt to doe it when they thinke they are not herde the rest I shall leve holy to you only the justices yet[?] to know his name I am insenced [i.e. unaware?] of your jusdement & your parts [?] may better for all things but them that know yo^u. My deare Granfether sigeneffinge in istemed great respect.

Your faithfull humble servant
Pembroke & Mont[gomery].

[1669]

Long. W.P. xx, 153.

PENDLEBURY, William. A Merchant Taylor of London; an acquaintance of Mr and Mrs George Cokayn (q.v.), of Mr and Mrs Samuel Wilson (q.v.) and of John Wildman (q.v.). He paid several visits to Whitelocke at Chilton Lodge. Whitelocke refers to bonds he signed to Pendlebury and to his difficulty in repaying the loans, *Diary* 2 Sept. 1673 with note; 14 Nov. 1674, *passim*. The jewel or decoration of the Order of Amaranth (the Order of Knighthood which Whitelocke received from Queen Christina, q.v.) was deposited with Pendlebury in London, presumably by way of security, ib. 16 Feb. 1670/71. Other references to Pendlebury and his loans occur in University of Reading, Archives Dept., BER 36/5 Nos. 29–30; 34–38.

PENINGTON (PENNINGTON), Alderman Isaac, MP (*c.*1587–1661). *D.N.B.*; M.F.K.; A.B.B. MP for London from 1640 to 1653 and 1659 to 1660. A Puritan, a friend of John Milton (q.v.) and of John Goodwin (q.v.), and a strong supporter of Parliament in the City. Prime Warden of the Fishmongers' Company in 1640; Lord Mayor of London and Colonel of a City Regiment in 1642. He raised large loans in the City, to enable Parliament to pay the Army. Appointed as one of the King's judges, he was on the Council of State from 1649–1652. His name appears at an earlier date, with others, on a writ of habeas corpus for one Thomas Jennings [1639], Cal., Long. W.P. vii, 355v. Whitelocke mentions Penington: (1) in connection with £2,500 arrears owed to Colonel Bulstrode (q.v.), which Penington (spelt Pennington by Whitelocke, but not by the Alderman himself) had failed to pay, *Diary* 23 June 1649; (2) when he surrendered, as one of the King's judges, ib. 15 June 1660. Pennington's plea of not guilty was rejected, and he died in the Tower at the end of the following year.

PENN (PEN), William (1644–1718). *D.N.B.*; *Papers of William Penn* vol.i.1644–1679 (ed. M.M. Dunn & R.S. Dunn. University of Pennsylvania Press. 1981); J. Aubrey *Brief Lives* (ed. O. Lawson Dick. Peregrine Books. 1962); *Pepys* x. Founder of Pennsylvania; the son of Vice-Admiral Sir William Penn. To his father's regret he became a convinced Quaker, while in Ireland in 1667. Several times he suffered imprisonment in London for his beliefs and for his publications. A few days before his imprisonment in the Tower, under a warrant of 12 December 1668, he sent Whitelocke a fee of £1.2s.0d., *Diary*. 9 Dec. 1668, with note. He was released at the end of July 1669 and preached in Ireland, but was imprisoned in Newgate in August 1670, and again in February 1670/71. On his release, he went to Holland and Germany, and returned to England at the end of 1671.

He sent Whitelocke 'a Civill letter & a booke', ib. 19 June 1673 and, after announcing that he would preach at Chilton Lodge on the next Lord's Day, he duly arrived and 'preached admirably' to a large congregation in Whitelocke's study, 'butt the fewer bicause it was very wett', ib. 10, 12 Oct. 1673. The service was interrupted by a local parson, Dr. Hungerford. Whitelocke's entry for that day ends ambiguously '. . . God direct me to the trueth'. The fact that Whitelocke, a staunch Independent (or Congregationalist), welcomed a Quaker into his house, and apparently told his neighbours of the visit in advance, suggests that he was distinctly sympathetic towards the despised and persecuted sect.

Years later, Penn wrote the introduction to a small volume of Whitelocke's sermons, and published it under the title *Quench not the Spirit* (London. 1711), 2nd edition 1715; two companion volumes survive in manuscript in the British Library, both bearing the title 'Lectures Uppon perticular Occasions By a Father to his Family', dated 1666 and 1667, Add. Ms 59780 and 53728. Some passages in Whitelocke's sermons are very appealing and have a distinct flavour of Quaker teaching. Penn wrote the biographical introduction to Whitelocke's *Memorials of the English Affairs from the Suppos'd Expedition of Brute to this Island to the End of the Reign of King James I* (London. 1709) – not to be confused with the better-known *Memorials of the English Affairs* . . . (covering the reign of Charles I, the Interregnum and the Restoration), which had been published earlier; to lessen this confusion the 2nd edition of the history from early times was renamed *History of England; or Memorials of the English Affairs* . . . (1713). Penn referred to Whitelocke as:

> one of the most accomplish'd Men of the Age . . . [he recalled] Being with him sometimes at his own House in Berkshire [Chilton Park] when Whitelocke said to him [in words which might well have been spoken by a Quaker] I ever have thought . . . there has been one true Religion in the

World, and that is, the Work of the Spirit of God in the Hearts and Souls of Men. There has been . . . divers Forms and Shapes of Things . . . but the old World has had the Spirit of God . . . and the New World has had the Spirit of God, both Jew and Gentile . . . And I myself must say, I have felt it from a Child . . . and it has often given me a true Measure of this poor World . . . I can say, since my Retirement from the Greatness and Hurries of the World, I have felt something of the Work and Comfort of it . . . So . . . my Religion is the good Spirit of God in my heart . . . [Penn also recalled how] After a Meeting at his House, to which he gave an entire Liberty, for all that pleased to come, he was so deeply affected . . . that . . . he rose up, and pulled off his Hat, and said, "This is the Everlasting Gospel I have heard this Day; and I humbly Bless the Name of God, that he has let me live, to see this Day, in which the Ancient Gospel is again preached to them that dwell upon the Earth" . . .

A Collection of the Works of William Penn . . . (1726) i, 431–432.

PENNINGTON, Alderman Isaac, see PENINGTON.

PERIAM, Lady Elizabeth (d. 1621). Her effigy, with a book in her hand, and a Latin inscription is in St. Mary's Church, Henley-on-Thames; the *D.N.B.* (entry for Sir Nicholas Bacon) refers to a daughter Elizabeth by his first wife. She was therefore a half-sister (rather than sister, as shown on the monument) of Lord Chancellor Francis Bacon. A patron of learning, she married: (1) Robert D'Oiley (D'Oyly), of an older generation than that of members of the family who appear in *The Diary*; (2) Henry Nevile (Neville); (3) Sir William Periam, knighted in 1592. Lady Periam founded a famous school in Henley for 20 poor boys and also endowed a fellowship and two scholarships at Balliol College, Oxford. Whitelocke probably never met her but he appears to have been a Governor of the Lady Periam School, see receipt 28 May 1640, Long. W.P. viii, 15; *Diary* 18 May 1665.

PETER (PETERS), Hugh (1598–1660). *D.N.B.*; R.P. Stearns *Strenuous Puritan* (University of Illinois. 1954). A Cornishman, of Flemish descent on his father's side, he studied at Trinity College, Cambridge, from 1613, and developed a life-long belief in the Independent (Congregational) style of church government, but without wishing to abandon the established Church. After leaving college he became a school master in Essex. In 1623 he was ordained Priest by George Montaigne, Bishop of London. He was to make his mark not only as a Minister and preacher but also as a social, economic and religious reformer, and as a champion of religious toleration – but only between protestants. In November 1626 he prayed publicly for the young catholic Queen, Henrietta Maria (q.v.), 'that God would remove from her the Idols of her father's House, and that she would forsake the ... superstition wherein she was and must needes perish if she continued in the same', *Strenuous Puritan* (above) p.41. For this, he was interrogated by Bishop Montaigne. He escaped punishment, for the time being, supported by his puritan patron, Robert Rich, 2nd Earl of Warwick (q.v.), and by using casuistry as a means of survival, when confronted by a questionnaire about his belief in the Church. In spite of this, his licence was revoked in December 1627 and he could no longer preach in England.

He escaped to the Dutch Netherlands. Returning to England, from time to time, he was imprisoned on one occasion for preaching unlawfully. After his release, he went back to the Netherlands and was eventually appointed Minister to the English colony in Rotterdam. In 1635, under pressure from Archbishop Laud (q.v.), Peter escaped to Massachusetts and was, in due course, appointed Minister in Salem. Back in England in 1641, he was made Chaplain to the forces to be sent to Ireland. Later, as a Chaplain in the New Model Army, he proved himself a powerful, often politically-motivated preacher. He favoured the King's trial and execution, and was made Chaplain to the Council of State in December 1650, in place of John Owen (q.v.). He strongly supported Oliver Cromwell (q.v.) but fell out of favour, briefly, after preaching and praying for peace during the Anglo-Dutch war, and appealing to Sir George Ayscue (q.v.) to refrain from fighting against his co-religionists. The matter was referred to Parliament and Hugh Peter was reprimanded.

Whitelocke's first mention of him is in connection with law reform. Peter had seen something of this both in Holland and in Massachusetts and he was one of a committee of 21, set up to reform the English law. Whitelocke wrote, however, that: 'none was more active in this business than Mr Hugh Peters the minister, who understood little of the law, but was very opinionative ...' *Memorials* iii, 388; see also *Diary* 31 Jan. 1651/52. This might seem to confirm the royalist stereotype of the man as a buffoon, but Whitelocke's criticism only applied to Peter the law-reformer: in the autumn of the following year, the Minister was the first named on Whitelocke's list of 'faithfull friends' who were to screen and then negotiate terms with the company chosen to escort Ambassador Whitelocke to Sweden, *Diary* 7 Oct. 1653 with note; moreover Hugh Peter, George Cokayn (q.v.) and Nathaniel Ingelo (q.v.), listed in that order, were the Independent Ministers who prayed and preached in Whitehall Chapel with Whitelocke and his company before the Swedish mission. After their safe return it was Peter who preached and prayed at a thanksgiving service in Whitelocke's house, *Diary* 27 Oct. 1653; 5 July 1654.

Some 20 years earlier, Peter had met Queen Christina's father, King

Gustav Adolf, in Germany and had served briefly in his Army. This may have emboldened him to send Christina a letter and presents. Whitelocke's engaging account, in dialogue, of her response appears in *Journal* i, 268–269, but his report of the incident in the original 'Journal' provides more information about Peter:

> The great Mastiffe dogge Lyon comming into the chamber after me[,] where the Queene was, she made much of him, & asked me if he were a good conditioned dogge, I sayd yeas, butt I did not well knowe whose dogge it was . . . some of my people informed me that one Mr Peters had sent him for a present to her M[ajes]^{ty}, she asked who that Mr Peters was, I sayd he was a gentleman of a good family & had been in all our Warres, & a Collonell, & was also an excellent preacher, she sayd that was much that he should be a preacher & a soldier, I tould her we had many who were so, then she sayd that Mr Peters had sent her a letter, I told her I heard so butt did not thinke it fitt to deliver either the letter or the Dogge from a private man . . . she sayd that . . . the dogge & the letter did belong to her and she would have them . . .'
> 30 Dec. 1653.
>
> Long. 124A fol. 60.

Peter had also sent her a great English cheese. Soon after this conversation, Whitelocke had the letter and the gifts delivered to the Queen, 3 Jan. 1653/54, ib. 64–64v.

There are a few more entries for Peter after 1654, including a reference to his telling Whitelocke about events in Mardyke and Dunkirk, where he had preached to the soldiers, *Diary* 8 July 1658. After the Restoration, Whitelocke refers to an order for Peter's arrest and to his capture, 'betrayed by his own servant', ib. 8 June, 3 Sept. 1660 (both entries being dated one day after the events occurred). Although not a regicide himself, Peter was sentenced to the grim death which many of them suffered. Despite his deep fear that his nerve might fail him at his execution, his gift for words did not desert him at the end, and he died courageously.

PETERBOROUGH, Henry Mordaunt, 2nd E. of (1623–1697). G.E.C. As a young man he fought for Parliament in 1642, and for the King in 1643 and 1644. He compounded for his estates in 1646 and again in 1649, after being involved in the Second Civil War, *Diary* 5 July 1648. After the Restoration he held a variety of posts at Court.

PETTUS, Sir John, Kt., MP (1613–1685). *D.N.B.*; *Hist. of Parl.* Of Chediston, Suffolk. Son of Sir Augustine Pettus of Rackheath, Norfolk. He was knighted in 1641. A Royalist, but related by marriage to Colonel

Charles Fleetwood (q.v.). He was imprisoned in 1650, for providing the exiled Charles Stuart with over £1,000 and for corresponding with him, but was released on bail of £4,000. Later, as an active member of the Society of Mineral and Battery Works, he assured the Protector that he would always be faithful to the government under which he lived, and he appealed against the decimation of his property. At around that time, having perhaps received help from Whitelocke, Pettus sent him 'kind letters', *Diary* 16 May 1655. He was elected MP for Dunwich, Suffolk, in 1670. His debts, and his wife's conversion to the Catholic faith, followed by her withdrawal to a convent abroad, combined to cause him considerable embarrassment.

PHELIPS (PHILLIPS), Sir Robert, Kt., MP (*c*.1586–1638). *D.N.B.*; *Shaw's Knights*; *Return of Members of Parliament*. Of Montacute, Somerset. He was knighted in July 1603; elected MP for East Looe, Cornwall, in 1604; for Bath in 1621, and for Somerset County in 1624, 1625 and 1627. Whitelocke's first experience as an MP was in Charles I's second Parliament, from February 1625/26 to June 1626. He stated that he came to know Sir Robert in the Commons at that time, *Diary* 1625.1626.fol.7. Sir Robert, however, although he was elected did not sit in that Parliament; having been very active in the previous one, he was pricked as Sheriff, to prevent him from serving as an MP. He and Whitelocke presumably met somewhere else at about that time. Phelips strenuously opposed the Duke of Buckingham (q.v.), but from about 1628 his allegiance shifted towards the court party. His sons, Edward and Robert, also became MPs; see M.F.K. for the elder son and *Hist. of Parl.* for both.

PHESANT, Judge Peter (*c*.1580–1649). *D.N.B.*; E. Foss *Judges of England*. Of Barkworth, Lincs. Entered Gray's Inn, 1602. A barrister in 1608; appointed a Judge of the Common Pleas by Parliament in 1645. Whitelocke disagreed with Phesant and Widdrington (q.v.), over an important but unnamed case, in which he was confident that he was in the right, *Diary* 12 Jan. 1648/49. After the King's execution, at the end of that month, Phesant was one of the six Judges who agreed (after essential adjustment to the laws) to continue in office, serving the Republic under the three 'Keepers of the Liberties of England', i.e. Commissioners of the Great Seal, of which Whitelocke was the most distinguished, ib. 9 Feb. 1648/49. Phesant was, however, in poor health and died later that year.

PHILIP IV, King of Spain (1605–1665). D.H. Pennington *Seventeenth-Century Europe, passim*; G. Masson *Queen Christina, passim*. Philip came to the throne in 1621, aged 16, the effective ruler of Spain being, for some years, Gaspard de Guzman, Count of Olivares. Philip was the first monarch to recognize the English Commonwealth and his envoy, Don Antonio Pimentel de Prado (q.v.), was the first diplomat to welcome Whitelocke as Ambassador Extraordinary to the Swedish Court. Queen Christina, moreover, proposed that the King of Spain should be included in the Anglo-Swedish treaty, *Diary* 30 Dec. 1653, but Whitelocke refused to countenance this addition, having no authority to agree to it; he was later informed, rightly or wrongly, that Pimentel had tried to sabotage the treaty, ib. 30 Mar. 1654. Another rumour, however, suggested that the Spanish envoy 'procured the alliance of Sweden with England', see the reference to *C.S.P. Venetian 1653–1654*, in the entry for PIMENTEL.

Despite his initial friendliness towards the English Commonwealth, it has been stated that in 1656 King Philip negotiated with Charles II (q.v.) in exile, offering him a pension and financial support for an invasion of England, also subsidizing plots against the Protector, J. Buchan *Oliver Cromwell* (Hodder & Stoughton. 1935) p.496 (no sources given). Philip is also said to have encouraged Charles Stuart with promises of 7,000 Spaniards to invade England, T. Carlyle *Letters and Speeches of Oliver Cromwell* ii, 500, *passim*. France, as Spain's enemy, solicited Cromwell's help and, in the Treaty of Paris, 1657, agreed that in return for the support of a fleet and 6,000 men, England should be granted Mardyke and Dunkirk when they were captured from Spain (see entries for: LOCKHART, Sir William, and WHITELOCKE, Col. Sir James). Sir John Holland (q.v.) sent Whitelocke news of four Kings, one of them being Philip IV of Spain, *Diary* 3 Apr. 1659.

PHILLIPS see PHELIPS, Sir Robert.

PICCART, Louis (Lewis). A Parisian goldsmith. Whitelocke met him in France and agreed to engage Piccart's son as a servant in England, some of the boy's duties being to play the lute and talk French with his master, *Diary* 1633.1634.fol. 27v. Earlier, Whitelocke wrote from France to his apprentice clerk, Thomas Napper (q.v.), about the Piccarts, father and son, 20 May 1634, Long. W.P. vi, 97, and more fully to his reliable friend and servant, John Cely (q.v.); he explained that the Frenchman was bringing the letters to London and intended to inquire about his (that is Whitelocke's) suitability as a master:

... I like the boy well, and will intertaine him if his father thinke good, pray talke with him what you thinke fit about it, and tell him that if he returne out of England before I come home, if he will leave his boy at my house in Salisbury Courte he shall be well there w[i]ᵗh my servants till my comming ... if the boy be left there I would have him ly by himselfe and diet and be there as my servant, we are agreed already uppon the termes, butt I beleeve he desires to enquire of [i.e. about] me, which I doe not mislike in him ... 20/30 May 1634.

Ib. vi, 96 (Whitelocke's autograph letter.)

Young Piccart duly joined the household; he is not mentioned again by name, but makes one more appearance. After Whitelocke's first encounter with Frances Willoughby, who became his second wife, he wrote defensively that he had been so far from any thought of courtship that he went to her aunt's house wearing rough clothes, his hair and beard overgrown, and looking about 50 years old (he was under 30 at the time). He added: 'only my horse was very hansome & my french boy, which waited on me, was in plush & Sattin', Add.Ms 37343 fol. 2v., 1634; *Diary* 1634.1635. fol. 30.

A receipt signed by one Hector du Mont, for £20 paid to him by Whitelocke, stated that the money was to be returned to Louis Piccart of Paris for Whitelocke's use there, 19 Aug. 1634, Long. W.P. vi, 123 (yet Whitelocke had returned to England some three months earlier). A receipt for £15.11s.6d. relates to money paid by Whitelocke to du Mont for Piccart's own use, 5 Feb. 1635 [probably new style], ib. vii, 10.

PICKERING, Sir Gilbert, Bt., MP (1613–1668). *D.N.B.*; M.F.K.; *Extinct & Dormant Baronetcies*; *Pepys* x. Appointed as one of the judges for the trial of Charles I, he was a close friend and supporter of Cromwell. Pickering and Whitelocke were sent with two other MPs, to meet Cromwell near Aylesbury and congratulate him, from Parliament, on his success at the Battle of Worcester, *Diary* 10 Sept. 1651 with note. Diary references to Pickering relate to his part in appointing Whitelocke Ambassador Extraordinary to Sweden and, at a later date, to their duties as two of the four Commissioners who were to treat with the Swedish Ambassador, Christer Bonde (q.v.). In December 1657 he was called to Cromwell's 'Other House'; he was also made Lord Chamberlain to the Protector. The last entry for Pickering refers to his being 'made incapable of any office', ib. 9 June 1660, with note.

PIERREPONT, Hon. William, MP (*c.* 1607–1678). *D.N.B.*; M.F.K.; *Hist. of Parl.* Second son of the 1st Earl of Kingston-upon-Hull. MP for

Shropshire in the Short Parliament, April 1640, for Much Wenlock in the Long Parliament, November 1640, and for Nottinghamshire in 1654 and 1660. He served as one of Parliament's Commissioners with Whitelocke at the Oxford and Uxbridge peace negotiations, and showed himself a good friend to Whitelocke after the Savile affair, *Diary* 2 Aug., 12 Dec. 1645. Active among the moderates, early in the Civil War, he was later a prominent radical, but broke with that group over Pride's Purge and the King's trial and execution. A Presbyterian Elder, he supported Cromwell but refused to sit in his House of Lords. Serving in the Convention Parliament, after the Restoration, he was suspected by some Royalists of being, at heart, a Cromwellian. He and Whitelocke remained on good terms. Their last meetings are recorded in ib. 15 Jan. 1662/63 and 21 May 1666. A daughter of Sir John Evelyn (q.v.) married Pierrepont's eldest son, Robert. Sir John Evelyn and his brother Arthur (q.v), Governor of Wallingford garrison, are referred to in connection with Pierrepont, ib. 31 Mar., 2 July 1648.

PIGOTT, Sir Richard, KB, MP (d. 1684). Of Dothersol, Bucks. (Doddershall House and Park, west of Quainton). He was made a Knight Bachelor in 1630. In 1642 he was appointed, with Whitelocke and four others, to serve on the Midland Association for maintenance of defence etc., *V.C.H. Bucks.* iv, 536, *passim*. Pigott sent a gift of venison to Whitelocke, *Diary* 21 Dec. 1645. He was elected one of five Knights for Buckinghamshire, to sit in Cromwell's second Parliament, ib. 21 Aug. 1656; (no return has been found for Buckinghamshire in that Parliament, see *Return. Members of Parliament.*) Between August 1653 and March 1659/60, he sat on more than a dozen committees for Buckinghamshire, C.H. Firth & R.S. Rait *Acts and Ordinances of the Interregnum*, *passim*.

PIKE (PYKE), George. Father of Mary Pitcher (or Pitchard) of Trumpington Hall, Cambs., who later married Whitelocke's son James, see WHITELOCKE, Lady Mary jun. (2). Pike negotiated his daughter's second marriage with a portion of £2,000, in addition to the jointure from her former husband, *Diary* 22 Jan., 2 Mar. 1656/57.

PILE (PYLE) family (below). *Extinct & Dormant Baronetcies*; *Complete Baronetage*; *V.C.H. Wilts.* ii, iv, ix, xii; Long. W.P. ix, 168–175, *passim*; a memorial in the church of Collingbourne Kingston, Wilts., erected in 1646, commemorates earlier generations. Members of the family were landowners in Berkshire with property in Compton Beauchamp and Okemarsh (the latter untraced), and in Wiltshire, at Axford, Clyffe Peppard, with nearby Bupton Manor, and Netheravon etc. Connected by marriage with the families of: Popham (q.v.) of Littlecote, in Wiltshire; Moore (q.v.) of Fawley in Berkshire, and with the Whitelockes at Chilton Park, west Berkshire, on the border of Wiltshire, through the marriage, near the end of Whitelocke's life, of his daughter Frances to Francis Pile (q.v.). Entries concerning the Pile family only start after Whitelocke moved to Chilton Lodge, *Diary* 22 July 1664. It is clear, however, that there was a connection with the family many years earlier, when Whitelocke wrote:

> Sir
> I take the boldnes being your auncient acquaintance & friend to intreat your assistance in a buisnes concerning my selfe. I have agreed w[i]'h S[i]ʳ Humphrey Forster [q.v.] for the purchase of the Mannour of Watchfield [the sale did not, it seems, go through] where I understand you have been formerly the Steward & I desire you would continue that Imployment & take order that a Courte may be kept there . . .

Whitelocke asked for valuations and details of the 'demesnes and coppy holds' of the Manor, 19 Sept. 1648, Long. W.P. ix, 168 (draft). The former steward replied courteously, enclosing the required details with the comment: 'I must desire this favour . . . that the name of the informers may be concealed according to their owne desire.' He wrote that he was most willing to serve Whitelocke in any way he could. The letter is signed 'Francis Pile', 16 Oct. 1648, ib.175. This appears to have been the 2nd Baronet (*c.* 1617–1649), owner of Compton Beauchamp, Berkshire (now Oxfordshire), near Shrivenham, a few miles south of Watchfield (above); he had been admitted to the Middle Temple in 1637.

PILE, Lady Elizabeth. Wife of Sir Seymour Pile, 3rd Baronet (q.v.), and sister of Sir Henry Moore, the 2nd Baronet (q.v.). Elizabeth's sister, Frances Moore, married Gabriel Pile (q.v.). This was one of many cases in the 17th century in which two sisters married two brothers.

PILE, Frances (b. 1655). She was Whitelocke's fourth child by his third wife (not by his second wife, as shown in *Complete Baronetage)*. Frances was named after Whitelocke's second wife and after a daughter of that marriage, who had died. She was known in the Whitelocke family as 'Frank' or 'Franke'. Scorning the first suitor approved by her parents, *Diary* 14 Oct., 22 Nov. 1668; 14 May, 22, 23 June 1669, she later married Francis Pile (below), the future 4th Baronet. The marriage was planned and negotiated by her parents but proved, on Whitelocke's own admission, to be an unhappy one, ib. 27 Jan., 6, 12 Feb. 1672/73, *passim*.

PILE, Francis, later 4th Bt. (d. *c.*1689). Son of Sir Seymour Pile, 3rd Baronet (q.v.). He married Whitelocke's daughter Frances (above). The reference books show the date at which he inherited the title as '1670?' but his father, the 3rd Baronet, was still alive and calling on Whitelocke five years later, *Diary* 22 Mar. 1674/75. The 4th Baronet probably succeeded to the title in about 1681, see details under his father's entry.

PILE, Gabriel. Difficult to identify in a flock of Gabriel Piles, but Whitelocke refers unambiguously to Sir Seymour Pile using his brother, Mr. Gabriel Pile, as mediator after a family brawl, ib. 14, 15 July 1674. It may be supposed from this that Sir Seymour's brother Gabriel, of Okemarsh, although shown by Burke (above) as dying in 1634, died much later, perhaps in 1684. He married Frances Moore (see entry for Moore family), sister of Elizabeth Pile (q.v.). This Frances was probably the 'aunt Pile' referred to in ib. 11 Sept. 1672.

PILE, Jane, Lady. (*c.* 1618–1692). Daughter of John Still, Bishop of Bath and Wells. Second wife and (when Whitelocke knew her) widow of Sir Francis Pile, 2nd Baronet, of Compton Beauchamp (*c.* 1617–1649), and sister-in-law of Sir Seymour Pile, 3rd Baronet (below). A match was proposed between her daughter (Sir Seymour's niece) and Samuel Whitelocke, but after some encouraging talk about the marriage portion during a first meeting at Collingbourne, Wiltshire, Lady Pile became 'much more reserved' and, while insisting that she took no exception to Sam or to his substantial estate, she told James Pearson (q.v.), the Whitelockes' tutor, that she must be excused from treating further for her daughter's marriage having 'perticular reasons' for this, which she declined to divulge. The Whitelockes were not unduly disappointed, having learned that the young lady 'was not of any great capacity and understanding', ib. 10, 23 Oct. 1671.

PILE, Sir Seymour, 3rd Bt., JP (*c.*1618–*c.*1681). Of Axford Manor near Ramsbury, Wilts. He inherited the title from his brother Francis, in about 1649. From 1664 onwards, Sir Seymour hunted with Whitelocke, sent him the occasional gift of trout or of partridges, became father-in-law to

Whitelocke's daughter Frances (q.v.), and the two often visited each other and dined together. Clearly, however, Whitelocke did not altogether like Sir Seymour. Early in their acquaintance the Baronet arrived on a visit 'halfe tipsy', 22 July, 2 Sept. 1664; 19, 28 June 1665, *passim*. After news of the Fire of London reached Whitelocke in Wiltshire, he happened to meet Sir Seymour, who gave him an outrageous account of what had happened and of what was likely to happen to people like Whitelocke and his foreign man-servant. A more sober and accurate report from Colonel Popham (q.v.) 'proved ... the fiction of S[i]ʳ Seymour, who had too much wine & too little grace, & in the midst of this sad judgem[en]ᵗ [i.e. the Fire] this godly Magistrat [Sir Seymour] was drunke & swearing & lying att almost every word.' Two days later, the godly Magistrate 'excused his mistake' about the news, ib. 7, 9 Sept. 1666.

As shown in the entry for his son Francis, 4th Baronet (q.v.), the reference books on Baronets suggest that Francis inherited the title in '1670?' but *The Diary* shows that Sir Seymour was active in 1675 and *V.C.H. Wilts.* xi, 49 states that his Will was proved in 1681. His wife Elizabeth (q.v.) also appears in *The Diary*; they proposed a match between their daughter Mary and Whitelocke's son Sam as well as that between their son Francis (q.v.) and Whitelocke's daughter Frances (q.v.), *Diary* 13 Aug. 1671. Nothing came of the first proposal and they then propounded a match between Sam Whitelocke and Sir Seymour's niece (which also came to nothing). This could have been the daughter of Gabriel Pile (q.v.) and his wife Frances, née Moore, but since only the mother is mentioned it is assumed that the niece was the daughter of the widow Jane, Lady Pile (q.v.).

PIMENTEL (PIEMENTELLI) de PRADO, Sir Antonio (b. 1604). G. Masson *Queen Christina* (Cardinal edn. Sphere Books. 1974), *passim*; *Catalogue, Christina Exhibition* Nos. 393, 473; S.I. Olofsson *Efter Westfaliska Freden: Sveriges Yttre Politik 1650–1654* (Almquist & Wiksell. 1957), *passim*. A soldier and diplomat; Spanish Governor of Nieuport in Flanders; he was sent from the Spanish Netherlands as Envoy Extraordinary to Sweden, representing Philip IV (q.v.). In 1652 he arrived in Stockholm with an impressive retinue, having travelled with Conrad van Beuningen (q.v.), the new Dutch Ambassador to Sweden. Pimentel soon endeared himself to Queen Christina, partly by his enthusiasm for entertainments at Court. By the time Whitelocke arrived as Ambassador Extraordinary, in December 1653, Pimentel was established as one of the Queen's favourites. At a Twelfth Night ball, at the beginning of that year, Christina had founded the Order of Knights of the Amaranth, and Pimentel was among those whom she had knighted. The insignia of the Order included two letters *A*, which it is thought may have stood for 'Amarantea' (the shepherdess played in a masque by Queen Christina) and for Don Pimentel's first name, 'Antonio'. (Whitelocke's knighthood was of the same Order.) Pimentel acted as a discreet go-between in connection with the Queen's plan to become a Roman Catholic, and later he was one of the few witnesses at the secret ceremony in Brussels, when she was received into the Catholic Church.

Pimentel was the first diplomat to send Whitelocke a message of welcome to Uppsala in December 1653, his master having been the first monarch to recognize the English Commonwealth. Whitelocke shrewdly decided to get on good terms with the Spaniard 'bicause he understood him to be a man of good parts, & in great favor w[i]^{t}h the Q[ueen,] & his M[aste]^r was a friend to the Commonwealth of England . . .', *Diary* 24 Dec. 1653. Pimentel proved to be an invaluable colleague, passing confidential information between the Queen and Whitelocke, and keeping the latter up to date on rumours and trends at Court. He left Uppsala before Whitelocke, and the last diary reference to him concerns a letter reporting his safe arrival in Flanders, *Diary* 29 Apr. 1654.

There is no mention of a letter which Pimentel wrote to Whitelocke, after completing his journey to Hamburg '. . . with much happinesse, which Journey I continue to morrow towards Brussells', there '& in all other parts, . . . I shall meet with yo[u]^r Exc[cellenc]^{ies} com[m]ands . . .' Pimentel also reported on a visit from Count Hannibal Sehested (q.v.), '. . . a Person whom undoubtedly for his singular merit yo[u]^r Exc[ellen]^{cy} hath had notice of [;] the great reputation yo[u]^r Exc[ellen]^{cy} hath in the world, makes this gentleman very desirous to bee knowne to yo[u]^r Lo[rdshi]^p & I beleeve yo[u]^r Lo[rdshi]^p will take much pleasure in this Conversac[i]on, for that besides his great knowledge of affaires in the world hee is of much Quality & gallantry . . .' $\frac{9}{19}$ May 1654, Long. W.P. xv, 168 (in Spanish, followed by a clumsy, contemporary translation), ib. 170. On his journey home via Hamburg, Whitelocke met Sehested, a Dane, and they subsequently came to know each other in England.

A letter in the Venetian Archives, referring to Pimentel, states dogmatically: '. . . the Spanish ambassador in Sweden procured the alliance of Sweden with England', adding more tentatively: '. . . perhaps [he] gave the impulse to the Swedes to undertake the invasion of Denmark . . .', *C.S.P. Venetian, 1653–1654* p.23, 12 Nov. 1653 *(sic)* [N.S.]. (It seems that the year was misread and the letter wrongly calendared, for the Anglo/Swedish Treaty was agreed in 1654, while the Swedish Army did not invade Denmark until 1657.)

The text of an interesting letter from Pimentel to his brother, Don Juan

Pimentel de Prado, some weeks after Whitelocke's arrival in Uppsala, appears in Add.Ms 14010 fols. 311–312, 15 Jan. 1654 [N.S.] (in Spanish. Copy.) Whitelocke issued a 'passport' to Pimentel, to protect a ship carrying the Spaniard's furniture, silver vessels, tapestries, clothes etc. to Dunkirk – '*à present sous l'obeissance de sa ditte majesté le roy d'Espagne*' – against piracy by English sailors, *Journal* ii, 476–477, 1st edition (this does not appear in the 2nd edition.), 4 Apr. 1654. A letter in Spanish from Pementel (*sic*) to Whitelocke concerns a 'passport' enabling the English Ambassador to return to England, partly overland, ib. 489. The warrant for a licence from the Protector and Council, permitting Don Pimantelli (*sic*) to export six horses from Dover, was issued at Whitelocke's request, *C.S.P. Dom., 1654* p. 440, 21 Aug. 1654.

PITT, George, MP, JP (1625–1694). *Hist. of Parl.* A wealthy Royalist, of Stratfield Saye, Hants (some seven miles south of Reading) and of Duke Street, Westminster. His father had bought the Hampshire estate in 1629 and his grandfather had acquired extensive property round Wareham, Dorset. Pitt himself came into property in Gloucestershire through his marriage to Jane, widow of the 6th Lord Chandos of Sudeley. (She was previously married to Sir William Sedley.) Pitt had been at the Middle Temple in 1652 and the Inner Temple in 1654. He is reputed to have been of an avaricious temperament. Whitelocke was acquainted with him before the Restoration: Pitt wrote to him about the elections at Wareham, *Diary* 7 Jan. 1658/59; he was elected for that borough in 1660 and 1661. (*Return. Members of Parliament* i, 522, note 5, states that there was a double return for Wareham, 9 Apr. 1661, which was declared void by the House of Commons on 15 June 1661.)

Pitt's offices included those of Gentleman of the Privy Chamber from 1660 and Comptroller to the Duke of York (q.v.), a post which he bought in 1674. He was called upon as an arbitrator on behalf of John, 2nd Lord Lovelace (q.v.), in the Baron's dispute with Whitelocke over Blunsdon (Blundesden), in Wiltshire, north-west of Swindon, *Diary* 17 Jan. 1661/62. There was a distant, perhaps irrelevant, connection in that the estate had belonged to Lord Chandos in the reign of Queen Elizabeth, see entry for LOVELACE. Whitelocke's kinsman and arbitrator, the Royalist Adrian May (q.v.), reported that Pitt 'would consent to nothing', ib. 21 June 1662. This non-co-operation was probably inspired by Lovelace, who had forbidden his arbitrator to meet any more on the Blunsdon business, ib. 17 Jan. 1661/62.

PONDER (Nathaniel). J. Brown *John Bunyan, his Life, Times and Work* (London. 1885) *passim*; G.L. Turner *Original Records of Early Non-conformity under Persecution and Indulgence* (Fisher Unwin. 1911), i, 318, *passim*; iii, 485–490 (an outline of Ponder's activities), *passim*; and 791–792 (concerning Whitelocke and James Pearson, q.v., at Chilton Lodge). Brown, p.263, describes Ponder as 'an agreeable man to have dealings with' and quotes from John Dunton: 'He has sweetness and enterprise in his air'; Turner iii, 485, describes him as a 'Puritan printer, or more strictly publisher ... or bookseller'; (the term 'printed for' was used in the 17th century rather than 'published by'). In the modern usage, Ponder published John Owen's Greek-titled book on the Holy Spirit in 1674, and his *Treatise on Schisme* in 1684. On 10 May 1676 he was imprisoned for publishing a pamphlet 'tending to Sedition and Defamation of the Christian Religion' but later that month he paid the fine, entered into a bond for £500, made the requisite abject apology, promising never to offend again in the same way, and was released from the Gate House. In 1677, after Dr. John Owen (q.v.) had helped secure Bunyan's release from Bedford Gaol, Bunyan showed Owen the manuscript of 'Pilgrim's Progress', then took it to the publisher. The 1st edition of part 1 states that it was 'printed for Nath. Ponder at the Peacock in the Poultrey, nr. Cornhil, 1678.' Ponder also published Bunyan's *Life and Death of Mr Badman* in 1680 and *Pilgrim's Progress* part 2 in 1684/85. The publisher came to be known as 'Bunyan Ponder'. The 1st edition of Whitelocke's *Memorials* ... was also 'Printed for Nathaniel Ponder, at the Sign of the Peacock, in the Poultry, near the Church', in 1682.

This posthumous publication was not Whitelocke's only connection with Ponder. After the Fire of London the Whitelockes, coming up from the country, 'took lodgings att Mr Ponders', *Diary* 10 Nov. 1666. On the following day they heard Dr. Owen preach, probably in Ponder's house. They stayed with Ponder again on visits to London in the next two years, ib. 15 Jan. 1666/67; 24 Mar. 1667/68; 5 Nov. 1668. Whitelocke refers to his wife, Mary, who was ill, being disturbed by 'disorderly persons' at a 'victualling house' nearby, most of them being the Judges' and Serjeants' men from Serjeants' Inn. Ponder, as master of the house in which the Whitelockes were lodging, did what he could to prevent their being disturbed 'having served formerly under Whitelocke', ib. 12 Dec. 1668. There is no indication as to when, where, or in what capacity he had served.

In 1672 Ponder was very active in applying for licences to preach, on behalf of Nonconformist Ministers. Most of these were Independents and the majority were in Northamptonshire, where he probably had relatives, but he also applied for licences on behalf of preachers in other counties.

These included one for James Pearson, the Whitelocke family's tutor at Chilton Lodge, Berkshire (shown as Wiltshire in the application, the village of Chilton Foliat being in that county), and another for John Whitman (an Elder of the Bedford Church) to preach at the house of George Cokayn (q.v.) at Cotton End, Bedfordshire, where Whitelocke stayed with Cokayn's parents, Turner (above) iii, 790–791; 489.

Evidence which helps to confirm the identity of Whitelocke's Mr. Ponder is found on a bond for £600 to William Pendlebury (q.v.); Whitelocke's signature is witnessed by Nathaniel Ponder, 21 May 1667, Long. W.P. xx, 131. Whitelocke was staying in London at that time. (See *Diary* 10 Dec. 1668 for another financial transaction.)

POPHAM family (below). *Historical Manuscripts Commission* No. 51, *Report on Mss of F.W. Leyborne Popham* (H.M.S.O. 1899); J. Burke *History of the Commoners* (London. 1835) ii; J. & J.B. Burke *Dictionary of the Landed Gentry* (London. 1846) ii; J. Le Neve *Pedigrees of the Knights* (ed. G.W. Marshall. London. 1873) viii; *V.C.H. Wilts.* xii; *Berks.* iv; *Som.* ii & iv; numerous B.L. Mss. Sir John Popham MP (*c.* 1531–1607), of Balliol College, Oxford, and the Middle Temple, had been Lord Chief Justice in the reign of Queen Elizabeth. A wealthy man, he built a large mansion in Wellington, Somerset, which, after his lifetime, was destroyed in the Civil War. He had acquired estates in several counties, among them Littlecote, on the Kennet, north-east of Marlborough, in Wiltshire. Sir John's son, Sir Francis Popham MP, lived at Littlecote, as did his grandson, Colonel Alexander Popham. The Colonel and his brother, Admiral Edward Popham, both feature in *The Diary*. Colonel Alexander's son was another Sir Francis Popham MP, whose son was another Alexander. The family was economical in the choice of first names, both for sons and daughters.

POPHAM, Col. Alexander, MP (*c.* 1605–1669). M.F.K.; *Hist. of Parl.*; *D.N.B.* (in the entry for his father, Sir Francis Popham MP, sen.). He studied at Balliol, his father and grandfather's College, matriculating in July 1621, seven months after Whitelocke had matriculated at St. John's. The two young men were also contemporaries at the Middle Temple. Popham was elected MP for Bath in the Short and Long Parliaments. He supported Parliament in the Civil War and, although a Presbyterian Elder, sat in the Rump Parliament after Pride's Purge, but did not take a very active part in it. He was opposed both to the execution of the King and to the setting up of the Protectorate. In spite of this, he was again elected MP for Bath in Cromwell's first Parliament, in 1654; he represented Wiltshire in 1656, and Minehead in 1659, having earlier declined Cromwell's invitation to sit in the newly-constituted 'Other House'. Although regarded as a Republican in the 1650s, he established himself as a Royalist in time for the Restoration, and waited on Charles II with about 100 gentlemen from the West Country, *Diary* 2 June 1660. Once again, he had been elected MP for Bath, serving in successive Parliaments from April 1660 until his death. It seems that he owned Houndstreet, 10 miles from Bath, but in his last years, and probably for most of his life, he lived at Littlecote, near to Whitelocke's last home, Chilton Lodge.

The earliest diary references to Alexander Popham concern proposals for a match between his niece and Whitelocke's son James (q.v.), but these came to nothing, ib. 25 May, 14 July 1656. The two men presumably knew each other at the Middle Temple and in Parliament, but there is no diary reference to this. That they knew each other in the 1650s is, however, confirmed in a letter from 'Lytellcott' sent by Alexander Popham to Whitelocke; in it the Colonel refers to '. . . the many reall Noble favors' he had received from his friend '. . . and were it not for plunginge my self into that loe [i.e. low] thynge caled [i.e. called] crevorie [fulsome praise?] I should make large expressions of thankfulnes . . .' after referring to a financial transaction he continued: 'My wife [his second wife, Letitia, according to *Hist. of Parl.*; elsewhere Letitia is shown as his first wife] and the poor widow [Letitia's sister Anne, widow of Admiral Edward Popham, below] present ther searvis to your good Lady [Whitelocke's third wife, Mary]', 20 Jan. 1652/53, Long. W.P. xii, 150.

Alexander Popham entertained Charles II handsomely at Littlecote in 1663. Unlike some of Whitelocke's supposed friends from earlier decades Popham, although a newly converted Royalist, was consistently cordial towards his old friend and new neighbour after the Restoraton: he invited the Whitelockes to stay, *Diary* 20 Oct. 1663 and to dine, 21 July 1664, *passim*. It was to Popham (perhaps in his capacity as an MP, or as a Deputy-Lieutenant of the County) that Whitelocke turned for reliable news about the Fire of London and its implications, ib. 7 Sept. 1666, and it was Popham who sent him news of Chancellor Clarendon's fall from power, ib. 28 Aug. 1667.

Two of Popham's daughters appear in *The Diary*: (1) Letitia, ib. 26 July 1667. After she had rejected Lord de la Warr's son, ib. 18, 27 Apr. 1670, she married (in 1674) Edward Seymour, MP (q.v.), later 4th Baronet, of Maiden Bradley, Wiltshire (2) Anne or Anna, ib. 28 May 1666. Whitelocke was consulted about the settlement when she married William Ashe of Heytesbury, Wiltshire (within riding distance of Maiden Bradley), and she sent him a fee of £2., ib. 2, 6 July 1670.

POPHAM, Admiral and General-at-Sea, Edward, MP (c. 1610–1651). *D.N.B.* Brother of Colonel Alexander Popham (above). He too fought for Parliament. He was elected MP for Minehead in 1646 and, like Alexander, continued to sit after Pride's Purge. On 27 February 1648/49 the Council of State appointed him, with Robert Blake (q.v.) and Richard Deane (q.v.), as 'commissioners for ordering and commanding the fleet during the coming year'. When Admiral Popham died of fever, Whitelocke was chosen by the Council of State to report this to Parliament, and he and Sir Henry Vane (q.v.) were then sent to condole with the Admiral's widow, *C.S.P. Dom. 1651* p.354, 22 Aug. Whitelocke, with Speaker Lenthall (q.v.), Cromwell (q.v.) and others, attended the funeral procession from Exeter House to Westminster. Although this is, in fact, the only diary reference, the entry states that by the Admiral's death, Whitelocke 'lost a kind friend', *Diary* 24 Sept. 1651. The widow, another Anne (d.1692), was a daughter of William Kerr or Carr (a Groom of the Bedchamber to James I), and sister of Colonel Alexander Popham's wife. In 1661 she married Philip, 4th Lord Wharton (q.v.) as his third wife. She too appears in *The Diary*.

POPHAM, Sir Francis jun., MP (1646–1674). *Hist. of Parl.* First surviving son of Colonel Alexander Popham (q.v.). He studied at Christ Church, Oxford. In 1669 he was returned unopposed as MP for Bath, the seat left vacant by his father's death, and he held it until his own death in his late 20s. He married Helena Rogers of Cannington, Somerset, probably in 1669. The marriage settlement comprised £10,000 and several manors, including those of Chilton Foliat, Littlecote (with the house), Rudge (south-west of Littlecote), North Standen and Oak Hill (both south-west of Hungerford), with further property in Chilton Foliat, Hungerford and nearby Froxfield and Ramsbury. Helena's portion was £4,000, Wilts. R.O. 488/9, Serial No. 9 1668/69. Popham's wife, Helena, came to Littlecote a few months before the death of her father-in-law, Colonel Alexander Popham, *Diary* 1 May 1669 with note. She herself died before her husband and her funeral was something of a local event, ib. 12 Mar. 1671/72; 1 Apr. 1672. Sir Francis Popham was on cordial terms with Whitelocke, his father's contemporary. As the new master of Littlecote, he sent welcome gifts including half a doe, half a buck, and a 'very fatt side of venison', ib. 22 Jan. 1671/72; 26 June, 16 July 1672. He also paid several substantial fees for legal advice, two of them for £10., ib. 15, July 1672; 8 May 1674, *passim*. His early death from smallpox is recorded with the brief comment that he was 'meanly buried', ib. 13, 28 Aug. 1674.

PORTLAND, Charles Weston, 3rd E. of (*c.* 1639–1665). G.E.C. Son of Jerome Weston, 2nd Earl of Portland (below). Styled Lord Weston until he succeeded to the title in March 1662/63. He and his father appear in *The Diary* in connection with Whitelocke's friend and physician for some three years, Dr. Thomas Winston (q.v.). On his deathbed the doctor sent for a scrivener, dictated a new Will, made some amendments to the document and signed it. Because of the alterations he asked the scrivener to write it out again, but before the fair copy was finished he died, *Diary* 24 Oct. 1655. Some of those present at his death tried to have the new, signed Will burned, but the scrivener resisted them. Among other bequests, Dr. Winston left land in Raunds and Hargrave, Northamptonshire, with Blunts Hall, Witham, in Essex, to the 2nd Earl of Portland and his son Charles Weston, for their lives, with reversion to Whitelocke's son Bulstrode. Whitelocke attempted to buy out the life interest, agreeing to pay £1,000 to the 2nd Earl and an annuity of £200 for life to the future 3rd Earl; to this end bonds were duly sealed, ib. 20 Dec. 1655. After the Restoration, however, Whitelocke found once again (as in his dealings with Lord Lovelace q.v.), that Royalists who signed and sealed contracts in the 1650s were disinclined to honour them in the 1660s; indeed, it was rumoured in 1662/63 that the 2nd Earl of Portland was planning to sue for possession of Dr. Winston's land. In spite of his legal acumen, Whitelocke was in a very weak bargaining position and decided, for his son's sake, to re-negotiate the settlement with the 2nd Earl and to have the deal confirmed by Act of Parliament. The new agreement was reached a few days before the Earl's death on 17 March 1662/63; ib. 13 Jan., 19, 20, 26 Feb., 11 Mar. 1662/63.

On 2 April 1663, a few weeks after Charles Weston succeeded to the title, a Bill was read for the first time, not in the Commons but in the Lords, since it concerned a Peer, *L.J.* xi, 504. It embodied an agreement between Francis Lord Willoughby of Parham (q.v.), and his brother William Willoughby (q.v.) of the one part, as uncles of Whitelocke's son Bulstrode (an 'infant' i.e. minor, aged 15) and Charles, Earl of Portland of the other. It allowed for the sale by trustees of part of Dr. Winston's legacy in Northamptonshire, in order to raise money to pay Portland the agreed lump sum of £3,700 (of which, the Bill stated, £1,500 'or there abouts' had already been paid), plus an annuity for life of £300. (If Whitelocke could have known that two years later the young Earl was to die, fighting the Dutch off Lowestoft, he need not have gone to such lengths.) Included in the Bill were unrelated bequests to two of Whitelocke's other sons; one concerned a legacy from Henry Dixon (q.v.) to Willoughby, and named Thomas Dixon, perhaps 'Nephew Dixon' (q.v.), who may well have disputed the bequest; the other related to Whitelocke's young son Carleton, and a legacy promised by the astrologer, William Lilly (q.v.).

For details see the Act 'For settling an Annuity on the Earl of Portland', Record Office, House of Lords, 15 Charles II, No. 30 (1663). The Bill was read in the Commons, 29 April, 7, 14 May, and the Royal Assent, to this and other Bills, was read in the Lords, with the Commons present, on 3 June 1663.

PORTLAND, Jerome Weston, 2nd E. of (1605–1663). G.E.C. Ambassador to Turin, Venice, Florence and Paris in the 1630s. He succeeded to the Earldom in 1635; held a number of offices, including those of Keeper of Richmond New Park in June 1637, and joint Lord-Lieutenant of Hampshire in 1639. The family's connection with Dr. Winston has not been traced. Negotiations over the doctor's legacy were nearly all conducted between Whitelocke and the 2nd Earl, but are outlined above in the 3rd Earl's entry, since they were incorporated in the Act bearing his name. Weston served as Governor of the Isle of Wight from November 1633 to August 1642, when Parliament cancelled his patent, but this was renewed after the Restoration. He was also joint Lord-Lieutenant of Hampshire in the 1630s, with his brother-in-law, the Duke of Lennox.

A Mr. Weston, brother of the 2nd Earl, makes just one appearance in Whitelocke's record, intervening on his nephew's behalf over payment of the agreed annuity, *Diary* 10 Oct. 1657. He was probably Thomas Weston (1609–1688), who succeeded as 4th Earl when his nephew was killed at sea.

POTLEY, Andrew. Son of Christopher Potley (below). One of Whitelocke's retinue on the Swedish Embassy, described as 'a Young Gent[leman]. Kinsman of Wh[itelocke], of very good parts, and Stout [i.e. courageous], he spoke High Du[t]ch [i.e. German] perfectly; & had the French Tonge. Gent[lema]ⁿ of the 1st degree', Add.Ms 4995, appendix 5 fol. 12v.; he is also described as a gentleman at Whitelocke's table. His father having links with the Swedish Court, Andrew Potley stayed on in Sweden, after Whitelocke's Embassy, with no less a host than General Wrangell (q.v.), as a letter in Latin from the General shows, 5 June 1655, Long W.P. xvii, 56.

Later, Potley spent some time in Hamburg, *Diary* 23 Mar. 1658/59. He kept in touch with Whitelocke, sending news of political events overseas. The early letters were sent from Stockholm: the first to be traced refers to 'great talke of a warre with the Muscovites' under the bellicose King Charles X of Sweden (q.v.) who, having succeeded Queen Christina (q.v.) at her abdication, was confronted by financial problems and unrest, 16 Dec. 1654, Long. W.P. xvi, 162–162v. A few days later Potley wrote:

a Diet is to bee kept here the 22th [*sic*] of February, & then many things to bee reformed both in Court & State[;] care to bee taken how debts maye bee payed on all sides & a warre to be undertaken to the profit of this Nation[,] as some thinke with the Moscovites . . .
23 Dec. 1654

ib. 168.

The next letter reported that the King of Sweden had withdrawn, to be out of the way of solicitants and to acquaint himself with the country. His Queen, Hedwig Leonora, was recovering from measles and the Polish envoy had arrived, 15, 26 Jan. 1654/55, Cal. Long W.P. xvii. Three months later, Potley explained that he had been ill, which was why he had not been more diligent in writing:

The great sea preparations they talke off heere will not amount much above 40 main shippes; the King goes in the Scepter[.] Our Lord Wrangell as Admirall off the fleete goes in the Crowne, to w[hi]^{ch} must bee added 8 gunns more to make up the number of 80 w[hi]^{ch} will make it a very considerable Vessell; The Court here is jealous [i.e. suspicious] as if the Hollander should bee willing to defend the Prussians by Sea as Saving great benefit off trade from thence – to wit from Danzig and Queensborough, and not lyable to pay such Customes as the Swedes would make them paye if they were Masters there, it is not above 3 weekes since the King hath caused the Customes to bee raised [:] a Shippound off iron w[hi]^{ch} for[m]erly [paid] 1 Christina or 16 Steurerspice, now payes 4 Christinas, a Shippound off Copper formerly 4 now 14 Rixdollers[;] a piece off Cloath formerly 2 now 6 Rixdollers; The Embassader Mr Bonde [q.v.] its thought will not goe from hence at the dissolution of the Parlia^m[en]^t here, they say he is to demaund a round summe off money off the English, for spoiles & losses their shipps have sustained passing through the Channell[,] having beene arrested by our shipps, & againe they will proffer a free trade unto the English to erect 3 staples in any off their sea Townes and none to buye their Commodities off them but the English, & they to rent them to other Nations at their pleasure . . .
Apr. 1655.

Long W.P. xvii, 43–43v.

After Wrangell's letter, referred to earlier, which commended Potley to Whitelocke (not knowing, presumably, of the young man's candid letters reporting on Swedish affairs), Potley wrote from Elsinore, saying that he had arrived there the previous day with Ambassador Bonde, bound for England. In the course of their eight day voyage through the Baltic, they had encountered the Polish Ambassador, bound for Stockholm, and had subsequently learned, in Elsinore, that the Ambassador had been well received by the King of Sweden (who, incidentally, invaded Poland later the same year). He concluded with a cryptic 'longing desire to

communicate some particulars to my Lord Protectour & your Lords[hi]p
... The 30th of June [1655] at Elsineur', ib. 68–70v.

By 14 August 1655 Andrew Potley was in Hamburg, pleading for the
release from prison of one Henry Harleff, ib. 84. On 13 January 1655/56,
Sir George Fleetwood (q.v.) wrote, in a postscript to a letter, asking
Whitelocke to persuade Colonel Christopher Potley (below) to relieve his
son's necessity, ib. 135.

POTLEY, Col. Christopher. Father of Andrew (above). He married
Whitelocke's cousin, a daughter of Richard Whitelocke (d. 1624), who had
been a merchant in Elbing (Elblag), south-east of Danzig. Potley had
served for some time in the Swedish Army, during the Thirty Years War.
Returning to England, he fought for Parliament in the Civil War;
Whitelocke recorded that when two of the City Regiments were ordered to
join Sir William Waller, 'the major general of his army was colonel Potley,
an old soldier under the king of Sweden, Gustavus Adolphus', *Memorials*
i, 211; the rank of Major-General may only have related to one campaign.
Whitelocke usually referred to his kinsman as Colonel Potley.

After the execution of Charles I, the Council of State despatched Potley
to Denmark and Sweden 'to send us from those parts intelligence, and we
gave him 200 l. in hand, and promised him 100 l. more for one year's
entertainment ... He was as fit as any man for this service, had lived long
in those countries a soldier, well ... esteemed by the grandees, especially
in Germany and in the court of Sweden: I recommended him to this
employment, which was of great consequence to us' ib. iii, 5, 31 Mar. 1649.
A warrant was issued for his pass, permitting him to embark for Hamburg
and Sweden on business of state, *C.S.P. Dom. 1649–1650*, 12 Apr. 1649.
He was still in Sweden two years later, when it was resolved to pay him 'for
his service in Sweden for 18 months, at the rate of 300 l. a year', ib.*1651*, 16
Jan. 1650/51. Three days after this resolution was passed, Potley sent news
from Stockholm, in an unsigned letter endorsed by Whitelocke 'cousen
Potley': Lord Montrose (who had been in northern Germany, in Denmark
and in Sweden, trying to raise ships, arms and ammunition for the royalist
cause), had left Gothenburg bound for the 'Ills of Orthe' (i.e. Isles of Orkney)
and so into Scotland 'with his officers and soulders being about 1200 of all
natures' but because of freezing conditions he was unlikely to achieve his aim
during the winter. Montrose had received no assistance from the Swedes,
'neither do they intend to meddle w[ith] foreign affairs that concern them
not.' He had, however, found a good friend in Gothenburg, a wealthy
Scottish merchant named John Mackcleare, who had supported his plans
with about 60,000 crowns, 19 Jan. 1650/51, Long. W.P. xi, 18.

Colonel Potley was a natural choice as a leading member of Whitelocke's retinue for the Swedish Embassy, and 'was the more willing to attend Wh[itelocke] hoping to obtain the Easier way for some of his arre[a]rs there . . .'; he was 'well acquainted with the Government of Sweden; and had the High Du[t]ch Tongue perfectly', Add.Ms 4995 appendix 5, fol. 12.

POVEY, Thomas, MP (1615–c.1702). *D.N.B.*; *Pepys* x. Of Grays Inn. Elected a recruiter member of the Long Parliament for Liskeard, Cornwall, in March 1646/47. In spite of falling under suspicion of disloyalty to the Council of State, in 1650, he served on the Council for the Colonies in 1657, and was elected MP for Bossiney, Cornwall. He had a London house in Lincolns Inn Fields, built in 1657, and a country house, the Priory, Hounslow (sold in 1671), to which he invited Whitelocke, *Diary* 4 July, 3 Sept. 1656. Whitelocke only seems to have known him slightly, but Povey helped to obtain a Cornish seat for William Whitelocke (q.v.), ib. 1, 6 Jan. 1658/59, see also entry for BULLER, Francis. Soon after this election, General George Monck wrote about Povey finding a seat in Scotland, ib. 1 Feb. 1658/59. Povey does not appear in *The Diary* after the Restoration, when he was appointed Treasurer of the Duke of York's Household and to various trade and colonial committees; his accounts were muddled and Pepys had a very poor opinion of his gifts in business, but he was a man of taste who appears to have influenced his nephew, William Blathwayt, in collecting furniture, pictures and books, see *Dyrham Park, Gloucestershire* (National Trust. 1967).

PRATT, Sir George, 2nd Bt. (c.1605–1673). *Complete Baronetage.* Of Coleshill, Berkshire. Studied at Magdalen Hall, Oxford, and Grays Inn. He married, in or before 1647, Margaret, daughter of Whitelocke's friend Sir Humphrey Forster, Bt. (q.v.). Whitelocke describes Lady Pratt (d.1699) as 'excellent ingenious company, butt not equally yoaked', *Diary* 16 Sept. 1647. She occasionally reappears in the record, socially or as a client, up to 26 Aug. 1669, but Sir George is only mentioned again once, as Whitelocke's client, ib. 24 Mar. 1662/63.

PRIDE, Col. Sir Thomas (d.1658). *D.N.B.*; D. Underdown *Pride's Purge*, *passim*. Regicide. A wealthy brewer, who fought for Parliament. 'Pride's Purge' took its name from the Colonel who, acting under military orders on 6 December 1648, prevented those MPs who planned a settlement with Charles I from entering Parliament, and indeed arrested some of them.

Pride is only referred to twice in *The Diary*: in connection with the Purge and (posthumously) after the Restoration, when the 1st Earl of Berkshire (q.v.) referred contemptuously to members of Cromwell's Other House as 'base mechanicke fellowes'; challenged on this by Whitelocke, the Earl admitted that there had been some gentleman among them, but that he was thinking of men like Pride and Hewson (q.v.), *Diary* 7 June 1660. Pride had bought himself the considerable estate of Nonesuch, Surrey, and served as Sheriff of that County. In 1656 he was knighted by Cromwell but the next year, true to his republican principles, he opposed the plan to make Cromwell King.

PRIDEAUX, Sir Edmund (Edmond), 1st Bt., MP (1601–1659). *D.N.B.*; *Extinct & Dormant Baronetcies*; *Complete Baronetage*; M.F.K. A distinguished Inner Temple barrister; a West Country man, he sat as MP for Lyme Regis, Dorset, in five Parliaments between 1640 and his death in 1659. He was a religious Presbyterian but a political radical; he served as one of the Commissioners of Parliament's Great Seal from November 1643 for three years, and was appointed by Parliament, in 1644, as Master of the Posts, Messengers and Couriers. Like Whitelocke, he was sent as one of Parliament's Commissioners to the Uxbridge negotiations in January 1644/45; he was created a Baronet in May 1658. Whitelocke was on good terms with him and refers to dining with him frequently at Kew, accompanied by Sir Thomas Widdrington (q.v.), and other lawyers, and to being 'highly feasted', *Diary* 11 May 1648; 18 Aug. 1649. Prideaux served as Attorney-General from April 1649; after his death, Whitelocke described him as a generous person, faithful to Parliament's interest, a good Chancery man and his friend, ib. 19 Aug. 1659.

PRUJEAN (PRUGEAN, PRIDGEON), Sir Francis, MD (1593–1666). *D.N.B.* He was Whitelocke's physician for some years, *Diary* 23 Sept. 1645; 9 May 1649. President of the College of Physicians from 1650 to 1654; he was knighted by Charles II in 1661.

PRYCE (PRYSE, PRICE), family (below). *Extinct & Dormant Baronetcies*; *Complete Baronetage*. Of Gogerddan, north-east of Aberystwyth; from an old Welsh family. Two of Whitelocke's daughters, Elizabeth and Hester, married two brothers, Sir Richard Pryce, 2nd Baronet, and Carbery Pryce. The marriages resulted in much work and anxiety for Whitelocke. Sir Richard Pryce sen. (created 1st Baronet in 1641) does not appear in *The*

Diary, but papers from about 1640, concerning his sale of land in Montgomeryshire to Sir John Wittewronge (q.v.) are in Long. W.P. viii, 60.

PRYCE, Carbery (d. *c*.1668). Youngest brother of Sir Richard, 2nd Baronet (below), and of Sir Thomas, 3rd Baronet. He married, before 21 March 1665/66, Whitelocke's daughter Hester (1642 – *c*.1694); Whitelocke's sister, Elizabeth Mostyn (q.v.), living in Wales, warned him that the marriage was impending, and he no doubt echoed her views in describing Carbery as 'a man of no fortune & of much disorder', *Diary* 17 Feb. 1661/62; his attempts to get Hester away from Carbery failed, ib. 26 Apr., 6 Oct. 1662; The couple married without the consent of the bride's father, and without his knowledge they went to Barbados, ib. 21 Mar. 1665/66. Against Whitelocke's advice they returned to England, ib. 22 Mar. 1666/67. By the following year, Carbery was dead. Neither Carbery's brother, Sir Richard Pryce (below), nor Hester's sister, Lady Pryce, would do anything for the young widow, ib. 2 Feb. 1668/69. She later married a Welshman, Taylor (?) Scawen. Carbery, the son by her first marriage, succeeded his uncle Thomas, becoming 4th Baronet in 1682 and MP for Cardiganshire in 1690.

PRYCE, Sir Richard, 2nd Bt., MP, JP (*c*.1630–*c*.1675). *Hist. of Parl.* (as Pryse). Eldest son of Sir Richard Pryce, 1st Baronet; he succeeded to the title and land in 1651. In 1653 he married Whitelocke's 15-year-old daughter Elizabeth (b.1638), with her father's consent. From the age of 11 (a few months after her mother's death) Elizabeth had been brought up in Wales by her aunt, Elizabeth Mostyn (q.v.), *Diary* 6 Oct. 1649. As a very young wife she lost several children at birth or by miscarriage; on one occasion Whitelocke recorded that she 'miscarryed through discontent', ib. 12 Dec. 1656. He very seldom referred to 'son Pryce' (the recognition he gave to his other sons-in-law) but gave him the title 'Sir Richard', perhaps with tongue-in-cheek. The young man frequently turned to him for help, for example in a long-standing legal dispute with Colonel John Jones of Nanteos (q.v.) over some land in Cardiganshire. With Whitelocke's help this was resolved: Articles of Agreement were drawn up, supported by a bond in £4,000 and a deed of covenant, for producing certain deeds mentioned in the Agreement, both signed by Colonel Jones, 22 July 1654, Long. W.P. xvi, 81–86; *Diary* 18, 20, July 1654. At the same time, Sir Richard was at odds with Sir John Wittewronge (q.v.), ib. 21, 26, 28 July 1654. Elizabeth had written begging her father to help her husband, ib. 20

June 1656, *passim*. Two years later Sir Richard, newly appointed as Sheriff of Cardiganshire, wrote in some agitation to his father-in-law about a religious demonstration in his area:

> There mett me som two miles of my house at least 400 persons out of ... Wales commanded in chief ... by Mr Vavasor Powell [a leading Fifth Monarchist and a former Chaplain in Parliament's Army] ... I sent my deputy Sheriffe ... to know uppon w[hat] scor this convened ... [and received] this answer ... th[a]ᵗ they mett to breake breade, and intended a merghing[?] of part of severall congregations' Churches of Wales, at our parish Church this last Lords Day[.] W[hat] their intentions were, or may bee I cannot conjeture ... I doe humbly desire your Lords[hi]p to move his Highnesse [Cromwell] (if you see fitt) ... to know his pleasure whether such tumultuous assemblyes bee allowed or not ...
> Gogerthan
> 12 July
> [16]56
>   Bodleian Ms Rawl. A. 39 fol. 274.

There were many more occasions on which Whitelocke's busy public life was interrupted by Pryce's urgent appeals for help. Pryce was returned as MP for Cardiganshire on 11 July 1660. A derisive appraisal by a Royalist, written in about 1661, describes:

> Sir Richard Price, a young gentleman not of full age, in the tyme that the discovery of principles was most dangerous, and it is conceived he hath not as yet any that he is too much obliged unto. He ranne through several publique offices under all the governments that have been from 1652, to this tyme; but probably more by the direction of his father-in-law, Mr Bulstrode Whitlock [*sic*], than by his own desires.
> Quoted by S.R. Meyrick *History and Antiquities of the County of Cardigan* (1907) p.308.

PRYNNE (PRINNE, PRIN), William, MP (*c*.1602–1669). W. Lamont *Marginal Prynne* (Routledge & Kegan Paul. 1963); *Hist. of Parl.*; *D.N.B.*; J. Aubrey *Brief Lives* (ed. Oliver Lawson Dick. Peregrine Books. 1962). Of Swainswick, north of Bath. A Lincoln's Inn barrister, and a prolific pamphleteer. Prynne's ferocious attack on stage plays in *Histriomastix* was punished by: a fine of £5,000, having part of his ears cut off in the pillory and by life-imprisonment, the sentence being imposed by the Star Chamber. His subsequent pamphlets against bishops led to a repetition of the punishment with the addition of 'S.L.' ('Seditious Libeller') being branded on his cheeks. The Royal Masque *The Triumph of Peace*, in which Whitelocke was responsible for the music, was presented in 1634 by members of the Inns of Court, to dissociate themselves from their fellow lawyer's condemnation of masques. Whitelocke's connection with the performance may well have initiated Prynne's dislike for him, but on Whitelocke's own admission Prynne bore another grudge against him: in November 1648, Prynne was elected a Recruiter Member of the Long Parliament for Newport, Cornwall. In the Commons he opposed the Army, favoured a compromise with Charles I, and was consequently secluded (the month after his election) in Pride's Purge, and was imprisoned without trial for three years. While in Parliament he had quoted inaccurately from records and precedents, and was corrected by Whitelocke. (Aubrey confirms that 'He was a learned man ... but is much blamed for his unfaithful quotations.') As MP for Bath, after the Restoration, he took his revenge, as Whitelocke describes in *Diary* 1 June 1660. His malicious attempt, however, to have Whitelocke excepted from the King's pardon failed. Later, he tried to damage Whitelocke by opposing the Earl of Portland's Bill on the grounds that Whitelocke, having been a rebel, deserved no favour; but again he failed, ib. 29 Apr. 1663.

Whitelocke's papers include notes on two charges against William Prynne: the first concerned Prynne's alleged libel against the late Attorney-General William Noy (q.v.), in an anonymous tract which was attributed to Prynne, in view of the contents and the person against whom part of it was directed. It was entitled 'A Divine Tragedy ... Examples of God's Judgment upon Sabbath-breakers', and Noy's death was cited as an example. It was Noy who had instituted the harsh proceedings against Prynne in the Star Chamber; after watching the inhuman sentence carried out, on 7 May 1634, as did William Laud (q.v.), Noy had suffered a vesical haemorrhage. A few months later he arranged for Prynne's further confinement, then went to drink the waters at Tunbridge Wells; he was suffering severely from stone and from haemorrhages, and died in Brent on 9 August 1634. The second charge against Prynne concerned 'Newes from Ipswich', 1636, which attacked Bishop Wren (q.v.) of Norwich. The notes in Whitelocke's papers connected Prynne with the 'Newes' because he had publicly denied the lawfulness of bishops and priests officiating in the Church of England 'w[hi]^{ch} is the chiefe scope of that Libell'; also because he had absented himself from Church on fast-days, and because the lack of sermons on fast-days was 'a mayne matter of exception in this Libell.' A further 'proof' against him was: that 'hee hath frequent conference in the Tower with M^r H[enry] Burton' (who had been pilloried along with Prynne and Bastwick, in June 1637), and 'Because ... Mr Prynne's man used to take notes of Mr Burtons sermons and to bring them to his Master.' Moreover, 'the stile and quotations in this Libell are agreable to the rest of Mr Prynnes Bookes.' There was further evidence that 'Newes from Ipswich' had been delivered by a Mrs. Fleet, living in the Tower, to a Mr. George Pancooke, 'a dutch Gentleman'. Besides this, Prynne and Burton frequently met in the Tower and 'consulted of the divulging (if not the making) of one or both the aforesayd Libells', [1637?], Long. W.P. vii, 209–209v.

PUCKERING, [Jane]. Daughter of Sir Thomas Puckering, Bt. (d.1636), of Weston, Herts. She sent a petition to Parliament, which the Commons referred to the Commissioners of the Great Seal, with 'all other Cases of like Nature', *C.J.* vi, 491. Whitelocke, as one of the Commissioners, recorded that the case was between Puckering and Welch and concerned a forced marriage, *Diary* 7 Mar. 1650/51.

PULESTON, Judge [John] (1583–1659). E. Foss *Judges of England*. From Emral, Flintshire. A Middle Temple lawyer. After the King's execution, Puleston replaced one of the Judges who refused to act, becoming a Justice of Common Pleas on 1 June 1649. Earlier, he offered Whitelocke his Middle Temple lodgings and the offer was gratefully accepted, *Diary* 30 Mar. 1649. Puleston's son married Whitelocke's great-niece, daughter of Roger Mostyn (q.v.), of Cilcain, Flintshire (now Clwyd), ib. 15 Feb. 1658/59.

PUREFOY family. *Complete Baronetage*; *V.C.H. Berks.* iv. George Purefoy of Wadley and Wicklesham near Faringdon, Berks. (now Oxon.), was Sheriff of Berkshire in 1640. He was probably the Colonel Purefoy who was appointed by the Council of State (with Whitelocke and Mr. Love) to serve on a committee to consider repairs to Windsor and Wallingford Castles, 24 Aug. 1651, Long. W.P. xi, 49. In or before 1655, George Purefoy married Catharine, widow of Sir James Bellingham, 2nd Bt. MP (d.1650). The Purefoys' son, Henry (c.1656–1686), was created 1st Baronet as a child, in 1662. In the last years of Whitelocke's life, these three members of the Purefoy family paid fees to him for legal advice. George Purefoy is shown as sending two fees of £1, *Diary* 17, 28 Oct. 1670. These may have been in connection with his Will, for Catharine is described two months later as 'widdowe to Mr Purefoy', ib. 17 Dec. 1670. In that (and in a later entry) Whitelocke reverts to her former title of Lady Bellingham, but identifies her son as the young Baronet, Sir Henry Purefoy, ib. 30 Apr. 1673.

PYE, Sir Robert, Kt., MP, sen. (1585–1662). M.F.K.; *D.N.B.* (in the entry for his son and namesake); G.E. Aylmer *King's Servants* pp. 311–313 and *State's Servants, passim*; D. Underdown *Pride's Purge, passim*. Admitted to the Middle Temple in 1607. He bought the Manor of Faringdon, Berks. (now Oxon.) in 1623. An office-holder, initially under the patronage of the 1st Duke of Buckingham (q.v.), he was elected MP for Bath in 1621 and 1624, and for other seats in 1625 and 1626, representing Woodstock in the Long Parliament, from 1640 until Pride's Purge in 1648. It was probably he, rather than his son (below), who often invited Whitelocke to his house, *Diary* 14 Dec. 1647.

PYE, Sir Robert, MP, jun. (*c.*1622–1701). *Hist. of Parl.*; *D.N.B.* Son of Sir Robert (above). He married, in about 1641, Anne, daughter of John Hampden (q.v.). Pye was a cavalry officer in Parliament's Army and MP for Berkshire in 1654 and 1660. Whitelocke only refers to Pye being commited to the Tower after petitioning the Speaker for a free Parliament, and to his release a month later, *Diary* 25 Jan., 21 Feb. 1659/60.

PYLE family, see PILE.

PYM, John, MP (*c.*1584–1643). J.H. Hexter *Reign of King Pym* (Harvard. 1941); *D.N.B.*; M.F.K. He studied at the Middle Temple. Served as MP for Calne in Wiltshire in 1621 and for Tavistock, Devon, in 1624, 1625, 1626, 1628, April 1640 (Short Parliament) and November 1640 (Long Parliament) until his death. From early in his political career he opposed court policies and voiced grievances; he actively supported the impeachment of the 1st Duke of Buckingham (q.v.), 'the cause of all these grievances', and helped to promote the Petition of Right. In the Short Parliament it was he who vigorously proclaimed the nation's grievances and (partly as a consequence) he became Parliament's unofficial leader in the Long Parliament. He was a prime mover in the impeachment of the Earl of Strafford (q.v.), and promoted the Grand Remonstrance in November 1641. Inevitably, he became a marked man: he was one of the five MPs whom Charles succeeded in having impeached on 3 January 1642, but the King failed, on the following day, in his attempt to have these members arrested in the House. Two months later, Pym played a major part in preparing the Militia Ordinance and the 19 Propositions. His negotiations with the Scots led to the signing of the Solemn League and Covenant in September 1643. Three months later he died of cancer.

Whitelocke, as a very young MP, first encountered Pym in Charles I's second Parliament, summoned in February 1625/26. Pym must, undoubtedly, have played a major part in choosing Whitelocke (still a relatively inexperienced lawyer and MP) as Chairman of the committee which was to manage the evidence against the Earl of Strafford, in 1641. True to his father's teaching, Whitelocke openly refused to join with any faction or party in the months leading up to the Civil War: he kept on good terms both with the Earl of Essex (q.v.) and his supporters, and also with Hampden and Pym and their militant 'company', being welcomed (as he records) with friendship by both sides, *Diary* 1641.1642. fols. 53v.–54.

PYNE, Col. John, MP (1600–1678). M.F.K. Of Curry Mallet, Somerset, south-east of Taunton. After studying at the the Middle Temple with his cousin, Alexander Popham (q.v.), and Whitelocke, he sat as MP for Poole, Dorset, in 1625, 1626, 1628 and from 1640 until 1653. Pyne's mother had been a Hanham; soon after Whitelocke was called to the Bar, Pyne 'being in love with a gentlewoman of Dorset [his cousin Eleanor, daughter and heiress of Sir John Hanham] & with her fortune . . . & she having a good affection for Mr Pyne', Whitelocke agreed to help him to win her. This meant outwitting the young lady's guardian (her uncle, Thomas Hanham), who had a financial interest in her remaining single. Whitelocke played the part of a rival suitor, which did not, apparently, displease the guardian. After delivering a note to the house Whitelocke returned the next day in a coach; he and the young lady took leave of her guardian, and shortly afterwards John Pyne married her. With hindsight, Whitelocke commented that when Pyne (although a Presbyterian Elder) became one of the 'more rigid party' (who promoted the Civil War and supported Pride's Purge), he repaid Whitelocke's earlier help by showing his enmity, Add. Ms 53726 fols. 32–32v.; *Diary* 1626.1627. fols.7v.–8. The only other reference to Pyne in this work occurs 45 years later, when he asked another favour, wishing Whitelocke to come up to London from Chilton Park as a witness, on his behalf, in a dispute with his eldest son, ib. 22 May 1671.

RALEGH (RALEIGH), Col. Carew, MP (1605–1666). *D.N.B.* (in the entry for his father, Sir Walter). He was born and brought up in the Tower of London (where his father was imprisoned in the Bloody Tower, attended by his wife and servants). In 1618, the year of his father's execution, Carew Ralegh became a student at Wadham College, Oxford. He served as MP for Haslemere, Surrey, from 1648–1653 and in the restored Rump of May 1659. Soon afterwards, he supported plans for the

Restoration, and Monck (later Duke of Albemarle, q.v.) had him appointed Governor of Jersey, *Diary* 29 Feb. 1659/60. The *D.N.B.*'s suggestion that he may never have gone to Jersey can perhaps be questioned, in view of a 'Licence for Col. Carew Raleigh, Governor of Jersey, to send hence 6 horses to complete his troop there', *C.S.P. Dom. 1659–1660*, 11 May 1660.

Ralegh owned the Manors of East and West Horsley, north-east of Guildford, Surrey. He settled the West Horsley estate on his sons, Walter and Philip, but when Walter died, in about 1663, the property was put up for sale. Whitelocke and his wife and two of his sons went to view the house, when they were staying with Ruth and William Lilly (q.v.), at Hersham, *Diary* 24 Apr. 1663. The Manor was sold two years later to Sir Edward Nicholas (q.v.) for £9,750.

RANELAGH, Elizabeth Jones, later Viscountess, then Countess of (d.1695). G.E.C. Second daughter of Whitelocke's brother-in-law Francis, Lord Willoughby of Parham (q.v.). She married the Hon. Richard Jones, later 3rd Viscount (q.v.).

RANELAGH (RENNELAGH), Lady Katherine or Catherine (1614–1691). G.E.C.; *D.N.B.*; C. Webster *Great Instauration. Science, Medicine and Reform, 1626–1680* (Duckworth. 1975), *passim*; N. Canny *Upstart Earl. A Study of the Social & Mental World of Richard Boyle, first Earl of Cork, 1566–1643* (C.U.P. 1982), *passim*; C. Hill *Milton and the English Revolution* (Faber. 1977), *passim* (in the entries for her husband Arthur Jones, 2nd Viscount Ranelagh, d. 1670, who was described as 'the foulest Churle in the world' with the 'one [very doubtful] vertu that he seldom cometh sober to bedd', G.E.C. p. 731, note d). Lord Ranelagh does not appear in *The Diary*. Lady Ranelagh was the fifth daughter of the 1st Earl of Cork. Whitelocke knew her brothers, Robert Boyle (q.v.) and Lord Broghill, later Earl of Orrery (q.v.). She was highly regarded by John Milton (q.v.), Bishop Gilbert Burnet and by many others. The Bishop recalled in 1692 that:

> ... she made the greatest figure in all the Revolutions of the Kingdoms for above fifty years, of any woman of our age. She imployed it all for doing good to others ... she was indefatigable as well as dextrous in it ... her great understanding ... made all persons ... desire and value her friendship ... G. Burnet *Lives Characters and a Sermon preached at the funeral of the Hon. Robert Boyle* ... (Dublin. 1815), p. 269.

Whitelocke's first reference to her occurs in *Diary* 29 May 1659. Later, when her elder brother the Earl of Orrery was impeached, she sent

Colonel Kiffin (q.v.) with a letter appealing for Whitelocke's help, ib. 2 Dec. 1669. The following month, when Whitelocke and Colonel Kiffin (q.v.) dined with her, the conversation turned to liberty of conscience '. . . to w[hi]ᶜh she was a great friend . . .', ib.20 Jan. 1669/70; a fortnight later she sent a Sedan to bring Whitelocke to her house, ib. 3 Feb. 1669/70.

RANELAGH, Hon. Richard Jones, MP, later 3rd Viscount, then E. of (c.1638–1712). *Hist. of Parl.*; G.E.C.; *D.N.B.* Son of the 2nd Viscount and Lady Katherine Ranelagh (above); Richard's mother appointed John Milton as his tutor. Realizing, no doubt, that the young man had more of his father than of his mother in his make-up, Milton wrote a wise and kindly letter of advice to his former pupil when the latter was up at Oxford, *Prose Works of John Milton* (ed. C. Symmons. London. 1806) vi, 132–133, 21 Sept. 1656 (Latin). Richard became a highly successful man, full of wit and charm and well-liked by Charles II, but he adopted an extravagant life-style and proved to be dishonest in handling public money.

RAVIS (RAVIUS), Professor Christian (1613–1677). *Alumni Oxonienses*; *Journal* i, 281–283, 438–439, *passim.* Born in Berlin, he came to England for sanctuary and 'for the freedom of his conscience and religion.' He taught Oriental languages in London in 1642, was made a Fellow of Magdalen College, Oxford, in 1648 and, according to Whitelocke, was appointed a Professor at the University. A salary of 500 rix-dollars tempted him to accept a Professorship at Uppsala. As 'Dr' Ravis, he was granted a pass to travel to Sweden with his servants and books, being described as Professor of 'the Oriental tongue', 9 Jan. 1650, *C.S.P. Dom. 1649–1650.* If Whitelocke was correct, however, Ravis was Professor of Hebrew. The Professor called on Whitelocke in Uppsala and gave him useful information about prominent people in that city, and their attitude towards the Embassy and Whitelocke's negotiations. On finding that Ravis's salary was much in arrears and that he was in serious need, Whitelocke sent a gift of £5 by his senior Chaplain, Nathaniel Ingelo (q.v.), which was gratefully accepted. Whitelocke gives a brief account of this in *Diary* 3 Jan. 1653/54, *passim*, and a detailed account in *Journal* (references above).

READE (READ), Sir John, 1st Bt. (c.1616–c.1694). *Complete Baronetage; Extinct & Dormant Baronetcies; V.C.H. Herts.* iii; ib. *Berks.* iv; ib. *Oxon.* x. The Reades were distantly related to the Whitelocke family, through the marriage of Henry Bulstrode (q.v.) to Mary Read (*sic*), of Barton, *Liber*

p. 28, *passim*. The family owned Barton Manor near Abingdon, Berks. (now Oxon.), also Duns Tew, south of Banbury, Oxon., and Brocket Hall near Welwyn, Herts.; this last had come into the family through the marriage of Sir Thomas Reade, Kt., to Mary, daughter of Sir John Brocket. John Reade was their third or fourth son, and he inherited the Brocket Hall estate. In 1632 he was admitted to Lincoln's Inn. It is not clear how he spent the next 10 years, but in March 1641/42 he was knighted by Charles I, and was created a Baronet four days later. The title not being recognized under the Protectorate, he was again created a Baronet (this time by Cromwell) in 1656. He was Sheriff of Hertfordshire from 1655–1656, and again from 1673–1674. His sister Anne was the wife of Whitelocke's friend Richard Winwood (q.v.). Sir John Reade evidently received some help from Whitelocke, in response to which he sent a letter with the gift of a doe, *Diary* 7 Nov. 1652. A transcript of his abjectly grateful letter, written 10 days later from Brocket Hall, appears in the 'Annales'; Whitelocke introduced it with the comment that he did not accept provisions for his table from friends if they had a Chancery suit pending, or business coming before Parliament, Add.Ms 37345 fol. 240.

Whitelocke and the Winwoods dined with Sir John and his second wife, widow of the Hon. Francis Pierrepont, at Duns Tew; (the couple were married in January 1662/63). When the Reades returned the visit an attempt was made, not for the first time, to reconcile Sir John and his wife, *Diary* 13, 20 Mar. 1665/66. A note in *Complete Baronetage* throws light on this episode: quoting from a family history, Burke states that Sir John '. . . kept a mistress in his house and encouraged her to insult his wife'. The couple separated about three and a half years after their marriage, and Lady Reade retained Whitelocke to act on her behalf against her husband, ib. 28 Jan. 1666/67.

REDDING, [Thomas]. Of Windsor, Berks. One of Whitelocke's two Lieutenants in Windsor Forest, *Diary* 12 May 1656, *passim*, to 9 June 1659. Redding sent details of an agreement with a Mr. Richard Rider in the parish of St. Martin-in-the-Fields, who contracted to buy some of Whitelocke's timber (presumably from Windsor Forest), which was stored at Water Okeley wharf on the Thames. The rate agreed was 100 loads at 30s. a load, with other timber at 26s. and 25s.'. . . alloweing two load of timber over'; £50 was to be paid by 24 February, and the balance when the contract was completed, not later than 31 March. Mr. Rider could choose his timber out of some 250 loads at the wharf, dated 12 Jan. 1656/57, Long. W.P. xviii, 1.

REYNARDSON, Sir Abraham, Kt. (1590–1661). *D.N.B.*; C.M. Clode *London during the Great Rebellion being a memoir of Sir Abraham Reynardson* ... (London. 1892); A.B.B. ii. A Royalist. As Lord Mayor of London in 1648, he opposed any involvement by the Corporation in the trial of the King. Refusing to proclaim the abolition of the kingly office and of the House of Lords, in April 1649, he was examined by Parliament, dismissed, fined £2,000 and committed to the Tower. He was knighted in 1660. Whitelocke only refers to his activities by way of news items.

REYNOLDS, Dr. Edward (1599–1676). *D.N.B.*; *Alumni Oxonienses; Walker Revised.* He studied at Merton College, Oxford, and was later appointed as one of the King's Chaplains; a member of the Assembly of Divines in 1643. Dean of Christ Church, Oxford, from 1648 to 1651, when he was ejected; later he replaced Dr. Owen (q.v.) in that office, *Diary* 3, 13 Mar. 1659/60. He preached to the Lords and Commons at St. Margaret's, Westminster, ib. 25 Apr. 1660. As Bishop of Norwich, after the Restoration, he was exceptionally gentle towards puritan Dissenters. Nothing in *The Diary* suggests that Whitelocke knew him personally.

REYNOLDS, Col. Sir John, Kt. (1625–1657). *D.N.B.*; *Register of Admission to the Middle Temple.* Younger brother (his date of birth suggests that he was, perhaps, a half-brother) of Sir Robert Reynolds (below). Admitted to the Middle Temple in August 1642 and called to the Bar in 1647, he fought for Parliament in the Civil War and was knighted by Cromwell in 1655. His wife's sister married Henry Cromwell (q.v.), who had a high regard for him. In 1657 Oliver Cromwell appointed Reynolds Commander-in-Chief of the forces sent to support the French Army in Flanders. After the capture of Mardyke, Reynolds was made Governor of the English garrison there. Sailing for England on a visit, his ship was wrecked on the Goodwin Sands and he was drowned. Whitelocke described him as a 'kind & good friend', *Diary* 16 Dec. 1657. Strangely, there are only two entries for this friend.

REYNOLDS, Sir Robert, Kt., MP (*c*.1601–*c*.1661). *D.N.B.*; Brunton and Pennington *Members of the Long Parliament* (Allen & Unwin. 1954); M.F.K.; *Register of Admission to the Middle Temple.* Second son of Sir James Reynolds, Kt., of Castle Camp, Cambridgeshire. Elder brother of Sir John Reynolds (above). Admitted to the Middle Temple in February 1619/20, six months after Whitelocke; a Bencher in 1648 and Treasurer in

1651. MP for Hindon, Wiltshire, in the Long Parliament, he also sat in Richard Cromwell's Parliament, in the restored Rump Parliament of 1659, and again in 1660. He was nominated as one of the King's judges but, like Whitelocke, refused to serve. In spite of this, he was appointed Solicitor-General in 1650, and Attorney-General in January 1659/60; the King knighted him in June 1660. He seems to have been a fair-weather friend to Whitelocke, *Diary* 5 July 1645; 10 Jan. 1647/48; 8 Apr. 1648; 27 Dec. 1659, *passim*.

RICH, Lady Mary (d.1666). G.E.C. and *D.N.B.* (entries for her father and her husband). Third daughter of Henry Rich, 1st E. of Holland (q.v.), who was executed in 1649. She consulted Whitelocke about her estate, *Diary* 10 June 1657; six months later, she married John Campbell as his first wife. After her death he was created Viscount, then Earl of Breadalbane (*c*.1635–1717).

RICH, Col. [Nathaniel], MP (d.1701). *D.N.B.* A Gray's Inn lawyer, who fought for Parliament. His first wife was the sister of John Hampden (q.v.). A Republican and a Fifth Monarchist, he lost the command of his regiment and was taken into custody when he openly opposed the Protectorate in 1655. His rank was restored to him in 1659. White-locke only records three events concerning Rich: his helping to reduce Portsmouth and being thanked for this service by the Commons, *Diary* 21, 29 Dec. 1659 (*C.J.* vii on the previous day); and the House approving his arrest for opposing moves towards the Restoration, *Diary* 7 Mar. 1659/60.

RICH, [Robert] (1634–1658). G.E.C. Grandson of Robert Rich, 2nd E. of Warwick (q.v.). One of three train-bearers at Cromwell's second inaugura-tion as Protector, *Diary* 26 June 1657. In November that year Rich married Cromwell's youngest daughter, Frances; he died three months later, his father and grandfather surviving him, the latter by two months.

RICHARDSON, [Thomas], MP, Lord (as he was commonly called), otherwise CRAMOND, Thomas Richardson, MP, 2nd Lord (*c*.1627–1679). *Hist. of Parl.* as Richardson; G.E.C. as Cramond. He succeeded to the Barony in 1651. The first-named of three gentlemen who brought 'The Declaration of the Gentry of . . . Norfolk' to Parliament, asking that the secluded MPs be readmitted, or that elections be held for a free Parliament, *Diary* 28 Jan. 1659/60.

RICHELIEU, Cardinal Armand Jean du Plessis, Duke of (1585–1642). French statesman and Cardinal. Secretary of State for War and Foreign Affairs, 1616. Chief Minister from 1624 until his death. Referred to in *The Diary* between 1624 and 1632.

RICHMOND, James Stuart, D. of (1612–1655). G.E.C. A Royalist, he held high office under his relatives, James I and Charles I. Inheriting the Dukedom of Lennox (and other titles) from his brother in 1623/24, he was created Duke of Richmond in 1641. He came to London with the Earl of Southampton (q.v.), for negotiations between them, as the King's representatives, and a Committee of the Lords and Commons, *Diary* Dec. 1644. fol.70v.; Whitelocke encountered him from the opposite side of the table both then and at the Uxbridge negotiations of 1644/45.

The Duchess (Mary, the dowager), was Whitelocke's client on 25 Nov. 1663; her parents were the 1st Duke of Buckingham (q.v.) and Katherine, daughter of the 6th Earl of Rutland, so she was distantly related to Whitelocke by marriage, his second wife, Frances, being a cousin of the Duchess of Buckingham (q.v.).

RIVERS, Thomas Savage, 3rd E. of (c.1628–1694). G.E.C.; T. Langley *History . . . of the Hundred of Desborough* (London. 1797). Reference is made to Mr. Green (q.v.) writing 'to further his [presumably Whitelocke's] buying the L[ord] Rivers his wood', *Diary* 7 Apr. 1657. This was evidently part of the Manor of Hambleden, Buckinghamshire, near to Whitelocke's Manor of Fawley and his house, Fawley Court. Rivers' first wife, whom he married in 1647, was Elizabeth Scroope (*sic*), the second of three illegitimate daughters of Emanuel Scrope, Earl of Sunderland (d.1631). The sisters had inherited as much of their father's estate as he was free to dispose of away from his wife Elizabeth; according to Langley (above), Hambleden Manor (presumably including the woodland) came to the Earl of Rivers through his wife. Whitelocke's neighbour, the dowager Countess of Sunderland (q.v. for details) had moved into New House (now the Manor of Hambleden), where Whitelocke met and courted her niece Frances Willoughby, who became his second wife.

ROBARTES (ROBERTS), John, 2nd Baron; later E. of Radnor (1606–1685). G.E.C. (as Radnor); *Pepys* x (as Robartes). A Presbyterian, he fought for Parliament in the Civil War but supported the Restoration, and was subsequently appointed Lord Deputy of Ireland and Lord Privy Seal; he was created Earl in 1679. He is only referred to twice, *Diary* 10 Aug. 1660; 12 Dec. 1666. The second entry indicates that he and Whitelocke were acquainted. Lord Robartes's son Robert (1633–*c.*1682) was mentioned with Robert Rich (q.v.) as a train-bearer at the Protector's second inauguration ceremony, ib. 26 June 1657.

ROBERTS, Elizabeth. One of three washerwomen in Whitelocke's retinue for Sweden, Long. 124A. fol. 361v. Whitelocke's practical wife, Mary (q.v.), wrote to him in Sweden: 'Pray bid Besse Roberts sow your dyamond hatband to your hat for if it be not sowed the waite of it will make it fall of', ib., fol. 42v. (transcript). Besse was still a member of the household 13 years later, when she and Bulstrode jun. managed to save two loads of her master's goods from the Fire of London, *Diary* 10 Sept. 1666.

ROBINSON, Alderman Sir John, 1st Bt., MP (1615–1680). *Hist. of Parl.*; A.B.B.; *Complete Baronetage*; *Pepys* x. Clothworker. An Alderman, then Sheriff of London during the Protectorate, and after the Restoration Lord Mayor from 1662–1663. He had been appointed, on 22 December 1659, to the Common Council Committee, to draft their reply to a letter from George Monck (later Duke of Albemarle, q.v.). Significantly, on that same day Robinson went to see Whitelocke on urgent business; he was accompanied by: Major-General Richard Browne (q.v.), also of the City and a future Lord Mayor (with whom Robinson had been associated that year in a royalist plot); by Whitelocke's brother-in-law Francis, Lord Willoughby of Parham (q.v.), and by Mr. Loe (q.v.). They 'confirmed his [Whitelocke's] suspition' as to Monck's design, prophesying that the General would 'bring in the King ... without any termes for the Parlem[en]ᵗ party', whose members would face disaster. They persuaded Whitelocke to go to Charles Fleetwood (q.v.) and urge him that he and his friends should make their own terms for the King's restoration, *Diary* 22 Dec. 1659. After an encouraging start, this came to nothing. Within four months, Robinson was supporting Monck so loyally that he was described as the General's favourite. In May 1660 he was one of the Commissioners sent from the City to the King at Breda; he was knighted, created a Baronet and appointed Lieutenant of the Tower in the same year.

Robinson's only recorded speech in the Convention Parliament was made on Whitelocke's behalf, asking for his inclusion in the Bill of Indemnity, *Hist. of Parl.* p.341.

Pepys despised Robinson, describing him as 'a talking bragging Buffle-head', who led his city colleagues 'as oxen and Asses' and took the credit for other men's achievements; 'as very a coxcomb as I could have thought had been in the City', *Pepys* iv, 77 with note, *passim*.

ROBINSON, Luke, MP (1610–1669). *Hist. of Parl.*; *Pepys* x. An ardent Parliamentarian and revolutionary, he became an equally ardent Royalist in time for the Restoration, and although 'formerly a most fierce man ag[ains]ᵗ the King, did now ... magnifie his grace & goodnes', *Diary* 1 May 1660.

ROBINSON, Major William (1620s?–c.1673). G.E. Aylmer *State's Servants* pp. 239–241, and 406 note 44; 'Check-List of Central Office-holders' (compiled by G.E. Aylmer. 1976). Secretary to the Generals-at-Sea and notably to Edward Popham, 1649–1650. Council Clerk in July 1659, he continued as Clerk to the Committee of Safety in October 1659, *Diary* 1, 20, 30 Nov. 1659. Whitelocke's last entry for the Clerk refers to him as Jo Robinson, but this was probably a slip of the quill.

ROCHFORD, John Carey, Viscount (1608–1677). G.E.C. (see entries both for Rochford and for Dover). A Royalist; styled Viscount Rochford from 1628–1666, when he succeeded his father as 2nd Earl of Dover. Rochford, accompanied by Lord Willoughby of Parham (q.v.), dined with Whitelocke, *Diary* 1 May 1662. Colonel William Willoughby, later 6th Baron Willoughby of Parham (q.v.), had bought Hunsdon House, near Stanstead Abbots, in Hertfordshire, from Henry Carey, 1st Earl of Dover, in 1653, G.E.C. Willoughby p.709, note f.

ROGERS (ROGER), [Francis] (Baptized 1615). Parish Register, Hambleden, Bucks. Son of Francis Rogers, gent. As young men, he and Whitelocke were hunting companions, sharing their beagles, *Diary* 1632. 1633. fol. 18v. Rogers was a kinsman of old Lady Scrope; when she died at 'Hambleden new house', now the Manor House, her daughter-in-law, the dowager Countess of Sunderland (q.v., aunt of Whitelocke's wife Frances) moved in, the house being part of her jointure. At that point, Francis Rogers moved out, Add.Ms fol.53726 fol.82.

ROGERS, Henry (d.1672). *V.C.H. Somerset* v, 89–90. Of Cannington, Somerset, north-west of Bridgwater. His niece Helena Rogers married Sir Francis Popham (q.v.) and Whitelocke was consulted on the legal aspects of the match. Henry Rogers' name appears on the settlement, see entry: POPHAM, Sir Francis, jun., also *Diary* 20 May 1670 with note; 10 June 1672. After Helena's early death, Whitelocke was consulted by Sir Francis Popham, jun., about Henry Rogers' estate, ib. 31 Jan. 1673/74, *passim*.

ROLLE (ROLLES), Judge [Henry], MP (*c*.1589–1656). *D.N.B.*; E. Foss *Judges of England* vi. An Inner Temple lawyer. He sat in all the Parliaments of the 1620s. Whitelocke, as a young MP, no doubt met him in Charles I's second Parliament, 1625/26, in which Rolle supported the demands for redress of grievances. In 1648, having served as a King's Bench Judge, Rolle was appointed Chief Justice of that Court. For a time, he served uneasily under Cromwell. Whitelocke referred to him as his 'brother in law' (denoting a professional not a family relationship), when consulting him as to whether or not to continue to serve in Parliament under duress, after Pride's Purge; Rolle and others advised him to continue and not to desert his trust, since no force had been used against him personally, *Diary* 6 Dec. 1648. The other entries also concern professional matters.

ROLT, Major [Edward] (*c*.1629–1698). 'Check-List of Central Office-holders' (compiled by G.E. Aylmer. 1976); *Pepys* x. Rolt served as an Officer in the Eastern Association; he was a Gentleman of the Bedchamber to his kinsman the Lord Protector in 1655, and was sent to Poland in November that year, as Envoy to King Charles X of Sweden (q.v.), *Diary* 8 Nov. 1655. From Hamburg, Major-General Edward Massey (q.v.) wrote sourly to Sir Edward Nicholas (q.v.) that he had heard from a Cavalier, who had been with the Swedish Army, that Rolt was '... magnificently entertained ... having a coach and 6 horses to attend him, and goes the next coach to the King, and has all imaginable honour, which sticks much in my stomach ...', *C.S.P. Dom. 1655–1656* pp.50–51. Rolt's mission to Sweden and to the Baltic States, from 1655-1656, was followed by his appointment as Gentleman of the Robes in 1658.

ROOS (ROSSE), John Manners, MP, Lord (1638–1711). G.E.C. (under Rutland); *Hist. of Parl.* (under Manners). Of Belvoir Castle, Leicestershire.

Son of John Manners, 8th Earl of Rutland (q.v.), whom he succeeded as 9th Earl in 1679; created Duke of Rutland in 1703. Whitelocke refers to him in connection with a *cause célèbre*, namely Roos's parliamentary 'Bill for divorce' (as Whitelocke called it) on grounds of his wife's adultery, *L.J.* 5, 17 Mar. 1669/70; 'An Act for Lord Roos to marry again' was duly signed by the King, ib. 11 Apr. 1670. Charles II, with a personal interest in divorce, requested Whitelocke to prepare notes on the legal aspect of the case, and Dr. Owen (q.v.) on its religious implications, *Diary* 15 Apr. 1670 with note. See also *Hist. of Parl.*, in the entry for Lawrence Hyde.

ROUS, Francis, MP (1579–1659). *D.N.B.*; M.F.K.; A. Woolrych *Commonwealth to Protectorate* (O.U.P. 1982) pp. 128–129, 151–152, *passim*. After studying at Oxford and Leyden, he was admitted to the Middle Temple in 1601. He was appointed Provost of Eton from February 1643/44. A learned and a tolerant man; he represented several West Country constituencies between 1625 and 1656 and was created one of Cromwell's Lords in 1657. As Speaker in Barebone's or the Little Parliament of 1653, Rous gave Whitelocke the commission, credentials and instructions for the Swedish Embassy, *Diary* 29 Oct. 1653. Later, Whitelocke applied for the post of Provost of Eton in succession to Rous, as 'a thing of good value, quiet & honourable & fitt for a Schollar' but he found that Cromwell was using the appointment 'as a baite' for others. When recalling this rebuff Whitelocke wrote, incorrectly, that Rous was dead by that time, ib. 25 Oct. 1657; on the day after Rous actually died, Whitelocke again recorded the death, ib. 8 Jan. 1658/59.

RUDYERD (RUDYER, RUDGIER, RUDYEARD), Sir Benjamin, Kt., MP (1572–1658). *D.N.B.*; M.F.K. Of St. John's College, Oxford, and the Inner Temple. A politician and poet; Surveyor of the Court of Wards from 1618 until its abolition in 1647; a moderate, he sat in all Parliaments from 1620 to the Long Parliament of 1640. Rudyerd took Whitelocke to dine with their friend Philip Herbert, 4th Earl of Pembroke (q.v.), and showed Whitelocke great kindness, *Diary* 10 Oct., 9 Dec. 1645, *passim*. His widow Elizabeth, née Harrington, a kinswoman of the Earl of Pembroke's, was possibly the 'Mrs Rudgier' who consulted Whitelocke at Chilton Lodge, ib. 13 Oct. 1674, for although Whitelocke's meetings with Rudyerd had all been in London (except for one at Phyllis Court), Rudyerd's country home, where he died, was in West Woodhay, Berks., a few miles south-east of Hungerford and within riding distance of

Whitelocke's last home, near Chilton Foliat. Yet it is curious, if so, that Whitelocke did not refer to her as 'Lady' Rudyerd.

RUPERT, Prince (1619–1682). *D.N.B.*; *Pepys* x. Count Palatine of the Rhine. Nephew of Charles I (q.v.). As headstrong and quarrelsome by nature as he was skilful and daring, he became a dominant figure in the King's Army during the Civil War, and later in the Navy. In spite of tensions between the Prince and his cousin Charles II (q.v.), Rupert was appointed First Lord of the Admiralty, serving from 1673–1679. The first diary reference to him describes the capture of Whitelocke's house, Fawley Court, in 1642, when royalist soldiers ransacked the place and made a present of his hounds and of his tame hind to Prince Rupert, *Diary* 1642.1643. fol.58. The following year, Rupert was with the King in Oxford when Parliament's Commissioners, including Whitelocke, came to negotiate. In the garden at Christ Church, he graciously allowed the Commissioners to kiss his hand; noticing that Whitelocke was (no doubt conveniently) caught in the throng, he made a point of going over to him, enabling the man whose estate his soldiers had plundered to pay homage like the rest. Whitelocke records the incident without comment, ib. fol.60. There are a few more entries concerning Rupert, before a critical reference to his conduct at the Battle of Naseby, ib. 14 June 1645. After that he is not mentioned in *The Diary* for over 20 years: having been appointed Constable of Windsor Castle, 29 September 1668, he turned to Whitelocke (who had held the post under Cromwell) for advice as to his rights in that office, ib. 28 Feb. 1668/69; 14, 15, 17 June 1671 with notes.

RUSHWORTH, John, MP (*c.*1612–1690). *Hist. of Parl.*; *Pepys* x. *D.N.B.* A public servant, both before and after the Restoration. Famous for his massive *Historical Collections*, which Cromwell ordered him to show to Whitelocke (as far as they had been assembled) before the work went to press, *Diary* 1 Jan. 1657/58. This first part was published in 1659 and dedicated to Richard Cromwell. Earlier, when Rushworth was Secretary to his kinsman General Sir Thomas Fairfax (q.v.), then commanding the New Model Army, Whitelocke wrote soliciting his help:

> ... I am very gladd that the Generall hath given order for the sliting [i.e. slighting, levelling or in this context dismantling] of my house att Fillis [i.e. Phyllis] Courte [fortified as Henley Garrison, of which Whitelocke was by then Governor], butt some of the Com[mit]^tee of Oxon have bin so unkind ... as to appoint the doing of it att this time[,] the middle of the [judicial] Terme, when they know I cannot be there my selfe (which is very necessary I

should be) ... I intreat you ... to procure an order from the Generall to stay the sliting of the house until I may be ... present ... which will be ... the more fitt bicause the house of Commons have referred it to my care by a late order ...

9 June 1646 Sloane Ms 1519 fol. 135.

Rushworth was MP in six Parliaments between 1657 and 1681 (inclusive). He and Whitelocke were still in touch a decade after the Restoration, *Diary* 5 Sept., 7 Nov. 1671.

RUSSELL, Col. Frauncis (Francis), MP, later 2nd Bt. (*c.*1616–1664). C.H. Firth & G. Davies *Regimental History of Cromwell's Army*; *Hist. of Parl.* (in the entry for his younger brother Gerard Russell, MP); *Extinct & Dormant Baronetcies*; *Complete Baronetage*. Of Chippenham in Cambridgeshire, north-east of Newmarket. Eldest son of Sir William Russell, 1st Baronet, who was Treasurer of the Navy from 1618 to 1627 and 1630 to 1642, see G.E. Aylmer *King's Servants, passim*. The Colonel was elected MP for Cambridgeshire in November 1645, serving until 1653, and again in the two Protectorate Parliaments. In 1642 Russell was marching to join Parliament's Army and stopped off at Fawley Court. Whitelocke described him as being '... well armed, & 12 of his servants in scarlet cloakes well horsed & armed. He only called ... to give me a visit & finding uppon what service I was ingaged, he accompanied me ...', Add. Ms 37343 fol.255v. and *Diary* Aug. 1642, fol.56v. They marched together, with a company of horsemen from the neighbourhood, under Whitelocke's command, to support Lord Say & Seale (q.v.), against Sir John Byron (q.v.) who was defending Oxford. In 1644 Russell is shown, by Firth (above), as a Colonel of Foot. He was appointed Governor of Ely in 1645. His daughter married Henry Cromwell (q.v.) and Russell sat in Cromwell's House of Lords. (He and his father should not be confused with their contemporaries Sir William and Sir Francis Russell, also 1st and 2nd Baronet, but of Worcestershire.)

RUTHVEN, Gen. Patrick. See FORTH and BRENTFORD, E. of.

RUTHVEN (RUTHEN), Patrick, self-styled 'Lord'. (b.*c.*1628). *D.N.B.* (in the entry for his grandfather William, 4th Lord Ruthven & 1st E. of Gowrie); see also entries for his ill-fated uncles: John, 6th Lord Ruthven & 3rd Earl of Gowrie (1577–1600) and Alexander Ruthven (*c.*1580–1600), shown as Master of Ruthven (in *D.N.B.*), Master of Gowrie (in G.E.C.); see also G.E.C. for John Ruthven, 3rd Earl of Gowrie (above), with entries under both his titles; *Papers relating to William, First Earl of Gowrie, and Patrick Ruthven* [sen.] ... (privately printed. 1867). These sources outline the background to the so-called 'Gowrie conspiracy', essential to an understanding of Whitelocke's entries for 'Lord' Ruthven. Ruthven's two uncles mentioned above were assassinated before he was born: John, 3rd Earl of Gowrie, aged 23 or 24, and Alexander Ruthven, about three years his junior. They were killed at Gowrie's house in Scotland, in August 1600. King James VI of Scotland (soon afterwards James I of England) had dined at the house and then retired with Alexander Ruthven to a turret on 'a quiet errand'. There was a commotion: Alexander was killed and so was John, Earl of Gowrie, when he rushed up to the turret. Both young men were assassinated by the King's servants and in his presence. Whether or not the murders were planned, and whether they were prompted by homosexual, financial or other considerations has never been established. Three months after the killings, the murdered Earl was pronounced guilty of high treason: both bodies were quartered and stuck on poles in different Scottish towns; forged letters and what appear to be fantastic lies were accepted in evidence; the family was deprived of all offices, honours and Scottish lands, and the name of Ruthven was abolished. It appears that the King's embarrassing debt to Gowrie of over £80,000 (based on a debt to the Earl's father) was liquidated. The proceedings were regarded by many contemporaries in Scotland and in England as a massive cover-up.

The two surviving brothers, at school in Edinburgh at the time, were advised to get away: William Ruthven went abroad. Patrick, the youngest brother (father to Patrick of this entry), escaped to England; in April 1603 he (the father) was arrested by order of King James (who was travelling south to become King of England), and was imprisoned in the Tower of London for 19 years; in 1616, while still a prisoner, he received a grant of £200 a year for clothes and books; in 1622 he was conditionally released (see letters to Dudley Carleton, 10 and 13 Aug. 1622, *C.S.P. Dom. 1619–1623* pp.439, 440). An allowance of £500 a year was settled on him. Under Charles I, the arbitrary actions taken against the family in 1600 were toned down by a Scottish Act of Parliament, dated 17 November 1641. The family was once again permitted to enjoy Scottish lands, offices and pensions and the name of Ruthven was restored, although not the Barony of Ruthven. The family, however, affected to believe that they were restored to the peerage. Patrick Ruthven sen. died in 1652.

Victims of Stuart oppression were viewed sympathetically by the Protector and his circle, so 'Lord' Patrick Ruthven jun. was on firm ground in approaching Whitelocke for relief of his poverty, *Diary* 12 May 1656. Later that year, Ruthven and his first wife 'Dame Sarah' (married in July

1656) petitioned the Protector for help, and Whitelocke pleaded his case. This is wrongly entered in *The Diary* as 3 Nov. 1657 instead of 1656 (the date shown at the end of the petition, also in the *D.N.B.*, under William, 4th Lord Ruthven); the error may have been picked up from Whitelocke's *Memorials*. Confusingly, 'Lord' Ruthven (grandson of William, 1st Earl of Gowrie) described himself, according to this copy letter, as:

> Grandsonne [instead of nephew] to John Earle of Glowry [*sic*] whose life[,] hono[u]ʳ & estate were sacrificed to the Courte p[r]ᵉtence of a Conspiracy . . . [In pursuit of that oppression] the Infancy & Innocency [of] the pet[itione]ʳˢ father [Patrick Ruthven, sen.] suffered 19 years Inprisonm[en]ᵗ in the Tower of London till the late King was pleased to enlarge him with 500ˡ p[er] Ann[um] out of the Excheq[ue]r [this firmly identifies the petitioner as the murdered Earl's nephew]. And in the parliam[en]ᵗ of Scotland 1641 restored him to the Barony [of] Ruthven . . . notwithstanding it were the whole visible pension the pet[itione]ʳˢ father had for the support of his family[,] . . . the distractions of their times obstructed his due paym[en]ᵗ & Involved him into inevitable debts which cast him into prison where he died[,] leaving the pet[itione]ʳ & another sonne in a . . . lamentable Condic[i]on . . . [Ruthven wrote that he had never done anything against the Protector's interest; that there was nearly £5,000 in arrears due to his late father; that he himself] might have long since perished had he not been releived by his life [a copying slip for 'wife'] who is not able longer to contribute . . . [He begged that Cromwell] would be pleased[,] if not to restore him to his familyes former splendour yet to such a subsistance as may not altoge[th]er misbecome the Quality of a Gent[leman]. Honor with Beggary being an insupportable Afflicc[i]on . . . [Below. In the same hand, except for Cromwell's signature]
> Oliver P
> Wee referre this . . . to our Councell
> desiring a tender & speedy Considerac[i]on
> thereof may be had
> Whitehall the 3[r]d of November
> 1656

Long. W.P. xvii, 211 (evidently copied by a clerk).

No order for payment of arrears has been traced; indeed, Whitelocke received a 'sad letter' from Ruthven, asking if he might borrow £5, which Whitelocke sent to him, *Diary* 24 Apr. 1658. There was a further petition for maintenance, ib. 16 Sept. 1659.

RUTLAND, Frances, Countess of (d.*c.*1656). G.E.C., in the entry for her second husband, George Manners, 7th Earl of Rutland (below), whom she married in 1605. Daughter of Sir Edward Carey of Aldenham, in Hertfordshire, the Countess appears to have been an unpretentious woman; she is described by Whitelocke (when he and his second wife stayed at Belvoir Castle, near Grantham) as showing them more than ordinary civility, and as being 'a Lady more humble then high, & more religious then Stately', *Diary* 1634.1635. fols.37v.–38.

RUTLAND, George Manners, MP, 7th E. of (*c*.1575–1641). G.E.C.; *D.N.B.* The date of birth is usually given as '*c*.1580', but Whitelocke wrote in *Diary* 1634.1635. fol.38 (July 1635), that the Earl was then about 60. Manners had studied at Cambridge; he was knighted in 1599, when serving as a volunteer in Ireland under the Earl of Essex; he and his brother Roger, 5th Earl of Rutland, were implicated in Essex's plot against Queen Elizabeth in 1601; moreover, Whitelocke's dashing uncle, Captain Edmund Whitelocke (q.v.), a convivial friend of the brothers, was charged at that time with high treason but was later cleared, *Liber* pp.8–9. Sir George Manners sat as MP for Grantham or for Lincoln in all Parliaments from 1604 to 1625, before inheriting the title from his brother Francis, the 6th Earl, in 1632. Two of the 7th Earl's sisters, Frances and Elizabeth, married respectively William, 3rd Lord Willoughby of Parham, and Emanuel Scrope, Earl of Sunderland. (Both sisters were widowed by the time Whitelocke met them.) In 1620, one of the Earl of Rutland's nieces, Katherine (q.v.), married the 1st Duke of Buckingham (q.v.); another niece, Frances (q.v.), daughter of Lady Willoughby, fell in love with Whitelocke (who had recently lost his first wife), and he with her. Her uncle the 7th Earl of Rutland, a none-too-scrupulous executor to her father's Will, tried to prevent her marrying a commoner, but Whitelocke discovered that 'love is a subtle & working passion', Add.Ms 37343 fol.8, and he successfully staged a runaway marriage on 9 November 1634. Resigning himself to the *fait accompli*, Rutland eventually accepted Whitelocke as a member of the family, but when this barrister-nephew pressed for payment of his wife's portion of £2,000, under her father's Will, the Earl resorted to genial delaying tactics. Whitelocke and Frances were invited to stay at Belvoir Castle, where they were handsomely entertained, but the full £2,000 was not forthcoming.

Whitelocke gives a more vivid portrait of the Earl than any in the reference books above: by 1635, according to *The Diary*, Rutland was a man with a stoop. Once good-looking, he was disfigured by the loss of an eye. He:

> ... understood buisnes well, & managed it prudently when he would be troubled with it, butt (like other great men) he trusted his servants & minded more his pleasures which were hunting, hawking, bowling, racing, & such sports ... [He enjoyed playing cards and watching] young people daunce & be frollick wherin he would somtimes goe too farre in example.

Even when the Earl's Agent, Mr Beresford (q.v.), arrived and they settled down to business (between bouts of sport), there were disputes, and after Whitelocke left, he still 'received from them [the executors] good words & delayes . . .'; Rutland, nevertheless, retained Whitelocke as his Counsel and paid him good fees, *Diary* 1634.1635. fol.38; 1635.1636. fol.40v.; 1636.1637. fol.43v., *passim*; also Add. Ms 37343 fols. 133v.–134v., 25 and 26 July 1635 (transcripts). The incompletely-paid marriage portion re-appears in entries for the 8th Earl (below). For Articles of Agreement, dated 12 May 1635, see Long. W.P. vi, 212v.–213; for Bartholomew Hall's report from Belvoir Castle after examining the estate accounts of William, Lord Willoughby of Parham, 10 August 1635, see ib. 251v.–256; for Whitelocke's undated demand for payment of the balance of his wife's portion, see ib. vii, 306–306v.

RUTLAND, John Manners, MP, 8th E. of (1604–1679). G.E.C. Cousin of the 7th Earl (above). He studied at Cambridge and at the Inner Temple, and served as an MP, in 1626 and in the Short Parliament of 1640, before succeeding to the title in 1641. He sat in the House of Lords as a moderate in the Civil War. Belvoir Castle was seized by the Royalists in 1643, then captured and garrisoned by Parliament's Army in November 1645; the garrison was not dismantled until May 1649. The Earl received £1,500 in compensation, and rebuilt the Castle after the Restoration.

There are several diary entries for him: he consulted Whitelocke about business and Whitelocke helped him, *Diary* 17 Sept., 19 Oct. 1645. Whitelocke's friends advised him to prefer a bill in Chancery for recovery of the balance of his wife's marriage portion (see 7th Earl, above); when Whitelocke tried to speak to the 8th Earl the latter avoided him, ib. 13 Jan. 1647/48; 3 July 1648. (At that date only £700 had been paid of the £2,000 portion bequeathed to her by her father.) Eventually, after Frances Whitelocke's death in May 1649, an undated, draft receipt records a payment 'in full satisfaction of the remainder of the portion of Fraunces my late wife deceased & of all interest money & dammages for the forbearance therof . . .' The receipt names John, Earl of Rutland, executor to George, late Earl of Rutland, Long. W.P. Parcel 4, No. 23. This was more than 20 years after Lord Willoughby's death.

RYLEY (RILEY), [William, sen.] (d.1667). *D.N.B.*; *Pepys* v, 149 with note 1. He studied at the Middle Temple, was Clerk of the Records at the Tower of London from about 1620, and Keeper of the Records from 1644. Appointed: Bluemantle Pursuivant of Arms, 1633; Lancaster Herald,

1641; Norroy King of Arms, 1646; Clarenceux King of Arms, 1659. In September 1646 he was chosen by Parliament, with two others, to arrange the state burial of the Earl of Essex (q.v.); he assisted at Oliver Cromwell's funeral and at Richard Cromwell's installation as Protector. Yet just before the Restoration he was one of three Heralds who, by command of Parliament, proclaimed Charles II at the Gate of Westminster Hall, on 8 May 1660. After the Restoration he was demoted, when William Prynne (q.v.) was appointed Keeper of the Records on a salary of £500. (Ryley's salary for that post had been £100.) He and his son became Prynne's discontented deputies, as Pepys recorded. Earlier, when Whitelocke was at the Treasury, Ryley asked for money to pay his own salary and those of his Clerks, promising great service by way of calendaring the records, *Diary* 17 July 1658.

SABRAN (SABRON), Melchior de. '*Negociations de Mons[ieu]' de Sabran en Ang[leter]'* en l'année 1644', Add.Ms 5460, 5461; I.D'Israeli *Commentaries on the Life and Reign of Charles the First* (London. 1831) v, 167, chapter 7 'The Two French Residents' (D'Israeli made some use of the important, but largely neglected, '*Negociations*' above; a further edition of the *Commentaries* ... was published by his son Benjamin Disraeli in 1851); *Historical Mss Commission*, 7th Report p.112, *passim*; *Hist. of Parl.* (entry for Lancelot Lake q.v.). De Sabran had served France as a diplomat in Italy, at the Emperor's Court, and at Geneva. He was a Gentleman of the Bedchamber and was appointed a member of the French Council of State. In 1644 (King Louis XIV being about five years old), de Sabran was chosen by the Queen Regent to go to England as French Resident or Agent. He was to be briefed by Cardinal Mazarin (q.v.). His instructions were to offer France's mediation between the King and Parliament, but not to take sides. He was given an outline of the legal and traditional relationship (as understood in France) between the English King, Parliament and the people. This, and much more, is recorded in the two large volumes of the '*Negociations*'.

The numerous references to de Sabran in the *C.J.* and *L.J.*, between 1644 and 1646, do not amount to much, so a letter to Whitelocke from Sir Philip Stapleton (q.v.) and others, is of some interest:

> The French Resident has made his address to both houses ... his [purpose?] is said to be such as many hope peace will be p[r]ocured, if we [i.e. Parliament] bee not wantinge to our selves ... those who affect the good of the kingdom should not Loyter ...

9 Aug. 1644.   Long. W.P. ix, 27.

While in England, de Sabran married Mary, only daughter of Sir Arthur Lake who (on the death of his elder brother, Sir Thomas Lake) became heir to the Manor of Canons, Middlesex (of which more later). At the end of a frustrating term of office, de Sabran took Mary back to France, where their eldest son Renée (*sic*) was born in about 1652.

There are only three diary entries for de Sabran, and they occur within six weeks, between 1 Jan. and 7 Feb. 1656/57. It is clear, however, from de Sabran's first letter (extracts below), that he and Whitelocke knew each other quite well; indeed, they could hardly have failed to meet during the Civil War years, when de Sabran was French Resident. The letters concern the vexed question of young Renée's inheritance from his English mother, who had recently died. Some of de Sabran's communications are undated, but it is clear, from various references in them, that they were written before the Restoration, and probably around the date of the references to him in *The Diary*, early in 1656/57.

The first letter traced, congratulates Whitelocke on the honour of his appointment as acting-Speaker (see *Diary* 27 Jan. 1656/57), '*le chef de cett Illustre companie qui compose le parlement*', this confirmed de Sabran in his belief that: '*l'homme propose mais Dieu despose*', for he recalled that when last they met, Whitelocke had shown a disposition to retire and work for himself, but now, as de Sabran had prophesied, Whitelocke was forced to return to state duties and to devote his service to the public good; the Frenchman rejoiced with all his heart at the glorious violence – '*cette gloireuse violence*' done to Whitelocke's plans, which compelled him to continue '*au dedans*' (i.e. in Parliament) and in the most important office of the Republic (de Sabran avoided the word 'Protectorate'), 7 Feb. 1656[/57], Long. W.P. xviii, 7.

An undated, rather confused, letter from de Sabran was presumably written while Whitelocke, as acting-Speaker, was still entitled by his office to receive the substantial fee of £5 a head from everyone naturalized by Act of Parliament, *Diary* 18 Feb. 1656/57: de Sabran's letter solicited Whitelocke's help in persuading Parliament to retain his cause, Long. W.P. xviii, 17 and 18 (French). From what follows, the cause may be assumed to have been that of Renée's naturalization. This was the subject of a prolonged and bitter contest between the Frenchman, acting on behalf of his small son, and Lancelot Lake (q.v.), a Royalist and the youngest of three brothers. Mary de Sabran, daughter of Sir Arthur Lake, was Lancelot's niece, and Renée was his great-nephew (referred to in documents as his nephew). Mary had inherited from her father the Rectories of Castle Martin and Melrose, but she only took possession after a long suit in Chancery against Lancelot Lake. After her early death, Lancelot was determined that Mary's little French son should not inherit the estate of Canons (Edgware), in the parish of Stanmore, Middlesex. It may be relevant to point out that a few years earlier, in another context, Lancelot Lake had been accused of trying to bribe witnesses to leave their homes until a court case affecting him was over, and later of threatening witnesses with whipping, the pillory etc., 5 Mar. 1650; 14 Jan. 1652, *Calendar of the Committee for Advance of Money* p. 1206. His objections to his great-nephew's naturalization were set out in a petition:

S[i]ʳ Thomas Lake the Elder haveing 3:sonnes

> S[i]ʳ Thomas Lake
> S[i]ʳ Arthur Lake
> Lancellott Lake
> [knighted 1660]

Did amongst div[er]se other Landes Settle the Capitall messuage & mann[o]ʳ of Cannon Comitatu Midd[lese]x (being his cheife seate) Upon S[i]ʳ Thomas Lake his eldest Sonne and the heires of his body, the Remainder to Sir Arthur Lake and the heires of his body [Mary and her son Renée]. The remainder to Lancelott Lake and his heires &c ... [Lancelot claimed that some 16 years earlier his eldest brother, Sir Thomas Lake, jun., had sold the property to a stranger and levied a fine to bar his own issue from the inheritance] and did Covenant to make over other Lande for Collatterall security, untill Recovery were suffered or an Acte of Parlaim[en]ᵗ passed, to Barre the remainders to S[i]ʳ Arthur and his heire[s] &c ...[but he had died before achieving this.]

Lancellott Lake after 14: yeares spent in suite to p[re]serve the said Capitall messuage and Mann[o]ʳ in his fathers family (being the flower of his Estate) did at last submit the matter ... to Referrence, where hee was Ordered to pay 15250ˡ; to Redeeme the same out of the hande of the Purchasor, which he hath ... payd but hath yett noe Recov[er]y nor Acte of Parliament nor Collatterall Security, to Barr the heires of the body of S[i]ʳ Arthur Lake ... [Renée's grandfather; Lancelot claimed that his father, Sir Thomas Lake sen., had settled other lands to the value of £150 p.a. on Sir Arthur and his heirs, and, in default of such heirs, on Lancelot.] S[i]ʳ Arthur Lake dyed ... some 23: yeare[s] since Leaving one only daughter [Mary] who about 7: yeare[s] agoe [c. 1650? or was this petition written before 1657?] married Mounseir Sabran by whom shee had Issue (dureing the late breach betweene England & Fraunce) [the strained relations around 1650–1652?] a sonne borne in Fraunce and there shee dyed about a yeare since [1656?], after whose decease Lancellott Lake [,] being advised that her Issue borne beyond the seas had never any inheritable blood in him, and therefore there was noe heire of the body of S[i]ʳ Arthur Lake[,] did ... Enter uppon the Land ...

Mounseir Sabran a French man is now lately come out of Fraunce, and hath obtayned his Highnesse [i.e. Cromwell's] Letters Pattente for his sonnes denization, and says he will endeav[ou]ʳ to have him Naturallized by Acte of Parlaim[en]ᵗ ...

It is Prayed no such may Passe: Because:

1º ... noe sonne of a french man borne in fraunce was e[ve]ʳ naturalized, and there is the lesse motive in this case[,] his sonne being borne an alien Enemy in the time of warr:

2° It would make way to defeate a Purchasor whoe hath paid soe greate a consideration as aforesaid ...

Itt would p[re]ferre an alien ... (whose father hath already Transported out of this nation 1700ˡ which hee had of his wives portion) before a naturall borne Subjecte, and bee a p[re]sident [i.e. precedent] of Ill Consequence ... [1657?]   Long. W.P. xviii 106v.–107.

Lake's square brackets have been altered to round ones, to avoid confusion with editorial additions.

The most interesting of de Sabran's communications with Whitelocke is written in English but not in his own hand; it was probably composed by his Counsel. It is an answer to Lake's objection but not, it seems, to those in the above petition, which do not refer to religion, nor to de Sabran's political sympathies:

An Answer to Mʳ [not yet 'Sir Lancelot'] Lakes Objections against Mʳ René [sic] de Sabran his [great–]Nephew. Lancelot Lake having procured a meeting of the Committee for Naturalization[,] without any notice given to the child or any defence made for him, sayd ... in opposition to his naturalization That it was a Generall Rule in the Parliament not to naturalize the sonne of a Roman Catholick.

That by the Law hee [Lancelot Lake] was heire of the mother [his niece], and was In possession of an Estate which would be thus taken from him beeing a Protestant, to be given to a Catholick. That Mons[ieur] [Melchior] de Sabran had been ill affected to the Parliament when he was Resident here for the King of France etc. All which allegations are neither grounded uppon fact nor uppon practice, nor uppon truth. he [Lake] can not produce an Example of a Denyall of naturalization because of Religion, to a child of 4. or 5. yeares old, that hath none [i.e. religion], because he is the sonne of a french Catholick who offers to see him brought up in the protestant Religion[,] to make profession of the same within the time allowed by the law, and which [i.e. French Catholicism] ought to be distinguished w[i]ᵗʰ great difference from the English, Irish, Scottish or Spanish Catholicks that are declared Enemies of this Commonwealth ... the french are the onely fryends that this state hath joyned with them In union by the peace [Mar. 1657], and ... are as much enemies to the Spaniard; the Libertie of the two Religions Is such in France that families are commonly mixed with both, the protestants being admitted Into all kinds of Imployments even ... the highest places both of the Crowne and of the Chyefe Command in the Armies and also Into the Secret [Service?] abroad, seeing the french Ambassadors Secretary is a Protestant.

The Refusall of naturalization to this child after the free denizing granted unto him by his Highnes [Oliver Cromwell] by the recommendation of the King of france [Louis XIV, b. 1638], after the streyght union ... betweene the two nations And the taking away of Escheatages in the behalfe of the English onely, which Confiscat[e]s the estate off Strangers Dying in France, this Denyall I say can not be favourable to the English that shall have recourse unto his Ma[jes]ᵗʸ [of France] or his Counsell, for any Grace or favour.

As for the Law, there is none that gives to a Kinsman the Estate of a Mother[,] her child being alive: ... if he [Lancelot Lake] pretends to it to the prejudice of the young pupill his [great-]nephew as being an alien for want of naturalization, hee knowes full well that the Law is not for him In that Case, ... it provides better for the child[,] allowing him to be 14 or 15 yeares old before he makes profession of the Protestant Religion[,] which if he doth ... not within that time, let him undergoe the Penalty of an English Catholick[,] since ... by his naturalization he shall become a subject of this Commonwealth[.] But all the Aime of the sayd Lancelot is to exclude this poore Innocent Babe from the hopes that he may have of the bloud of his Mother ... having but lately gotten back into his owne hands the Dowry of his Grandmother [the £1,700 referred to in Lake's letter?].

These are the groundlesse objections which he hath alledged ... with his counsell before the Com[m]ittee, without any Defence made on the childes part, uppon ... which neverthelesse the Com[m]ittee hath voted him Incapable of being naturalized[,] without giving him any Audience, though much sought after ... nor making any Report to the Parliament ... [de Sabran stressed that the King, Louis XIV, had entreated the Protector on the child's behalf, and that any help would be reciprocated] so much tendernes and bounty hath his Ma[jes]^{ty} expressed for the sonne of a gentleman who hath served him these 40 yeares, and is a Councell[o]^r of state ...

The production of ... two witnesses against Mons[ieu]^r de Sabran[,] Alledging that he was ill-affected to the Parliament when he was Resident here ... shewes that he [Lake] is faine to make use of anything to Maintaine an ill cause. But there are above two hundred men that will beare witnesse of the letter of the last King [Charles I], to the Queene [Henrietta Maria] his wife, that was found in his cabinet taken at Naseby field, wherein he did complaine of Mons[ieu]^r de Sabran[,] Declaring unto her the reasons that he ... [did] so suspect and mistrust him[,] advising her withall not to trust him with her letters[,] which letter the Parliament, out of their love, sent unto him [the French Resident] by two of their Members; and the free passe for 12 horses which they were pleased to give him at his departure, with their appointing the Viceadmirall to carry him back into france, are more certaine markes of their liking of his service and ... approbation of his good Carriage.

ib. 19–20 [1657?]

The contest continued after the Restoration: the Bill for Renée's naturalization, with amendments, reached its third reading in the Lords and was delivered to the Commons for their concurrence. There it was read twice, amended in committee, the amendments were approved by the Commons, and after debate the Bill was recommitted. At that point, Lake asked to be heard by Counsel at the Bar of the House. He was, by that time, an MP and a Knight. The Bill was quietly dropped, L.J. xi, 79, 135, 154, 165, 177, 178, 191, 30 June – 24 Nov. 1660; C.J. viii, 191, 257, 264, 284, 290, 24 Nov. 1660 – 4 July 1661. Later, an Act for confirming a contract between Sir Lancelot and the child Renée de Sabran came to nothing, L.J. xi, 659, 17

Feb. 1664/65. We are left with the impression that skulduggery was rewarded.

SADLER [John], MP (1615–1674). *D.N.B.*; *Calamy Revised*; A. Woolrych *Commonwealth to Protectorate* pp.203–209, *passim*. He studied at Emmanuel College, Cambridge, and at Lincoln's Inn. A scholar and administrator, a man of versatile and distinguished gifts, with a great capacity for hard work. A friend both of Cromwell and of Milton; independent in mind as in politics. A Master-in-Chancery from 1644 to 1660 (*Calamy Revised*), or from 1649 to 1656 (E. Foss *Judges of England*). Town Clerk of London from 1649 to 1660 and Master of Magdalene College, Cambridge, from 1650 to 1660; he was also Master of Requests to Oliver Cromwell from 1655 to 1656. Very active as an MP for Cambridge in Barebone's Parliament, 1653; he sat for Yarmouth, I.O.W., in Richard Cromwell's Parliament, 1659.

It was in his capacity as Town Clerk of London that Sadler's name was put forward by Sir John Danvers (q.v.), to serve on the Hale Commission on Law Reform, set up by the Rump early in 1652. Danvers nominated several men, giving their credentials; he described Sadler as '. . . now towne Clerke of the Citty of London, and Secretary for the Parlem[en]'[,] eminently knowne for his Abilities and integrity . . .'; he suggested that Sadler might also 'bee appointed to collect the register[,] the sense and Arguments inducing such Conclusions, as may be thought fitt to bee presented to the Parlement . . .', 26 Dec. 1651, Long. W.P. xi, 159–159v., (unsigned but endorsed by Whitelocke 'S[i]ʳ Jo Danvers[.] Law'). Later, the 15 members of the Committee, including Sadler, were appointed Judges for the Probate of Wills and for Administration (unpaid), G.E. Aylmer *State's Servants* p. 42; *C.J.* vii, 658, 19 May 1659.

After his ejection at the Restoration, Sadler went to Whitelocke for legal advice, *Diary* 10 Nov. 1660. He retired to his wife's home in Warmwell, north-east of Weymouth, Dorset, but in view of his being known to Whitelocke and their having much in common he, rather than Richard Sadler, was probably the Mr. Sadler who preached both at Whitelocke's lodgings in London, and at the home of Samuel Wilson (q.v.), ib. 24 Jan. 1668/69; 24 Oct. 1669.

ST. ALBANS, Henry, cr. Baron Jermyn in 1643 and later E. of (*c.*1604–1684). G.E.C.; *D.N.B.*; *Pepys* x. Created Earl on 27 April 1660. Ambassador to France in 1644, 1660 and from 1667 to 1669. Only referred to once, in connection with his second Ambassadorship, *Diary* 18 July 1660.

SAINT CLARE, Lord John, see SINCLARE.

ST. JOHN, Oliver, MP (*c.*1597–1673). *D.N.B.*; M.F.K.; B. Worden *Rump Parliament, passim*; E. Foss *Judges of England* vi, 475–489; *Pepys* x; G.E. Aylmer *State's Servants, passim*. Of Lincoln's Inn. Well known to Whitelocke, who was eight years his junior; they had many professional encounters: in 1637 Oliver St. John was Counsel for John Hampden (q.v.), supporting his stand against paying Ship Money and distinguishing himself in his opposition to the claim by the Crown; Whitelocke, too, was one of Hampden's legal advisers in the case. In January 1640/41, hoping to disarm St. John with a favour, Charles I appointed him Solicitor-General, but the lawyer was nobody's 'creature'; he became an active member of the select committee, under Whitelocke's chairmanship, which was to handle evidence for the impeachment of the Earl of Strafford (q.v.), and he promoted the Bill of Attainder against the Earl, with some venom. Both St. John and Whitelocke were among the Commissioners sent by Parliament to negotiate with the King or his Commissioners at Oxford and Uxbridge. Both men served in the highest legal office, as Commissioners of Parliament's Great Seal.

In 1648 St. John was appointed Chief Justice of the Common Pleas. Like Whitelocke, he refused to have any part in the King's trial. In his domestic life, like Whitelocke, he had three wives; the first two, in his case, were related to Oliver Cromwell, the second being Cromwell's cousin. From about 1648, St. John's views began to differ from Cromwell's and he edged away from politics, but he was one of the Judges who continued to serve after the King's execution. In March 1651, St. John was chosen joint-Ambassador with Walter Strickland (q.v.) to seek a close alliance with the United Provinces, but the circumstances were against him and he failed to come to terms with the Dutch, returning to England angry and disappointed; (two years later Whitelocke, a more gifted diplomat and in an easier setting, achieved a treaty of amity with the Swedes and came home triumphant). In September 1651, St. John and Whitelocke, with John Lisle (q.v.) and Gilbert Pickering (q.v.), were sent by Parliament to meet Cromwell at Aylesbury, and to congratulate him on his victory at Worcester. As lawyers, both men were suspicious of the Protectorate as an institution, its powers and limitations being untested by the law of the land, and since English laws and liberties had been built round the monarchic principle, they favoured the abortive attempt to make Cromwell King.

Unlike Whitelocke, St. John later supported demands for a 'free Parliament' and Monck's plans for the Restoration, but they were both marked men, who had done conspicuous service for the Commonwealth.

After the Restoration St. John appealed for help (as Whitelocke's wife did) to William Prynne (q.v.) and was received with more courtesy than that shown to Mary Whitelocke, *Diary* 1 June 1660. Both men proceeded to circulate papers they had prepared, justifying their activities during the Interregnum: a printed tract, *The Case of Oliver St. John Esq* (1660), and copies of a manuscript, 'The Case of Bulstrode Whitelocke K^t'; the former is in the British Library; the text of the latter is in *Diary* 2 June 1660. Whitelocke, who was good company and who had regularly befriended people of different convictions from his own, could muster more support in both Houses than could his fellow lawyer. Clarendon described St. John as: 'reserved, ... of a dark and clouded countenance, very proud, ... conversing with very few, and ... very seldom known to smile ...'(quoted in *D.N.B.*). In spite of the close resemblance between their careers, both in the service of Parliament and in the Courts, St. John and Whitelocke's fate at the Restoration differed, at least in theory. St. John's name was included in the Second Exception to the Pardon, which excluded him from ever holding office again. (A different account is given in *Judges of England*.) Whitelocke, despite his enemies' efforts, was not excluded from the Act of General Pardon and Oblivion; yet in the event, he never held office again. The King even had him and John Thurloe (q.v.) ousted from the Governing Body of Sutton Hospital (Charterhouse), as unfit to serve, commenting at the same time that Oliver St. John and William Lenthall (q.v.) were already disabled from serving, *Diary* 22 Jan. 1660/61.

There are numerous entries for St. John in *The Diary* but, despite the parallels and close contacts in their lives, it is only St. John's actions which emerge from Whitelocke's record, not the man himself.

SALISBURY, William Cecil, MP, 2nd E. of (1591–1668). Of Hatfield House, Herts. Studied at St. John's College, Cambridge, and Gray's Inn. He travelled abroad, then sat as MP for Weymouth from 1610 to 1611, before succeeding to the title in 1612; he was made a Privy Councillor in 1626. After the abolition of the House of Lords, he sat for King's Lynn from 1649 to 1653. He is referred to only three times in *The Diary*: as one of the four Lords sent as Commissioners, by Parliament, to negotiate with the King at Oxford, and with the King's Commissioners at Uxbridge, ib. 1642.1643. fol.60; 1644.1645. fol.71 (Jan. 1642/43; Jan. 1644/45). On both occasions Whitelocke was a Commissioner from the Commons. The third entry records that the Earl, unaccountably, sent Whitelocke 'a fatt Doe', ib. 22 Dec. 1647. Lord Salisbury's wife Catharine (married in 1608), was a daughter of Thomas Howard, 1st Earl of Suffolk. For some reason she informed Whitelocke that his widowed sister, Elizabeth Mostyn (q.v.),

had married Owen Wyn, 'a man of no fortune', ib. 7 Nov. 1648. Years later
Lady Salisbury came to Whitelocke as a client, ib. 20 Jan. 1662/63.

SALMON, Col. Edward [Edmund?]. C.H. Firth & G. Davies *Regimental
History of Cromwell's Army* ii, *passim*. He was at the siege of Oxford in
1646, as a Lieutenant-Colonel; he then served in the West Country, but
resigned from his regiment in 1649 to become Deputy-Governor of Hull;
he was made Colonel of a regiment in Scotland, where the Presbyterians
attacked him for encouraging Independent preachers, and was appointed
an Admiralty and Navy Commissioner from 1653 to 1656, and Supervisor
of Hospitals, in 1658, see G.E. Aylmer 'Check-list of Central Office-
holders, 1649–1660.' Five Companies of his Regiment took part in the
siege of Dunkirk in 1658. He signed the Declaration from Charles
Fleetwood (q.v.) and others, inviting the Rump to return, *Diary* 6 May
1659. Supporting the Army against Parliament, he was subsequently a
signatory to the letter from the Council of Officers to General George
Monck (later Duke of Albemarle, q.v.), pressing him to approve their
actions of 20 Oct. 1659, and he was one of those who signed the letter to
Whitelocke informing him that they, the 'General Council of the Army'
had 'thought fit to appoint a Committee of Safety for the preservation of
the Peace, and Management of the present Gouvernement thereof . . . also
for . . . preparing a forme of a future Gouvernm[en]ᵗ . . . upon the
foundation of a Commonwealth or free State'; the letter also informed
Whitelocke that he had been nominated to serve on the Committee, Long.
W.P. xix, 90; *Diary* 27 Oct. 1659 (transcript) with note. Salmon was
arrested in April 1660, suspected of being involved in Lambert's rising, and
lost his Regiment to Colonel Arthur Evelyn (q.v.). Whitelocke records
that Salmon was 'discharged uppon security', ib. 7 May 1660; he was,
however, re-arrested in about December 1661, on suspicion of helping to
lead another conspiracy.

SALWEY, Major Richard, MP (1615–1685). *D.N.B.*; D. Underdown
Pride's Purge, passim; B. Worden *Rump Parliament, passim*; A. Woolrych
Commonwealth to Protectorate, passim; G. Davies *Restoration, passim*.
Fourth son of Humphrey Salwey, an MP in the Long Parliament. Richard
Salwey was apprenticed in London and became a grocer; he is said to have
been a spokesman for the City apprentices when petitioning the Long
Parliament; a friend of Sir Henry Vane, jun. (q.v.). Salwey was elected
with Henry Ireton (q.v.) as an MP in the Long Parliament for Appleby in
Westmorland (now Cumbria), October 1645. A few months earlier he sent

Whitelocke details of an alleged parliamentary scandal on the day the news broke. His letter supplements the information given in the *Commons Journal*:

> The 10. June. 1645
> This day about halfe an hour after 12. a clock Mr James Cranford (minister) came to the E[x]ch^a[nge] in London and did there openly declare & affirme that there was discovered to the parlyam[en]^t a great Treachery in the Com[m]ittee of both kyngdomes [the High Command, including the Scots], some wherof had assum[e]d to themselves power to bee a subcom[m]ittee and had for about 3. monthes last past Treated secretly w[i]th the kyng for the p[ro]curing and makying theire owne peace and for the surrendring & delyvering up of the parlyam[en]^{ts} Forts Castles & Garrysons[,] and that the houses of parlyam[en]^t had chosen a Com[m]ittee of 7 Lords & 14 Com[m]oners to search out this Treason, and th[a]^t there were dyvers amongst them who were of the former SubCom[m]ittee that treated w[i]th the kyng; & Mr Cranford being askt whether this w[hi]^{c}h he reported was certayne & true, hee affyrmed it was & sayd Let it flye as farre as it will for it is true.
>   This wee doe declare & affyrme to bee the substance of Mr Cranfords speech to us & dyvers others . . .
>
>   Richard Salwey
>   Jo[hn] Greensmyth
> d^r Alston
> Col. Gower
> Cptn Venner   } can give further
> Mr Ballowe   } information about this matter
> Mr Lane
> Mr Alexander [these two in another hand].
>
>   Long. W.P. ix, 43.

See also plans to interrogate James Cranford (or Crawford) on the 'great treachery . . .' 11 June 1645, ib. 45.

Salwey's letter to Whitelocke coincided with one from Sir Philip Stapleton (q.v.) to the Commons, on the same subject. The House promptly appointed a committee to investigate the charges brought by Cranford (transcribed as Crauford), *C.J.* iv, 172, 11 June 1645. Whitelocke, presumably as Chairman, reported after a preliminary meeting, ib. 174, 14 June 1645; see P. Crawford *Denzil Holles* p.115, *passim*; for James Cranford, see A.G. Matthews *Walker Revised* p.45.

Later, Salwey was appointed as one of the King's judges but refused to serve. He opposed Cromwell's dissolution of the Rump on 20 April 1653, yet he was nominated to sit in Barebone's Parliament which met on 4 July; the following month (according to the *D.N.B.*), he was invited to go as Ambassador to Sweden, but declined. At the end of August, Whitelocke was offered the Ambassadorship and some weeks later, under pressure from Cromwell, he reluctantly agreed to go; he recorded that Viscount Lisle (q.v.) had refused the appointment, but made no mention (perhaps he did not know) of Salwey's having turned it down. In 1654 Salwey went as Ambassador to Constantinople. Before the Restoration he was invited to serve on the Committee of Safety – indeed, Whitelocke was urged to serve on it as a moderating influence over Vane, Salwey, and others suspected of having revolutionary designs. In the event, however, Salwey refused to serve, but agreed to discuss a future form of government with the Committee, *Diary* 26, 27 Oct., 1 Nov. 1659. After the Restoration he was arrested, more than once, but was not imprisoned for long.

SANDWICH, Gen. Edward Mountagu (Montague), MP, later 1st E. of (1625–1672). G.E.C.; *Hist. of Parl.*; *Pepys* x. Mountagu fought for Parliament in the Civil War, supported the Protectorate and finally worked for the Restoration; through the good offices of his first cousin twice removed (also named Edward Mountagu, q.v.), he made his peace with the King and resumed a successful career. He had fought at the battles of Marston Moor and Naseby. In 1656 he was appointed General-at-Sea jointly with Robert Blake (q.v.); in February 1660 he was re-appointed in the same capacity with George Monck (later Duke of Albemarle, q.v.), and in May 1660 it fell to him to bring Charles II back to England in his flagship the *Naseby*, tactfully renamed the *Charles*.

Details of Sandwich's character, reputation and career are recorded in the above sources. Whitelocke's entries refer to him as Colonel and later as General Edward Mountagu. These begin the day after both men were appointed as Treasury Commissioners, the event being recorded in *Diary* 4 Aug. 1654; the last entry occurs on the day the Earl of Sandwich left the Commons (where he had represented Weymouth) and took his seat in the Lords, ib. 26 July 1660. (Whitelocke confused the creation of the Earldom, two weeks before, with the date on which Sandwich took his seat in the Lords.) Earlier, Whitelocke recorded that Mountagu read the Declaration of Breda to the ships' officers, then fired the first gun himself, which was answered by all the ships around him, with loud acclamation and cries of 'God blesse the K[ing],' after which the General regaled the men with two pipes of Canary wine, ib. 5 May 1660. (One pipe contained 105 gallons.)

SANDYS, Sir Edwin, MP (1561–1629). *D.N.B.* Second son of Archbishop Edwin Sandys. Studied at Corpus Christi College, Oxford, and at the Middle Temple. A man of liberal convictions, both in religious and in secular matters. He sat in every Parliament from 1589 to 1626, except for that of 1601. Whitelocke records that as a young man, sitting in his first Parliament (and Sandy's last), he was 'admitted into perticular acquaintance' with Sir Edwin Sandys and a dozen other prominent men, including Sir John Eliot (q.v.), John Pym (q.v.) and John Hampden (q.v.), *Diary* 1625.1626. fol.7.

SANDYS (SANDES), Thomas, MP (*c.*1601–*c.*1659). M.F.K.; D. Underdown *Pride's Purge* p.396 note 25; *Register of Admission to the . . . Middle Temple.* Probably the son of John Sandys or Sandes (see M.F.K. para 2), of Little Pachesham (formerly Pachevesham) also known as 'Randall's estate' near Leatherhead, Surrey, *V.C.H. Surrey* iii, 296–297, *passim.* He was admitted to the Middle Temple in 1617 and became a Bencher, as Whitelocke did, in 1648; MP for Gatton, Surrey, in the Long Parliament. He is referred to as Whitelocke's kind friend, Diary 6 Mar. 1647/48.

SANDYS, William, MP (*c.*1607–1669). M.F.K.; *Hist. of Parl.* A Royalist. Great-nephew of Archbishop Sandys. He sat for Evesham in the Short Parliament of April 1640, and briefly in the Long Parliament, from November 1640 until he was ejected, as a monopolist, in January 1641; he served again as an MP from 1661 to 1669. Because of his obsession with schemes for drainage and inland navigation, he came to be known as 'Waterwork Sandys'. Whitelocke describes Sandys as his friend from the Middle Temple, and records that he, Whitelocke, was among those who were persuaded to invest in Sandys' ambitious project to make the river Avon navigable as far as Worcester. Whitelocke lost nearly £1,100 in the venture, but put this down to the troubled times which followed. Sandys sent a gift of four brace of deer to help stock the deer park at Fawley, but Whitelocke noted, making a rueful pun, that they 'proved deer Cattle', *Diary* 1639.1640. fol.47v. See also ib. Sept. 1644 fol.66v.

SAVILE, Lord, see Sussex, E. of.

SAY, William, MP (1604–*c.*1665). *D.N.B.* He studied at University College, Oxford, and at the Middle Temple. A recruiter member of the Long Parliament, from April 1647, and a regicide. He is referred to by Whitelocke as working against Lady Katherine Scot (q.v.), *Diary* 21 May

1655. Say was chosen as acting-Speaker of the House of Commons when William Lenthall (q.v.) was ill, ib. 13 Jan. 1659/60. After the Restoration, he escaped to the Continent.

SAY & SEALE (SAYE & SELE), William Fiennes, 1st Viscount (1582–1662). G.E.C.; *D.N.B.*; *Hist. of Parl.* (entry for his son James Fiennes, q.v.). Of Broughton Castle, south-west of Banbury, Oxon. He was subtle, able and ambitious, with a strong sense of rank. From his early years he opposed court policies, yet, through the influence of the 1st Duke of Buckingham (q.v.), he was created Viscount in 1624. In spite of this inducement to conform, he refused to pay the forced loan in 1626 and later resisted the Ship Money levy. Parliament appointed him Lord-Lieutenant of Oxfordshire in 1642. He was refused a safe-conduct by the King, in 1643, when Parliament proposed sending him to Oxford to negotiate with their other commissioners.

Earlier, when Whitelocke decided to stand for Oxfordshire, in November 1640, contesting the seat against Lord Say's son James Fiennes and others, the noble Lord (known as 'Old Subtlety') expressed surprise that an 'Upstart Lawyer' should oppose his son. Whitelocke sent a sharp rejoinder that he honoured his Lordship as a Peer and a patriot, but as to being called an 'Upstart Lawyer', his own forebears had lived as gentlemen in Oxfordshire before the name of Fiennes was known in those parts. On the advice of his friends, however, Whitelocke withdrew from the contest and was soon afterwards elected MP for Great Marlow, *Diary* 1640.1641. fol. 49v. The 'strangeness' or estrangement which followed, between Lord Say and Whitelocke, was still evident when Whitelocke, as a Deputy–Lieutenant for Oxfordshire, was sent with others to support Say & Seale in recapturing Oxford from Sir John Byron (q.v.): Whitelocke's far-sighted advice that they should garrison the city for Parliament was ignored by Lord Say, ib. 1642.1643. fols. 56v.–57. Shortly afterwards it fell to the King and became his headquarters.

Lord Say reappears in the record, encouraging 'though underhand' Lord Savile (Earl of Susssx, q.v.) to press charges of treachery against Denzil Holles (q.v.) and Whitelocke; the two accused MPs even suspected that the 'design against them . . .' came 'from the advice if not contrivance of the L[ord] Say', ib. 5, 8, 14 July 1645. If this was indeed true, it did not inhibit Lord Say from writing, later, about a case to be heard in Chancery between his cousin, William Croker, and 'that unworthy fellowe Wise'. He appealed to Whitelocke (who, years earlier, had been concerned with the case when it was heard in the House of Lords) to allow his (Lord Say's) son Nathaniel Fiennes (q.v.), to consult him about the 'unjust, base, vile and cosening carriage thereof.' The letter is signed 'Your Lo[rdshi]^{ps} very lovinge Friend and Servant W[illiam] Say & Seale. 9 June 1656. Broughton. Long. W.P. xvii, 166.

Later still, Say wrote begging Whitelocke to help save the life of Sir George Booth (q.v.), *Diary* 29 Aug., 12 Sept. 1659. This is not mentioned in the reference books listed above, although Sir Charles Firth, in the *D.N.B.*, noted that in 1658 a royalist agent described Say as being favourable to the King. In the first of the two letters, Say wrote that Booth had married his grand-daughter (Catherine Clinton, daughter of the 4th Earl of Lincoln; she had died in 1643 and Booth had married again in the following year). Say asked Whitelocke to try to obtain a pardon to save Booth from execution, since he had always been faithful to Parliament; greater offences than Booth's had been pardoned, and if he were treated harshly, that might be used as a precedent, bringing the same treatment upon others if events changed, as had often happened before, 29 Aug. 1659, Long. W.P. xix, 82. Another letter from Broughton Castle, of the same date, is unsigned. It refers to Sir George Booth having brought himself to the condition of being Whitelocke's enemy and then his prisoner; (Whitelocke was Lord President of the Council at the time of the rising). The anonymous writer refers to being a near relative and formerly a particular friend of Booth's. Few of the King's party, he wrote, had suffered the death penalty in the First Civil War for a first offence; Booth's was a first offence, and he had previously given eminent service to the public. However mistakenly, he had acted in obedience to his conscience and not for selfish ends, 29 Aug. 1659, ib. 80. The writer was probably either Whitelocke's colleague, Nathaniel Fiennes (q.v.), or the unidentified 'Sir L.D.' (or 'L.O.') mentioned in *Diary* 29 Aug. 1659. Whitelocke's reference to a letter from Lord Say & Seale of 12 September, on the same subject, may have been a slip: in fact, Say wrote on that date appealing to Whitelocke on behalf of New College, Oxford (where Say had been a student); this concerned an impropriation at Hornchurch, Essex, which the Committee of Plundered Ministers were likely to take from the College. Lord Say begged that the College might not be denied a trial at which to assert their rights, 12 Sept. 1659, Long. W.P. xix, 84.

SCOBEL, Henry (d. 1660). G.E. Aylmer *State's Servants* pp.256–258, *passim*; *D.N.B.* Clerk of the Parliaments from 1648, in succession to Henry Elsing (q.v.). Appointed for life but later ousted. He also served as a Clerk to the Protectorate Council. He is only mentioned in his official capacities by Whitelocke.

SCOT (SCOTT), Lady Katherine (Catherine), (d. 1686). T. Burton *Diary* i, 204–206, 265, 297–298, 334–337, 352; *C.J.* vi, 473, 479, 482, 576, 588 (referring to her as 'Mrs' Scot). Lady Scot's father was the Royalist, George Goring, Earl of Norwich (q.v.); she derived her title from him, not from her husband. Whitelocke received a letter from her about the ill-treatment she had suffered at the hands of her husband, made worse by William Say MP (q.v.) who, she reported, used his great influence with John Lisle MP (q.v.), to her detriment, *Diary* 21 May 1655. Lady Scot's letter of that date does not mention the two MPs, but describes her desperate poverty and inability to pursue her suit against her 'seduced husband', without ruining herself. She had been unable to examine her witnesses, 'those smalle sums which your L[ordshi]^{ps} [the Keepers of the Great Seal?] allowed me for expences, being disbursed for necessary bread'. Her husband and his friends '. . . themselves enjoy an estate of att least 2100^l a year', but had allowed her not a penny, in the past 15 years, 'save onely two fifty pounds & 40^l . . . in almost six years . . . for expences of the suit, this is the trueth of my perishing condition . . .', Add. Ms 4992, 124v.–125 (transcript).

Lady Scot's husband was Captain Edward Scot, of Scot's Hall, Smeeth, Kent, between Ashford and Hythe. Earlier, Scot had petitioned the Long Parliament: gossips had linked his wife's name with that of Prince Rupert (q.v.). Thomas Burton recorded what ensued, in his parliamentary *Diary* (refs. above); the original 'Diary of Parliament' is in the B.L., Add. Ms 15859–15864. On 22 Dec. 1656 another petition from Scot was read, alleging that his wife had 'eloped from him and at Oxford, and other places, had children by other men', and that she had also incurred heavy debts from which he wished to be relieved. He appealed for divorce and to have her children declared bastards. Anticipating the petition, Major-General Thomas Kelsey (q.v.) came to Parliament with a Bill ready to be enacted. Sir Thomas Wroth supported him: 'It is not every man's luck to have a good wife. No man in this House has so bad a wife. The Lord Chief-Justice has settled alimony upon her, but she deserves no more than a dog.' He proposed that the Bill be read. But Walter Strickland (q.v.) argued: '. . . for us to judge parties unheard, is very unequal. By this means any man that is weary of his wife may be quit of her by petition.' Scot was described by another MP as '. . . a very weak man and under some restraint'. His subsequent appearances showed that the weakness was in his head; it would be interesting to know who put him up to presenting the petition. A Colonel sprang to Scot's defence: 'As weak as he is reported to be, he has been a captain in your Service.' Another MP said it would be unparliamentary procedure to bring in a Bill 'under colour of a petition . . .' and agreed with Strickland that it would be 'very unequal to condemn, before parties are heard on both sides.' Finally, the business was referred to a Committee which was to examine the opposing parties. The Committee met on 27 December 1656 and adjourned until 3 January 1656/57, but still could not proceed, for lack of evidence. Lady Scot's Counsel requested that Scot should pay for his wife's defence, which would include bringing witnesses from far afield; he pointed out that similar payments by husbands were allowed in the law courts, adding persuasively: '. . . it is likely to be the last time her husband shall be troubled with her, if the matters be proved as . . . set forth in the petition. If she can vindicate herself, it ought to be his rejoicing as well as her's [sic], and he will not grudge the charges.' The Committee then fixed a date on which evidence was to be brought and Counsel was to be heard for both parties.

On 10 January 1656/57, the Committee learned that Mr Scot refused to pay his wife's costs, although even his own Counsel had tried to persuade him to pay her £1 a day. 'Her simple husband could not utter his mind in a word of sense.' A Mr Lee took notes for Lady Scot, but denied that he was retained by her. The first witness for the petitioner was a Mr Timothy Rookes, an old retainer at Scot's Hall, who 'ripped up the whole course of her elopement . . .' He stated that the couple had been married for 25 or 26 years; that only £1,500 of her £3,000 portion had been paid; that Lady Scot had lived with her husband for about two years and then, saying that she wished to go to London for three weeks or so, had stayed away for three years. Another time she had pretended to visit her brother 'who had a sore foot' and again, a proposed absence of three weeks had been extended to three years. Later, asking leave to go to London for a month and 'promising upon her honour to return within six weeks' she was away for yet another three years. 'Still the poor man was content, from time to time, to receive her and all her faults . . .' but when Scot sent his wife £40 for her journey home, she 'set sail another way, for Oxford, where she was all the time of the siege . . .' The witness further alleged that after her return to London she met 'five or six lusty fellows, whom she had to a tavern' and that she hired them to abduct Scot and rush him up to London; that she paid them £15 in advance, with a promise of £100 when they had finished the job. Rookes did not explain the purpose of this enterprise, but it was supposed that the object was to lock Scot up with his wife so that (rather late in the day) 'the bold-face might have the more colour for fathering upon him those children, which, in all probability, were gotten in adultery.' On Cromwell's orders, Scot was set free and some of the young 'blades' were arrested.

The next witness for the petitioner was Major Riswick, an impoverished German, on crutches, who had served in Parliament's Army. He gave evidence on two 'remarkable passages' of Lady Scot's life, but Burton wrote: '. . . one could scarce understand him, for he spoke pitiful English';

an MP protested that he 'could not understand a word' and that this witness should stand down and be heard at the end, with an interpreter. The Committee, however, did not agree to this so the German Major continued, but the 19th century editor decided it was 'not proper for publication'. The following week, the Committee heard five witnesses for the petitioner who were said to prove the petition, but again several pages of the manuscript were suppressed.

A good scandal brings colour into the lives of politicians and the public alike, not least if the lady happens to be well-connected, and Scot's case was no exception. Burton records: 'It was a great Committee; there were above one hundred people present, besides pickpockets ... They said there was one under the table ... I took not much notice (nor nobody else) what other Committees sate.' Whitelocke was not appointed to the Committee. The petition for divorce and to bastardize the children, seems to have faded out and, astonishingly, not long before his death Edward Scot acknowledged the eldest son, Thomas, as his heir and, to Pepys's surprise, left Thomas a substantial estate. This transformed the young man into a desirable bachelor: Sir George Carteret (q.v.) swiftly arranged a match between his little daughter and Thomas Scot, before Whitelocke's distant kinsman, Sir Henry Benet (later Lord Arlington, q.v.) had time 'to get this gentleman for a sister of his', *Pepys* iv, 254 with note 2, 30 July 1663.

Notes on the family pedigree and arms appear in Mss Rawl. B.82, 62v. and C.678, 32.

SCOTT, Thomas, MP (d. 1660). *D.N.B.*; D. Underdown *Pride's Purge* pp. 34, 339, 396 note 26, *passim*; B. Worden *Rump Parliament, passim*; Mss Rawl., *passim*. He lived in Lambeth and at Little Marlow, Bucks., north-east of Marlow. Whitelocke, living nearby at Fawley Court, was elected MP for Marlow in the Long Parliament. Scott, an attorney and later Recorder of Aylesbury, made a name for himself as Treasurer of the County Committee for Buckinghamshire, from 1644 to 1646. He was elected a member of the Long Parliament for Aylesbury in December 1645. A regicide and a staunch republican, he worked closely with Sir Arthur Hesilrige (q.v.). He was one of a handful of people, including Bishop Sheldon (q.v.) and John Lisle (q.v.), whom Whitelocke actively disliked.

The first reference to Scott concerns a request, from some gentlemen of Buckinghamshire, that Whitelocke should act against him (probably to hinder his election), but Whitelocke was ill at the time and did nothing, *Diary* 21 Sept. 1645. Less than two months later a petition from

Buckinghamshire was prepared, opposing the new election, and Whitelocke appeared for the petitioners, which '. . . made Mr Scott & his party to hate him', ib. 7 Nov. 1645. There was further friction when Scott tried to impose a rigid Presbyterian Minister on the congregation in Marlow, and Whitelocke recommended someone else to fill the vacancy, ib. 8, 9 Apr., 25 May 1655. Adding fuel to the fire, Whitelocke arranged for his son James to contest Scott's seat at Aylesbury, ib. 21 Dec. 1658; 14 May 1659. Scott responded swiftly, with an unsubstantiated report from an Irish friar that Whitelocke was corresponding with Charles II (in Europe) and with Edward Hyde (later 1st Earl of Clarendon, q.v.), ib. 18 May 1659. Scott's indignation was renewed, a few months later, by Whitelocke serving with the army officers on the Committee of Safety; when Parliament reassembled, Scott and others made threats against Whitelocke's life, with Scott declaring that Whitelocke should be hanged with the Great Seal round his neck, ib. 27 Dec. 1659.

By the beginning of 1660, Scott was riding high: he was made *Custos Rotulorum* of Westminster, and Secretary of State, ib. 11, 14 Jan. 1659/60. He and Luke Robinson (q.v.) were even sent to greet General George Monck (later Duke of Albemarle, q.v.) at Leicester, on his journey to London, ib. 16 Jan. 1659/60. Scott, unlike Whitelocke, totally misjudged the General's intentions. Monck, with unwonted subtlety, showed every courtesy to the regicide. The fact that Charles II was shortly to be restored to the throne did not dawn on Scott for some weeks: '. . . the great turne, & the design of Moncke' became apparent (when the General insisted that the secluded members, Royalists and supporters, should be readmitted to the restored Rump Parliament), ib. 18 Feb. 1659/60. Scott's appointment as Secretary of State was repealed, ib. 23 Feb. 1659/60, and within six weeks he signed an Engagement to the Council of State not to do anything to disturb the peace, '& his great friend Moncke began to be more reserved towards him then formerly', ib. 31 Mar. 1660. After the Restoration, Scott's name was omitted from the Act of General Pardon and Oblivion, ib. 6 June 1660. He tried to escape abroad, but was recognized under his disguise and was persuaded to give himself up and return to England. At his trial as a regicide, he vainly pleaded parliamentary privilege. He went to his execution with defiant courage.

SCROPE (SCROOPE), Col. Adrian (1601–1660). *D.N.B.*; E. Ludlow *Voyce from the Watch Tower* (ed. A.B. Worden), pp.245–248, *passim*; *Pepys* i, 232–233 with note. A regicide. He studied at Harts Hall, Oxford, and at the Middle Temple; fought for Parliament and was made a Colonel in 1647. Governor of Bristol Garrison from 1649 to 1655. He is referred to three times in *The Diary*: (1) in the Second Civil War, when he and Major Gibbons captured the Earl of Holland (q.v.) and other Royalists, *Diary* 5 July 1648; (2) when the House of Commons voted to impose a fine on him, but not to except him from the Act of Indemnity, ib. 9 June 1660 (this was in accordance with the pardon promised in the King's proclamation to regicides who surrendered); (3) when, according to Whitelocke, Scrope and two others surrendered, ib. 19 June 1660 (in fact he had surrendered on 4 June); on 20 June Scrope was discharged on parole. The House of Lords, however, opposing the Commons, insisted that all those who had judged the King must be arrested. The Commons resisted, but gave way on 28 August 1660. Scrope was imprisoned again, then tried and condemned in October, largely on the word of the former parliamentarian Major-General Richard Browne (q.v.). A most endearing description of Scrope's character, written by an enemy, is recorded in *Voyce from the Watch Tower* (reference above). Ludlow also tells of Scrope's peace of mind: how on the very eve of his execution he slept soundly, snored loudly and even had to be woken the next morning; also how, in a speech from the scaffold, he forgave all his enemies including (without naming him) 'the worst of his enemyes', who was surely Richard Browne.

SCUDAMORE, Lady [Jane?]. She paid Whitelocke three fees of £1 each, *Diary* 12, 15, 25 Nov. 1669. This was a fee such as well-to-do clients paid him at that time. His women clients were usually widows, or women involved in matrimonial disputes. It has not been possible to identify this woman with certainty: the title could have been from her father, or acquired through marriage to a peer, baronet or knight. John, created 1st Viscount Scudamore of Sligo in 1628, is ruled out as the husband, since he was a widower by 1669. His son James Scudamore MP (1624–1668), see G.E.C. and *Hist. of Parl.*, died before him, and had no claim to a courtesy title (as with higher grades in the peerage), but this fact might have eluded Whitelocke. Two points lead to the supposition that 'Lady' Scudamore may well have been James Scudamore's widow, Jane (*c.*1629–1700): (1) Jane was the eldest daughter of Richard Bennet (*sic*) of Kew (Whitelocke's relative by his first marriage); moreover, she was married from the Benets' house in Babraham, Cambridgeshire, a place which features in *The Diary*; (2) the consultations took place about a year after Jane's husband died.

SEDGWICKE, [Robert?] (b. *c.*1641). Mr. Sedgwicke and Mr. Thankful Owen (q.v.) consulted Whitelocke on legal matters, *Diary* 2 Nov. 1660.

Sedgwicke was perhaps Robert, whose father Obadiah (d.1658) had been a well-known puritan divine, see *D.N.B.*; Sedgwicke may, however, have been Obadiah's brother, William (Will proved in November 1663), see *Calamy Revised*.

SEHESTED (SESTED, SCHESTEDT), Count Hannibal (Hanibal), (1609–1666). *Dansk Biografisk Lexikon*; *Journal* ii, 368–369, 391–393; G. Masson *Queen Christina* (Sphere Books. Cardinal edn. 1974) p. 221. One of the wealthiest and most influential Danes of his day; a statesman, diplomat and courtier. He had matriculated at Oxford University in September 1629, had been on several embassies and had served as Governor of Norway for the Danish crown, until he fell out of favour with his wife's half-brother, King Frederick III of Denmark. His wife's sister was married to Count Corfitz Ulfeldt (q.v.), who had been one of his most bitter opponents in Denmark. (Whitelocke knew Ulfeldt in Uppsala; by that date, 1653–1654, Ulfeldt too was in deep disgrace with his wife's half-brother, the King of Denmark, and was prepared to betray his country to the English or to the Swedes.) Sehested's fall from power was said, by Whitelocke, to have been occasioned by 'jealousies (particularly . . . in some matters of mistresses)', *Journal* ii, 368; members of the Rigsråd envied his power and wealth, and accused him of avarice.

   Don Antonio Pimentel de Prado (q.v.) wrote from Hamburg that 'the Excellent Signior Don Hanniball Seastett' was eager to meet Whitelocke; he extolled the Dane's 'singular merit', 9/19 May 1654, Long. W.P. xv, 168 (Spanish), 170 (English). When Whitelocke stopped in Hamburg, on his journey home from Sweden, Sehested called on him more than once. Whitelocke summed him up as '. . . a gentleman of excellent parts [who] had gained perfectly the French, Italian, Dutch, English, and Latin tongues', *Journal* ii, 368; *Diary* 13 June 1654. The exiled Dane expressed a desire to go to England and serve the Protector, but he wished this to be kept a secret. A week later, Whitelocke was on board ship (surrounded by his small fleet and waiting for a favourable wind before sailing for England) when Sehested arrived uninvited, 'about five o'clock this morning (an unusual hour for visits)'. They had '. . . much discourse together, wherein this gentleman is copious, most of it to the same effect as at his former visits in Hamburg . . .' After trying, unsuccessfully, to pick Sehested's brains about troop movements in Lower Saxony, Whitelocke entertained him to breakfast and Sehested 'fed and drank wine heartily'. Finally, Whitelocke paid his departing guest the surprising compliment of a 21–gun salute (as if Sehested had still been Governor of Norway), ib. 20 June 1654; *Journal* ii, 391.

Three months later Count Montecuccoli (q.v.), who kept a journal of his travels, recorded meeting Queen Christina in Antwerp, 16 Sept. 1654, *I Viaggi* (Modena. 1924); on being invited into her coach, Montecuccoli found the Prince of Lüneburg and Count Sehested already ensconced. Some three weeks later, Christina wrote to Whitelocke in most gracious terms, reminding him of their earlier friendship, hoping that his feelings towards her had not changed, and asking him to sponsor Sehested at an audience with the Protector (French text in the entry for CHRISTINA, Queen of Sweden). Whitelocke had already arranged a free pass, signed by Cromwell, for the Dane to come to England, 21 Aug. 1654, Ms Rawl. A 328 fol. 119 (copy). He had sent it in the diplomatic bag, care of Richard Bradshaw (q.v.), the Resident in Hamburg; for this he received a letter of thanks from Sehested, Antwerp 27 Sept./7 Oct. 1654, Long. W.P. xiv, 61 (copy, in French – as are all the letters which follow in this entry).

On arrival in London, two weeks later, Sehested wrote obsequiously that he had not presumed to trouble Whitelocke, beyond inquiring when he might pay his respects and hand over a letter from Queen Christina (probably the one referred to above), ib. 62; 11/21 Oct. 1654. Two months later, Sehested notified Whitelocke that the Danish Envoy had arrived, to ratify the Anglo-Danish Treaty (which followed the Anglo-Dutch Peace Treaty). This Envoy (who appears to have been H. Willemsen Rosenwinge, see *Thurloe S.P.* iii, 31) intended to dispatch the business quickly. Sehested entreated Whitelocke to see them both together, about a recommendation of benefit to himself. This was at the Envoy's own suggestion, and Sehested was confident that, backed by the Protector's recommendation, the Envoy would do everything possible to secure his (Sehested's) reinstatement, 11 Dec. 1654, Long. W.P. xiv, 62v.

Within a week, Sehested wrote expressing his deep indebtedness to Whitelocke for having spoken on his behalf to the Protector. He would not fail to visit Whitelocke on the following evening, to receive his advice. (It seems that he enclosed a draft statement about his qualifications) ... If there appeared to be a touch of vanity in his self-praise, Sehested assured Whitelocke that this was far from his usual style but he was compelled, in this case, to adapt to the practice of society. He told Whitelocke to alter and add to the statement as he thought fit, and then to arrange for it to be delivered to the Envoy, before the latter left London. The Envoy had already promised Cromwell his loyal assistance in bringing the matter before the Danish King, and Sehested had no doubt whatever but that he would keep his word ... , 17 Dec. 1654, ib. 66.

The next month he wrote a long, unhappy letter saying that the greatest of all misfortunes had befallen him: earlier, when he had collapsed under the blows of fate, he had accepted the loss of all his possessions, of his public office and of the King's favour, facts which he said were only too widely known. He had thought at that time to cure his affliction by absenting himself and, with the King's permission, had set off to seek his fortune elsewhere; but now he had suffered a relapse, and did not know by what desperate expedient he might escape the misfortune which pursued him everywhere ... He recalled their conversation on Whitelocke's last visit; Sehested had then complained of suspicions current at the Danish Court. These concerned: firstly his negotiations in England, which arose from Queen Christina recommending him to Cromwell, and secondly some non-existent correspondence between himself and his brother-in-law, which was supposedly secret, cunning and to the detriment of the Danish King and his dominions. Because of these suspicions, Sehested again begged to be allowed copies of the Queen of Sweden's letters, both to Cromwell and to Whitelocke (having already asked for these in earlier letters). He appealed to Whitelocke to testify that his business and inquiries in England had been in no sense prejudicial to the King of Denmark nor to his dominions; that, on the contrary, he had always spoken of the King in terms of humble respect and devotion, desiring a firm and good friendship between Denmark and England ... , Feb. 1655 (New Style), ib. 85, 85v.

Whitelocke replied sympathetically; it was true that misfortune comes unbidden. This was something we experienced from time to time, but the greater the wrongs and difficulties, the greater was the glory in overcoming them; it was not without reason that the poet [Ovid] wrote:

> Qua[e] latet inq[ue] bonis cessat non cognita rebus apparet Virtus arguiturq[ue] malis.
> [When times are good virtue lies hidden, out of view,
> When things go wrong, its proven worth shines through.]

The malice, envy and calumny of enemies only reflected their own folly ... truly noble souls, who honoured and respected justice, would not ... be prejudiced by hearsay. For himself, Whitelocke would not be swayed by partiality ... if he had to testify to the Dane's innocence, he would willingly bear witness that ever since he had known him and been his friend, he had observed nothing in him but honour and virtue, nothing for which to make excuses nor at which to be even remotely shocked ... Far from Sehested showing venom, craft or evil intent in word or in deed against the King of Denmark, Whitelocke had proof only of his dutiful respect towards his King. If there were any need to bear witness to this he, Whitelocke, would always be ready in that (as in everything else) to prove himself Sehested's very humble and affectionate servant ... Chelsea, 16 Feb. 1655 (N.S.), ib. 86.

An undated letter from Sehested concerns his passport etc., ib. 87. Finally, he wrote about a note which had just reached him, apparently while he was on the highway, which he enclosed. Having no other support than Whitelocke's kindness to console and help him, Sehested craved his sympathy and asked when he might call in person, to discuss how to rid himself of the troubles, which tormented him all the more because he was destitute of any other friendship and advice, 3 Mar. 1655 (N.S.), ib. 87v. The editor's assumption that the date 1655 (shown on the later letters) was new style, cannot be confirmed from diary entries. Strangely, neither this correspondence nor the meetings in London are mentioned in *The Diary*, although they must have been a burden on top of Whitelocke's public duties. Indeed, the only reference to the Dane's visit to London occurs four months after the date of the last letter (above), in an entry which summarizes several encounters: it states that Count Sesthed (*sic*), whom Whitelocke had met in Germany, had come to England; that Whitelocke took him to visit and to offer his services to the Protector, '... who seemed delighted w[i]'h his Company ... butt the Prot[ecto]ʳ afterwards understanding that he was a debauched person, he would have no more converse w[i]'h him', *Diary* 8 July 1655.

It was one of Whitelocke's endearing characteristics that, throughout his life, he stood by his friends and acquaintances, regardless of how they were judged by those in power. Sehested's letters give ample proof that all his other acquaintances in London had dropped him. Perhaps Whitelocke's support was of some long-term use in seeing him through a bad time. Not long after his unceremonious departure from England, Sehested was made very welcome in the Netherlands by Charles II. He then served as a General in Spain, returning to Copenhagen for his mother-in-law's funeral, when he met the Danish King but was still neither trusted nor reinstated. In the Swedish/Danish war, when Denmark was over-run and much of the country was occupied, Sehested was captured by the Swedes. After making some abortive attempts to negotiate a peace settlement, he returned to Denmark in April 1660 and led the negotiations, obtaining better terms for his countrymen than they had hoped for. This led to his full reinstatement. He became Lord Treasurer, and by 1665 was active as a reforming minister and diplomat, still under Frederick III. He died in Paris in 1666.

SELDEN, John, MP (1584–1654). *D.N.B.*; M.F.K.; Clarendon *The Life by Himself* (1843) p. 923; Aubrey *Brief Lives*; B.L. Mss, Index. A distinguished Inner Temple lawyer, scholar, antiquarian and orientalist, also a versatile and learned writer. The obscure style of his writing has been criticized but his spoken word was clear and witty, as is shown in his *Table*

Talk. Clarendon wrote of Selden's ability to 'make hard things easy'. As an MP in the 1620s he defended the liberty of the subject and rights of the Commons: in 1626 he was active in the impeachment of the 1st Duke of Buckingham (q.v.); in 1627 he refused to pay the forced loan; he opposed imprisonment without charge, and refusal to obey writs of *habeas corpus*. In 1629, he himself was one of nine MPs imprisoned, under harsh conditions, during the King's pleasure, and he was not released until 1631, when the Earl of Arundel and Earl of Pembroke (q.v.), who needed his legal services, appealed on his behalf. He subsequently served in the Long Parliament.

Edward Hyde (later 1st Earl of Clarendon, q.v.) and Whitelocke were at one in their admiration for Selden. They both came under his influence when they were students at the Middle Temple. Clarendon's glowing description (quoted at length in the *D.N.B.*) starts: 'Mr Selden was a person whom no character can flatter, or transmit in any expressions equal to his merit and virtue ...' Whitelocke's account indicates some of the things he learned from Selden:

> I was brought acquainted with Selden, that admirable learned man ... & from him received good counsell & incouragement in my studyes, amongst others, he gave me this rule ...
>
> That I should not neglect to study men as well as bookes, & as often as I could, to be in the Company of ingenious, & learned men, by whom I might gaine more by conversation, then I could by study. yett though I should be in Company late att night, he advised me att my returne home to reade somwhat, that there should be *nulla Dies sine linea*.
>
> That I should likewise be carefull in the choice of such bookes to reade, as not to wast my time about common knowne, or impertinent [i.e. irrelevant] matters, butt to study the choicest & most profitable learning, & ... to indeavor to gayne more speciall knowledge then what was commonly studied, not neglecting the usefull & generall points also.
>
> That what I read & judged usefull I should bee sure to bee Master of it, & not slightly to passe it over[,] & to take such course & notes, that I might find it agayne when I had occasion to make use of it.
>
> He likewise especially recommended to me the study of the English history, & of records, & antient manuscripts, & to compare them with the year bookes, & printed Histories ...
>
> He further gave me instructions concerning the Oriental tounges ... & so well liked my company, that he gave me the freedome of his rare library, the which I did often resort unto, & had the incomparable learned conversation & direction of himselfe, ... a great contentment & furtherance to me in my studyes ...
>
> Add. Ms 53726, 11–11v.

There are numerous diary entries for Selden between 1623 and 1654, the year in which he died. There is also material connected with him among

Whitelocke's papers: the first document is a Brief in Attorney-General Sir Robert Heath's case against Selden, in the Star Chamber; the charge was that Selden had planned to further and cherish seditious rumours against the King, by copying and publishing the Proposition ... (May 1629?) Long. W.P. iv, 11v. This is followed by a demurrer, ib. 12; examination of Selden, 18 January, ib. 14; depositions and proofs, followed by the examination of Selden's friend Robert Cotton and others, 11 November, ib. 16.

Selden was Solicitor and Steward to Henry Grey, 8th Earl of Kent (d. 1639), and was regarded as a friend, staying with him in Wrest, between Luton and Bedford, with freedom to follow his scholarly pursuits. If Aubrey is to be believed, Selden and the Countess (q.v.) were more than good friends. Whitelocke links their names on many occasions (see entry for KENT, Elizabeth Grey, Countess of). In his late sixties, Selden wrote to Whitelocke from The Carmelite (or Whitefriars), the Countess's town mansion near the Temple, which she put at his disposal:

> My Lord
> I heare that my deere freind S[i]^r Th[omas] Cotton is named in the bill for sh[e]rif[f]e of Bedf[ordshire] ... [This precluded him from standing for Parliament at the next election.] I can not think but that your great interest [i.e. influence] in that county may get him by & save him. I beseach you do so with timelynesse. You see you can never be rid of the importunities of
> Your L[ordshi]^{ps} most affectionat,
> obliged & humble ser[va]^{nt}
> J. Selden.
> 4 Nov. 1652.
>
> Long. W.P. xii, 177.

Almost on the eve of Whitelocke's departure for Sweden, Selden wrote again, insistently, apparently on the same theme, although without naming Sir Thomas Cotton.

> ... I thought it my duty to put your L[ordshi]^p in mind of that which[,] among your so pressing occasions, may possibly slip your memory. The old suit in behalf of my deere friend, which concernes the shrifalty of Bedf[ordshire]. [Selden appealed to Whitelocke to secure his friend against] that inconvenience which he extremely desires for the present to decline ...
> Westminster. 25 Oct. 1653
>
> ib. xiv, 134.

A letter from Selden to Whitelocke in Sweden contains no news of events in England, other than comments on the cold winter, but it goes on:

> ... The best news I have heard since I had the honour to see you, and that which brought me ... an ample store of gladness, was the assurance of your

Excellence's safety, which a false rumour with great confidence had utterly destroyed here. There is none living can with more hearty affection wish all happiness to you and good success . . . than doth most really,
            your Excellence's most obliged and most humble servant
                                  J. Selden
Whitehall. 10 Feb. 1653[54]

Journal ii, 37–38.

Queen Christina had questioned Whitelocke extensively about Selden, *Diary* 31 Dec. 1653; when Whitelocke wrote reporting this to his old friend, ib. 3 Feb. 1653/54, Selden replied, with immoderate elation, that the letter brought him '. . . so unexpressible a plenty of the utmost . . . happiness . . . as that nothing . . . will equal or come near it.' He expressed his deep regard for the Queen, who was '. . . justly acknowledged with the height of . . . admiration by all that . . . love arts or other goodness . . .' He was profoundly flattered that she should 'descend to the mention of my mean name . . . [and make] inquiry of my being and condition with such . . . gracious expressions . . . the danger is, that your noble affection rendered me far above myself . . .' He begged that if her Majesty and Whitelocke happened to speak of such a trifle as himself again, Whitelocke would express Selden's humble thanks and devotion to the Queen, *Journal* ii 234–235, 2 Mar. 1653[54]. The heavily amended draft of this letter is in Add. Ms 32092, fol. 328.

The Countess of Kent had died in 1651, leaving Selden her personal estate, with various leaseholds and a life-interest in her lands in Leicester and Warwick. Shortly before his own death, Selden sent for Whitelocke and consulted him about selling his estate. He also discussed changing his Will and making Whitelocke one of his executors, but he became too weak to carry out these plans, *Diary* 10 Nov. 1654. When Selden died, a few months later, Whitelocke referred to him as

That incomparable person . . . a great & intimate friend . . . or rather a father . . . & most affectionately kind, his funerall sermon was preached [by] the Primate of Armach Dr Usher [q.v.] who gave him his deserved prayse as a prodigy of learning & hospitality, he was no lover of the Clergy & their pride & greatness & he was true to Parlem[en]^{ts} interest . . .

ib. 20 Mar. 1654/55.

SEYMOUR, Edward, MP, later 4th Bt. (1633–1708). *D.N.B.*; *Hist. of Parl.*; *Complete Baronetage*; *Pepys* x. Of Maiden Bradley, Wilts., and Berry Pomeroy, Devon. MP for Hindon, Wilts., south-east of Warminster, and later for constituencies in Devon. A powerful and adroit Speaker of the House of Commons from 1673 to 1679. Treasurer of the Navy from

1673 to 1681. Described by Pepys as 'a most conceited fellow'. He succeeded to the Baronetcy in 1688. His second wife was Letitia Popham, daughter of Whitelocke's friend and neighbour at Littlecote, Alexander Popham (q.v.), in whose entry she appears. According to J. Le Neve *Pedigrees of the Knights*, and *Complete Baronetage* (above), they married in 1674. The Popham connection may explain why Edward Seymour (who is mentioned only once) visited Chilton Lodge with his wife, *Diary* 11 July 1675, only two weeks before Whitelocke's death.

SEYS (SISE, SIZE), [Evan], MP (*c*.1604–1685). *Hist. of Parl.*; J.H. Baker *Order of Serjeants at Law* (Selden Society. London. 1984). Son of Richard Seys of Swansea. Admitted to Lincoln's Inn, Feb. 1623/24. A Parliament-arian in the Civil War, he was made a Serjeant-at-Law under Parliament's Great Seal in 1649. He is referred to twice by Whitelocke: (1) when Seys was appointed second Justice of the North Wales circuit, according to *Hist. of Parl.* in 1658/59, but in *Diary* on 14 Mar. 1659/60; (2) after the Restoration, when he and others were again made Serjeants, ib. 23 June 1660 (writs issued during the Interregnum being treated as invalid). Selections from treatises on the Star Chamber, borrowed from and probably written by Seys, are in Ms Rawl. C. 358, 43v., 55v. (copy).

SHARPE family. Francis and his bother Nathaniel, are first mentioned when they served as grooms on Whitelocke's Swedish Embassy, but they seem to have been in his service before that. From 1656 onwards, Francis appears as Whitelocke's tenant, woodman, and (officially or unofficially) as his land-agent or Steward at Fawley, filling the gap left by the death, in 1653, of William Cooke (q.v.). When Whitelocke was in London, Sharpe wrote keeping him up to date with news of the estate, with notes on the debauchery or death of tenants, advice on cutting trees, on sale of timber etc., *Diary* 3, 27 Oct. 1656; 7 Jan. 1656/57; 5 Dec. 1658; 13 Apr., 24 May 1661, *passim*. 'Old' John Sharpe and his wife, probably the parents of Francis and Nathaniel, died within a week of one another, ib. 26 Dec. 1661. 'Young' John Sharpe came from Chilton Foliat to Fawley, in his wagon, ib. 30 Apr. 1667. Finally, George Sharpe (who witnessed Whitelocke's last Will with his mark) was presumably the servant, referred to only as 'George', who was in Whitelocke's household at Chilton Foliat, ib. 13 Oct.1670, *passim*; surprisingly, George paid Whitelocke 20 shillings to renew his copyhold at Fawley, ib. 1 Apr. 1674.

SHAW, Sir Jo[hn], Bt., MP (c.1615–1680). *Hist. of Parl.; Complete Baronetage; Pepys* x. Elected MP for Lyme Regis in 1661. Knighted in July 1660; created a Baronet in April 1665. A successful office-holder. After his second marriage (to the widow of the 4th Viscount Kilmorey), he bought a crown lease of the Great Park at Eltham, Kent, for £3,700, where the architect, Hugh May (q.v.), built him a fine house in the Dutch style. May took Whitelocke to see the house, *Diary* 1 May 1665. (Whitelocke was related to the May family through his first wife, Rebecca, née Benet.)

SHEAFE (SHEAF), the Revd. Grindall, DD (d. 1680). *Alumni Cantabrigienses.* Of Welford, Berks. An Eton scholar, he went on to study at King's College, Cambridge, matriculating in 1626/27; appointed Rector of Horstead and Coltishall, Norfolk, in 1649, he was later Vicar of Westerham, Kent, from which parish he was ejected. He served as Archdeacon of Wiltshire from 1660 to 1680; DD in 1661. Dr. Sheafe was also Rector of Chilton Foliat, Wiltshire; Whitelocke sometimes attended his church and heard 'the Dull D^r' preach, *Diary* 4 Sept. 1664; 25 June 1665. Returning the compliment, the Rector sent a spy to one of Whitelocke's conventicles at Chilton Lodge, ib. 17 June 1666; he and his wife, a daughter of Dr. Mundy (q.v.) of Welford, visited Whitelocke from time to time, sometimes joining him for Sunday dinner (perhaps to inspect the latest dissenting preacher), ib. 2 June 1667; 2 Nov. 1673.

SHELBORNE, see SHILBORNE.

SHELDON (SHELDEN), Archbishop Gilbert, DD (1598–1677). *D.N.B.* A fervent, anti-puritan Royalist and a friend of Edward Hyde (later 1st Earl of Clarendon, q.v.). He was Warden of All Souls, Oxford, from 1626 until he was ejected in 1648, but was reinstated in 1659. An attested copy of an Order from Parliament, issued after Sheldon's ejection and while he was imprisoned in Oxford, reads:

Oxonio Visitato
A[t] the Com[m]ittee of the L[or]^{ds} and Com[mon]^s for
Referma[ti]on of the U[niversity] of Ox̄on
Whereas Dr. Shelden was com[m]itted to Prison in Ox̄on by t[h]^e Lo[rd] chancel[lo]^r of Ox̄on and visitors for his contempt of their aut[h]ority. This Com[m]ittee takeing it into considerac[i]on if his continuance there may bee of dangerous consequence in regard of the greate resort of Persons to him, doe think fitt and order th[a]^t the said Dr Shelden be removed fro[m] Ox̄on

and conveyed sutely (i.e. subtly: in a manner that defies observation] to Wallingford Castle there to be kept in safe custody by the Governor of the sayd Castle til further order . . . 30 May 1648
Long. W.P. Parcel 2, No. 8 (a small folder of papers).

After the fall of Oxford, in 1646, Colonel Arthur Evelyn (q.v.) had succeeded the Royalist, Colonel Thomas Blague (q.v.), as Governor of Wallingford. Perhaps from religious scruples, Evelyn refused to accept Dr. Sheldon and his friend Dr. Henry Hammond, as prisoners. (Hammond had been a Canon of Christ Church and Public Orator at the University of Oxford, until the City surrendered to Parliament.) Sheldon was released, conditionally, before the end of 1648. He withdrew to the Midlands and did little to trouble the Commonwealth and Protectorate governments, apart from raising funds for Charles II in exile.

At the Restoration, Sheldon met the King at Canterbury. He was made Bishop of London in October 1660. Understandably, the new Bishop wished to recover the Manor of Fulham (later Fulham Palace) which, by tradition, had been the Bishop of London's residence until the deprivation of Bishop William Juxon (q.v.), in 1649. Sheldon spoke about this to Chancellor Hyde, who sent an urgent message to Whitelocke via Bartholomew Hall (q.v.), *Diary* 1 Nov. 1660. Whitelocke was involved because his young daughter Cecilia, and her husband Samuel Harvey (q.v.), were living in the Manor of Fulham; it had been bought, with its lands, for £7,617.2s.10d. by Colonel Edmund Harvey (q.v.), one of the King's judges, and a man with a bad record. Harvey had settled the Manor on any children of Sam and Cecilia Harvey's marriage. He himself was, by that time, in prison.

Whitelocke went to see Chancellor Edward Hyde (who was created a Baron two days later, and 1st Earl of Clarendon in April 1661), and assured him that the Manor would be restored without a contest. Hearing this, Hyde said he would be a friend to Colonel Harvey. Whitelocke's attempt, a few days later, to obtain a pardon for Harvey, ib. 9 Nov. 1660, was no doubt prompted by Clarendon's promise and by the Bishop's claim on the Fulham estate. In the meantime, Whitelocke took his young son-in-law, Samuel Harvey, to see the Bishop who was very civil and suggested that, in case of difficulty, Whitelocke's 'old friend', as he called the Chancellor, should act as referee. Whitelocke assured him that there would be no occasion for this. He found the Bishop so affable that he asked a favour: Cecilia was expecting her first baby. She was a sensitive, nervous young woman and her father asked that, if possible, the estate should not be handed over until after the baby was born; if, however, the Bishop wanted it sooner, Whitelocke entreated him to send a message, but not on any account to send in soldiers to evict the couple. The Bishop promised that no officers or soldiers would be sent and nothing would be done to frighten Cecilia, ib. 3 Nov. 1660. Despite his promise, on Sunday, 23 December, Bishop Sheldon sent a band of officers and men to take possession. No warning was given. They forced an entry, plundered the house, and even went off with the baby linen. Sam Harvey was out and Cecilia was terrified, ib. 24 Dec. 1660.

Whitelocke had a further encounter with the Bishop, again arranged by the Chancellor, who remarked, as an opening gambit, that he was sorry to hear that Whitelocke was 'head of the Phanatickes [i.e. Dissenters] in the Citty'. Whitelocke dealt with the charge adroitly. Most of the interview is recalled in dialogue; it reflects the hostile atmosphere and the Bishop's indignation. This was caused by Whitelocke having advised clients in two parishes (ib. 8 Feb. 1660/61 and 15 Oct. 1661 with notes) that a Commission from Sheldon, enabling a group of parishioners approved by him to set themselves up as a Vestry (or Parish Council), was illegal, since such a body should have been elected democratically by the parishioners themselves. With the icy courtesy of a learned Counsel, Whitelocke proved that the Bishop, not he, was in the wrong. He did nothing to save Sheldon's face, ib. 7 May 1662.

Four months earlier, Whitelocke wrote that his son-in-law, Sam Harvey, had died of a broken heart, through the 'barbarous usage of himselfe & his wife by the B[isho]ᵖ of London & his Agents', ib. 8 Jan. 1661/62. They had lost the baby, and some three weeks after Whitelocke's sharp interview with Sheldon and the Chancellor, Cecilia died at her father's house in Coleman Street. Whitelocke wrote at length about her and her little family, ending bitterly: 'all their blood lyes att the doore of this B[isho]ᵖ', ib. 27 May 1662. There is no entry in *The Diary* to report Sheldon's appointment as Archbishop of Canterbury, in June 1663.

Not surprisingly, Whitelocke was blind to Sheldon's good qualities: his scholarship, his acknowledged generosity and his courage, for example in rebuking the King for his adultery, and in remaining at Lambeth Palace during the Plague. His teaching that the chief point of religion lay in living a good life could only have increased Whitelocke's anger. Significantly, Bishop Burnet referred to Sheldon appearing 'not to have a deep sense of religion, if any at all' and to his speaking of religion as 'an engine of government and a matter of policy.'

SHEPPARD (SHEPHEARD, SHEPHARD), William (c.1596–1674). N.A. Matthews *Cromwell's Law Reformer* (C.U.P. 1984); *D.N.B.*; J.H. Baker *Order of Serjeants at Law* (Selden Society. London. 1984); *Register of Admission to the ... Middle Temple*. Son and heir of Philip Sheppard of

Horsley, Gloucestershire, south-west of Nailsworth. He was admitted to the Middle Temple in November 1620 (the year after Whitelocke's admission) and was called to the Bar in 1629. Besides having a large and successful country practice, he was a prolific writer on legal and religious subjects. Cromwell persuaded him to come to London to serve as a Clerk of the Upper Bench (as the King's Bench was named during the Interregnum). Sheppard was made a Serjeant-at-Law in 1656. Whitelocke refers to Sheppard's appointment as a Judge in Wales, *Diary* 29 Sept. 1659; this was in Carmarthen, where he served from 1659 to 1660. Sheppard dined with Whitelocke in London, *Diary* 25 Jan. 1666/67.

SHERWYN (SHERWIN), Richard, MP (d. 1675). G.E. Aylmer *State's Servants* pp. 99, 253–254, 399, 409–410 with note 63 (sources). He was Treasurer of Goldsmiths' Hall from 1652 to 1655 and (overlapping with this) Secretary to the Treasury Commissioners from 1654 to 1660. He is referred to by Whitelocke in this second capacity, as 'an able man in that buisnes', *Diary* 2 July 1655. Whitelocke, by then a Treasury Commissioner, makes a number of other references to Sherwyn between 1655 and 1658. In the latter year, he recommended Sherwyn as a parliamentary candidate for Ludgershall in Wiltshire, ib. 30 Dec. 1658; Sherwyn was elected and sat in Richard Cromwell's Parliament, from January 1658/59 to April 1659.

SHILBORNE (SHELBORNE) Mr. (d. 1656). R.H. Whitelocke *Memoirs ... of Bulstrode Whitelocke* (Routledge. 1860) pp. 461–462. Schoolmaster of 'Grandon' (Grendon, east of Northampton). Whitelocke's four eldest sons (q.v.), James (by his first marriage), William, Willoughby and Bulstrode (sons of his second marriage) were educated at Mr Shilborne's establishment. James and William were there together when 'Mr Shilborne my sons school-master came to Towne & brought to me, good Latin & Greek verses made by James, & a good Latin Epistle made by William ... & I ... returned tokens to them', 28 Dec. 1647, Add. Ms 37344, 126v.; *Diary*, same date. James 'came from Mr Shilbornes school a well grounded Schollar', ib. 20 Oct. 1648. Willoughby and Bulstrode jun. attended the school some eight years later, and Mr. Shilborne wrote of 'their health and proficiency in learning', ib. 26 Aug. 1655. They left abruptly when Shilborne died in May 1656, see *Memoirs ... (above)*.

SIDNEY, Col. Algernon, see SYDNEY.

SINCLARE (ST. CLARE, SAINTCLARE), Lord John (c.1610–1674). G.E.C. A Royalist, he was captured at the Battle of Worcester in September 1651 and, according to G.E.C., was confined in Windsor Castle for nearly nine years. Whitelocke refers to MPs enquiring as to the reason for the imprisonment of Sinclare and Sir George Booth (q.v.), the latter captured in 1659, and of three others, *Diary* 21 Feb. 1659/60. The Lord Keeper of Windsor Castle was required to provide this information concerning Sinclare, *C.J.* vii, 848 (date as in *Diary*). Soon afterwards, Sinclare and some other prisoners were released, *Diary* 3 Mar. 1659/60; *C.J.* vii, 860 (date as in *Diary*).

SINDERCOMBE (SYNDERCOMBE), Miles (d. 1657). *State Trials* (compiled by T.B. Howell. London. 1816); *D.N.B.* After being apprenticed to a surgeon in London, he joined Parliament's Army and became Quartermaster in Colonel Sir John Reynolds' regiment. Having Leveller sympathies, Sindercombe took part in his regiment's mutiny in May 1649; he was imprisoned, but escaped and joined a regiment of horse; he was cashiered by George Monck (later Duke of Albemarle, q.v.), who viewed him as a trouble-maker.

Colonel Edward Sexby (alias Hungerford and Brookes, see Ms Rawl. A. 28, 27, *passim*, and *D.N.B.*) had distinguished himself in Parliament's Army, but was bitterly opposed to the Protectorate. From Flanders, he misguidedly picked Sindercombe (whose record he knew) as the man to assassinate Cromwell. Sindercombe was probably a sincere Republican. As a hired assassin, however, with orders to kill the Protector, he was a disaster. Funds were raised by Sexby in Flanders, supported by exiled Royalists and also, it was said, by Spain, see T.B. Howell (above) p. 843; so Sindercombe and his accomplices received undreamed of supplies of money.

State Trials (above) provides a jumbled, documentary account of the expensive bungle which followed: Sindercombe (alias Fish) and a fellow-conspirator, John Cecil, passed themselves off as clerk and coachman to a fictitious Mr Havers of Norfolk. A large trunk arrived from Flanders, filled with guns, harquebusses and pistols, loaded with lead bullets and iron slugs. The conspirators collected some of the weapons in a viol-case. They rented rooms in a well-placed house, planning to shoot Cromwell on 17 September 1656, as he went from a service in Westminster Abbey to the opening of Parliament; the conspirators innocently believed that 'in the disorder the people would rise, and so things might be brought to a commonwealth again.' A marksman placed on the garden wall was, however, distracted by people coming into the garden. Since money was no object, the amateur assassins next rented a house on the right-hand side, entering Hammersmith from London; it had a small 'banqueting house' built on the wall, which overlooked the road down which Cromwell travelled for Hampton Court. Sindercombe purchased the services of John Toop, one of Cromwell's life-guards, who kept him informed about the Protector's movements. (The inducement was a promise of £1,500 and a troop of horse, plus the expectation that he would be a Colonel of horse within six months.) Unaccountably, the Hammersmith venture came to nothing, so Sindercombe invested in some of the fastest horses that money could buy: a bay from the Earl of Salisbury's stables, costing £80; a fine black horse at £75 and others at £42, £34 and £30.

Toop continued to supply news of Cromwell's journeys, and opportunities for the murder occurred in Kensington, Hyde Park, Turnham Green, Acton and once again in Hyde Park. On the last occasion, Cromwell dismounted and asked John Cecil who owned the horse he was riding. It was the ideal moment, but Cecil 'doubted his horse, having at that time got a cold.' The conspirators decided to postpone the assassination until the Spring but, presumably to show their paymaster that they were still earning their keep, they decided first to set fire to Whitehall, where Cromwell was in residence. An explosives expert arrived from overseas, bringing 'a firework in a hand-basket' which he left at Toop's lodgings. Sindercombe collected the bomb and took it to Cecil's lodgings. He met Toop at the Ben Johnson tavern in the Strand to discuss their current plan. Clearly they had no intention of killing Cromwell in the explosion: they would set fire to Whitehall 'and then defer the other business until the spring.' Sindercombe, Cecil and Toop then met at the Bear Tavern, in King Street, and agreed to plant their primitive time-bomb in the chapel at Whitehall. This was done early in January 1656/57. It was put in position at about 6 o'clock one evening, with two 'matches' of rope on either side, more than a yard long, which were intended to burn slowly and ignite the 'firework' of gunpowder, brimstone etc. The explosion was timed to occur between midnight and 1.00 a.m. Instead, the plot was discovered.

Sindercombe was captured and brought before a Jury in the Upper Bench, where Cecil and Toop gave 'accomplice evidence'. Sindercombe was found guilty of high treason and was sentenced to be hanged, drawn and quartered. He attempted to bribe his way out of the Tower and, when that failed, to obtain poison. On the eve of the execution he was closely guarded, visitors were not left alone with him and his room was searched. Yet he died in mysterious circumstances. Later, there were reports from the guards of his heavy snoring; of his vomiting, kicking and snorting; of his 'snuffing' a poisonous substance. Friends suspected that he had been suffocated, to avoid public disorder at the execution. An autopsy was carried out on his body by two Wardens from the Company of Surgeons with Mr Laurence Loe (q.v.). Their signed statement records that they could find no sign that death had been caused by poison, but the swelling of the brain and of the vessels in the head, with much coagulated blood, suggested to them that the prisoner had used 'some extraordinary means' to hasten his death. Two physicians, one of them Reader in Anatomy at Gresham College, opened the head and found extensive damage: '. . . the effect of some very violent and preternatural cause . . .'; it was like damage 'caused by contusion, and other . . . extraordinary violences.' The inquest was adjourned from Saturday 14 to Monday 16 February 1656/57. On the Sunday, the prison-keeper and others conveniently discovered a suicide note, said to be in Sindercombe's hand; it did not explain how he was going to kill himself, but it was enough to satisfy the Jury that he had done so and (despite the medical evidence of 'contusion' and signs of 'extraordinary violence') they 'verily believed the same to be by poison.' This highly dubious verdict has commonly been accepted in books of reference.

Whitelocke, who was acting-Speaker at the time, recorded the discovery of Sindercombe's plot to set fire to Whitehall and to kill the Protector, *Diary* 19 Jan. 1656/57; he also wrote of the day of thanksgiving for Cromwell's deliverance, ib. 18 Feb. 1656/57. Elsewhere, he recorded that Sindercombe was tried at the Bar of the Upper Bench, and sentenced for high treason; he explained that since high treason against a Protector was not known to English law, a statute from the time of Edward III had been invoked, which made it high treason 'to compass or imagine the death of the chief magistrate, by what name soever he was called', *Memorials* iv, 285.

SKIPPON, Major-General Philip, MP (d. 1660). *D.N.B.*; C. Firth and G. Davies *Regimental History of Cromwell's Army*. Having served as a soldier abroad in the 1620s and 1630s, Skippon returned to England in about 1639. In January 1641/42, the Common Council of the City of London appointed him to command their Trained Bands and to provide a guard for Parliament; this followed the King's attempt to arrest the five MPs. Whitelocke described Skippon's friendly, informal style of encouraging his men when the Trained Bands joined Essex at Brentford, against the King's Army, see *Memorials* i, 190, and, more briefly, *Diary* [Nov.] 1642, fol. 58v. Skippon showed both courage and humility during a distinguished military career, serving in the Civil War and under the Commonwealth and Protectorate. He was elected a recruiter MP for Barnstaple, in April 1647, and later sat in the Rump Parliament and in Cromwell's Parliaments of

1654 and 1656. He was a member of four Councils of State during the Commonwealth, and of two Councils under Cromwell. Unlike Whitelocke, in the debate on the alleged blasphemies of James Nayler (q.v.), Skippon supported the brutal hard-liners with the words: 'If this be liberty, God deliver me from such liberty ... the more liberty the greater mischief.'

The Diary has half a dozen entries for Skippon. In one, Whitelocke refers to his own enemies wishing to have him appointed Lord Chief Justice of Ireland, in order to be 'honorably quitt' of him; 'Field Marshall Skippon' who a month earlier had, with the greatest reluctance, accepted command of military affairs in Ireland, 'desired much to have Wh[itelocke] with him into Ireland', but Whitelocke refused to go, *Diary* 25 May 1647.

There is only one entry for this officer of a non-professional nature: Whitelocke records that Skippon recommended him as a suitor to Mary Wilson (the wealthy young widow of Colonel Rowland Wilson), *Diary* 12 June 1650. A few months later, Whitelock married her – twice.

Only one letter from Skippon to Whitelocke has been traced. He wrote about the death of his son-in-law, Captain Rolfe or Rolph (who had been accused of plotting in 1648 to assassinate Charles I). He also explained that illness affecting his wife, three of his children and five servants accounted for his absence from Parliament. The letter ended with greetings addressed, curiously, 'to my hon[our]ˢ Land lady [Whitelocke may have been staying at his wife's house in Bishopsgate Street; there is, otherwise, no greeting to Mary] and good young Landlord [Samuel, their firstborn, nearly 18 months old, or their newborn son Carleton? It was not unknown to write of a toddler as a "young Landlord"] and all yours [Mary's 10 stepchildren], and true respects to good Mʳ Cockayne [George Cokayn q.v.] and his good wife and Mʳˢ Carleton [q.v., Mary's mother]', Foulsham [Norfolk], 22 Oct. 1652, Long W.P. xii, 174.

SLINGSBY, Col. Sir Henry, Bt., MP (1602-1658). *D.N.B.*; *Complete Baronetage*; *State Trials* (collected by T.B. Howell. London. 1816); M.F.K.; *Diary of Sir Henry Slingsby* ... (ed. D. Parsons. London. 1836). A staunch Royalist; of Scriven, Yorkshire, north-east of Harrogate. He studied at Cambridge; was elected MP for Knaresborough, Yorkshire, in 1625, and also sat in the Short and Long Parliaments of 1640, serving until he was disabled in December 1642. A man of strong convictions: he voted with the minority against the attainder of the Earl of Strafford (q.v.); he maintained it was unlawful for Parliament to try to reform the country by force of arms; he refused to compound for delinquency, so his estate was sold (although not to his disadvantage); he fought in the King's Army and was with the King at Oxford and elsewhere. After being involved in plans for a royalist rising in Yorkshire, in March 1655, he was arrested and imprisoned in Hull Garrison. There, he naively attempted to bribe Major Waterhouse, and other parliamentary officers, to support plans for a landing of Charles II's forces in Hull. The officers appeared to be amenable, but when they had collected evidence of the conspiracy they handed Slingsby over to the so-called High Court of Justice in London, set up by the Protector's previous Parliament to conduct treason trials. As a Treasury Commissioner, Whitelocke was appointed to the Court ex officio, but he refused to serve. Slingsby challenged the legality of the Court and demanded to be tried by a jury, only to be told that those in the Court were both judge and jury. He pleaded not guilty, but the evidence against him was overwhelming and the plea that he had been joking to the officers was naturally dismissed. Special courts set up for treason trials do not lean towards mercy. Slingsby was duly sentenced, and he and Dr. Hewet (q.v.) were beheaded on Tower Hill, *Diary* 8 June 1658.

SMITH (SMYTH) [John?] (1). 'Mr Smith' wrote, as Clerk to the Committee for the King's trial, summoning Whitelocke to attend the Court (as one of the King's Judges), *Diary* 26 Dec. 1648. He is identified here with some diffidence as John Smith, who was appointed Clerk of Parliament in 1657/58 and 1658/59, see G.E. Aylmer 'Check-list of Central Office-holders'. It seems unlikely that young Henry Smith MP (*D.N.B.* 1620–c.1668), a future regicide, would have served both as Clerk and as a Judge at the trial.

SMITH, [John] (2) of Tidworth. *Hist. of Parl.* (in the entry for his son, also named John Smith, b. 1656, who entered Parliament as a Whig supporter in 1679). John Smith (2) bought the Manor of South Tidworth, south-west of Ludgershall, Wiltshire, in 1650. He was appointed a Militia Commissioner in 1659. A friend of Whitelocke's brother-in-law Samuel Carleton, *Diary* 30 July 1666, he appears to have consulted Whitelocke several times, being identified, on the first visit, as 'Mr Smith of Tidworth' (some 15 miles south of Chilton Lodge), ib. 27 May 1668. On that occasion Whitelocke took no fee. For subsequent advice, 'Mr Smith' (presumed to be the same client) paid fees of 10s., £1 and once even £4, ib. 13 Aug., 17, 20, 23 Oct. 1668; 5 Feb. 1671/72; 20 Jan. 1672/73.

SMITH, John (3). Listed as one of the 'Musitians & servitors' in Whitelocke's retinue for Sweden, *Diary* 26 Oct. 1653, and elsewhere as one of the 'Gentlemen and servants of the second ranke' who accompanied him on the Embassy; he is described as 'an honest civill man, and very skillful in all kinds of musicke'. Assumed by Dr. Ashbee to be the John Smith who, at the Restoration, was appointed a violist in the King's Music but who was replaced in 1673 when, Smith alleged, he was forced to resign because of his religious convictions. The Test Act may well have forced his resignation. A claim for arrears of salary was presented to the King for consideration, as late as December 1687, see A. Ashbee 'A Not Unapt Scholar: Bulstrode Whitelocke (1605–1675)', *Chelys* xi (1982) pp. 28–29.

SMITH, the Revd. Canon [Sebastian]. Canon of Peterborough; Rector of Hambleden, Bucks., 1661–1665, to whom Whitelocke paid a tithe for 'Longdoles', one of the fields at Fawley Court, *Diary* 19 Apr. 1664, with note.

SMITH, [William]. Marshall of the prison in Oxford Castle, during the Civil War. When Whitelocke, as one of Parliament's Commissioners, was negotiating with the King in Oxford, Charles I instructed Smith to allow Whitelocke and Sir John Holland (q.v.) to visit members of Parliament's Army, imprisoned in the Castle. In his letter-book and journal (which has recently come to light), compiled during these negotiations, Whitelocke named the nine Captains he visited as: Wingate, Walton, Scrope, Fleming, Lilborne, Austen, Catesby, Lidcote and Vivers. 'They told us', he recorded, 'they might have anything for their money, butt their imprisonm[en]t was close . . . They did not complaine of ill usage from the Provost Marshall', 24 Mar. 1642/43, Add. Ms 64867 fol. 4. To Whitelocke's amusement, this visit by himself and Holland occasioned a rumour in Oxford, to the effect that Parliament's Commissioners had so offended the King that he had sent two of them to the Castle, where they were seen in the Marshall's custody, *Diary* 1642.1643. fol. 62. Smith had the reputation of being a sadistic gaoler, but this is not borne out by Whitelocke's report.

SMITH, Dr.—. Probably a Doctor of Divinity. Son of Edward Smith of the Middle Temple, a Counsellor at Law, and brother of Sir Edward Smith, Chief Justice of the Common Pleas. Dr. Smith is referred to by Whitelocke as a brother of the Countess of Nottingham (q.v., Arabella née Smith). At the age of 17 Charles Howard, later Earl of Nottingham, 'a wild young scholar at Oxford', was married to Arabella by his tutor, without banns being read; when his mother threatened to reject him, Howard deserted his wife (G.E.C. entry for Charles Howard, 3rd Earl of Nottingham, with notes). It may have been in this connection that, years later, Whitelocke helped the Countess and her brother. In return for unspecified services, Dr. Smith sent him a richly bound English Bible and an 'ingenious' (i.e. intelligent or discerning) letter, *Diary* 6 Oct. 1649. A few months later, 'M^r' (*sic*) Smith, 'brother of the Countess of Nottingham', wrote to Lambert Osbaldston (q.v.) expressing hopes for Whitelocke's success if he stood for election as Chancellor of Oxford University, against Sir Thomas Fairfax (q.v.) and John Bradshaw (q.v.), ib. 19 Feb. 1649/50.

SMITH(S), unidentified. A Mr. Smith wrote about the purchase of Hockwold in East Anglia, *Diary* 5 Feb. 1662/63; perhaps the same Mr. Smith sealed a lease of ejectment to test the title of the lands in Northamptonshire, bequeathed by Dr. Winston (q.v.), ib. 17 June 1663.

SOLME (SOLMES), Richard (d. 1657). A.R. Ingpen *Middle Temple Bench Book* (London. 1912). Son and heir of George Solme of Hornchurch, Essex. He was admitted to the Middle Temple in 1616, three years before Whitelocke's official date of admission, but was called to the Bar only one year before him, in 1625; a Bencher in 1648. Whitelocke, although admitted in 1619, did not start his legal studies until 1622, but he came to know Solme at that time; 16 years later, visiting him at his home in Hampshire, Whitelocke 'was heartily wellcomed ...', *Diary* 1637/38 fol. 45v.; in the early summer of 1638, Solme and two other friends were bound with Whitelocke for the purchase of Henley Park and of Sir John Miller's interest in part of the Phyllis Court estate, ib. fol. 46. There is no further mention of Solme until 19 years later when, in the year of his death, he lent Whitelocke £1,500, ib. 10 June 1657.

SOMERSET, John Seymour, 4th D. of (c.1633–1675). *Hist. of Parl.*; G.E.C.; *C.S.P. Dom. 1672–1673* pp. 193–195, Apr. 1672. Styled Lord John Seymour from 1640 until, on the death of his nephew, he succeeded to the Dukedom in 1671; MP for Marlborough from 1661 to 1671. He owned extensive lands in Wiltshire, yet suffered from chronic debts. Admitted to Gray's Inn, October 1666, he was, curiously, made a Bencher 'and to be Assistant thereto' only three months later, *Pension Book of Gray's Inn* p. 453. He proceeded to hide in his lodgings at Gray's Inn, to evade his creditors. His wife Sarah (whose dowry was £10,000), attempted to clear his debts, but these increased on his succession to the Dukedom.

His boon companions assured him that his wife was managing his affairs too much, that she added water to his wine etc., so he turned her out, accusing her of taking his Will, stealing his plate and of incurring most of his debts., *C.S.P. Dom.* (above). She was a daughter of Sir Edward Alston MD (q.v., President of the College of Physicians), and the widow of George Grimston, eldest son of Whitelocke's friend and kinsman, Sir Harbottle Grimston, 2nd Baronet (q.v.).

Whitelocke was not displeased when the Duke invited his young sons to dine with him in Wiltshire, *Diary* 16 July, 30 Dec. 1672, nor when the Duke sent him the warrant for a buck from Savernake Forest, ib. 26 Aug. 1673. It was another matter when Samuel (q.v.) and the delinquent Bigley (q.v.), without even mentioning it to their parents, dined with the Duke and returned home to Chilton Lodge at two o'clock in the morning. Whitelocke then described the Duke's establishment as 'a house of debauchery', ib. 10 Nov. 1673. In spite of his debts, the Duke considered buying some of Whitelocke's land on the borders of Berkshire and Wiltshire, ib. 26 May, 9 Nov. 1674. He died the following year, four months before Whitelocke, who was nearly 30 years his senior.

SOUTHAMPTON, Thomas Wriothesley, 4th E. of (1608–1667). G.E.C.; *Pepys* x. A Royalist. He inherited the title in 1624. Studied at St. John's College, Cambridge, from 1625 to 1626. A Gentleman of the Bedchamber from January 1641/42. Whitelocke met him when they were Commissioners, on opposite sides, at the Oxford and Uxbridge negotiations of 1643 and 1644/45. There are several references to the Earl in that context, and in connection with his safe-conduct to London, *Diary* 1642.1643. fol. 60v.; 29 Nov., Dec. 1644, fols. 70, 70v.; 4 Feb. 1644/45. At the Commons' enquiry into the Earl of Sussex's charge against Whitelocke and Denzil Holles (q.v.), that they had negotiated secretly with Royalists, it was stated that they had visited the Earls of Southampton and Lindsey, ib. 2, 12 July 1645. The only other diary reference to Southampton occurs when he was appointed Lord Treasurer, ib. 30 Aug. 1660, an office which he held, without distinction, until 1667.

SPELMAN, Sir Henry, MP (*c*.1564–1641). *D.N.B.* A scholar, writer and antiquarian. Brought up in Norfolk, he studied at Trinity College, Cambridge, and at Lincoln's Inn. He moved to London for his researches and died at his house in the Barbican. When Whitelocke was in Sweden, years after Spelman's death, he gave books from his own library to the

University Library in Uppsala, including some by John Selden (q.v.) and some by Henry Spelman.

SPENCER, Sir Edward, Kt. (b. c.1595). *Alumni Oxonienses*. Son of Lord Edward Spencer. He studied at Corpus Christi College, Oxford, was admitted to Lincoln's Inn, 1612, and was knighted in 1625. When publishing his edition of Boethius's *De Consolatione* (London. 1654), '*Anglo-Latinæ expressus*', he wrote an odd but interesting dedicatory epistle to the 4th Earl of Southampton (q.v.): '. . . Be pleased to accept . . . my Boethius, whom I by many reasons may cal mine, having studied him at least these forty yeares, and used as many meanes and helps of Commentators and Interpreters as I could get, to make him wholly mine.' After referring to the Earl's parents and to a manuscript translation he once saw, which was dedicated to the Earl's mother, he recalled some of the distinguished men who had studied at Lincoln's Inn, 'And I, quoth the dog, may come in the reere . . . who have beene a Dunce there, because I never gate money by the Law, ever since 1612 . . .' After hinting that times had changed, he remarked out of the blue, 'Yet I hope to make them [the Inns of Court] more glorious when they are made Academies of Musicke, and all the Musicke of the world shall be made English.' Referring to some new work he had in hand, he wrote: 'I hope my friends will not pronounce mee an absolute Dance [i.e. Dunce?] . . . though neither by this [the new project] doe I intend to get money. I am in love with God and goodnesse and not with Mammon . . .' dated 12 Sept.1654. Two weeks later, he sent Whitelocke 'a letter w[i]ʰ a booke of his making', *Diary* 26 Sept. 1654; this is the only diary reference to Sir Edward.

SPILMAN, Captain-Lieutenant [Thomas]. C.H. Firth & G. Davies *Regimental History of Cromwell's Army* i, 258, 260. Made Captain-Lieutenant under John Lambert (q.v.), in June 1659. He was sent to give a full account of Lambert's proceedings to the House of Commons, *Diary* 23 Aug. 1659; this report concerned Lambert's success in crushing the royalist revolt inspired by Sir George Booth (q.v.).

SPRINGALL, Mr.—. Whitelocke's vociferous neighbour and tenant in Fawley, possibly a lawyer. He 'declared the trust' of Greenland, which had previously been part of Whitelocke's property, *Diary* 31 May 1667; some months later he pressed Whitelocke, who was patron of the living at Fawley, to appoint Knollys Kitson (q.v.) as parson, and was angry when his candidate was not chosen, ib. 24 Mar. 1667/68; 25 Jan. 1668/69. From 1662 onwards, Springall's name appears in connection with the tenancy of Fawley Court Farm, ib. 22 Dec. 1662; 4 May 1663, *passim*. He quarrelled with Jonathan Up (q.v.), ib. 24 Aug., 30 Sept. 1670, *passim*, but in the end he and Up seem to have held a joint tenancy of the home farm, ib. 7 Nov. 1670.

STAFFORD, Lady [Mary] (*c.*1621–1694). G.E.C. (entry for STAFFORD, William Howard). Presumably this was the Lady Stafford mentioned in *The Diary*. The sister and sole heir of Henry Stafford, 5th Baron, she was created a life-Baroness and her husband Baron Stafford, in 1640; in the same year, he was created Viscount. Their estate was sequestrated for his delinquency and recusancy. He was arrested by order of the Elector Palatine, was imprisoned in Heidelberg from 1652 to 1653, and was then imprisoned in Holland (for his father's debts) in 1655/56. These family crises point to it being this Lady Stafford who applied to Whitelocke for help, *Diary* 6 Dec. 1656; she made a further approach to him concerning a Treasury case, he being one of the Treasury Commissioners, ib. 2 Jan. 1656/57.

STAINES (STANE), [William], MD, MP (*c.*1610–1680). W. Munk *Roll of the Royal College of Physicans*; *Alumni Cantabrigienses*. Of Essex; MP for Thetford, Norfolk, in January 1658/59. He was appointed Censor, then Registrar of the College of Physicians, a few years after the Restoration. He prescribed medicine for Whitelocke's stone, *Diary* 25 Nov. 1669. He was buried in Westminster Abbey.

STAMFORD, Henry Grey, 1st E. of (*c.*1600–1673). G.E.C. Studied at Cambridge and at Gray's Inn. He fought for Parliament in the Civil War, but when his son-in-law, Sir George Booth (q.v.), led the royalist rising of August 1659, Stamford declared for the King. Earlier that year, he wrote to Whitelocke complaining of being dropped from the Commission of Peace, with other 'persons of quality', and of their being replaced by 'mean men ... who insult over their betters ...'; all good men (he wrote flatteringly), rejoiced that Whitelocke was, once again, appointed a Commissioner of the Seal, and the Earl desired him to put these matters right, *Diary* 14 Feb. 1658/59. No evidence has been found that Whitelocke helped this haughty Earl.

STAPLETON, Col. Sir Philip, Kt., MP (1603–1647). *D.N.B.*; M.F.K. As an Officer in Parliament's Army and a vigorous Presbyterian, he was a close friend of the Earl of Essex (q.v.), at whose house Whitelocke sometimes met him, *Diary* Dec. 1644, fol. 70; 21 Dec. 1645. He staunchly supported Whitelocke and Denzil Holles (q.v.) in the Savile affair, ib. 2, 5 July 1645, *passim*. As one of the 11 MPs impeached by the Army on 16 June 1647, Stapleton withdrew from the House of Commons and tried to escape to France, but was captured near the French coast. He was taken ill, died and was buried in Calais.

For the main theme of a letter he wrote to Whitelocke and Denzil Holles (q.v.), concerning the French Resident's address to both Houses, see SABRAN, Melchior de; the letter continues: '. . . my Lo[rd] Generals condition requires his freinds being heere, wherfore w[i]thout delay, fayle nott to hasten hyther, where y[o]^u are much wanted, and ernestly expected . . .' 9 Aug. 1644, Long. W.P. ix, 27. This was shortly before the Earl of Essex (q.v.) and his Army were trapped in Cornwall by the Royalists. The letter was countersigned by two other moderates, Sir John Clotworthy (q.v.) and Robert Reynolds (q.v.).

STAPYLTON (STAPLETON), [Robert]. One of Whitelocke's retinue on the Swedish Embassy. There is no indication that he was Robert, second son of Sir Philip Stapleton (above). It seems more likely that he was related to Robert Stapylton, one of Cromwell's favourite Chaplains, see T. Carlyle *Letters and Speeches of Oliver Cromwell* (ed. S.C. Lomas), i, 359–360. Carlyle attributed 'a copious despatch concerning the Battle of Worcester' to this Chaplain; Whitelocke gave the text of the letter (which was addressed to the Speaker of the House of Commons and contained fervent expressions of piety, followed by detailed information), see Add. Ms 37345 fols. 148v.–149 (transcript); printed in *Memorials* iii, 345–346. It seems possible that the letter, signed 'Robert Stapleton', was written not by the Chaplain but by Whitelocke's subsequent Gentleman of Horse in Sweden. It is difficult to explain Stapylton's appointment to this responsible post and, still more, his easy familiarity with Cromwell (which appears below), if he had not had some standing in the Civil War.

When Stapylton was appointed to the retinue, Whitelocke described him as the 'Gent[leman] of Horse . . . an ingenius Civil person, very sober and discreet, a good Scholar, and able to pray and preach well, he had the Latin Tongue very well, and was good at governing those under his Charge and the rest of the Family' (i.e. household), Add. Ms 4995, appendix 5 fol. 11. Stapylton was responsible for having Whitelocke's horses and coaches shipped across the North Sea, in the specially equipped *Adventure*.

This amounted to over 30 horses, including six large black coach horses (plus two in reserve) for the ceremonial coach, which was lined with red velvet, and the same number of bays for the travelling coach, which was lined with blue velvet, *Journal* i, 106; 5 Nov. 1653, *passim*. After a few days' respite in Göteborg (Gothenburg) Stapylton supervised the transport, including the hire of local post-horses, carriages and waggons, for the diagonal journey across Sweden, from Göteborg to Uppsala. Such a journey, undertaken in December, was hard both on men and horses, and no doubt on the laundry-women, of whom we hear little. Riding far ahead of the Ambassador, at first, Stapylton kept him informed of the convoy's progress. The following letter shows his awareness of the need to economize:

... Wee have made a shift to come up thus farre with the goods, that were yesterday left behind at Houva [Hova]; The country men here are in a better forwardnesse, soe that, I suppose, we shall bee fully furnished for to morrow's march without any staying for them. I suppose, we shall reach noe further to morrow night, then Blacksta [Laxå? in fact, they appear to have reached Vretstorp; see below] where I would willingly rest on the Sabbath day, if it be a convenient place, and alsoe convenient for the Countrey people ... Your Excell[en]^{cy} may be pleased to inquire of Mr Barkman [q.v.] concerning it; ... if it could possibly bee, I should desire, that the Countrey men may have notice not to come in to morrow night, but on the Sabbath day at evening; when I would load the goods for an early march on munday ... I shall not bring the carriages to lodge at all in Erburgh [Örebro]; for I well remember, that it is a City, and we must pay almost double the price for our horses from thence then from a Countrey village; soe that in all our marches I shall bee sure to avoid these chargeable City's. I have bin inquiring concerning our next stage ... I understand that it is cal'd Glanshamber [Glanshammar] ... a Swedish mile from Erburgh. There are other city's, which your Excell[en]^{cy} is to lye at the next weeke, I shall endeavour to avoid them ... Your Excell[en]^{cy} may bee pleased to keepe those stages, as they are set downe in the paper given in by the Cindick [the Syndic of Göteborg, Haquinus Lidenius q.v.], and wee shall bee not farre from you ...
Wedestorpe [Vretstorp?]
Dec[em]^{ber} the 9th   Ro[bert] Stapylton
[1653]

Long. W.P. xiv, 227.

By the time Stapylton wrote again, five days later, the Ambassador's carriages had overtaken him, and although he planned to catch up with them, he was frustrated by the country people's refusal to allow their horses to be put at risk. He wrote, with some lack of sympathy:

... though we intreated them, and told them ... we would have paid for any of their horses, that should have miscarried by soe long a journey ... our

intreaties were to noe purpose; soe churlish, and unciville were the countrey people. And there being none of the Governours here to command them, we have bin enforced to make our stay here for this night. And 'tis to be doubted, whether wee shall bee able to remove ... hence to morrow: For I cannot learne that the Countrey have notice to come in with their carriages ... It will now be hard for us to reach Upsale by Satturday night; For I perceive the Countrey hereabouts are more stubborne, then in the places, where we have bin before ... I am sorry that wee are thus backward, wherby your excell[en]$^{cy's}$ servise is retarded ...
Quarna [Rekarne?]
December the 15th
1653

ib. 230.

The following month, Stapylton wrote a long letter to Cromwell, in the confident terms of friendship. The news and comments he sent were interspersed with religious exhortations. He wrote that: 'After a tedious, and most chargeable journey of three weekes ...' they had arrived safely in Uppsala. 'Wee had (considering the time of the yeare) a very fine season for our journey, far beyond expectation ... but our expences were very vast, and ... wee were not ... without ... difficulties and hardshipps.' After describing the great honour shown to the Ambassador on his arrival at the outskirts of Uppsala, Stapylton complained bluntly of a mistake made over the Queen's title in Whitelocke's credentials, and hinted that information was being leaked to the Dutch (with whom England was then at war); the text of this complaint is given in a note to *Diary* 21 Dec. 1653. The letter ends with a plea for more money '... That my Lord Ambassadour, who has undertaken nott onely a chargeable, but a perillous negotiation, for the good of his country, may not thereby impoverish his family', 23 Dec. 1653, *Thurloe S.P.* i, 645–646; original, Ms Rawl. A9, 144.

Whitelocke was well satisfied with Stapylton's service in Sweden, although less pleased when he and the Steward, John Walker (q.v.), caused unpleasantness because the gold chains with the Queen's portrait on a medal, which Christina sent them as a parting gift, were slightly shorter and of less value than the chains she gave to some other gentlemen of the household, *Journal* ii, 201–202; *Diary* 6, 7 May 1654. Despite this, Stapylton was among those who were chosen to preach and pray at the service of thanksgiving for their safe return, held at Whitelocke's house in Chelsea, ib. 5 July 1654. A few months later, Stapylton wrote an elegy to Whitelocke's daughter Frances, who died of smallpox in December 1654; it appears in the collection *Piscatoris Poemata* (1655); he wrote to Whitelocke, perhaps on the same subject, 'w[i]'h as high expressions of respect as could be, yett forgotten afterward', *Diary* 17 Feb. 1654/55; that is the phrase commonly used by Whitelocke for those who preferred not to know him after the Restoration.

STARKEY (STARKIE), [George], MP. Of Windsor, Berks. A Gray's Inn lawyer, and the father of Samuel Starkey, MP (see *Hist. of Parl.*). George Starkey was Steward of the Windsor Castle Court during the 1650s, when Whitelocke was Constable of the Castle; he was elected MP for Windsor in Richard Cromwell's Parliament, and resigned the Stewardship of the Castle to Whitelocke's son William, a few months later, *Diary* 25 June 1659. Some years earlier, he wrote very respectfully to Whitelocke about some property he had been asked to inspect at Swinsley-Payles in the Windsor area, where the tenancy was recovered after the death of a Mr Madeson. He urged Whitelocke not to re-let in a hurry, until he knew the value of the farm, since there was no fear of him not finding a tenant. He referred to coming to see Whitelocke in London, with a bond and the Seal of Windsor Castle, and wrote: 'I know noe reason why you should not make some p[ro]fitt of Crambourne [Cranbourne, west of Windsor Great Park] worth 50^l p[er] an[num] rather then p[er]mitt a straing[e]^r (not coming in by yo[u]^r favour) to goe away w[i]^{t}h it . . .' Writing down the side of the letter, he reported that there were no deer left and the rails (i.e. railings) were down in many places, 15 Oct. 1652, Long. W.P. xii, 171.

STEDMAN, [James?]. *Lincoln's Inn Admissions Register*. Presumably James Stedman of Stratton on the Fosse, north-west of Frome, Somerset, who was admitted to Lincoln's Inn, April 1649. Steward of the Chilton (Wilts.) Court, *Diary* 9 Oct. 1668. Whitelocke met him socially with Sir Seymour Pile (q.v.), and both socially and professionally with Col. Alexander Popham (q.v.) of Littlecote, ib. 28 June 1665; 27 Aug. 1666. At other times, Whitelocke was in touch with Stedman over legal matters affecting himself, ib. 8 May 1666; 2 Sept. 1670.

STEELE, Judge William, MP (*c*.1610–1680). *D.N.B.*; *Alumni Canta-brigienses*; E. Foss *Judges of England* vi, 489–492, in 'Biographical Notices of the Judges in the Interregnum'. He studied at Caius College, Cambridge, and at Gray's Inn. Steele was appointed Attorney-General in 1649; Recorder of London from August 1649; elected MP for the City of London in 1654; he served as Chief Baron of the Exchequer from 1655 to 1658, and as Lord Chancellor of Ireland from 1656 to 1660. He is mentioned four times in *The Diary*, first on 18 Aug. 1649 and finally on 15 Apr. 1670. He took refuge in Holland after the Restoration, but was back in England by 1670, when Whitelocke and Dr. John Owen (q.v.) consulted him about the notes on legal and theological aspects of divorce, which they were asked to prepare for the King, ib. 15 Apr. 1670.

STEWARD (STEWART), [Dr. Richard] (c.1595–1651). *Alumni Oxonienses.* Studied at Magdalen Hall. A Fellow of All Souls in 1613; DCL in 1624. Vicar or Rector successively of four parishes in the south of England, during the 1630s. His career points to his being the Dr Steward, a Royalist, who argued against Presbytery and in favour of Episcopacy at the Uxbridge negotiations, *Diary* 31 Jan. 1644/45.

STONEHOUSE (STONHOUSE), Sir George, Bt., MP, JP (1603–1675). M.K.F.; *Hist. of Parl.*; A. Baker *Historic Abingdon* (1963). Of Radley, near Abingdon, in Berkshire (now Oxfordshire); he married Margaret, daughter of Richard, 1st Lord Lovelace of Hurley, near Henley-on-Thames. Elected MP for Abingdon, in the Short and Long Parliaments of 1640, he was disabled, as a Royalist, in 1644. Elected to the same seat in 1660 and 1661, he served as MP for Abingdon until his death. Urged by Edward Hyde (later 1st Earl of Clarendon q.v.), and encouraged by supporters in Abingdon, Whitelocke had contested the seat when the King's 11 years of personal rule were coming to an end, but he was defeated by Stonehouse, the local Squire and JP who, as shown above, was elected to the Short Parliament. According to Whitelocke's account he, the young lawyer, had the support of the Mayor and Bailiff and most of the leading burgesses, but Stonehouse went for the popular or 'vulgar' vote, using his butcher, brewer, vintner, tailor, shoemaker and others: '. . . above all other arguments, he prevayled by his beefe, bacon & bagge pudding' and by allowing as many voters as chose 'to be drunke att his charge, att the Town Alehouses . . .'; with these inducements he 'convinced their judgements that . . . he was the ablest person to serve as their Burgesse . . .', *Diary* 1639. 1640. fols. 47v., 48.

STONOR family. *V.C.H. Oxfordshire* viii, 142–143, 223, *passim*; R.J. Stonor *Stonor: a Catholic Sanctuary in the Chilterns from the Fifth Century till Today* (R.H. Johns. 1951). Of Stonor Park near Henley-on-Thames, and Watlington Park; they also owned other land in the area. Whitelocke's young neighbour, Francis Stonor (1623–1653), sent him a doe on two occasions, *Diary* 27 Oct. 1648 and (no date) in Nov. 1652, fol. 124. It is assumed that both gifts were sent by the same 'Mʳ Stonor'; a letter referring to the second doe and signed 'Francis Stonor', from Watlington Park, 23 Nov. 1652, is transcribed in Add. Ms 37345 fols. 240–240v. The presents were probably intended as inducements. Whitelocke introduced the letter as coming from 'my great neighbour in Oxfordshire, Mʳ Stonor'; in the diary reference, he observed to his children that it was his custom to refuse gifts if the sender had a case coming up in Court. In fact, a month after the second doe was dispatched, numerous petitioners claimed against the estates of different members of this recusant family, including Francis and his younger brother Thomas (whose father, William Stonor, died in 1651); their mother Elizabeth was the daughter of Sir Thomas Lake (see LAKE, Lancelot, and SABRAN, Melchior de. It is interesting that two women in the staunchly Protestant Lake family married Catholics).

The intense financial pressure on the Stonor family is shown in *Calendar of the Committee for Compounding* pp. 3070–3071, 24 Dec. 1652. On the same day, Francis Stonor arranged to let Stonor, and other properties, for eight years to a fellow Catholic, Sir George Symeon.

STRAFFORD, Thomas Wentworth, MP, 1st E. of (1593–1641). G.E.C.; *D.N.B.*; C.V. Wedgwood *Thomas Wentworth First Earl of Strafford* (Cape paperback. 1964). A brother-in-law, by his second marriage, of Denzil Holles (q.v.). Of the Inner Temple and St. John's College, Cambridge. He sat for Yorkshire in the 'Addled' Parliament of 1614; in subsequent Parliaments, 1620, 1623/24, 1625 and 1627/28, he again represented Yorkshire or, on one occasion, Pontefract. He was imprisoned for refusing to pay the forced loan, in 1627, yet was created Baron Wentworth in 1628, and Earl of Strafford in 1640. He held profitable offices, including those of Lord President of the Council of the North from 1628, Lord Deputy General of Ireland from 1632, and Lord Lieutenant of Ireland in 1640. He was a powerful and ruthless administrator. His impeachment by the House of Commons, early in the Long Parliament, was brought before the Lords in March 1641. In this notorious trial, largely planned by John Pym (q.v.), when it became clear that the impeachment would fail, the dubious, antiquated device of a Bill of Attainder was introduced. The Bill was enacted against a background of wild rumours, violent popular demonstrations against the Earl, and rescue attempts by the Court. Strafford was sent to the block.

Whitelocke claims that at the age of 20, when serving in Charles I's second Parliament, summoned in February 1625/26, he was 'admitted into perticuler acquaintance with [among other distinguished MPs] S[i]ʳ Thomas Wentworth afterwards Earle of Strafford ...', *Diary* 1625.1626. fol. 7. Whitelocke may well have known him outside the Commons at that time, but in fact Wentworth was pricked as Sheriff and so rendered incapable of sitting in that Parliament. Some 15 years later, as an up-and-coming lawyer, Whitelocke was chosen by Pym, John Hampden (q.v.) and others as Chairman of the Select Committee which was to prepare the Articles and manage the evidence for Strafford's impeachment. Whitelocke claims that he tried to resist the appointment and that it was 'a buisnes of great trouble' to him, ib. 1640. 1641. fol. 51, *passim*. Strafford told a friend that whereas John Glyn (q.v.) and John Maynard (q.v.) behaved towards him like advocates, Geffrey Palmer (q.v.) and Whitelocke 'used him like gentlemen', yet without weakening their case against him, *Memorials* i, 124.

STRAFFORD, William Wentworth, 2nd E. of (1626–1695). G.E.C. Son of Thomas Wentworth (above); grandson of the 1st Earl of Clare and a nephew of Denzil Holles (q.v.). After his father's execution and the forfeiture of all the family's titles and honours in May 1641, William Wentworth was created Earl of Strafford by the King, in December 1641. He obtained a pass to leave the country, in November 1642, and spent nine years abroad. His father's Attainder was revoked soon after the Restoration, and William succeeded to his titles. He is only referred to indirectly in *The Diary* when Whitelocke's sister, Elizabeth Mostyn (q.v.), asked her brother to assist the Earl over the matter of a living he had given to her Chaplain, *Diary* 18 June 1658.

STRICKLAND [Walter], MP (c.1598–1670). *D.N.B.*; A. Woolrych *Commonwealth to Protectorate*. Admitted to Gray's Inn, 1642. He was appointed Envoy from the Long Parliament to the Netherlands in 1642, on a salary of £400 a year. Returning to England in 1648, he was sent back to Holland the same year, at a salary of £600 a year. He was recalled in 1650. The following year, he accompanied Oliver St. John (q.v.) on a joint Embassy to Holland to negotiate an alliance or, if possible, a political union. Strickland wrote a long letter to Whitelocke from The Hague, Add. Ms 32093, fols. 276–277. The mission was a total failure. This may explain why, after Whitelocke's successful Embassy to Sweden, Strickland tried to catch him out when they were both appointed Commissioners to treat with the Swedish Ambassador, Christer Bonde (q.v.), *Diary* 13 May 1656.

Strickland had been elected a recruiter MP for Minehead, Somerset, serving in the Long Parliament and Rump from 1646 to 1653; he also served in Barebone's Parliament and on the Council of State; he was elected to the Protectorate Parliaments of 1654 and 1656, sat on the Protector's Council, and was called to Cromwell's Other House in 1658; he was in the restored Parliament of 1659 to 1660. During the 1650s he showed (as Whitelocke did) his humanity and sense of justice in the cases of James Nayler (q.v.) and of Lady Scot (q.v.), despite fierce opposition.

Earlier, when Whitelocke was selecting his large retinue for Sweden, Strickland wrote recommending Samuel Morland (q.v.), who was reputed to be a good scholar and an excellent mathematician, 21 Sept. 1653, Long. W.P. xiii, 217; Whitelocke engaged this distinguished mathematician. Strickland being at that time President of the Council of State, he signed Whitelocke's private instructions for the Swedish Embassy, *Diary* 29 Oct. 1653. Besides indicating how Whitelocke should proceed with the Treaty, and the extent of his powers, Strickland required him to buy a quantity of guns (which he specified), on behalf of the Commonwealth; Whitelocke was to have them shipped to London, charging them to the Commissioners of the Customs or the Treasurer of the Navy, *Journal* i, 89–92 (originals: Long. W.P. xiv, 144, *passim*).

Whitelocke wrote to Strickland from Göteborg, three days after landing there. He described: the stormy crossing; the anxiety of his company, many of whom had been seasick, to go ashore without delay; the Governor's lengthy apology because, as a result of this hasty arrival, the City had not welcomed the Ambassador Extraordinary with as much ceremony as they would have wished. There were no guns to be had in Göteborg but Whitelocke assured Strickland that he would look into this matter when he reached his destination, 18 Nov. 1653, ib. 186–186v. Three days after arriving in Uppsala, he ordered the guns through a Mr. John Clavering, 23 Dec. 1653, ib. 231.

The only other material traced among Whitelocke's papers, consists of Strickland's notes, written in a clumsy and ill-formed hand, about meeting Ambassador Christer Bonde (q.v.), 4, 5 Dec. 1655; ib. xvii, 106.

STROUDE (STRODE), William, MP (*c.*1599–1645). *D.N.B.*; M.F.K. Studied at Exeter College, Oxford, and the Inner Temple. MP for Bere Alston, Devon, North of Plymouth, in all Parliaments from 1624 until his death. He supported Sir John Eliot MP (q.v.) in 1628, rejected the Star Chamber's attempts to judge him for words spoken in Parliament, and suffered imprisonment in the King's Bench prison, the Tower and the Marshalsea; he was released in 1640. The Long Parliament confirmed his assertion that the Star Chamber action was in breach of privilege. His sufferings inflamed him against the King's supporters: as one of Whitelocke's committee which managed the charges and evidence for the impeachment of the 1st Earl of Strafford (q.v.), Stroude even proposed that the Earl should not be allowed counsel to defend him.

SUFFOLK, James Howard, 3rd E. of (1620–1689). G.E.C. Styled Lord Howard of Walden from 1626 until he inherited the Earldom in 1640. He supported Parliament during the Civil War and was appointed a Commissioner from Parliament to the King at Newcastle, in July 1646. He was impeached by the Commons, with six other Peers, in September 1647, but these proceedings were dropped in June 1648. The Commons were approached to offer him the Stewardship of Greenwich, but they refused to act in Whitelocke's absence and without his consent, since he held that office, *Diary* 27 July 1648. Although Whitelocke did not relinquish the Stewardship at that time, the Earl of Suffolk was well disposed towards him, on account of help Whitelocke gave him over the impeachment. For some months after the death of his second wife, Frances, Whitelocke suffered from fever and acute depression. When the crisis of the fever was past, his doctors recommended country air and gentle exercise; at that point, Edward Eltonhead (q.v.) conveyed an invitation to Whitelocke from the Earl of Suffolk to go to his splendid house, Audley End, near Saffron Walden, in Essex. Whitelocke accepted. Although not in residence there, the Earl sent word to his servants to look after his guest, as if he were there himself, ib. 30, 31 Dec. 1649; 3 Jan. 1649/50. Four years later, Whitelocke took the opportunity of helping the Earl's brother, Thomas Howard, in Holland, ib. 3 Sept. 1654. The Earl's letters acknowledging favours and professing faithful friendship to Whitelocke (referred to in ib. 24 Jan. 1656/57), have not been traced.

SUNDERLAND, Elizabeth, Countess of (d. 1654). G.E.C. (entry for Scrope). Third daughter of John Manners, 4th Earl of Rutland, and sister of George, 7th Earl of Rutland (q.v.). She married, before Michaelmas 1609, Emanuel, Lord Scrope, of Bolton Hall, Yorkshire, who was created Earl of Sunderland in 1627. His appointments as Lord Lieutenant of Yorkshire and Lord President of the Council in the North were terminated in 1628, ostensibly on grounds of his 'indisposition', but actually because of corrupt administration. The dismissal was disguised by a payment of £3,000 from the King. In May 1629, just a year before the Earl's death, he quietly made over large estates in Yorkshire, Nottinghamshire and Buckinghamshire, to his four illegitimate children by a servant in his household, Martha Janes (James, Jeanes or Jones, otherwise Sandford, a tailor's daughter); the children did very well for themselves socially, see entry for RIVERS, Thomas Savage, 3rd Earl of; and G.E.C. Scrope p. 551 note d. The Archbishop of York's belated sentence, not on Sunderland but on his 'concubine, Martha James', followed by her submission, was pronounced in 1630, the year of Sunderland's death, Ms Rawl. C. 54 fols. 92–92v. and 177.

The childless Dowager Countess, who appears quite frequently in the early part of *The Diary*, seems to have been singularly unembittered, judging by Whitelocke's account, which makes no mention either of the servant or of the children. Lady Sunderland lived at the New House, Hambleden, in Buckinghamshire, which was part of her marriage settlement. It was a short ride away from Fawley Court and it was at the New House that Whitelocke fell in love with and ᵥ ooed his second wife, Frances Willoughby (q.v. under WHITELOCKE, Hon. Frances, sen.), the Countess's niece, *Diary* 1634.1635. fols. 30–31v., *passim*. During this courtship, the Countess escorted the young couple when they went fishing from a wherry on the Thames, and she joined them for musical evenings at Fawley Court, but she also had the tact to leave them alone together, ib. and Add. Ms 37343 fol. 5v. After Frances Willoughby's uncle, George, Earl of Rutland (q.v.), had descended on Hambleden to break off the match, it fell to the Countess to inform Whitelocke that he was no longer *persona grata*; it was from the Countess's house that Frances left on 9 Nov. 1634, ostensibly to go for a walk with a maidservant and two elderly gentlemen of the household, but in fact to jump into Whitelocke's coach, get married secretly in his private chapel, and escape with him to London for a honeymoon at a tavern in Fleet Street. When the bride's family had recovered from their indignation, the Countess welcomed them back. A few years later, Lady Sunderland addressed a business letter to Whitelocke as her '. . . very loving Nephew'; in it she entreated him, as a favour, to let his servant pay £40 (which she had entrusted to Frances) 'to the Receiver Generall of the Court of Wardes'. She asked for a receipt, adding 'I had sent it up sooner, butt I had not a safe messenger till now, so being sorry your occasions detaines you from us heer, I rest in hast Your affectionate friend . . .', 1638, Add. Ms 37343 fol. 147v. (transcript).

A later receipt for £40, from Sir William Fleetwood (q.v.), Receiver-General of the Court of Wards and Liveries, acknowledges a payment by the Countess for one half year's rent of the lands of Emanuel, late Earl of Sunderland, 12 Jan. 1642/43, Long. W.P. ix, 1. Earlier, Whitelocke signed a bond to the Countess for £400, 23 Apr. 1641, ib. viii, 116. After her death, her executors demanded repayment of a £200 loan, which Whitelocke duly paid, although believing it had been intended as a gift to his late wife Frances, *Diary* 21 Apr. 1655. Later, the Countess's nephew (Whitelocke's brother-in-law), Colonel William Willoughby (q.v.), a beneficiary under the Will, wrote asking Whitelocke to pay £300, owed to the Countess's estate, ib. 5 Nov. 1656. *The Diary* suggests that Whitelocke had been on good terms with the Countess, and the tone of her letter of June 1642, when the country was drifting into Civil War, was very cordial:

Good Nephew, I thanke you for yo[u]ʳ letter & papers, w[hi]ᶜʰ reading, I see mans inventions [unspecified] will never have end, I wish you could have written me word of hopes of agreement betweene the King & the Parliament, for as yett it seemes there is none ... [after referring to better prospects of success for the English in Ireland, she continued] I hope the next good news will bee of ... reconciliation betweene the King & p[ar]liament heere ... & th[a]ᵗ speedily, that y[ou]ʳ wife may have yo[u]ʳ company at Fawley, she was heere upon Friday, & very well but now dares not stirr noe more in a Coach [being pregnant with her seventh child, Hester, born 8 Aug. 1642], I have not beene abro[a]de since my deare sisters death [Frances' mother, the dowager Lady Willoughby of Parham] but now[,] y[ou]ʳ wife being alone[,] I intend to ayre my Coach horses (if Mʳ Emot will give me leave) who like a worthy freind & servant waited upon y[ou]ʳ sister Mosten [Elizabeth Mostyn q.v.] as far as Nettlebed, where he mistooke his way, & so returned to Hambleton ... [Down the margin she wrote mischieviously] we want yo[u]ʳ company to sing Mass Songes if you dare.
20 June 1642, Hambleden [Bucks.].

Long. W.P. viii, 229.

A family tree for the Scropes of Bolton, Yorks., with arms and a genealogical note, are to be found is Mss Rawl. B. 314 fol. 60; B. 82 fols. 79–82v.; B. 278 fol. 216.

The Earl of Sunderland's rather bland Will bequeaths annuities or lump sums, ranging from an annuity of £10 p.a. to legacies of £20 to £200, to servants and to a godson, also to the poor of Hambleden and of Eastbolton, Yorks. The remainder of his goods and chattels was left to his widow. The Will does not name his illegitimate children (or their mother), to whom most of his lands had already been conveyed, but his nameless 'heirs' were to make and receive certain payments. The Countess was appointed executrix of his 'anuncupative' (i.e. nuncupative or oral) Will, dictated on 26 May 1630, four days before he died. It was apparently written up, in the past tense, on 16(?) October 1630. The Will, parts of which are missing, is in the University of York, Borthwick Institute of Historical Research. The dowager Countess's Will states that she wishes to be buried in Langar Church, Nottinghamshire, beside her husband. Her legacies included £200 each to Whitelocke's wife Frances and her sister Elizabeth, and to the Countess's god-daughter Cecilia Whitelocke, with £100 each to other god-children, and various sums of money to servants. The residue (including jewellery) was left, after payment of debts and funeral expenses, to Whitelocke's younger brother-in-law, Colonel William Willoughby (q.v.), P.R.O. Prob. 11/239.

SUSSEX, Thomas Savile, MP, 1st Viscount Savile, and E. of (c.1590–1659). G.E.C. (with useful sources on p. 531 note j, passim); P. Crawford

Denzil Holles (R. Hist. S. 1979) pp. 114–118, *passim.* G.E.C. quotes, in a footnote, a description of the Earl of Sussex by Clarendon (q.v.) as: 'a man of an ambitious and restless nature, of parts and witt enough, but . . . so false that he could never be believed or depended upon.' He had been MP for Yorkshire and for York in 1624 and 1628. The Earl (usually referred to by Whitelocke as 'Lord Savile', but in the first and last entries as 'the L[ord] Savile . . . E[arle] of Sussex') wavered in his allegiance between the King and Parliament. The first diary reference to him occurs when he went out of his way to befriend Whitelocke and Holles, during the negotiations between Parliament's and the King's Commissioners at Oxford, *Diary* Nov. 1644 fol. 68v. Parliament knew enough of Sussex's character to be suspicious when, a few months later, he deserted the King and came to London, where he was examined first by a Committee of the House of Lords, but failed to convince them of his bona fides, ib. 19 Mar. 1644/45; 31 Mar. 1645. In the summer of political rumours, smears and scandals which followed (see SALWEY, Major Richard), Thomas Savile, Earl of Sussex, played his part by accusing Whitelocke and, more powerfully, Denzil Holles (q.v.), of having had secret dealings with King Charles (q.v.) and the Royalists, ib. 2 July 1645, *passim.* These charges and the successful defence put up by the two MPs have been analysed by P. Crawford in 'The Savile Affair', *E.H.R.* 354 (1975) pp. 76–93. Sir William Lewys (q.v.), supporting Whitelocke and Holles in a debate on the supposed scandal, argued that Lord Savile had already changed sides two or three times and that this time he was '. . . sent perhaps as a service for his new honor [he had been created Earl of Sussex at Oxford in May 1644] to cast a bone among them' i.e. in Parliament, *Diary* 2 July 1645. Part of the Earl's motive for including Whitelocke's name in the allegations against Holles, may have been a belief that the best form of defence is attack: Whitelocke had been very active as Chairman of the Committee of both Houses which had investigated, among other matters, Savile's charge that Holles was sending a weekly report of events to Oxford, and was corresponding with Lord Digby. Moreover, a few days before he was himself accused, White-locke had received an Order, signed by Henry Elsynge, sen. (q.v.), to attend, that afternoon, the Committee of Lords and Commoners appointed to examine Lord Savile's business, 26 June 1645, Long. W.P. ix, 41v. White-locke's notes of the Committee's proceedings, earlier that month, touch on the revelations made by James Cranford, and on Savile's reference to Lady Temple (q.v.), and on his refusal to identify the writer of a letter stating that Holles was corresponding with Lord Digby (it was, in fact, Katherine, Dowager Duchess of Buckingham, q.v.), June 1645, ib. 47, *passim.* Further notes concerning meetings of the Committee on 12, 14, 16, 17, 19, 26 and 28 June are written in Willis shorthand, ib. 48–51, 53–58v., 59v.–60.

Following the debates and final rejection of the Earl's allegations, Sussex was imprisoned in the Tower from 1645 to 1646, for Contempt of Parliament in withholding the name of his informant. He compounded for his delinquency and then took the Covenant. Some years later he had the audacity to write humbly and in flattering terms, to ask for Whitelocke's assistance in a Treasury matter, and Whitelocke 'w[i]'hout rancor or revenge did him right & favor ...', *Diary* 29 Nov. 1655.

SUTTON, Lord Robert. Otherwise Robert Sutton, MP, 1st Baron LEXINTON of ARAM, now Laxton and Averham, Notts. (*c*.1594–1668). G.E.C. (under Lexinton); *D.N.B.* and M.F.K. (under Sutton). Elected MP for Nottinghamshire in 1624, and in 1640 both to the Short and Long Parliaments. As a Royalist, he was disabled in December 1643. He contributed extensively to the garrisoning of Newark and was created Baron in November 1645. Impoverished by sequestration, he pleaded inability to pay the decimation tax in 1655, and appealed to the Protector. Perhaps in connection with his financial difficulties, he entreated Whitelocke to recommend him to Lord Broghill (later Earl of Orrery, q.v.) and to others, *Diary* 1 Apr. 1657.

SWINTON, John, MP, 19th Baron (*c*.1621–1679). *D.N.B.* A.Woolrych *Commonwealth to Protectorate*. Lord Swinton of Swinton's title (a Scottish one), is only mentioned indirectly among sources in the *D.N.B.*, but Whitelocke refers to him as 'Lord Swinton'. Swinton and his brothers fought with the Scottish Royalists until 1650 when he, the eldest, transferred his allegiance to Parliament. In consequence, he was sentenced to death (in his absence) by the Scottish Parliament and was excommunicated by the Kirk. Ironically (in view of this) after Parliament's victory at Worcester, he was appointed by the English as a Commissioner for the administration of justice in Scotland, one of his colleagues being William Lockhart (q.v.). He served in Barebone's Parliament and in subsequent Protectorate Parliaments. Cut off (through his excommunication) from the Presbyterians, he joined the Quakers in 1657, and it was in the house of a Quaker that he was arrested on 20 July (*Diary* 21 July), 1660. He was charged with high treason, but escaped with his life.

SWYFT (SWIFT), William (d. 1658). G.E. Aylmer 'Check-List of Central Office-holders'. He was already in Whitelocke's service (as Clerk to the Lords Commissioners of the Great Seal, for the taking of fines etc.), before the Swedish Embassy; besides this, he acted as a 'good intelligencer', sending news of riots in London, *Diary* 27 July 1647. He was chosen as second Secretary for Whitelocke's Embassy, from 1653 to 1654, the first Secretary being Daniel Earle (q.v.). Swyft was, in his master's opinion: '... of as good abilities for that place as any one in England, he spake French well, and wrote and spake good Latin and wrote a singular good hand, he had the faculty to draw up the sence of what was said to him in a most exact Way. He was a faithful, Loving and able Servant', Add. Ms 37346 fols. 30v.–31, also ib. 4995 fol. 11.

In Uppsala, Swyft attended Whitelocke at the first public audience with Queen Christina (q.v.), *Diary* 23 Dec. 1653; on the day before the Treaty of Amity between England and Sweden was signed, Whitelocke sent his son James and both Secretaries to examine and correct the Articles, ib. 27 Apr. 1654; *Journal* ii, same date.

The Swedish experience and his natural ability made Swyft eligible for work with other overseas missions. The year after the Swedish Embassy, he wrote to Whitelocke from Hamburg, where he was in the service of Major Edward Rolt (q.v.), English Envoy to King Charles X of Sweden (q.v.), who was with his Army in Poland. Swyft wrote describing their terrible crossing during which, as he recorded, '... wee were ... forc'd to loose our mainemast[,] foretopmast[,] two of our best Cables and anchors and to throwe severall ... Guns overboard.' They had drifted in a tempestuous wind off the west coast of Freezeland (Friesland, in the Netherlands); early on the Sunday morning the weather had improved, the storm having raged since the Friday night, and with only four sail they had managed to steer their course; at about 6 a.m. they '... made Highlogah Land [the small island of Heligoland] ... where a ship of any considerable burthen hath not binn seene during the memory of any man living ...' They had then embarked 'on a small Hoigh' (or coaster) bound for Hamburg; '... upon the viewe [i.e. inspection] of the Company ... wee found that Severall ... were soarely weather beaten and much bruised and that the Horses and some of our baggage was quite spoyld ... in this sad manner[,] very weary and sick with the Sea[,] wee sett sayle for this Towne.' On arrival, Swyft was sent to see the English Resident, to whom he delivered a message from Whitelocke, introducing Major Rolt; after that, the Envoy and his party were feasted at the Merchant Adventurers' house, and the citizens welcomed them with Rhenish wine. From Hamburg, 14 Aug. 1655, Long. W.P. xvii, 82. The Resident, Richard Bradshaw (q.v.), had entertained Whitelocke and his retinue very handsomely the previous year, on their journey home from Sweden, so Swyft must already have made his acquaintance.

Swyft's next (and last) appointment was with Sir William Lockhart (q.v.), Ambassador Extraordinary to France. He went with the Ambassador to Dieppe and on to Paris, where Whitelocke's son James (q.v.) accompanied Lockhart to the French Court. Whitelocke had, in fact, sent Swyft to look after James, *Diary* 11, 12 May 1656. The question of who was employing him, Whitelocke or Lockhart, is clarified in the correspondence.

Swyft's letters to Whitelocke, reporting events in France, may be read alongside those in the entry for James Whitelocke around the same dates. The background to the early letters was the proposed military pact planned by Cromwell and Mazarin, which culminated in the Treaty of Paris, in March 1656/57. England agreed to send a fleet and 6,000 men to support the French in attacking the Spanish Netherlands; the port of Gravelines was to be captured for France, while the ports of Mardyke and Dunkirk were to be England's prize; (Spain had offered only Calais in return for England's possible support against France). Mardyke fell in October 1657 and, after a siege and the Battle of the Dunes, Dunkirk surrendered in June 1658. The French Army was led by Marshall Turenne, and the English by their Ambassador, Colonel Lockhart.

When James Whitelocke returned to England, *Diary* 7 Jan. 1656/57, Swyft stayed on to serve the Ambassador in France, dying shortly after the capture of Dunkirk. He wrote several interesting letters to Whitelocke between July 1656 and March 1658. The first, which is undated, gives news of the war and finishes with a paragraph about his salary, which makes it clear that he was no longer on Whitelocke's payroll:

> About a fortnight since[,] I writ unto yo[u]ʳ Lo[rdshi]P to acquaint you with Cap\[t] Whitlocks [i.e. James's] going to the French Army. I received a Letter from him yesterday which did importe that hee had binn at the Camp [Valenciennes near Mons, south-west of Brussels, see Colonel James Whitelocke's letters of June & July 1656] with Mareschal Turenne (by whom hee was friendly received) & was retired from thence to Quesnoy, a Guarrison within 2 or 3 Leagues of Valencien, where hee intended to reside for his better Security till the Siege were over. All are in expectation here what will bee the issue of that Siege, the Towne being very strong, ... the defendants very resolute.
>
> The French have (as tis reported) allready lost between 3 & 4000 men before itt. But they (having daily greate Supplyes of men; & Provisions sent into them) abate not in theyr Courages. five or six daies more will put an end to that businesse ... I perceive the Cardinals [i.e. Mazarin's] Answer to the English Negotiations here [in Paris] doth much depend upon the Successe of the Kings Army before that Towne ...
>
> The Court & Cardinal have binn very kind to Coll Lockhart, & to our Nation, having favourably dispatch'd severall Letters on the behalfe of the English Merchants ... for a Reliefe upon theyr several Greivances.
>
> I have nothing more of the publique businesse, ... concerning myselfe I have ... binn now a whole yeare out in the States service, am a twelve month

behind in receiving my Salary from Whitehall, have expended that little all I saved from the place your Lo[rdshi]P^s favour continued to mee in the Chancery, am left poore, still imployed[,] without any encouragement, or advantage. This ... I thought fitt ... to acquaint your Lo[rdshi]P with (having had the honour of being eleaven years your servant, & all the time [receiving] a Subsistence for myselfe & family through your Sole Goodnesse) ... if your Modiation doe not ... prevent itt, I shall even loose the benefitt of what I had reserved [i.e. saved] whilst I was wholly commanded by your Lo[rdshi]P. But this ... I doe unfainedly professe[,] that whither you can prevaile for mee or not[,] I shall never bee wanting in any duty ...

[In a postscript] Pray my Lord bee pleased to escuse this rough[,] ill writt Letter. hast[e] having spoyld both the style & Character wherein I ought to have written ...',

[Paris. July 1656?]

Long. W.P. xvii, 188–188v.

A letter of the same month referred to Ambassador Lockhart and Captain James Whitelocke attending the French Court; Swyft went on:

This summer will showe the English how farr they may trust the Cardinal [Mazarin] who pretends to doe something ... to expresse how much he values the Amity of England.

The French have left their design on Valenchiennes & with itt about 10000 men, & much wealth & Baggage ... [Swyft concluded, ambiguously] The Cardinal expresseth much kindnesse to Coll[onel] Lockhart, to whom hee hath offered greate civilities, would the Coll[onel] accept of them ^{16}/$_{26}$ July 1656. Chaulny [Chaulnes, east of Amiens? or Chauny, north–east of Compiègne?]   Add. Ms 32093 fols. 343–343v.

Twelve days later Swyft wrote: 'Coll[onel] Lockhart still continues his kindnesse unto Capt[ain] Whitlocke & his favours unto mee ...' he referred to his previous letter, which could be collected from Mr Firbancks, in Secretary Thurloe's office, then returned to the previous theme: Lockhart had several times expressed a wish to find

an opportunity wherein hee might testify his affection to you by some good office towards your sonne, Hee pretends [i.e. professes] that both himselfe & the Scottish Nation have binn much oblieged to you formerly for your equall and just endeavours [unspecified] on theyr behalfe ... [This, Lockhart told him, was one among many reasons for his respect.]

In relation to myselfe, hee hath binn pleased to write a Letter to Mr. Secretary [John Thurloe q.v.] whereof the enclosed is the Copy, which if your Lo[rdshi]P shall vouchsafe to second, for a recompence in present money, or for some beneficiall place, something may bee done for the advantage of your poore Servant.

There is nothing of newes ... more then ... that the Duke of Orleans is after 5 years retirement now att Court, where hee hath binn highly welcom'd ... by the King[,] Queene & Cardinal:

I believe his comming . . . hath given an alarum & jealousy . . . to England and other Protestant countries (being a profesd stickler for the Romish, & Gallicane Church, as for the-much-spoke-of-generall Peace). But whosoever considers well the Cardinals Interest will not have any greate reason of Suspecting an Accord betweene France & Spaine, Since not only the Arrears of the Souldiery, but the excessive pillage of the people, & all other inconveniences that have hapned to France during his Ministry will fall heavily upon his shoulders, & if there was nothing more then the dissatisfaction of the nobles that, & a generall peace would ruine him for ever. This the Cardinal being very sensible of[,] hee will bee necessitated to a good Correspondency with our Nation, although itt may bee, much against his will . . .

I had almost forgot one thing which might have . . . given us a jealous [i.e. suspicious] apprehension of the Cardinals proceedings (and turnd my . . . arguments for him out of dores) which is this. Hee lately & privately sent one Mons[ieu]^r de Lyonnes towards Madrid to have spied out the Spanish inclinations to a Generall Peace[.] But hee being returned . . . itt will abate much of our Feares.

I cannot perceive by those persons . . . I have had the hono[u]^r to converse withe . . . that the Cardinal (being a man of a very high Spirit) will ever condiscend to a peace with Spaine unlesse hee bee able to bee Master of his own Conditions . . .

. . . I write imperfectly & confusedly[,] for my present hast[e] . . . made mee express very ill that little I have said . . . [He gave news of James, in a postscript.]

Chaulny, 7 Aug. 1656 (new style)

Long. W.P. xvii, 183–184.

Three months later, he wrote that he would have sent a letter (which he enclosed) sooner, but James's servant had left suddenly, without taking the letter. Swyft had received Whitelocke's letter of 9 Oct. and congratulated him and his wife (Mary) on the happy delivery of another son (John, born 26 Sept. 1656). Swyft wrote that he had received £50 from Lockhart, to see him through his immediate needs, and thanked Whitelocke for approaching Thurloe on his behalf. He interpreted Lockhart's kindness towards himself as being conferred on Whitelocke's account:

God I hope will reward your Charity unto mee. My poore old parents, and the rest of my little household doe continually pray for your prosperity, being sensible that through your Goodnes to mee, they subsist . . .

Paris, 22 Oct. (old style) 1 Nov. (new style) 1656

ib. 209.

In April 1657 Swyft wrote again, enclosing reports from Paris:

. . . I dare not give my poore Intelligence any better name . . . [he sent other pieces of information] concerning the late differences betwixt the French & Dutch. [The Treaty of Paris had been signed, and France was spoiling for a fight] . . . the Dutch vessells being seised on in all ports of this Nation, as allso

all theyr goods & bookes of Accompt. The Dutch Ambassadour desired Audience from the King [the young Louis XIV] & (itt being graunted ...) did declare (the Duke of Anjou, Cardinall [Mazarin] & other Peeres being in presence) that the States [General] had received very unkind usage from the King in the arresting [of] Ships &c ... [He appealed to Louis to halt the action until he heard from the Ambassador's Masters in the States General, who he did not doubt] would call in question any of Theyrs who had acted anything to the disturbance of the Amity betweene this Kingdome & theyr Commonwealth & did wish that his Ma[jes]^{tie} had none about him who did ill advise him as to his ... severe procedure against the Dutch. The King ... replyd that nothing had binn done without his speciall order: & that the Dutch should not putt any affront upon him ... by sea or land ... The Cardinal, the Duke of Anjou, & others likewise answered the Dutch Ambassad[o]^r very sharpely ... [Next day, the Ambassador thought to] mitigate the passions of this Court against his Masters & himselfe by ... applications to the Queene [i.e. the Queen Mother, Anne of Austria, 1601–1666, Regent from 1643 to 1651] ... But shee refused to see him[,]saying that she would have nothing to doe with one *Qui avoit parlé si mal a propos a son Fils.* Soe that there is noe Reconcilement likely ... I am confident the French will labour a difference twixt England & Holland if this difference bee not speedily made up ... [Ambassador Lockhart was calling him to close his packet, so he begged Whitelocke's] pardon for this scrible ...
Paris. ¹⁵/₀₅ Apr. 1657

ib. xviii, 37–36v.

Three days later, acknowledging a letter dated 26 March, Swyft apologized again for his recent letter which he had dispatched in such a hurry that he did not have time to peruse it. Reverting to the Dutch news, it was being said in Paris that:

... the Cardinal never acted soe ... vigorously against the Hollander ... untill the English Ambassad[o]^r came to this Court, and ... will have itt an English designe carryed on by the French ... they expect a second Warr betwixt England and Holland; concludeing that the French (who are not potent in shipping) durst not[,] but upon an English Accompt[,] have provoked the Hollander to a dispute att Sea. And ... will ... further argue that ... if the English intend (as the world begins ... to expecte) to assist the French, this summer, with theyr Fleete[,] the Hollander is likely to growe a Thorne in the English sides[,] Generall Blake being obliged to watch the Spaniard in the Mediterranean Sea, & an other parte of our shipping being as farr off as Jamaica. Soe ... they will have the Dutch to take us ... unawares: the Hollander haveing prepared ... a very greate strength of shipping to sett forth, this Spring ...
[Others believed that the recent seizure of Dutch vessels was intended] to satisfye for the Affront given by the dutch to the French King in theyr takeing two of his ships. And these will ... have itt [i.e. the French fleet] Superio[u]^r to that of the Dutch ... Whither the Dutch are likely to sit still or ingage in a warre with France or England is a Question ... for a better judgement then

myne to determine, however 'tis probable ... that the Dutch (who are a provident and thrifty Generation) will endeavour rather to regaine 3 or 400 ships & theyr Ladding [i.e. cargo] by Treaty rather then, by a Reengagement against England & a warre with France[,] run the hazard of a greater Losse (... especially when they are thought to bee much in debt to theyr owne pocquets)[.] And if soe, England will bee capable (tis sayd as wishd) ... singly or jointly to carry on this Summers Affaires against the Spaniarde [in the Netherlands] without a Dutch interruption.

Thus ... I doe (instead of newes) present you with my thoughts and (what is allmost as much a Trifle) the discourse of the people ...

Since the difference betwixt the French and Dutch[,] My L[or]^d Lockhart hath visited the Dutch Ambassad[o]^r, condoled with him for the present misunderstanding ... and strives by ... civilities and respects to establish in him a Faith of a continuall good Intelligence, & inviolable Amity betwixt us & Holland. But my Lords many Arguments, although ... prudently urged, are noe butter-pills for they will not [go] downe with ... Borrell [William Boreel] (a Greate Stickler for the Orange partye, and a man jealous even of o[u]^r thoughts) who pretends to have binn allready informed that the English have picked up severall Vessells ... & have carryed them to the Downes ... [Swyft had given Whitelocke's letter to the Ambassador and wished that the newly-knighted James Whitelocke had also written to Lockhart (who had presumably recommended him for the honour). As for himself, he was so sensible of Whitelocke's protection, bounty and charity, that no day had passed] for above eleaven yeares wherein I have not had occasion to prayse God for your Goodnesse towards mee...

Paris, $^{18}/_8$ Apr. 1657

ib. 40–41.

Swyft's (apparently) last letter to Whitelocke, records Ambassador Lockhart's audience with the King and Queen in Paris, 17 Mar. 1657/58, ib. 119–120.

Shortly after the capture of Dunkirk, and the handing over of the keys by Louis XIV to Lockhart, Whitelocke received the following letter from the Ambassador:

My Lord
Poore Mr Swift is dead[.] I feare he hath not left his wyfe very rich[.] I have desyred my wyfe to importune your Lo[rdshi]^{pp} in her behalf and I begg she may be favorably heard, I shall entertaine Mrs Swyft in my family till she can be better provyded for, and I hope his high[ness] will extend his charity towards her[,] since her husband died in his service, and tho their [i.e. there] might be abler men then he[,] I am confident their was not a more faithfull even harted man living, I have taken one Mr Cooke in his rowme [i.e. room or place] who is a very ingenios and as I hope honest man, tho I have ever observed that roule [i.e. rule] that my secretary could not doe my Master nor me any Considerable injury tho he showld design it ...

Dunkirk. 6 July (new style) 1658

Ms Rawl. A 59 fol. 250.

Swyft had, in fact, died during the Siege of Dunkirk. Whitelocke had already heard of this from Swyft's mother, who petitioned for the continuation of her pension, *Diary* 7 June 1658; this was followed up, ib. 2, 5 Mar. 1658/59; 2 May 1659. There are numerous entries for Swyft himself between 27 July 1647 and 10 Feb. 1657/58.

SYDENHAM, Sir Edward, Kt. *Shaw's Knights*; *Calendar of the Committee for Compounding, Domestic. 1643–60* p. 1,257. Of Giddy Hall, Essex. Knighted in 1642. Whitelocke helped him, and other Royalists, in connection with his composition for delinquency, *Diary* 18 June 1649.

SYDENHAM, [Thomas], MD (1624–1689). *D.N.B.*; W. Munk *Roll of the Royal College of Physicians*. Born in Winford Eagle, Dorset, north-west of Dorchester. He started his studies at Magdalen Hall, Oxford, in 1642, but these were interrupted by the Civil War, in which he fought for Parliament. He was elected a Fellow of All Souls in 1648, replacing a Royalist. Resuming his studies, having decided to become a doctor, he was awarded an MB in Oxford; many years later he took his MD at Cambridge, in 1676. He had been admitted a Licentiate of the College of Physicans in 1663; he published a number of medical treatises and was highly thought of, both personally and professionally; Sydenham has even been described as 'the father of English medicine'. He consulted Whitelocke about his brother's Will, *Diary* 1 Feb. 1661/62; this was presumably his eldest brother, Colonel William Sydenham (entry below); the Colonel, who was one of Whitelocke's Treasury colleagues, died in July that year, after suffering severe losses at the Restoration. Five brothers, in all, had survived infancy but two of them, Major John and Major Francis Sydenham, died in battle.

SYDENHAM, Col. William, MP (1615–1661). *D.N.B.*; A. Woolrych *Commonwealth to Protectorate*, *passim*; G.E. Aylmer 'Check-list of Central Office-holders'. Eldest brother of Dr. Thomas Sydenham (above). After active service in Parliament's Army, which included the Governorship of Weymouth, Colonel Sydenham was elected an MP for Weymouth and Melcombe Regis in November 1645; he was Governor of the Isle of Wight from 1649 to 1660 (jointly, until 1651, and then on his own), sat in Barebone's Parliament in 1653, represented Dorset County in 1654 and 1656, and served on the Protectorate Council from 1653 to 1659. He was made a Commissioner of the Treasury in August 1654 and Whitelocke joined him, as a fellow Commissioner, in July 1655. They must already have known each other in Parliament, and appear to have been on good terms; Whitelocke compared favourably the atmosphere at the Treasury, where colleagues were courteous, with that in Chancery where he had been conscious of envy and animosity, *Diary* 30 Oct. 1655. Although Sydenham had occasionally been ruthlessly cruel in the Army, as an MP he joined Whitelocke in opposing the excessive punishment that Parliament wished to mete out to James Nayler (q.v.). He was summoned to Cromwell's House of Lords and served on Richard Cromwell's Council, but in April 1659 joined the officers in the Wallingford House group, who planned Richard's downfall. Like Whitelocke, he served with the officers on the Committee of Safety in October 1659, for which they both suffered when the Rump Parliament was restored. Sydenham was expelled from Parliament and lost his regiment, early in 1660. At the Restoration he was incapacitated from ever holding office again, ib. 13 June 1660. He died a year later.

SYDNEY (SIDNEY), Col. Algernon, MP (1622–1683). *D.N.B.*; E. Ludlow *Voyce from the Watch Tower* (ed. A.B. Worden), *passim*. Son of Robert Sydney, 2nd Earl of Leicester, and brother of Philip, the 3rd Earl. He fought in Ireland and at Marston Moor; was appointed Governor of Chichester in 1645, and elected a recruiter Member of the Long Parliament for Cardiff Borough in 1646. Although a staunch Republican, Sydney would have nothing to do with the trial and execution of Charles I, and despite his hostility to the Protectorate, he took no part in republican conspiracies against Cromwell. When, after Richard Cromwell's fall, the Rump Parliament was restored under the Commonwealth, on 7 May 1659, he took his seat again, and a week later was elected to the Council of State. On 9 June he was appointed, with three other Commissioners, to mediate in the Swedish/Danish war. The Copenhagen Peace Treaty, eventually signed on 27 May 1660, was made possible by the death of the warlike Charles X of Sweden (q.v.).

England in May 1660, swamped by Restoration fervour, was no place for an ardent Republican, so Sydney travelled on the Continent, suffering financial hardship as well as attempts on his life by Royalists. He returned from exile in 1677 (two years after Whitelocke's death) and was befriended by, among others, William Penn (q.v.) and John Wildman (q.v.). His republicanism, coupled with his hatred of Roman Catholicism, caused him to be caught up in the Exclusion Crisis of 1678–1681, which aimed at preventing James Duke of York (q.v.) from succeeding to the throne. After the Rye House Plot was uncovered, Sydney was arrested, tried by Judge Jeffreys, sentenced on 26 November and executed on 7 December, 1683. He vainly appealed to Charles II. Strangely, although it was eight years after Whitelocke's death, Sydney's petition, begging to be admitted to the King's presence, is among Whitelocke's papers, Long. W.P. xx, 176. Sydney went to his death with dignity and with no histrionics. He was a man of great ability and relentless integrity.

Whitelocke's references to Sydney are comparatively few in number: the Colonel visited him at Chelsea and tried to persuade him to undertake the Swedish Embassy, which his brother Philip, Viscount Lisle, had already turned down, *Diary* 4 Sept. 1653 and (more revealingly) *Journal* i, 11–12, on the same date. The two men must already have known each other in the Long Parliament. The remaining references concern Sydney's activities as a mediator between the Kings of Sweden and Denmark, *Diary* 5 June, 26 July 1659; 15 Mar. 1659/60. For the background to these negotiations, see G. Davies *Restoration* pp. 203–207 and M. Roberts *Essays in Swedish History* pp. 171–172, *passim*. There was talk of Whitelocke himself going as one of the Commissioners, but he was unwilling to do so, especially since Colonel Sydney and Sir Robert Honywood would expect precedence over him, although he had been Ambassador Extraordinary to Sweden; he '... knew well the over ruling temper and height [i.e. haughtiness] of Col[lonell] Sidney ...' He put forward his old age and infirmity as an excuse for declining, *Diary* 5 June 1659.

The Colonel's long letters from Denmark show that he, for his part, was well disposed and respectful towards Whitelocke. On 20 July 1659 the Commissioners from England joined Mountagu, the 4th Commissioner, who was commanding the English fleet. Eight days later, Sydney wrote to Whitelocke:

> ... The difficultyes that I ... forsee in ... our businesse heare ... make me hartily wish your Lord^s[hi]^P could soe have accomadated your owne affaires ... that ... you might have made this journey, wee shall often want your ... ability and experience, and though wee receave very great helps from Gen[eral] Montaigue [Admiral Edward Mountagu, later 1st E. of Sandwich q.v.], I feare many difficultyes may arise out of which wee shall hardly bee able to extricate our selves...

He reported that they found the English fleet (which had been sent to the Sound by Richard Cromwell), was strong and loyal to the restored Parliament. (There had been some doubts in England as to Mountagu's loyalty, after the collapse of the Protectorate.) Sydney wrote reassuringly of the officers expressing great readiness:

> to pursue the English interest against forrainers or old enimyes at home, and very much to slight any family interest [i.e. Cromwellian or Stuart] that should endeavour to set it self up against that of England [which was once more a Republic] and in all things to behave ... faithfully ... [,] making noe

use of the power ... put into theire hands for any other end then the publike good ... [There would be] an ocasion of trying theire temper to morrowe by offering the newe engagement unto them upon the receipt of theire commissions ...

This referred to their pledge of loyalty to the restored Commonwealth Parliament. Sydney was confident that this would be accepted unanimously. He continued with news that the King of Sweden, Charles X (q.v.), had left Denmark the day before they arrived, to visit his latest conquest and settle its affairs:

> ... it is sayed his health is disturbed, by which his comming hither is retarded, but I doubt that is but a pretence, and that in truth he doth not like the conferences wee have had with the Dutch and French ministers, before we had audience from him, which I confesse is contrary to the ordinary way of ceremony ... [The Dutch, French, English and others were determined that Denmark should not be annexed by Sweden, thus destroying the balance of power in the Baltic. Sydney continued] the tow [i.e. two] Holland fleets having joyned with the Dane, [have] taken in the four thousand men formerly brought from Holland, gathered together above 200 boats and barques of all sorts to transport horse and foot, and ... prepared for a great expedition, ... wee thought [this] might be to the prejudice of the Swede unlesse they weare diverted by us, wee thought it best to use the way of treaty, waving all ceremony, wheareby wee have engaged ... that theire fleet shall not stirre untill wee can prepare ... for the 1st dayes treaty ... Wee have in our letters to the Par^l[iame]^nt and councell sayed all that I knowe of publike businesse and being all most blind with writing, I can adde ... only the assertion of a very great truth, that I am
>   your Lord^s[hi]^ps most humble and
>   obliged servant
> Elsinore   Al. Sydney
> July 28 [1659]
> Newes is common this day that Capt[ain] Cox[,] sent by the King of Sweden into the Belt[,] hath taken four Danish ships[,] sunk and destroyed many barks.

Long. W.P. xix, 66–66v.

Towards the end of the next month he wrote from Copenhagen. He disguised his indignation at the withdrawal (on orders from England) of Mountagu and the fleet; this was in breach of an undertaking given to the Dutch, and it undermined the English Commissioners' position as nego-tiators. (Whitelocke was, by that time, Lord President of the Council and was busy dealing with Booth's royalist rising.) The letter runs:

> The only consolation that I find heare[,] in a businesse full of thorns[,] is to find I am not forgotten by all my freinds in England, and your Lord^s[hi]^ps of the 3 of Aug: gives me a very pleasant assurance, of the continuance of your

... memory of and favour unto me. Wee had somme hopes of a good and speedy conclusion of the treaty ..., if [our] ships had bin kept heare to see it executed according to the agreement at the Hague, and the orders wee receaved from the councell ... in our instructions and [in] tow [i.e. two] letters ... but now that our whole fleet goes away[,] the businesse will I feare be much disturbed, if not overthrowne, the Hollanders will take advantage of our ... breach with them, in that[,] instead of joyning forces with them, in forcing the refusing king unto such conditions as wee should jointly propose[,] wee leave them engaged in a warre with the king of Swede or at liberty to make what ... conditions they please with him for themselves, which certainely may be very great, for he knewe that whilest wee had a force heare, and they [the Dutch] ... could not act without us, wee should ... have bin a balance ... and though wee should be forced to deale roughly with him [Charles X] he could at any time make his peace with us ... by signing the treaty whereas wee retiring[,] he is ... abandoned unto them whoe are likely to make ... use of theire force ... [to] theire owne advantage, and hatred unto him ... [In a confused sentence, Sydney seems to say that the Dutch hatred of the Swedish King, and the fear that he might weather the storm had made them apprehensive that the dispute could continue, unresolved, until the spring; that the English might feel forced, at great expense to themselves, to send him assistance] and though the Hollanders complaine of this[,] I am confident they are hartily glad of it. Your Lord^s[hi]^p may ... ask why I did not hinder this resolution, which I take to be a breach of the publike faith of the Parl[iame]^{nt} ... [It had been agreed at The Hague that the peace negotiations should be backed up by both the Dutch and the English fleets.] I returne this short answeare, that I did all that was possible ..., [and] prevailed soe farre as to change the resolution once[,] as is mentioned in our last dispatch to the councell of the 12 of this moneth ...

In the time spent 'considering and debating', the greater part of the fleet could have been sent home, leaving (as he would have wished) 15 or 16 vessels, but in the end they concluded that the fleet only had enough victuals to carry them home. They could have victualled the ships, locally, at a cost of £1,500 for almost three weeks, plus a month's 'sea provisions' which, on short rations, would have lasted for six weeks, by which time they could have made better provision or received supplies from England or, if so commanded, they would have sent back the remaining ships. But General Mountagu

having only ... power to charge the treasury with mony, and refusing to doe it, though a merchant heare offered to furnish him, and S[i]^r Robert Honniwood and myself offered to engage our selves with him ..., all was broken for that want, which wee ... could not supply without him in a country wheare wee have soe littell credite, thus ... I have only the liberty of declaring my dissent to what was done both publikely and privately ... [He saw danger, too, in] bringing soe great a fleet all together into England without victualls or mony, in a time of soe great disturbances [i.e. the royalist risings] that I doubt it will be hard to provide for them ... [He prayed, ominously, that this course might be less dangerous than he thought.] Wee heare many rumors of partyes rising in England[,] Charles Steward being gone unto them, Coll[onel] Okey [q.v.] ... being killed, Major Gen[eral] Lambert [q.v.] marched out with a small force against a numerous enimy, Chester surprized and many other things, which I hope are all false ... it is very uneasy ... to be ... treating of peace betweene tow [i.e. two] forraine Kings, when I think I might ... be a littell more serviceable at home. Wee are wearied to death with all the tedious and frivolous disputes of theis northerne people about formes and titles in the safe conducts for the Com[missione]^{rs} ... [As to the treaty, they had persuaded Frederick III of Denmark] to declare his minde upon every point ... [before the views of Charles X were known, which would greatly displease] the Imperialists, Polanders, and Austrians ... [the Swedish King could] noe longer deferre declaring himself ... [nor could the Commissioners defer blaming him for] refusing peace ... [Sydney asked Whitelocke to show his letter to Sir Henry Vane (jun. q.v.)] Copenhagen 24 Aug. [1659]

Long. W.P. xix, 74-75v.

Nearly three months later, when England was in turmoil, Sydney wrote:

Since your Lord^s[hi]^{ps} of 28th of Sept. I have receaved noe letter from England but such as have comme ... by chance from persons soe farre from the knowledge of businesse that they did not knowe of the liberty granted unto us by the Parl[iamen]^t and councell to returne home ... [He had to pick up news of what was happening in England, from the Dutch.] I was never more surprized with any thing then the votes and acts of the Parl[iamen]^t upon the petition of the fifth of the last moneth ... [see Diary 5, 12, 13, 21, 22, 26 Oct. 1659, passim, for the friction between the Army and Parliament, leading to the military coup, to the forcible disbanding of Parliament and to the officers setting up the Committee of Safety.] the contents of it [the Army's petition] being soe modest, ... for ought I can see they gave a very faire ... opportunity unto the Parl[iamen]^t of gratifying them and composing their differences ... I cannot imagine what could put them upon soe contrary a course, destructive unto themselves, and dangerous to our Long defended cause ...
Elsinore. 13 Nov. [1659]

Add. Ms 32093 fols. 416-417v.

Sydney's final letter to Whitelocke in the Longleat collection, may well have been written before he knew that Whitelocke had been serving with the officers on the Committee of Safety:

... I write theis few lines ... in great hast[e] while the ships are under saile[,] to tell you that the Swedes having severall times since theire defeat in Funen [Denmark], promised ... to assent unto the conditions agreed at the Hague ... theire Com[missione]^{rs} came unto us the last night with a frivolous desire that wee would goe to Copenhagen, make an overture of a treaty with the

Danes, and agree upon time and place for the meeting of Com[missione]^{rs} ... wee returned answeare[:]

That the Danes having long since declared theire assent to the agreements of the Hague[,] wee did not knowe upon what they could treat untill the King of Sweden did [the] like, and untill that weare done wee did believe the Danes would not treat at all[,] being assured of the assistance of the tow [i.e. two] Commonwealths while the Swed[e]s denied what they had accepted ... [Relying on promises made by the Swedes, the Commissioners had given an undertaking to the Danes] that a declaration should be brought unto them ... [but if they now went to the Danes without it, they would lose credibility and be unable to assist the King of Sweden, as they desired. They excused themselves from going] unlesse what was promised weare performed

Elsinore. 4 Dec. 1659

Long. W.P. xix, 94–94v.

Unlike the old Cromwellians, Sydney was, at heart, sympathetic to the Danes. For two prominent Danish negotiators, see the entries for SEHESTED and ULFELDT.

TALBOT, Col. Thomas. *Restoration* pp. 110–111, *passim*; C.H. Firth & G. Davies *Regimental History of Cromwell's Army*. A Yorkshireman. He served under Fairfax in the Civil War, and was appointed by Cromwell to succeed Colonel Matthew Alured (q.v.), in commanding a Regiment of Foot. Whitelocke refers to 'M^r' Talbot and later to 'Col.' Talbot writing to ask his opinion on 'matters of antiquity' relating to the Talbot family, and on unspecified 'matters of antiquity', *Diary* 1 Feb. 1656/57; 10 May 1657.

TAYLOR, [John]. A Gentleman of the Bedchamber (Gentleman of the second rank) on Whitelocke's Swedish Embassy, Long. 124A fol. 361v. He was capable of leading debates in Latin (for the diversion of members of the retinue) during the long winter evenings in Uppsala, *Diary* 22 Mar. 1653/54, with note. Whitelocke entrusted him with the command of a ship which was to carry a consignment of copper (a gift from Queen Christina, q.v.) and baggage, from Stockholm to London, ib. 26 May 1654.

TAYLOR, [Nathaniel], MP (*c.*1620–1684). *Alumni Cantabrigienses*; G.E. Aylmer 'Check-list of Central Office-holders' and *State's Servants* pp. 88, 371 note 40; A. Woolrych *Commonwealth to Protectorate*. A Lawyer and a friend of Whitelocke's friend, the Independent Minister, George Cokayn (q.v.), whose church he attended. Recorder of Colchester. He sat for Bedford in Barebone's Parliament of 1653 and appears also to have sat in

Cromwell's first Parliament, in 1654; Clerk of the Commonwealth (in Chancery) from 1655–1660; he is mentioned by Whitelocke in that capacity, *Diary* 17 Sept. 1656. He is also assumed to be the Mr. Taylor referred to in ib. 29 Nov. 1659; 2 June 1660.

TAYLOR, Mr.—, of Henley-on-Thames. He appears only once, when he purchased the Phyllis Court woods from Whitelocke's son William (q.v.), *Diary* 5 Dec. 1672.

TEMPLE, [Christian], Lady (d. 1655). *Complete Baronetage*. Wife of Sir Peter Temple, 2nd Bt., MP (1592–1653), of Stowe, Bucks., (see M.F.K.; also *D.N.B.*, entry for Sir Richard Temple, 3rd Bt.). Lady Temple was the step-daughter of Thomas, Lord Savile, Earl of Sussex (q.v.); see *E.H.R.* 354, 1975, P. Crawford 'The Savile Affair' p. 78, including note 3, *passim*. In Savile's attack on Denzil Holles (q.v.) and on Whitelocke, '... the Lady Temple was a great Soll[i]citrix against them'; she also acted as Savile's 'Messenger & Agent'. In the same context, Lord Say & Seale used 'the buisy Lady Temple for his Agent', *Diary* 5, 8, 14 July 1645. Her husband, although an MP, seems to have kept clear of the Savile affair.

TEMPLE, Col. James, MP (*fl.* 1640–1668). *D.N.B.* A regicide. Elected an MP for Bramber, Sussex, south-east of Steyning, in 1645. Cousin of Sir Peter Temple, 2nd Bt., MP (see previous entry). He is mentioned only when he gave himself up, *Diary* 16 June 1660. He escaped with his life, but was imprisoned for some years in the Tower, and later in Jersey.

TEMPLE, Col. Peter, MP (1600–1663). *D.N.B.*; D. Underdown *Pride's Purge* p. 387. A regicide. Of Temple Hall, Leicestershire. An MP for Leicester in 1645. Referred to only after he gave himself up on 12 June (*Diary* 13 June) 1660; he died in the Tower. Temple Hall was confiscated and given by Charles II (q.v.) to his brother James, Duke of York (q.v.).

TEMPLE, Col., later Sir Purbeck, Kt. (*c.*1623–1695). J.G. Nichols (ed.) *Herald and Genealogist* (London. 1866) iii, 542–544; J.A. Temple *Temple Memoirs* (London. 1925) pp. 55–57. Fourth son of Sir Thomas Temple. He served in Parliament's Army as a Captain at Edgehill in 1642, as a Major under Colonel John Fiennes, at the siege of Banbury, in 1644, and was proposed as Governor of Newport Pagnell until denounced by three Captains for showing cowardice at Banbury. The charge was not pursued, but neither was the appointment as Governor. He was, however, appointed Governor of Henley Garrison (Whitelocke's house, Phyllis Court, being the Garrison), *C.J.* 9 Aug. 1645; *Diary* 2 Sept., 9 Nov. 1645. His wife Sarah, née Draper, came from Remenham, Berks., less than two miles from Henley, across the Thames. At some point, he abandoned his allegiance to Parliament. He acquired an estate in Addiscombe, Surrey, was knighted by Charles II in September 1660, and served as one of the Gentlemen of the Privy Chamber.

TEMPLE, Col. T[homas]. Referred to only once, in connection with a legal matter, *Diary* 11 Apr. 1662 with note; this concerned a warrant for his title as a Baronet of Nova Scotia.

THIJSSEN (THYSON) Ankarhielm, Admiral [Martyn] (d. 1659). *Svenska Adelns Ättartavlor*; H. Almquist *Göteborgs Historia* i, 550–551, *passim*. Born in Zeeland, in the Netherlands; Dutch in origin, he was sent to help break the Danish blockade of Gothenburg (Göteborg) in Sweden, 1644. He was given the Swedish title of Ankarhielm in the same year, and appointed Admiral of the Fleet in the cosmopolitan port of Göteborg in 1645, under the Swedish Crown. By 1654, he was serving as Vice-Admiral under Carl Gustaf Wrangel (q.v.). Thijssen (referred to by Whitelocke as Vice-Admiral Thyson) paid a courtesy visit to welcome Whitelocke as Ambassador Extraordinary, when the latter arrived in Göteborg, but when Thijssen started talking about the Anglo/Dutch war (which was still being fought), and 'under valuing the English ... Wh[itelocke] answered him roundly'. Thijssen complained afterwards that the English Ambassador 'had disparaged the Dutch Nation'. In spite of continuing friction, Thijssen (and other local officials) dined with Whitelocke and 'dranke freely of his English beer & wine', *Diary* 15, 24 Nov. 1653; *Journal* i, 139, 162–163, *passim*. The Vice-Admiral lodged a complaint against Captain Welch who had gleefully, if undiplomatically, captured two Dutch ships and brought them, as 'prize', into Göteborg harbour. Thijssen's attempt to have some of the Englishmen imprisoned failed, as the Swedes checked with the Ambassador that they were part of his fleet, and the case was dismissed, *Diary* 27 Nov. 1653; *Journal* i, 167–168, 173–174. By the time Whitelocke and Thijssen met in Stockholm, at the end of the Embassy, the war was over and their encounters were entirely amicable, *Diary* 23, 27 May 1654; *Journal* ii, 297–298, 307.

THOMKINS (TOMKINS), [Nathaniel]. M.F.K. (in the entry for Thomas Tomkins). Clerk of the Queen's Council. John Aubrey states (in *Brief Lives*, entry for Waller) that Thomkins was a 'cosen germane', i.e. brother-in-law, of Edmund Waller (q.v.), with whom he conspired in a royalist plot to seize the City of London. When the plot was discovered, Waller betrayed his associates and Thomkins was hanged for high treason. He is referred to only in passing, *Diary* 1642.1643. fol. 60.

THOMLINSON (TOMLINSON), Col. [Matthew], Kt., MP (1617–1681). *D.N.B.*; A. Woolrych *Commonwealth to Protectorate*; E. Ludlow *Voyce from the Watch Tower*. A prominent soldier in Parliament's Army, he was put in charge of Charles I, from 23 December 1648 until the execution the following month when, at his prisoner's request, Thomlinson accompanied him as far as the entrance to the scaffold; he received a legacy from the King of a gold tooth-pick, in a case. Thomlinson was co-opted as a member of Barebone's Parliament in 1653, and later was nominated to Cromwell's House of Lords. A member of the Irish Council from 1654 to 1657 and in 1659; he and others were arrested in Ireland on suspicion of supporting the Army against Parliament, 13 December 1659, and he was impeached for high treason, *Diary* 19 Jan. 1659/60. Returning to England, however, he took the Engagement not to interfere with the civil government, and the proceedings against him were dropped. He escaped the worst rigours of the Restoration by recalling the favour shown to him by Charles I, and by giving evidence against Colonel Francis Hacker.

THOMOND, Barnabas O'Brien, MP, 5th E. of (c.1590–1657). G.E.C.; J. Lodge *Peerage of Ireland* (Dublin. 1754); *D.N.B.* (These sources offer some conflicting information.) O'Brien studied at Brasenose College, Oxford; was elected MP for Coleraine in 1613; he succeeded his brother as 5th Earl (of the second creation) in 1639; Lord Lieutenant and *Custos Rotulorum* of County Clare from 1640 to 1641. He attempted to remain neutral at the outbreak of the Irish Rebellion; at some point he joined the King at Oxford, but later declared for Parliament. He wrote about 'a great buisnes', which was referred by the Protector to Whitelocke and others, *Diary* 4 Aug. 1655. (Cromwell's first Parliament had been dissolved in January 1654/55, and his second Parliament did not assemble until September 1656.) A few months before his death, the Earl approached Whitelocke on a matter of concern to himself in Parliament, ib. 12 May 1657; the following month his wife Mary (c.1592–1675) née Fermor, widow of the 8th Lord Crichton of Sanquhar, wrote asking Whitelocke to support her husband, ib. 13 June 1657; see also (after his death), *C.J.* vii, 792, 5 Oct. 1659. The Earl's petition was read on 26 June 1657, *C.J.* vii, 576. These petitions probably related to Thomond's earlier appeals for support, in which he claimed: that he had lost £2,000 when he surrendered Bunratty Castle to Parliament's Army; that his Irish estates were in the hands of the rebels, and that he had spent £16,000 on Parliament's behalf. The earlier appeals are briefly referred to in ib. vi, 279, 15 Aug. 1649; 427, 20 June 1650, and 445, 23 July 1650; on that last date, Parliament had voted him £500 towards the Commonwealth's debt to him of £2,812. Whitelocke was appointed to the Committee for Irish Affairs, ib. vii, 427, 23 Sept. 1656.

THOMSON, Lady Elizabeth, née Warner. A grocer's daughter, as was Whitelocke's third wife, Mary. Elizabeth's husband was Sir William Thomson, MP (1614–1681), son of Robert Thomson, sen., of Cheshunt, Herts.; see *Hist. of Parl.* and *Pepys* x for his successful career and interests in the City, both before and after the Restoration. Despite his earlier sympathies, Thomson was knighted by Charles II at The Hague, ¹⁶⁄₂₆ May 1660, *Shaw's Knights.* Lady Thomson visited the Whitelockes at Chilton Lodge, on her journey to and from the Spa at Bath, *Diary* 7 July, 12 Aug. 1673.

THOMSON (Thompson), Col. George, MP (*fl.* 1643–1663). *D.N.B.*; G.E. Aylmer 'Check-list of Central Office-holders'; *Pepys* x. Brother of Major or Colonel Robert Thomson, jun., MP (q.v.), a Navy Commissioner, and of Sir William Thomson, MP (referred to above). The Colonel lost a leg in the Civil War, fighting for Parliament. Despite his handicap, he was elected an MP for Southwark, in about 1645; he served in the Rump and (after Richard Cromwell's fall) in the restored Parliament of May 1659. A Councillor of State from 1651 to 1653 and 1659 to 1660; Admiralty and Navy Commissioner, 1652 to 1653, and again from 1659 to 1660. He was out of Parliament and out of office during the Protectorate. When serving in Parliament again, he kept Ambassador Sir William Lockhart (q.v.) informed of royalist risings and their suppression, *C.S.P. Dom.1659–1660* pp. 88, 113, 136, 158, in letters dated 8, 15, 22, 29, Aug. 1659. In spite of Colonel Thomson's wooden leg, the Council instructed him to raise a regiment of volunteers in the City of London, ib. p. 124, 18 Aug. 1659. The numerous letters addressed to him with the Admiralty Commissioners, suggest that he was an active administrator, ib. *passim.* He was chosen, with others, to direct and order the forces (vetting men who were to receive commissions from the restored Rump), *C.J.* vii, 797, 26 Dec. 1659. After the Restoration, he concerned himself for a time with anti-royalist pursuits. His brother Robert (q.v.) sat on the Committee of Safety.

THOMSON (THOMPSON), John. G.E. Aylmer 'Check-list of Central Office-holders'. Auditor-General, Scotland, from 1653 to about 1658; co-Secretary of State, from February to May 1660. Whitelocke refers to Thomson's joint appointment (above) with John Thurloe (q.v.), *Diary* 27 Feb. 1659/60.

THOMSON, Oliver. A servant of Whitelocke's who sent him information about events in London, *Diary* 25 Aug. 1658.

THOMSON, Col. (?) Robert. *Restoration* p. 158 with note 48; C. Firth *Ludlow's Memoirs* ii, 131 note 1. Brother of Colonel George Thomson (q.v.). A Navy Commissioner; he served on the Committee of Safety, *Diary* 26 Oct. 16 Nov. 1659.

THORNHILL (THORNHULL), Capt. [William]. He and Whitelocke's son William (q.v.), where chosen by the Mayor and Aldermen of Reading to stand as burgesses for Richard Cromwell's Parliament, but the Committee of Privileges reported a double return for Reading, and the House ordered, on 1 February 1658/59, that Henry Nevill (q.v.) and Daniel Blagrave (Blagrove) be returned, *Diary* 4 Jan., 1 Feb. 1658/59; *Return: Members of Parliament* i, 507, note 1.

THORPE, Judge Francis, MP (1595–1665). *D.N.B.*; E. Foss *Judges of England* vi, 492–494; G.E. Aylmer 'Check-list of Central Office-holders'. Of Gray's Inn. Recorder of Beverley, Yorks., from 1623 to 1649, and of Hull, from 1639 to 1648. He attained the rank of Colonel in Parliament's Army. An MP for Richmond, Yorkshire, in 1645; he represented Beverley in Cromwell's first Parliament, 1654, and was elected for Yorkshire, West Riding, in 1656, but was excluded by Cromwell for having shown royalist leanings. In spite of this, he took his place in the restored Rump Parliament of 1659.

Earlier, he had been named as a Commissioner to try Charles I; although he never attended the Court, he afterwards attempted (using considerable invective), to justify Parliament's proceedings which had led to the King's execution. Whitelocke refers to a rumour that Thorpe was to be appointed a Commissioner of the Great Seal, *Diary* 13 Jan. 1648/49; in fact, the Yorkshireman was made a Baron of the Exchequer from 1649 to 1655. He was dismissed from this post 'for disobeying the Prot[ecto]^{rs} command', ib. 9 May 1655, but was reinstated as a Baron of the Exchequer, ib. 18 Jan. 1659/60.

THROCKMORTON (THROGMORTON), [Joseph]. *Pepys* x. Whitelocke's client; presumably the merchant of that name who was at one time in partnership with Whitelocke's relative, Samuel Wilson (q.v.), *Diary* 10 Oct. 1660. A year earlier, Throckmorton had been invited to send two well-manned and well-armed frigates to France, bound for Portugal, '... who, by the way, can make very good purchase both of the Spaniards and Hollanders ...', *C.S.P. Dom.* 1659–1660, p. 136, $^{Aug.\ 22}/_{Sept.\ 1}$ 1659, Paris. (Wilson, a vintner, showed his eagerness to seize opportunities for piracy against enemy or rival fleets.) Throckmorton was knighted in 1661.

THURLOE, John, MP (1616–1668). *D.N.B.*; G.E. Aylmer *State's Servants* pp. 258–260, *passim*; *Thurloe State Papers*. Son of an Essex parson. A mature entrant to Lincoln's Inn, 1646; an office-holder in Chancery, 1648; called to the Bar in 1653. Thurloe had been, for some years, in the service of Oliver St. John (q.v.), through whose recommendation he was appointed one of the Secretaries to Parliament's Commissioners at Uxbridge in January 1644/45. Whitelocke, as one of the Commissioners, would undoubtedly have encountered him there, and probably helped in drafting papers sent by Parliament's Commissioners to those of the King. This might explain Whitelocke having, among his papers, a collection of queries and statements which passed between the secretaries on both sides; those sent by the Royalists are originals, and those from Parliament's secretariat are rough drafts, some of which are initialled by Thurloe, Long. W.P. ix, 196–256v., including some blank folios.

Thurloe attended Oliver St. John and Walter Strickland (q.v.) in 1651, as Secretary, on their ill-fated mission as Ambassadors Extraordinary to the Netherlands. He was Secretary to the Council from 1652 (later styled Secretary of State and given a seat on the Council). Thurloe served as MP for Ely, Cambridgeshire, in Oliver Cromwell's Parliaments of 1654 and 1656, and in Richard Cromwell's brief Parliament of January 1658/59.

The first diary reference to Thurloe appears three years after the Uxbridge negotiations. Thurloe had a post in Chancery, as Clerk of the

Cursitors' fines (i.e. fees), and in that capacity paid Whitelocke his 'divident' or share of the fees, *Diary* 9, 21 June, 13 July, 19 Dec. 1648. Two years later, when Whitelocke was courting Mary Wilson (who became his third wife), he learned that Colonel Charles Fleetwood (q.v.), Major-General Philip Skippon (q.v.) and John Thurloe were among those who had 'given a great commendation' of him to the young widow and advised her to accept him, ib. 12 June 1650.

In the eventful months between November 1653 and May 1654 (when Whitelocke, as Ambassador Extraordinary to Sweden, was out of the country), Thurloe, as Secretary of State, wrote to him every week, the letters taking between 20 and 34 days to reach Uppsala. The originals of nearly all these letters are in Long. W.P. xv. They run from 13 January 1653/54 to 18 May 1654 (except for that of 21 April, of which there is a transcript). The original letters to Whitelocke between 10 November 1653 and 6 January 1653/54 have not been traced but copies exist, starting 10 November 1653, in Long. 124A fol. 40. These are probably the most reliable of the several transcripts, since that manuscript is the original, on-the-spot 'Journal of the Swedish Embassy'.

Whitelocke expressed surprise that Thurloe should have enclosed, in his first letter, 'a character to write Secret things', i.e. a number code, *Diary* 10 Dec. 1653. He might well be amazed, in view of Thurloe's own skill in having enemy correspondence intercepted. For the key to the code see plate 12. No letters or transcripts have been found for the weeks of 24 November, 9 or 16 December. Most of Thurloe's letters to Whitelocke are transcribed in Add. Mss 4991A and 4991B (Whitelocke's later accounts of the Swedish Embassy); these 24 transcripts are, however, neither complete nor entirely accurate; 23 of them are printed (in English) by S. von Bischoffshausen in the appendix to *Die Politik des Protectors Oliver Cromwell in der Auffassung und Thätigkeit seines Ministers des Staatssecretärs John Thurloe* (Innsbruck. 1899). I am grateful to the late Commander Philip Aubrey for bringing this book to my notice.

The following extracts and summaries are chosen to suggest both the tone and the content of the letters. The first one starts:

> ... I am sorry I was not able to serve your Lo[rdshi]PP in your dispatch to Sweden, ... I should have ben glad of all opportunities to manifest the just sence I have of all the many obligac[i]ons your Lo[rdshi]PP hath laid uppon me ...

(none is mentioned in *The Diary*). After referring to the number code which he enclosed (and which Whitelocke used the following month, in a letter to the President of the Council, Long. 124A fol. 365), Thurloe continued with news of peace negotiations between Barebone's Council of

State and the Dutch Deputies; the Dutch were demanding an answer to their queries, but

> ... what resolution the Councell will take ... is very doubtfull being not come yet to any, nor have given on[e] lyne to the Deputies since Newports [i.e. Nieuport, the Dutch diplomat's] last coming ...
> 10 Nov. 1653.
>
> lb. fol. 40.

Later, Thurloe wrote about a murder which was to raise questions of diplomatic immunity:

> Heere hath happened a very strange accident this weeke between some English gentlemen and the Ambassador of Portugall his gentlemen upon the New Exchange ... as they walked togeather[,] uppon an accidentall rustle and words w[hi]^{ch} followed[,] ... they fell to blowes and one Gerrard[,] an Englishman[,] was wounded, but ... the Portuguese had the worst, w[hi]^{ch} to revenge[,] the Ambassadors brother Don Pateleo (who was in the former Scuffle) tooke w[i]th him about 40 of the family [i.e. household] the next night[,] all armed w[i]th swords[,] pistolles and gauntletts ... bringing w[i]th them alsoe Grandees w[i]th ... powder in a granado [grenade?], and as soone as they came into the Exchange drew their swords, and fell upon the next they mett ...
> No date; c. 17 Nov., rec^d 18 Dec. 1653.
>
> lb. fols. 43–43v. (transcript).

The rest of this letter is lost and no other copy has been found. The next letter traced starts:

> ... I hope my 3 former Letters are come safe to hand ... [This was a refrain in several of Thurloe's letters. The treaty with Holland was proceeding] but ... we want [i.e. lack] your helpe to debate w[i]th the Deputies the rights of those Seas, & in p[ar]ticuler that of the fishinge ... very little of moment is agreed ... as farr as I understand it, I doe not see that the Deputies have any greate desire to conclude a peace ... [The letter reported trouble in the Highlands, and new plans for stationing the English Army] in such manner ... that those beginnings may be nipt in the bud ... [Chanut had been sent as French Ambassador to The Hague, where he] made a plausible speech expressinge great desires that the 2 Comonwealths [England and Holland] were [i.e. might be] agreed but it is certaine that his instruc[ti]ons are to hinder the peace, for w[hi]^{ch} he is to move every stone ... Chanut hath Instructions to enter into a League offensive and defensive against England and to include the King of Scotts [Charles II] therein ...
> 2 Dec., rec^d 31 Dec. 1653.
>
> lb. 60v.–61 (transcript).

The most interesting of Thurloe's letters concern the dissolution of Barebone's Parliament, the abrupt take-over by Cromwell as Protector, and the responses (as Thurloe saw them) which followed. The original letter telling of these events has not been found; most of it is transcribed in the on-the-spot version of the 'Journal' but the opening passages are taken from yet another transcript:

> ... The Parlement [Barebone's, whose 164 MPs were selected, not elected] finding their Constitution ... such ... that they could never carry on the affaires of these Nations, the Major part of them [i.e. Cromwell's supporters] did[,] uppon the 12. instant[,] resigne up their powers & authorities to my L[or]ᵈ General, by a writing under their hands. Wheruppon the soldiers & severall members of Parlement, desired his Ex[cellen]ᶜᵉ to take uppon him the governement & protection of these Nations, & presented him with a forme of governement to be observed for the future ... [this extract is taken from Add. Ms 37346 fol. 173v.–174v., an edited version of the full letter. On 16 Dec. 1653, Cromwell] was accompanied to Westm[inste]ʳ Hall w[i]ᵗʰ the 2 Commission[e]ʳˢ of the Seale[,] the Judges[,] the Lord Mayor and Aldermen, the officers of the Army & very many other gentlemen of quality, and the forme of the Gov[e]ʳnem[en]ᵗ ... beinge publiquely read in Chancery, he tooke an Oath w[hi]ᶜʰ was administered by the Lorde Commission[e]ʳˢ of the Greate Seale ... [the Seal and the Lord Mayor's sword were formally delivered to him, and when he had handed them back, the officials proceeded to Whitehall by coach and] waited uppon him ... into the Banckettinghouse, where was a sermon, and soe w[i]ᵗʰ many great Acclamac[i]ons the Ceremony ceases; This change[,] though somwhat varying from that w[hi]ᶜʰ seemed to be the former intensions of the State, ... hath a very generall acceptance, especially amongst the Lawyers[,] the Ministry and the me[r]chants, who conceived themselves most in danger from the temper of the Last Parlam[en]t [notably from its fanatical Fifth Monarchy Men], who seemed to be resolved to take away all the Law ... the mayntenance of the Ministry ..., & to make warr w[i]ᵗʰ all the World[,] w[hi]ᶜʰ would have broken all the mᵉ[r]chants ... sober Christians were afraide of impositions upon their Consciences and every body of having arbitrary power sett up over their estates to the destruction of all their liberties, ... therefore ... the Souldiery were resolved to breake through all formes of govᵉ[r]nem[en]ᵗ ... [rather] then ... loose the substance, ... the people [are] ready to Comply w[i]ᵗʰ them therein. Only some of the old last Members [republicans] being discontented endeavored to dissaffect some of the people, who are apt to be led into actions of zeale w[i]ᵗʰout knowledge ... Mʳ Feake [Christopher, a leading 5th Monarchy Man] whome your Lor[dshi]ᵖ left preaching ag[ains]ᵗ the Last Parlam[en]ᵗ[,] hath now turned his Cannon against the p[r]ᵉsent govᵉ[r]nem[en]ᵗ ... w[i]ᵗʰ Mʳ Vavasor Powell [Welsh preacher and 5th Monarchy Man, formerly a supporter of Barebone's Parliament] who both prophecie the downfall thereof in a very short tyme ... [The new Council had intervened, and both preachers had been committed to the Serjeant-at-Arms and were being examined] but I Conceave they wilbe sett at liberty againe uppon promise of being more moderate for the future ... & ceasing to meddle w[i]ᵗʰ ... affairs of State, w[hi]ᶜʰ they understood not, Mʳ Cokayne [q.v.] hath alsoe ben to blayme in these things, but nothing is yet said unto

him ... [Thurloe considered it] a very ill Juncture of affaires for this State to make a peace w[i]^th the Low Countries, espetially seeinge that the Deputies have a very great apprehension [i.e. opinion] of our disorder at home, as likewise of the Enemies power in Scotland[,] though they are very much mistaken in both ... rest assured that [in] the affaires of Scotland it is rather a stealing & robbing buisines on their p[ar]^te then a warr ...

23 Dec. 1653, rec^d 13 Jan. 1653/54.

Long. 124A fols. 72–73.

Another incomplete transcript of this letter appears in Add. Ms 4991A fols. 125v.–126v.; see also *Journal* i, 313–318, for Christina's response to the news.

Six days later, Thurloe wrote again, mainly about the proposed Anglo/Dutch Treaty, disagreement over sovereignty of the seas, and Holland's wish to include Denmark in the Treaty, '... It will be seen by Monday whither there will be a conclusion or an utter breaking of[f].' He recorded: 'Harrison [Major-General Thomas, q.v., a 5th Monarchy Man] is putt from his commaund ... Feake & Powell [see previous letter] are sett att liberty ...', 29 Dec. 1653, rec^d 26 Jan. 1653/54 (transcript), Add. Ms. 37346 fols. 225v.–226.

Thurloe started his next communication with the hope that the letters he had sent to Whitelocke every week had arrived safely. The Dutch deputies had gone home to consult their superiors. With the partisan smugness common during negotiations, Thurloe wrote that the English were satisfied that they had done all in their power to reach a settlement: '... so ... in case the Treaty make not peace, it will have the good effect of making everybody unanimous in the Warre ...' Having intercepted the diplomatic mail of Coenraad van Beuningen (q.v., Netherlands Ambassador to Sweden, and Whitelocke's enemy in Uppsala), Thurloe summarized the Dutchman's report to his masters, 6 Jan. 1653/54, Add. Ms 4991A fols. 157v.–159 (transcript).

The next extracts are taken from Thurloe's original letters:

... My Lord Protector spends much of his tyme in setlinge the Courts of Justice, w[hi]^ch he intends to fill w[i]^th the best and most Learned men, he can finde in England, w[hi]^ch every body rejoyceth in, ... satisfied that they shall now be governed noe more by arbitrarye Com[m]ittees, but by the Lawes of the Land. The Governem[en]^t hath acceptance beyond what was expected, Engagements are every day sent unto his Highnesse from the Souldi[er]^s both in the field & in Garrison, as alsoe from the Fleet, that they will live, and dye in the maintenance of it, & severall of the Congregationall churches have beene w[i]^th hym, to expresse their satisfaction ...; both the universities have likewise sent their Orators to congratulate; Mr Powell[,] Mr Feake (I will not mention Mr Cockayne) [see earlier letters] w[i]^th some few ... follow[e]^rs expressed discontent, but their numbers are very inconsiderable, & their

creditt & esteeme light ... my Lord [Protector] chooses patience towards
them, rather then severitie, & they begin already to be wearye of their owne
excesses ... [The letter gives extensive news of Dutch and Scottish affairs.]
13 Jan., rec^d 9 Feb. 1653/54.

Long. W.P. xv, 6–6v.

In his next letter, Thurloe welcomed the first letter Whitelocke had written
to him from Uppsala, dated 22 December. He prayed that the Ambassador
might accomplish his task and return home with honour, but '... The
Dutch are very confident of the Contrary ...' He knew this from letters
intercepted by his agents in the previous two or three weeks. He believed
that the new powers and credentials sent to Whitelocke in the Protector's
name would be of no disadvantage to the Embassy:

> ... the Governement beinge setled upon a surer foundation then formerlye,
> & noe question will be a better Invitation to the Queene to make an Alliance
> ... then the Incertenities your Excellency left us in[,] upon your departure
> ...; Every body here lookes towards a Settlement, and are glad to be quiet
> ... [Every day, men holding command in civil or in military matters pledged
> their support. The Protector's] Cheife Care is to settle the Courts of Justice,
> beinge resolved to put noe body in there, but persons of Learneinge &
> reputation ... [This was made easier since] the Judges have declared their
> patents to bee all voyed upon this alteration ... yet his Highnes findes very
> great difficultie to finde fit persons ... [The Great Seal remained as it had
> been when Whitelocke left England] the breaches wilbe repayred, & the
> people governed by the good old Lawes, and all arbitrarines in Governement
> layd aside, w[hi]^ch I confesse I never lookt for in this nation againe. His
> highnes takes the like Care of the ministrye, providinge equally for its
> Reformation, as for its establishment. Soe that the hearts of manye w[hi]^ch
> were saddend revive againe ... [Thurloe described aspects of foreign policy
> and trade, reporting that] the orange partie [in the Netherlands] are much
> greived at the likeliehood there is of a peace, & will use their utmost
> Endeavours to hinder it ... [Cromwell had told the Dutch deputies, on their
> departure,] that he tooke the Treatie to be quite broken of[f] ... [England
> now had 60 or 70 ships at sea and hoped soon to have 100; the Dutch, too,
> were preparing for war but had no warships at sea] nor dare come into the
> Chanel w[i]^th any merchants ships but by stealth, soe perfectly is this state
> masters & Lords of the narrow seas ... [Because there had been a strong
> probability that peace would be declared between the English Commonwealth
> and the United Provinces,] the french Kinge hath made very many
> applications to his Highnes, and offers of very great Consequence ... [and
> the French Ambassador was] pressinge very hard for us to enter into a
> Treatie ... Yesterday, the Com[missione]^rs ... of his Highnes met ... the
> Ambassadour of the Kinge of Spayne, & entred into a treatie w[i]^th hym
> upon the Articles of peace formerlye propounded to hym by the [Barebone's]
> Councell of State, ... [he] is exceedinge desirous to come to a conclusion ...
> [The Portuguese Ambassador continued to solicit on behalf of his brother

PLATE 9

Archbishop William Juxon.

PLATE 10

Archbishop Gilbert Sheldon.

PLATE 11

John Thurloe, by Thomas Simon. Gold Portrait medallion.

PLATE 12

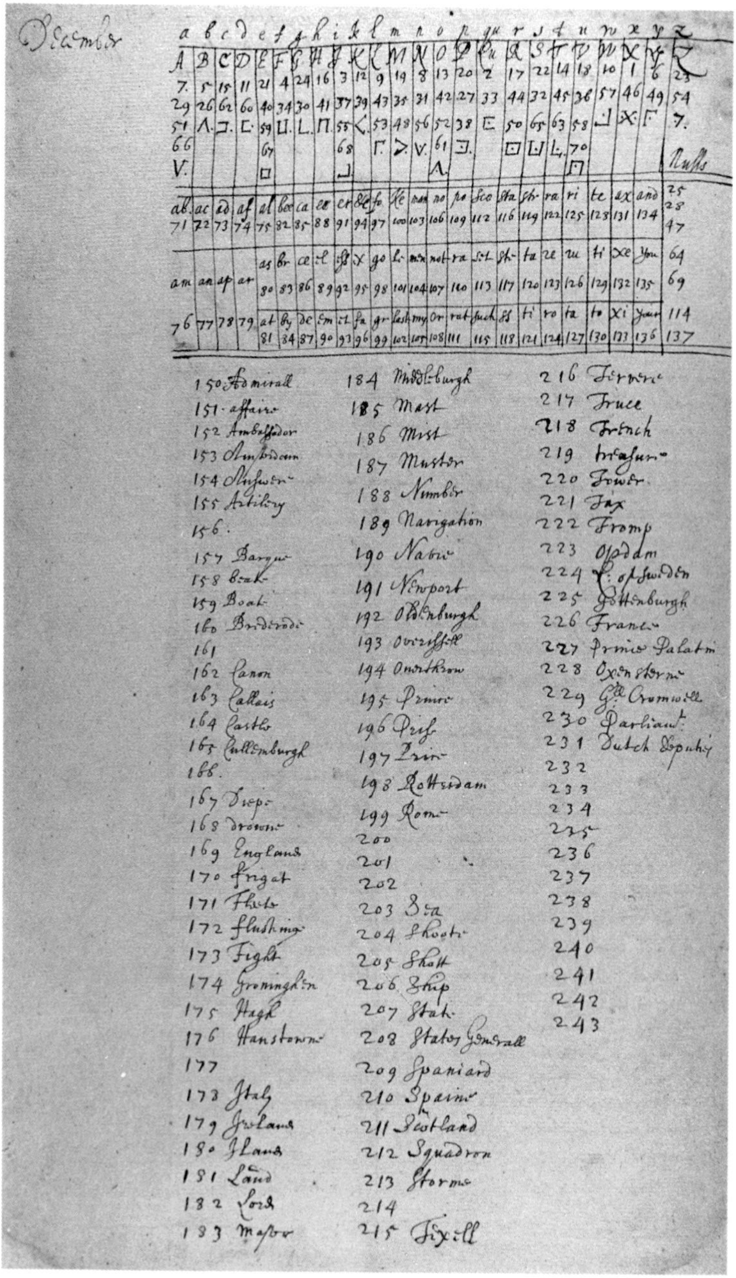

Decembr

	a	b	c	d	e	f	g	h	i	k	l	m	n	o	p	qu	r	s	t	u	w	x	y	z
	A	B	C	D	E	F	G	H	I	K	L	M	N	O	P	Qu	R	S	T	V	W	X	Y	Z
	7.	5	15	11	21	4	24	16	3	12	9	19	8	13	20	2	17	22	14	18	10	1	6	23
	29	26	62	60	40	34	30	41	37	39	43	35	31	42	27	33	44	32	45	36	57	46	49	54
	51	Λ.	⊐.	⊏.	59	⊔.	L.	Π.	55	<.	53	48	56	52	38	⊏	50	65	63	58	┘	X	Γ	7.
	66				67				68		Γ.	>.	V.	61	⊐.		⊡	⊔	L.	70				Nulls
	V.				□				┘					Λ.						Π				

ab. 71	ac 72	ad 73	af 74	al 75	be 82	ca 85	ee 88	er 91	&c 94	fo 97	he 100	man 103	no 106	po 109	sco 112	sta 116	sh 119	ra 122	ri 125	te 128	ax 131	and 134	25 28 47
am	an	ap	ar	as 80	br 83	ce 86	el 89	iss 92	x 95	go 98	li 101	mix 104	not 107	ra 110	sit 113	sh 117	ta 120	re 123	in 126	ti 129	xe 132	you 135	64 69
76	77	78	79	at 81	by 84	de 87	em 90	it 93	fa 96	gr 99	lash 102	my 105	or 108	rat 111	such 115	ss 118	ti 121	ro 124	ta 127	to 130	xi 133	your 136	114 137

150 Admirall
151 affaire
152 Ambassador
153 Amsterdam
154 Answer
155 Artillery
156.
157 Barque
158 Beat
159 Boat
160 Brederode
161
162 Canon
163 Callais
164 Castle
165 Cullemburgh
166.
167 Diepe
168 drowne
169 England
170 frigat
171 Fleete
172 flushing
173 Fight
174 Groninghen
175 Hagh
176 Hanstowne
177
178 Italy
179 Ireland
180 Iland
181 Land
182 Lord
183 Master
184 Middleburgh
185 Mast
186 Mist
187 Muster
188 Number
189 Navigation
190 Navie
191 Newport
192 Oldenburgh
193 Overyssell
194 Overthrow
195 Prince
196 Prise
197 [illegible]
198 Rotterdam
199 Rome
200
201
202
203 Sea
204 Shoote
205 Shott
206 Ship
207 State
208 States Generall
209 Spaniard
210 Spaine
211 Scotland
212 Squadron
213 Storme
214
215 Texell
216 Terveere
217 Truce
218 Trench
219 treasure
220 Tower
221 Tax
222 Tromp
223 Opdam
224 K: of Sweden
225 Gottenburgh
226 France
227 Prince Palatin
228 Oxenstierne
229 Gen: Cromwell
230 Parliament
231 Dutch Deputies
232
233
234
235
236
237
238
239
240
241
242
243

Key to John Thurloe's number code.

who was still in prison, having escaped and been recaptured, see Thurloe's letter of about 17 Nov. 1653. The Judges advised that in the case of murder, even though committed by an Ambassador's brother, the culprit must] be tryed by the lawe of the land ... [and] could have noe priviledge ... [nevertheless,] the Ambassad[o]^r is very importun[at]e ...

The Protector had, that week, been congratulated by all the foreign Ministers, with the exception of the Swedish Commissary, Benjamin Bonnel (q.v.). Papers of intelligence from France and Flanders were enclosed. The letter finished with news of events in Scotland and an assurance to Whitelocke that, in sending him to Sweden, there was no intention that he should bear the cost himself, 21 Jan., rec^d 16 Feb. 1653/54, ib. 27–29.

The next week Thurloe acknowledged Whitelocke's letters of 30 Dec. to Cromwell, to the 'late parlament' (Barebone's) and to their Council of State. 'I perceive you have to doe w[i]th a wise woman [Queen Christina] ... wise persons in any buissines sooner understand one another then others of lesse understanding, and knowledge in affaires.' The letter gave detailed news of the Dutch (with whom Thurloe had no doubt there would be peace), and of Denmark and France. At home, only (Christopher) Feake and John Sympson had been imprisoned 'for preachinge soe insolently against the Government ...' these were men who 'curse when all else blesse ...' Thurloe prayed for Whitelocke's safe return from his 'great[,] difficult, & tedious ymployment ...' at which no-one would rejoice more than himself. After signing, he wrote: 'I am almost tyrd, & ... begg yo[u]^r ... pardon for this confused letter', 27 Jan., rec^d 26 Feb. 1653/54, ib. 31–32.

The next week's letter acknowledged Whitelocke's letter of 4 January, from which Thurloe perceived that the Queen was waiting for advice from her Chancellor (Axel Oxenstierna, q.v.), before proceeding with the Anglo/Swedish Treaty:

> ... if any credit be to be given to the [report of the] 17.40.32.3.11.21.8.14.13. 4.208.10.37.45.41. [code for: Resident of States General with] the 224 [Q: of Sweden]; The 224 [Q: of Sweden] will make but an ordinary 75.9.6.7.8.15.21. [alyance] and is fixed upon her Neutralitie ... [He wrote, obscurely,] ... although the 224 [Q: of Sweden] speakes of the 22.13.18.31.11. [Sound] as that w[hi]^{ch} 22.16.21.57.37.9.7.22.32.3.65.14 [she wil (sic) assist] to open[,] I suppose her ... Intentions will scarce lye that way, if they doe your Excellencye will have opportunitie to 22.21.40. [see] the 5.13.14.14.42.19. [bottom i.e. reality] and may 22.21.56.11 [send] them hither, for further Consideration ...

(Earlier, Christina had enquired of Whitelocke whether England would help her to free the Sound – the entrance to the Baltic – from the Danish and Dutch stranglehold on trade, *Journal* i, 258–260, 29 Dec. 1653; the next day, Whitelocke had recorded that he reported this, in code, to the Council, ib. 264; the Queen had raised the matter again on 5 Jan. 1653/54, ib. 288–290.) The rest of Thurloe's letter dealt with the usual topics; he believed that England's proposed Treaty with Sweden would not conflict with a peace Treaty between England and the Netherlands, 4 Feb. 1653/54, Long. W.P. xv, 39–39v.

For some reason, the next letter was written in far-from-classical Latin. It acknowledged a letter of 13 January, which caused Thurloe to refer to 'the uncommon friendship I have always experienced from Your Excellency'. He described in detail the event of the week: the City's great banquet, held at Grocers' Hall, in honour of the Protector. It was presented in royal style, and with tight security. Translated, the letter records that the Protector

> ... rode in a coach to Temple Bar. Besides his own coach he was attended by 30 coaches, 14 or 15 of them drawn by six horses each. In addition, there were 200 mounted men, for the most part in splendid attire, and private persons of high birth ... the chief Officers of State and the ... Life-guard. The Lord Mayor and City Council met him at Temple Bar and there he mounted his horse and rode through the centre of the City to Grocers' Hall, where he was welcomed by the Lord Mayor. The Lord Mayor ... went before him, with head uncovered, bearing the sword. On either side where he passed, all was shut and barred and in front of the closed doors stood, in ranks, the Common Council and members of the Livery Companies, wearing their robes. So great was the concourse of people, both in the street and at the windows, that the like had scarcely ever been seen. Yet everywhere the utmost peace and quiet prevailed.

To put it another way, there was 'not a single cheer', C. Hill *God's Englishman* (Pelican. 1972) p. 140. John Evelyn was horrified that, contrary to 'all custom and decency', the usurper feasted on Ash Wednesday, *Diary of John Evelyn* 8 Feb. 1654. Undeterred by such thoughts, Thurloe continued:

> By order of the City Council, apprentices [known for organizing hostile demonstrations], and servants, were all given a holiday in honour of the solemn ceremony, all places of business were closed and though no keepers of the peace were posted, there was not the least disorder anywhere. Indeed, never before has the City been disposed to a more perfect obedience. And it is worthy of note that all parties concurred in this ... without any doubt this will exercise a powerful influence on the whole nation ...

As usual, Thurloe went on to give an account of the Dutch negotiations, and of the situation in France, where '... the Cardinal [Mazarin, q.v.] is displeased'. He believed that Holland was exceedingly unwilling to make peace and was not acting in the matter with any firm purpose; but the Cardinal (Mazarin) had decided to send a high ranking envoy as soon as possible. The Scots were withdrawing to the Highlands, 'broken in spirit'. A postscript recorded that the Lord Mayor of London was knighted by the Protector, also that England was prepared for war with a fleet of 100 ships at sea, 10 Feb., rec^d 2 Mar. (with the letter of 4 Feb.) 1653/54, Long. W.P. xv, 50–50v. (Latin).

Six days later, Thurloe acknowledged Whitelocke's letter of 20 Jan., in which he had complained that Swedish ships were still being held by the English prize office; even a ship with the Queen's pass, carrying 'bales of goods of the Queenes & ... one of her wardrobe'; these vessels should have been restored before Whitelocke left England; he had asked Thurloe to be 'instant with the Councell in this buisnes' since 'both the honnour of my Nation & the successe of their buisnes heere is concerned ...', 20 Jan. 1653/54, Ms Rawl. A. X fols. 312–318. In his reply Thurloe assured the Ambassador:

> ... a due care wilbe taken of that buissines, aswell for Justice sake, as that your present buissines be not hindred ... [The two professionals understood each other's problems in dealing with their masters' ineptitudes. The letter went on] it is taken for granted that a peace wilbe concluded ... that Holland fully intends it; & will breake through all difficulties to effect it ... [England had] about 100 sayles of good Ships of Warre at sea, & ... [the Dutch] have not any Fleet out as yet ... they goe on to build the 30 new ships w[hi]^{ch} they order[e]d to be built some tyme since ... which gives w[i]^{t}h other thinges great grounds of Jealousie. Thinges heere ... continue very peaceable ... & satisfaction dayly growes amongst them who were most dissatisfied ... [If Whitelocke had heard rumours that the Protector had not been proclaimed in Ireland, they were false.] He hath beene proclaymed all over that dominion ... [News from Scotland showed] the badnes of the Enemies condition.

A postscript reported that K.C. (or possibly R.C.), i.e. Charles II in exile, had left Paris for Cullen (Cologne); also that the Council had ordered an additional £1,500 to be paid to Whitelocke. Finally, Thurloe enclosed a letter (or perhaps a copy of one) sent by Ambassador Beuningen (q.v.) from Uppsala, to his masters, the States General, 16 Feb., rec^d 15 Mar. 1653/54, Long. W.P. xv, 54–55v.

The next two letters are printed in *Thurloe S.P.*, ii, 113, 135–136. The originals are in Long. W.P. xv, 57–57v., dated 24 Feb., rec^d 23 Mar. 1653/54 and ib. 74–74v., of 3 Mar., rec^d 30 Mar. 1654 (this last arrived on the same day as the next letter). In a postscript to the letter of 3 March Thurloe wrote that he had not failed to write every week, and he hoped that all his letters had arrived safely.

Thurloe had little of interest to report in his next letter: the Dutch negotiators were objecting to an Article in the (draft) Treaty '. . . although it was fully agreed at their last being heere, but surely they will not think fitt long to insist upon it . . .' In spite of peace being so near, both Commonwealths 'prepare their Fleetes as if the Warre were to continue.' After giving other news from abroad, Thurloe observed, once again, that he had written every week but that Whitelocke made no mention, in his last two letters, of receiving any of these letters, 10 Mar. 1653/54, rec^d 30 Mar. 1654, ib. 80–80v. Thurloe enclosed the Council's reply to Benjamin Bonnel (q.v.), the Swedish Resident, who had objected to the continued detention of several Swedish ships and their cargo, captured at sea. The Council had declared as far back as 1 April 1653 that, to avoid the obstruction to trade, all ships truly belonging to Queen Christina, or her Swedish subjects, should carry certificates from the Queen or from a Chief Magistrate. Although 'a forme of passport & Certificate' to prevent 'frauds & collusion' was to have been prepared within the three months that the Order was in force, nothing had yet been agreed, but since it was not the intention that Swedish ships should suffer, Cromwell was renewing the earlier Declaration. He had also ordered the Judges in the Admiralty Court to discharge immediately any Swedish ships that were brought in, provided there was no 'fraud or deceit' in their documentation, 10 Mar. 1653/54, rec^d 30 Mar. 1654, ib. 82–82v.

The remaining letters contain less interesting news than the early ones: 'It is wonder[e]d here, what the Queenes [Christina's] desyne is, in offeringe to lay downe her Governement[.] I have heard of it, these three months past, but did not beleeve it to be in earnest till now . . .' Thurloe ended apologetically: 'It is near midnight, & I am extreame weary . . .', 15 Mar. 1653/54, rec^d 6 Apr. 1654, ib. 88–88v.

The next letter recorded: '. . . This day we have had a fast for the great drought. my lady [Mary Whitelocke] was here w[i]th me yesterday, to hasten yo[u]^r returne, wherein I shoulde be glad to be instrumentall . . .' A postscript in the margin told Whitelocke that there was no truth in a letter to the Protector from Uppsala (presumably from one of the Embassy staff), implying that Whitelocke had been removed from his post as a Keeper of the Great Seal. Cromwell had asked Thurloe to assure Whitelocke 'that there are noe such intentions, but much the contrary . . .', 24 Mar. 1653/54, rec^d 13 Apr. 1654, ib. 97.

A week later, Thurloe wrote that England had neither been beaten nor frightened into the impending Peace Treaty, to be signed on the following Monday, 31 Mar., rec^d 21 Apr. 1654, ib. 104–105; *Journal* ii, 141–143.

By the next post came the long-awaited news, which had delayed the signing of the Anglo-Swedish Treaty: 'the dutch Treatye . . . is fully concluded . . .' On the domestic front, Cromwell being 'very much resolved upon a solid & good reformation of the lawe ...' had entrusted this to various distinguished lawyers, 'to give the learned gentlemen of the robe [i.e. lawyers] the hono[u]^r of reforminge their owne profession ...', 7 Apr., rec^d 4 May 1654, ib. 117–117v.

The next letter told Whitelocke that when he had brought his negotiations to a conclusion, and if no further problems arose, he would be 'at libertie to returne home ... w[hi]^{ch} I can assure y[ou]^r execll[en]^{cy} yo[u]^r friends and Serv[an]^{ts} very much long for ...' Thurloe hoped the Treaty would be concluded before the Coronation of Charles X of Sweden, as that would cause further delay '... but in truth wee cannot beleive (not w[i]thstandinge all that is sayd) that her Ma[jes]tie will quit her Crowne, beinge soe well qualified in all respects to governe as shee is, and seems to be very well accepted of her people ...' He reaffirmed that at home: 'satisfaction in the Govern[men]^t encreaseth dayly ...' Congratulations were coming in almost every day: 'Upon Wednesday there came one from the County of Bucks, & some days before, others from Yorkshire, Herefordshire[,] as that I beleeve he [Cromwell] will very shortly have the unanimous Consent of the people ...', 13 Apr., rec^d 11 May 1654, ib. 135–135v.; (extract from the letter in *Journal* ii, 232). The original of the next letter has not been found and the transcript is of little interest, 21 Apr. 1654, Long. 124A fols. 280–281.

In an unusually short letter, Thurloe wrote:

> ... The peace [with the States General] was proclaymed upon Wednesday by the Heraulds, with the Solemnities used in the like cases, yesterday the Ambassadors were all feasted by the Protector at his owne Table ...

They had requested that the time limit for cessation of hostilities should be shortened and it was agreed that anything captured by either side after 4 May must be restored, 28 Apr., rec^d 25 May 1654, Long. W.P. xv, 139.

The last three letters in the series reached Whitelocke at Lübeck on his journey home. The first congratulated the Ambassador on the success of his mission, assuring him

> ... of the good acceptance of it here, and of your prudent conduct of this affaire, w[hi]^{ch} hath been attended with soe great difficulties ... I need not tell you how much your returne is wisht and prayed for ... his Highness ... yesterday gave order for 2 of the Ships to goe unto Hamborough [i.e. Hamburg] to meet your Excell[enc]^{cy} ...
> 5 May, rec^d 7 June 1654.

Ib. 162.

With this letter came another, reporting again on the aftermath of the Dutch Treaty; Thurloe wrote, down the side of the letter, an acknowledgment of Whitelocke's 'great favour & civility' to him, 12 May, rec^d 7

June 1654, ib. 180–179v. (*sic*).

The last letter of this series commented that:

> ... The Peace w[i]th the lowe Countryes is enterteyned here w[i]th all satisfaction; It is not soe on the other side, espetially because of the secret Articles w[hi]^{ch} exclude the house of the Orange Family from beinge stadhold[e]^r of the United Province or any of them ...
> 18 May, rec^d 7 June 1654.

lb. 186.

Whitelocke and Thurloe remained on friendly terms for the rest of their lives, the last entries appearing in *Diary* 22 May, 14 Dec. 1667; Thurloe died in February 1667/68.

THYNNE, [Theodosia?]. Identified by Whitelocke as a kinswoman of Elizabeth, Countess of Sunderland (q.v.), who was a sister of Roger, Francis and George Manners, 5th, 6th and 7th Earls of Rutland (q.v.). Mistress Thynne is also described by Whitelocke as a cousin of Katherine, Duchess of Buckingham (q.v.), who was a daughter of the 6th Earl of Rutland, *Diary* 1634.1635. fols. 33, 43v. The case for supposing that Mistress Thynne was Theodosia, daughter of Roger Manners, 5th Earl of Rutland is, on the face of it, a strong one: Theodosia married Edward Thynne, one of the younger sons of Sir John Thynne of Longleat (1515–1580), see *Genealogy of Family of Thynne* (1741) and B. Botfield *Stemmata Botevilliana* (1858); the maiden name and married name tally, and Theodosia was indeed the Duchess of Buckingham's cousin. The only stumbling–block is that Theodosia's father, the 5th Earl of Rutland, married Sir Philip Sidney's daughter before 15 March 1598/99, when she was about 13, so their daughter Theodosia (the Countess of Sunderland's niece) hardly fits Whitelocke's description of Mistress Thynne as 'an antient gentlewoman' of the Countess's household: in 1634, Theodosia was, at most, in her mid-thirties. She was active in helping Whitelocke when his courtship of the countess's niece, Frances Willoughby, was forbidden, and she even travelled from Hambleden to London to join in planning the young couple's runaway marriage. 'Antient' might have been a joke, or the 29-year-old Whitelocke, deeply in love, might have seen a 35-year-old widow in that light, viewed beside Frances, his young bride-to-be.

TICHBORNE, Benjamin. *Middle Temple Admission Register.* Son and heir of Sir Walter Tichborne, Kt., of Aldershot, Hants. He entered the

Middle Temple in May 1616 and was called to the Bar in May 1623, shortly after Whitelocke began his studies there. Whitelocke makes no reference to him after *Diary* 1622. 1623. fol. 5, although he borrowed money from him in 1639 and 1640, see *Diary* above, note.

TICHBORNE (TICHBURN), Col. Sir Robert, MP (*c.*1609–1682). *D.N.B.*; B. Worden *Rump Parliament*; A. Woolrych *Commonwealth to Protectorate*. A London linen-draper. One of the regicides. He was appointed to serve in Barebone's Parliament of 1653, representing the City of London; a Customs Commissioner from 1649–1656; knighted by Cromwell in 1655 and appointed to the Protector's House of Lords in December 1657. He had been a highly successful Lord Mayor of London in 1656. Serving with Whitelocke on the Army's Committee of Safety from October 1659, these two were chosen, with a few others, to frame a new constitution for a commonwealth (i.e. a republican) government of the three Nations, *Diary* 1 Nov. 1659. A few days later Whitelocke, Tichborne and two others, warned the City of General Monck's disguised plan (i.e. to restore the monarchy), and of the danger of a new Civil War, ib. 4. Nov. 1659. After the Restoration, when writing his own defence, Whitelocke stated that Alderman Tichborne could testify: (1) that Cromwell 'bare him no favour', and had sent him across the North Sea (to Sweden) in November 1653; (2) that he (Whitelocke) had refused to seal writs on behalf of the Committee of Safety (in 1659), to summon a new and illegally constituted Parliament, ib. 2 June 1660.

Whitelocke referred to Tichborne giving himself up, ib. 16 June 1660. The regicide escaped execution by pleading ignorance, at the time of the King's trial, both of law and of government, but he was imprisoned for life.

TOMBES (TOMES), [John] (*c.*1603–1676). *Calamy Revised.* An Anabaptist preacher, mainly working in Herefordshire and Wiltshire, but preaching in and around London in 1645, when he was Master of the Temple. Whitelocke, who referred to him mistakenly as 'Thomas' Tombes, heard him preach and took down the sermon in shorthand, reading it afterwards to his family; later in the same year Maynard (possibly John, q.v.) also read notes of one of Tombes's sermons to the Whitelocke household, *Diary* 24 Aug., 28 Dec. 1645.

TOTT, Count Klas (1630–1674). *Catalogue, Christina Exhibition* p. 214; G. Masson *Queen Christina, passim.* Swedish courtier and diplomat. After spending some time abroad, including a spell in Paris, Tott (still in his early 20s) became a member of Queen Christina's Court in 1651; the next year he was created Count of Karlberg, and soon afterwards was appointed Lord Steward and Captain of the Queen's Guard, then a Councillor of the Realm and the Queen's Master of the Horse. According to Whitelocke, Tott was also the First Gentleman of her Bedchamber, *Journal* i, 256. After Christina's abdication, the Count was sent as Ambassador to Paris in 1657, and served there again, two years before his death.

After arriving in Uppsala on 20 December 1653, Whitelocke quickly discovered that Tott and the Spanish Envoy, Don Antonio Pimentel de Prado (q.v.), were the Queen's favourites and he set about cultivating their friendship. The young Count obligingly acted as go-between, arranging appointments with the Queen and bringing messages from her to the Ambassador, *Diary* 24, 28, 29, 30 Dec. 1653, *passim*. He was rewarded by Whitelocke, at the end of the Embassy, with the gift of an English gelding, ib. 19 May 1654.

TOWNSHEND (TOWNSEND), Sir Horatio, Bt., MP (1630–1687). *Complete Baronetage*; *Complete Peerage*; *Hist. of Parl.* A Royalist, of Raynham, Norfolk. MP for Norfolk in 1656, 1659 and 1660. Whitelocke refers to Townshend and two other men bringing an address from Norfolk, and petitioning for the readmission of the secluded MPs to a Free Parliament, *Diary* 28 Jan. 1659/60. In April 1661 Sir Horatio was created Baron Townshend of Lynn Regis (King's Lynn), Norfolk.

TRAPHAM, [Thomas], jun., MD (c.1633–c.1692). *Alumni Oxonienses*; W. Munk *Roll of the Royal College of Physicians*. His father embalmed the body of Charles I and became Surgeon-in-Chief to Oliver Cromwell. Whitelocke consulted Dr. Trapham jun. about his piles, *Diary* 29 May, 8 July 1665, and he and his wife, Mary, were Trapham's patients, ib. 4, 5, 9 Dec. 1665; 26 Jan. 1665/66; 14 Feb.1667/68. Trapham is believed to have died during an earthquake, in Jamaica.

TREVOR, Sir John, sen., Kt., MP (d. 1673). *D.N.B.* (in the entry for his son, of the same name and title, who predeceased him by one year). His son was not knighted until some years after the Restoration, which confirms that Whitelocke's Sir John was the father, *Diary* 8 Jan. 1658/59; 24 June 1659.

TRIPLET, Thomas, DD (1603–1670). *Alumni Oxonienses*; J. Aubrey *Brief Lives*; K. Weber *Lucius Cary, Second Viscount Falkland* (Columbia U.P. 1940) pp. 143–156; *Clarendon State Papers* xix, xx, *passim*. A staunch Royalist and supporter of Archbishop Laud (q.v.); appointed Vicar of Woodhorn, Northumberland, in 1630; Rector of Whitburn, Co. Durham, 1631; of Washington, in the same county, 1640; Canon of York in 1641, etc. Having been plundered by the Scottish Army, he left the North East to teach in Dublin, then ran a school in Hayes, Middlesex, south-east of Hillingdon, where he treated his pupils with the brutality he himself had suffered at St. Paul's School.

After transcribing one of Triplet's effusively grateful letters, Whitelocke wrote of the Doctor:

> This gentleman was of my acquaintance in Oxford, a great schollar & witt & highly now of the kings party, butt not active to disturbe the governement, uppon his applications to me I protected him from trouble & from imprisonment, & did him many kindesses which afterwards in the change of times were forgotten
> 15 July 1655.
>
> Add. Ms 4992 fol. 127.

This hindsighted comment on Triplet's ingratitude is echoed in *Diary* 13 Aug. 1649, *passim*. The tone of a letter from Triplet to Archbishop Laud suggests a man of rigid beliefs, with a malicious contempt for men whose convictions differed from his own, *C.S.P. Dom. 1639–1640*, pp. 515–520. This did not, however, inhibit him from pestering Whitelocke, a Dissenter, for help; this is shown in a number of entries in *The Diary* between 13 Aug. 1649 and 12 Aug. 1659, and is confirmed in the following extracts from letters written in Hayes:

> Though it were but a short journey, 12 little miles, & my pace very easy & slow, when I wayted on y[ou]^r L[ordshi]^p on Thursday morning, yet at my return I made bloody urine, as I doe allmost upon any ryding [He suffered, as Whitelocke did later, from stone] … the physitians forbidding it, … may be y[ou]^r L[or]d[shi]p may Spare me this journey, … by causing Mr Swift [SWYFT, William q.v.] to write me an answer of that le[tter], or by telling Mr Mede, who brings this to y[ou]^r L[ordshi]^p, w[ha]^t return I shall make; but if y[ou]^r L[ordshi]^p had rather I should come my selfe, I will goe gently to Braynford [Brentford] & from thence take a boate, & go w[i]^{t}h as little violent motion as I can …
>
> Y[ou]^r L[ordshi]^{ps}
Most Bounden
>
> Hayes   Triplet
> Jul. 16. 1652
>
> Long. W.P. xii, 158.

A few months later, he wrote asking Whitelocke to see him 'for an quarter of an hower' about a letter; he had already spoken to Whitelocke's Secretary, William Swyft, about a suitable time and place, 28 Jan. 1652/53, ib. xiii, 4.

The next letter was clearly written in a state of panic and confusion:

I have no cause to fear more then all Sequesterd persons have, & that beeing now cause enough, because I see so many secur[e]d, that p[er]haps know as little by themselves as I do by myself, I am bold to fly to y[ou]ʳ L[ordshi]ᴾ as to my *Anchora Sacra*; knowing that it is farr easyer for y[ou]ʳ L[ordshi]ᴾ to prevent y[ou]ʳ S[e]rv[an]ts danger, then to redeem him out of actuall trouble ... my humble suit is, if it may be, that y[ou]ʳ L[ordshi]ᴾ will be please[d] to think of some way to protect me, in case Soldiers should by vertue of some generall com[m]ission come to gather me up among the rest. If y[ou]ʳ L[ordshi]ᴾ please to putt in a good word for me, & if need be to give y[ou]ʳ word, having now known me for 6 & twenty yeares, that as I have done hitherto, so I shall for the future live peaceably under the present Gover[n]m[en]ᵗ, I will by Gods Lawe neyther shame nor betray my Security; & w[ha]ᵗsoever my private opinions be, I will ever be true to the protection I live under ... [Thanking Whitelocke for his] great civilityes & kindnesse [he was (as usual) Whitelocke's] Bounden Triplet. [After signing, he added] If y[ou]ʳ L[ordshi]ᴾ please to return any answer to Mʳ Mead at the black Lyon at Temple Gate it will come safely to me.

9 July 1655.

(See *Diary* 12 July 1655.)

lb. xvii, 76.

TULL, [Jethro] (*c.*1615–1691). N. Hidden 'Jethro Tull I, II, and III', *Agricultural History Review*, 1989, pt. I. Great-uncle of the famous Jethro Tull III (1674–1741), the agricultural writer and innovator, who invented the farmer's sowing drill (for whom see *D.N.B.*; *V.C.H. Berks.* ii, 220); this youngest Tull (son of Jethro Tull II and his wife Dorothy), conducted his later experiments at 'Prospers', 'Prosperent' or 'Prosperous Farm' (as it is now known), south of Hungerford, in Berkshire. His great-uncle, Whitelocke's acquaintance, had owned the farm, and was agent to the trustees of Thomas Hussey, who had owned, among other properties, Hungerford Park, south-east of Hungerford, also Chilton Park (including Chilton Lodge), north of Hungerford.

Tull I took Whitelocke to view Chilton Park, with Hayward Farm and Hidden, *Diary* 10, 11 June 1663. After various negotiations, the sale of the Chilton Estate to Whitelocke went through, ib. 13 July 1663; 7 June 1665, *passim*. Tull appears to have been on good terms with Whitelocke, who visited and probably stayed with him, ib. 27, 29 July 1663; later, Tull dined

TULLY   385   TURNER

with the Whitelockes at Chilton Lodge, ib. 10 Sept. 1664; they signed
bonds together, ib. 30 Aug. 1664; 18, 24 May, 7 June 1666. Whitelocke did
not prepare us for his abrupt entry: 'More of Mr Tulles being broke', ib. 1
May 1674, *passim*. This financial disaster meant that Whitelocke and
others who had been bound with Tull for various debts, were left to pay
them, ib. 17, 19 June 1674. Tull, for his part, transferred his interest in
Prosperous Farm to his nephew and namesake, and sold his property in
Kintbury, Inkpen, Shalbourne etc. to Sir William Jones (q.v.) in 1674 and
1677, Wilts. R.O., Burdett Papers 1883/127; (the catalogue for these
manuscripts identifies that Tull as *father* of the agricultural writer, but in
view of the financial crisis in the older Tull's affairs in 1674, it seems more
likely that Whitelocke's friend, the *great-uncle*, was the vendor).

Tull's wife Mary, who appears several times in *The Diary*, was the widow
of Vincent Goddard; her daughter, Mistress Elizabeth Goddard, appears
in *Diary* 30 July 1671.

TULLY, Dr. [Thomas] (1620–1676). *D.N.B.*; *Alumni Oxonienses*. Studied
at Queen's College, Oxford, of which he later became a Fellow. He was
appointed Principal (or, according to Whitelocke, 'President') of St.
Edmund Hall, Oxford, from 1658 until his death. He was, simultaneously,
Rector of Grittleton, Wilts., north-west of Chippenham, and died at the
Rectory. Although a strict Calvinist, he became a Chaplain-in-ordinary to
Charles II. Sam and Carleton, Whitelocke's eldest sons by his third
marriage, studied at St. Edmund Hall under Dr. Tully, their tutor being
John Marche (q.v.), *Diary* 30 June 1668; the Hall was an obvious choice
because of its noconformist tradition.

TURNER, Dr. [Samuel], MP (d. *c.*1647). *D.N.B.*; M.F.K. Studied at
Oxford and Padua. He represented Shaftesbury, Dorset, in King Charles
I's second Parliament, of 1625/26. Whitelocke's first experience as an MP
was in that Parliament, and he was present when Turner, among others,
attacked the Duke of Buckingham (q.v.) as the chief cause of the public
grievances, S.R. Gardiner *History of England 1603–1642* vi, 76; see also
Add. Ms 53726 fol. 17v., *passim*, and University Library, Cambridge, Ms
Dd 12.20–22, *passim*.

Whitelocke and Turner served together, briefly, in the Long Parliament,
but by that time the Doctor had become a staunch Royalist, and he was
excluded from Parliament in 1641. In the Civil War he was commissioned
as a Captain in the King's Army. He also spent some time with the King at
Oxford, as one of his physicians. When Whitelocke (one of Parliament's

Commissioners negotiating with the King) was taken ill at Merton College, and had two physicians at his bedside, Dr. Turner called unexpectedly; his oaths, and loud assertions that 'these fellows' would kill Whitelocke, drove them out of the sickroom. With something less than the conventional bedside manner, Dr. Turner paced up and down, smoking his pipe and hurling political abuse at his patient. Despite this, Whitelocke maintained that the Doctor was 'a very able man in his profession . . . much addicted to drollery or raillery & plain speaking'; he added that they had often met each other with Mr. Selden (q.v.), at the London house of the Countess of Kent (q.v.), *Diary* 1642.1643. fol. 61. The conversation between doctor and patient is given in Add. Ms 37343 fol. 265v.–266; most of it appears in R. Spalding *Improbable Puritan* pp. 91–92. After telling Whitelocke he was a rogue, a rebel and a traitor, who did not deserve to live, Turner wrote him a prescription and said, reassuringly, that there was no poison in it, although he insisted that Whitelocke deserved poison rather than physic. Friends urged Whitelocke not to have the prescription made up, but understanding Turner's style better than they did, he disregarded their advice, took the medicine and quickly recovered.

TURNER, Susan. One of three washerwomen on Whitelocke's Embassy, Long. 124A fol. 361v.; *Diary* 26 Oct. 1653. The three women sailed to Sweden in Whitelocke's frigate, the *Phoenix*, ib. 6 Nov. 1653.

TURNER ——. Presumably a vintner, since he was in partnership with Samuel Wilson (q.v.), *Diary* 10 Feb. 1661/62, *passim*. He was Whitelocke's client, both at that time and later. Elizabeth Turner was probably his daughter. Wilson attempted to negotiate a match between her and Whitelocke's son Samuel (q.v.). Unfortunately the young lady had a 'preingagem[en]t' to a Mr. Bodenham, which had to be broken off before any progress could be made; moreover, Samuel Wilson's gout, coupled with his unwillingness to proceed unless what Whitelocke termed his 'unjust accounts' were settled, meant that nothing came of the proposal, ib. 25 July, 1, 18, 26 Aug., 10, 20 Sept., 23 Oct., 11 Nov. 1671.

TURNOR (TURNOUR, TURNER), Judge Sir Edward, MP (c.1617–1676). *Hist. of Parl.*; *D.N.B.*; E. Foss *Judges of England* vii, 177–179. Of Little Parndon (or Paringdon), west of Harlow, Essex. He studied at Queen's College, Oxford, and at the Middle Temple. Was elected MP for Essex in 1654, 1656 (excluded), 1659 and 1660, and for Hertford (near his Essex home) from 1661. Whitelocke's brother-in-law Francis, Lord

Willoughby of Parham, was one of Turnor's clients before the Restoration. After the Restoration, Turnor was chairman of the committee which examined Lord Willoughby's claim for recompense, and which recommended a payment to him of over £2,000. Turnor was knighted in July 1660, appointed King's Counsel and sat in judgement on the regicides. He served as Speaker of the House of Commons from May 1661 to May 1671. Despite allegations of corruption made against him, he was appointed Chief Baron of the Exchequer in May 1671. Whitelocke refers to Turnor once before the Restoration, commending his conduct at the Assizes in Reading as 'civill & just', *Diary* 26 Feb. 1647/48. After the Restoration, Speaker Turnor was helpful to Whitelocke over the Bill moved in the name of the Earl of Portland (q.v.) which was, in effect, largely Whitelocke's Bill, ib. 28, 29 Apr., 13 May 1663. Later, Whitelocke visited Turnor to enquire about 'Britridge', presumed in the context to be Valentine Greatraks, the famous Irish 'stroker' and faith-healer, who visited London that year, 1 May 1666, R. Spalding *Improbable Puritan* pp. 234, 298 note 5. Whitelocke also found the Speaker sympathetic over the loss of his Middle Temple Chambers, *Diary* 26 Apr. 1668.

TWISDEN, Judge Sir [Thomas], Bt., MP (1602–1683). *Hist. of Parl.*; E. Foss *Judges of England* vii. Studied at Cambridge and the Inner Temple. MP for Maidstone, Kent, from 1646 until Pride's Purge; he was readmitted in February 1660 and sat again from about April to July 1660. Having served, reluctantly, as Serjeant-at-Law under the Protectorate, he resigned at the Restoration but was reinstated (with others) as Serjeant, *Diary* 23 June 1660; he was sworn in as a King's Bench Judge on 2 July 1660, was knighted on the same day, and created Baronet in 1666. There is only the one entry for him in *The Diary*.

TYRRELL, Col., later Judge Sir [Thomas], Kt., MP (c.1594–1672). *Hist. of Parl.*; E. Foss *Judges of England* vii. Third son of Sir Edward Tyrrell, Kt. (who died in 1606), of Thornton, north-east of Buckingham. He studied at the Inner Temple. In 1642, Lord Paget (q.v.) appointed Tyrrell, Whitelocke, John Hampden (q.v.) and others, as Deputy Lieutenants for Buckinghamshire; shortly afterwards, Paget went over to the King. Tyrrell became a Colonel in Parliament's Army, serving under the Earl of Essex (q.v.); he was elected MP for Aylesbury in Richard Cromwell's Parliament of 1659, and sat for Buckinghamshire from April to July 1660; a Commissioner of the Great Seal from June to October 1659, and January to May 1660; appointed a Judge of the Common Pleas and knighted in July

1660. The numerous references to him in *The Diary* are of a factual, impersonal nature.

TYRINGHAM (TYRRINGHAM, TERINGHAM), Col. [William], KB, MP (1618–1685). *Hist. of Parl.* (as Tyringham); *Return of Members of Parliament* (as Tyrringham); *V.C.H. Bucks.* iv, 121 (see the Tyringham family and Tyringham Manor, Emberton, north of Newport Pagnell, Bucks.). He sat as MP for Buckinghamshire from 22 August 1660 and in 1661. *Hist. of Parl.* states: 'As a Cavalier, Tyringham was ineligible at the general election of 1660' i.e. in the month before the Restoration. He won the seat soon afterwards, however, at a by-election caused by Sir Thomas Tyrrell (above) resigning from Parliament on his appointment as a Judge of the Common Pleas. Whitelocke (in his only reference to Tyringham) reports that at the general election of April 1660, Colonel Tyringham and Sir William Bowyer were returned '... butt indifferent [i.e. impartial] men affirmed that Mr Wynwood & M^r [Richard] Hampden had many more voices [i.e. votes] then the other two ...', *Diary* 8 Apr. 1660.

ULFELDT (WOOLFELDT, in Whitelocke's bizarre spelling), Count [Corfitz] (1606–1664). *Dansk Biografisk Leksikon* (1983); *Catalogue, Christina Exhibition* pp. 198, 219; *Journal* i, 270; ii, 184–186, *passim*. There is a remarkable similarity between the careers of Count Corfitz Ulfeldt and Count Hannibal Sehested (q.v.): both were very prominent Danes, holding high office; both married half-sisters of King Frederick III of Denmark; both, independently, incurred the King's wrath, ostensibly by their alleged corruption. Ulfeldt (who had been *Rigshofmester* or Chancellor) fled to Holland and then, in September 1651, to the Court of Queen Christina of Sweden, where Whitelocke met him in 1653. Sehested (who had been Governor of Norway) escaped to Germany and then to England, where Whitelocke befriended him in 1654 and 1655. Both men were reinstated in time to assist with the peace negotiations after the Swedish/Danish war, and they helped to obtain better terms for their country than the Danes had thought possible. After that, however, while Sehested remained in high favour, Ulfeldt was found guilty of high treason, became a fugitive abroad in terror of extradition, and died in a boat on the Rhine.

At the Court in Uppsala, Whitelocke decided soon after his arrival to cultivate Ulfeldt's acquaintance, believing that the dissident Dane could supply him with useful information, Denmark and England being enemies at the time, *Diary* 24 Dec. 1653. Ulfeldt, who was in favour with Queen

Christina, proved useful, but Whitelocke was taken aback when he actually volunteered advice on how Oliver Cromwell could capture Elsinore and even Copenhagen. When Whitelocke expressed surprise at such treachery, the Dane insisted that a conquest by England would save Denmark from the tyranny of Frederick III, *Journal* ii, 91–96, 5 Apr. 1654; *Diary*, same date, only gives a discreet reference to an unnamed 'Danish Lord of great quality' (clearly Ulfeldt) who provided information '... of great consequence, especially to England.' Ulfeldt was a good linguist, widely travelled, and (like Melchior de Sabran, q.v.) he had been to England in the 1640s, trying to mediate between the King and Parliament.

USSHER (USHER), [James], DD (1581–1656). *D.N.B.* Born in Dublin. A student, Professor and later Vice-Chancellor of Trinity College, Dublin; appointed Archbishop of Armagh in 1625. He was influential in England (where he often stayed, studied and preached) as well as in Ireland. He endeared himself to Royalists by his opposition to the execution of the Earl of Strafford (q.v.) and by his belief in the Divine Right of Kings. His churchmanship was as 'low' as that of Archbishop Laud (q.v.) was 'high', yet they were on cordial terms. He was a man of rigid and intolerant but deep convictions, a great scholar and lover of antiquities. In September 1643, Parliament voted him an allowance of £400 a year, two years after Irish 'rebels' had destroyed all his property, except for his great library. This allowance or 'pension' was not, however, paid until December 1647; Whitelocke records helping Ussher 'for continuance of his allowance of 400^l ...', *Diary* 2 July 1649. When he was in Sweden, Whitelocke gave 20 books to the University Library in Uppsala, identifying only three of the authors: the Primate of Armagh, John Selden (q.v.) and Sir Henry Spelman (q.v.), ib. 22 Apr. 1654. In the only other reference to Ussher, Whitelocke noted that he preached the sermon at the funeral of their friend John Selden (q.v.), praising him for his learning and hospitality, ib. 20 Mar. 1654/55. It is remarkable that, despite holding some strongly royalist views, Ussher was given a public funeral in Westminster Abbey, by order of Oliver Cromwell (q.v.).

VALE (VAL), Sir Gustav du, see DUWALL, Marshall Sir Gustav.

VANDERLIN (Whitelocke's spelling), see LINDE, Erik von der.

VANE, Sir Henry, Kt., MP, the elder (1589–1655). *D.N.B.*; M.F.K. Of Gray's Inn. For Whitelocke's spirited encounter with the irascible Comptroller of the King's Household (appointed in about 1629), concerning production requirements for the Royal Masque, see *Diary* 1633. 1634. fol. 20, with note. The *D.N.B.* gives the background to the elder and younger Vanes' motives and involvement in the impeachment of the Earl of Strafford (q.v.), and in the Bill of Attainder which followed. Whitelocke was concerned, as Chairman of the Committee which drew up evidence against the Earl, and was greatly troubled when Sir Henry Vane's vital notes disappeared; a copy was later found in the King's cabinet, after the Battle of Naseby, transcribed in the handwriting of George Digby, later 2nd Earl of Bristol (q.v.). When Vane was dismissed as Secretary of State, in November 1641, he threw in his lot with Parliament. His subsequent acitivites are not mentioned in *The Diary*. He sat in every Parliament from 1614 to 1654.

VANE, Sir Henry, Kt., MP, the younger (1613–1662). V.A. Rowe *Sir Henry Vane the younger* (Athlone Press. 1970); *D.N.B.*; B. Capp *Fifth Monarchy Men*, *passim*. A far more gifted, complex and likeable character than his father (above). As a young man, he had spent some years among Puritans in New England, gaining useful if traumatic experience in administration, as Governor of Massachusetts; he had returned to England in 1637. Although a zealous Millenarian, unlike many fanatics of his own and of other centuries, he believed passionately in toleration and, which was even more rare, he extended this to Roman Catholics. In 1659 he demanded justice both for Fifth Monarchists and for Royalists.

Although a Republican he was not a regicide, yet after the Restoration he was executed for high treason. Vane and Whitelocke must have been acquainted in the Short Parliament and they met in the Long Parliament in connection with Strafford's impeachment (see Henry Vane the elder, above, and *Diary* 1640.1641. fol. 52v.). Vane represented Wilton, in Wiltshire, in both Parliaments. He and Whitelocke were Commissioners together at the Uxbridge negotiations in January 1644/45. Between 1642 and 1645 Vane received a large income of £3,000 a year, from fees as Treasurer of the Navy; this was then reduced to £1,500, by the Self-denying Ordinance. Whitelocke had done Vane a service in drafting the Ordinance for this post, on the strength of which he approached Vane to lend him (and his family) the Navy House at Deptford, which they found 'a pretty place for the Summer ...', ib. 1643.1644. fol. 65. They were in Deptford when news reached Whitelocke that a charge of high treason was being brought against both him and Denzil Holles (q.v.) by Lord Savile, Earl of

Sussex (q.v.). Vane and Oliver St. John (q.v.) were among those most active in pressing the charge against them in Parliament. When Vane's old Headmaster at Westminster School, Lambert Osbaldston (q.v.), appealed to him and others not to pursue the charge, Vane indicated that it was Holles whom they wished to ruin, but because of Whitelocke's involvement they were obliged to destroy him too, ib. 2, 7, 11 July 1645. After the two accused men had been cleared by the Commons, Vane turned Whitelocke out of the Navy House, on the grounds that his wife wanted it back, ib. 12 Aug. 1645. Yet two months later, Whitelocke found himself being treated kindly by Vane and his friends, ib. 20 Oct. 1645, and three years later Vane insisted that Whitelocke should both draft and present to the Commons an Ordinance for his resignation as Treasurer of the Navy, '... none butt Wh[itelocke] must doe this service for him, & he was very courteous & Civill to him', ib. 28 Dec. 1646. The next year, Vane and Henry Elsynge (q.v.) came to Whitelocke for advice, ib. 9 Sept. 1647.

When, without legal authority, the Army set up the Committee of Safety, Whitelocke joined it reluctantly, being persuaded that he should serve on it to balance radicals like Vane, ib. 27, 28, Oct. 1659. Some years after Vane's execution, his widow Frances, Lady Vane, came to Whitelocke as a client to consult him about her daughter Albinia's marriage to Alderman John Forth (q.v.); she paid a fee of £10, ib. 26 Mar., 17 Apr. 1668.

VAUX, Sir [Theodore] de, MD, Kt. (c.1628–1694). W. Munk *Roll of the Royal College of Physicians*; *Shaw's Knights*. Son of Thomas de Vaux of St. Paul's, Covent Garden. No doubt Dr. de Vaux knew Whitelocke through his brother William de Vaux (below). The Doctor was named after his famous godfather, Sir Theodor de Mayerne, MD (q.v.). De Vaux was of Middlesex and Guernsey. He studied at Padua, became a Fellow of the Royal Society, physician to Charles II and was knighted in 1665. Whitelocke refers to him in connection with a dispute between de Vaux and another Doctor, Sir John Colladon (q.v.), in which Whitelocke acted as mediator, *Diary* 27, 28 Feb. 1660/61.

VAUX, William de (d. 1657). *Alumni Oxonienses*; *Middle Temple Admission Register* (Wood and Whitelocke spell the name as in the heading. The above sources and the man himself spell it DEVAUX, but Whitelocke's spelling has been used to keep this entry next to that of William de Vaux's brother). De Vaux studied at Christ Church, Oxford, obtaining his BA in 1652, having been admitted to the Middle Temple in 1651. He was appointed a Gentleman of the Bedchamber for the Swedish

Embassy, when Whitelocke described him as: 'an honest and affectionate
... Servant to him[;] he spake good French and Latin, and was ingenius for
Business', Add. Ms 4995 appendix 5, fol. 12v. Three years after the
Embassy, de Vaux accompanied Colonel Sir John Reynolds (q.v.) on the
English expedition to support the French, and to capture Mardyke from
the Spanish. He wrote five letters from abroad:
(1) He described the English infantry's progress from Boulogne to join the
French Army, 15/25 June 1657, Long. W.P. xviii, 68.
(2) He begged for the encouragement of knowing that Whitelocke did not
grudge sparing a moment from his weightier employment to read his letter,
and sent further news of the Army's progress, 19/29 June 1657, ib. 70.
(3) Another letter described how disease had swept through the English
Army; their discipline, however, was much admired by the French. Army
grievances were being sent to England, 23 Aug./2 Sept. 1657, ib. 80.
(4) The next letter told of the capture of Mardyke by the French and
English which gave, among other things, access to the English fleet.
Continous rain was delaying further progress; the soldiers were growing
very weak and sick, and needed winter quarters, 27 Sept./7 Oct. 1657, ib. 88.
(5) The last letter, written from Mardyke 'Fort', told of an unsuccessful
attempt by Spanish forces, on the previous night, to recapture Mardyke.
De Vaux claimed that the 'King of Scots' (Charles II, q.v.), James Duke of
York (q.v.) and others were present with the Spaniards during this
attempt. In the morning, the enemy had retreated in great confusion,
24 Oct./3 Nov. 1657, ib. 90.

William de Vaux accompanied his master, Colonel Sir John Reynolds,
the newly-appointed Governor of Mardyke, when he sailed for England,
but they were both drowned off the Goodwin Sands. Recording this
disaster, Whitelocke recalled that this young man, who had been a good
scholar, when he had been in great danger of drowning on the voyage
home from Sweden, had then said that if ever he went to sea again he
would be content for God to let him drown, *Diary* 16 Dec. 1657.

VAVASOUR, Thomas. A member of Whitelocke's retinue for Sweden,
described as an '... ingenius. Gent[lema]ⁿ of 1st degree', Add. Ms 4995,
appendix 5 fol. 12v., and as '... son of S[i]ʳ W[illia]ᵐ Vavasour', Long.
124A fol. 361v. He appears in the list of Gentlemen at Whitelocke's table,
Diary 26 Oct. 1653.

VENNER, [Thomas], (d. 1661). *D.N.B.*; B. Capp *Fifth Monarchy Men*. A
wine cooper and Fifth Monarchy preacher; known as a fanatic, who had

threatened the life of the Protector and plotted a rising against Parliament in 1657. He was imprisoned in the Tower. After the Restoration, he continued to preach a bloody revolution to bring in the Kingdom of God, the Fifth Monarchy, with the love-your-enemy slogan: 'King Jesus, and the heads upon the gates.' On 6 January 1660/61, he preached at a Meeting-house in Coleman Street and stirred some 50 men to join him in overthrowing the government. After an encounter with the City's Trained Bands, Venner and his men withdrew; they reappeared in the City three days later, when they were all killed or captured by the King's Guards. Venner was tried, then hanged and drawn outside the Meeting-house, see *Pepys* ii, 18, 20 (with notes), 19, 21 Jan. This 'rising' provided an excuse for Royalists and Anglicans to repress Dissenters i.e. 'fanatics'. Whitelocke, who had moved to Coleman Street (an area favoured by 'fanatics'), was not in London at the time of the riots, but recorded the news, *Diary* 10, 11 Jan. 1660/61. His Coleman Street address was held against him in high places, ib. 17 Jan. 1660/61, *passim*.

VILLIERS, Lord Francis (1629–1648). *D.N.B.* (in the entry for George Villiers, 1st D. of Buckingham). Third son of the 1st Duke (q.v.), he was born after his father was assassinated. His mother was Katherine, Dowager Duchess of Buckingham (q.v.), his maternal grandfather Francis Manners, 6th Earl of Rutland. Whitelocke was distantly related, through his second wife Frances, née Willoughby, a niece of the 6th and 7th Earls of Rutland. Villiers joined in the Second Civil War with his brother, the 2nd Duke of Buckingham (q.v.), *Diary* 5 July 1648; his short life ended in a battle near Kingston, Surrey.

WAITE (WAYTE), Col. [Thomas], MP (*c*.1617–*c*.1668). *D.N.B.* A regicide. MP for Rutland 1646–1653 and 1659–1660. Referred to only when he and two others surrendered, *Diary* 13 June 1660. He escaped execution.

WALE, Alderman, Sir [William], Kt. (d. 1676). A.B.B. ii, *passim*; *Pepys* x. A City wine merchant. George Monck (later Duke of Albemarle, q.v.) moved his quarters into the Alderman's house (near Drapers' Hall), *Diary* 15 Feb. 1659/60. Wale went to the King at Breda with the City's delegation, and was knighted on 26 May 1660. He became purveyor of wines to the King in the same year, and gave a banquet for Charles II (q.v.) and James, Duke of York (q.v.) in London, ib. 17 July 1660. Father-in-law of Edward Seymour (q.v.).

WALKER, [Sir Edward?] (1612–1677). *Pepys* x. Garter King of Arms. From the context, it seems that Whitelocke's 'Cousen' Walker may have been Sir Edward, although no relationship has been established and the identification is tentative. Whitelocke, with his wife and children, went to their 'Cousen Walkers house' to see the King and his nobles and the Knights of the Bath 'going in great gallantrie' from the Tower to Whitehall, *Diary* 22 Apr. 1661. This was the day before the Coronation of Charles II.

WALKER, John (b. *c*.1619). *Alumni Oxonienses*; *Middle Temple Admission Register*. Son and heir of William Walker of London. He studied at University College, Oxford, was admitted to the Middle Temple in 1648 and called to the Bar in 1653. Later that year, he was appointed Steward of Whitelocke's household for the Swedish Embassy, and was described, in that capacity, as: '... an honest Gentleman, and a Barrister at Law. He had something of the French, High Dutch, and Latin, was faithful in his place ...', Add. Ms 4995 appendix 5 fol. 11. There are several references which indicate his efficiency as Steward. Less acceptable was his behaviour when, at the end of their stay in Uppsala, Queen Christina sent him a gold chain with her portrait on a medallion, and a similar one to Robert Stapylton (q.v.), Master of the Horse; on finding that other gentlemen in the household had been give chains with more links in them they were both 'discontented', *Diary* 6 May 1654. One letter from Walker has been traced; it concerns practical arrangements for sailing from Gravesend, at the start of the mission, 5 Nov. 1653, Long. W.P. xiv, 179.

WALKER, Sir Walter, LL D. (*c*.1600–1674). *Alumni Oxonienses*; *Pepys* x. Of Staffordshire, also Bushey Hall, Herts., and Stretham, Isle of Ely. He studied at Oriel College, Oxford; later at Christ's College, Cambridge and, according to the first source above, at the Inner Temple, although this has not been traced in the *Register* (which has an entry for his son and heir). An advocate in Doctors' Commons in 1657; after 10 years' service he was dismissed as Judge Advocate (of the Admiralty Court), *Diary* 3 Mar. 1659/60; see G. Davies *Restoration* p. 202. He was knighted in 1661.

WALLER, Edmund, MP (1606–1687). *D.N.B.*; *M.F.K.*; *Hist. of Parl.*; *Aubrey's Brief Lives* (ed. O. Lawson Dick), pp. 359–362. Of Beaconsfield, Bucks. He studied at Eton, at King's College, Cambridge, and at Lincoln's Inn. A wealthy man and a poet of some quality; he was MP for six different constituencies between 1624 and 1685 inclusive. Sent by Parliament, with

Whitelocke and 10 others, to negotiate peace propositions with the King at Oxford, from 21 March 1642/43 to 13 April 1643. Whitelocke overheard the King's welcoming words to Waller, whose plot for a royalist rising in the City was uncovered shortly afterwards. Waller saved his own life by betraying his bother-in-law, Nathaniel Thomkins MP (q.v.), and others, and (according to Aubrey) by his excellent rhetoric and by bribing the whole of the Commons '. . . which was the first time a house of Commons was ever bribed . . .' After spending some months in the Tower, he paid a fine of £10,000 and was banished, but was granted a pardon under the Great Seal in 1651 and allowed to return to England, when he wrote suitable verses in praise of his relative, Oliver Cromwell. After the Restoration, he paid the same compliment to Charles II, and soon managed to endear himself at Court, and to be elected again to Parliament.

Earlier, when his plot was discovered, Waller was questioned as to whether Whitelocke, John Selden (q.v.) and William Pierrepont (q.v.) knew about it. Bearing in mind his readiness to implicate accomplices to save his own skin, it is clear that they were innocent, for he replied that he had intended to consult them '. . . & began to mention such things in generall, butt they all inveyed so much against anything of that nature as basenes & treachery . . .' that he said no more, and was almost put off from pursuing the plot himself, *Diary* 1642.1643. fol. 63.

WALLER, Major-General Sir Hardress, Kt., MP (*c.*1604–*c.*1666). *D.N.B.*; *Pepys* x. A regicide. First cousin of Sir William Waller (below), and related to Edmund Waller (above). Knighted in 1629. After his marriage he settled in Castletown, County Limerick, in about 1630. Eleven years later, he lost most of his property in the Irish rebellion, but subsequently received grants of Irish lands from Parliament, having fought in the New Model Army and in Ireland. He sat as MP for Kerry, Limerick and Clare Counties in 1654, 1656 and probably in 1659; he was appointed Governor of Cork, and later of Dublin Castle. Describing Waller's conduct at the end of 1659 as 'ambiguous', the *D.N.B.* records that Edmund Ludlow (q.v.), on being recalled to England, declined to leave the government of the Army in Waller's hands. After this, Waller refused to allow Ludlow to land in Ireland. Whitelocke tells a little of Waller's activities at around that time, but there is no suggestion that they ever met; he records that Officers from Ireland brought letters to Parliament from Sir Hardress and two fellow officials, containing Articles of Treason against Ludlow and three other former Commissioners for Ireland, and that Parliament then appointed new Commissioners, Sir Hardress being one of them, *Diary* 19 Jan. 1659/60. (Whitelocke was in hiding at the time, and probably received the news from his wife, Mary, who trudged through the dark and the dirt to visit him, near Tower Hill). Later, Sir Hardress fled to France, but returned to give himself up (and to stand trial as a regicide), ib. 20 June 1660. His life was spared, but he was imprisoned for life in the Tower and in a castle in Jersey.

WALLER, Major-General Sir William MP (1598–1668). *D.N.B.*; *Hist. of Parl.* A rigorous Presbyterian. He studied at Magdalen Hall, Oxford; was knighted in 1622, and elected MP for Andover in the Short Parliament of April 1640. He and Whitelocke were urged, by friends, to stand for Oxfordshire in the elections for what was to become the Long Parliament, *Diary* 1640.1641. fol. 49; Add. Ms 37343 fols. 206v.–207. In the event they both withdrew, and Whitelocke was elected for Great Marlow, taking his seat on 5 Jan. 1640/41; Sir William was elected (again for Andover) in May 1642, but was excluded at Pride's Purge. He had been very successful in some areas as a Colonel of Horse, then as Major-General for Parliament in the Civil War, resigning his commission, with relief, at the time of the Self-denying Ordinance in December 1644. Earlier, Whitelocke had recommended his relative, Christopher Potley (q.v.), to his 'Noble Friend' Sir William, under whom Potley was appointed a Major-General, *Diary* 1643.1644. fol. 63v. There are two further references to Waller: these record his courtesy towards Whitelocke, and his coming to Whitelocke for legal advice, ib. 11 Sept., 2 Oct. 1645. *The Diary* tells nothing of Sir William's disputes with Parliament and the Army, of the gradual transfer of his allegiance from Parliament to the King, of his arrest at the time of Sir George Booth's royalist rising in 1659, nor of his election to the Convention Parliament of April 1660, as MP for Middlesex; in 1654 he had bought Osterley Park, in that county.

WALLOP, Robert, MP (1601–1667). *D.N.B.*; M.F.K.; *Hist. of Parl.* A substantial landowner. Of Hurstbourne Priors, Hants. Appointed as one of the King's judges, he attended the Court only on three days. He was elected MP for Hampshire or Andover in 11 Parliaments, from 1621 to 1660. Whitelocke referred to him twice: when Parliament (newly restored) ordered that thanks be given to Wallop, among others, for good service at Portsmouth on their behalf, *Diary* 29 Dec. 1659; and when Wallop was incapacitated from sitting in Parliament or from holding any other office, ib. 9 June 1660 (in a very long entry for that day; the date of the resolution was, in fact, 11 June, *C.J.* viii, 61). Wallop was imprisoned for life.

WALTON (later Bishop), Brian, DD (c.1600–1661). *D.N.B.* Studied at Magdalene College and Peterhouse, Cambridge. A Royalist and follower of Archbishop William Laud (q.v.). He investigated underpayment of tithes in London, but lost his living there after being accused of 'popish innovations' etc., and was imprisoned as a delinquent in 1642. On release, he joined the Royalist at Oxford, where he studied Oriental languages. He compounded for his delinquency in 1647. Despite this background, his plan to publish a Polyglot Bible, using nine languages (funded by public subscription), was warmly approved by the Council of State in 1652. They allowed him paper for the publication, duty-free, and lent him books and manuscripts from government libraries, including the four-volume manuscript of the 'Tecla Bible', the great 'Codex Alexandrinus' (a copy of the Bible in Greek, from the first half of the fifth century, see R. Spalding *Improbable Puritan*, pp. 228, 296 note 16). This was in Whitelocke's care and the receipt to him for it, dated 15 Aug. 1653, is in Add. Ms 32093 fol. 308. There is also an undated petition to the Council of State regarding the 'Privilege of the Polyglot Bible' (i.e. licence to publish it), with a note that it was approved by James Ussher (q.v.) and John Selden (q.v.) and endorsed by Whitelocke, ib. 333. The subscription raised £8,000, subscribers of £10 receiving a copy of all six volumes. These appeared between 1654 and 1657, inclusive. Whitelocke was appointed chairman of a large sub-committee of the Grand Committee for Religion, which met at his house in Chelsea to examine and report on the translations; these learned men also discussed faults in the existing English translation, *Diary* 6 Feb. 1656/57. Dr. Walton wrote acknowledging Whitelocke's help over the publication of the *Polyglot Bible*, sending him the six volumes and offering his opinion on plans for a new English translation, ib. 17 Feb. 1656/57.

WALTON (WANTON), Col. [Valentine], MP (c.1594–c.1661). *D.N.B.*; *M.F.K.* A regicide, he married Margaret, a sister of Oliver Cromwell; sat as MP for Huntingdonshire from 1640 to 1643 and 1659 to 1660. Apart from the first reference to Walton (when he was appointed by Act of Parliament as one of seven Commissioners to govern the Army), *Diary* 12 Oct. 1659, Whitelocke consistently spelt the name 'Wanton', which the editor has amended, see ib. 25 Nov. 1659, note. Other entries refer to: (1) letters to the City from Walton, Sir Arthur Hesilrige (q.v.) and Colonel Herbert Morley (q.v.), after they and others had occupied Portsmouth on behalf of Parliament, declaring against the army leaders, ib. 22 Dec.; (2) Monck's letter confirming their authority, ib. 27 Dec. Three days after Parliament was once again restored (following its interruption by the Army) the same trio strode into the House in their riding habits, to receive the thanks of the House for their part in holding Portsmouth, ib. 29 Dec. 1659, *passim*. Walton's elation was to be short-lived. He held the army post only until 21 February 1659/60. At the Restoration, being hunted as a regicide, he escaped abroad where (according to Anthony Wood) he worked as a gardener.

WARCUP (WARCUPP), [Edmund], JP (1627–1712). *Pepys* x; *E.H.R.* XL (1925) 'Journals of Edmund Warcup, 1676–84' pp. 235–260; this includes an outline of his life. He was a member of an Oxfordshire family, one of 21 children of Samuel Warcup, and a nephew of Speaker Lenthall (q.v.). As Secretary to the parliamentary Commissioners to the King on the Isle of Wight, in 1648, Warcup kept some of the papers from the negotiations (now in the Bodleian Library), much as Whitelocke kept some of those from the Uxbridge negotiations (now at Longleat, see entry for THURLOE, John). By 1651 Warcup was describing himself, perhaps fancifully, as of Lincoln's Inn; his name does not appear in their *Admissions Register*, but the name of a brother does, admitted on 26 Jan. 1637/38: 'Robert Warcopp [*sic*], 2nd son of Samuel W., arm., at request of Wm. Lenthall, now reader', ib. i, 234.

Warcup was concerned in the 1650s with 'litigation, trusts, Welsh land, and dealings in coal', *E.H.R.* (above) p. 237. He was perhaps the Mr. Warcup who sent Whitelocke a gift of venison, *Diary* 11 Nov. 1648; there are three references, in the 1650s, to Lieutenant-Colonel Warcup, ib. 1 Sept. 1651; 26 Mar., 16 Apr. 1659. Edmund claimed to have served as a Captain in the regiment of Ashley Cooper (q.v.). He was employed by George Monck (later Duke of Albemarle, q.v.) in 1660, became a magistrate in 1664, and succeeded his father as Bailiff of Southwark. When Whitelocke wrote his own defence (shortly after the Restoration) he claimed that Lieutenant-Colonel Warcup and Captain Warcup could testify to his motives in agreeing to serve, from October 1659, on the Committee of Safety, ib. 2 June 1660. The last entry for Warcup tells of his giving a banquet to the Dukes of York, Gloucester and Albemarle, ib. 20 Aug. 1660; only then does Whitelocke describe him as his 'old servant', but without explaining in what capacity. (The Warcup entries may perhaps refer to several different members of that large Oxfordshire family.)

WARISTON (WARRISTON, WARESTON), Archibald (Archibold) Johnston, Lord; otherwise Sir Archibald Johnston, Laird of Wariston (1611–1663). *D.N.B.* (as Johnston); *Diary of Sir Archibald Johnston of Wariston* (eds. G.M. Paul, D.H. Fleming and J.D. Ogilvie. Edinburgh

University Press. 1911,1919,1940). Johnston was educated at the University of Glasgow and in France. A very able man, but a grim Presbyterian with a fanatical horror of toleration; a powerful advocate and statesman; in 1643 he was one of three Scottish laymen in the Westminster Assembly of Divines. He proved an unsympathetic King's Advocate (appointed by Charles I when he was held by the Scots at Newcastle, in October 1646). He was appointed Lord Clerk Register, in charge of Scottish records, from March 1649 until the Battle of Dunbar in September 1650, when the records were seized by the English; Cromwell reinstated him in July 1657, and in November that year appointed him a Commissioner for the Adminstration of Justice in Scotland, shortly afterwards calling him to his 'Other House', in January 1657/58. This was despite Wariston's stern disapproval of the Protector's religious principles.

When the Rump Parliament was restored in 1659, Wariston was among those chosen by ballot to serve on the new Council of State, over which he often presided. At the 'interruption' of Parliament by the Army, he presided over the Committee of Safety. Whitelocke, who also served on the Committee which took over the Government, refers to their Orders being signed 'A. Johnston President', *Diary* 11, 19 Nov. 1659. There are several entries for 'Wareston' (*sic*) in Whitelocke's *Diary* at about that time. Correspondingly Wariston, in his *Diary*, has numerous entries for Whitelocke; these occur between July 1659 and the end of January 1659/60; in the entry for 1 Nov. 1659, Wariston stated that he saw Sir Henry Vane's draft constitution for a new government, that he 'disliked the foundation of it and toleration in it' and that he discussed the matter with Salwey (q.v.), Whitelocke and Ludlow (q.v.), *Diary of ... Wariston* (see above) iii, 150.

After the Restoration, Whitelocke (writing his own defence) named Lord Wariston as one of those who could confirm that he (Whitelocke) had angered the Army Officers on the Committee of Safety, when he was Keeper of the Great Seal, by refusing to seal writs to summon a new, unlawful Parliament, *Diary* 2 June 1660. Whitelocke's last entry for Wariston refers to a £100 reward being offered in Scotland for his capture, ib. 31 July 1660. Wariston had escaped to Hamburg and moved on to Rouen, where he was arrested and brought back to England. He was imprisoned in London, then in Scotland, and was hanged for high treason at the Market Cross in Edinburgh. Ostensibly, his crime was that, having acted as the King's Advocate, he later consented to serve in Cromwell's House of Lords: the comparatively flimsy charge and evidence seem to have been tainted by the powerful animosity that Charles II felt against him. Years earlier, Wariston had lectured the young man on the subject of his sexual behaviour.

WARNER, Alderman [Francis], MP (d.1667). A.B.B. ii, 91, *passim*. A Master Leatherseller, he represented Tiverton, Devon, in Richard Cromwell's Parliament of 1659. He came to Whitelocke as a client, *Diary* 24 Oct. 1660. Later, Whitelocke was involved in financial dealings with the Alderman, ib. 31 Dec. 1665; 18 Oct. 1670. Whitelocke and the family tutor, James Pearson (q.v.), signed a promissory note to pay Warner arrears of an annuity of £300 (referred to on 31 Dec. above), 13 Feb. 1671/ 72, Long. W.P. xx, 166.

WARR (WARE), Charles West, 5th Lord de la (1626–1687). G.E.C. He inherited the title when he was two years old. In 1646 he was sent as one of Parliament's Commissioners to treat with the Scots, but was later implicated in the royalist rising led by Sir George Booth (q.v.), and was imprisoned, *Diary* 13 Aug. 1659. Whitelocke encountered him briefly in 1670, when one of de la Warr's sons, 'a very sober fine gent[leman]', was a suitor for the hand of Letitia Popham (q.v., in the entry for her father, Alexander Popham). This was probably the eldest son, the Hon. Charles West, MP (1645–1684), of Wherwell, south of Aldershot, Hants, see *Hist. of Parl*. Whitelocke took considerable trouble in drafting a settlement and inspecting a deed of jointure held by West's grandmother Isobella, the Dowager Lady de la Warr; she would not permit him to borrow the document, but allowed him to study it at her house. When he had satisfied himself that everything was in order, Letitia Popham wrote instructing him not to proceed; he considered that she 'stood in her own light', ib. 18, 19, 20, 27 Apr. 1670. In 1674 she married Edward Seymour MP (q.v.), later 4th Baronet and Speaker of the House of Commons. The Hon. Charles West married Elizabeth, daughter of Sir Edmund Pye, Bt., in 1678.

WARWICK (WARWICKE), Robert Rich, 2nd E. of, formerly MP (1587–1658). G.E.C.; *D.N.B.* He studied at Cambridge and the Inner Temple; succeeded to his father's title in 1619, and had many overseas financial interests. He became a staunch Puritan and Parliamentarian; in 1643 he urged Whitelocke to help his brother Henry Rich, 1st Earl of Holland (q.v.), who had also been 'a favourer of the Puritans', *Diary* 1634. 1635. fol. 32, but who had turned Royalist, ib. 1643. 1644. fol. 64. Warwick was Commander-in-Chief of Parliament's Navy, from 1642 to 1645, and 1648 to 1649; he is mentioned in connection with the fleet, ib. 8 Aug. 1648. He supported the Protectorate and played a leading part at the second inauguration of Cromwell as Protector, when he carried the Sword of State, ib. 26 June 1657.

WEEDON, [Robert]. A shadowy figure, apparently from the Fawley, Bucks., area, referred to as bringing letters from Royalists, which Whitelocke handed over to the Committee of Examinations in London 'for his indempnity' (or protection), not long after the Savile affair, *Diary* 30 Sept. 1645. Weedon's first name and residence (presuming he was the same man) are taken from a paper concerning the Manor of Bosmore, north of Fawley village with, it seems, land to the east of the neighbouring village of Hambleden, in Buckinghamshire, purchase price £6,057.16s.8d., in 1651, Long. W.P. xi, 240. Later, Weedon was brought in to help when Whitelocke considered making a purchase of property in Hambleden but, according to Whitelocke, he dealt dishonestly, *Diary* 13 July 1658, with note. The Mr. Weedon, a client, who paid fees of £2 and £1, may have been someone else, since by then Whitelocke was living at Chilton Lodge, in west Berkshire, ib. 11 June 1669; 31 Aug., 7 Sept. 1670.

WENMAN, Thomas, 2nd Viscount, MP (*c*.1596–1665). G.E.C.; *D.N.B.*; M.F.K.; *Hist. of Parl.* Of Twyford, south-west of Buckingham, and Thame Park, Oxfordshire, the latter a longish ride from Whitelocke's houses, Fawley Court and Phyllis Court near Henley-on-Thames. Wenman and Whitelocke often visited and dined with each other. Wenman sat in eight Parliaments, for Brackley (Northamptonshire) or for Oxfordshire, starting in 1621 and finishing in 1660. He supported the peace party in the Long Parliament, and was one of Parliament's Commissioners, with Whitelocke and others, in Oxford, *Diary* 1642.1643. fol. 60 and at Uxbridge, where '... quarter [was] hard to be gott ...' and they had to share a room, ib. 1644.1645. fol. 71. Whitelocke was lent an army field bed (or camp bed) and a quilt, so he did not have to share a bed, as he had done at Merton College with Sir John Holland (q.v.), during the Oxford negotiations.

Some months after Uxbridge, Wenman spoke up for Whitelocke in the Savile affair, ib. 5, 12 July 1645. They continued to meet socially and to talk politics at intervals. Over dinner, Wenman and his guests expressed fears that there might be another war, ib. 28 Dec. 1647. The next year, he entertained Whitelocke and his wife on what turned into a very wet and windy summer's day, in a notably wet summer, D. Underdown *Pride's Purge* p. 106. When the Wenmans 'very slenderly' invited their guests to stay the night, they preferred to ride home some 12 miles to Phyllis Court in the pelting rain. As a result, Frances '... tooke a great cold, which scarse left her till she dyed ...' nearly 10 months later. Whitelocke was taken aback at such unkindness, *Diary* 31 July 1648. In September, Wenman was sent as one of Parliament's Commissioners to the King at Newport, Isle of Wight, and in due course was excluded from Parliament at

Pride's Purge and kept prisoner, with others, in most unpleasant conditions, from 6 to 20 Dec. 1648, *Pride's Purge* (above) p. 153, *passim*, and p. 168 note 71. After his release and during the King's trial, Lord Wenman and his wife Margaret (d. 1658), 'came now & often' to visit the Whitelockes at Phyllis Court, *Diary* 16 Jan. 1648/49. (Their other house, Fawley Court, had been seriously damaged in the Civil War.) After that, there is one more entry: Wenman wrote from Thame Park, invoking their old friendship and entreating Whitelocke to help Sir Anthony Morgan (q.v.), ib. 17 July 1659.

WENTWORTH, Sir Peter, KB, MP (1592–1675). *D.N.B.*; M.F.K. He studied at Oxford and Lincoln's Inn; represented Tamworth, Staffs., in the Long Parliament, sitting until 1653. A radical, he gave Whitelocke a hard time in the cross-examination over the Savile affair, *Diary* 7, 10, 17 July 1645. A friend of Henry Marten (q.v.); when Cromwell forcibly dissolved Parliament he stared at Wentworth and Marten, declaring that some Members of the House were whoremasters, ib. 20 Apr. 1653.

WENTWORTH, Thomas, see STRAFFORD, 1st E. of.

WEST, [Edmund], MP (c.1608–1683). D. Underdown *Pride's Purge* pp. 34, 389, *passim*. An MP for Buckinghamshire in 1645, and one of the lesser gentry, with radical leanings, who took over power from the major gentry on the Buckinghamshire County Committee. Whitelocke said he was ill, when some of the county gentry asked him to 'serve ... [their] desires' against West and Thomas Scott (q.v.), *Diary* 21 Sept. 1645.

WHALEY (WHALLEY), Col., later Major-General Edward, MP (d. c.1675).*D.N.B.*; T. Carlyle *Letters and Speeches of Oliver Cromwell, passim*. Active in the Civil War. He, with his regiment, was in charge of Charles I at Hampton Court in 1647, and sent news to his cousin, Oliver Cromwell (q.v.), of 'the least incident in the king's life, his walks, his conversations, the visits and the proceedings of his councillors, the indiscretions of his servants ...', F. Guizot *History of the English Revolution* (London. 1846) p. 350. See a letter from Whaley reporting on the King's activities, J. Rushworth *Historical Collections*, second edition (London. 1721), vii, 795. A regicide, he sat as MP for Nottinghamshire in Cromwell's Parliaments of 1654 and 1656, and was summoned to his 'Other

House' in January 1657/58. He is referred to twice by Whitelocke: (1) when Whaley and his son-in-law, William Goffe (q.v.) with two others, were sent to General Monck (later Duke of Albemarle, q.v.) to appeal to him to prevent further 'effusion of blood', *Diary* 1 Nov. 1659; for the background to these talks, see *Restoration* p. 175, *passim*; (2) when a reward of £100 was offered to anyone apprehending Colonel Whaley and Colonel Goffe, *Diary* 22 Sept. 1660. Even before this Proclamation was made, the two regicides had reached the safety of Boston, Massachusetts. Despite attempts to capture them, they were given asylum in New England.

WHARTON, Philip, 4th Lord (1613–1696). G.E.C.; G.F. Trevallyn Jones *Saw-pit Wharton* (Sydney University Press. 1967). He succeeded to the Barony on the death of his grandfather in 1625, when he was 12; studied at Exeter College, Oxford, and entered Lincoln's Inn, January 1637/38. He was wealthy, but neither extravagant nor corrupt; a Puritan with austere religious principles; he married three times; the harsh discipline he imposed on his sons had precisely the opposite effect on their morals to that which he intended (see *Hist. of Parl.* for his three MP sons, the Hon. Goodwin, Henry and Thomas Wharton). He was present with his regiment at Edgehill and served several times as Speaker of the House of Lords. Although very critical of monarchy, he was, nevertheless, dismayed by the King's execution. Although a friend of Oliver Cromwell's, he was highly critical of the Protectorate. He withdrew from the political scene from the time of Pride's Purge, in December 1648, until after the Restoration which he welcomed in a lavish style.

Whitelocke's only entry for Wharton, before 1670, refers to his appointment as Lord Lieutenant of Buckinghamshire in 1642, *Diary* 1641.1642. fol. 54v. In 1661 Wharton married his third wife, Anne (d. 1692), widow of General Edward Popham. The Popham family (q.v.) lived at Littlecote in Wiltshire, on the river Kennet; Whitelocke and his wife Mary (living nearby at Chilton Lodge), met Anne when they visited Colonel Alexander Popham (q.v.), and found her very courteous, *Diary* 26 July; she called on them six days later, ib. 1 Aug. 1665, *passim*. Five years later, she and her husband visited Whitelocke in London; he recorded that Wharton often came to consult him about liberty of conscience, 'to w[hi]^{ch} he was a friend', ib. 14 Apr. 1670 with note. Details of Lady Anne Wharton's considerable estates, released to her by Trustees (mainly between 1663 and 1675), around Chelworth, Christian Malford, Seagry etc. (to the north-east and south-east of Malmesbury) may be found in the Wiltshire R.O., Trowbridge, 212B/1604.

WHETHAM, Col. [Nathaniel]. *Restoration* pp. 179–181. Governor of Portsmouth. A friend of George Monck's. He had fought for Parliament since 1642. Referred to twice by Whitelocke: (1) when, as Governor of Portsmouth Garrison, Whetham, supported by Colonel Herbert Morley (q.v.), declared for the restoration of Parliament, at which the Committee of Safety sent forces to capture Portsmouth, *Diary* 5 Dec. 1659; (2) a few weeks later, when the Speaker of the restored Parliament thanked Whetham and his officers for their services, ib. 29 Dec. 1659.

WHICHCOTE (WHITCHCOTT), Col. [Christopher]. *V.C.H. Berks.* iii, 17–19; C.V. Wedgwood *Trial of Charles I, passim.* He succeeded Colonel Venn as Governor of Windsor Castle in June 1645. Before that, Whichcote had been in touch with a parliamentary committee, set up to inquire into treasure found in Windsor Castle. It was reported that a: 'Collar SS [i.e. of Esses], a Garter & George, much spoyled in the Earth' had been dug up in the Castle in January 1645/46, but it seems that nothing more was unearthed. Excavations were also made in the house of one Dr. Giles, but the rumours about this supposed treasure trove came from John Marston Clarke; Whichcote wrote of this informant that he had:

> ... not only betrayed his ... malign[an]^t nature & ignoble Disposition to his owne friends (the Enimies of the Parlam[en]^t) at Oxon: But allsoe ... w[i]th mee, seeinge he Could not bringe his owne Ends about to obtayne some reward from mee[,] w[hi]ch he Endeavoured to have gayned, If I would have Concealed the Jewels[.] And then I conceave he would have returned to his owne p[ar]ty at Oxon ... [Marston Clarke had written] the book Intituled the City Complaint, & is a man Double harted, & very ungratefull to that Civill respect he hadd from mee ...
> Windsor Castle, 16 Mar. 1645/46.
>
> Long. W.P. ix, 79–79v.

As Governor, Whichcote showed great respect for Whitelocke and his wife when they stopped at Windsor on their journey, by boat, up the Thames from London to Phyllis Court, near Henley-on-Thames, *Diary* 17 July 1648. After Whitelocke's appointment as Constable of the Castle, in 1649, with authority over the Governor, Whichcote wrote several letters to him concerning Windsor Forest, a few of which are mentioned in ib. 12 May, 18 June 1656, 9 June 1659.

Whitelocke was non-committal as to the Colonel's character, but the letters reveal aspects of it. In one, Whichcote expressed a pious hope that the Lord would 'so[o]ne put an End [to], and lay our Enemies[,] such catterpillers[,] in the dust', so that His people and the Commonwealth might have more rest and an opportunity to praise His name. He thanked

Whitelocke for the tender care shown when 'wicked raunting Levilling sperits are set a worke to Scandalise my Integrity ...' and he finished as '... a true servant of this Com[m]onwealth of England ...', 1 Sept. 1651, Long. W.P. xi, 52. A complaint was sent to Whitelocke that the Governor and his colleague, Thomas Redding (q.v.), had cut down 100 trees and sold all the young beech trees around Bearwood (west of Wokingham), 30 May 1656, ib. xvii, 160. (The identity of this Bearwood is confirmed in a complaint against Humphrey Broughton, a great drinker, night-walker and poacher, living at Bearwood Lodge, in the parish of 'Okingham', i.e. Wokingham, Berks., 7 July 1658, ib. xviii, 135.) See also the entry for YOUNG, Francis, 'wood-warden' of Windsor Forest, who later moved into the poacher's run-down lodge.

On another occasion, Whichcote wrote acknowleding Whitelocke's letters and an Order, from the Protector, for timber to be sent from Windsor Forest to fence 40 acres of Whitelocke's land at Fawley (probably in compensation for the destruction of his deer park, years earlier, by Prince Rupert's soldiers, *Diary* 1642.1643. fol. 58). The Colonel was too respectful to query the Order, but he pointed out that the timber already cut was unsuitable for the purpose, and that the season for felling and carting was past. He therefore asked Whitelocke to postpone the business until the following April. He also asked Whitelocke to obtain money from Parliament for repairs to Windsor Castle; they had timber, bricks, lime and sand on the site, but needed funds to carry out the work, 30 Sept. 1656, Long. W.P. xvii, 199. Some 18 months later, he sent proposals as to how best to cut the palings for Whitelocke, bearing in mind the need for conservation; this followed a new Order of 8 April; he gave particulars of how the timber might be brought to the waterside – the Thames – with proposals for felling, squaring and carting it; the letter was signed both by Whichcote and Thomas Redding (q.v.), 14 Apr. 1658, ib. xviii, 127.

After Richard Cromwell's fall and the return of the Rump Parliament, Whichcote showed increasing anxiety: he sent Whitelocke a detailed account of his stewardship of the Forest between 1653 and 1659, itemizing, among other things, timber supplied to Hampton Court, used within Windsor Park, sent for use in Whitelocke's park and for unexplained underground services at Kingston. There were accounts for loads of timber, and a reference to wood supplied to Whitelocke apart from that in the original Order; again, the letter was signed with Redding, 16 June 1659, ib. xix, 24v.–25; Parliament evidently suspected that timber which should have gone to the Navy had been misappropriated: no more trees were to be felled except for the use of the State, and three officers were appointed to oversee the work. This appears in an Order of 15 June 1659 (which clearly inspired the above account), also in a nervous covering letter from Whichcote and Redding, in which they protested that the timber felled by order of the late Protector was, in general, not of the type that would be useful to the Navy, 21 June 1659, ib. xix, 28; Order, 15 June 1659, ib. fol. 30.

Another defensive letter hints at the possible damage to Whitelocke (as well as to Whichcote and Redding) resulting from complaints brought to the Committee by the Forester, Francis Young (q.v.), for his own ends, 18 July 1659, ib. 55.

Colonel Whichcote may well have felt relieved when he surrendered Windsor Castle to Major Wildman (q.v.) and a troop of 300 volunteer horsemen, 'for the use of the Parlem[en]', *Diary* 28 Dec. 1659.

WHISTLER, Daniel, MD (1619–1684). W. Munk *Roll of the Royal College of Physicians*; *Pepys* x. Studied at Oxford and at Leyden, where he qualified in 1645, having his medical degree incorporated at Oxford in 1647. A man of many talents, he was appointed Gresham Professor of Geometry in 1648, and was recommended by 80-year-old Dr. Winston (q.v.) for appointment as Whitelocke's physician for the Swedish Embassy. Whitelocke described him at that time as:

> ... of excellent Knowledge and Successe in his Faculty, he had been formerly imployed by the Parliament and gained great Experience about their Seamen [in the Dutch war], ... he had as much Ellegancy both in Speaking, [and] especially in writing of Latin, as any person whatsoever, he spake good French, and understood the High Dutch [i.e. German] & Italian and was exceeding tender, and Careful of Wh[itelocke]; and of all his Company.
>
> Add. Ms 4995 appendix 5, fol. 11.

Elsewhere, after referring to Whistler's good disposition and 'generous conversation', Whitelocke expanded his earlier reference to the Doctor's care of seamen, saying that this had been an obstacle to Whistler undertaking the journey to Sweden, since he was in the State's service, tending the sick and wounded and, of necessity, practising both as a surgeon and as a physican. Moreover, he would not desert his post without permission from the State; this, Whitelocke obtained from the Barebone's Council of State and, by way of compensation, paid Whistler an advance of £50, Eg. Ms 997 fols. 64–64v.

The Order for Whistler's release, signed by John Thurloe (q.v.), in October 1653, is in Long. W.P. xiv, 1, 3. His experiences with the Navy soon proved useful: travelling along the frozen Swedish roads, he had to set a broken arm and a broken leg, and to treat head injuries, when one of the party was kicked by a horse, *Diary* 3, 4, 9 Dec. 1653. Later, Queen Christina (q.v.) consulted him about her indisposition (unnamed), ib. 6

Feb. 1653/54; after talking to Whistler on other subjects, she 'gave him the character of a learned, able scholar and physician', *Journal* i, 395. At Hamburg, on the journey home, when Whitelocke believed he had been poisoned at a reception, Whistler gave him a powder in a drink and quantities of oil of sweet almonds, to very good effect. The friendship which developed between Whitelocke and his physician during the Embassy, continued until Whitelocke's death. Some time after the Embassy, Whistler wrote expressing profuse gratitude to Whitelocke:

> more then I can expresse ... butt I am not satisfyed with ... useles returnes, butt labor under the panges of a frustrated violent spirit, till I am instrumentall to some advantage to your L[ordshi]^P, if your L[ordshi]^P give me your hand, to pull me up the staires[,] I hope it is not above my meanness of condition to become a footstool to your ... advancement ...
> Gresham College, London, 12 Mar. 1655/56.
>
> > Add. Ms 4992, 145v. (transcript); *Diary* same date.

Neither source tells in what way Whitelocke had promoted the Doctor's career. A few years later, Whitelocke put Whistler's name forward for election as MP for Thirsk, in Yorkshire, but without success, ib. 3 Jan. 1658/59. Whitelocke took no fee when Whistler consulted him on a legal matter, ib. 7 Nov. 1660. After that, numerous entries tell of Whistler being called in or simply arriving to give medical advice to Whitelocke, his wife or the children; his diagnosis was usually less alarming and the treatment he prescribed less drastic than that of his fellow doctors. On one occasion he declined a fee from Whitelocke, but was quite prepared to accept £10 from Mary, ib. 24 Sept., 1 Oct. 1661; 30 Apr. 1664; 13, 22 Mar. 1664/65; 29 Mar. 1665; 26 Sept., 30 Nov., 18 Dec. 1668; 3, 6 Jan. 1670/71, *passim*. When consulted by Whitelocke at Chilton Lodge, Whistler stayed with a kinsman, Mr. Whistler of Combe, in west Berkshire, ib. 3 Jan. 1670/71.

In 1683, Whistler was elected President of the College of Physicians, eight years after Whitelocke's death. This was a disaster: although he had married a rich widow, Whistler was in debt. He proceeded to defraud the College, and the year after his appointment he died in poverty and disgrace. The proceedings (in Latin) of an Extraordinary Meeting of the College, held two days after his death, record 'the remarkable, fraudulent activity of Daniel Whistler the President, who recently died'. The meeting was adjourned to 24 May, when the officials impounded certain valuables until the executor to Whistler's Will arrived (see W. Munk, above). It was a shameful end to the career of a likeable and gifted man.

WHITELOCKE family. *D.N.B.*; J.S. Burn *History of Henley-on-Thames* (Longman. 1861) with a two-page family tree (not wholly reliable), following p. 248; B. Burke *History of the Landed Gentry of Ireland* (Harrison. 1904) under 'Lloyd of Strancally Castle', pp. 346–348; *Alumni Oxonienses, passim*; *Merchant Taylors' School Register*; *Middle Temple Admission Register*; J. Whitelocke *Liber Famelicus* (Camden Society. 1858); Chart prepared by Peter Whitlock of Port Coquitlam, B.C., Canada, for 'Whitlock Genealogical Research'. Dates and information in these sources are valuable, but do not always tally with each other, nor with material in parish registers, Record Offices and in *The Diary*. A family tree is given between pp. viii and ix of this volume.

Whitelocke's three wives and 17 children appear in his *Diary*, living at or visiting Fawley Court or Phyllis Court (both near Henley-on-Thames) or, towards the end, at Chilton Lodge near Chilton Foliat (on the Berkshire/ Wiltshire border, near Hungerford). Those daughters and granddaughters whose marriages are recorded by Whitelocke are cross-referred, and appear under their married names; otherwise they appear under their maiden names.

WHITELOCKE, Anne (fourth daughter of Whitelocke's second marriage), see HILL, Abraham.

WHITELOCKE, Anne (Ann) (d. 1736). J. Burke *Extinct & Dormant Baronetcies*. Whitelocke's granddaughter by his son, Sir William Whitelocke MP (q.v.) and his wife Mary (q.v.), née Overbury, of Phyllis Court. As a child Anne, with her parents, stayed with her grandfather at Chilton Lodge, *Diary* 14 Sept. 1671; 30 Aug. 1672. She subsequently married Sir Thomas Noel Bt., of Kirkby Mallory, Leicestershire. (Her brother William married Ann Noel, daughter of Edward Noel; this has sometimes led to confusion between the two 'Ann Noels').

WHITELOCKE, Bigley (1653–1686). The third son of Whitelocke's third marriage. On the night before Whitelocke set sail for Sweden he was aboard the frigate *Phoenix*, anchored near the mouth of the Thames, when news reached him of Bigley's birth, *Diary* 7 Nov. 1653. The baby, named after his maternal grandfather (Bigley Carleton, a grocer), seems to have been rejected by his mother at birth, as appears in her grief-stricken letter to her husband of 25 Nov. 1653, see entry for Whitelocke's wife, Mary. Moreover, Bigley's conduct as an adolescent suggests that something had gone wrong. After the record of his birth, there is nothing more about him until he was nearly nine years old, when Whitelocke mentions that Carleton and Bigley were ill but that they recovered, *Diary* 21, 27 Sept.

1662; later, there is news of Bigley catching 'smallpox' (probably chicken-pox) and of his speedy recovery, ib. 4, 11 Dec. 1664.

His next appearance is at the age of 16, when his father apprenticed him to a French merchant in London, for one or two months on trial. Within a month Bigley was dismissed for bad behaviour. His father dealt with the disgrace obliquely, appealing to his son to disappoint his 'ill willers' by reforming, and Bigley promised to do so, ib. 4, 6, 25 May, 15, 17, 19, 21, 23 June 1670. A very good master was found nearer to Chilton Lodge, although Whitelocke considered a fee of £200, as well as the provision of all Bigley's clothes, to be high terms for an apprenticeship in Bristol. This time the young man was commended for his diligence and, with parental consent, was promoted to go as a factor (i.e. agent) to Malaga; but again he misbehaved and was sent home. James Pearson (q.v.), the sturdy and long-suffering tutor, tried to smooth things over, but Bigley refused to go back to Bristol, ib. 30 Sept. 1670; 4 July 1671; 23, 26 Oct. 1672; 20 Sept. 1673, *passim*. He stayed away from home and consorted with 'evill company' in Marlborough, about 10 miles west of Chilton Lodge, and when his bother Samuel (q.v.) persuaded him to come home, the pair of them slipped out one evening to dine with the Duke of Somerset (q.v.), in his 'house of debauchery', without telling their parents, and distressed their mother even more by coming home at 2 o'clock in the morning, ib. 5, 6 Oct., 10 Nov. 1673, *passim*. Bigley then set off for London, where he enlisted in the Earl of Carlisle's Company, and went to Holland as an Ensign, ib. 15 Dec. 1673; 11, 21 Mar. 1673/74.

It is characteristic of Whitelocke, that in his last Will, having little money or land left to bequeath, he only named the following three children: to his reliable son Carleton (q.v.), a trustee to his Will, £50 p.a. (Carleton had been promised, and later received, a substantial legacy from William Lilly, q.v.); to Bigley and to Hester £20 p.a. each; yet they, of all Whitelocke's 17 children, had caused him the most sorrow and anxiety (apart perhaps from James, q.v., the spoiled son and heir). The remaining children and the grandchildren were each to receive a ring costing £1. According to Burn, *History of Henley-on-Thames* (above), Bigley was buried at Chilton [Foliat], 12 May 1686 (aged 32).

WHITELOCKE, Sir Bulstrode, Kt., MP (1605–1675). *The Diary* (so-called) tells the story of his life, from birth until six days before his death; 'The Annales' (published as *Memorials ...*) cover his life up to 1660, sometimes in greater detail; his ambassadorship, 1653–1654, is related colourfully, much of it in dialogue, in his *Journal of the Swedish Embassy*, the first edition being fuller and better than the second; the on-the-spot manuscript of this 'Journal' is in the Longleat Collection, while two other versions, carefully edited by Whitelocke (perhaps with a view to their publication), are in the British Library (see Manuscript Sources).

Whitelocke was a tireless writer; he prepared a lengthy 'History of England' which continued up to the early years of his life, and he also wrote different versions of the events (both public and private) of his own day, as well as a 'History of Persecution', and works on government and on religious toleration. A hitherto unknown manuscript of Whitelocke's was auctioned at Sotheby's in December 1987, and bought by the British Library. It gives an account of the Parliamentary Commissioners' negotiations with Charles I at Oxford, March 1642/43 to April 1643, with a letter-book from that time. This material supplements the diary account, giving (among other details) some terse comments by the King, with questions he put to the Commissioners and their replies; it also names the nine Captains from Parliament's Army, imprisoned in Oxford Castle, whom Whitelocke visited, Add. Ms 64867; (see SMITH [William] for the prisoners' names).

A glance at his enormous output, listed among Manuscript Sources, makes one suspect that Whitelocke sat up half the night studying and writing, and that he could manage on very little sleep; it is justly observed in the preface to the first edition of his *Memorials of the English Affairs* ... (1682), that he 'was ... so much in Business [parliamentary and legal], one would not imagine he ever had leisure for Books; yet who considers his Studies, might believe he had been always shut up with his Friend Selden [q.v.], and the dust of Action never fallen on his Gown ... few Mysteries of State could be to him any Secret. Nor was the Felicity of his Pen less considerable than his Knowledge of Affairs ...'

Whitelocke was also an active letter-writer, and kept rough drafts or copies of much of his correspondence. Some of his letters appear in the entries of the people to whom they were sent. These, with the letters addressed to him by all manner of people, tell us a good deal about his nature, generosity, and the respect and affection in which he was generally held. There is a mass of other material among his papers, including Charges to Juries, briefs and other legal material; political and religious notes, sermons he preached in conventicles, papers on the Merchant Adventurers and News Letters, some from abroad. Many of these papers are referred to in footnotes to *The Diary* and in this volume. There are also numerous financial papers; a few small samples from this last group are given below, starting with items which reflect Whitelocke's daily expenditure and life-style as a Middle Temple student, between November 1628 and January 1628/29:

17 [Nov. 1628]	For new cloth & making ... Cuffs	0 - 0 - 6
	Att the black fryars playhouse	0 - 1 - 6
18	to the boyes boxe att the dauncing schoole	0 - 0 - 3
	Att the Taverne	0 - 0 - 4
21	For musick att the Dauncing schoole	0 - 1 - 6
22	For carriadge of a loade of billetts from the wharfe to the Temple	0 - 1 - 0
	For exceedings [i.e. extra provisions for festive occasions] in the Temple hall	0 - 1 - 0
24	For mending my Stockins	0 - 0 - 6
26	For boat hire	0 - 0 - 4
	For new soling a pr of bootes	0 - 1 - 2
	For mending my shoes	0 - 0 - 3
	For my place in the Starr Chamber M.T. [i.e. Middle Temple?] cā͞r [i.e. carriage?]	0 - 5 - 0
27	Att the rose Taverne	0 - 0 - 6
28	For ribbon for mending my stockins	0 - 0 - 4
	For my supper att Mrs Percyes [his landlady]	0 - 1 - 2
29	For carriadge of 68^{l[b?]} of hopps by Gresford Carrier	0 - 5 - 9
	For carriage of letters	0 - 0 - 10
27 [sic]	For washing some linnen of mine the last circuite[?]	0 - 1 - 0
	For a pr of kidde leather gloves	0 - 1 - 4
28	To my bawbers [i.e. barbers?] boy	0 - 0 - 5
30	For apples & sugar & nuttmegg & ale att my fire	0 - 1 - 2
	Dec. 1628	
1 [Dec.]	For beere & sugar & a rolle	0 - 0 - 6
	To a poore boy for going uppon errands	0 - 0 - 1
2	For postage of letters	0 - 0 - 3
	For wine in the Temple hall	0 - 0 - 3
	Lost att Gleeke [a card game for three players]	0 - 2 - 0
3	Payd my Temple Commons from the 11 of Octb until the 30 November	2 - 10 - 10
9	Lost att Gleeke	13 - 8
10	Lost att Gleeke	0 - 3 - 0
	For a fustian wastcott, cloth, & making & tape for things	0 - 6 - 0
15	For mending a pr. of grey stockins	0 - 1 - 4

All but two entries from 16 to 30 December, concern playing at cards, showing a net loss of £1. 4s. 0d., apart from 16s. 8d. lost earlier at Gleek. On 22 December, Whitelocke paid 1s. 0d. to have his 'viola & other things from London', so evidently much of the card-playing took place at Fawley Court, over Christmas. He managed to raise a New Year's gift of 10s. for

Mr. Emot (q.v.), and on 9 January 1628/29 paid his father's servant, Adrian Gray, 2s. 6d. for escorting him back to London. There were more visits to the Playhouse; Whitelocke paid 3d. for a wax candle, 3d. for an almanac and 6s. 6d. for 'a pr of Spanish leather shoes & galoshes'. Dinner and wine at the Castle Tavern cost 4s. 6d.; the weekly payment to his landlady of 8s. 6d. covered his 'commons' (or food) and fires. He paid a cutler 8s. 6d. for resetting his sword hilt, securing the blade and supplying a new scabbard etc., Long. W.P. Parcel 5 (at the time of writing, these papers are unnumbered).

The accounts tell little of Whitelocke's extravagance as Master of the Revels, before Christmas that year, or of the debts in the New Year which he did not dare report to his father, *Diary* 1628.1629. fols. 9–10v., *passim*. His 'quarteridge', or quarterly allowance from his father, was £90, 26 Dec. 1630, Long. W.P. iv, 270. Larger bills, not shown in the petty cash accounts, include one from his tailor for £31. 9s. 2d., June 1630, ib. 135v., and one for a horse, £5, plus extras for it amounting to £1. 2s. 0d., 23 July 1630, ib. 138. After Whitelocke's parents died, he invested in a coach, built by Stephen Wilkinson, costing £30 'for . . . all the timber[,] iron[,] silke and all worke whatsoever about it', 28 Feb. 1632/33, ib. vi, 11. At about the same time he paid £4. 10s. 0d. to his tailor for an Athens suit and hose, with all buttons, taffeta, ribbons, sewing silk etc. itemized, Mar. 1632/33[?], ib. v, 212; he also ordered liveries, including a cloak for his coachman and a suit for the footboy, totalling £5. 5s. 0d., 22 June 1633, ib. vi.

Later, a paper endorsed 'grosers bill for frutes 19 of november 1638', totalling £10. 2s. 0d., gives an aspect of the family's eating habits. It includes: 86lb. each of currants and raisins at 5d. and 4½d. per lb. respectively; 40lb. of prunes at 2½d. per lb., nutmegs, large maces, milled mace, cloves, Jordan almonds, rice, dates, French barley, olives, capers, anise, liquorice, white wine vinegar etc., Long. W.P. vii, 294; the hamper, runlets (or casks), two barrels, bags and boxes were returnable to Robert Martyn, the grocer. The next month, household accounts included a dozen candles for 5s. 0d., two pairs of worsted stockings 13s. 0d., tobacco pipes 2d., a hat for Master James (aged 7) 4s. 6d. and 1s. 6d. for dressing Whitelocke's beaver (hat), 8 Dec. 1638, ib. 296. There is a receipt for an ornate bridle and saddle supplied by John Fletcher, in July 1651, costing £6. 3s. 6d., ib. xi, 51.

A teasingly large account, prepared by Whitelocke's secretary, Daniel Earle (q.v.), and showing his master's transactions, deserves closer attention than space and time can allow to it here. It amounts to over £12,000 in money received and paid out between May and November 1652; among other substantial receipts, Earle showed: £2,066. 13s. 4d. from (presumably the estate of) Rowland Wilson jun. (q.v.) of Martin Abbey, probably a legacy to his widow Mary, who was by then married to Whitelocke; from the Guinea Company at 'Mr Abbotts' (again, Martin i.e. Merton Abbey) £1,552. 10s. 0d., and from Whitelocke's kinsman by marriage, the merchant Samuel Wilson, £500; there were undefined payments for as much as £2,000 from Sir Humfry Foster *sic*, (q.v. as Humphrey Forster), and from a Mr. Bailie and others, ib. xii, 181v.–182.

When Whitelocke was a Commissioner at the Treasury, he kept a copy of Treasury Estimates for the year to 1 November 1657, totalling £2,326,989 with revenue to £1,743,478, ib. xvii, 218; also accounts of cash in the Exchequer and 'Pressing payments' at 10 Mar. 1656/57, ib. xviii, 27–28, with further Treasury accounts at 7 Apr. 1657, ib. 38–39; 19 May 1657, ib. 51–52; 7 July 1657, ib. 73; 9 Mar. 1657/58, ib. 121–122.

Whitelocke himself seems to have been a big spender; his bonds to friends and to various wealthy men appear in most decades of his life, not least in the last years, when his income had dwindled to a trickle of small fees for legal advice and rents from tenants. His Will, referred to in the entry for his son Bigley (above), shows that the once properous man of property had, by the time of his death, made over his estates to his elder sons and had spent his money (apart from his extravagant outlay on new buildings, in his last years) on the education and training of his sons, and on dowries for his daughters. There was very little left to bequeath.

WHITELOCKE, Bulstrode, jun. (b. 1647). Born 17 Nov. and baptized in the dining-room of Whitelocke's Middle Temple Chambers, *Diary* 17, 30 Nov. 1647; Add. Ms 37344 fol. 123; or baptized 1 Dec., according to *Register of the Temple Church, London* (Harleian Society New Series i. 1979). Bulstrode was the ninth and last child of Whitelocke's second marriage. He inherited, perhaps by accident, the reversion of lands in Essex and Northamptonshire, under the Will of Dr. Thomas Winston (q.v.), *Diary* 24 Oct. 1655; 27 Feb. 1662/63, *passim*. His father and stepmother (Mary, q.v.), both believed that the Doctor had intended to leave his property to one of her small sons (i.e. a child of Whitelocke's third marriage), since she was an old friend of the Doctor's and had introduced him to Whitelocke. The legacy resulted in lengthy negotiations and an Act of Parliament in the name of the Earl of Portland (q.v.), ib. 19, 26 Feb. 1662/63.

Whitelocke was at Chilton Lodge, in west Berkshire, at the time of the Fire of London; his son Bulstrode, aged nearly 19, was at their Fleet Street house, where he and a servant, Elizabeth Roberts (q.v.), salvaged two loads of his father's goods, ib. 10 Sept. 1666. In 1668, young Bulstrode started studying medicine at Leyden, under the distinguished Dr. Boerhaave; (the University attracted students from all over Europe, but especially from England and Scotland). When he was taken ill in Utrecht, young Bulstrode was befriended by James Desborough (kinsman of John Desborough, q.v.), ib. 26 Oct. 1669, with note. He recovered and came home, ib. 13 July 1670. The following year he wrote home from Leyden, ib. 30 Jan. 1670/71 and from Paris, ib. 6 July 1671. Two years later, Whitelocke was troubled to receive letters from his son in London 'demanding his money' and 'earnest for money', ib. 26 Apr., 7 May 1673. When young Bulstrode and his brother William visited their father at Chilton Lodge, 'Bul' (*sic*) was 'very garish', ib. 22 Sept. 1673; in spite of this, he was regarded as sufficiently reliable to accompany the tutor, James Pearson (q.v.), on his mission to get 'Bul's' half-brother, Bigley Whitelocke (q.v.), away from evil company in Marlborough, ib. 5 Oct. 1673.

WHITELOCKE, Bulstrode (grandsons). Three of Whitelocke's grandsons (sons of James, William and Sam), were named after him. The first appears in *Diary* 2 Apr. 1658, 13 June 1659, 20 June 1671; he entered the Middle Temple on 1 May 1676, see *Admission Register*. The second namesake, apparently a son of Sir William (q.v.) of Phyllis Court, was shot dead by Captain Lorange, at the King's Head, Cirencester, in 1688; he had been marching with Lord Lovelace to join William of Orange. The third was born in 1678, three years after Whitelocke's death, and died in 1737; his memorial bust may be seen over the south door inside Chilton Foliat Church. The name has recurred down the centuries, in many generations of the Whitelocke family.

WHITELOCKE, Carleton (1652–1705). *Alumni Oxonienses*. The second child of Whitelocke's third marriage, coming between Samuel (q.v.) and Bigley (q.v.). Carleton was given his mother's maiden name (just as his half-brother, Willoughby, and their father, Bulstrode, were given their mothers' surnames as Christian names). Carleton was already a sickly child, at the age of nine, when his young tutor Ichabod Chauncy (q.v.), struck him on the head with a heavy book. Whitelocke was fair-minded enough to write that he could not say whether it was this that caused the boy to suffer violent attacks of nose-bleeding, but he dismissed the tutor, *Diary* 23 Aug. 1657; 6 Jan. 1657/58; 14 Aug., 16 Sept. 1661, *passim*. Various forms of treatment were used in the attempt to cure Carleton's nose-bleeding: medicines were prescribed; he was let blood; fingers were pressed up his nostrils to stem the bleeding, after which he was given a purge to clear the accumulated blood from his stomach; he also had bruised nettles pushed up his nostrils, ib. 1 Oct. 1661; 9 Aug. 1662.

A few years later, Carleton and his elder brother Sam studied together at St. Edmund Hall, Oxford, ib. 16, 30 June 1668. The next year, Whitelocke was 'full of trouble' on hearing that his sons at Oxford 'were not so studious & thrifty as they should be', ib. 24 July 1669. They both went on to study at the Middle Temple, and Carleton was called to the Bar in May 1673. He returned to his parents at Chilton Lodge, where he sometimes read his father's sermons to the family, at Conventicles, ib. 16 Aug., 11, 18 Oct. 1674. He became Steward of the Manor at Hidden cum Iddington on the Chilton Park estate, and held the Court Baron there during his father's lifetime, ib. 15 Oct. 1674; 9 Apr. 1675. He continued to serve as Steward after his brother Sam became master of Chilton Lodge, see a document of 17 Apr. 1677, Long. W.P. xx, 171; also Wilts. R.O. Apr. 1692, 212B 3458 (H.1-10), *passim*. For further details of Carleton's Stewardship see N.F. Hidden *Manor of Hidden* (privately published. 1987) p. 93, *passim*.

Carleton inherited substantial property in Hersham, Surrey, from the astrologer, William Lilly (q.v.), whom Whitelocke had helped years earlier when Lilly was in prison, *Diary* 12 Oct. 1658; 27 Feb. 1662/63; 25 Apr. 1663. He married: (1) Catherine or Katherine Henley of Bramshill, Hampshire, in 1678; (2) Mary née Alwyn (or Aylwin), widow of Thomas Kitchell of Greyford, Kent. He was probably the most reliable of Whitelocke's sons, for he was chosen as a trustee to his father's Will; the text of the Will is given in R. Spalding *Improbable Puritan* p. 254. (Carleton's son, John Carleton Whitelocke, served as an Officer in the King's Army in Ireland; he settled in Priorswood, a house outside Dublin, taking with him a number of family heirlooms, and headed the Irish line of the Whitelocke family.) Carleton edited his father's *Essays Ecclesiastical and Civil* for publication; when it appeared, in 1706, it contained a printed note 'from the Bookseller to the Reader', indicating that Carleton had died before the work appeared.

WHITELOCKE, Cecilia, a daughter of the second marriage; see HARVEY, Cecilia.

WHITELOCKE, Capt. Edmund (1565–1608). *D.N.B.*; *Liber Famelicus* pp. 7–11 with notes, *passim*; *Historical Manuscripts Commission Hatfield House*, parts 10, 12, 14, 17, 18, *passim*; ib. for *Duke of Rutland*, Belvoir Castle, iv, *passim*. The most extraordinary member of the family.

Whitelocke's uncle and godfather. He was educated at Merchant Taylors' School, under Richard Mulcaster; then at Christ's College, Cambridge, where he studied 'liberall sciences' and continued with his Greek, Latin and Hebrew; subsequently at Lincoln's Inn where (according to his youngest brother, Whitelocke's father) he 'spent his time among to [i.e. too] good companions'. At 23 he left England to study, in turn, at the Universities of Rostock, Wittenberg, Prague, Rome and Paris. He was away for nearly 12 years and his family did not know whether he was alive or dead. How his lengthy studies and expensive tastes were financed is not explained; his youngest brother, Judge Sir James Whitelocke, described him as 'prodigall and wastefull in his expence ...'

When Edmund came back to England, with the rank of a Captain in the French Army, his polished manners and speech were such that he was sometimes taken for a Frenchman. With his quick wit and racy sophistication, he charmed his way into aristocratic circles and managed to live, without working, in the houses of various noblemen, who favoured him 'by reason of his experience in foreyne affayres, his knoledge in the tongs [i.e. tongues] ... pleasant behaviour, and ... wit in his conversation, according to the Frenche fashion ...', *Liber* p. 8. Captain Whitelocke's friends and benefactors included: Secretary of State Sir Robert Cecil, created Earl of Salisbury in 1605 (with whom Edmund corresponded when in trouble); Henry Percy, 9th Earl of Northumberland (who apparently granted him a pension of £40 a year, later increased to £60, see below); Roger Manners, 5th Earl of Rutland (with whom he lived much of the time); this Earl's disbursements on his behalf for some two years from January 1598/99 included payments for cloth boot-hose, for his doctor's fees and apothecary's bills, and 'Defrayments for diet at London', *H.M.C. Duke of Rutland* (above) iv, *passim*.

On two occasions, Edmund's friendship with noblemen led him into grave danger, purely by association. He was arrested after the 2nd Earl of Essex's conspiracy against Queen Elizabeth was discovered. His youngest brother gives an account of this in *Liber* pp. 8–9; he himself gives a slightly different version, in a letter to Sir Robert Cecil, which explains that on Sunday 8 Feb. 1600/01, he followed the Earl of Rutland to Essex House, where he found him with a crowd of gentlemen who were all setting off for the City, on what Edmund thought was 'some private quarrel'. He accompanied Rutland, wishing to support him because of the many courtesies he had received from that quarter. When, however, Edmund heard the Queen's name mentioned as a party to the dispute he left hurriedly, and hid in the house of a citizen 'of good account', from 1.0 p.m. on the Sunday until the Monday morning. He was falsely accused to Cecil's brother, Lord Burghley (who had been in the City), of persuading Essex's company 'to persist in their rebellion'; but he claimed that, on the contrary, some people suspected him of trying to keep Rutland away from Essex, *H.M.C. Hatfield House*, part 10, pp. 40–41, endorsed 11 Jan. [a slip for Feb.?] 1600/[01]. He was accused of high treason and was imprisoned, first in Newgate and then in the Marshalsea, but was finally discharged.

Much the same misfortune befell Edmund as a result of his dining at Syon House with the Earl of Northumberland and Thomas Percy on 4 Nov. 1605, the very eve of Guy Fawkes's Gunpowder Plot, in which Percy was a prime mover. On that occasion he was arrested, sent to the Tower and then to the Fleet but again, after a long spell of imprisonment, he was released since once more there was no evidence against him. Four days after the Gunpowder Plot was uncovered, Sir Walter Ralegh (who was in the Tower for an alleged conspiracy against King James I, and was assumed to be in sympathy with the conspirators) wrote to the Council defensively: 'I have not had any other affair with Captain Whitlock than familiar and ordinary discourse, neither do I know any other cause of his coming unto me than to visit me, having not much wherewith to busy himself . . .', *H.M.C. Hatfield House* part 17, p. 480, 9 Nov. 1605. In the same month, an anonymous writer reported a meeting in Lent, the previous year, at the Horns Tavern in Carter Lane, when various men (including Catesby) had been present; the writer did not name Edmund as being among them, but went on to state, darkly: 'Whitlocke, that is now in the Tower, was in the beginning of Summer last in the Archduke's country as he confessed himself [presumably this implied a 'popish plot']; and often afterwards came to the Tower after his return and there accompanied Sir Walter Raughley', ib. p. 522.

In an undated letter, endorsed 1605, Edmund wrote to the Earl of Salisbury from the Tower, objecting to the Council saying, in his hearing, that he had not been truthful about Sir Walter Ralegh. He went on to ask for 'liberty of this house [the Tower] like other prisoners' and for an opportunity to clear his name of 'confederacy with these wretched men that have gone about so unchristianlike to destroy the King and his realms. I shall behave myself in such sort that you shall hear no complaint of me' (this sounds like legal advice from his young brother, James), ib. p. 646, endorsed '1605'. A note from Will Julian (apparently a personal servant) refers to 40s. od. received for Captain Whitelocke, half of which Julian had kept for his board, wages and lodgings. 'I have sent you this morning ½ ounce of "tobbaca" price 3s. I know not how you will like it, but I take it to be good'. He reported that the Lieutenant's man had locked up Edmund's desk, but 'without perusing anything'. A message to the Earl of Salisbury, at the foot of the letter, indicates that this note was intercepted, ib. 517, 27 Nov. 1605. Asking a favour of the Earl of Salisbury, the next year, the

Captain referred to 'the errors I came into unawares', for which he made no excuse. He was still anxious to be allowed freedom within the Tower, this time in order to visit Henry Percy, 9th Earl of Northumberland (imprisoned there in June 1606), who was 'settling his estate'. Edmund's presence, as a dependant, was required; 'admittance will assuredly help my fortune, my absence peradventure may lose it', ib. part 18 p. 453, endorsed 1606. Northumberland, who remained in the Tower for 16 years, had an extensive library in his quarters and employed a fleet of research assistants, see *D.N.B.*; Edmund, widely travelled and cultured, may well have been one of them.

Bulstrode Whitelocke's christening had taken place at the Church of St. Dunstan in the West, less than three months before the Gunpowder Plot. The godfathers were his uncles, Henry Bulstrode (q.v.), and Captain Edmund Whitelocke. Perhaps it was his gift for pleasing those he was with, that prompted Edmund to name the infant 'Bulstrode'; when challenged, he declared that the parson could choose between Bulstrode and Elizabeth, but he was resolved the child should have one of its mother's names (and the Parson chose the lesser of two evils), *Diary* 1605.1606. fols. I–IV.

Edmund was staying at New Hall, Essex, with Robert Radcliffe, 5th Earl of Sussex, when he died in the hot summer of 1608. Apart from his reputation as a sociable and witty companion, Edmund seems to have earned his keep in that household by singularly unsavoury means: it is recorded that he was hired by the Earl of Sussex to regale the Countess with tales of the clothes lavished by her husband on one of her former gentlewomen, the Earl's mistress, who later became his second wife, see Manningham's *Diary*, quoted in G.E.C. under 5th Earl of Sussex p. 527 note a. Edmund's charm (coupled no doubt with his services to the Earl) earned him a burial place in the Sussex family vault, under their Chapel in Boreham Church, Essex.

WHITELOCKE, Elizabeth, sen. (1575–1631). *Liber, passim.* Bulstrode Whitelocke's mother. Born at Hedgerley Bulstrode, south-west of Gerrards Cross, Bucks.; daughter of Edward Bulstrode and his wife Cecill, née Croke, she married James Whitelocke sen. (q.v.), later a Judge and a Knight. The marriage settlement was executed between Elizabeth's widowed mother, acting with her son Henry Bulstrode (q.v.), and the prospective husband, James Whitelocke, of the Middle Temple. Basically, it amounted to a dowry for Elizabeth of £500, with clothing and jewellery 'fittinge for her place and degree' and the couple's free board and lodging for a certain length of time, left vague in the settlement, but shown as 18 months by James Whitelocke, *Liber*, p. 15; for the original settlement, see Long. W.P. i, 37–37v.

Whitelocke described his mother as being, in times of illness, 'full of skill . . . [and] tenderness . . . She did much good . . . by her extraordinary skill in physicke & Surgery, wherby . . . she did many great Cures in her own family & uppon her sicke friends & neighbors . . . & most uppon poor people who had not means to gratify a Doctor . . .', Add. Ms 53726 fols. 4v.–5. When Whitelocke, aged nine, was kicked in the mouth by a horse, his mother sewed up his lip and it healed, slowly and painfully, leaving only a scar, ib. fol. 7. His parents supplemented his school work with (among other subjects) religious instruction, and his mother was the 'the more zealous . . . , being of that perswasion . . . which was then in scorne termed Puritanisme . . .', ib. Earlier, when he was four years old, she had taught him to read and to begin to study, 'being herselfe well furnished with learning, she had read much, & was able to make use of it, especially she was expert in the french Language', *Diary* 1609.1610. fol. 1v., with note.

Elizabeth was also an effective organizer: once, when she and her husband were walking round the Fawley estate, he said he wished they could build a new barn in place of the old one. When he went away as a Circuit Judge, 'she caused timber to be cutt down & framed, & all preparations to be ready for the building', and '. . . had a fayre barne newly built & finished, before harvest'; when her husband returned 'he wondred, & took great contentment, att the setting up of a new barne, which he only wished & it was done', Add. Ms 53726 fol. 55v. On the eve of Whitsun, in the following year, Elizabeth (who had been taken ill in London), travelled to Fawley Court with her son. She knew it was to be her last journey and, weak though she was, she insisted on alighting from the coach and walking, with her son's help, up the avenue of elms to the house. The account of her last contented and even cheerful hours, is touchingly told, ib. 58–58v.; also in *Diary* 1630.1631. fols. 12v.–13v.

WHITELOCKE, Elizabeth, jun. (1) (b. 1638), a daughter of Whitelocke's second marriage; see PRYCE, Sir Richard.

WHITELOCKE, Elizabeth, jun. (2). Née Gough or Goffe. (See entry for the GOUGH family.) Of Vernham, Hants, some 12 miles from Chilton Lodge. Joint heiress, with two sisters, she married Samuel (q.v.), eldest son of Whitelocke's third marriage. Elizabeth's marriage portion was £3,000, with the promise of a share in her father's estate at his death, *Diary* 8 Nov., *passim*, 22 with note, 23, 26, 27 Dec. 1671, *passim*. After the wedding, the couple lived in their own quarters at Chilton Lodge, the property which Sam was to inherit. Whitelocke became apprehensive, on

hearing that his new daughter-in-law was pleading for 'patches (fashionable in the 1660s) to wear on her face, also for paint (i.e. make-up), and
that she was expressing a wish to live in London and to go and see plays.
(This last should not have shocked Whitelocke, in view of his own frequent
visits to the Playhouse when he was a Middle Temple student, as the
accounts in his entry show; perhaps as an old man he considered the
Playhouse unsuitable for young ladies.) There was also discontent over
Sam's (quite substantial) side of the marriage settlement, ib. 5 Feb., 6
Mar., 1671/72, both with notes. Elizabeth went on her own to stay with her
father, and seemed not to want her husband's company, ib. 8 Oct. 1672;
she even took her horse and a groom and went to Vernham without telling
Sam or his friends, 'an unusual & unhansome freake', ib. 10 Mar. 1672/73;
she was nearly three months pregnant at the time. The same occurred on
20 Apr. 1674. When her daughter Mary was born at Chilton Lodge, her
sisters, Mrs. Godfrey and later Mrs. Forster, rallied round '& there was
trouble enough, as is usual at such times', ib. 30 Sept., 3, 18 Oct. 1673,
passim. When Elizabeth's brother-in-law, Mr. Forster, arrived 'there was
much whispering between him & his Sister Wh[itelocke], though her
husband & others were by', ib. 13 Jan. 1673/74, and there was the same
lack of discretion even on Christmas Day, ib. 25 Dec. 1674. The last entry
concerning this daughter-in-law states briefly: 'My Son Sams wife gave me
trouble', ib. 19 May 1675. It may or may not be relevant, that this was two
days after Whitelocke signed his last Will.

WHITELOCKE, the Hon. Frances, sen. (1614–1649). Daughter of
William, 3rd Lord Willoughby of Parham, and sister of Lord Francis and
the Hon. Colonel William Willoughby, the 5th and 6th Barons (q.v.).
Whitelocke, as a young widower, first set eyes on Frances when he called
on her aunt, the dowager Countess of Sunderland (q.v.), whose home
(New House, Hambleden, Bucks.) was a short ride from Fawley. The
courtship started at once and flourished, with the consent of Frances's
widowed mother, and under the approving eye of the Countess, with the
added bonus that James Whitelocke, junior (aged three), took to Frances,
calling her 'his Lady', *Diary* 1634.1635. fols. 30–33, *passim*; Add. Ms 37343
fol. 5v. Whitelocke was obliged to go to London briefly, on professional
business, and took the opportunity both to have his hair and beard
trimmed and to order smart coloured clothes from his tailor, with a 'falling
band' at the neck (as his portrait shows), instead of the old-fashioned ruff
of the earlier portrait. At that point Frances Willoughby's brother, Lord
Willoughby of Parham, and her uncle, the 7th Earl of Rutland
(q.v.), descended on Fawley; (as an executor to her father's estate,

Rutland controlled Frances Willoughby's marriage portion). They made enquiries about Whitelocke's income and standing, even having the effrontery to question tenant-farmer William Cooke (q.v.) about his landlord's finances. The Earl then announced that his niece could not be allowed to marry a commoner. His unfortunate sister, the Dowager Lady Sunderland, was instructed to convey this information to Whitelocke who learned, on his return, that he was no longer welcome at New House. But 'love', as he wrote, 'is a subtle & a moving passion', ib. fol. 8. He had an ally in a gentlewoman of the Countess's household, Theodosia Thynne (q.v.), and in William Cooke's wife, who carried his letters to Frances, hidden in the baskets of provisions she took to New House. A letter declaring his love, dated 23 Sept. 1634, with a covering note to Mrs. Thynne, is in Long. W.P. vi, 129.

The ban on the courtship led to a runaway marriage, carried out with the connivance of Mrs. Thynne, who acted as go-between. It is remarkable that this gentlewoman of the household managed to slip away and join Whitelocke and some stalwart young friends of his in London, to devise the campaign. Everything went according to plan, and after a secret wedding in Whitelocke's private Chapel at Fawley Court, the couple were driven at top speed to London for a honeymoon at the Ship, in Fleet Street. There, Whitelocke indicates, the Almighty made it up to him for his earlier, disastrous marriage, *Diary* 1634.1635. fol. 30–34; more fully in Add. Ms 37343 fol. 9v., *passim*. The Lord Chamberlain (the 4th Earl of Pembroke, q.v.), and even King Charles I (q.v.), spoke favourably of the marriage; Bishop Williams (q.v.) wrote a helpful letter commending Whitelocke, and gradually the bride's aristocratic family accepted the inevitable and received the young lawyer into their circle.

It was clearly a love match, untainted by other considerations. Frances, an uninhibited young woman, free from ladylike constraints, would (as Whitelocke wrote) meet him when he came home from work 'leaping, & rejoycing to ... wellcome me'. Until her last illness, she always sat up for him when he was out late. They had three sons and six daughters, and Frances died when she was six months pregnant with a 10th child. Her death was no doubt speeded by the bizarre series of treatments recommended by a team of well-known physicians, in consultation with the famous doctor, Sir Theodor Mayerne (q.v.). They prescribed bleeding, a laxative drink, cordials, vomits, suppositories, and the application of pigeons, slit in half and bandaged to the soles of the patient's feet, *Diary* 27 Apr. to 16 May 1649, *passim*.

The 'Annales' version gives a more detailed account of Frances's character and family; of Whitelocke's astonished delight that a woman, with no political experience, could give him such wise advice; of the medical treatment given to her; of her passionate desire, at one point in her pregnancy, to eat a sweet lemon, and at another time to devour some pomegranates; of Frances's illness and death and of Whitelocke's almost demented grief. He gives a vivid, if sometimes incoherent, picture of a very fine woman. Whereas he was frank, in *The Diary*, about occasional difficulties at home with his first wife, Rebecca, and with his third wife, Mary, of Frances he wrote that they had met 'uppon termes of affection only, without consideration, of portion or Estate, or settlem[en]^{ts}, or those ... provisions, & discreet cares of friends ... she trusted me only, & marryed me for no other reason butt bicause she loved me, the same were my motives for marrying with her.' After referring to her family and descent from the Plantagenets he described her, recording that she was:

> ... taller then most woemen, her person ... streight & exceeding beautifull, her Countenance with a mixture of modesty & cheerfullness, of a most lovely aspect ... Her discourse, was ... serious, wise, & godly, & att fitt times full of ... mirth ... In the most perplexed & difficult matters, which befell me, in my publique imploym[en]^{ts}, I received sound & wise Counsell from her, beyond imagination to come from a woemans braine, unexperienced in such affayres. When she saw me troubled ... she alwayes ministred to me comfort & courage, & cheered me up in all difficulties. She was constantly, & in all the time of the War ... most firme to the Parlem[en]^{ts} interest, and to the Army, & uppon any doubts in my selfe ... she would still confirme me to goe on, & joyne with them in the cause of God, which she tooke to be the Parlem[en]^{ts} cause ... she was much unsatisfyed with the Kings proceedings, butt more with the finall proceedings ag[ains]^t him. In all companies, she would maintain the justnes of the Parlem[en]^{ts} cause, & would shew more then ordinary passion ag[ains]^t those who did traduce or censure them ... & in all trouble there never was a truer comfort then this woman ... her counsell ... was alwayes backed with solid reason ... I injoyed the blessing of her society 14 years, 6 moneths, & 6 dayes, in all which time, I never heard an ill worde from her to me or any other nor [saw] an unworthy or ill action done by her ... she had bin bredd as high & plentifully with her Mother, & afterwarde with her Aunt the Countess of Sunderland as any young woman, yett she was as humble, as little expensive or addicted to gadding or gallantrye, & as well contented in my poor house[;] & when the troubles drove us ... thence, in a meane Temple chamber ... in all the troubles & changes ... and ... after our plate [was] solde & the money spent, & nothing comming out of our estate ... & smalle hopes of getting more, to buy bread for us & our children, yett ... was she not one jot discouraged, or lesse cheerfull ... And when I was in my great trouble, upon the accusation of my L[ord] Savile [Earl of Sussex, q.v.] ag[ains]^t Mr Hollis [q.v.] & me, when she was told that my life & fortune would be taken away from her & her children, she was not troubled ... butt did greatly incourage me, & cheer me, & sayd she was confident of Gods mercy ... [He described her gifts at running their home] she would see her house to be neate, sweet, & cleanly

... certainly, never husband, children, friends, servants, fed att any table with more contentm[en]ᵗ, plenty, cheerfullnes, & freedom, then her table did affoarde, & ... with farre lesse charge, then reasonably could be imagined. With so much ... wholsomness, & orderlyness of dyet, that seldome any of our family ... were in sickeness, though so full of children & servants ... [She herself was never ill until struck down by the sickness from which she died. She had always been a good traveller; before a journey] she would be the first ready, & the last weary, never (as the custome of Ladyes is) would she make the Company waite for her, ... she commonly waited for the Company. She loved good horses ... & would herselfe oversee the feeding & dressing of her horses ... [She had a rare gift of love] & her wisdome was seen, in her admirable education & governm[en]ᵗ of her children & serv[an]ᵗˢ[,] who all, did beare her as great awe & love togither as was possible. She would tell any of them their faults, with some quicknesse, butt would soone be meeke & loving agayne, she never did strike any serv[an]ᵗ, & very rarely a childe, yett they all stood in as much awe of her eye, or worde, as of any correction ... [Whitelocke wrote of her familiarity with the humblest servants in the house, of her giving them good counsel] & if any of them were sicke, she was very tender of them ... [Her children lacked nothing,] butt she did not like to keep them in any height, rather lower then their condition, knowing there were many of them to be provided for ... [yet she never opposed] any charge for my eldest Son [James, the spoilt son and heir] though not her own ...

She had put in order the house, gardens and walks at Phyllis Court, and finished what had to be done to her husband's Middle Temple Chambers, including his study, furnishing and equipping it all to his great satisfaction, and she had effected the move from a house near Temple Bar to his new Chambers; with 'great care & providence, she had caused my last debt[,] which was to Mʳ Tichborne [q.v.], to be discharged.' When she had seen to all these matters, 'as if she had done all she could thinke of, for my content & good ... she tooke herselfe to her new chamber in the Temple, & there she dyed.' In his distress, Whitelocke believed it was his sins that had 'brought this terrible judgm[en]ᵗ' on him. The elaborate arrangements for the funeral cortège from London to Fawley (where Frances was to be buried in the Whitelocke vault), were made by Lady Elizabeth Willoughby (q.v.); the funeral address was given by Mr. Hanserd Knowles or Knollys (q.v.). Near the end of his moving recollections of his wife, Whitelocke wrote: 'In all the time of our being togither, there never past an ill or harsh word between us, all our worldly care was to please one another, & to injoy our selves, in the mercyes which God bestowed ...', 27 Apr. to 18 May 1649, Add. Ms 37344 fols. 286–300v. (The Diary gives 17 May as the day of the funeral, but 18 May is the more likely date.)

Only two letters from Frances have been traced, of March 1647/48, Add. Ms 37344 fols. 136 and 136v. (transcripts). Elaborately inscribed verses to her, entitled 'Carmen Congratulatorium', were probably written soon after the runaway marriage; a pattern of green leaves encircles two hearts, with the words 'Honour' in one heart, 'Love' in the other, and 'Fidelity' between them. In the verses below these emblems, the initial letters of the odd-number lines spell BULSTRODE WHITELOCKE (in red) while the even-number lines, which are indented, read FRANCES WHITELOCKE (in blue), Long. W.P. Parcel 4, No. 23 (3 papers clipped together). An Elegy to Frances, with heavy black borders, is in the same Parcel. Whitelocke also wrote two versions of 'A dialogue betweene a Disconsolate husband, and sorrowful child ...', i.e. Frances Whitelocke, jun. (1), the original being in ib. Parcel 5. Fuller details of this are given in the entry for their daughter Frances (below).

WHITELOCKE, Frances, jun. (1) (1635–1654). First child of Whitelocke and his second wife, Frances (above). Early in her life, when she was subject to fainting fits, her parents discovered that, in their absence, she was being badly treated by Mrs. Letitia Hungerford (q.v.), her mother's 'waiting gentlewoman', Diary 29 Sept. 1648. She was sturdy enough, at 12 years old, to ride 'in a day singly [a single day? or was she alone?] on horsebacke, from Phillis Court [Henley-on-Thames] to London', ib. 16 Oct. 1648. She comes across as a warm-hearted, mature child: in the last months of her mother's life, young Frances tended her with 'all diligence, carefullnes & willingnes', and waited on her 'w[i]'h great affection & care' (her mother being pregnant), ib. 8, 21 Mar. 1648/49. After her mother's death, this 13-year-old seems to have been responsible for the house-keeping; her duties included bringing her father accounts of the money she spent on her sisters and brothers, as her mother had done, ib. 21 June 1649. When Whitelocke became ill with grief, he was supported by many kind friends 'Butt his daughter Frances was beyond all', ib. 19 Dec. 1649. In the verse dialogue between the bereaved husband and his child (referred to in the entry above), Frances recalled her mother with the words:

> ... her household disciplined to all
> her children, servants, ready at her call ...
> her government of love was such
> none thought their busines servile or too much ...
> [her mother had shown]
> a meaknes in prosperity
> a manly courage in adversity ...

The original version of this dialogue, in Long. W.P. Parcel 5, was improved by Whitelocke in a second version, which appears in his record of 'September 1653', Add. Ms 53727 pp. 30–40. (At the time of writing, this manuscript, which is one of the four volumes found by the editor in Ireland, has not been foliated, so Whitelocke's paging is given.) Although undistinguished as poetry, some of the lines express Whitelocke's love and anguish. A conversation (recorded in the second source) led to Whitelocke allowing Frances to see his verses, and after reading them she asked if she might keep them. Before reading the poem she spoke of Mary, her stepmother (or 'mother in law' as she called her), and said with the worldly-wise candour of a teenager: 'we might have had a froward, proud, expensive[,] carelesse mother in law, who would not have regarded you or your children, butt her own humor.' Whitelocke knew by then (2 September 1653) that he might be compelled to go as Ambassador Extraordinary to Sweden (where he would be in grave danger of assassination); he told Franke (as he called her) that she and her brothers and sisters must treat Mary with love and respect, during his absence. Frances endearingly described her stepmother as 'our best friend, for so she testifies her selfe to be, & ... none could discerne by her actions butt that she were our own mother', ib. pp. 25–29.

   Some months later, when Whitelocke was in Sweden, Queen Christina (q.v.) questioned him about one of his daughters (namely Frances) who, she had heard, although 'of a good spirit ... was averse to marryage', *Diary* 30 Jan. 1653/54. Not long after Whitelocke's return from Sweden, Frances (who had turned down a match with the heir to a large estate, ib. 27 Oct. 1651), was betrothed to a son of Serjeant Bernard and was soon to have married him, but she died of smallpox in Whitelocke's Temple Chambers, ib. 2 Dec. 1654. For details of an elegy written in her memory, see the entry for STAPYLTON, Robert.

WHITELOCKE, Frances, jun. (2) 'Frank', see PILE.

WHITELOCKE, Hester, see PRYCE, Carbery.

WHITELOCKE, Judge Sir James, MP (1570–1632). *D.N.B.*; *Alumni Oxonienses*; J. Whitelocke *Liber Famelicus* (Camden Society. 1858), reprinted (Johnson Reprint Corporation, U.S.A. 1968); the manuscript of this book, Add. Ms 53725, contains many of the Judge's accounts which are omitted from the printed text. The father of Bulstrode Whitelocke, James Whitelocke, sen., was the youngest son of a youngest son. His father, Richard Whitelocke (merchant), of Thames Street, London, died aged 37 on a business trip to the Bordeaux vineyards, three weeks before

James and his twin brother, William, were born in the Thames Street house, which had passed to their mother. James's eldest brother was Whitelocke's godfather, the unpredictable Captain Edmund Whitelocke (q.v.). The boys' mother (Whitelocke's grandmother) was Joan, née Colte, daughter of a tenant farmer in Little Munden south-east of Stevenage, Herts.; she was executrix to her second husband's Will, and proved herself an astute administrator. She showed less talent, however, in the choice of her third husband, Thomas Price (merchant), who was described by his stepson, James, as 'a notable unthrift, and a verye unkinde and insolent husband'. James went on to describe the 'extraordinarye providence and patience' with which his mother, 'by meanes underhand', preserved the £150 allocated from their father's estate to each of her four sons; how she bought up 50-year leases in the parish of St. Dunstan's in the East, managed the inheritance skilfully and, in spite of being 'so afflicted withe the dayly miseries wroughte to her from her husband', gave all her sons a good education. After she had buried her husband, Thomas Price, she sold the leases at a profit, kept a portion for her own needs, and distributed the rest among her sons, *Liber* pp. 6–7.

James, the youngest and, on the evidence, the most gifted and reliable of the four boys, went from Merchant Taylors' School, to St.John's College, Oxford, then, in 1590 to New Inn and in 1592 to the Middle Temple. He was called to the Bar in 1600, appointed Land Steward of his old College in 1601, and he married Elizabeth Bulstrode (q.v. as Elizabeth Whitelocke, sen.) in Beaconsfield Church, Bucks., in 1602. They had seven children, of whom three survived infancy: Elizabeth (q.v., who married Thomas Mostyn), Bulstrode (the diarist) and Cecilia (q.v. who married Edward Dixon). Their father, James, was appointed Steward and Counsel of Eton College in December 1609, and joint-Steward of Westminster College (of which Westminster School was and is a part) in the following May. He was elected MP for Woodstock in February 1609/10 (where he had served as Recorder from 1606) and he sat for the same constituency in 1614 and 1621/22. During his first year in the Commons, he challenged the legality of the King's impositions on imports, and in particular the increased duty on currants in Bate's case (four years earlier) when James I had quietly increased the duty from 2s. 6d. to 7s.6d. a hundredweight. The new MP for Woodstock, being an experienced lawyer, argued that such impositions could only be authorized by the sovereign power of state, and that by himself the King lacked such power; only the King in or with his Parliament wielded sovereign power, G.W. Prothero *Select Statutes and Other Constitutional Documents*, fourth edition. (O.U.P. 1913), pp. 351–353; *Liber* p. 24, *passim*. This was significant as a 'dummy-run' for challenges to the royal prerogative, made later by Sir John Eliot (q.v.) and John Hampden (q.v.).

Some three years after the contentious debates on impositions, James Whitelocke was warned by Sir Humphrey May (q.v.) that the King had taken grave exception to his parliamentary speeches and that he had done himself serious damage by the line he had taken; Sir Humphrey predicted, moreover, 'that sum ill mighte befalle ...' as a result, and James Whitelocke wrote: 'this he did continually inculcate unto me after the parliament ended, untill ill happened in deed', *Liber* pp. 32–33. In due course, James was confronted by a trumped up charge, was summoned to the Council Chamber in Whitehall, and was committed to the Fleet. After a month in prison, he made the necessary, abject apology, in writing, and was released on the King's order, ib. pp. 38–40 and *D.N.B.* Despite this contretemps, in 1620 James was appointed Chief Justice of the Court of Session for the County Palatine of Chester, he was knighted in the same year and made a King's Bench Judge in 1624.

In 1632, about a year after his wife's death, Judge Sir James Whitelocke caught a heavy cold and sensed that he was dying, but he remained active almost to the end. His death is described in detail, as are his legacies and his character, *Diary* 1631. 1632. fols. 14v.–16, and more fully in Add. Ms 53726 fols. 67–70v. This second version gives the text of: the Judge's Deed of Gift in his son's favour; his Will; and the Latin epitaph (for his wife and himself) which he wished his son to place on the monument to be built in Fawley Church. These documents were locked in a cabinet of private papers. Whitelocke wrote: '... I also found his Liber famelicus, the short story of his own life ...' ib. 70v. (see above). Whitelocke gives a list of the Judge's household, ranging from nine gentlemen, including the organist, who attended him (and some of whom kept their own servants and horses), to the 'Butler, the Cooke, the Baylife, the Gardiner, the Coachman, the Groome & the footman, & many chairefolkes continually about the house, his men servants were about twenty', ib. 69. When he was convinced 'that his death was drawing on, he spred all his sayles to gaine this harbour'.

A long description of the Judge in the same manuscript tells us:

> His stature was tall & proper. His person straight & somwhat corpulent ... His Countenance serious & smiling ... His mind, stout and pittifull [i.e. compassionate] ... His voyce was sweet & musicall. His speech rownd, & significant. His complexion sanguine, & healthfull. His temper was somwhat subject to Chollar ...

Whitelocke illustrated this last point with the story of a servant, Mr. Bull, who had been with James Whitelocke for 40 years, but who irritated him so much one day that the Judge:

> bad[e] him gett out of his house [Bull however did not go, and when the Judge asked him why not, he replied] If you doe not know when you have a

good servant, I know when I have a good Master, & therfore I will never leave you. which soft & drolling answear, pacifyed the Masters wrath, & reconciled him, to his old servant, who left him not, till he left this world.

Sir James was a scholarly man, with fluent Latin (which he spoke on one occasion for the benefit of some foreigners attending his Court of Law); he also had a good knowledge of Greek and Hebrew and of History:

> He was provident in his hous[e]hold affayres, & expences, & by his own industry ... raysed his own fortune & family, yett he was of a very generous mind in his intertainment of friends, & [showed] old English hospitality, & though he loved not feasting, ... yett his housekeeping was ... att all times free & liberall ... He was a most laborious student in his younger dayes, as I have heard from those that knew it, & ... in his latter dayes, he seldome neglected one hower of leisure, butt ... betooke himselfe to his study ...
>
> ib. 68–69.

The copy of a letter from Whitelocke to his sister, Elizabeth Mostyn (q.v.), endorsed '... *sur la mort de mon père*' has more immediacy:

> ... none of us had any fear of daunger. I my selfe was that day he dyed[,] which was last Thursday about 6 a clocke after noon [,come] from London [to Fawley] ... I think, at the instant I alighted from my horse the breath went out of his body for ... I ... ran unto his Chamber & kissed his warm flesh ...
>
> Long. W.P. Parcel 6 (in a vellum folder).

The same folder contains another long description by Whitelocke of his father. Three paragraphs, endorsed 'My Father[s] love of music', tell how the Judge's servants, Chaplain and clerks provided him with 'a consort of voyces in his owne house'; they were accompanied by an organ and other instruments, with 'himselfe bearing his parte among them', ib. xxiv, 239.

Many of the Judge's most valuable books and manuscripts were destroyed by the royalist soldiers who plundered Fawley Court, *Diary* 1642. 1643. fol. 58; Oct. 1644 fol. 67. Among the manuscripts which escaped their attention and were not used as spills for lighting their pipes, are: a bond from Thomas Shakespeare of Lutterworth to James Whitelocke, for 26s. 8d., 27 Nov. 1600, Long. W.P. i, 47; James Whitelocke's marriage settlement, ib. i, 37–37v. (damaged); sundry legal papers, including petitions, e.g. one concerning a staple for Welsh cloth at Oswestry, with an appeal that drapers at Shrewsbury might be allowed to sell existing supplies of cloth there, 13 Sept. 1622, ib. ii, 70; lists of prisoners awaiting trial, with the charges against them and marginal notes on the outcome, in Leicester, Warwick, Northampton, Rutland, Lincoln etc., between 1625 and 1627, ib. ii, 181, 182, iii, 6, 8, 10, *passim*. There is also a petition and a protest to Judge Whitelocke of 1624 and *c.* 1630, in Long. Coventry Papers xiii, 27; cxi, 32. A letter to James Whitelocke from

Sir Humphrey May (who had earlier warned him of King James's displeasure) reported that Charles I had referred to him (James Whitelocke) as '. . . a stout[,] wise & learned man; . . . I think you have the prime opinion w[i]'h him of all the Judges in England . . .', 8 May 1629, Long. W.P. iv, 9. Among the financial papers is a bond from the Judge's bargeman promising a payment of £16 for 32 loads of faggots, 14 June 1631, ib. v, 170. Political papers of some interest include: one from the House of Commons to James I, on the right to debate the question of impositions; another, concerning the perusal of records on that subject, housed in the Tower; a third is the King's reply to the Commons' grievances, 24 May, ib. i, 90; 12 June, ib. 92 and 10 July 1610, 94v. The warrants have survived relating to James Whitelocke's imprisonment in the Fleet, 18 May, ib. 166; and to his release, 13 June 1613, ib. 167. Later papers include one with a reference to a silver mine in Cardiganshire, July 1622, ib. ii, 64. For correspondence on various legal matters, see entry for: WILLIAMS, Archbishop John.

WHITELOCKE, Col. Sir James, MP (1631–1701). *D.N.B.* (in his father's entry); parish register, Trumpington, Cambs. Whitelocke's eldest son; the spoilt, only child of the unhappy first marriage. James and his eldest half-brother, William (q.v.), attended the boarding-school of a Mr. Shilborne (q.v.) at 'Grandon', i.e. Grendon, Northamptonshire, to which school Whitelocke later sent his sons Willoughby (q.v.) and Bulstrode (q.v.), R.H. Whitelocke *Memoirs . . . of Bulstrode Whitelocke* (Routledge. 1860) pp. 461–462. Once, during the Civil War, James and William were snatched away from school by an acquaintance of their father's for fear of their being seized by royalist soldiers, *Diary* 29 Sept. 1645. While still at school, they were formally admitted to the Middle Temple on 4 June 1647, *Middle Temple Admission Register* (or some months later, according to *Diary* 29 Oct. 1647). Whitelocke also recorded that he sent both boys to Oxford University (no College is mentioned), ib. 27 May 1648; no confirmation has been found that William ever studied there, but James Whitlock (*sic*) is shown as a 'Fellow' of All Souls from 22 Jan. 1648/49, *Alumni Oxonienses*; his father's entry shows this three days earlier, *Diary* 19 Jan. 1648/49; that was probably the day on which James set off for Oxford. The previous autumn, he had left school 'a well grounded Schollar', ib. 20 Oct. 1648, but that is the last we hear of his scholarly gifts.

From 17 May 1649 (nearly four months after the King's execution), Fairfax, Cromwell and other Army Officers, stayed in Oxford for several days, at All Souls; they were handsomely entertained and were awarded honorary degrees by the University. Speeches appropriate to the occasion were given by James Whitelocke's tutor, the newly-appointed Proctor, Jerome Zankey (q.v.), Fellow and Sub-Warden of All Souls, T. Carlyle *Letters and Speeches of Oliver Cromwell* i, 442. Two months after these celebrations, Zankey was accompanied by his pupil, James, as far as Bristol, where he and many others embarked for Ireland, under the command of Cromwell, the new Lord Lieutenant. Zankey served in Ireland as a Major and later as Colonel. Whitelocke was still stricken by the death, two months earlier, of his wife Frances (q.v.), when he received letters from Zankey, saying that James wished to volunteer for service in Ireland. This was 'altogither unexpected' and Whitelocke was deeply troubled at the news. James arrived in London, begging for his father's permission and stressing that Cromwell himself had invited him to go to Ireland, with promises of favour and preferment. Whitelocke, who was most reluctant to let him go, 'layd before him the daungers & hardships', as well as the fact that it would disrupt his studies at Oxford; but, as usual, James (backed by his uncle Richard Benet, q.v.) had his own way, having virtuously 'commended the sobriety & good company of the Officers of the Army' and the 'good example they gave', in contrast to 'the debauchery of the University', *Diary* 22, 24 July 1649; Add. Ms 37344 fols. 322–323, *passim*.

James's career in the Army was very successful; he proved to be courageous and a good comrade. Whitelocke recorded that he would not write (as some friends suggested) asking Cromwell to give the boy a commission:

> I thought it more proper, as it was more suitable to his owne desires, [for him] to goe over in a private capacity, & first to ride in the L[ieutenan]ts Regim[en]t as a Trouper ... which ... procured him the more credit among the soldiery, who love to have their officers to rise to commaunds by degrees & not *per saltum* [in one leap].

Whitelocke did, however, write asking Cromwell for his favour and care of James 'in respect of his Youth' (he was just 18), and expressed the hope that if, later on, his son 'should deserve his spurres & win them' Cromwell would then 'preferre' i.e. promote him. Cromwell replied that James was:

> the only gentleman of England that came as a volunteer [presumably a trooper volunteer as distinct from an officer] to serve under him in this expedition, & that he would have a very perticular care and respect towards him.

In due course, James was commissioned as a Standard-Bearer, as a Captain and finally (before the battle of Worcester), as a Colonel. His promotion laid a heavy financial burden on his father, who had sent him to Ireland with a servant, 'my 2 black saddle Nagges, & a wat[c]h & 15ˡ in gould in his pocket, with letters of credit for money both for England &

Ireland', Add. Ms 37344 fol. 326v. Even before he was commissioned, James borrowed £15 from Colonel Nathaniel Goffe, in Ireland, to buy himself a bay nag, with a bridle and saddle, writing confidently under his note of the debt: 'I have written to my father the L[or]^d Com[m]issioner Whitlocke [*sic*] to pay the sayd sum[m]e to his brother Collonel Goffe on sight of my letter ...', 14 Nov. 1649, Long. W.P. x. 44. He wrote from Cork, asking his father to pay £12 to Captain William Hind, 5 Jan. 1649/50, ib. 113. A few days earlier, he wrote announcing that Cromwell had appointed him Cornet (i.e. Standard-bearer) to his Life Guards; James mentioned, in passing, that he would need money to equip himself as an officer. It was perhaps the only occasion on which he showed a glimmer of self-doubt, writing of his commission: 'I hope the Allmighty providence will inable me to shew myselfe worthy of it, & hide my weakness[es] so, as they may [not] be ridiculous, nor offensive to any ...', 1 Jan. 1649/50, Add. Ms 37345 fols. 36v.–37, (transcript).

As a newly-commissioned officer, James assured his father that his promotion would be:

> an ease to you for the future, in maintaining me heere ... [although initially] a great charge to you, in putting me into an Equipage suitable to my condition. I have therfore taken up an hundred powndes, of M^r [Francis] Harvey, the deputy Commissary of our Army, to be repayd by you (if you please) in London ... [He stated that he had also borrowed £30 from the bearer of his letter, for clothes and lodgings, and continued ingratiatingly] Deare Father I hope you will not take it ill, that I thus farre presume on your paternall care ... You ... may understand from this bearer, that this is the least charge I could putt you unto ... [He ended with a pious hope that in future he would have] little or nothing att all to burthen you with the like loade of expences ...
>
> 4 Mar. 1649/50
>
> ib. fols. 53–53v. (transcript).]

Three months later, however, we read that bills of exchange had been presented totalling some £1,500, and that Whitelocke had settled them on James's behalf:

> ... which large expence of his (as I was informed) was not by debauchery, butt kind heartedness to his fellow soldiers, lending money to the officers & relieving the wants of the private soldiers. This & his own too free expences gained him, the love of the soldiers butt it was too much for my estate to beare, & therfore I wrote to him this admonishing letter ...

The copy of a stern if loving letter followed, in which Whitelocke pointed out that he had to consider the needs of his other children, and warned that he would not go on paying James's debts, *Diary* 20 June 1650; Add. Ms 37345 fol. 79v., (transcript of Long, W.P. x, 149). This, however, did nothing to stem James's extravagance and Whitelocke, predictably, failed to carry out his threat: James signed a bill of exchange committing Lord Commissioner Whitelocke to pay £30 to Major Anthony Morgan's wife, Elizabeth, 15 July 1650, ib. 156; receipt of 13 Sept. 1650, ib. 165. Another bill of exchange on Whitelocke, for payment of £60 to Edward Francklin, milliner, of the New Exchange, was duly paid, 12 Nov. 1650, ib. 202. £100 borrowed from Robert Turner of Clonmel, 11 Aug. 1651, ib. xi, 46, was receipted, 3 June 1652, ib. 46v. A debt of £120 to Richard Goldsmith was also presented, dated 2 Jan. 1651/52, ib. xii, 1, and was paid 2 June 1652.

James's reckless spending is a constant refrain in *The Diary*, with begging letters, importunate messages and, in later years, news of hasty trips abroad to escape from creditors. This eldest son was, however, not without ability, and was evidently very good company. He and William had the valuable experience of escorting their father on his Swedish Embassy, 1653–1654. James was well received at Court and could be trusted, with Whitelocke's two experienced Secretaries, Daniel Earle (q.v.) and William Swyft (q.v.), to examine and draft Articles for the Anglo-Swedish Treaty, *Diary* 11, 27 Apr. 1654. Returning to England on 1 July 1654, Whitelocke promptly used his influence to obtain a seat for his eldest son in the first Parliament of the Protectorate. A letter from James, addressed to his father at Chelsea, with the command 'Haste, haste', reported that he had been elected, with Charles Fleetwood (q.v.), Robert Jenkinson, Nathaniel Fiennes (q.v.) and William Lenthall (q.v.), the former Speaker (by then Master of the Rolls), to represent Oxfordshire, *Journal* ii, 462, 12 July 1654. Whitelocke himself was returned both for the City of Oxford and for Buckinghamshire, and decided to serve for the latter, when Parliament met in September. His son James was in France when elections were held for Cromwell's second Parliament.

James's experience on the Swedish Embassy stood him in good stead, for he was appointed to the retinue of Ambassador William Lockhart (q.v.) and accompanied him to France; moreover, the Ambassador wrote about him to Whitelocke in glowing terms, see entry: LOCKHART. Whitelocke sent William Swyft (q.v.) to keep an eye on his son, and when James himself wrote home from Dieppe, he referred to Swyft's care of him, *Diary* 11 May 1656. He did not state that he was already in the Ambassador's service, nor indeed is Lockhart's Embassy mentioned in *The Diary* until later. Swyft wrote sending news both of James and of events in France, ib. 12 May, 26 July 1656, *passim*; extracts from Swyft's letters appear in his entry.

In James's first letter from Paris, he referred back to Dieppe, writing that the Ambassador

... leaving that place the 26th of the last month [i.e. April] and declining the great roade to Roan [i.e. Rouen] came a more private and neerer way by Flory [i.e. Fleury] ... [to Paris] the country affording many delightfull prospects togeather with the sweetnes of the season contributed a greate deale of pleasure to our journey.

On the day that James wrote, Lockhart had made an approach to the Cardinal (Mazarin), and James promised to give an account of the Cardinal's reply in his next letter; he was confident it would be a civil one, since Mazarin had recently displayed great respect for the Ambassador '... by a late com[m]and which he sent in the kings [Louis XIV's] name to the English court [i.e. the Court of Charles II in exile] ... to forbeare all occasions of dispute or quarrell with the Embassador or his retinue'. General Turenne was to leave the Court within a few days, 'to take the field with his army', and it was rumoured that the French King intended to invade Italy, with a very powerful army; some people thought the intention was not only to 'amuse' (i.e. divert the attention of) the Spaniards, but also 'to draw better tearmes from my L[or]^d Protector', and to gain support for the war against Spain in Flanders. The French clergy, on the other hand, 'excited by the pope' had lately petitioned their King against the protestants; 'glancing ... at the Cardinall, the pope in his L[ette]^{rs} calling him a turbulent Minister of State ...' Mazarin's reply had displeased the clergy, for he told them he perceived their projects 'to tend extremely to the dishoner and disadvantage of this crown' by attempting to bring about a union 'with the broken and allmost desperate Spaniard', under colour of a Catholic league. James finished, characteristically, by saying that the Ambassador had been extremely civil to him '... espetially as to matter of charges: which[,] if you please to take notice of by a L[ett]^{re} to him[,] it may be a future advantage to mee'. After signing, and sending a message from William Swyft, whom he commonly referred to as 'WS', James sent a humble greeting to his (step)mother and 'best affections to my [half-] brothers and sisters ...', Paris [May 1656], Long. W.P. xvii, 148–148v.

James's next letter recorded that Ambassador Lockhart had arrived in Paris on 5th May and had an audience with King Louis XIV and Cardinal Mazarin, on the afternoon of 8th May, 'all in the space of two houres'. James enclosed a copy of the Ambassador's speech to the 18-year-old King

... whose reply (to tell you the truth) was but in two words spoken to the Interpreter which were: How does his Highnesse [i.e. the Protector] doe [?], and Does not the Embassador Speake French[?].

Lockhart and Mazarin had proceeded to spend an hour and a half together, with no-one else present. The atmosphere had been very cordial and, in

James's opinion, it promised well for the negotiations. It was generally believed that King Louis intended to move to 'Campeigny' (i.e. Compiègne, north-east of Paris), within a few days, 'in order to take the feild with his army' and make a sudden attack on Flanders; the 'prince' of Turenne had already been dispatched

> to draw the army to a Rendezvous ... at Marles [i.e. Marle, north-east of Compiègne]. The difference between the king and Parliament about the price of mony is now accomodated: upon the parl[iament] accepting ... the kings ingagement to bring the mony to the old rates after five months.

The sessions of the Assembly of Clergy 'which made such a noise here by their stickling for a generall peace ...', presumably with Spain, had been moved to Soissons (east of Compiègne), where it was thought Mazarin would 'not want [i.e. lack] an artifice to dissolve them ...', Paris, 10 May 1656, ib. 150–150v.

Still with his ear to the ground, James wrote that the Prince of Condé (who supported Spain against France in the Netherlands) had appeared with 10,000 or 12,000 men before (la) Bassée (south-east of Calais), which was held by the French. Condé's move had caused the King and the Cardinal to leave Paris on the following day, to support the French Army. The English Ambassador, who had not had an opportunity to speak to either of them since the first audience, in spite of several requests, '... received nothing but excuses and a desire from the Cardinal to march with the king into the feild, which he is forc[e]d to doe ...' James feared that, because of this, he himself would have little opportunity to write, but he hoped that his father would send '... a line or 2' about his own health, which would give 'infinite satisfaction'; Whitelocke's letters could be addressed to him at Colonel Lockhart's lady's lodging, near Charing Cross, 'at one Malhues house', Paris, 17 May 1656, ib. 156.

James entrusted his next letter home to William Swyft, who returned to England on a brief visit. James wrote informing his father that the Ambassador continued to be '... very kind and friendly' to him and 'remembers you with tearmes full of respect'. As to Swyft, James commended his 'devotion and true affection' towards Whitelocke, '... manifested by many offices of friendship and intimate kindnesse shewn to me ... in this journey'. He ended mysteriously: 'I have desired him to acquaint you with some particulars relating to my selfe not fitt to com[m]itt to paper', Compiègne, 19 May 1656, ib. 158.

A letter acknowledging his father's reply (which Swyft had brought back) gave confident estimates as to the strength of the French cavalry and infantry at some 15,000 each; he dismissed the Spanish forces as being not more than 4,000 horse and 2,000 foot, writing from Chauny (north-east of

Compiègne, or possibly Chaulnes, north of Compiègne; see the spelling of the place name after his letter, below), 1 June 1656, ib. 162.

James's next letter announced: that the city where he was stationed was very large and rich, with a sizeable population, but not well fortified; that French forces under Turenne were standing ready to besiege Valenciennes (south-west of Mons). He continued to keep up his spirits with the age-old folly of belittling the enemy's strength, Chauny, 9 June 1656, ib. 164.

News of the Spanish Army 'defeating a greate part of the French army' (outside Valenciennes), brought more realism to his next letter, with an account of how the French had suffered, encamped on either bank of the river Escaut, which flowed through the town; the enemy had shut the sluices and raised the level of water in the dams, then they had suddenly released the water to cause flooding and destroy bridges, to the detriment of the French cavalry. Many Frenchmen were drowned, while General Turenne, with 18,000 men, '... made a very honorable retreate[,] marching off with bag and baggage and many of his greate guns ...', Chaulney, 10 July 1656, ib. 174–174v.

James's next letter acknowledged one from his father of 9 July (Whitelocke's were dated in the old style, whereas James used the new style, being abroad). Whitelocke's letter concerned a possible wife for James's consideration, and enquired whether he wished to stand as a candidate for the next Parliament. James thanked his father for his care with regard to a match; as to standing for election, that would depend on support by his father's friends; if he came over and was not chosen, 'it would be no small disgrace,' but if his father thought otherwise and let him know, he would return before the elections. His pass would expire at the end of September, which would compel him to go home, and he thought that would then be 'time enough' to think about marriage. The French Ambassador to England, M. Antoine de Bordeaux, had told him of plans to send over English troops (in support of the French). If this happened, James assumed that Ambassador Lockhart would command them, and he hoped that he himself would be given the command of a regiment, which would be 'much better then my present [unspecified] imployment'. He also wrote that Lockhart begged Whitelocke not to heed reports that 'the French had been baffled in Italy and forc[e]d to raise their Seige before Valen[cienne]s with the losse of 2000 men ...', 16 July 1656, ib. 177–177v.

A note introducing its bearers, Colonel Donnell and Mr. John Cooke, was sent from 'Chaulny' (perhaps Chaulnes, north of Compiègne, rather than Chauny, to the north-east, as clearly written in earlier letters), 8 Aug. 1656, ib. 186.

In the last letter of this collection, James thanked his father for approaches made to the Protector on his behalf, and for speaking to friends about his re-election to parliament. '. . . I must confesse I am not without my ambition to be of the house, not so much from any fancy that I shall . . . make my selfe considerable[,] either by doing his Highnesse any greate service or my country much right, (though no man can bring better affections to boath those ends) but . . . as an opportunity to gaine experience and knowledge . . .' He wrote that Queen Christina (q.v.) was expected in Paris that week; they said at Court that her journey was delayed by some malady contracted in Italy, where the Pope had given her the title of 'Christianissima' and 'other pledges of his affections': it was hoped (unrealistically) that he had also furnished her with 'a new pretention to the crown of Sweden' (preferable, in French eyes, to having the Lutheran and warlike Charles X on the throne); preparations for her visit to Paris were 'very magnificent'. The news there was that the King of Sweden had 'bitterly defeated the polish Army'; also that 'The Titular Duke of York' was going to Flanders, to his brother (Charles II in exile), where the French Army was 'very potent & desirous to fight', but James thought 'the cautious Spanyard' would try to avoid an encounter. William Swyft sent his humble thanks for letters from Whitelocke, and would write at the next opportunity, but just then he was: 'very much ingaged in running up and down the town about Coll[onel] Lockarts busines . . .', Paris, 20 Aug. 1656, ib. 194–194v.

Whitelocke referred to two more letters from James in Paris, Diary 21, 29 Oct. 1656. The originals of these have not been traced; the first contained a characteristic request to his father to send him some horses.

James returned to England before the New Year, and was promptly knighted by the Protector, ib. 7 Jan. 1656/57. Later that month, he 'tooke an affection' for a wealthy young widow who had two small children. She was Mary Pitcher (or Pychard), née Pike, to Trumpington Hall, near Cambridge, see: WHITELOCKE, Lady Mary jun. (2). In this matter, young Sir James followed the advice of his uncle Richard Benet (q.v.), who lived nearby at Babraham, in Cambridgeshire, rather than that of his father, Diary 22 Jan. 1656/57. The couple were married in London that summer, ib. 27 June 1657, with note. The entry is oddly vague as to the date, but is more precise on details of the settlement. Whitelocke noted that James and Mary 'lived high' and that, although they had an income of £1,200 a year, James still 'did not keep w[i]'hin Compasse, debts and high living are not agreeable [i.e. compatible]', ib. 1 July 1657. For his part, the new Master of Trumpington Hall wrote with elation of distinguished guests visiting the Hall and boasted, accurately enough: '. . . this is a place where we shall never want company till we want means', ib. 8 July 1657. Whitelocke and his wife, Mary Whitelocke senior., were cordially invited to Trumpington: James's uncle Richard Benet, and father-in-law George

Pyke (q.v), had business of importance to discuss, and they evidently considered that Whitelocke's position and experience could by useful to them. Whitelocke and his wife were 'intertained w[i]ᵗh cheerfullness by his son', ib. 23, 28 Sept., 4 Oct. 1657.

Three months after that visit, James asked Whitelocke to make his excuses to Fleetwood (q.v.) for being absent from his troop, ib. 10 Jan. 1657/58. Later that year, James and his wife brought Whitelocke's first grandson, Bulstrode (q.v.), to visit the family at Chelsea and at Fawley Court, ib. 2 Apr. 1658. Whitelocke was soon busy trying to have James and William elected to Richard Cromwell's Parliament, ib. 4, 10, 15, 16, 21, 22, 23, 24 Dec. 1658. When James was returned as Burgess for Aylesbury, ib. 30 Dec., he neglected to attend the House regularly, ib. 1, 22 Mar. 1658/59.

There is little direct news of James in *The Diary* (apart from the efforts to win him a seat in Parliament) between the entry on 2 April 1658, referred to earlier, and that on 29 May 1659, when he wrote that he was continuing his command of a troop under Fleetwood. This gap may be significant: on 3 June 1658 the Royalist, John Mordaunt (later 1st Lord Mordaunt, q.v.), had been narrowly acquitted on a charge of treason, brought before the High Court of Justice. Despite this verdict, he was detained in the Tower (G.E.C. entry for Mordaunt p. 200, text and note d.); at the request of Lord Francis Willoughby (q.v.), Whitelocke had helped to obtain Mordaunt's release, *Diary* 5 June 1658. Undeterred by his imprisonment and trial, as early as 19 May 1659 (three months before Sir George Booth's rising) Mordaunt was writing to Charles II in exile, with plans for him to make a surprise landing at Lynn (i.e. King's Lynn, Norfolk). Once again Whitelocke's brother-in-law, Lord Willoughby of Parham (q.v.), was involved; he believed that the operation was feasible and declared that if he were with the King, he himself would be prepared to undertake it, with as few as 500 foot-soldiers, but preferably with 1,000, supported by an officer who understood such a mission. At high tide the invader could sail right into the town in three vessels, bringing an army of 1,000 men, of whom 100 should be 'firelocks' (i.e. musketeers). There were only 120 foot-soldiers in the town, and 'one troop of horse which Mr. James Whitlock commands; this is the person hath made his addresses to Sir H. Bennet [q.v. BENET, Henry or Humfrey?] and offers himself to be ready at any time to serve you ...' This information appears in a letter from Mordaunt to Charles II in exile, Clarendon *State Papers* (Clarendon Press. 1786) iii, 472–473; see also *Letter-Book of John Viscount Mordaunt 1658–1660* (ed. M. Coate. Camden 3rd series. 1945) p.18, note 6; quoting from C. Firth *Regimental History*, i, 98, M. Coate states that James Whitelocke was actually in command of the garrison, but that Mordaunt was 'uncertain how long [James] Whitelocke will be there [at Lynn] in command'.

It seems clear that Whitelocke knew nothing of James's negotiations with the Royalists; had he known, he would surely have made use of the fact later, when applying for a Royal Pardon on behalf of himself and James, because they had both served in the Army against the King, *Diary* 29 May 1660. James's brief bout of royalism, however, did nothing for his career at and after the Restoration. By the end of the year he was in France, avoiding his creditors and appealing to his father for money, ib. 1 Dec. 1660. Later, he visited the regicide Edmund Ludlow (q.v.), by then a refugee at Vevey on Lake Geneva, E. Ludlow *Voyce from the Watch Tower* (ed. A.B. Worden) pp. 14, 67; *Diary* 24 Sept. 1669.

The remaining diary entries concerning James tell of his disastrous debts, which even jeopardized his annuity from the Fawley Court estate, ib. 13 Jan. 1662/63; 29 Apr. 1668, *passim*. Although he was the heir to Fawley Court, James had the effrontery to speak of claiming a 'right' in the adjoining estate of Phyllis Court, with was William's inheritance, ib. 24 May 1671.

James, the pampered product of an unhappy marriage, was indulged all his life by his father. He became a successful, if extravagant, soldier; he was intelligent and (it seems) likeable, but in relation to his father he remained to the end an indisciplined, demanding child. For his own children, see the entry for his wife, Lady Mary Whitelocke, jun. (2).

WHITELOCKE, John (b. 1656). Fourth son of Whitelocke by his third wife, Mary. Born in Bishopsgate Street, London, in the house of Mary's brother-in-law, Samuel Wilson (q.v.). There are diary entries for his birth, both on 26 September and on 26 October 1656. The first date is crammed in as an afterthought, and is confirmed by Whitelocke's letter, see SWYFT p. 354. Whitelocke records little about John, beyond mentioning his frequent illnesses; there is also a reference to his lucky escape, when he was nine years old and his horse bolted, *Diary* 4 Dec. 1664; 23 March 1665/66, *passim*. He was presumably educated at home by the family tutor, James Pearson (q.v.). John was 19 when his father died, and his subsequent career has not been traced with any certainty.

WHITELOCKE, Mary, sen. (d. 1684). *D.N.B.* (entry for Colonel Rowland Wilson); R.H. Whitelocke *Memoirs . . . of Bulstrode Whitelocke* (Routledge, Warne, & Routledge. 1860) pp. 283–288, *passim*. Daughter of Bigley Carleton, a London grocer. She married (i) Rowland Wilson jun.

(q.v.) in 1634; (ii) Bulstrode Whitelocke (twice) in 1650 (secretly on 5 August and openly on 5 September, see *Diary*). Her first marriage had been childless; the second produced seven children, half-brothers and -sisters to Whitelocke's other 10 children. In Mary's 'Diary' (untraced), part of which is transcribed in R.H. Whitelocke's *Memoirs* ... (above), she described her brief first widowhood and Whitelocke's courtship; later, she told of the birth of their first child, Samuel (q.v.). The extract starts with an account of how, on the night that her husband Colonel Rowland Wilson died (19 Feb. 1649/50), his father and mother were moved to pity her, but how the next day, on discovering that their son had left her, a childless widow, all of his considerable estate, 'they did foam and rage both against me and him ...' Mary's father-in-law came to her bedside expressly to tell her she should not have one penny more than the extremity of the law would give her. Yet she viewed this cruelty as a blessing: 'For if it had not been for his hard usage, I think I should have sunk under my ... unspeakable loss'. As it was, she got up from her bed and went out to take legal advice; she wrote that even her father-in-law's lawyers 'gave their judgment for me, but my father[-in-law] would be ruled by none'.

A number of suitors appeared, almost immediately, and a lawyer 'highly commended the widdow & her fortune' to Whitelocke, who learned that she was 'well spoken off, by all that knew her, for her disposition & godlines' and that she would be good to his children, but he entreated one of her Trustees, with whom he discussed the lady, not to mention his name until after her husband's funeral, *Diary* 12, 22 Feb., 1 Mar. 1649/50. (The entry for 12 Feb. conflicts with the date of Wilson's death, quoted above, as shown in the *D.N.B.*) Even after the funeral (vividly described in *Diary* 5 Mar. 1649/50), Whitelocke thought it untimely to make an approach, but he soon learned that other suitors had no such scruples. Friends suggested he might go to a service at Pancras Church, Soper Lane, in order to have a look at the widow, '... butt he held that time & place unfitt for such buisnes', ib. 9, 17 Mar. 1649/50. Fortunately, however, Mary was advised to take the inheritance dispute to the Chancery Court (where Whitelocke, as the First Keeper of the Great Seal, sat as principal Judge). She made enquiries as to whether he took bribes, for she believed these would be offered by her father-in-law; her Chaplain, George Cokayn (q.v.), looked into the matter and was able to assure her that Whitelocke would scorn to take bribes, and 'would doe right & justice'. Cokayn then did his best to promote the match, ib. 3, 5 Apr. Whitelocke and Mary did not actually meet until the following month, ib. 28 May 1650.

Mary gives an account, in her 'Diary', of the hesitation she felt at the prospect of marrying a man with 10 children, but she was encouraged by the Psalmist's view of having children (or, more precisely, sons): 'happy is the man that hath his quiver full of them ... they shall speak with the enemies in the gate' and 'Thy wife shall be as a fruitful vine ..., thy children like olive plants round about thy table, thus shall the man be blessed ...', Psalms 127, verses 4 and 5; 128 verses 3 and 4. She wrote: 'I durst not refuse a man for having ten blessings ... And in marrying him, I thought I might be in a capacity to do some good amongst those children', R.H. Whitelocke (above).

The courtship is described in *The Diary*. At one point, Whitelocke (who had been visiting Mary at the house in Bishopsgate Street, *Diary* 5 June 1650) wrote a distinctly crisp love letter, saying that he had hoped to visit her, but finding her gone to Martyn (or Martin) Abbey (now Merton, Surrey, see entries for WILSON, Rowland sen., Rowland jun. and Samuel), he thought it inconvenient, imagining that she would be 'assaulted with sundry objections ...' against his suit 'truely in my heart there is no roome for any distrust of your constancy in affection being once setled, as I hope yours is, & cann assure you of my owne ...' He did not believe she would countenance arguments or information 'depending uppon perticular interests not agreeable unto yours'; they would easily be answered by her own judgement and, above all, by her affection, 25 June 1650, Long. W.P. x, 155 (copy).

In due course, the secret wedding was celebrated at Bromham, in Bedfordshire; this was followed by a festive, public wedding at St. John's Church, Hackney, after Mary's brother-in-law, Samuel Wilson (q.v.), had given his consent. Almost on the eve of the London marriage, mischief-makers tried to prevent it with reports that Whitelocke had debts amounting to £4,000. Mary, a straightforward woman, asked him to tell her the truth, saying that if he was in debt the two of them must find a way of paying his creditors, but he was able to assure her that he only owed £20 or £30, for household bills, *Diary* 3 Sept. 1650.

Mary's name appears countless times in *The Diary*. In the next 25 years she and Whitelocke supported each other in sickness and in health (particularly in sickness), for richer and, in the last years for poorer, with affection, patience, and their share of bickering. Mary was an admirable stepmother, '... so carefull & tender of his children, that a stranger could not observe butt that she was their own Mother, only in some things she was more indulgent to them then an own Mother would have bin ...', ib. 17 Sept. 1650. (Later confirmed both by James and by his half-sister, Frances.)

Mary was at once hard-headed, strong-minded, courageous and highly emotional. She wrote in a basically italic but rather unformed hand, almost without punctuation. In a businesslike letter, she told Whitelocke that if he planned to buy Toddington Manor, Bedfordshire (from Thomas

Wentworth, 1st Earl of Cleveland, q.v.), that was 'a contracting day' and if he missed his 'right of prehemsion [i.e. pre-emption]' it might cost him £1,000. Mr. Hodgekins (evidently the Earl's agent), did not wish him to 'put things of[f] to the last day for feare some others step betweene you and it . . .', Apr. 1652(?), Long. W.P. xii, 101.

When Mary was six or seven months pregnant with her third son, Bigley, Cromwell and the Council decided to send Whitelocke as Ambassador Extraordinary to Sweden. The danger of his being assassinated by Royalists was considerable; Dorislaus and Ascham, representing Parliament, had been murdered in other countries, following the King's execution. Mary pleaded with her husband to refuse the appointment, arguing that Cromwell wanted to be rid of him, Add. Ms 4902 fols. 6–6v.; *Journal* i, 17–22, 6 Sept. 1653. Whitelocke recorded a conversation with Mary, in which she made the earnest request: '. . . that you would accept of my Company in your journey'. He replied that the only reason why he was unwilling to take her was because of the hardship and danger 'bejond the strength & constitution of women [apart from that of the four washerwomen who accompanied the party,] especially of one in your condition'. Mary insisted that many Ambassadors' wives had gone to foreign parts on Embassies, and others with Armies, and that she herself had accompanied her former husband abroad; she would not fear the danger. Whitelocke pointed out that she would be in great danger if she fell into labour on the journey. Mary retorted that no country was unacquainted with women in labour; if she was brought to bed, they could leave her behind on the journey, for a short time, and she would soon follow after him. She was undaunted by her husband's talk of passing near England's enemies, the Dutch and the Danes, saying: 'I could beare that or any thing . . ., better then the losse of your Company'. His argument that their poor children needed her guidance at home was dismissed, with a further proposal that as many as were fit should accompany them, while the little ones could stay with her mother and sister. Whitelocke directed her thoughts towards two-year-old Samuel, her beloved first-born, who 'will not stay behind you, & is too young to carry with you'. Mary thought that he was strong enough to travel, and Whitelocke agreed that, for his age, he had 'strange affections.' Then he tactfully suggested they should wait until they knew when he was likely to be sent on his mission, 16 Sept. 1653, Add. Ms. 53727 (not foliated at the time of writing), pp. 221–228.

After some stormy, emotional scenes in the following weeks, Whitelocke had a painful parting from Mary and the children, 'full of griefe & passion' but, finding two of the ships at Gravesend were not ready to sail, with endearing affection he took a boat back up the Thames (secretly, so that the Council should not hear of it), and said another good-bye. This time

Mary controlled her grief and was very loving, *Diary* 3, 4 Nov. 1653; *Journal* i, 98–101, 103–104. Three days later, the small fleet lay at anchor near the mouth of the Thames, waiting for a favourable wind; at about midnight, letters were brought by watermen, with news that Mary had been safely delivered of a son, *Diary* 6, 7 Nov. 1653.

Eighteen days after Whitelocke set sail, Mary wrote him a long letter, full of grief, with signs of post-natal depression; there are hints, too, that she was rejecting the new-born son, Bigley: 'I longe very much for the tyme wherein I may enjoy thy good company ... men did act very unkindly in hastning you away at such a tyme when nether men nor Shipps were ready.' She reminded him of how much grief she would have been spared if he had been ruled by her; she wrote of her great affection for him, recording that she could 'doe little else but weepe night and day'. He and others might remind her that it was a common thing for husbands to have to go away, and that wives had to be contented, but her grief was the worse, since other women could bear the separation while she could not, '... oh my deare instead of blayming me[,] pitty me ...' The letter is full of regret that:

> I did not goe w[i]th you to Gravesend[,] there to have ben brought to bed and soe to have [page torn: been] carried in my bed on Shipboard, by that meanes I should have left my child behind and ... prevented the greatest sorrow that ever I knew ... I cannot but daylie envie the meanest servant in thy house for I could willingly doe their work[,] soe that I might enjoy your good company, my heed [i.e. head] is daily workinge w[hi]ch way to come to you ...

She feared she would not know how to do this but begged him, as he tendered her life, if he had ever loved her, to hasten his return, '... or else sende for me to come to you ...' After her signature she wrote that six of the children were with her, and that 'Franck [Frances, jun. (1), q.v.], & Moll [Mary, later married to George Nevill, q.v.] & Nan [Anne, later Hill, q.v.] & Cell [Cecilia, later Harvey, q.v.] & Sam [her eldest son q.v.] and [a blank; probably one-year-old Carleton]' remembered their duty to him.

> Samm [aged two-and-a-half] is very fond of you and rides every day a horseback to [meet] dad in the boate for he sayes dad is gon in the boate to fawly Court[.] H[e] speakes often of you, but will not come neere me[,] he sees me soe malencholly, he says he will have a new Mum ...

After further news and messages she sent love from her mother to Whitelocke, and her own love to her two sons (i.e. stepsons), James (q.v.) and William (q.v.), and greetings to Mr. de la Marche (q.v.) whose wife (Mary wrote) went out three days after her child was born, whereas she herself, one day under three weeks since her baby's birth, had still not walked the length of her room. Finally, she sent a practical message about Whitelocke having his diamond hatband sewn on by their servant, see entry for ROBERTS, Elizabeth, 25 Nov., recd. 17 Dec. 1653, Long. 124A fols. 42–42v. (transcript).

Another letter is written in rather odd French, starting:

> Cher coeur
> J'ay un extreme desir d'entendre de tes nouvelles . . . cher coer . . . je Langui en attendant le retour du vendred[i]; pour t'escrire.

She was afraid of troubling him, but she could neither think nor write of anything but what was in her heart, which was full of trouble and sadness . . . she begged him to pray that she would not be crushed under her heavy and distressing affliction . . . Her sorrow was increasing daily and she could not sleep at night. If she slept, however briefly, she was terrified by dreams . . . then her strength was so much dissipated that she could hardly talk to friends who visited her the next morning. Her visitors, and those close to her, attributed this melancholy to her staying in bed. Although she did not agree, to please them she did not go to bed for four consecutive nights, after which they were convinced that she was the embodiment of weakness – 'je suis la faiblesse mesme . . .', London, 2 Dec. 1653, Long. W.P. xiv, 225 (transcript). The original may or may not have been in French.

Mary pulled herself together enough to attend to business matters while her husband was in Sweden, signing, for example, a receipt for his quarterly allowance, a modest £67.4s.9d., sent by Sir William Allenson, Clerk of the Hanaper, 27 Feb. 1653/54, ib. xv, 62. Another receipt, also signed by Mary, for the quarterly allowance to 25 March, is for £62.11s. 4d., 26 May 1654, ib. xvi, 1. George Cokayn (q.v.) referred to her in one of his letters as the 'faithful casheere'.

Four months after Mary's dismal letter, quoted above, she wrote at great length and in more positive terms: 'My deare Heart. Having opportunity I could not forbeare writing to you by the ship . . . the goulden Hawke[,] by Mr Dickenson'. She sent four pairs of silk stockings for Whitelocke's pages and sent her love to her 'two sons' (i.e. stepsons), with a small token for each of a pair of silk stockings. She wrote that on the previous Friday, she had sent to John Thurloe (q.v.) to ask if the Dutch negotiations were concluded; he had replied that they were as good as concluded, and that he would send Whitelocke word by the same post, so that the Ambassador might start preparing for his return home. Every day seemed to her like a year, waiting to hear of his return:

> . . . I never did so much instruct other women, to love & prize their husbands, as when I was a widdowe, & now, in your absence, if they doe att any time fall out . . . I tell them many times with tears, if their husbands were in

Sweden, they would prize them more, . . . & resolve to beare & forbeare any thing that might displease them . . . this you may be sure of, you have my love & heart . . . my Deare as our lives have bin happy in each other, so I hope it shall increase in joy & comfort . . .

She blessed God daily to hear that Whitelocke was not tempted to sin against Him, among 'people, who walke so loosly' towards Him and she prayed that they might see the evil of their ways. It was sweet to live a life of faith. After a number of religious exhortations she asked her husband to forgive her for writing of such things: 'I know you are more able to teach me in these things, then to learne of me'; she asked him not to think her letters were too long. Nothing pleased her so much as writing to him 'seeing I cannot talke with thee face to face, lett my pen speake for me . . .' After other devotional passages, she ended with the good news: 'All our children are well from the biggest to the leastle', 3 Apr., recd. 25 May 1654, Add. Ms 37347 fols. 235–236, London (transcript).

After the Restoration, Mary stood up to hard times at home with considerable fortitude. She was buried at Chilton Foliat in 1684, Wilts. R.O. 735/4.

WHITELOCKE, Mary, jun. (1), Whitelocke's third daughter, see NEVILL.

WHITELOCKE, Lady Mary, jun. (2), (d. 1715). *V.C.H. Cambs.* viii, 253. Whitelocke's daughter-in-law. The daughter of George Pike (q.v.), she first appears in *The Diary* as the wealthy widow of Thomas Pitcher, sen. (otherwise Pitchard, Pychard etc.), former owner of Trumpington Hall, near Cambridge. She had two young sons by her first marriage, Thomas Pitcher, jun., and John. (An 18th century letter states, without supporting evidence, that she had been Pitcher's servant; it quotes a report that after marrying him, she had Pitcher's estate settled on her, then poisoned him and buried him privately, Add. Ms 5819 fol. 59v.; the letter was addressed to the Revd. Mr. Cole of Milton, near Cambridge, and was signed S. Peck, from Trumpington, 8 Sept. 1776.) Clearly Whitelocke knew nothing of any such gossip when his eldest son, Sir James (q.v.), 'tooke an affection' for the 'young Widdow' who was 'given out to have a very great fortune, & was hansome & ingenious' yet he 'was not well satisfyed w[i]'h this Match'; but James consulted his uncle Richard Benet (at Babraham, near Trumpington) more than his father, and the widow's father agreed to a satisfactory marriage settlement, *Diary* 22 Jan., 2, 5 Mar. 1656/57, *passim*.

The marriage settlement is, at the time of writing, in private hands at Fawley. It is dated May 1657 and was witnessed by Bartholomew Hall (q.v.) and Richard Whitelocke (presumably the physician and clergyman of that name, q.v.). Shortly before the wedding, Richard Benet invited Whitelocke and his wife 'to a great intertainem[en]ᵗ att his house' for the young couple at which, according to *The Diary*, 'Mʳˢ Pitcher carryed herselfe & was attended with more state then befitted her condition'; this ostentation made Whitelocke even more dubious about her suitability as a wife for his (already extravagant) son James, 'butt he [James] was too far ingaged to her' and the couple were married soon afterwards in London, ib. 17, 27 June, with note, 1657. Their extravagant life-style at Trumpington Hall, and continuous problem with creditors is suggested in James's entry. In 1676 the male heirs of Mary's first marriage sold the reversion of Trumpington to Lord Chief Justice Sir Francis Pemberton; Mary outlived James and, having a life-interest, remained in the Hall until her death.

James and Mary appear to have had three sons: Whitelocke does not mention their births, but refers to seeing his young grandson, Bulstrode, when James and Mary came to stay at Chelsea and Fawley, ib. 2 Apr. 1658; perhaps the name was inserted with later knowledge, when copying *The Diary*, for James's wife later wrote of naming the child 'Bulstrode', ib. 13 June 1659; he is referred to as being ill, ib. 20 June 1671, when he would have been about 13, but the dates of his birth and baptism have not been traced, nor has any other information about him come to light. 'The Bishop's Transcripts', among the Diocesan Records, Cambridge University Library, give the following information about Sir James and Mary Whitelocke's children: James, baptized 19 Nov. 1662, buried 24 Jan. 1662/63; George, baptized 23 Jan. 1664/65; another James (Jeames, *sic*), baptized 7 Mar. 1666/67 and Caelia Mary, baptized 9 July 1668. None of these children is named in *The Diary*; perhaps their grandfather was too much occupied with saving his son and daughter-in-law from impatient creditors, to record their birth. There are, however, some general references to James and Mary's children, *Diary* 20 June 1671, *passim*. George and the surviving brother James later studied at Oxford, the one at Pembroke and the other at Merton, *Alumni Oxonienses*. This source shows that they both matriculated in December 1682, but it confuses the issue by showing them both as aged 17; yet, in view of the two-year gap between the dates of their baptism, it seems unlikely that they were twins.

George Whitelocke, unlike his father, had money to give away, and in his Will of 1724 (the year in which he died) he endowed the Whitelock (*sic*) Charity in Trumpington to provide, originally, coal for 34 poor households, coats and caps yearly for eight poor boys, 20 cottages to be let to poor people, etc., see *V.C.H.* (above) and *Report of the Commissioners for the County of Cambridgeshire, 1815–1839* pp. 185, 186. The bequest has been adapted, and survives to this day in the form of old people's flats in Trumpington, on the road to Cambridge.

WHITELOCKE, Mary, jun.(3), later Lady, (bur. 1711). Another daughter-in-law of Whitelocke's. Sister of Thomas Overbury, jun. (q.v.), who was knighted in 1660, of Bourton-on-the-Hill, Glos. Related to the D'Oiley family (q.v.), of Greenland (adjoining Whitelocke's Fawley Court estate), and of Chislehampton, Oxon. Mary Overbury married Whitelocke's second son, William (q.v.), at Bourton, on 19 May 1659. For details see entry: WHITELOCKE, Sir William. Their children seem to have been: Bulstrode (Whitelocke's second grandson of that name), apparently the one who was shot dead in Cirencester in 1688, see entry: WHITELOCKE, Bulstrode (grandsons); Overbury; William jun., who married Anne (or Ann) Noel; John; Mary; Elizabeth, who married William Wiseman; Hester; and finally Anne (q.v.), who married Sir Thomas Noel. Some of these children appear in *The Diary*, on visits to their grandfather, but only Anne is named, *Diary* 28 May 1667; 14 Sept. 1671, *passim*. Whitelocke does not record any of their births, apart from that of an unnamed granddaughter, ib. 2 May 1661.

WHITELOCKE, Mary, jun. (4), (b. 1673). First child of Samuel (q.v.) and his wife Elizabeth (q.v.), née Gough. Whitelocke and Mary's granddaughter, *Diary* 30 Sept., 1 Oct. 1673.

WHITELOCKE, Rebecca, sen. (1609–1634). Add. Ms 53726 fols. 53v.–54v., 102v.–103, *passim*. Daughter of Alderman Thomas Benet (Bennet), Sheriff of London (who had bought the Babraham estate, south-east of Cambridge), and of Dorothy Benet (q.v.) the sister of Sir Humphrey May (q.v.). Mrs. Benet had a house in Cheapside, London, and one at Mortlake in Surrey. Rebecca was a sister of Sir Thomas Benet, Bt. (q.v.) and of Humphrey Benet, later Kt., MP (q.v.). She was Whitelocke's first wife; they were married in her mother's private Chapel at Mortlake, in June 1630. This disastrous marriage was negotiated by Whitelocke's father and Rebecca's widowed mother; the latter provided a marriage portion of £3,000. When the young couple met they appear to have liked each other, but on the wedding day, before the ceremony, Rebecca had an attack of hysterics; she recovered well enough to go through with the marriage service, which was followed by a great feast with music, dancing and revels, but when the bride was put to bed and her husband came to her 'expecting marryage joyes', she had a worse attack of hysterics and the young bridegroom was obliged to call for help, believing she was going to die, *Diary* 1629.1630. fols. 11, 11v. Some weeks later the marriage was consummated, and their only child, James (q.v.), was born in July 1631.

Rebecca did not like the country so they moved to London, but her neurotic condition grew worse and, on her mother's advice, Whitelocke sent her for six months to Dr. Bartlett (q.v.) in Bow (where her sister was also being treated). The Doctor insisted that none of her family should visit her, while she was in his care, and advised Whitelocke to go abroad, which he did. When Rebecca's condition was improving her mother, Mrs Benet, insisted on seeing her and talked to her privately. After that visit, Rebecca stopped eating and died soon afterwards. Whitelocke could never discover what it was that his mother-in-law had said at the private meeting, but he may well have had a suspicion that she had told her daughter he had gone to France and deserted her, ib.1633.1634. fol. 24v.

WHITELOCKE, Rebecca, jun. (Rebekah), often referred to as 'Beck' or 'Becke' (b. 1658). Whitelocke's 16th child, the sixth of his third marriage. Rebecca's mother, Mary Whitelocke, sen. (q.v.), evidently accepted, with her usual generosity, not only that her eldest daughter should be named Frances (after Whitelocke's beloved second wife and their daughter who had died), but also that her other daughter should take the name of the neurotic first wife. Whitelocke recorded Rebecca's birth and her childhood illnesses, including an attack of measles when she was 16. She was very ill and the family tutor, Dr. James Pearson (q.v.), sat up with her for two nights, *Diary* 14, 16 Mar. 1673/74. This seems to have awakened something in the 40-year-old bachelor, for the following month, 'Dr Pearson went to London & in a frollick carryed with him Beck whom he calles wife'. Her parents clearly hoped this would develop into more than a 'frollick': they viewed the versatile tutor, preacher, physician and family friend as an eligible suitor but (to their annoyance) Beck's sister, Frances Pile (q.v.), and her brother Sam's wife, Elizabeth, jun. (2), (q.v.), set her against him, ib. 10 Apr., 8 June 1674.

WHITELOCKE, Richard, sen. (1565–1624). *Liber, passim.* One of Whitelocke's uncles. He left England to become a merchant, living near the Baltic, at Danzig and later at Elbing, where he married a woman of property. He sent one of his sons, James, to England in September 1620, to be provided for and to be entered at Magdalen Hall, Oxford, by

Whitelocke's father, James Whitelocke, sen. (q.v.). Richard Whitelocke's daughter married Colonel Christopher Potley (q.v.), who had served the Swedish Crown and who, with his son, accompanied Whitelocke (his wife's cousin) on the Swedish Embassy, *Diary* 1643.1644. fol. 63v.; 31 Mar. 1649; 26 Oct. 1653, *passim*.

WHITELOCKE (WHITELOCK), Richard, jun. (b. *c.* 1616). *Alumni Oxonienses*. Studied at Magdalen Hall, Oxford; BA in 1635; Fellow of All Souls, 1638; BCL and Doctor of Physic in 1640. He appears to have been the 'kinsman' or 'cousin' of Whitelocke's, who preached the monthly Fast Sermon to the Commons, *Diary* 28 July 1647, and who later sent a copy of his book *Zootopia: or Observations on the present manners of the English* ... (1654), which Whitelocke found 'ingenious & usefull & in good language', *Diary* 26 Oct. 1655, *passim*. Dr. Whitelocke also wrote thanking his kinsman for '. . . disposing him for the Ministry, & giving his wife to him, & procuring a benefice for him, & an augmentation to it, & for many other favours', ib. 19 Nov. 1657. He seems to have proceeded, after the Restoration, to the living of Stowe, Buckinghamshire, in 1661, and then of Ashford, Kent, in 1662, but by then his correspondence with Whitelocke had ceased.

WHITELOCKE, Samuel, usually referred to as Sam (1651–1690). *Alumni Oxonienses*. The first child of Whitelocke's third marriage. Mary, Samuel's mother, had previously been married to Colonel Rowland Wilson (q.v.), for 14 childless years. She recalled Hannah (in *The Bible*) who, after many barren years, had a son whom she called Samuel, the answer to her prayers, 1 Samuel 1,v.20. The women attending at Samuel Whitelocke's birth feared that the baby was going to die, until someone had the idea of blowing tobacco (presumably smoke) into his face, at which no doubt he gasped for breath, cried out, and recovered, *Diary* 30 May 1651. Samuel was baptized on 18 June 1651, J.E. Cox *Annals of St. Helen's Bishopsgate* (Tinsley Brothers. 1876) p. 94. The early entries about him concern childhood illnesses, enlivened, when he wäs 10 years old, by news of his writing Latin verses, inspired by the new tutor, James Pearson (q.v.), as a New Year's gift to his father, *Diary* 1 Jan. 1661/62. Later, Sam studied with his younger brother, Carleton (q.v.), at St. Edmund Hall, Oxford. They were both registered as entering the Middle Temple in January 1666/67 but, unlike his brother, it is doubtful whether Sam studied law.

After several attempts at match-making by his impoverished parents, Sam married Elizabeth Gough, see WHITELOCKE, Elizabeth, jun. (2).

Whitelocke's last home, Chilton Lodge, with a large part of the Chilton Park estate, was settled on Sam, *Diary* 22 Dec. 1671; a footnote gives details of the settlement. After the wedding in Vernham, Hants, south of Hungerford, ib. 27 Dec. 1671, Sam's parents had serious misgivings about the match; then there was a mistake in the draft conveyances of the property, for which Whitelocke had to 'justefy himselfe', after which Sam's wife and her friends grumbled at the smallness of the estate, although the terms had been accepted in the original agreement, ib. 19, 29 Feb., 5, 6 Mar. 1671/72. Whitelocke was unwell, suffering a good deal of pain, and very ready to find fault, so when Sam and Elizabeth went to London, for a visit, this was condemned as 'an unnecessary expence'.

The terms of the settlement allowed Whitelocke and Mary to continue living as before in Chilton Lodge, with suitable rooms designated to the new owner and his wife; this afforded ample opportunity for Whitelocke and Mary to disapprove of the wife they had chosen for Sam, ib. 6 May, 22 June 1672. Sam was probably Mary's spoilt eldest son, for whom no wife would have been good enough, much as James (q.v.) was to Whitelocke. Understandably, Sam's wife Elizabeth sometimes stayed at her father's house without her husband, 'whose company she seemed not to desire' – more probably, however, she was escaping from the company of her in-laws, ib. 8 Oct. 1672; 28 Jan. 1672/73.

Sam and his wife must have suffered intense irritation from living under the same roof as his parents who, it seems, failed to notice that he was no longer their cherished child, but a young married man in his early 20s. There are entries such as 'Sam was late att Miles his house', and 'He went to Vernham not acquainting me with it, nothing butt trouble'; or, Sam being out, Elizabeth took her horse and one manservant '& without acquainting her husband or his friends went to Vernham. an unusuall & unhansome freake' (perhaps this *was* rather bold), ib. 26, 27 Feb., 10 Mar. 1672/73. Six months later, Sam and Elizabeth's first child was born, and christened Mary (q.v.), ib. 30 Sept., 1 Oct. 1673. When Sam, by that time a father, took his brother Bigley to dine with the Duke of Somerset (q.v.) at his 'house of debauchery', he omitted (for obvious reasons) to tell his parents, and the young men came home at two o'clock in the morning, ' . . . att which mother was much grieved', ib. 10 Nov. 1673. When Sam, quite properly, negotiated with Farmer Dore (a tenant on his estate) about a new lease of Heywood Farm, Whitelocke felt he 'was in a manner sett by' for it seems that Sam only consulted his father-in-law; Whitelocke felt better about it when he was drawn into a general discussion, but soon afterwards he thought himself 'little regarded', ib. 17, 19 Dec. 1673; 20 Jan. 1673/74. It is hard to hold high public office for many years, and then to be a nobody at home.

Whitelocke feared that Sam was drinking too-much, and this led to an unpleasant exchange one night when Sam threatened to sue his father, but he apologized for this the next day, ib. 23 Dec. 1673; 19 Dec. 1674.

After Whitelocke's death, when Sam was entirely his own master, he made good as owner of Chilton Lodge. The 'Parish Register' at Chilton Foliat (transcript), which is not given to eulogies, states that Samuel was buried on 26 May 1690, having been 'the best neighbour unto the poor in the parish & a man in much Esteem with the rich'. His son, Samuel, jun., also of Chilton Lodge (baptized at Chilton Foliat 23 Dec. 1675, buried there 23 Apr. 1743), was married twice, the second time being in Westminster Abbey, to Katherine Dolben, granddaughter of John Dolben, Archbishop of York. They had three sons (one named Samuel, baptized 1709, Wilts. R.O. 'Chilton Foliat Register, 1705–1764') and nine daughters; the male descent of that branch died with the three sons, W. Money *Historical Sketch of the Town of Hungerford* (Blacket. 1894) pp. 24, 25. A wall tablet in the Church, quoted by Money, names seven of the daughters (probably those who survived infancy), of whom Mary died in 1802 aged 91, widow of George Garrard, Judith (or possibly Edith) died in 1807 aged 84, and (Mrs ?) Mulso Whitelocke in 1812, aged 97.

WHITELOCKE, Stephen (Steven) (b. 1659). Whitelocke's 17th and last child. Apart from mentioning Stephen's other childhood ailments, his father recorded that when he was nearly six the boy suffered a fall which made him lame, *Diary* 8 Sept. 1665. Characteristically, his parents went to great pains to try and have the injury put right: Mr. Ivy, a bonesetter, treated the thigh bone, which he said was out of joint, but he only caused a great deal of anguish, leaving Stephen in a worse condition than before the treatment; Mr. Carden, a surgeon, reported that there was no bone out of joint, and this opinion was confirmed by Mr. Turland, another bonesetter, *Diary* 29 Nov. 1665; 9 Mar. 1665/66. Valentine Greatrakes or Greatrix (mis-heard by Whitelocke as 'Britridge'), the famous 'Stroker' and healer (on a visit to England from Ireland) said he could do little good, because Stephen's hip had been dislocated, ib. 1 May with note, 2, 9 May 1666; the next year the parents consulted another surgeon, Mr. Fothergell, ib. 4 May 1667. There is no further information about Stephen's leg, but this youngest son came in for two friendly gifts: (1) when making a token payment of £2 for legal advice, Whitelocke's Cousin Fettiplace (q.v.) 'directed' (i.e. addressed) the fee to 14-year-old Stephen, ib. 29 Nov. 1673; (2) the final entry for Stephen concerns his receiving from trustees the reversion of a lease (after two lives) for his lifetime, from the estate of Sir Francis Popham (q.v.), who had died some three months earlier, ib. 11 Nov. 1674.

WHITELOCKE, Sir William, Kt., MP (1636–1717). *Hist. of Parl.* (spelt WHITLOCK). Whitelocke's eldest son by his wife Frances. William was educated with his elder half-brother, James (q.v.), whose entry contains references to their going to school together and later accompanying their father on his Swedish Embassy, 1653–1654; but their paths had begun to diverge when James went up to Oxford and William to the Middle Temple, which he entered in 1647. William was called to the Bar in 1655; a Bencher in 1671; one of the City of London's 'counsel at large' in 1673; later, Reader and Treasurer of the Middle Temple. He took silk in 1689, 14 years after his father's death; in the same year he was knighted by William of Orange, whom he had entertained on the new King's march to London.

As a young man, he had been an irregular attender in the Commons as MP for West Looe, Cornwall, in Richard Cromwell's Parliament, *Diary* 22 Mar. 1658/59, being preoccupied at that time with his forthcoming marriage. Years later, he sat for his father's old constituency of Great Marlow in 1689 and 1690, and in the next century, for Oxford University. For some years a Whig, he ultimately turned Tory.

He married Mary Overbury, see WHITELOCKE, Mary jun. (3), later Lady. The year of the marriage was wrongly shown on the family tree in R. Spalding *Improbable Puritan* as 1671, following that in J.S. Burns *History of Henley-on-Thames* (and in later sources), but it is shown by Whitelocke to have taken place 12 years earlier, on 19 May, 1659 (*Diary* 20 May); that date is confirmed by the Bourton-on-the-Hill parish register, Gloucestershire County Record Office, P54 IN 1/1. This confusion may have originated through an indenture of agreement and a deed, both concerned with the marriage settlement, and dated respectively 1 Jan. 1670/71 and 3 July 1671, Oxford Record Office? (reference untraced for this transcript). Their agreement and the diary entries refer to Mr. Overbury or (from 1660, when he was knighted) to Sir Thomas Overbury as Mary's *brother*, who paid £2,000 as his sister's portion. In some sources he is mistakenly shown as Mary's *father*. The deed of 1671, mentioned above, recalls the terms agreed upon (12 years earlier) for William's marriage, in which Whitelocke 'did settle ... or intend to settle' on his son the manors of Henley and Phyllis Court, with their woods, lands, tenements etc. It appears, however, that James Whitelocke (heir to the adjoining estate of Fawley Court, living with a wealthy wife at Trumpington Hall in Cambridgeshire, but chronically in debt and scrounging on his father) had joined with Whitelocke in mortgaging portions of William's estate, which Whitelocke evidently still controlled. It was discreditable on both their parts, and when the 'mortgage became forfeited ... Doc[to]^r Colston [*sic* in transcript; possibly Dr. Colladon, q.v.] the surviving Mortgagee obtain'd a Decree in the High Court of Chancery' against Whitelocke and James. In obedience to the decree, James 'granted & confirm'd s[ai]^d premises to W[illia]^m'. There are entries in *The Diary* which lead up to this trouble, for example, the disagreement between Whitelocke and William over the estate of William's brother Willoughby (q.v.) who died young; his father had provided money to ensure an inheritance for Willoughby, at whose death Whitelocke, being very short of funds, hoped to recoup something, but William, an astute lawyer, made good a claim to be his young brother's heir, *Diary* 16, 17 Mar. 1670/71.

Not long afterwards, James made an indefensible claim to a right in the Phyllis Court lands, ib. 24, 25 May 1671. William and his wife had wisely decided to move into Phyllis Court five years after their marriage, ib. 28 May, 20 Oct. 1664, Whitelocke having bought for himself the Chilton Park estate, with Chilton Lodge, in July 1663. There were further discussions and exchanges of letters (some now in private hands of a descendant, through a female line) between Whitelocke and William, ending in a dispute over woodland on the Phyllis Court estate, ib. 16, 18, 20 Sept., 1, 19, 21, 28 Oct., 1, 11, 13 Nov. 1671; 4, 24 Sept., 5 Dec. 1672, *passim.* William probably had a strong case and knew how to go through the proper channels, as when he obtained a licence 'to grub up the underwood on certain parcels of ground ... about 100 acres in Henley parish ... and convert them into tillage', *C.S.P. Dom.* 1672–1673 p. 219.

Whitelocke was not always tactful with his children, but his letters to William are reasonable and affectionate. He had paid heavily to rear a family of 17 children, and had little to live on after the Restoration, apart from rents and modest fees for giving legal advice. In a letter to William he indicated that he could only live by borrowing money and paying interest on it, but that William must keep this information to himself. The children had their own problems, and none of them appears to have eased things for their father. The relationship with William, however, which had been good during most of the 1660s, improved again in Whitelocke's last years, ib. 26 Aug., 22, 23 Sept. 1673; 17 Aug. 1674; 20, 22 Mar. 1674/75.

WHITELOCKE, Willoughby (1645–1670). Whitelocke's eighth child by his second wife, Frances, was given his mother's maiden name. An entry in the 'Annales' is engagingly confused: 'My son Willoughby was borne in my lodgings in the Temple about Dec. 23. 1644. & baptized att St Dunstans Church Dec. 28. 1644. butt I doubt this yeare is mistaken & I must referre you to the next year for more certainty ...', Add. Ms 37343 fol. 350v. In view of this, the diary version is probably correct; it states that Whitelocke came home at about 10 p.m. to find Frances very ill, and that she gave birth to their son Willoughby during the night, *Diary* 7 Oct. 1645.

Willoughby and his younger brother, Bulstrode, jun. (q.v.), were sent to Mr. Shilborne's school at Grendon, where James, jun. (q.v.) and William (above) had been before them, *Diary* 26 Aug. 1655, but they left suddenly in May 1656, when Mr. Shilborne (q.v.) died, see R.H. Whitelocke *Memoirs of Bulstrode Whitelocke* ... (1860) pp. 461–462; he quotes a passage about the schoolmaster's death, from a Whitelocke manuscript which has not been traced. The three estates, Fawley Court, Phyllis Court and Chilton Lodge, being earmarked for the eldest sons by each of his three wives, Whitelocke was anxiously concerned to provide for his other children. In Willoughby's case, he lent £1,400 to Henry Dixon (q.v.), whose son Edward (q.v.) had married Whitelocke's sister Cecilia (q.v.). It is not clear whether the debt was repaid or was even meant to be repaid. The purpose of the transaction was that Dixon should, after leaving a life interest to his widow, Anne Dixon, bequeath property in Wandsworth and in Braughing, Hertfordshire, to young Willoughby, as indeed he did. When Dixon died in 1656, the house in Wandsworth was worth £32 a year and the lands in Braughing, £90, *Diary* 12 Jan. 1655/56.

Willoughby had his quota of childhood ailments, duly recorded by his father, and he also hurt himself falling into a cellar, ib. 3 June 1661. When Willoughby was 16, Samuel Wilson (q.v.) to whom he had evidently been apprenticed in the wine trade, wrote that he wished to send the boy to the Canaries, and Whitelocke thought it best to give his consent, ib. 25 Aug. 1662. Willoughby stayed overseas for three years, writing home occasionally, and Whitelocke also had news of him from some Spaniards, in London, ib. 5 Jan. 1662/63. The boy returned home, ib. 24 Jan. 1664/65. After two interviews with his master in Oxford, ib. 10 Oct., 25 Nov. 1665, things seem to have gone wrong for Willoughby: reading between the lines, he lost his job and Whitelocke thought Samuel Wilson treated him badly, ib. 30 June 1666. There was talk of his finding a new job as a factor (or agent) with the East India Company, ib. 27 Dec. 1667, but Willoughby had thoughts of going to his uncle, Lord William Willoughby (q.v.), in Barbados, and 'missed of the factors place ... by his loytering w[i]'h that ill company [James's friends?] att Fawley Court, & by Mr Willsons ill character given of him ... an ill requitall for his service,' ib. 10 June 1668.

Whitelocke worked hard and even paid £100 to get his son a place, with prospects, as assistant to a marine factor in the Turkey Company, and Willoughby was duly appointed, ib. 1 Dec. 1669; 21 Jan., 8, 18, 23 Feb., 3 Mar. 1669/70. Then 'Brother Willson' made trouble about Willoughby's 'buisnes & writings', probably his apprenticeship contract, ib. 10 May 1670. Whitelocke was ill with dropsy and stone when news arrived that Willoughby had died, within a week of arriving in Iskenderon, ib. 4 Feb. 1670/71. He was deeply grieved, and further upset by 'harsh letters' from

William, who claimed (successfully) that he was the heir to his young brother's estate. In the end, William agreed to allow his father £500 out of the estate, ib. 16 Mar. 1670/71; 19 Oct. 1671; 4 Sept. 1672, with note.

WHITFIELD, [Thomas?] (d. c. 1666). *Students admitted to the Inner Temple 1547–1660* (London. 1877). Probably Thomas, son and heir of John Whitfield of Worth, east of Three Bridges, Sussex. Admitted to the Inner Temple in 1632. He acted as Counsel to John, 2nd Baron Lovelace (q.v.), against Whitelocke, *Diary* 17 Jan. 1661/62. Later, Whitelocke wished to use Whitfield's services against John Green (q.v.), but learned that he was already acting for Green, ib. 21 Nov. 1662, *passim*. His death is mentioned indirectly, ib. 11 May 1666.

WIDDRINGTON, Sir Thomas, Kt., MP (c.1600–1664). M.F.K.; *Hist of Parl.*; *D.N.B.*; E. Foss *Judges of England* vi; *Pepys* x (in the entry for Widdrington's younger brother Ralph, who was Pepys's tutor at Cambridge). He studied at Christ's College, Cambridge, and Gray's Inn; married, in 1634, Frances (d. 1649), sister of Sir Thomas Fairfax, later 3rd Baron (q.v.). Widdrington's many political and legal appointments are enumerated in the sources above. Whitelocke encountered him: as a fellow MP from 1640; as a colleague in Chancery, when they were both Commissioners of the Great Seal (both before the King's execution and during the early part of the Protectorate); and with some tension when Widdrington, the Speaker of Cromwell's Parliament in 1656, fell ill and Whitelocke was appointed acting Speaker. Whitelocke was told by the Commons that, during the Speaker's absence, he was to receive the profits due to the office, *Diary* 27 Jan. 1656/57. The friction began when Sir Thomas 'in his love of money, claymed all the profitts'. These were considerable, since the Speaker was entitled to receive fees for naturalization, for which there were almost 100 applicants in one parliamentary Bill at that time, *C.J.* vii, 487 (second reading), 7 Feb. 1656/57.

Some months later, Widdrington attempted to smooth things over by sending a jewel worth £50 or £60 to Whitelocke's wife Mary (q.v.), but she refused it; finally, he sent his colleague £100, which Whitelocke accepted for the sake of peace, although he considered he should have been paid four times that sum, ib. 14 July 1657. He seldom held a grudge for long unless he felt seriously wronged, and in both the early and again the later stages of their working together, he described Widdrington in glowing terms, as: '... a gentleman of known integrity, & great abilities in his profession ...', recalling that when they were both Commissioners of the

Great Seal they '. . . did seldome interpose or interrupt one another' and when they had been working in Chancery they were accustomed '. . . to take the aier att Hampstead Heath' together, ib. 2 Mar. 1647/48; 14 Apr., 15 June 1648. They supported each other in refusing to have any part in the King's trial; some days before the first session of the High Court of Justice on 8 Jan. 1648/49, Whitelocke took Widdrington in his coach to Phyllis Court, Henley-on-Thames, to be out of town. Shortly after this Whitelocke concealed himself, for a few days, in Widdrington's house, ib. 26 Dec. 1648; 4 Jan. 1648/49. Later they joined forces again, in (unsuccessfully) opposing Cromwell's plan to dissolve the Rump, ib. 19 Apr. 1653. Despite the friction between them as Speaker and acting Speaker, recorded above, a year later Whitelocke was referring to Widdrington as his 'Collegue & friend', and wrote that he, with others, recommended Widdrington for appointment as Chief Baron (i.e. the Presiding Judge of the Exchequer), ib. 26 June 1658.

The only letter traced from Widdrington to Whitelocke was written during the Swedish Embassy, when both lawyers were reappointed Commissioners of the Great Seal, this time under the Protectorate. After the King's execution, Widdrington had pleaded ill-health and a troubled conscience, to avoid appointment to the Seal under the Republic. When the Protectorate was established, however, he wrote that, despite his former resolutions and considerations of repose and profit, he had been moved by the Protector's commands and persuasion to accept the office, and to serve with Whitelocke and Richard Keble (q.v.). He continued with surprising diffidence:

> I know my owne unfitnesse, but my unhappinesse is that others will not believe it till they learne it afterwards out of my actions . . . I have but one Single encouragem[en]ᵗ[,] w[hi]ch is that I shall have the honour & comfort to by joyned w[i]th y[ou]r L[ordshi]ᵖᵖ, who are able alone to manage that busines . . . [although he was only a 'Cypher' in the number, Whitelocke's presence would complete it, besides which] the affection & Friendship w[hi]ch I have ever found from y[o]ᵘ adds to that encouragem[en]t . . . [he ended with hopes for Whitelocke's early return from Sweden] w[hi]ch . . . I assu[re] y[ou]ʳ L[ordshi]pp is as much desyred by me as by any p[er]son living[,] unlesse it be by y[ou]ʳ Lady . . .
> 14 Apr. 1654.
>
> Long. W.P. xv, 137.

Without any spectacular compromise on his part, Widdrington was accepted by Royalists after 1660, although deprived of his former offices. He served as an MP in 1660 and 1661, and on the Committee for the reception of Charles II, etc. There is no entry to suggest that he and Whitelocke ever met after the Restoration.

WILDE (WYLDE, WELDE), Judge John, MP (1590–1669). *D.N.B.*; M.F.K.; E. Foss *Judges of England* vi. He studied at Balliol College, Oxford, and at the Inner Temple. Served as MP for Droitwich, Worcestershire, in the last years of James I's reign, and the first years of Charles I's, also in the Short Parliament, April to May 1640; he represented Worcester County in the Long Parliament (continuing in the Rump), and represented Droitwich again in Richard Cromwell's brief Parliament from January 1658/59 to April 1659, resuming his seat in the restored Rump in the summer of that year. In January1659/60, Parliament (restored yet again) reinstated him as Chief Baron of the Exchequer, the appointment which he had held from October 1646 and after the King's execution; he had been put out of office during the Protectorate, from 1654, and was finally ousted in 1660, at the Restoration.

Earlier in his legal career, it was at his suggestion that the Long Parliament had a new Great Seal struck, after Lord Littleton (q.v.) had sent the existing one to the King, and Wilde was then appointed one of the six Commissioners of the new Seal (two from the Lords and four from the Commons), in November 1643. At the trial of Archbishop Laud (q.v.), in March 1643/44, Wilde made accusations against him which are described in the *D.N.B.* as 'more conspicuous for political and religious rancour than for argument and good taste'. The charges were, indeed, colourful and extravagant, including the suggestion that Laud had been making a ladder up which he could climb to the papacy; but more realistically, he accused Laud of cruelty and oppression, *State Trials* (ed. T.B. Howell. 1816), pp. 353–363. The peevish antiquarian, Anthony Wood, 'who never spake well of any man' (*D.N.B.*, Wood) wrote of Wilde's corrupt pronouncements as an Assize Judge in 1645 (quoted in the *D.N.B.* entry for Wilde).

Whitelocke entertained Wilde at Phyllis Court, when it was Henley Garrison, and was indulgently amused by the Judge's signs of timidity, wrongly entered in *Diary* 28 July 1646 (Whitelocke noted at the end of the passage that this entry should have been made before the fall of Oxford and Wallingford). Later, Whitelocke made the formal speech when Wilde was sworn in as Chief Baron, ib. 15 Nov. 1648. When Wilde was replaced in that office he wrote an unhappy, undemanding letter, welcoming Whitelocke home from the Swedish Embassy; he recorded that after all the work he had done for the country and the Commonwealth, and after suffering great losses in the service of the public and in discharging his duty, 'a dark shadow' was cast on him 'with . . . sad consequences . . . to me and mine, and many others that have dependence on me . . .' In this connection, Whitelocke described Wilde as '. . . very laborious in the service of the Parliament, and stiff for them', he had 'sustained great losses and hatred by adhering in all matters to them. He was learned in his profession, but of more reading than depth of judgement ...' Whitelocke had 'never heard of any injustice or incivility of him. The Parliament made him Lord Chief Baron of the Exchequer, which place he executed with diligence and justice ...' yet, when Cromwell assumed power as Protector, Wilde was set aside. Whitelocke appealed unsuccessfully to Cromwell on the Chief Baron's behalf: '... the Protector having a dislike of the Sergeant, but the ground thereof I could not learn', *Journal* ii, 460–461. Clarendon (q.v.), judging Wilde from the Royalist viewpoint, described him as an 'infamous judge'.

WILDMAN (WILDEMAN, alias WENMAN), Major John, MP, knighted in 1692 (*c.* 1624–1693). M. Ashley *John Wildman* (Jonathan Cape. 1947); *D.N.B.*; *Hist of Parl.*; *Pepys* x. Son of Jeffrey Wildman, yeoman, of Wremingham, south-west of Norwich; he bought Beckett (or Becket) House, Shrivenham (formerly in Berkshire now Oxfordshire), in about 1655. Earlier, it had belonged to the regicide, Henry Marten (q.v.). During Whitelocke's lifetime, Wildman was active as a Leveller, republican conspirator, land-speculator and briefly, after the Restoration, as a top official in the Royal Post Office (becoming Postmaster-General in 1689); he was also business adviser to the 2nd Duke of Buckingham (q.v.), who described him as 'the wisest statesman in England', quoted by M. Ashley (above) p. 198.

Whitelocke's first reference to Wildman concerns the Leveller being taken into custody (details below) when, interestingly, Whitelocke describes himself as 'a favourer of him', *Diary* 18 Jan. 1647/48. Part of Wildman's offence was that some months earlier he had helped to frame and had promoted a seditious (i.e. a democratic republican) petition on behalf of the soldiers, 'The Case of the Army truly stated', M. Ashley p. 30. This was a forerunner of the two versions of 'The Agreement of the People', Oct. 1647 and Jan. 1648/49, see S.R. Gardiner *Constitutional Documents* pp. 333–335 and 359–371. Briefly, these stated the principles for which radicals in the Army felt they had fought, and the future style of government which they envisaged as a result of the Civil War. Wildman was active in the Putney Debates with Cromwell and other Officers, who were boldly criticized in the Army's petition. The Levellers maintained that 'Every [male] person in England hath as clear a right to elect his representative [i.e. MP] as the greatest person in England.' Wildman saw it as an undeniable maxim that 'all government is in the free consent of the people' and that a man could not justly be bound by law if he had not consented to 'such persons' (i.e. MPs) making laws for him, M. Ashley p. 37, *passim*. Wildman followed up 'The Case ...' and 'The Agreement ...'

with a pamphlet entitled *Putney Projects* or *The Old Serpent in a New Form*, showing how the Army's political cause had been betrayed by Cromwell and Ireton.

Besides issuing pamphlets, in January 1647/48, Wildman (with John Lilburne) held a meeting at Smithfield, to propagate republican and democratic beliefs. The Serjeant-at-Arms was instructed by the Commons to arrest them, and bring them before the Bar of the House. They duly appeared there on 19 January 1647/48, made long speeches, and the Commons, in vague terms, referred their cases to be tried in the King's Bench, then proceeded to send Lilburne to the Tower and Wildman (alias Wenman) to the Fleet prison (where they remained for over six months without a trial), *C.J.* v, 437–438; 18, 19, 20 Jan. 1647/48. Fortunately for them, Sir John Maynard (q.v.) had been arbitrarily imprisoned in the Tower in September 1647, by order of the Commons, and was released on 3 June 1648; resuming his seat in the House, he compared the committal by the Commons, without trial, of men who were not MPs, to the actions of the old (and execrated) Star Chamber, M. Ashley (above) pp. 58–59. Events had moved against Cromwell and the Officers, and the Republicans were set free. It was Whitelocke who actually obtained the Order for Wildman's release, *Diary* 2 Aug. 1648.

Undeterred by his spell in prison, a few years later Wildman was plotting to overthrow the Protectorate, and was again arrested. He was caught drafting a paper which was headed uncompromisingly: 'The declaration of the free and well-affected people of England now in arms against the tyrant Oliver Cromwell, esq.' The text of this unfinished document, which Whitelocke transcribed, is strong stuff. The declaration foresaw that those who took up arms for the defence of their native rights would be branded rebels and traitors, or be misrepresented by the Army and the City as disturbers of the public peace, as arbitrary cavaliers, or levellers and so on, but Wildman contended:

> The whole Christian world knows that our English earth hath been drunk with blood these twelve years through the great contest for right and freedom, and the whole treasure of the nation exhausted in that quarrel ... [People had suffered years of oppression, arbitrariness, and tyranny ... with a burden of excise and taxes such as England had never known before, and had been fed with] specious pretences and most alluring promises ... [of liberty and impartial justice] by him that now calls himself Lord Protector, and his army ... [They could not have believed that] a man of such a mean quality and estate ... should aspire to make himself an absolute lord and tyrant over three potent nations ... [Wildman referred scornfully to Cromwell's] professions of godliness, simplicity, and integrity ... his dissembled humility and meekness, and his frequent compassionate tears upon every occasion ... these things rocked us ... asleep with the pleasant

dreams of liberty and justice . . . [until Cromwell sacrificed the people's] laws, liberties, and properties unto his own ambition . . . [He, who had formerly protested before God and the Long Parliament that he and his Army would be subject to the civil authority, now exercised absolute dominion over the laws of the three nations] what patron in Algier ever claimed more mastery over his slaves bought in the market than . . . Cromwell extends . . . over us? . . . The patron can but give the slave his laws, his clothes, his meat, his life . . . all those Cromwell owns to have given to us, only he speaks it in such language as sounds not so harshly . . . [Wildman appealed to the conscience of all honest men to consider arming themselves in defence of their] ancient laws and dearest birthrights.

He proceeded to set down five demands to be made concerning their rights and liberties. He was still dictating when the soldiers arrived to arrest him, *Memorials* iv, 183–187, Feb. 1654/55. This inflammatory declaration was sent to the Protector. Some days later, Whitelocke too received a copy; although as a Commissioner of the Great Seal he was working for the Protectorate, it is clear that, as a citizen, he disliked the new alternative to monarchy, and considered that 'there was . . . much of reason & trueth' in Wildman's declaration, *Diary* 20 Feb. 1654/55.

Two years later, Wildman was involved behind the scenes with Edward Sexby, in the conspiracy mismanaged by Miles Sindercombe (q.v.), to assassinate the Protector. In his comments on Wildman's activities (other than the assassination attempt), Whitelocke showed a marked preference for a republican style of government, rather than for a Protectorate.

Although the fact is not referred to until later, Whitelocke and Wildman, with others, were required by Charles Fleetwood (q.v.) to draft the constitution of a 'Free State' i.e. a Republic. This was evidently while the Committee of Safety was operating, some six months after the Protectorate had ended with Richard Cromwell's Declaration, *C.J.* vii, 664–665, 25 May 1659. John Aubrey described how, in the autumn of that year, James Harrington (author of *The Commonwealth of Oceana*) and a crowd of his 'disciples', including John Wildman, met every night at the 'Turke's head in New Palace-yard'; there they drank coffee and conducted brilliant discussions. At about that time, Harrington published his pamphlet *Divers modells of Popular Government*, see Harrington's entry in *Aubrey's Brief Lives* (ed. A. Clarke. Clarendon Press. 1898) i, 289–290; Harrington's was a property-owner's republicanism, C. Hill *Puritanism and Revolution* (Mercury Books. 1958), chapter 10. By the time Parliament resumed power from the Army, on 26 December 1659, Whitelocke was convinced that Monck's undeclared intention was to restore Charles II to the throne. As Constable of Windsor Castle, Whitelocke had refused the command of 3,000 – no doubt fictitious – horsemen, offered to him by Wildman if he would defend the Castle (against Lambert and the Army), and declare for a free Commonwealth. By that stage he 'saw no likelyhood' of effecting this; but when Colonel Sir Henry Ingoldsby (q.v.) and Wildman arrived before the Castle, with a troop of 300 volunteer horsemen, Whitelocke's subordinate, Colonel Christopher Whichcote (q.v.), Governor of the Castle, surrendering it without a fight, they were duly thanked by Parliament, *C.J.* vii, 798; *Diary* 28 Dec. 1659. Earlier in the same long and confused entry, Whitelocke, who had been collaborating with the Officers on the Committee of Safety, was apprehensive that the Castle's surrender to Parliament 'might bring his name in question' since he was its Constable, and worse still, that Wildman might divulge the part they had both played in drafting the constitution for a Republic (on orders from the Army). To his relief, however, 'Wildeman carryed himselfe prudently & faithfully', ib.

A fragment of a manuscript in Whitelocke's handwriting is headed:

> The Great Statute of the freedome and Governement of the Commonwealth of England, Scotland, & Ireland, & the Dominions & Territories therunto belonging

This is calendared as probably having been prepared for use after the execution of Charles I, but it is almost certainly the beginning of Whitelocke and Wildman's draft of around November/December 1659. The text of the document starts:

> for the better securing of the good cause of the Parlement so long contended for . . . & for the better conservation of the freedome & Governement of this Commonwealth The Parlement have thought fitt [or Fleetwood and the Officers intended them to see fit, when they were allowed to reassemble] to assent unto . . . & enact the ensuing Articles . . .

The surviving Articles lay it down that: (1) the supreme, delegated power residing in the people's trustees (i.e. MPs), is limited by certain fundamentals which are not to be dispensed with or altered; (2) supreme, delegated power is reposed in Trustees by the people, for the people's preservation, not for their destruction; (3) it would be destructive to the people's right and freedom, to which they had been restored, ever to admit or receive any earthly King or single person, whoever it might be, to be Chief Magistrate (this suggests that they had been suffering under a Protector), to exercise power in governing the Commonwealth, Long. W.P. xxiv, 399, 400.

It was probably early in 1660 that Whitelocke (who had been on the run and in hiding during most of January 1659/60) sent a note to Wildman who, unlike many supposed friends, had evidently stood by him when political fortunes changed. Whitelocke wrote appreciatively of 'the expression of your hearty love & friendship . . . especially att this time when I have so much neede of it'; he wrote that he could only return his hearty thanks and entreat

Wildman's advice and continued favour (Feb. 1659/60?) ib. xix, 126, in Whitelocke's hand (a draft or copy).

For over a year after the Restoration Wildman was a successful man of affairs, with an influential appointment at the Post Office. Chancellor Clarendon (q.v.) discussed Wildman with Whitelocke, who praised his abilities as a public servant and his trustworthiness in anything he undertook, but Whitelocke observed that the Chancellor was no friend to Wildman, *Diary* 3 Aug. 1661. A few days after this interview, Whitelocke consulted Wildman about his difficulty in obtaining money due to him from the 2nd Duke of Buckingham (to whom Wildman was, surprisingly, a trustee and adviser), and Wildman told him to 'gett what he could w[i]'h expedition', ib. 9 Aug. 1661. Some three months later, Wildman was charged as an accomplice in a republican conspiracy against the government. A list of questions to be asked at his examination was drawn up. Basically, these enquired:

Did he know of current designs to disturb the peace or alter the government?
When was he last in Mr. Harrington's company; where did they meet and who was present? etc.
Were Alderman Love and Alderman Fowke and Ireton present?
At a meeting in Millbank, was Mr. Pretty present? Did Wildman know him?
Was an Oath of Secrecy proposed? Did they agree to choose a Committee of '7 ... to ripen [the] business'? Who were the 7? How often did they meet? Did Wildman know Mr. Barebone? Major Haynes? Samuel Moyer? John Portman etc.
Had he ever met Mr. Nevile, Mr. Moyer and Mr. Barebone at the Tavern in St. Martin Le Grand etc? Had there been a communication about reviving the Long Parliament?
Who else had he conferred with about a petition for taking away the Excise and about not retaining a Standing Army? etc.
Did he know of any invitation sent to disbanded Officers to meet in London before 10 Dec.?
Did he know of any plan to seize the gates of the City? etc.
26 Nov. 1661.

Eg. 2543 fols. 65–66v.

Wildman was imprisoned successively in the Tower, on the Scilly Isles and in Pendennis Castle, until shortly after Clarendon's fall in October 1667, when the Duke of Buckingham helped to obtain his adviser's release. In the early months of Wildman's imprisonment, Whitelocke learned (from Geffrey Palmer, by then Master of the Rolls) that the reason why Clarendon did not find him, Whitelocke, an appointment was because he was too friendly with Wildman, *Diary* 2 Jan. 1662/63. This warning, however, did nothing to dampen his friendship with Wildman: they visited each other once Wildman was released, and exchanged gifts of vension from Becket House, and trout, tame rabbits, crayfish and melons from Chilton Lodge, during the remaining years of Whitelocke's life, ib. 19, 21, 24, 26 July 1669; 27, 28 July 1671, *passim*; while Wildman was in prison, Whitelocke had kept in touch with his second wife, Lucy, daughter of Lord Lovelace, ib. 4 July 1660 with note; 13, 14 Sept. 1667. The last entries concerning Wildman refer to his dining at Chilton Lodge, and to George Cokayn (q.v.) going to Wildman's home, ib. 2, 5 May 1674.

After Whitelocke's death, Wildman continued his activities as a conspirator, from time to time; he resumed his work at the government Post Office, became an MP, and was eventually knighted by King William III, whom he had supported.

WILKINSON [Henry] DD (1610–1675). *Calamy Revised; D.N.B.* Known in Oxford as 'Long Harry', to distinguish him from the younger Henry Wilkinson, 'Dean Harry', Principal of Magdalen Hall. 'Long Harry' Wilkinson was appointed, by Parliament, a Canon of Christ Church, Oxford, and became Lady Margaret Professor of Divinity in 1652. After his ejection, in July 1660, he preached in and around London; a Conventicle in Camberwell, at which he was preaching in 1665, was broken up. He appears in *The Diary* when he and Dr Owen (q.v.), and others, visited Whitelocke who was ill in London, *Diary* 21 Nov. 1667. Because of his London connections after 1660, it seems likely that this was 'Long Harry', not the Dean (who, after his ejection, withdrew to Leicestershire and later to Essex).

WILKINSON, Dr [Samuel], STP, i.e. *Sacrae Theologiae Professor* (c. 1600–1669). R. Davies *Chelsea Old Church* (Duckworth. 1904) pp. 185, 194. The date of birth is given on the presumption that this was Samuel Wilkinson of Sussex, who was made a Canon of Chichester in 1660 and of St. Paul's in 1668, *Alumni Oxonienses*. His first name is not given in *The Diary*, but appears on receipts for quarterly tithes of £1, for Whitelocke's share of the park and gardens of Beaufort House, Chelsea (sequestrated from the 2nd Duke of Buckingham, q.v.); these receipts, dated 3 Jan. 1651/52 and 1 Apr. 1652, are in Long W.P. xii, 2 and 88. The house was leased to Whitelocke and John Lisle (q.v.), Commissioners of the Great Seal, as their London residence, Diary 20 July 1649; see entry: LISLE. Dr Wilkinson was Rector of Chelsea Parish Church from 1632. Whitelocke became his parishioner, living at Beaufort House at intervals during the 1650s, ib. 24 Mar. 1650/51, *passim*. The Rector is described mercilessly by Whitelocke:

I was with my wife & family att Chelsey Church, where preached, Dr Wilkinson the parson of the parish, not the other Dr Wilkinson his brother, who is a reverend pious & learned man, & an excellent preacher . . . this Dr Wilkinson . . . is a Dull, proud, scandalous, man, & a drye pittyfull preacher, yett being of the parish, I sometimes heard him . . . 12 June 1653.

Add. Ms 37345 fol. 275.

Some months after the Restoration, Wilkinson put in a demand for £18 as pew-rent, covering three years' use. Whitelocke noted bitterly that the Rector had freely offered him the pew, as he had another one for Mrs. Wilkinson and the family, and only thought fit to put in a bill when Whitelocke was 'under a cloude', *Diary* 14 Nov. 1660. A little earlier, Whitelocke had written to Wilkinson acknowleding a letter of 25 September 1660, which had informed him that 12 years' pew-rent amounting to £18 was due, as promised by Whitelocke, who replied firmly in the tones of a lawyer:

If I knew or remembred any such bargaine or promise, I should give you satisfaction . . . butt I doe not remember it, & it seemes the lesse probable, bicause in all that time it hath not bin demaunded either by your clerke or any other for you . . . [this was in spite of the fact that every quarter he had paid other monies to the Rector] butt though I doe not remember the bargaine you mention yett if you can prove it, I shall save you the trouble to recover it by law. It is not well to revile me (as I have heard hath bin done [)], & very undeservedly & improperly for a Churchman to his neighbour . . .

He went on to say that he had been 'no spoyler' of the Church, had never received 'rewards' from the Rector, who could not be more forgetful than Whitelocke was of courtesies done to him (i.e. Wilkinson, before the Restoration when the Churchman's position was perilous); '. . . I shall not be much terryfied by threats nor . . . backward to answer respects with . . . civility . . .' no date (Sept. or Oct. 1660), Long. W.P. xix, 132 (rough draft or copy). Confusingly, a receipt for £10 in full payment of the rent of a pew in the Chancel is signed 'Sam Wilkinson', dated 5 Feb. 1659/60, ib. 151.

WILLIAM I, King of England (1027–1087). C. Hill *Puritanism and Revolution*, chapter 3 'The Norman Yoke'. Duke of Normandy; the conqueror of 1066, who defeated Harold, at Hastings. 'The Norman Bastard' was a favourite scapegoat among republicans and underprivileged groups nearly 600 years later: he was the invader who had imposed tyrannical kingship and laws in foreign tongues (Latin and French), on the freedom-loving Anglo-Saxons, and the conquered people were still suffering. Whitelocke refers three times to King William: (1) in the

Commons, in November 1641, when he replied to assertions that Irish bitterness and rebellion against the English was comparable to that of the English against the Normans; he maintained that 'the English were never Conquered by Duke William ... butt received him by Compact as their King, that indeed he overthrew Harold the Usurper'; that he came to an agreement with the people of England and only the flattering monks styled him 'Conquerour' and, finally, that he claimed the crown by right under the Will of Edward the Confessor, 'from whom he received the lawes of England into Normandy ...', *Diary* 1641. 1642. fol. 53v. with note; (2) years later, in a long debate on translating the law-books into English, Whitelocke rejected the view that laws had been introduced by William; nevertheless, he voted in favour of their being translated into English, ib. 22 Nov. 1650 with note; (3) his final comment on the Norman King occurs in a letter to his brother-in-law, Col. William Willoughby (q.v.); in it, he compared the kindness and pardon he had received from Charles II with the conduct of William I, who conquered the bodies of some of the English, but pardoned all who submitted, and employed them (Whitelocke claimed) on an equality with the Normans, ib. 12 Nov. 1660.

WILLIAMS, Sir Abraham, Kt. G.E.Aylmer *King's Servants*; *Shaw's Knights*. After James I issued instructions that idle vagabonds were to be suppressed in the City of London and that licences must be issued to approved pedlars and petty chapmen (i.e. traders and hawkers), Williams (with other officials) wrote to the Lord Mayor reporting complaints received from shopkeepers, whose trade was endangered by these licences, July 1617, *Remembrancia* (London. 1878), iv, 361, No. 83. Williams was paymaster and agent to the Queen of Bohemia, was knighted in April 1625 by Charles I, and served as Signet Clerk. Many years later, Whitelocke escorted Christer Bonde (q.v.), the Swedish Ambassador Extraordinary, to a house in Westminster owned by Sir Abraham, *Diary* 29 July 1655. The Government hired the premises for the use of foreign diplomats, at a rent of £300, *King's Servants* (above) p. 204.

WILLIAMS, Adwyn, of Hungerford, Berks. He lent money to Whitelocke, who was living nearby at Chilton Lodge; Williams, however, was later described as unkind and greedy, *Diary* 30 Aug., 20 Sept. 1667; 25 Mar. 1673.

WILLIAMS, alias CROMWELL, Henry (d. 1673). *Bibliotheca Topographica Britannica* vii. Of Bodsey, Huntingdonshire, a large farm in the parish of Ramsey, worth £2,000 a year. A kinsman of Oliver Cromwell whose forebears, the Williamses, had assumed the name of Cromwell; some of the Protector's other relatives used this alias, T. Carlyle *Letters and Speeches of Oliver Cromwell*, i, 27–28. Whitelocke recorded that, during the Interregnum, Henry Williams had been very active against the King and his party, but that at the Restoration he was 'so much converted' that, with the King's permission, he altered his embarrassing name and signed himself only 'H. William', *Diary* 18 July 1660. *Bibliotheca* ... (above) quotes a letter of 1769, which stated that Henry Williams had dropped dead while carousing after the elections at Huntingdon – at which his party's candidate had been defeated.

WILLIAMS, Archbishop John, DD (1582–1650). B. Dew Roberts *Mitre & Musket* (O.U.P. 1938); *D.N.B.*; *Alumni Cantabrigienses*; A.G. Matthews *Walker Revised* (Oxford. 1948); *Liber, passim*. Second son of Edmund Williams and Mary, née Wynn. Sizar at St. John's College, Cambridge, in 1598. Ordained (according to *D.N.B.*) not later than 1605. Proctor of his University from 1611 to 1612. He held a string of ecclesiastical appointments under James I and Charles I, including those of Dean of Westminster, 1620–1642, Bishop of the (then) vast diocese of Lincoln, 1621–1642, and Archbishop of York, 1641–1649. He served as domestic Chaplain and, in effect, as trusted Secretary to Lord Chancellor Ellesmere from 1612. Ellesmere resigned in October 1616 and died five months later; he had encouraged Williams to study the law, and after the disgrace of Lord Chancellor Francis Bacon in 1621 (for accepting bribes) Williams was appointed, for a probationary three years, to the secular office of Lord Keeper of the Great Seal. His first speech in Chancery, when he was Bishop-elect of Lincoln, was made on 9 October 1621. He began modestly, expressing wishes that the former course of his life had qualified him for the great place in which he found himself 'by the will of God, and the spetiall favour of the Kinge ...' (James I); he then embarked on a long and learned disquisition, Bodleian Ms Rawl. D. 924 fols. 23–27. He lost this high office in 1625, soon after Charles I came to the throne, having offended both the new King and the 1st Duke of Buckingham (q.v.), and he then withdrew to his neglected Bishopric in Lincoln. Although still Dean of Westminster, he took no part in the Coronation.

Other papers in the Bodleian, relating to Williams, include his report on the local examination of Mr. Howe (shown as Mr. Tyler in *Mitre & Musket*, above), the young Vicar of Grantham, in the diocese of Lincoln.

Howe had outraged his parishioners, by moving the Communion Table from the body of the Church where it 'had stood time out of minde', up into the Chancel. One practical reason for this change was that 'Schoole-boyes threw their ... Hatts, and Bookes [on it] at Service, and Sermon Time'. The Vicar also wished to have the altar where the congregation could see it better. Bishop Williams's report explained, rather oddly, that Howe 'was indeed not at all Puritanically affected ... (as ... Strangers to those parts might easily suppose).' But his examiners were not satisfied; they spoke not of puritanism but of popery and idolatry (through his ranking the altar above the pulpit), and 'Hubbub followed', Ms Rawl. D. 353 fols. 139–142v. (See Bishop Williams *The Holy Table, Name & Thing*, written anonymously on this subject, in reply to Peter Heylyn's pamphlet *A Coal from the Altar*, which is mentioned in the Grantham report.) A further significant reference to Williams occurred years later, when the Bishoprics came under threat from Parliament. Ralph Brownrigg, Bishop of Exeter, wrote discerningly of John Williams: '... my Lord of York [as he was by then] doth putt off his clothes a little too soone ... if it be true w[hi]^{ch} they write of him.' He wished the Archbishop would remember St. Ambrose's reply to the angry Emperor: 'Were it mine owne house or goods w[hi]^{ch} you demand I would ... yeild it to you, but I may not surrender the house of God'. He feared that the Archbishop's possessions had 'beene a snare to him, & the keeping of them hath made him content to part with his calling', Ms Rawl. D. 1,104 fols. 4–4v., 28 May 1647 (copy).

Williams was a complex character: worldly-wise, ambitious and astute, sometimes devious, but both in political and church affairs a moderate man and a conciliator. In the earlier fury over the position of the altar, he advised young Mr. Howe that when he was more experienced, he would 'find no ... ceremony equal to Christian charity'. Unlike many of his contemporaries, he accepted differing points of view, and could support both the King and the Puritans. Yet even before the Civil War, he made a bitter enemy of Archbishop Laud (q.v.), and some of Laud's supporters.

Charges had been brought against Williams in the Star Chamber that, as a Privy Counsellor, he had betrayed secrets and suborned witnesses, and in 1637 he was heavily fined and imprisoned in the Tower, during the King's pleasure. Numerous documents in connection with the trial survive among Whitelocke's papers: some are concerned directly with the case, others with Williams's attempt to discredit witnesses; there is a copy of his pitiful petition to the King; an Order from Lord Keeper Coventry, etc., dated 3, 5 (twice) and 27 Apr. 1637, Long. W.P. vii, 103–104v., 105–106v., 107, 108–108v.; some of the following are dated May (1637), some are undated, ib. 118 and 119–200, 201v.–202, 203v.–204, 205v.– 206, 207v.–208. Soon after the Long Parliament assembled the Bishop was released, by order of the House of Lords. This enabled him to sit in the Upper House again, but he was one of the 12 Bishops impeached for high treason in December 1641, and was again sent to the Tower. He was released on bail in May 1642; breaking the conditions of his bail, he escaped to York where, in June, he was enthroned as Archbishop. In the Civil War, he garrisoned Conwy Castle for the King, and suffered sequestration as a Royalist.

Williams's friendship with the Whitelocke family had developed early in his career, when he was Lord Keeper. He wrote on behalf of various people, most of whom had Welsh connections, and sometimes he issued instructions: he recommended to the 2nd Earl of Northampton (Lord President of the Council of the Marches) and to Judge Sir James Whitelocke, with the rest of the Council, a Mr. Jenkin Gwyn, Utter Barrister of the Inner Temple, who hoped to practise before the Council and at various Assizes, 10 July 1622, ib. ii, 65; he wrote to Sir James Whitelocke and Sir Marmaduke Lloyd, Justices of Assize for Denbigh and Montgomery, on behalf of two fatherless children in his care, who he claimed were entitled to a grant, 9 Apr. 1623, ib. 85; he wrote from Westminster College, as Keeper of the Great Seal, directing the Earl of Northampton and others to dismiss a case in which the offence (if there was one) had been committed in Chancery (his godfather, Sir John Wynn, was one of the defendants), 5 June 1623, ib. 97; he asked James Whitelocke to help the guardians of two other children, by ensuring that funds were paid for their maintenance and education (one of the guardians was Robert, son of Sir John Wynn), Westminster College, 26 June 1624, ib. 137.

Williams also wrote to Sir James Whitelocke, by then Chief Justice of Chester, about £30 due to Richard Price (Muster Master for Montgomeryshire) from John Blaney (County Treasurer), 9 July 1624, ib. 150. It was evidently in his capacity as Lord Keeper that he wrote about the animosity which had developed between the Earl of Northampton and Judge Whitelocke; the solution was reached by King James appointing Sir James Whitelocke as a King's Bench Judge, 3 Oct. 1624, ib. 172; an account of the trouble and a transcript of John Williams's friendly letter announcing Justice Whitelocke's promotion are given in *Liber* pp. 95–96. Williams also wrote supporting his 'freynd & chaplayne', whose case was coming before the Derbyshire Assizes, and asking James Whitelocke and the other Circuit Judges 'to protect him from beinge wrought upon or oppressed, as you shall finde, the Justice of his cause shall deserve. Beyond those Limitts it becommeth me not to enlarge my Request ...', 7 July 1626, 'Bokden' (i.e. Buckden, near Huntingdon, the Bishop's House), Long. W.P. iii, 50. (Williams was by then writing as Bishop of Lincoln but no longer as Lord Keeper.)

Bishop Williams came to consecrate Judge James Whitelocke's private Chapel, at Fawley Court, on 27 Dec. 1631 (Fawley, Bucks., being at that time in the diocese of Lincoln), *Liber* 110–111; he and his considerable 'train' stayed for two nights. Whitelocke stated that at that point, shortly before his father's death, he himself 'grew into great favour with the B[isho]p', *Diary* 1631.1632. fol. 14v.; a much fuller account of the Bishop's visit is given in Whitelocke's 'Annales' where he recorded that the Bishop came from London '... purposely to consecrate the Chappell, he would not doe it by Commission [i.e. by sending a deputy] to so good a friend ... No ceremony was omitted, they said a prayer, in every part & pew of the chappell'. Dr. Warre, the Bishop's Chaplain, preached; the music consisted of 'a very good Organ', with music from lutes, viols and a harp, played behind a curtain in a gallery or 'upper room' at the back of the Chapel. The Bishop and his company were 'liberally feasted'. Some of the guests in the small congregation objected to the altar and pulpit being level with each other, instead of in the new style, with the altar on the east wall and the pulpit taking second place; they also objected to there being no pictures or crucifixes on the walls or in the windows. Puritanical friends, on the other hand, doubted the legality of having music in the Chapel. The Bishop, for his part, approved of all the arrangements and observed that Sir James 'had the best musicke in his Chappell, of any subject in Christendome ...' On more worldly matters, he told Sir James (who lent him a coach and driver) that the Fawley Court coachman 'drove as furiously as if he had bin a younger son of Nimshi' (i.e. a brother of the reckless Jehu, son of Nimshi, 'for he driveth furiously', *Bible*, 2 Kings 9, verse 20). Undeterred by this, when the Bishop left Fawley he sent his own coach ahead and travelled in his host's for part of the journey to London, Add. Ms. 53726, fols. 64–66.

The friendship established between Williams and young Whitelocke at that time bore fruit after the Judge's death. Following Whitelocke's runaway marriage to Frances Willoughby, in November 1634, her aristocratic relatives, stunned by her marrying a commoner, were not prepared to receive him, until the Bishop wrote a diplomatic and flattering letter to the bride's mother, the dowager Lady Willoughby (q.v.), and succeeded in reconciling the Willoughby family and George Earl of Rutland (q.v.) to the young lawyer, Long. W.P. vi, 157; part of the letter is transcribed in R. Spalding *Improbable Puritan* p. 65.

A few years later, Williams was in trouble with Laud (who had been consecrated Archbishop of Canterbury in 1633), over his controversial book *The Holy Table, Name & Thing*, referred to above. Whitelocke commented that the book, which favoured placing the Communion Table level with the pulpit, was better liked than was Laud's order to have the table placed 'Altar wise' against the east wall, *Diary* 1636. 1637. fol. 42.

When, as Archbishop of York, Williams was out of favour for his royalist activities in Wales, he wrote from 'Gwyder' (home of the Wynn family), in the Vale of Conwy, North Wales, asking a favour for William Mostyn (q.v.), a scholarly preacher (and relative of Whitelocke's sister, Elizabeth Mostyn, q.v.), who had been ejected, ib. 15 Sept. 1649 with note; Add. Ms 37345 fol. 14; original in Long. W.P. x, 30. He wrote again on behalf of a friend, whom Whitelocke was able to help, *Diary* 4 Jan. 1649/50. A few months later, Whitelocke learned of the Archbishop's death and described him as 'a kind & great friend', ib. 22 Apr. 1650. Williams's relationship with the Wynn family made him a kinsman, through marriage, of the Mostyn family, into which Whitelocke's elder sister had married. The Archbishop was looked after, during his last illness, by Lady Mary Mostyn, daughter of old Sir John Wynn, at Gloddaeth, between Llandudno and Colwyn.

WILLIS, Thomas, MD, FRS (1621–1675). *D.N.B.*; W. Munk *Roll of the Royal College of Physicians; Alumni Oxonienses*. A royalist physician. Born in Great Bedwyn, Wilts., south-west of Hungerford, Berks. His father, also Thomas, had been a farmer in Long Hanborough, north-west of Oxford, and was later appointed Steward to Sir Walter Smith in Wiltshire. Thomas Willis, jun., studied at Christ Church, Oxford. During the Civil War he served in the university legion, while studying medicine, and later practised as a physician. After the Restoration he was appointed Sedleian Professor of Natural Philosophy, in June 1660, and four months later was created MD (Doctor of Medicine). After extensive research, he wrote on the anatomy of the brain and on the nervous system. He was elected a Fellow of the Royal Society soon after it was founded, and a Fellow of the College of Physicians. As a distinguished physician, Willis was consulted, with other doctors, by James, Duke of York (q.v.), but he was too candid in commenting on the likely effects of the future King's promiscuity, and was consequently dropped.

Whitelocke summoned Willis on several occasions when Mary was ill; once he sent a messenger to Oxford to bring him to Chilton Lodge, but learned that he was not there, *Diary* 4 Dec. 1665. When Willis attended Mary in London he prescribed medicines for her and, with Dr. Whistler (q.v.), allayed Whitelocke's fears that Mary was suffering from cancer of the womb, as diagnosed by another doctor, ib. 20, 21, 28, 30 Nov. 1668. When Willis failed to visit his patient as often as the family expected, he excused himself by saying that he did not wish to put Whitelocke to unnecessary expense, but he made up for his absence by prescribing 'some Chimicall medicines', which proved effective; the Doctor then said that there was a good prospect of Mary recovering, ib. 15, 27 Dec. 1668; 2 Jan. 1668/69. Willis also treated Whitelocke for stone. He finally advised Mary to go into the country for a change of air, ib. 7 Jan., 18 Feb. 1668/69.

WILLOUGHBY OF PARHAM, family (below). G.E.C.; Lincolnshire Archives, *passim*; *Lincolnshire Pedigrees* (Harleian Society. 1904), lii, 1088–1089. Whitelocke's second wife, Frances (q.v.), was a daughter of William, 3rd Baron Willoughby of Parham, who had died in 1617; her mother, the Dowager Lady Willoughby, was Frances née Manners (q.v.); this Lady Willoughby and her sister Elizabeth, Dowager Countess of Sunderland (q.v.), initially approved of Whitelocke courting young Frances. Their brother, however, George Manners, 7th Earl of Rutland (a trustee for the 3rd Baron's Will), descended on Fawley from Belvoir Castle when Whitelocke was away in London, made enquiries about the young lawyer's financial position and announced that the match must be broken off. The runaway marriage which followed, on 9 November 1634, brought Whitelocke into the reluctant bosom of two aristocratic families. Partly through the good offices of Bishop John Williams (q.v.) and Edward Hyde (later Earl of Clarendon, q.v.), both families decided to make the best of an alliance that they could not alter; they received the intrusive lawyer (although a commoner) into their homes, and made full use of his professional skills, and later of his political position, *Diary* 1634. 1635. fols. 30–34, 36–40v., *passim*. George, Earl of Rutland, discovered quite soon that his niece's husband, being an astute and tenacious barrister, required him to pay the full dowry for his niece Frances, as laid down in her father's Will (which had been proved 16 years earlier, in November 1618). Yet, in spite of continuous pressure, the final instalment of the dowry was not paid until after Frances' death in 1649, and then by the Earl's successor, John, 8th Earl of Rutland (q.v.). A dubious executorship document (concerning the estate of the 3rd Lord Willoughby) had been signed by George Manners and the two other Trustees, in 1620; in it, the three agreed to submit accounts to one another twice yearly, and 'to save each other harmless' from the late Baron's children, Lincs. Archives YARB 3/6/1. They had reckoned without Whitelocke, who also fought them on behalf of his wife's sister, the Hon. Elizabeth Willoughby (q.v.).

WILLOUGHBY, Anne, later Lady (*c.* 1615–1672). Third daughter of Sir Philip Carey and niece of Henry, 1st Viscount Falkland. She married the Hon. Colonel William Willoughby, later 6th Lord Willoughby of Parham (q.v.). They had 14 children between 1638 and 1656, born variously: at

PLATE 13

Count Klas Tott.

PLATE 14

Sir Thomas Widdrington, Speaker of the House of Commons.

PLATE 15

John Wildman.

PLATE 16

Francis, 5th Baron Willoughby of Parham.

Belvoir Castle, west of Grantham (the Earl of Rutland's home); in London, at the Savoy and at a house in Aldersgate Street; at Stanstead Bury, north-east of Stanstead Abbots, Hertfordshire (where Colonel Willoughby was, for some years, a tenant of Edward Baesh), and finally at nearby Hunsdon House, between Harlow in Essex and Ware in Hertfordshire, which William Willoughby bought in 1653, H.C. Gibbs *Parish Registers of Hunsdon 1546–1837* (St. Catherine Press. Revised edition. 1918). Anne and her husband proved themselves good friends to their brother-in-law, Whitelocke: when he was in hiding before the Restoration and arrived, uninvited, to take refuge with them, he was generously welcomed at Hunsdon House, *Diary* 30 [31] Dec. 1659; 10 Jan. 1659/60. For later encounters, after William succeeded to the title, see William, 6th Lord Willoughby of Parham.

WILLOUGHBY, the Hon. Elizabeth (d. *c.* 1641). Sister of Whitelocke's wife Frances (q.v.), and of Francis, 5th Baron Willoughby of Parham (q.v.) and of the Hon. Col. William Willoughby (q.v.), later 6th Baron. She lived with her mother Frances, the Dowager Lady Willoughby (q.v.), in Lincoln, *Diary* 1634. 1635. fols. 36v.–37. Whitelocke described her as 'a gallant & beautifull young Lady' who wrote him 'very kind letters & desired him to take care of the buisnes of her portion as he did of her Sisters', ib. fol. 35v. This he did at Belvoir Castle, pressing the young women's uncle, the 7th Earl of Rutland (q.v.), as a Trustee of their father's estate, to pay Frances' dowry of £2,500, due under the terms of the Baron's Will, and Elizabeth's portion of £3,000, ib. 1635. 1636. fol. 40. In fact, their father's Will left £2,000 to Frances, Lincs. Archives Office (Wills) 1617/ii/ 261.

Elizabeth's handwriting and spelling are so immature that one could be forgiven for wondering whether, although 'gallant & beautifull', she was a little retarded. She wrote Whitelocke an extraordinary letter which starts, disconcertingly:

> Deare Husband ... [and goes on to report that she has recovered so well] that I could whis [i.e. wish] my Annt of Sunderland weare redy to take her jorny for hampleton [i.e. Hambleden] ... [She refers to her] tow Nefews [Frances and Whitelocke's son William, born in 1636, and his half-brother, James, and to her god-daughter, and thinks the boys will be grown men and] 'franck [i.e. Frances, born in 1635] a woman before I shall see them ... [The letter ends] w[i]th the true affection of a wife to a husband ...
> Your truly loving wife
> Eliza Willlughbye
> 19 Apr. [1638?]
>
> Long. W.P. vi, 200.

Even allowing for the fact that Whitelocke 'husbanded' her inheritance, the letter is distinctly odd.

It is not clear whether Elizabeth received her inheritance, before her early death; there is a receipt, bearing her signature, for £30 received from Whitelocke, for money due from George Earl of Rutland, by way of interest, 24 Dec. 1638, ib. vii, 297.

Whitelocke's only other references to Elizabeth occur in *Diary* 1634.1635. fols. 37, 41. Her Will was proved in July 1641, see G.E.C. entry for Willoughby, p.705 note b.

WILLOUGHBY of PARHAM, Lady Elizabeth (d. *c.* 1661). The third daughter of Sir Edward Cecil, who was created Viscount Wimbledon in 1626. She married Whitelocke's brother-in-law Francis, 5th Baron Willoughby of Parham (q.v.), in about 1629. Their eldest daughter, Diana, married Heneage Finch, 3rd Viscount Winchelsea (q.v.), and their second daughter, Elizabeth, married the Hon. Richard Jones and later became Countess of Ranelagh (q.v.). Lady Willoughby (at the Willoughbys' house in Covent Garden) acted as sole midwife to her sister-in-law, Whitelocke's wife Frances, at the birth of Anne Whitelocke (who married George Hill, q.v.), *Diary* 1639.1640. fol. 48v., Apr. 1640. She and the Whitelockes were on good terms. She and other ladies visited Whitelocke when he was ill, ib. 25 Sept. 1645; when her husband was in disgrace with Parliament, Whitelocke, Sir Henry Vane the younger (q.v.) and Henry Elsing (q.v.), advised Lady Willoughby to persuade him to keep away from London, which she did, but she was 'much afflicted att this Condition of her L[or]d ...' ib. 9 Sept. 1647.

Lady Willoughby attended the christening of Bulstrode, jun., ib. 30 Nov. 1647, and there are references to Whitelocke paying her several visits, alone or with his wife, ib. 10 May, 6 Aug., 22 Sept. 1648, and to her visiting and receiving help from him, ib. 28 Sept., 19 Dec. 1648. In view of her husband's change of loyalty from Parliament to the King, there was danger to the Whitelockes in receiving her as a guest, especially after Pride's Purge of 6 Dec. 1648.

When Whitelocke's beloved wife Frances was dying, he sent for Lady Willoughby, who frequently watched at her bedside, on one occasion sitting up with her all night. (Her husband, Lord Willoughby, was by that time overseas, with the exiled Charles II.) Frances Whitelocke begged her brother, Colonel William Willoughby, and her sister-in-law, Lady Willoughby, to be good to Whitelocke, and when Frances died Lady Willoughby (wrongly identified as William's wife Anne, in *Improbable Puritan* p. 119) took Whitelocke back to her house in Charterhouse Yard.

Probably anxious for his safety, in view of his distraught state, she gave him a ground floor bedroom, leading on to the garden. Lady Willoughby made all the complicated arrangements for the funeral procession and burial in Fawley, 'providing coaches, blackes [i.e. mourning] & necessaries for my wifes buryall', Add. Ms. 37344 fols. 288, 291v., 292v., 293v., 295, 295v., 298v.–299v. and, less fully, *Diary* 4, 15, 16, 17 May 1649.

Lady Willoughby was displeased when Whitelocke married again, in the following year, and brought Mary (whom she already knew quite well) to visit her, ib. 15 Sept. 1650, but later the Whitelockes were received with cordiality. Whitelocke helped Francis and Elizabeth Willoughby when they were under a cloud, before the Restoration; after it, when Whitelocke was in danger, Lord Willoughby in turn supported him, ib. 10 Jan. 1656/57; 4 June, 16 Aug. 1657, *passim*; 9 June 1660, *passim*.

WILLOUGHBY of PARHAM, Frances, Dowager Lady (1588–1642). Widow of William, the 3rd Baron. Whitelocke's mother-in-law. After she had been persuaded by Bishop Williams of Lincoln (q.v.) to forgive the couple for their runaway marriage, *Diary* 1634.1635. fol. 34v., Whitelocke and Frances visited her in Lincoln, where she 'lived in a house of her own', with her other daughter Elizabeth (q.v.), ib. fol. 36v. He had already summed her up as 'a Lady of great parts & honour, to whome multitudes of servants & pretended friends thronged for her favour & loafes, butt her estate wasting by improvident liberality when that decayed, her friends & alliances decayed with it . . .', ib. fols. 35v.–36. Later, Whitelocke brought about a reconciliation between the Dowager and her elder son, the 5th Lord Willoughby, which was appreciated by the family, ib.1635.1636. fol. 41. It is clear from various documents among Whitelocke's papers, that he advised her when she was in financial and legal difficulties, with actions against her for recovery of debts, e.g. for four debts of £40 each and for arrears of an annuity of £13.6s.8d. granted by her late husband, to be paid out of the Manor of Gateburton, Lincolnshire, June 1636, Long. W.P. vii, 57v.–72; 30 Oct. 1637, ib. 131v.–190; there is also a receipt for £9 received from Whitelocke for the Dowager's use, to sue out a pardon of alienation and an Order in the Exchequer, 14 Feb. 1637/38, ib. 258. After her death in June 1642, Whitelocke described the Dowager, generously but realistically, as 'a woman of a great & Noble Spirit, & of good parts, she had not bin Carefull of her Estate, yett was discreet & rationall in other matters', *Diary* 1641.1642. fol. 55v.

WILLOUGHBY, the Hon. Frances, see WHITELOCKE, the Hon. Frances, sen.

WILLOUGHBY of PARHAM, Francis, 5th Lord (c.1613–1666). G.E.C.; D.N.B. On the day that his sister Frances ran away from New House, Hambleden, where she had been living with their aunt, the Dowager Lady Sunderland (q.v.), the indignant 21-year-old Baron pursued her and Whitelocke to London. He tracked the couple down to their lodgings at the Ship tavern, in Fleet Street, where he enquired of his sister 'whither the buisnes were past recovery or not' and when she informed him that it was, and that they were married, 'he seemed much offended' and totally ignored Whitelocke when the latter tried to speak to him, *Diary* 1634.1635. fol. 34; Add. Ms 37343 fol. 9. Within a few days, however, Edward Hyde (later 1st Earl of Clarendon, q.v.) effected a reconciliation, and soon afterwards Lord Willoughby and his wife Elizabeth (q.v.) entertained the couple at Knaith, north-west of Lincoln, *Diary* 1634.1635. fol. 37.

Whitelocke's pressure on the Earl of Rutland and his fellow trustees, to pay the legacy due to the Hon. Elizabeth Willoughby (q.v.) and to her sister Frances Whitelocke (q.v.), from their father's estate, no doubt inspired their brother to take the trustees to court, demanding an account of their father's estate. The brief for this case, dated 1637, was probably prepared by Whitelocke; this, with the evidence, is in Long. W.P. vii, 219v.–248.

Willoughby had objected, in 1636, to what he saw as partiality in the assessment of the Ship Money levy for Lincolnshire. It has been suggested that this shaped his attitude, both before and in the early stages of the Civil War: on 5 Mar. 1641/42, Parliament (having failed to obtain the Royal Assent for the Bill) passed their Militia Ordinance; for its text see *Constitutional Documents of the Puritan Revolution 1625–1660* (ed. S.R. Gardiner. O.U.P. 1962) No. 50, p. 245. This was in open defiance of the King who, following precedent, claimed control of the country's forces although the Commons had to foot the bill. A few months later, Charles I denounced the Ordinance in his own Proclamation, 27 May 1642, ib. No. 52, pp.248–249; on 4 June Lord Willoughy, who had been appointed by Parliament as Lord-Lieutenant of Lincolnshire, on 26 March 1642, proceeded to execute the Militia Ordinance, by summoning the County's Trained Bands. On the day they were to assemble, however, he received a letter from the King warning him not to obey instructions which came:

... under pretence of an Ordinance of Parliament, whereunto We have not given Our Consent ... [to forestall Willoughby from later pleading ignorance, the King expressly commanded him to desisted from raising, mustering, training, exercising, or assembling the Trained Bands of the County, promising] we shall pass by what you have already done ... [provided that, on receipt of this letter] you ... give over medling any further with any thing belonging to the Militia of our County ... [otherwise] We are resolved to call you to a strict Account for your Disobedience ..., [and proceedings would be taken against him] as a Disturber of the Peace of Our Kingdom ...
The Court at York, 4 June 1642.
J. Rushworth *Historical Collections* 2nd edition (London. 1721) iv, 676–677.

Some phrases in the letter echo those in the King's Proclamation, referred to above.

Willoughby replied deferentially, while holding his ground: '... there can be nothing of greater Heaviness to me than to receive a command from your Majesty whereunto my Endeavours cannot give so ready an Obedience as my Affections ...', but he pointed out that he was in a difficult position: the Ordinance of Parliament, which he was carrying out, had been voted for by Lord Littleton (q.v.), and other Lords 'better vers'd in the Laws than my self'; they considered it to be legal; moreover (if he were not mistaken) their view was shared by His Majesty's Chief Justice, Sir John Bankes (q.v.).

... If the Opinion of those great Lawyers drew me into an Understanding unsuitable to your Majesty's liking, I hope the want of Years will excuse my want of Judgment ... I am now so far engaged in their [i.e. Parliament's] Service as the sending out warrants to summons the Country [i.e. County] to meet me this day at Lincoln and afterwards at other places ...

He begged the King not to cause him to be false to those who relyed on him, and ended with profuse assurances of loyalty, Rushworth (above), 677.

Like many others caught up by conflicting demands for loyalty, at the start of a revolution that was none of their making, Lord Willoughby tried to placate both sides; he promptly wrote to a member of the House of Lords giving the exuberant and rash assurance:

... my Heart ever was, and shall ever be ... ready to obey their Lordships' Commands in all things both with Integrity and Industry. And God's curse light upon him and his that carries any other Heart about him.

He referred to the letter received that day from the King, saying he felt it his duty to acquaint the House with it. In a postscript, he praised Lincoln's Trained Bands as being far beyond his expectations, in view of the sickness in Lincoln at that time; moreover, the numbers had been kept up by a company of volunteers '. . . equal in number and goodness of Arms to the Trained Bands', 6 June 1642, ib. 676. The Lords and Commons concurred in a Resolution commending Lord Willoughby's efforts, ib. 677, 678.

Willoughby served as Colonel of a regiment of horse under the Earl of Essex (q.v.), from the autumn of 1642 until 9 Jan. 1642/43, when he was given the chief command of Lincolnshire. In that capacity, he captured Gainsborough from the Royalists and lost it to them again a fortnight later, on 16 and 30 July, respectively, 1643. He then failed to defend Lincoln, and moved with his dejected and depleted forces to Boston. From there, on 5 August, he wrote to his

> noble Friend, Colonel Cromwell . . . since the business of Gainsborough, the hearts of our men have been so deaded that we have lost most of them by running away. So . . . we were forced to leave Lincoln upon a sudden:– and if I had not done it then, I should have been left alone in it.

Reporting that he was now in Boston, 'very poor in strength' he appealed for speedy supplies, without which he could not hold the town for long. He also warned Cromwell that if Boston fell into enemy hands, it would not be long before the Royalists entered Norfolk and Suffolk as well; Cromwell wrote supporting him, T. Carlyle *Letters and Speeches of Oliver Cromwell* i, 146–147. But Willoughby had failed in his County and when, on 20 September, Lincolnshire was absorbed into the Eastern Association (Parliament's Army drawn from Norfolk, Suffolk, Cambridgeshire, Essex, and Hertfordshire), he became an unwilling subordinate under the command of the Earl of Manchester. This was formalized in an Order of the House of Commons, *C.J.* iii, 373, 22 Jan. 1643/44. On the same day Whitelocke, Sir Henry Vane the younger (q.v.), Sir Arthur Hesilrige (q.v.) and others were appointed to a Committee which was to enquire into the 'Miscarriages informed of in the County of Lincoln'.

According to Whitelocke, his brother-in-law did gallant service for Parliament in the North, and kept up a constant correspondence with him (but this has not been traced), *Diary* 1643.1644. fol. 63v.; he does not, however, refer to Willoughby's shortcomings at that time. Willoughby appears to have been a charming, impetuous, self-opinionated and quarrelsome man, who could neither accept criticism nor endure being over-ruled. For a relative lightweight, in and out of politics, he drew quite a lot of attention to himself in Parliament: Cromwell (who had come to his assistance in Lincolnshire) complained, in the House of Commons, that Willoughby tolerated licentious and profane behaviour among his officers, and accused him of deserting both Gainsborough and Lincoln, and of leaving behind ammunition, to be seized by the enemy, J.W.F. Hill *Tudor and Stuart Lincoln.* (C.U.P. 1956) p. 156, *passim*; T. Carlyle *Letters and Speeches of Oliver Cromwell* i, 168, 19 Jan. 1644/45. Earlier, Colonel Bointon (who evidently shared Cromwell's view) had informed the House that William, Christopher and Theophilus Wray had invited him 'to drink a Pint of Wine' with them, but had proceeded to question him because he had spoken against Lord Willoughby; then two of them had held him, while the other one punched him twice on the head. For this, the three Wrays were designated delinquents, *C.J.* iii, 387, 3 Feb. 1643/44.

In the meantime, Willoughby had outraged both Houses by sending a challenge to his superior officer, the Earl of Manchester, ib. 384, 1 Feb. The Commons sent word of this to the Lords, saying that they considered this to be a breach of privilege; Willoughby was taken into custody by Black Rod. The Lords investigated the case, calling witnesses and hearing both parties; they found that the Earl of Manchester had only done his duty, and they expressed their disapproval of Lord Willoughby's action; they also commanded their two Members to do nothing further to 'prosecute this Difference'. This resolution was read to Willoughby, who undertook to 'submit to the Pleasure of this House', *L.J.* vi, 405, 414, 415; 1, 7 Feb. 1643/44.

In spite of his outrageous behaviour, three years later Willoughby was chosen to serve, briefly, as Speaker of the House of Lords, in place of the Earl of Manchester himself, *L.J.* ix, 358, 361, 363; 30, 31 July 1647. Earlier that year he had been appointed a member of the Committee for Compounding. (An inexplicable entry states that Whitelocke attended for Lord Willoughby's composition, *Diary* 3 Sept. 1645, but at that date Willoughby was still supporting Parliament; for his subsequent sequestration, see below. He had even been recommended by the Commons for promotion to an Earldom, ib. 1 Dec. 1645.)

As a moderate, who favoured compromising with the King, Willoughby was regarded by the Army and by radical MPs as a traitor; consequently he was impeached of high treason by the Commons, in September 1647. This alarming event was forecast to Whitelocke, in general terms, by the astrologer William Lilly (q.v.), ib. 6, 7 Sept. 1647. Whitelocke learned that Oliver St. John (q.v.) and his circle were incensed against Willoughby, whom they regarded as the ringleader of recent disturbances in the City. Yet at that point, Willoughby had the unlikely support of the radical, Sir Henry Vane the younger (q.v.) who, accompanied by Henry Elsing (q.v.), consulted Whitelocke about Willoughby's predicament. All three agreed that he would be wise to keep out of the way 'till the present heat & storm were a little over'. Whitelocke sent this advice to Lady Willoughby, probably at her house in Charterhouse Yard (see the end of the entry for Whitelocke's wife Frances), her husband being in Lincolnshire, probably at Knaith, ib. 9 Sept. 1647. Either the advice was ignored or Willoughby was compelled to return, for soon afterwards he was under house arrest in London, supervised by Black Rod. Whitelocke visted him frequently at Charterhouse Yard and pleaded his case in Parliament, ib. 3, 28 Oct., 2, 26 Dec. 1647; 27 Jan. 1647/48.

Willoughby and the six other Peers, arrested at the same time, were conditionally released on 19 January; this followed an appeal from six of the seven against their long restraint without trial. After debate, the Lords agreed that in future their members should not be held on a 'General Charge' for longer than 10 days, without trial. Willoughby and the others were ordered to attend and hear the Commons' charge of high treason against them, at the Bar of the House of Lords, on 4 February, and to produce bail of £4,000 plus £2,000 from sureties. They were then permitted nearly two weeks in which to prepare their defence, before a hearing on 16 February, *L.J.* x, 14, 15, 18. Whitelocke dined with Willoughby, *Diary* 6 Feb. 1647/48, no doubt to advise him before his appearance at the Bar of the House of Lords; but instead of appearing to hear the charge, Willoughby escaped to Holland, where he joined the Royalists. He left behind a letter to the Lords framed in terms that Whitelocke, as a lawyer, could hardly have condoned let alone inspired, *L.J.* x, 34, 8 Feb.

Willoughby remained abroad for some time. After the execution of Charles I, he supported Charles II in exile before the Restoration, and in England after it. In exile, knowing nothing of naval matters, he held the post of Vice-Admiral of the royalist fleet. He obtained a 21-year lease of the Caribbee Islands and, in 1650, was appointed Governor of Barbados. Sequestration proceedings against him, started in 1648, were long and complicated. With evident foresight (and possibly with Whitelocke's connivance), he had signed a deed on 20 August 1647, making over much of his property to trustees; those named in the deed included his brother William (q.v.) and Whitelocke; Lady Willoughby and her children, who were left behind in England, were acknowledged as having a possible claim on the estate, *Calendar of the Proceedings of the Committee for Compounding 1643–1660*, pt. 3. pp. 1838–1839; 20 Sept. 1650; *Diary* 28 Feb. 1655/56.

When Admiral Sir George Ayscue (q.v.) was sent by Parliament to capture Barbados, Whitelocke successfully appealed to him to negotiate reasonable terms with Willoughby so far as his duty allowed, *Diary* 12 May 1651; 15 Mar. 1651/52. In the event, Willoughby's surrender of the island in January 1651/52, was handsomely rewarded by the restoration of his English possessions without fine or composition, and free from any parliamentary encumbrances, *Calendar of the Proceedings of the Committee for Compounding* pp. 1840–1841, 1 Sept. 1652; 17 Mar. 1652/53; 24 June

1653. Papers concerning Lord Willoughby's activities as Governor of Barbados, both before its surrender and after his reappointment on 12 June 1663, may be found in Long. Portland Papers ix, *passim*; there is also a joint patent to him for sugar mills, of 1663, ib. xii, 47.

There are many and varied entries in *The Diary* concerning Lord Willoughby, including references to his foolhardy return to England in the 1650s (partly to support royalist risings), which led to his imprisonment in the Tower, *Diary* 24 June 1655, *passim*. Whitelocke acknowledged the services his brother-in-law performed on his behalf in the House of Lords, shortly after the Restoration, ib. 9 June 1660. He continued to advise Willoughby on business and legal matters, ib. 8 Mar. 1660/61; 12 Nov. 1662; 8, 30 May 1663, *passim*, and Willoughby went on writing after he returned to Barbados, ib. 8 Dec. 1663. The last entry refers to Willoughby being lost at sea in a hurricane, attempting to recapture St. Kitts (i.e. St. Christopher), one of the Leeward Islands, from the French, on 16 August 1666. The disaster is mentioned in *Pepys* vii, 390 with note 3, 29 Nov. 1666; *Diary* 24 Jan. 1666/67.

WILLOUGHBY of PARHAM, the Hon. George, later 7th Lord (1639–1674). G.E.C. Eldest son of Col. William Willoughby, 6th Lord (below), and nephew of Francis, 5th Lord Willoughby (above). Born at Belvoir Castle. Died at Knaith, in Lincolnshire, at the age of 35, having inherited the title only one year before. He is referred to five times by Whitelocke; the first entry was after Whitelocke (disguised in a heavy cloak and a large grey wig) arrived, without warning, at Hunsdon House and was protected by George's parents, he and his servant being given a secluded suite of rooms upstairs. Twenty-year-old George claimed that he knew the identity of this mysterious fugitive, but that he would take no notice, *Diary* 30 [31] Dec. 1659. The other four entries relate to a match proposed by Whitelocke's wife, Mary, between George and the daughter of Dr. Sir Edward Alston (q.v.), ib. 20 Sept., 9, 18, 28 Oct. 1661. Nothing came of this, however, and five years later George married Elizabeth, daughter of Henry Clinton (otherwise Fiennes) of Lincolnshire.

WILLOUGHBY of PARHAM, the Hon. Col. William, MP, later 6th Lord (c.1616–1673). G.E.C.; *Hist. of Parl.*; *D.N.B.* (end of the entry for his brother Francis, 5th Lord, q.v.). A good-humoured and cheerful man, some 11 years Whitelocke's junior. Usually referred to as 'brother Willoughby' until he succeeded to the title when (like his brother before him) he became 'Lord Willoughby' in *The Diary*. Early entries sometimes give him the title 'Col. Willoughby', but warrant for this rank has not been established. (Confusingly, a different Colonel William Willoughby appears in *C.J.* vi, 144, 16 Feb. 1648/49, *passim*, and in *C.S.P. Dom. 1648–1649* p.261, 31 Aug. 1648 and ib. 1651 p. 125, 2 Apr. 1651; this 2nd entry reports his death.)

At about the age of 18, Willoughby wrote from Italy congratulating his sister Frances (many months after her runaway marriage to Whitelocke), on her being both a bride and a mother-to-be:

I wish you fortune in both, and by report, cannot wish better to you, then the gentleman you have made choice of . . .
[by the time he arrived back in England, his sister would no doubt] so furnish me with Nephewes, & Nieces, that I shall be forc't for examples sake, to putt on an unknowne gravity. My curiosity & rambling humors are now both so well satisfyed [after the Grand Tour], that I am thinking of comming homewards . . . [hoping by Michaelmas] to present my service . . . to your selfe, & my un-knowne brother [-in-law] . . . should I begin to make an excuse for my neglect in not writing oftener, I should transforme this Epistle into a Volume, I am now att Rome, where pardons are plentifull & I hope, as free in your breast . . . 10 March 1636.

Add. Ms 37343 fol. 140 (transcript).

Years later he wrote to Whitelocke, starting the letter:

Deare Brother
That being a title, I shall ever take the privilege, & thinke it a happyness to begin with . . .
6 Oct. 1649.

Add. Ms 57345 fol. 20 (transcript).

A friendly, jocular letter to Whitelocke appears in *Journal* ii, 458, July 1654.

The deed under which William Willoughby, his cousin William Godfrey and Whitelocke were appointed trustees to Lord Francis Willoughby's estate (before the latter left Parliament to join the Royalists in exile), is referred to in the entry for Lord Francis Willoughby; see also *Diary* 18 Feb. 1647/48; 28 Feb. 1655/56; 10 Jan. 1656/57. A draft, in Whitelocke's hand, starts 'Gentlemen', with no other identification; it concerns a debt of £1,000 owed to William by his brother Francis, and refers to the possible sale of Parham (in Suffolk): 'which among other of my Lords fe[o]ffes I much desired might have bin sold[,] butt wee could not effect it . . . My Lord was pleased before his going beyond Sea to settle his estate on my selfe & some others of his neere friends for payment of his debts . . .' 11 Sept. 1648, Long. Parcel 4, No. 23. William Willoughby signed a bond, with Whitelocke, to 'William Poulteney' of the Inner Temple for £600, 11 Nov. 1656, Long. W.P. xvii, 212.

It was to William and his wife Anne (q.v.) that Whitelocke turned for refuge when he was on the run, and they were generous in giving him a hiding place, *Diary* 30 [31] Dec. 1659 to 11 Jan. 1659/60. After the Restoration, William defended Whitelocke in the Commons (as Francis did in the Lords), when the second exceptions to the Act of Pardon and Oblivion were being debated, ib. 9, 13 June 1660. William Willoughby and Whitelocke had numerous business and other dealings with each other during the next 13 years, ib. 30 May 1663 with note, *passim*.

William succeeded as 6th Baron Willoughby of Parham when his brother was lost at sea in 1666, and he assumed the Governorship of Barbados, ruling firmly but showing rather more consideration and humanity than Francis had done; he continued to carry out an aggressive policy against the French and the Dutch. When William returned to England for a year or more, ib. 7 Mar. 1668/69, Whitelocke dined with him, and had a long conversation 'about Liberty of Conscience to w[hi]ᶜh he seemed a good friend', ib. 28 Mar. 1670.

Recording William's death after his return to Barbados, Whitelocke referred to him as 'a loving true friend ... a gallant gentleman, butt not requited for his services', ib. 5 July 1673. William's body was brought home for burial at Knaith, in Lincolnshire. His wife Anne had been buried at Aldenham, Hertfordshire, in January 1671/72.

Papers concerning the 6th Lord Willoughby's activities in Surinam, Tangiers, Tobago and Barbados, between about 1668 and 1673, may be found in Long. Coventry Papers lxx, 17, 19; lxxvi, 169, 261–266, 279, 281, 282.

William was succeeded by his son George (q.v.).

WILMOT [WILLMOT]. There seem to be three Wilmots in *The Diary*. (1) Sir George Wilmot, Kt., of Charlton, Berks., knighted at Windsor in 1628, *Shaw's Knights* (Charlton, Berkshire, has not been traced; there are villages of that name in Wiltshire). Whitelocke met Sir George with his own 'cousen Willmot' when dining with Colonel Alexander Popham (q.v.) at Littlecote, near Chilton Foliat, *Diary* 22 Aug. 1666. (2) 'Cousen Willmot' (whose precise kinship with Whitelocke is not clear), evidently lived within riding distance of Chilton Foliat. On several occasions between 11 June 1666 and 4 June 1667, 'Cousen Willmot' and his wife visited and dined with the Whitelockes at Chilton Lodge; he sent a gift of venison, *Diary* 6 July 1666, and apparently consulted Whitelocke on legal matters, sending fees which ranged from £6 down to 10s., ib. 8 July 1668; 10 July 1675, *passim*. (3) There is also a well-to-do Richard Wilmot of Ipsden, in Oxfordshire. His first name is shown on a bond, from

Whitelocke, to him and Robert D'Oiley of Turville, Buckinghamshire, and on receipts for its repayment in 1636, Long. W.P. vii, 51, 53, 84. Many years later, Mr. Wilmot of Ipsden is described as 'a debauched man, & an e..nemy to Wh[itelocke] . . .', ib. 11 Nov. 1662. The Wilmots of Stadhampton and Chiselhampton appear to have been a prosperous family in the 17th century, *V.C.H. Oxon.* vii, 83; *Visitation of the County of Oxford* (Harleian Society. 1871) pp. 301, 302. A connection between them and Whitelocke's Wilmots is probable, but unproved for purposes of this entry.

WILSON, Rowland, sen. (d. 1654). *D.N.B.* (in the entry for his son and namesake, see below). Of Gresgarth, Kendal, in Westmorland (now Cumbria) and, from 1624, of Martyn (Martin or Merton) Abbey, Merton, see *V.C.H. Surrey*, iv, 66, 68. A wealthy merchant, described at his death on 16 May 1654 as a vintner, *Obituary of Richard Smyth* (ed. H. Ellis. Camden Society. 1849) p.37. His wealth was, however, probably derived more from the Guinea Company in Africa than from the wine trade. Whitelocke refers to both the Rowland Wilsons in an entry which states that his brother-in-law, Lord Francis Willoughby (q.v.), as Vice-Admiral to Prince Charles (in exile), had captured a ship from Guinea with a cargo of gold worth £20,000, '. . . most of it belonged to Mr Rowland Willson & his son, & their parteners'. He added, with hindsight, that later he himself had a claim to part of it, having married the younger Wilson's widow Mary in 1650, *Diary* 8 Aug. 1648 (the note for that entry shows that, in fact, he received over £3,500, partly from Rowland Wilson sen., and the rest from 'the Guyney Company at M[arty]^n Abbotts', i.e. Martyn Abbey, Long. W.P. xii, 181v., 182. For a letter concerning the Guinea Company's interests, signed by Rowland Wilson sen., with four others, and sent to Whitelocke in Sweden, see the entry for: WILSON, Samuel. Earlier, when Rowland Wilson jun. died (leaving Mary a childless widow) her father-in-law, Rowland Wilson sen., promptly told her she would receive nothing from her husband's estate, beyond what she could obtain by law, *Diary* 3 Apr. 1650, *passim*. In spite of this very unpleasant incident, after she had married Whitelocke, in 1650, they both dined with old Mr. Wilson at Martyn Abbey, where Whitelocke first met Dr. Thomas Winston (q.v.), ib. 9 July 1652.

Earlier, Martyn Abbey was believed, at one point, to be in danger of attack by Royalists, and a warning was sent to Mr. Wilson, desiring him to preserve it from being surprised by the enemy, *C.S.P. Dom.*, 4 July 1648. On the same day, the Commons sent an obscure Order to the Committee at Derby House about Martyn Abbey and 'other places of strength' in Surrey, *C.J.* v, 623.

After the death of Rowland Wilson sen., the estate descended, through the marriage of his daughter (another Mary, named after her mother), to Tobias Crispe, 3rd son of Ellis Crispe, *Collections Relating to the Family of Crispe* (privately printed. 1883) ii, pedigrees, 32–35. In 1662, the estate was conveyed to Elisha Crisp who sold it, six years later, to Thomas Pepys, *V.C.H. Surrey* ii, 367; ib. iv, 66, 68. (A genealogy which conflicts with this information appears in *Crispes Collection Relating to the Family.* New series. 1913.)

WILSON (WILLSON), Sheriff and Alderman, Col. Rowland jun., MP (1613–1650). *D.N.B.*; A.B.B. (the latter comments reassuringly that the *D.N.B.* contains 'a short but adequate article on Wilson, free from inaccuracies' and adds with feeling '*O si sic omnia!*' – Oh that they all were!). Son and partner of Rowland Wilson sen. (above), who outlived him. A member of the Vintners' Company, he fought for Parliament, served as a Lieutenant-Colonel of the London Trained Bands in 1643, and also served under the Earl of Essex (q.v.), after the Battle of Newbury. A recruiter MP for Calne, Wiltshire, in 1646. He refused to serve at the trial of Charles I, but took part in proclaiming the abolition of the monarchy. He was elected to the Council of State, early in 1649 and 1650.

Whitelocke referred to Wilson as heir (apparent) to an estate of £2,000 a year, yet Wilson's wife and other relatives could not dissuade him from marching with Essex to capture Newport Pagnell and Grafton House. For him it was a matter of conscience to exchange the best in food and drink for coarse bread, dirty water '& a very fowle pipe of Tobacco'. He and others of his conviction 'left their soft beddes & warme chambers to lodge ... uppon the cold & hard earth'; they exchanged the company and conversation of their wives, children and friends 'for the whistling of bulletts, & groanes of men dying att their feet ...', *Diary* 1643.1644. fol. 64. Later, when he died at his house in Bishopsgate Street, it was thought that the hardship he had suffered in the Civil War had shortened his life; he was described as a kind friend to Whitelocke, ib. 9 Feb. 1649/50. The funeral of Sheriff Wilson, a month after his death, was disturbed by a demonstration against Lord President John Bradshaw (q.v., one of the mourners), who was shouted at and abused as a king-killer, ib. 5 Mar. 1649/50.

George Cokayn (q.v.), Mary Wilson's Chaplain, had been a resident Minister in the house. He was active in promoting Whitelocke's courtship of Mary, in preference to that of other suitors who were quicker than Whitelocke in calling on the rich man's widow, ib. 3, 5 Apr. 1650, *passim*; Add. Ms. 37345 fol. 54.

WILSON (WILLSON), Samuel. A London merchant and vintner, of Hackney, Bishopsgate Street and Greenwich, with interests in the Canary and the Guinea Companies; he signed a document with Rowland Wilson, sen. (q.v.), and others concerning the Guinea Company (see below). No direct kinship has been discovered between him and the Rowland Wilsons, father and son; it seems more than a coincidence, however, that Samuel Wilson served, at one time, as their factor (or agent) in Spain, *C.J.* ii, 736, 25 August 1642 (petition to the Commons). Samuel is referred to as 'brother Willson' by Whitelocke, but Wilson signed his name with one 'l'; their kinship was not claimed through Mary Whitelocke's late husband, Rowland Wilson, jun., but through Mary's sister, Hannah, who was married to Samuel Wilson, *Diary*, 6 May 1650. Samuel was pleased at the prospect of his sister-in-law marrying Whitelocke, a man with influence. Not knowing that the couple had been married secretly in Bromham, Bedfordshire, he obligingly negotiated the marriage settlement (unwittingly approving the settlement already agreed upon in the country), before Whitelocke and Mary Wilson (née Carleton) were married again, this time in Hackney Church, in the presence of many friends, including the Speaker of the House of Commons, *Diary* 31 Aug., 5 Sept. 1650.

There are numerous entries for 'brother Willson', and several for his wife Hannah, with a few references to their daughters Lindley and Anne, ib. 2 June 1669; 1 Apr. 1670; 19 July 1671, *passim*. 'Brother Willson's' wife is not named in *The Diary*, but she appears as 'Mrs Hannah' on 28 Apr. 1654, in Add. Ms 37347 fol. 234. Writing with hindsight, Whitelocke was of the opinion that Samuel Wilson's cordiality and kindness towards him 'abated' when he, Whitelocke, no longer held a position of power and influence, *Diary* 26 Apr. 1651. Occasionally, when Whitelocke was still in office, Wilson supplied him with money or was bound with him to raise a loan; Whitelocke wrote to his extravagant son James (q.v.): '... I have bin much beholding to my brother Willson who furnished me with 1000^l ...' 3 Dec. 1655, Long. W.P. xvii, 105; *Diary* 20 Dec. 1655. Earlier, when Whitelocke was sent to Sweden, he accepted hospitality at the Wilsons' house in Bishopsgate Street for his wife Mary and five of the children, leaving others at their house in Chelsea and taking two sons with him; servants were instructed to look after the Fawley estate. He left to his wife 'the command of all ...' but under her, Samuel Wilson and John Carleton (q.v.), 'Marchants of good value & credit' were to deal with his correspondence and bills of exchange, Long. 124A fol. 361. Wilson, for his part, expected Whitelocke to support his commercial enterprises. The document referred to in para 1 above, signed by Rowland Wilson sen., Samuel Wilson, John Carleton and two others, was addressed to Whitelocke in Sweden. It shows a total callousness towards anyone, African or

Swedish, who stood in the way of their trade. The merchants referred respectfully to Queen Christina's promise to Whitelocke (about which he had written), that she would give them satisfaction for losses they had sustained in Guinea, under the pretence of a Swedish 'pattent' from a Mr. Degers of Amsterdam and his associates:

> ... who have underhand dealt w[i]th the Natives to dispossesse us of our Plantac[i]ons and houses, and hindred our trade, many thousands of pounds, As by the papers p^r[e]sented [to] your Ex[cellen]^{cie} at your dep[ar]ture appeareth ... [They wished him to do what, in his wisdom, he thought best] For the Companies right, and reposs[ess]inge us of our owne trade and houses againe.
> But as for buying the Sweades out[,] whoe have intrenched upon our Inheritance and right, We humbly conceave there is noe reason to give them any thinge. For soe other Nations may doe the like by us hereafter ...
> 6 Apr. recd. in Stockholm 4 May 1654
>
> ib. fol. 268v. (transcript).

Later, Wilson wrote thanking Whitelocke effusively for his 'loving letters & large expressions of love ... truely you are very much mist heere'. He believed that De la Vale (Duwall ? q.v.) and de la Barre 'have bin very great plunderers ...' (presumably of ships); he continued regretfully: 'Our trade some report is almost att an end in the Prize Office'; (Swedish ships could no longer be plundered, in view of the Treaty of Amity negotiated by Whitelocke). After expressing the hope that Spanish wines would sell, since he had a large stock of them, Wilson sent humble service and hearty thanks from 'Mrs Hannah', evidently his wife, 28 Apr. 1654, Add. Ms 37347. fols. 234–234v. (transcript).

When Dr. Thomas Winston (q.v.) died, Samuel Wilson sent a messenger to Chelsea, with news that the Doctor had made a substantial bequest, in a deathbed Will, to one of Whitelocke's sons. Wilson wrote that he rejoiced for his brother-in-law, adding: 'I neede not ... acquainte you my house is yo[u]rs ...', Bishopsgate Street, 24 Oct, 1655, Long. W.P. xvii, 95, 96; this was followed by further information about the Will, ib. 99, 100. Another letter from Wilson concerns payments made by a Mr. Noell totalling £500 towards a loan, also a full £500 in settlement of 'one of the Tallys' from a Mr. Prise, and an invitation to Wilson to collect 'the other thousand pounde. w[hi]^{ch} ... shallbe done'; Wilson undertook to wait on Whitelocke at Chelsea to receive his further commands, Bishopsgate Street, 7 Mar. 1656/57, ib. xviii, 25. Later that year, Wilson urged Mary Whitelocke to help him procure a profitable appointment; accordingly, Whitelocke used his influence to have his brother-in-law made one of the Commissioners for prize goods, *Diary* 19 Oct. 1657.

Wilson continued to prosper after the Whitelocke family fell on hard times. He still expected Whitelocke's help over business and legal matters: after the Canary Company was incorporated on 17 March 1665 (causing factions between rival merchants), Wilson failed to conform to the new patent and was taken into custody in Oxford; his wife hurried over from Oxford to Chilton Lodge, begging Whitelocke to intercede with the Chancellor (presumably the Earl of Clarendon, q.v., not the University Chancellor), to have Samuel released; Whitelocke at that time was too ill to travel, but he sent a letter on Wilson's behalf, which the Wilsons considered was not good enough, ib. 16 Nov. 1665. (For the Canary Company, its monopoly, and the subsequent revocation of the Charter, see *Pepys* vii, 314 note 2, 8 Oct. 1666.) Some years earlier, when Whitelocke went into hiding, Wilson had been helpful, *Diary* 30 Dec. 1659; 11, 16, 23 Jan. 1659/60, and the family was glad to accept the Wilsons' hospitality in Greenwich, ib. 15 June, 14 July 1661, *passim*. But when Whitelocke was desperate to borrow money, Wilson (and other close friends) would do nothing for him, *Diary* 14 May 1667.

Wilson was evidently an Independent by religion, and a friend of George Cokayn (q.v.), ib. 21 Jan. 1666/67; 3 Apr., 12, 19 May 1667, *passim*; Whitelocke heard various other Congregational Ministers preach at Wilson's house, including Dr. John Owen (q.v.), ib. 13 May, 22 Nov. 1666; 22 May 1667, *passim*.

Soon after the Restoration Whitelocke discovered, to his dismay, that 'brother Willson' was growing less friendly towards him, ib. 15 Oct. 1662; 31 Oct. 1663; 5, 7 Nov. 1666; 31 Oct. 1671, *passim*. There were subtle insults, as when (protecting Mary Whitelocke's money against the possibility of her husband squandering it), Wilson insisted that the proceeds from the sale of Blunsdon should be deposited with him, until it could be invested in a new property; Wilson, in the meantime, had the use of Mary's money until Whitelocke bought Chilton Park, ib. 3 June 1663. When Whitelocke, his wife and some of the children, stayed with the Wilsons and were very short of money, Mary's sister Hannah demanded £2 a week for their keep, despite the fact that they had brought provisions from the country, with plenty of wood both for their own fires and for those of the Wilson family; Whitelocke noted, sardonically, that Wilson hoarded some of the logs for future use; worse still, Wilson and his wife were 'discourteous & uncivill' to their paying guests, both at table and in private, ib. 23, 25 Jan. 1669/70. Nor was it just a vendetta against Whitelocke; Mary, with two sons, a daughter and James Pearson (q.v.), the tutor, were also 'unkindly entertained', ib. 11 May, 25 Nov. 1671.

The Wilson family, for their part (sometimes accompanied by George Cokayn's family and others), thought nothing of descending on Chilton Lodge to stay with the Whitelockes, ib. 6 Oct. 1665; 3 Apr. 1667; 25 Sept.

1668 and 2 June 1669, when about nine of them arrived, no doubt with servants in attendance. When Whitelocke's daughter Frances, jun. (1), fell ill, with suspected smallpox, 'her unkind Uncle Willson' would not hear of her being moved to a back room, but pushed her out of his house in very cold weather. Fortunately, George Cokayn and his wife gave her shelter in their home, ib. 30 Dec. 1669.

A disagreement between Whitelocke and Wilson, over an alleged old debt, led to their calling in two arbitrators on each side, ib. 12 May 1670; 31 May 1671; 11 with note, 13 Nov. 1671, *passim*. Whitelocke commented on his brother-in-law: 'he will take little pains for a friend', ib. 18 Oct. 1670. When some members of both families (on a journey from London to Chilton Lodge) set up 'in drollery' a 'Committee to order the housekeeping' and to share the expenses, this 'putt brother Willson into his Element'. On arrival, Wilson was afraid that he might not get a taste of venison; fortunately, however, Sir Frances Popham (q.v.) and another friend came to the rescue, each providing a fat buck, while Richard Winwood (q.v.) sent a side and a shoulder, so at the end of the visit Wilson was even able to take some venison home with him, ib. 19, 21, 22, 24 July 1671. On the Wilsons' last recorded visit to Chilton Lodge, Whitelocke entertained them with venison, but noted that Wilson was there to dun him for money which he still claimed was due, ib. 28 Aug. 1673.

WINCHILSEA (WINCHELSEA), Heneage Finch, 3rd E. of (1628–1689). G.E.C. Succeeded to the title in 1639. A Royalist. He married in March 1645 (as the first of four wives) Diana, eldest daughter of Whitelocke's brother-in-law Francis, 5th Baron Willoughby of Parham, and his wife Elizabeth; Diana died in March 1648. Some two years later, Winchilsea wrote to his 'Uncle', Lord Commissioner Whitelocke, thanking him for some favour in the matter of his estate (presumably over his sequestration), East[well], 5 Mar. 1649/50, Long. W.P. x, 125. Whitelocke had thoughts of visiting him at Eastwell, in Kent, but was prevented by illness from doing so; this prompted Winchilsea to write a sympathetic letter, regretting the loss of his company and presenting him with a buck, *Diary* 6, 7 Aug. 1657. Whitelocke recorded the Earl's appointment by Monck (later D. of Albemarle, q.v.), as Governor of Dover, ib. 11 May 1660.

WINSTON, Thomas, MD (1575–1655). W. Munk *Roll of the Royal College of Physicians* i, 160–162; *Alumni Cantabrigienses*; *D.N.B.* A carpenter's son from Painswick, Gloucestershire. He studied at Clare Hall,

Cambridge; graduated Doctor of Medicine at Padua, and was Professor of Physic at Gresham College, London, from 1615 to 1642. He is mentioned as physician to Edward Hyde in Clarendon's *Life* (O.U.P. 1857) i, 119. He had connections with the Virginia Company and through that and his earnings he evidently accumulated considerable wealth, much of which he invested in land, as appeared in his Will. Having, it seems, committed some political indiscretion, he left the country with a warrant from the House of Commons to travel abroad and take the waters for recovery of his health, accompanied by two servants, *C.J.* ii, 763, 13 Sept. 1642.

Winston appears to have settled in France. Returning to England in 1652, he found that his land had been sequestered and (not surprisingly) that he had lost his lodgings and professorship at Gresham College. Whitelocke's wife Mary (q.v.), who had known Dr Winston when she was married to Col. Rowland Wilson (q.v.), introduced the Doctor to Whitelocke at Martyn Abbey, the home of Rowland Wilson sen. (q.v.), Mary's father-in-law by her first marriage. Whitelocke promptly investigated Winston's case. Finding that there were no grounds for treating the Doctor as a royalist delinquent, Whitelocke had the property and post restored to him and sent a servant to give him the good news, *Diary* 9, 10 July 1652, *passim*.

When Whitelocke was appointed Ambassador Extraordinary to Sweden, Winston (being nearly 80) said he was too old to travel with him as physician, but at 2 o'clock one morning he scrawled a note saying that he had obtained the services of Dr Whistler (q.v.), to act as physician to Whitelocke and his retinue, Long. W.P. xiii, 277; *Diary* 3 Oct. 1653. When Whitelocke was in Sweden, Dr Winston looked after the family in England. He wrote reassuringly that whoever had frightened Whitelocke with news that Mary 'had a Cancer in her breast' had been quite wrong: she had had trouble with her head and eyes, from constant crying at his absence, and she had indeed developed a small pimple between her breasts, which she had shown to Dr Winston; someone had advised her 'to have opened the skine' (i.e. have it lanced), but he had recommended that she '... apply a little disolving plaster' and it had disappeared in six to eight days. 'I visit her commonly every morning', evidently at the house of her sister and brother-in-law, Hannah and Samuel Wilson (q.v.), in Bishopsgate Street (where she was staying with her younger children); besides this, every ten days he visited those of the Whitelocke family who had remained in Chelsea, and he was able to report: 'all are very well ...' London, 7 Apr. 1654, Add. Ms 37347 fol. 237v.; *Diary* 25 May 1654. The following year, Whitelocke gave an account of Dr Winston's last illness and death, and described him as 'indeed the kindest friend' he ever had, 22, 24 Oct. 1655. News of the death reached Whitelocke at Chelsea in a letter from Samuel

Wilson, who characteristically sent news of an important legacy: on his deathbed, Winston had sent for a scrivener (in this context a clerk), had cancelled his previous Will and dictated a new one, leaving his Manor of Blunts Hall, Witham, Essex, to Whitelocke's son Bulstrode, and also the reversion of his copyhold land in Raunds, Northamptonshire, south-east of Kettering, after the death of Jerome Weston, 2nd Earl of Portland (q.v.) and of his son Charles, later 3rd Earl of Portland (q.v.). Details of the protracted negotiations over this legacy are given in the 3rd Earl's entry. The new Will was amended and sealed by the dying man; then, because of the alterations, he instructed the scrivener to write it out again, but he died before it was finished. Those present tried to persuade the scrivener to burn the deathbed Will, but he refused: (1) believing it to be good in law; (2) out of respect for Whitelocke; (3) because his wife and Whitelocke's were related, *Diary* 24 Oct., 20 Dec. 1655; letters in Long. W.P. xvii, 95, 99, 105; the first two are from Samuel Wilson to Whitelocke, the third is a letter from Whitelocke to his son James (q.v.). All three concern Dr Winston's legacy. For the Will itself, see P.R.O. Prob. 11/246 and a copy in P.C.C. Wills (1655–1705) Aylett 190.

The author is grateful to Mr Ralph Hall for supplying details of the Raunds property, and to Mr Watkins Shaw for information about a paper in Whitelocke's hand, headed 'October. 1655', which describes (much as it is told in *The Diary*), Thomas Winston's death at his lodgings in Gresham College, and the preparation of his deathbed Will; this manuscript was among Sir Frederick Ouseley's papers in St. Michael's College (now closed), and has been moved to Hereford Cathedral Library, Ouseley Ms fol. 5; with it is a transcript of Judge James Whitelocke's *Liber Famelicus*, ib. fol. 6 (Sir Frederick claimed descent from the Whitelocke family, through his mother's father). The manuscript of October 1655 could well be an odd page of the original 'Diary', from which the first part of *The Diary* was copied by Whitelocke; another page has been traced, concerning the birth of one of his children.

WINTER (WINTOUR), Sir John (1600–*c*.1686). *Pepys* x; *D.N.B.* (the latter giving dates 1600?–1673?). Of Lydney, Gloucestershire, north-east of Chepstow. A wealthy Roman Catholic and Royalist. Cousin of Edward Somerset, 2nd Marquess of Worcester; he was related to Thomas Winter of the Gunpowder Plot, a fact which his enemies did not allow him to forget. Secretary to Henrietta Maria (q.v.) from 1638–1642, and again after the Restoration. In 1640 he bought 18,000 acres of the Forest of Dean, which he had formerly leased from Charles I (q.v.). He was active in selling timber and iron, until he was deprived of his estates in 1642, on account of his religious convictions; he was imprisoned more than once in the Tower, as a delinquent. Being released on 14 October 1653 (on condition he remained within 30 miles of London), he turned his technological skills to charking sea coal (i.e. turning it into coke) and to designing a new type of grate in which to burn it. Whitelocke thought this new fuel would damage the sale of timber, *Diary* 17 Aug. 1658. After the Restoration Winter obtained a monopoly for this process.

WINWOOD (WYNWOOD), Richard, MP (1609–1688). M.F.K.; *Hist. of Parl.*; *D.N.B.* (in the entry for his father); *V.C.H. Bucks.* iv, *passim*; *Visitation of Buckinghamshire, in 1634* p. 131, genealogy; a marble effigy in St. Mary & Holy Cross Church, Quainton, Buckinghamshire. Of Ditton Park, north-east of Windsor, and of Quainton, north-west of Aylesbury, Buckinghamshire. Eldest son of Sir Ralph Winwood MP, who was Secretary of State to King James I. Richard was educated at Eton; he was appointed a Deputy-Lieutenant for Buckinghamshire with John Hampden (q.v.), Whitelocke and others, *Diary* 1641.1642. fol. 54v.; an earlier entry shows that he and Whitelocke were already friends, ib. fol. 54. Winwood was MP for New Windsor in the Long Parliament, from about July 1641 until Pride's Purge in December 1648. He was readmitted to the Commons in February 1659/60 and served again (after Whitelocke's death) in 1679, 1680 and 1681.

Winwood's wife Anne (c.1616–1694) was the sister of Sir John Reade (q.v.), the unpleasant master of Brocket Hall, near Welwyn, Hertfordshire. His sister, another Anne, married Edward, 2nd Lord Mountague of Boughton (q.v.).

Winwood and Whitelocke were two of Parliament's eight MPs who were sent with four members of the House of Lords, to negotiate with the King at Oxford, ib. 1642.1643. fol. 60. Soon afterwards, Whitelocke and his wife decided that it would be healthier for them and for their children 'to be in the Countrey aier in the Summer' but not far from London, since he had to attend Parliament. They and the Winwood family combined to rent Sir Robert Payne's large house at Highgate, ib. 1642.1643. fol. 62v., '& ... enjoyed the contentment of one anothers society'. This provided a diplomatic excuse for Whitelocke to terminate the joint-tenancy of a house in Ivy Lane, which he had been sharing with his royalist friend Geffrey Palmer (q.v.). Winwood generously lent his coach to Whitelocke (who had suffered heavy losses when the King's forces ransacked Fawley Court) until a client, Sir William Drake (q.v.), settled his fees handsomely with the gift of a coach and pair, ib. 1643.1644. fol. 63. Later, after the Whitelockes had moved to the Navy House in Deptford, Winwood went to warn his friend of the treason charge brought against him and Denzil Holles by Thomas Savile, Earl of Sussex (q.v.); Whitelocke asked Winwood why he ventured his own life and fortune to bring such news. Winwood replied that he did so because Whitelocke was his friend and he loved him. As the case proceeded, he proved himself to be one of Whitelocke's 'very hearty friends', ib. 2, 5 July 1645. That same summer, the Whitelockes were made welcome at the house Winwood had presumably rented at Castle Beare, Acton (i.e. Castlebar, Ealing), ib. 7 Aug. 1645, and later, ib. 16 July 1647; 22 May 1648, *passim*.

There are numerous entries reflecting their friendship, both before and after the Restoration: at Winwood's request, Whitelocke saved him from being made Sheriff, ib. 20 Oct. 1656; 21 Nov. 1657; 15 Nov. 1664, and Winwood consulted him about the purchase of Fewcot near Bicester, for which service Whitelocke neither received nor expected a fee, ib. 17 May 1661, *passim*. Winwood was both rich and generous. He sent or brought gifts of venison, game or fowl some 40 miles, from Ditton Park or from Quainton to Chilton Lodge, ib. 16 Nov. 1664; 5 Aug., 1 Sept. 1666; 26 July 1667. When Whitelocke, by then very short of money, bought a second-hand, crimson-lined coach for £26, Winwood sent his six coach horses to London to bring Whitelocke and his wife to Ditton Park; Mary being ill, Mr and Mrs Winwood met them at the gate with servants and a chair (probably a sedan) to carry her to her room, ib. 18 Feb. 1668/69. Twice the Winwoods arrived with their own servants, to stay at Chilton Lodge, causing their friends some difficulty in accommodating 10 extra people and nine horses, but on both occasions Whitelocke recorded that they were very welcome, ib. 27 Feb. 1665/66; 23 July 1667. Just once, Whitelocke suspected that he and Mary were made less welcome than usual when visiting their friends, ib. 1 Nov., 1666. The Winwoods must have been famous for their hospitality, notably at Christmas time: on one occasion, 300 guests sat down to dinner at Ditton Park, and a few days later a great number of uninvited guests arrived for dinner, yet there was 'no debauchery nor swearing & they had good cheer', ib. 28 Dec. 1663; 1 Jan. 1663/64, *passim*.

Although Richard Winwood appears to have been a Presbyterian in the 1640s, after the Restoration he conformed to the Church of England; yet an ousted Minister, John Batchelor (q.v.), preached in Anne Winwood's room, ib. 26 May 1667, and Richard came to Chilton Lodge in order to be absent from home when the Second Conventicle Act was to be executed (and he took the opportunity to ask Whitelocke to draft his Will), ib. 23, 31 May 1670.

Winwood does not seem to have been a scholarly man, but at one point he wrote offering Whitelocke the use of any of his father's books, *Diary* 18

Feb. 1654/55. This may have been in lieu of paying a fee to a friend. The author is grateful to Dr. Alan Piper for drawing attention to a manuscript (and to its provenance) in the Durham University Library, Cosin Ms V, i, 13 fol. 3, with a Latin inscription which states that it was given to Whitelocke by his friend Richard Winwood, 5 June 1655. The main texts in the work are: Bernard on 'The Song of Songs', Origen on 'Joshua' and Henry Suso 'Horologium Sapienciae'. This manuscript was in the hands of the Revd. George Davenport (Chaplain to Bishop Cosin of Durham) in 1664. It seems likely that Whitelocke sold it after the Restoration, when he was short of money.

WITHERS, [Thomas], (d. 1668). Probably one of Whitelocke's tenants in Chilton Park, west Berkshire; described as of 'Chilton Foldat' (i.e. Foliat), in a promissory note from Whitelocke for £6 (with interest) 'for the beasts commons in Chilton Marsh', Oct. 1663; receipted Nov. 1668, Long. W.P. xx, 134, 134v. Withers signed the receipt with his mark. For the certificate of his burial at Charlton, Kent, in 1668, see ib. 150. When Whitelocke was obliged to send the family tutor, James Pearson (q.v.), to Oxford, with his sons Sam (q.v.) and Carleton (q.v.), to pay their arrears, he sold (the late) Thomas Withers' house to raise the money, *Diary* 9 Mar. 1668/69. Later, Mrs. Withers consulted Whitelocke and paid fees of 10s., ib. 20 Feb. 1672/73; 7 Apr. 1673.

WITTEWRONGE (Witterong), Sir John, Kt., later 1st Bt., MP (1618–1693). *Complete Baronetage; Extinct & Dormant Baronetcies; V.C.H. Herts.* ii, *passim; Alumni Oxonienses*; D.H. Boalch *Manor of Rothamsted and its Occupants* (Rothamsted Experimental Station. 1978) pp. 8–16, *passim*; Herts. County Record Office, Rothamsted Papers (a very large collection, with many items concerning the Wittewronge family), D/ELw, *passim.*

Of Rothamsted, south-west of Harpenden, Herts., and Stantonbury, Bucks., south-west of Newport Pagnell. John's grandfather, Jacques Wittewronghele, had come to London in 1564, a refugee from religious persecution in the Netherlands under Philip II of Spain; his father Jacob, educated at the St. Albans Free School and Magdalen College, Oxford, made two profitable marriages and became a prosperous brewer and an Elder of the Dutch Church in London. In 1611 Jacob obtained a mortgage on Rothamsted; he died at his house in Westham, Essex (i.e. West Ham, Greater London).

John himself, born in Barking, London, became the first of a succession of Wittewronges to live at Rothamsted, a large estate given to him by his mother; after his father's death in 1622, she married Sir Thomas Myddleton (Middleton), former Lord Mayor of London, who brought John up as if he were his own child, *Manor of Rothamsted* (above), p. 8. John studied at Trinity College, Oxford. After travelling abroad he married (in Chirk Castle, north of Oswestry) Mary Myddleton, his stepfather's grand-daughter, who died in 1640. He was knighted in 1641 and, in the same year, married Elizabeth Myddleton from Essex (a cousin of his first wife), and they moved to Rothamsted in the autumn. He was appointed: Deputy-Lieutenant of Hertfordshire in August 1642; Captain of the Trained Bands for the Hundreds of Caishowe and Dacorum in his county, and he appears to have been Governor of Parliament's garrison at Aylesbury, Buckinghamshire, from April to August 1643.

Wittewronge's second wife died in 1649, and he married Katharine Thomson, daughter of a London merchant. He was elected MP for Hertfordshire in Cromwell's Parliaments of 1654 and 1656, but was one of those excluded from sitting in the second Parliament: under the Instrument, the Protector had power to select from the elected representatives, and only those MPs who were handed certificates of admission (a sign of their moderation) could enter the House of Commons. Wittewronge was one of 98 MPs, headed by Sir Arthur Hesilrige (q.v.), who signed a long and trenchant protest, on the grounds that the Protector and his council

> ... boldly declare, that none of the people's deputies [i.e. elected MPs] shall meet in parliament unless they agree to the measure of their [the Protector and Council's] fantasies, humours or lusts; they now render [i.e. depict] the people such fools ... as know not who are fit to be trusted ... with their lives, estates, and liberties ... And if the people shall tamely submit ..., who can doubt but he [Cromwell] may pack such a number as will obey all his commands ... none of the most wicked kings, in their ... hope to erect a tyranny ... [had dared, since elected Parliaments began] to throw aside by force as many of the chosen members as they thought would not serve their ends ...

They protested that MPs who sat, knowing that others had been forcibly excluded, were 'betrayers of the liberties of England ...' For the petition and signatories see *Memorials* iv, 274–280, 22 Sept. 1656.

In 1658, Sir John was made High Sheriff of Hertfordshire. After the Restoration he was pardoned for his former activities, and was created a Baronet in 1662. He was High Sheriff of Montgomeryshire (where he owned property) in 1664 and, in that year, started a 'Memoir' of his forebears and of himself, printed in R. Clutterbuck *History and Antiquities of the County of Hertford* (London. 1815) i, footnote to pp. 407–410; see also a family tree, ib. 411. He had inherited £4,000 from his father, and his mother (as indicated earlier) had given him the valuable Manor of Rothamsted. He owned a brewery in London and in 1656 invested £1,000 in East India Company shares. He also owned lands near Rothamsted, and in Buckinghamshire, Lincolnshire and Montgomeryshire. In his last years, from 1684, he kept a meticulous and detailed five-year gardener's 'Diary', recording the weather and the progress of his crops, including his cherries, quinces, grapes and melons, peaches and Roman nectarines, artichokes and asparagus, Herts. C.R.O. D.E.Lw F19.

Whitelocke had a good deal in common with Sir John, but they only encountered each other in a matter of litigation between Whitelocke's son-in-law, Sir Richard Pryce (q.v.) and Sir John Wittewronge, over land in Montgomeryshire. In this connection, particulars of tenants and rents paid on land which Sir John bought from Richard Pryce, in 1640, may be found in Long. W.P. viii, 60–61, endorsed 'Aber Buchan' (or 'Bachan'). Whitelocke was brought into the dispute soon after his return from Sweden, Diary 21, 26, 28 July 1654; it seemed to be resolved, ib. 7 Oct. 1656; 11 Feb. 1656/57, but it broke out again, ib. 9, 15 Apr. 1657 and (in a different context), ib. 20 May 1662, the property being spelt this time 'Aber Bechan'. Whitelocke's only reference to Sir John which is unrelated to the land in Wales, concerns Wittewronge returning several pictures to the King, which he had bought from the State, ib. 3 July 1660.

WOGAN, [Capt. Edward], (d. 1654). C. Firth & G. Davies Regimental History of Cromwell's Army; D.N.B. A Captain in Parliament's Army until 1648, when he turned Royalist and took his troops with him, first to Scotland and then to Ireland where he joined James Ormond, later 1st Duke of Ormond (q.v.). There are only two entries for Wogan, occurring when it was reported from Ireland that Colonel Zankey (q.v.) had captured him, killing or taking prisoner many of his men at Passage Fort, near Waterford, Diary 31 Dec. 1649; 5 Jan. 1649/50. Wogan was imprisoned in Cork, but managed to escape. He accompanied Ormond to Brittany, but returned to England to fight with the Royalists at Worcester, in September 1651. Escaping to France, he later landed with troops at Dover, enlisted men for the Royalist cause and bluffed his way as far as Durham; these troops joined John Middleton's Highland forces in Scotland, where Wogan received a wound from which he subsequently died.

WOLSELEY (OULSEY), Sir Charles, 2nd Bt., MP (c. 1630–1714). A. Woolrych Commonwealth to Protectorate, passim; Hist. of Parl.; D.N.B.;

Complete Baronetage. Son of a Royalist, Sir Robert Wolseley, 1st Bt., Charles himself initially supported the King. In September 1646 (aged about 16) he succeeded to the title and, inheriting his father's sequestrated estate, he compounded for £2,500. Two years later he married Anne, youngest daughter of William Fiennes, 1st Viscount Say and Seale (q.v.) and became an ardent Cromwellian.

Wolseley's first parliamentary experience was in the nominated (unelected) Barebone's Parliament of 1653; in December 1653 he was active in promoting the dissolution of Parliament by its Members, and the handing over of supreme power to Cromwell. It was reported that, at their last session, Wolseley declared that 'he had lain a long time under the pressure of his own spirits, in sitting with those whose designs and ends were destructive to the Commonwealth ...'; he denounced their 'evil intentions' towards the Army in trying to curtail the greater part of their pay; they lacked 'the spirit of justice', moreover '... they intended to destroy the law, and to pull it up root and branch ...', as shown by 'their vote to take away chancery ...' without putting anything in its place. They also intended '... to take away all property ...', H.A. Glass *Barbone Parliament* (London. 1899) p. 113. His great satisfaction at the outcome (namely the setting up of the Protectorate) is shown in extracts from his letter to Whitelocke in Sweden, below. He subsequently served in the Protectorate Parliaments of 1654 and 1656, until called to Cromwell's 'Other House'. Later, he supported Richard Cromwell (q.v.), but in 1659 joined in a royalist conspiracy. He was elected MP in the Convention Parliament of April 1660, and was pardoned at the Restoration. During the enforced leisure which followed, while he was still in his 30s, Wolseley turned to gardening and writing. His pamphlets include two on liberty of conscience, dated 1668, and *The Case of Divorce and Remarriage*, following the sensational divorce petition of Lord Roos (q.v.). In later years he was active as a Whig.

Wolseley, 25 years Whitelocke's junior, was on cordial terms with the older MP. He is variously referred to in *The Diary* as Ousley, Oulsey, Ouseley – and occasionally Wolseley. It was as a member of the Barebone's Council of State that he leaked the information to Daniel Earle (q.v.), that Whitelocke had been chosen to go as Ambassador Extraordinary to Sweden, *Diary* 23, 25 Aug. 1653. This was followed by two visits to Whitelocke; the first of these led to his well-intentioned attempt to persuade the Council of State to postpone the Embassy until the spring, but the result was that the Council went into action, and despatched their Ambassador the following month, causing him to cross the North Sea and to travel across Sweden, with his large retinue, in the winter, ib. 15 Oct. 1653, *passim.* Whitelocke took the trouble to write, telling Wolseley of his safe arrival in Gothenburg. After acknowledging the letter with gratitude, Wolseley announced:

> ... the state & complexion of affayres are much altered heere since you left us & I thinke very much for the better: the Parl[iamen]ᵗ you left sittinge[,] the major part of them (Beinge Endeed grown soe injurious to magistracye[,] property & ministry that the safetye of the whole would not admitt them to sitt longer) delivered up their power to my L[or]ᵈ Gene[ral] from whence they received it: The Government now established is by a Lord Protector (who hath much the same power w[i]ᵗʰ the Kinge formerly) assisted w[i]ᵗʰ a Councell not exceeding 21 & Parliaments to be chosen triennially[,] who have the Legislature wholly in them[,] save for some time till the fyrst Parl[iamen]ᵗ be Elected ... The Nation is much generally satisfyed w[i]ᵗʰ it ... the Present Protector is my L[or]ᵈ Generall[,] whose personall worth I thinke I may say ... qualifyse him for the greatest monarch of the world[;] the succeedinge protectors are Elective by the Councell ...

In a message below his signature he told how the Dutch treaty 'hanges yet loose though Nothinge be in difference betweene us' but the Dutch would not sign the Articles without consulting their superiors, and the outcome was uncertain, Whitehall, 7 Jan. 1653/54, Add. Ms 32093 fols. 317–316v. (*sic*). Compare letters from John Thurloe and Marchmont Nedham, expressing a similar view of the Protectorate.

Whitelocke wrote that 'none was a more hearty friend to him & his buisnes then S[i]ʳ Charles Woulsey', Long. W.P. xiv, 254v. It was probably Wolseley who sent a very flattering Ode in Latin to Whitelocke ('Vitlock'), which the Ambassador showed to Christina (q.v.), knowing that 'such diversions were pleasing to the Queen' and in his 'leisure hours' he translated them into English verse; he told the Queen that they came from an English gentleman, his friend, *Journal* ii, 71, 72.

After Whitelocke's return to England, he used to meet Wolseley and a few others who were regularly called on to advise Cromwell; when the business was finished, they would relax with the Protector and, 'by way of diversion', write poetry and Whitelocke and Cromwell would smoke a pipe, *Diary* 2 May, 18 Oct. 1657.

Whitelocke's last recorded meeting with Wolseley was at the house of Samuel Wilson (q.v.) in Greenwich, when Dr. John Owen (q.v.) preached, John Thurloe (q.v.) and Sir Charles Wolseley being present at the Conventicle, ib. 22 May 1667.

WOLSTENHOLME, Sir John, Kt., later 1st Bt., MP (*c.*1596–1670). *Extinct & Dormant Baronetcies*; *Complete Baronetage*. Of Stanmore, Middlesex. He studied at Gray's Inn, was knighted in 1633, and was created a Baronet in 1665. He became, like his father (Sir John Wolstenholme Kt., d. 1639), a farmer of HM Customs. Sir John (senior or junior?) negotiated on Whitelocke's behalf with Sir John Meller (q.v.), over the purchase of Phyllis Court, *Diary* 1635.1636. fol. 41v. The other two entries occur after the elder Sir John's death: on receiving a letter from the younger Wolstenholme, probably in the autumn of 1641, Whitelocke did him some service in Parliament and in his County, ib. 1641. 1642. fol. 53v. Years later, after the Restoration, Whitelocke recorded that he dined with Sir John, who was his client, ib. 13 May 1664.

WOODSON (WODDESON), Jo[hn]. At one time a servant of Whitelocke's, he seems later to have defamed or 'scandalized' his former master, perhaps on account of his politics, *Diary* 3 Oct. 1645. This did not, however, deter Woodson from applying later to Whitelocke, as Constable of Windsor, for the post of Deputy, to keep the Windsor Court, 13 Jan. 1650/51, Long. W.P. xi, 14; still later, he wrote applying, more modestly, for a place as Clerk to the Windsor Castle Court, *Diary* 1 June 1659.

WOODWARD, the Revd. Samuel (d. 1687). Vicar of Aldworth, Berks. Inducted in December 1659; buried August 1687. He wrote about the giant 14th century monuments to Whitelocke's de la Beche ancestors, believed to have been damaged during the Civil War or the Interregnum, *Diary* 14 Dec. 1670 with note.

WOOLASTON (WOLLASTON), Alderman Sir John, Kt. (d. 1658). A.B.B.; G. E. Aylmer 'Check-list of Central Office-holders'. Prime Warden of Goldsmiths' College from 1639 to 1640, he was knighted in December 1641 and made Colonel of the Trained Bands in the same year; he 'feasted' Whitelocke and his wife Frances, in London, when the guest of honour was Sir John Holland (q.v.), *Diary* 5 July 1648. His name appears with those of Sir Maurice Abbot, Lord Mayor of London, and Alderman Isaac Pennington (q.v.), on a document concerning a Writ of Habeas Corpus for one Thomas Jennings (n.d.), Long. W.P. vii, 355v.-356, *passim*. Woolaston was co-Treasurer at Wars from 1645 to 1652; co-Treasurer for the sale of Crown lands from 1649, and Trustee for the sale of Church lands in 1646 and 1649. Although knighted in 1641, he was referred to as 'M^r' in *Diary* 5 July 1648.

WOOLFELDT, Count Corfitz, see ULFELDT.

WORCESTER, Edward Somerset, 6th E. and 2nd Marquess of; titular E. of Glamorgan (1603–1667). G.E.C.; *D.N.B.* (as Somerset). A staunch Roman Catholic and Royalist; he succeeded to the title in 1646. After the outbreak of the Civil War he acted as a go-between, transferring large sums of money from his father, the 1st Marquess, to Charles I. He appears to have been a man of conviction but of singularly poor judgement, and given to using forgery in what he considered a good cause, see his G.E.C. entry p. 860, note d. (The *D.N.B.* entry, less convincingly, rebuts the charge of forgery.) After a few weeks of imprisonment in Dublin Castle, from 26 December 1645, he escaped from Galway to join Queen Henrietta Maria (q.v.) in Paris. He was one of 12 men officially banished by the House of Commons and condemned to 'die without Mercy' if he ever returned, *C.J.* vi, 164, 14 Mar. 1648/49. Despite this, he came back in 1652 and was imprisoned in the Tower under tolerable conditions, until his release on bail in 1654. Oddly enough, in 1655 Cromwell granted him a pension of £3 a week. His sequestered estates were returned to him after the Restoration, but his claim that he was to have been created a Duke in the 1640s (based, according to G.E.C., on another forgery) was withdrawn when challenged. The more attractive side of the Marquess's character was his lifelong interest in mechanical experiments, carried out in a Vauxhall laboratory. He worked, for example, on a 'water-commanding engine', a calculating machine and had wild theories on how to make a man fly.

Whitelocke's only reference to him, *Diary* 19 Aug. 1658 with note, concerns the Marquess's letter asking for a favour. It started smugly: 'Remembring the kindnesse w[hi]^{ch} heretofore I endeavoured to shew you ...' In view of Worcester's troubles and spells in gaol, it is difficult to imagine what kindness he, a Royalist, had been able to show Whitelocke, but it is clear from the letter that they knew each other. He wished Whitelocke (as a Governor of Sutton's Hospital, i.e. Charterhouse) to find a place there for his cousin Quarterman, a man of 'very good family and allyed to the Percys and Veares as well as to my selfe, of Civile and good behaviour but in distresse ...' He ended the letter 'your Lo[rdshi]^{ps} affectionat Cosin and humble servant Worcester', 18 Aug. 1658, Long. W.P. xviii, 142.

No kinship with Whitelocke has been traced.

WORTLEY, Sir Francis, 2nd Bt. (d. 1665). *Complete Baronetage*; *D.N.B.* (entry for his father of the same name). Of Wortley, Yorks. Studied at

Gray's Inn. Succeeded to the title in 1652. Only referred to when he applied to Whitelocke over some business in Parliament, and a matter concerning recusants, *Diary* 1 Mar. 1656/57. It is not clear whether the application to Whitelocke was over two different matters. Parliament considered a Bill for Recusants, *C.J.* vii, 503, 509, 541; 14, 21 Mar. 1656/57; 28 May 1657, *passim*.

WRANGEL, General and Admiral Carl Gustav (1613–1676). *Svenska Män och Kvinnor*; A. Losman *Carl Gustaf Wrangel och Europa* (Almquist & Wiksell. 1980). One of Sweden's most distinguished commanders, both at sea and on land, in Sweden's 'age of greatness'. After travelling abroad, he entered the service of King Gustav Adolf II in 1631, and took part in the German campaign of the Thirty Years War, being present at the battle of Lützen in 1632, when the Swedish King was killed. Afterwards, serving in Johan Banér's Army, he was promoted to the rank of Colonel and later to that of Major-General. After Banér's death in 1641, Wrangel was one of three Generals in command of the Swedish Army in Germany. In 1644 he was in charge of the Swedish fleet based on Kiel, and the next year became Supreme Commander of the whole fleet. In 1646 he was Commander-in-Chief of the Swedish Army in Germany; he was appointed Governor of Pomerania, also Chancellor of the University of Greiswald; he was created an Earl in 1651 and made Vice-Admiral in 1653. After the abdication of Queen Christina (q.v.), he fought for King Charles X of Sweden (q.v.) in Poland and Denmark; appointed Admiral of the Fleet in 1657. He amassed great wealth, partly through the high offices he held, and partly by plunder. His castles included Skokloster (which he started to build in 1654); this is now a centre for Baroque culture, while 'Wrangel's Palace' in Stockholm is the High Court of Justice.

Whitelocke first encountered Wrangel in Uppsala, and later (on several occasions) in Stockholm; he gave a full account of their first meeting, with a description of Wrangel, in *Journal* ii, 33, 34, and a shorter entry in his other account, which indicates that the Vice-Admiral 'delighted much in Sea affayres & in . . . relations of the ships & battles in England', *Diary* 14 Mar. 1653/54. At their next meeting, Wrangel dined with Whitelocke and 'discoursed freely and much of the English fleet at sea'. Whitelocke showed him a 'draught' (or drawing) of the ship *Sovereign* 'with her dimensions, guns, and men', and of other ships; the Vice-Admiral had received orders to provide ships for Whitelocke and his company, for their voyage across the Baltic at the end of the Embassy, and another ship to transport the weighty gift of copper from the Queen, ib. 7 Apr., 26 May 1654, *Journal* ii, 102. Wrangel paid Whitelocke the compliment of inviting him to name a

Swedish ship which was to be launched in Stockholm. The choice of a name was rather embarrassing: the Vice-Admiral would not allow her to be called the *Wrangel*, as this might cause jealousy at Court; for similar reasons, the Ambassador would not agree to her being named the *Whitelocke*, nor would he call her the *Cromwell* or the *Protector*, because she only carried 30 guns. Fortunately, he spotted the mark of a falcon on the ship's guns and that being part of his Arms, he named her the *Falcon*, ib. 302–303, 25 May 1654; for a shorter version see *Diary*, on the same date. Whitelocke's last entry for Wrangel refers to the Admiral's gallantry in a sea battle against the Dutch who were attempting to relieve Copenhagen, *Diary* 8 Nov. 1658.

In the previous year, knowing that a new war was imminent, Wrangel wrote asking for Whitelocke's help in procuring two English horses for him, 28 May 1655, Long. W.P. xiv, 79. (Whitelocke had already made him a present of an English gelding before he left Sweden, *Diary* 19 May 1654.) Wrangel wrote another letter warmly recommending Andrew Potley (q.v.), who had been living in his house during the winter. The recommendation hardly seems necessary, since Andrew and his father, Christopher Potley (q.v.), were related to Whitelocke, and had both been in his retinue throughout the Embassy, 5 June 1655, Long. W.P. xvii, 56 (Latin).

WRAY, Sir Christopher, Kt., MP (1601–1646). M.F.K.; *D.N.B.* (in the entry for his father). He resisted the Ship Money levy in 1636; sat as MP for Great Grimsby in the Long Parliament, and was appointed a Deputy-Lieutenant for Lincolnshire and Commissioner of the Admiralty. He and the 4th Earl of Pembroke (q.v.) 'treated' (probably 'entertained') Whitelocke kindly, *Diary* 20 Dec. 1645. When Wray died shortly afterwards, in Parliament's service, on 8 February 1645/46, Whitelocke helped to procure an Ordinance to discharge Sir Christopher's heir (William Wray) from being a ward, ib. 24 Feb. 1645/46; *C.J.* iv, 452, same date. For the three Wrays' brawling defence of Lord Francis Willoughby, see that Baron's entry.

WREN, [Bishop Matthew], DD (1585–1667). Son of a London mercer. Educated at Pembroke Hall, Cambridge. Ordained priest in February 1610/11; Prebendary of Winchester in 1624; Bishop of Hereford, 1634, of Norwich in 1635, and of Ely in 1638. Rigidly anti-Puritan, he was impeached in 1641 and imprisoned in the Tower, from December 1641 to May 1642. After his release, he was rearrested in Ely and again committed to the Tower, without trial, from September 1642 until March 1659/60.

Whitelocke commented briefly: 'D^r [not Bishop] Wren discharged of his imprisonm[en]t', *Diary* 15 Mar. 1659/60.

WRIGHT, [Thomas] (b. *c.* 1604). *Alumni Oxonienses; Middle Temple Admission Register.* Son and heir of Sir George Wright, Kt., of Richmond, Surrey. A friend of Whitelocke's at St. John's College, Oxford; to save him from the consequences of some unnamed offence, Whitelocke risked punishment himself, *Diary* 1620.1621. fol. 3v. There is no reference to their being fellow law-students, although they were contemporaries at the Middle Temple.

WROTH, Sir Thomas, Kt., MP (1584–1672). *Hist. of Parl.*; *D.N.B.* Of Petherton Park, south of Bridgwater, Somerset. He studied at Oxford and at the Inner Temple. A recruiter Member of the Long Parliament; he had financial interests in the New England, Bermuda, Virginia and Eastland Companies. He is referred to only in connection with some unspecified kindness to Whitelocke, *Diary* 30 Dec. 1647.

WYLDE, see WILDE, Judge John.

WYNDHAM (WINDHAM), Judge Sir Hugh (*c.* 1603–1684). E. Foss *Judges of England; D.N.B.* He studied at Wadham College, Oxford, and at Lincoln's Inn, later serving as a Serjeant-at-Law and then as a Judge, both before and after the Restoration. Whitelocke formally records, in *The Diary*, the date of some of Wyndham's appointments and re-appointments under different governments, and gives fuller details in *Memorials*. *The Diary* gives no personal details of Wyndham as a man.

WYNN families, see *Dictionary of Welsh Biography.*

WYNN (WYN), Owen (1592–1660). of Gwydir, Caernarvonshire (now Gwynedd). It is possible that this was the 'Owen Wyn' described as 'a man of no fortune' and reported by Lady Salisbury (q.v.) as having married Whitelocke's widowed sister, Elizabeth Mostyn (q.v.), *Diary* 7 Nov. 1648, with note. Wynn had married a niece of Archbishop Williams (q.v.) in 1642, but may have been a widower six years later. The Mostyns and Wynns were already connected by marriage and this Owen could have been the 'Mr Wynne' from whom Whitelocke received news of his sister and daughter in Wales, ib. 26 July 1658. He was Sheriff of Caernarvonshire in 1653, and High Sheriff of Denbighshire in 1656.

WYNNE (WYNN), the Revd. Hugh, DD (1596–1670). Rector of Llantrisant and Llanyhyddlad, in Anglesey. Probably the 'Mr Wynne[,] a Minister', whom Whitelocke was asked to help by his own daughter Elizabeth, wife of Sir Richard Pryce (q.v.), *Diary* 8 May 1663.

WYNWOOD, Richard, see WINWOOD.

YATE [Thomas], see GATES.

YATES [Joseph]. *Calamy Revised.* A London Minister, 'silenced' in 1662. Samuel Wilson (q.v.), with his wife Hannah, came to see her sister Mary Whitelocke, who was ill, and brought with them Mr. Yates, who preached in the sick woman's room, *Diary* 5 Feb. 1664/65.

YORK, James Stuart, Duke of; later King James II (1633–1701). J. Miller *James II: a Study in Kingship* (Hove: Wayland. 1978); G.E.C.; *D.N.B.*; *Pepys* x, *passim.* Brother of Charles II. He led a colourful and disturbed life, both as a boy in England, before his father's execution in 1649, and as a young man in exile with his brother, during the 1650s, when he held commissions in the Navy and Army. Before and at the Restoration Whitelocke recorded: prayers for the King and Duke of York; money voted for the Duke by Parliament, £10,000 in all; and the landing near Dover, on 25 May, of the King and the Duke, *Diary* 9, 10, 26 May 1660, *passim.* He subsequently noted some of the banquets arranged by public bodies and by private people in honour of the King and the Duke, ib. 16, 23, 29 June, 17 July, 20, 31 Aug. 1660; Whitelocke also mentioned one of the Duke's new appointments, and money voted for him, ib. 3 July 1660; 30 Oct. 1665, *passim.*

After the Restoration, although Whitelocke was permanently out of office and under a cloud, the Duke of York (like the King and their cousin Prince Rupert, q.v.) respected his knowledge of the law enough to consult him on some legal matter, sending his Steward, Lord Berkeley, to ask for his opinion, ib. 21 April 1663. There is no hint that any of the three recompensed Whitelocke, in any way, for his advice. Six years later, Lord William Willoughby of Parham (q.v.) asked Whitelocke (his brother-in-law) whether, if he were sent for by the House of Lords, he would give his opinion on the Bill of Registers (to set up a register of land titles in England) about which the Duke of York, as a member of that House, desired his opinion, ib. 12 Nov. 1669. The Lords had been considering reasons for the fall in rents and decay of trade; some days after Lord Willoughby made his approach to Whitelocke, the Lords agreed: 'That One Cause of the Decay of Rents and Value of Lands is the Uncertainty of Titles of Estates . . .', and in view of this, they '. . . suggest there be a Bill of Registers . . .', *L.J.* xii, 274, 24 Nov. 1669. See J. Thirsk and J.P. Cooper *Seventeenth Century Economic Documents* (O.U.P. 1972) pp. 68–79, 174–175, *passim*. Although Whitelocke agreed to give his opinion, he was not called upon to do so.

The Duke of York's notorious affair with Anne Hyde, daughter of the Earl of Clarendon (q.v.), leading to her pregnancy, their secret marriage on 3 September 1660, the birth of their son who died in infancy, and to the subsequent acceptance of the Duchess in court circles, are told (with some inaccuracies) in *Pepys* i, 260–261, see note, 7 Oct.; 273 see note, 24 Oct.; 320, 21 Dec. 1660; ib. ii, 2–3, 1 Jan. 1660/61, *passim*; see also *Diary* 23 Sept. 1660, with note.

YOUNG [Francis]. 'Woodward' or head forester of Windsor Forest. The diary entries and the documents quoted below, concerning Young, indicate that Whitelocke's appointment as Lieutenant of the forest in March 1649/50 (and subsequently as Constable of Windsor Castle) was no sinecure. The considerable work entailed was in addition to his duties as a Commissioner of the Great Seal. The diary entries tell of: (1) the courteous welcome that Young extended to Whitelocke and Frances when they moved for a time into Manor Lodge, Windsor Park; (2) Young writing about Bearwood Lodge, west of Wokingham, in Berkshire, and about game in Windsor Forest, *Diary* 20 Mar. 1648/49; 29 July 1658. Many bridges had been destroyed during the Civil War and, by an Order of the Council of State, Young was required with two others, to assess what timber was required to repair bridges in Binfield, north-east of Wokingham, and to report their conclusions to Lord Commissioner Whitelocke. At about that time, Whitelocke was empowered to appoint a 'woodward' for the forest, 9 Mar. 1649/50, Long W.P. x, 127.

The following month, Young wrote to one Christopher Havergal (possibly related to Whitelocke's tenant Thomas Havergill, q.v.) asking him: (1) to remind Whitelocke to obtain an Order from the Council of State for fencing new ground in Windsor Forest; (2) to tell him that some 30 acres of the Forest, planted 200 years earlier, would (in his opinion) provide 1,000 trees suitable for ships timber, 4 Apr. 1650, ib. 136. He informed Whitelocke, among other matters, that soldiers had been placed in the Park 'for the care of the deare'; he also sent details of land that

Whitelocke could buy locally for a 'reasonable peneworth [i.e. pennyworth]', £9,000 was being mentioned, but if Whitelocke 'was not to[o] forward [i.e. not over-eager]', Young believed he could get it 'at a lower rate . . .', 18 Apr. [1650?], ib. 134.

Young wrote again saying that he had appointed three deputies to protect the timber in Windsor Forest; if the offenders (who had been despoiling it) were not punished, Whitelocke's authority would, in his opinion, be held in contempt and the State would suffer at the hands of 'fellowes that are in those ill offices as much out of malignity to the Governement as to benefitt themselves . . .', 9 June 1650, ib. 144. He enclosed a letter telling of trees being sawn down and taken away by one John Baithe and his servants, date as above, ib. 146.

The next letter brought some good news: 'We have bin abroade [i.e. out] w[i]th your hauke [i.e. hawk] and she proves a very good one . . .', more news of her on Wednesday. The forester had been troubled by a multitude of 'Ockingam' (i.e. Wokingham) men, who took up a mile of the pipes that carried water into Windsor Castle. He thought there were £400 to £500 worth of pipes still in the ground and (rather obscurely) recommended taking them and laying them into the Castle. He enclosed his copy of the decision concerning the petition from Binfield for the bridges, 21 Jan. 1650/51, ib. xi, 21–20 v.

Next, Young was troubled by four landowners who were enclosing parts of 'Barewood' (i.e. Bearwood). A lawyer who had examined the relevant documents in Court found nothing to justify enclosure of the land, and neighbours looked to Whitelocke, who had visited the area, to do something about it. New Lodge, where Young was living, needed £6 or £7 spent on new tiles etc., before the winter. Another letter reported on what Young clearly thought were dubious activities, in connection with a survey of the Dean and Chapter's houses, with other property in Windsor, n.d. (1651?), ib. 174. There had been 'a great faule [i.e. fall] of wood' in Bearwood, near Wokingham; more than 100 trees had been marked by a Mr. Halstead of Sonning (some five miles north of Bearwood), who wished to requisition it for repairing Sonning Bridge, which had been pulled down by 'the Kings p[ar]^{tie}', when the late King first came to Reading: 'They are all the best trees in beare wood'; if this action were sanctioned, the felling should be done at Halstead's expense, he being Lord of the Manor. Young asked Whitelocke to appoint a Commission (or Committee) of neighbours, to prevent the building of new cottages and the enclosure of land, n.d., ib. 176, *passim*. Further details of forestry matters are given in the entry for WHICHCOTE, Christopher, Governor of Windsor.

YOUNG, Patrick (1584–1652). *D.N.B.*; A.G. Matthews *Walker Revised.* Son of Sir Peter Young. He took Holy Orders and was appointed Chaplain of All Souls, Oxford. Librarian to Charles I at St. James's Palace and at Whitehall; a scholarly man. Whitelocke helped to promote an Order encouraging Patrick Young to publish the Greek translation of the Old Testament, from the 'Septuagint' (the first part of the 'Tecla Bible' or 'Codex Alexandrinus'), *Diary* 13 Mar. 1645/46 with note. The following year, Young appealed to Whitelocke to join John Selden (q.v.) in helping him to get the work printed, ib. 30 June 1647. The treasured manuscript, from the first half of the fifth century, was given to Charles I by the Greek Patriarch of Constantinople in 1627, and was housed in the library at St. James's Palace. After the King's execution it was entrusted to Whitelocke, with other treasures from the royal library; he refused to sell it overseas for £4,000, and ultimately restored it to Charles II, *Diary* 8 June 1660. (It is now displayed in the British Museum.)

After losing both his posts as 'Library Keeper', Young petitioned the Council of State (in a very small and neat hand, not easy to decipher) to compensate him and his father for money owed to them, and for loss of office. He had not been paid his salary as librarian since Michaelmas 1642; he was owed £195 from his post at St. James's Palace and £410 during the same period for his work in the library at Whitehall. He appears to have claimed £2,450, on behalf of his father, from the Exchequer and the Cofferer's Office. He pointed out that he had been loyal to Parliament, and had not gone to Oxford as required by the King's Proclamation, 1649, Long. W.P. x, 89.

ZANKEY (ZANCHY, SANKEY, SANCHY), Col. Sir Jerome (Hierome), DCL, Kt., MP (d. 1687). *Alumni Oxonienses*; C. Firth & G. Davies *Regimental History of Cromwell's Army*; *Pepys* i, 68, 69. Son of Richard Zankey of Shropshire. He studied at Clare Hall, Cambridge. Fellow and sub-warden of All Souls, Oxford, in 1648, where he was tutor to Whitelocke's eldest son, James (q.v.). Said by Whitelocke to be a good scholar. He was appointed University Proctor in 1649. When he was commissioned as a Major in Cromwell's Army, to be sent to Ireland, James Whitelocke accompanied him as far as Bristol; from there Zankey wrote telling Whitelocke that his pupil wished to join him in Ireland, *Diary* 22 July 1649. Whitelocke reluctantly gave his consent.

Zankey wrote further, from Ireland, telling of his successes against Edward Wogan (q.v.), who was hated for defecting from Parliament's Army, ib. 31 Dec. 1649; 5 Jan. 1649/50. His letters tell of further triumphs in Ireland, ib. 4 July 1651; 12 Apr. 1652. He commanded Parliament's

Cavalry there from 1654 to 1655, and was knighted by Henry Cromwell. He was also elected MP to sit in all the Protectorate Parliaments from 1654 to 1659, representing Tipperary and Waterford; Reigate, Surrey; and Woodstock, Oxfordshire. At the time of the royalist rising led by Sir George Booth (q.v.), Colonel Zankey and Colonel Axtell (q.v.), came over with their regiments to support John Lambert (q.v.), ib. 20 Aug. 1659. Yet Zankey, with two others, drafted the Derby Petition, without even consulting Lambert, *Restoration* p. 147; *Regimental History* (above) i, 89; *Diary* 22 Sept. 1659, with note. Zankey's was the second of 12 signatures on the letter which politely instructed Whitelocke to serve on the Committee of Safety, ib. 27 Oct. 1659; Long. W.P. xix, 90 (original). In spite of this, Zankey and his Irish Brigade (quartered soon afterwards in Berwick), accepted orders from George Monck (later Duke of Albemarle, q.v.), and he subsequently declared for Parliament, *Diary* 7, 24 Dec. 1659.

Glossary

ALLHOLLANTIDE	Around All Saints' Day, 1 November.
AMUSED	Puzzled, astonished.
ANSWEARABLE	Answerable: matching, suitable.
ANTIENT, AUNTIENT	Senior.
BARE	Bare-headed.
CARASS	Caress: show great respect for, make a fuss of.
CHIRURGEON	Surgeon.
CHIRURGERY	Surgery.
COUNTREY	Country, county.
CUSTOS BREVIUM ET RECORDORUM	Keeper of the writs and records.
DENY	Refuse, withhold.
DISGESTED	Endured, stomached (usually 'could not be disgested').
FADOM	Fathom.
FALL DOWN	Whitelocke uses the term for 'lie at anchor'.
FINE	A mode of conveyancing land; also a fee.
GENTILE	Well-born, having the rank of a gentleman.
GRANDEE	Person of the highest rank or position, used to describe leading men in the Commons and for Cromwell's circle. The word, with its Spanish connotation, was used disparagingly. (See Junto.)
GRAVE	A foreign Count.
HUMANE LEARNING	Classical literature etc.
I	Aye, ay.
INGENIOUS	Skilful, talented.
INTEREST	Personal influence.
JEALOUS	Suspicious, fearful.
JEALOUSY	Suspicion, mistrust.
JUNCTO, JUNTO	Pejorative name suggesting a secret Spanish conclave.
LEAGUER	Siege.

MAHEMED	Maimed, wounded.
PASSAGE	Incident, event.
PLAYSTERS	Medical plasters.
POLE	Poll: human head, referred to in counting voters and in poll-tax.
PURITAN	Offensive nickname from Queen Elizabeth's days, for those who believed that the Reformation had not gone far enough.
RUNDLET	Roundlet, runlet: a small cask, often containing wine.
SNEAKE	To cringe, be servile.
SURPRISED	Assailed.
TERTIAN AGUE	Acute fever, characterized by paroxysms every other day.
THEN	Than.
WHITHER	Whether.
WRASLE	Wrestle.

Select Bibliography

ALMQUIST, Helge, *Göteborgs Historia* (Göteborg. 1929)

AUBREY, J., *Brief Lives* (ed. Oliver Lawson Dick. Peregrine Books. 1962)

AYLMER, G.E., *The King's Servants 1625–1642* (Routledge & Kegan Paul. 1961)

AYLMER, G.E. (ed.), *The Interregnum: The Quest for Settlement 1646–1660* (Macmillan. 1972)

AYLMER, G.E., *The State's Servants 1649–1660* (Routledge & Kegan Paul. 1973)

BAKER, Agnes, *Historic Abingdon* (privately printed: Abbey Press, Abingdon. 1963)

BARTON, Morag E., *A History of Hamm Court Farm* (1972)

BEAVEN, A.B., *The Aldermen of the City of London* (London. 1908–1913) 2 vols.

BIRCH, Thomas, *A Collection of the State Papers of John Thurloe* (London. 1738–1753) 7 vols.

BOEHN, Max von, *Modes and Manners* (Harrap. 1935) 4 vols.

BOTTIGHEIMER, Karl, *English Money and Irish Land* (O.U.P. 1971)

BRETT-JAMES, N.G. *The Growth of Stuart London* (Allen & Unwin. 1935)

BURKE, J., *Extinct & Dormant Baronetcies* (London. 1844)

BURNS, J.S., *A History of Henley-on-Thames* (Longman. 1861)

CAMPBELL, Lord John, *Lives of the Chancellors and Keepers of the Great Seal of England* (John Murray. 1857)

CARLTON, William J., *Descriptive Catalogue of the Library of Samuel Pepys* Part IV Shorthand Books (Sidgwick & Jackson. 1940)

CARLYLE, Thomas, *Letters and Speeches of Oliver Cromwell* (3 vols. ed. S.C. Lomas, Methuen. 1904)

CATALOGUE, Christina Exhibition, Stockholm (Council of Europe. 1966)

CLARENDON, Edward, 1st Earl of, *The History of the Rebellion and Civil Wars in England* (1707–1759) 6 vols.

CLARENDON, Edward, 1st Earl of, *The Life of Edward Earl of Clarendon by himself* (O.U.P. 1842) 3 vols.

COKAYNE, G.E., *Complete Baronetage*. 6 vols. & index
COKAYNE, G.E., *Complete Peerage*. 12 vols.
COLLENETTE, C.L., *A History of Richmond Park* (Sidgwick & Jackson. 1937)
CRAWFORD, Patricia, *Denzil, First Lord Holles* Studies in History Series No. 16 (Royal Historical Society. 1979)
DAVIES, Godfrey, *The Restoration of Charles II* (O.U.P. 1969)
DEVILLE, A., *Tombeaux de la Cathédrale de Rouen* (Rouen. 1833)
DORMER, Sir Robert (attributed to), *Exceeding good news from Oxfordshire: being a relation of the ... apprehending of the Earl of Berkshire* (1642)
D'OYLY BAYLEY, William, *Account of the House of D'Oyly* (John Bowyer Nichols & Sons. 1848)
EVELYN, John, *Diary* (ed. E.S. de Beer. O.U.P. 1955) 6 vols.
FIRTH, C.H., *Cromwell's Army* (Methuen University Paperbacks. 1967)
FIRTH, C.H. and DAVIES, G., *Regimental History of Cromwell's Army* (O.U.P. 1940) 2 vols.
FIRTH, C.H. and RAIT, R.S. (eds), *Acts and Ordinances of the Interregnum* (London. 1911)
FOSS, E., *Judges of England* (London. 1857) 9 vols.
GARDINER, S.R., *History of England ... covering the years* 1603–1659 (Longman, Green & Co. 1863–1902) 10 vols.
GARDINER, S.R., *Constitutional Documents of the Puritan Revolution* 1625–1660 (O.U.P. 1962)
GOUGH NICHOLS, J. and BRUCE, J. (eds.), *Wills from Doctors' Commons* (Camden Society. 1863)
HENNING, B.D. (ed.), *History of Parliament. House of Commons* 1660–1690 (Secker & Warburg. 1983) 3 vols.
HILL, Christopher, *Change and Continuity in Seventeenth-Century England.* (Weidenfeld & Nicholson. 1974)
HILL, Christopher, *Milton and the English Revolution* (Faber & Faber Paperbacks. 1979)
HILL, Christopher, *Puritanism and Revolution* (Mercury Books. 1962)
HOPWOOD, C.H., *Middle Temple Records* (Butterworth. 1904)
JOSTEN, C.H. (ed.), *Elias Ashmole 1617–1692* (O.U.P. 1966) 5 vols.
KEELER, M.F., *The Long Parliament 1640–41* (The American Philosophical Society, Philadelphia. 1954)
LUDLOW, E., *A Voyce from the Watch Tower* Part Five: 1660–1662 (ed. A.B. Worden. Camden 4th Series vol. 21. Royal Historical Society. 1978)
MASSON, Georgina, *Queen Christina* (Sphere Books. 1974)
MATTHEWS, A.G., *Calamy Revised* (O.U.P. 1934)

MILNE, H.J.M. and SKEAT, T.C., *The Codex Sinaiticus and The Codex Alexandrinus* (Trustees of the British Museum. 1963)

MOORE, James, *Memorials of Charterhouse* (London. 1844)

MOSTYN, Lord, and GLENN, T.A., *Mostyn of Mostyn* (1925)

MUNK, W., *The Roll of the Royal College of Physicians of London* ... (London. 1878)

PENNINGTON, D.H., *Seventeenth-Century Europe* (Longman. 1970)

PEPYS, Samuel, *Diary of Samuel Pepys* (ed. Robert Latham and William Matthews. Bell & Hyman. 1970–1983) 10 vols. & index.

PIGGOTT, Stuart, *William Camden and the Britannia* (Reckitt Archaeological Lecture, from Proceedings of the British Academy vol. xxxvii. 1951)

RADFORD, P.J., *Antique Maps* (Garnstone Press. 1971)

ROBERTS, Michael, *Essays in Swedish History* (Weidenfeld & Nicholson. 1967)

ROBERTS, Michael (ed.), *Sweden as a Great Power* 1611–1697 (London. 1968)

ROBERTS, Michael (ed.), *Sweden's Age of Greatness* 1632–1718 (Macmillan. 1973)

ROBINSON, C.J., *Register of the Scholars admitted into Merchant Taylors' School* (Farncombe & Co., Lewes. 1882)

RUSHWORTH, John, *Historical Collections* viii 'The Tryall of Thomas Earl of Strafford' (London. 1680)

SHAW, W.A., *Knights of England* (Sherratt & Hughes, London. 1906) 3 vols & index

SOMERVILLE, Sir Robert, *Duchy of Lancaster Office Holders* (Phillimore. 1972)

SPALDING, Ruth, *The Improbable Puritan. A Life of Bulstrode Whitelocke 1605–1675* (Faber & Faber. 1975)

STOLPE, Sven, *Christina of Sweden* (Burns & Oates. 1966)

SVENSKA MÄN OCH KVINNOR (Bonniers, Stockholm. 1942–1955) 8 vols.

SVENSKT BIOGRAFISKT LEXIKON (Bonniers, Stockholm. 1977)

TANNER, J.R., *English Constitutional Conflicts of the Seventeenth Century* (C.U.P. 1961)

TAPSELL, Alan, (translator) *Guide to the materials for Swedish Historical Research in Great Britain* (P.A. Norstedt. 1958)

The Scientific American Cyclopedia of Formulas (The Standard Literature Co., Calcutta. 1946)

THIRSK, Joan, *Horses in early modern England: for Service, for Pleasure, for Power* Stenton Lecture 1977 (University of Reading. 1978)

UNDERDOWN, David, *Pride's Purge* (O.U.P. 1971)

WHITELOCKE, James, *Liber Famelicus* (ed. John Bruce, Camden Society. 1858; reprint: Johnson Reprint Co. 1968)

WHITELOCKE, R.H., *Memoirs, Biographical and Historical, of Bulstrode Whitelocke* (Routledge, Warne & Routledge. 1860)

WILLIAMS, John, *The Holy Table, Name and Thing* (printed for the Diocese of Lincoln. 1637)

WOOLRYCH, Austin, *Commonwealth to Protectorate* (O.U.P. 1982)

WORDEN, Blair, *The Rump Parliament* (C.U.P. 1974)

Index

Since Whitelocke's Contemporaries are arranged alphabetically, they do not appear in the index except where they feature in someone else's entry. Modern county boundaries and modern spelling of place-names are used throughout.